D1624051

DISCARDED

WIDENER UNIVERSITY

AMBIGUOUS

RELATIONS

AMBIGUOUS

RELATIONS

THE AMERICAN
JEWISH COMMUNITY
AND GERMANY
SINCE 1945

SHLOMO SHAFIR

WAYNE STATE UNIVERSITY PRESS   DETROIT

Published in cooperation with the
JACOB RADER MARCUS CENTER OF THE
AMERICAN JEWISH ARCHIVES,
CINCINNATI, OHIO

Copyright © 1999 by Wayne State University Press,
Detroit, Michigan 48201. All rights are reserved.
No part of this book may be reproduced without formal permission.
Manufactured in the United States of America.
03 02 01 00 99   5 4 3 2 1

Library of Congress Cataloging-in-Publication Data

Shafir, Shlomo.
    Ambiguous relations : the American Jewish community and Germany
since 1945 / Shlomo Shafir.
      p.   cm.
    Includes bibliographical references (p.   ) and index.
    ISBN 0-8143-2723-0 (alk. paper)
    1. Jews—United States—Politics and government.   2. Public
opinion—Jews.   3. Germany (West)—Foreign public opinion, American.
4. Holocaust, Jewish (1939–1945)—Germany (West)—Reparations.
5. Holocaust, Jewish (1939–1945)—Germany (West)—Influence.
I. Title.
E184.355.S53   1999
973'.04924—dc21   98-34526

WIDENER UNIVERSITY
WOLFGRAM
LIBRARY
CHESTER, PA

To Mina, Estee, and Ofra

CONTENTS

PREFACE

Fifty years after the end of World War II and the destruction of the major part of European Jewry, many American Jews still distinguish themselves from other Americans in their ambiguous and largely negative attitude toward the German state and its people. The half century that passed since 1945, however, has brought far-reaching changes in the status of Germany. From unconditional surrender and occupation of its territory, and a partition that lasted for forty years, it has reemerged as a first-rate economic power and a united country of close to eighty million inhabitants. Since the breakdown of the Soviet Union, Germany is now considered the strongest nation in Europe. Despite the remaining uncertainties about German national consciousness, the Federal Republic has proved to be the German people's most—or perhaps only—successful experiment in democracy and in sustaining a stable liberal parliamentary system. It has also evolved as one of the closest and most important allies of the United States.

Nonetheless, the trauma of the Holocaust became an important component of Jewish identity and continues to leave its mark on American Jewry's relationship with postwar Germany, despite the sociological and generational changes within the community. American Jews found themselves in a quandary soon after the war, having helplessly watched the murder of close to six million

9

fellow Jews, among whom were many of their own relatives. It was therefore not surprising that they favored a "hard" peace with the vanquished nation, in the internal American discussion about the postwar German settlement. Yet, because of the Cold War between the victorious allies, the larger part of Germany held by the United States, Britain, and France soon came to be regarded as a vital factor in the economic reconstruction of Western Europe, and subsequently in the political and military consolidation of the Western bloc. These political and strategic considerations coupled with the domestic anti-Communist hysteria contributed to a rapidly changing American posture toward Germany that clashed with Jewish demands, at first also shared by other liberals, for a far-reaching denazification of German society and a clean sweep of the German elites who had loyally served the Nazi regime. Furthermore, these demands spelled heavy punishment of all Germans involved in the warfare against the Jewish people.

American governmental records in the late 1940s and early 1950s clearly demonstrate the limits of direct and indirect Jewish pressure regarded as adverse to American national interest on Washington's German policy. Likewise, that pressure proved ineffective, more than thirty years later, during the Bitburg imbroglio, when President Ronald Reagan rebuffed strong Jewish protests against his visit to the military cemetery where a number of SS soldiers were interred.

However, the pluralistic character of American public opinion and its continuing impact provided American Jewry an opportunity to play a larger role vis-à-vis postwar Germany than on the level of policy formulation, where it was surpassed by much more powerful forces. Germany's concern with the hostile or at least critical attitude of a number of American Jewish organizations and influential individuals led it to attempt to soften this hostility. Conversely, constant Jewish reminders and criticism, though sometimes exaggerating the dangers of antisemitism and the revival of Nazism, may have contributed to German soul-searching about their past, and their historical responsibility as heirs of the perpetrators of the Holocaust. At the same time, Jewish discontent enabled American Jews to intervene in favor of legitimate Jewish demands such as the postponement and eventual abolition of the German statute of limitations in cases of murder. This resulted in the trial of more Nazi criminals who had been involved in Hitler's Final Solution.

The ambiguous relationship between the American Jewish community and Germany over the last fifty years cannot be scrutinized without taking into account the impact of Israel. The Six Day War and the Yom Kippur War further served to strengthen the identification of American Jewry with the Jewish state. Within the triangular relationship, the American Jewish community's skeptical approach toward Germany, based on memory and moral considerations, often bowed to Israel's pragmatic political and economic needs as a sovereign nation in hostile surroundings. The first example was the active role that the American Jewish community played in the common effort to secure reparations for Israel and its leading part in the Claims Conference. That partnership also affected subsequent dealings between organized American Jewry and the Germans.

In the first years after the war, American Jewish concern mainly centered on the rehabilitation and well-being of the Jewish survivors in Germany and the much larger number of East European refugees who assembled in the American occupied zone awaiting their immigration to Israel, the United States, and other countries overseas. Subsequently, American Jewry displayed its interest in the rights and safety of the surviving Jewish communities in Germany. However, until recently, the Jews there and their institutions played only a marginal role in the American Jewish–German relationship. In contrast, the German government and establishment, keen to present a demonstrative philosemitic stance, paid growing attention to the remaining Jews as compensation for the exterminationist antisemitism of the "Third Reich."

The above is a broad outline of the subjects, interactions, and developments to be discussed in this book, which has been arranged mostly in a chronological order. The monograph does not pretend to present a full overview of perceptions and reactions of American Jews in different walks of life. It mainly deals with organized Jewry, its major communal and religious groups, a few committed legislators and intellectuals, as well as a few outstanding individuals who were nevertheless connected to the community. The elements of both continuity and change in the major agencies have been elaborated, as have the different rationales of the agencies' attitudes toward Germany, the role of the survivors, and even the special case of professed pro-German lobbyists. A caveat must, however, be added: despite the traumatic and emotional effect of the Holocaust, the postwar American Jewish relationship with Germany was not a central issue. Israel, the fate of Soviet Jewry, and the domestic fight for civil rights were the lead items on the community's agenda.

A review of American Jewish attitudes toward the Federal Republic also requires a scrutiny of the handling of that complex relationship by both German conservative and Social Democratic-led governments, their different emphases and preferences, political aims and moral convictions. In this context, the recurrent efforts from the early 1950s of German diplomats in the United States to assuage American Jewish hostility are being explored. Again, a distinction must be made here between the responses of Jewish organizations, mainly voluntary elite groups and their leaders, as well as public figures, and the attitudes of Jews in general, most of whom seem to have remained more suspicious and negative.

Except for one chapter dedicated to American Jewry's attitude toward former Communist East Germany, this book deals mainly with the Federal Republic, which until 1990 comprised only Western Germany. American Jewish contacts with the East German Democratic Republic (GDR) were almost nonexistent for thirty years following the end of World War II for a number of reasons: the Cold War; the lack of American–East German diplomatic relations until 1974; the East Berlin government's refusal to refer directly to the Jewish angle of the Nazi crimes and to share the special historical responsibility of the German people for the Holocaust; its unreadiness to enter talks on restitution and compensation; and its hostility toward Zionism and Israel. Only in the last decade of its existence did a gradual change in East Germany's attitude take place, as an attempt was made to use Jewish influence to improve GDR relations with Washington and prepare the way for a state visit by Communist leader Erich Honecker. The fall of the Berlin Wall and the subsequent collapse of the East German regime prevented those aims from being achieved.

One of the conspicuous historiographic inadequacies of this study derives from the fact that American, German, and Israeli governmental records, which I used extensively, were open for research only until 1965, because of the customary thirty-year limit. Nonetheless, the records of major American Jewish organizations, a few important collections in Germany and Jerusalem, as well as available printed sources and memoirs, have enabled me to extend the monograph until the 1990s. Thus, such significant events are included as the impact of Israel's wars of 1967 and 1973, Bitburg, the U.S. Holocaust Museum controversy, the exchange programs between American Jewish organizations and German political foundations since the 1980s, and the momentous year of Germany's unification.

Some of the topics dealt with in various chapters of this monograph have been discussed in a number of studies that appeared in the last decades, some of which are listed in the select bibliography. These topics include the role of Henry Morgenthau Jr., Jewish concerns in occupied Germany in the first years after the war, restitution and reparations, the Eichmann Trial and its repercussions, Holocaust consciousness among American Jews, Bitburg, and the separate problems of East Germany. Since I began my research in the late 1980s, I have published several articles in English, German, and Hebrew on relevant subjects. In the first part of the introductory chapter, I mainly relied on the writings of historians such as Henry L. Feingold and David S. Wyman, who dealt with American Jewry and the Roosevelt administration. My own unpublished Ph.D. dissertation on the persecution of the Jews in Germany and American-German relations during the 1930s (Georgetown University, 1971) was also of help. Chapter 10 on the initial efforts of German diplomats in the United States to soften American Jewish hostility is based in great part on my essay published in the *YIVO Annual* 22 (1995) by Northwestern University Press.

Most of the main theses of this study were outlined in my expanded lecture, *American Jews and Germany: Points of Connection and Points of Departure*, American Jewish Archives Brochure Series #14 (Cincinnati, 1993). Sylke Tempel's Munich doctoral dissertation, which has since appeared in print, is an honest treatment of organized American Jewry's postwar relationship with Germany from a German viewpoint: *Legenden von der Allmacht: Die Beziehungen zwischen amerikanisch-jüdischen Organisationen und der Bundesrepublik Deutschland* (Frankfurt, 1995). The Israeli-born German Jewish historian Michael Wolffsohn also referred to the subject in his *Eternal Guilt? Forty Years of German-Jewish-Israeli Relations* (New York, 1993) and other publications, although I do not share his interpretation of the impact of the German–Israeli–American Jewish triangle and its repercussions.

This study was essentially completed in 1995, after the fiftieth anniversaries of the liberation of Auschwitz, Bergen-Belsen,

Buchenwald, and Dachau, as well as many slave labor camps; the Allied bombing of Dresden; Hitler's suicide; Nazi Germany's surrender; and the salvation of the surviving camp inmates by the advancing victorious armies in the East and the West. Despite the fear that the crimes of the Third Reich would be overshadowed after Germany's reunification by the confrontation over the Communist past of the GDR, the murder of the Jewish people in the 1940s still continues to occupy an important place in the mind and consciousness of the German public opinion-molding elites as evidenced by the many publications and public discussions in the media.

At the anniversaries mentioned above, almost all German leaders struck the right tone. Both in NATO and in the European Union, the Federal Republic continues to be a solid and reliable partner. In the long run, the recent emergence of a substantial conservative and right-wing trend in the nation's intellectual scene could, of course, have negative repercussions on Jewish-German relations. At this point, however, its impact on both the foreign policy of Germany and its political culture has been limited.

While it is not a historical study's task—or within its ability—to predict the future, the lessons of the developments since the end of World War II do depict the limits that will continue to affect the attitudes of American Jewry toward Germany and the Germans for years to come.

ACKNOWLEDGMENTS

After living in the United States from the mid-1960s to the early 1970s, I began work on this monograph during a two-month research period as fellow of the American Jewish Archives in Cincinnati in 1987–1988. In its initial stage, my research in the United States and Germany was facilitated by a three-month research grant of the Friedrich Ebert Foundation in Bonn. The Harry S. Truman Library Institute enabled me to spend a week of research at the Truman Library in Independence, Missouri. I am sincerely grateful to these three institutions for their financial assistance.

Since 1987—unfortunately with many breaks—I have carried out research in many archival collections, record centers, and libraries in the United States, Germany, and Israel, and I owe many thanks for assistance and advice to the directors and staff of the following institutions:

UNITED STATES

American Jewish Archives and Klau Library, Hebrew Union College, Cincinnati; American Jewish Committee Record Center and the Blaustein Library, New York; YIVO Archives, New York; Anti-Defamation League Archives and Resource Center, New York; Special Collections, New York Public Library, New York; Leo Baeck Institute Archives and Library, New York; American Jewish

Joint Distribution Committee Archives, New York; Columbia University Oral History Collection, New York; Herbert H. Lehman Papers, Columbia University, New York; Jewish Labor Committee Collection, Robert F. Wagner Labor Archives, Tamiment Institute Library, New York University, New York; American Jewish Historical Society Archives, Waltham, Massachusetts; Goldfarb Library, Brandeis University, Waltham, Massachusetts; John Fitzgerald Kennedy Library, Boston; Harvard University Archives, Cambridge, Massachusetts; Archives and Special Collections, Amherst College Library, Amherst, Massachusetts; U.S. National Archives, Diplomatic Branch, Washington, D.C.; Washington National Records Center, Suitland, Maryland; Manuscript Division, Library of Congress, Washington, D.C.; B'nai B'rith Archives, Washington, D.C.; Jewish War Veterans Archives, Washington, D.C.; Franklin Delano Roosevelt Library, Hyde Park, New York; Harry S. Truman Library, Independence, Missouri; Manuscripts and Archives, Sterling Memorial Library, Yale University, New Haven, Connecticut; Seeley G. Mudd Manuscript Library, Princeton University, Princeton, New Jersey; Wilson Library, University of Minnesota, Minneapolis.

GERMANY

Bundesarchiv Koblenz; Politisches Archiv, Auswärtiges Amt, Bonn; Friedrich-Ebert-Stiftung, Archiv der sozialen Demokratie und Bibliothek, Bonn; Ludwig-Erhard-Stiftung, Bonn; Konrad- Adenauer-Stiftung, Archiv für Christlich-Demokratische Politik und Bibliothek, St. Augustin; Archiv des Deutschen Liberalismus, Friedrich-Naumann-Stiftung, Gummersbach; Deutsche Bibliothek und Deutsches Exilarchiv 1933–1945, Frankfurt/Main; Max Horkheimer Archiv, Stadt-und Universitätsbibliothek, Frankfurt/ Main; Institut für Zeitgeschichte, Archiv und Bibliothek, Munich; Deutsches Literaturarchiv, Marbach a.N.; Hessisches Hauptstaatsarchiv, Wiesbaden; Baden-Württembergisches Hauptstaatsarchiv, Stuttgart; Landesarchiv Berlin, Berlin; Stiftung Archiv der Parteien und Massenorganisationen der DDR im Bundesarchiv, Berlin; Archiv Stiftung Bundeskanzler-Adenauer-Haus, Rhöndorf.

ISRAEL

Israel State Archives, Jerusalem; Zionist Central Archives and Library, Jerusalem; Hebrew University Oral History Collection,

Hebrew University, Jerusalem; Ben-Gurion Archive, Kiryat Sdeh Boker; Israel Labor Party Archive, Beit Berl; National and University Library, Jerusalem; Ayala and Zalman Abramov Library, Hebrew Union College, Jerusalem; Wiener Library, Tel Aviv University, Tel Aviv; Bar-Ilan University Library, Ramat Gan.

ENGLAND

Board of Deputies of British Jews, Archives, London; Institute of Jewish Affairs (now defunct), London.

I owe special thanks to Dr. David Singer of the American Jewish Committee for granting me access to recent records of that organization. Thanks are also due to Mr. Alan Schwartz of the Anti-Defamation League of B'nai B'rith for enabling me to make use of the ADL foreign correspondence files.

Last but not least, I am particularly indebted to Professor Jonathan D. Sarna and Dr. Abraham J. Peck, who read the manuscript before it was submitted to Wayne State University Press and made a number of important suggestions regarding its structure and content. I appreciate the comments and advice given by Professor Alfred Gottschalk, chancellor of the Hebrew Union College, who has served for many years as a member of the U.S. Holocaust Memorial Council. Dr. Ofer Shiff, my son-in-law, made fruitful suggestions on the chapters dealing with the impact of the Holocaust on American Jewry.

Both Mrs. Dena Matmon in Israel and Mrs. Eleanor M. Lawhorn in Cincinnati did an excellent job in typing the final draft to which Mrs. Jean Peck supplied editorial help. The copyeditor, Ms. Tammy O. Rastoder, meticulously prepared the manuscript for publication. I owe many thanks to all of them.

The book is dedicated to my wife, my beloved lifelong companion, and to both my daughters and their families in the United States and Israel.

PART 1

████

EARLY
POSTWAR
CONCERNS

████

1

American Jews and the German Problem Until the End of the War

From the inception of the German Nazi regime in January 1933, Adolf Hitler's persecution of the Jews became a permanent and pervading issue on the American Jewish agenda, causing a fundamental change in the attitude of American Jews toward Germany.

Many of the German Jewish elite in America still maintained an attachment to the cultural heritage of their former homeland at the end of the nineteenth and beginning of the twentieth century, although these links began to weaken as rapid assimilation in America and the impact of antisemitism in Germany took hold.

However, quite a number of American Jews of German origin continued to visit the old home; a few studied at German high schools, earned degrees at German universities, and intermarried with German Jewish sons and daughters. Before World War I, despite the semiautocratic traits of the Wilhelmian Empire and the antisemitism of its society and establishment, Germany was regarded as the lesser evil as compared to czarist Russia. Thus, in response to the discrimination against Jews in Russia, German-born Jacob Schiff, one of the most prominent figures in the Jewish community, played a leading role in the campaign for the abrogation of the eighty-year-old American-Russian treaty of commerce. After the outbreak of the war in Europe, Schiff at first refused to float Anglo-French loans because of the partnership of the Western nations with Russia. The masses of recent Eastern European immigrants loathed the czarist oppressor of their fellow Jews; whereas some of the socialists opposed both sides in the conflict because of their pacifist convictions, others cherished the strength of the German Social Democratic party, the strongest in Europe.[1]

Nonetheless, this partly emotional preference of some American Jews for Germany and the Central Powers came to an end with the Russian revolution and the breakdown of the czarist regime in March 1917. From the moment of President Woodrow Wilson's declaration of war in April 1917, the community fully endorsed the United States' active partnership in the anti-German alliance. In addition, the hostility of the Turkish empire to the small Jewish settlement in Palestine and Zionist expectations of British support for their aims reinforced the pro-Allied trend among American Jewry. After the end of World War I, American Jews took notice of the social and cultural achievements of German Jewry under the short-lived parliamentary democratic government; both individual and organizational contacts between the two communities were fostered. Beginning with the late twenties, however, the major American Jewish organizations watched with growing concern the increasing antisemitic agitation of the Nazis and the implications for Germany's Jews during the tottering Weimar Republic.[2]

After Weimar's collapse in 1933, the American Jewish community became a consistent anti-German factor on the American political scene. Admittedly, serious tactical and ideological differences existed among American Jews on how to confront the Nazi danger abroad, as well as the rise of antisemitism at home. On the one hand, activists of the American Jewish Congress and the Joint Boycott Council, which included the Jewish Labor Committee (JLC), as well as the Non-Sectarian Anti-Nazi League to Champion Human Rights, favored public appearances and boycotting German products. On the other hand, the prestigious, moderate American Jewish Committee (AJC) and in part B'nai B'rith preferred quiet backstage efforts and concentrated on information and on educational activities. Beside the rise of Nazism and fascism in Europe, the depression and the increase of antisemitism at home also enhanced pro-Communist influence among the Jewish population. Altogether, Jews of liberal, democratic, and leftist convictions and different political orientations tried to present national socialism as a threat not only to themselves but

22

to all Americans and to world peace. However, ethnic feelings and fear of the Jewish masses, of first- and second-generation citizens, persisted. Many of these Jews had family in the "old countries" of the European continent who could not be brought over because of the economic crisis and the nation's restrictionist immigration policy.[3]

To most American Jews, President Franklin Delano Roosevelt represented the great antagonist to Hitler, even during the early years when he still refrained from challenging the nonintervention-ist policy of his predecessors. Quite naturally, with few exceptions, they supported President Roosevelt's shift toward confrontational policies aimed at "quarantining" the aggressors before the United States' entry into the war against Nazi Germany and its allies. Sub-sequently, they unconditionally endorsed FDR's leadership during the war years and the priority he attached to victory over Hitler, the arch-enemy of the Jewish people. In their great majority, they remained an anti-German element after the end of the war, when, because of the East-West conflict, Washington's attitude toward the former enemy nation was reversed and the United States began to regard West Germany as a potential ally against the Soviet-led Eastern bloc. However, in contrast to the direct and indirect con-tribution of American Jewry to shifting American public opinion from isolationism to facing the Nazi threat, the Jewish community did not influence the making of wartime policy, and its impact on the handling of Germany was rather marginal.

The main exception in that context was the role of Henry Morgenthau Jr., secretary of the Treasury Department since 1934. But the secretary acted as a member of the administration and not as a spokesman for the Jewish community.[4]

The continuous support of American Jews for Roosevelt origi-nated from his domestic, social, and economic policies that ben-efited many of them, and in which a number of Jewish brain trusters were involved. FDR's anti-Nazi stand increased his popu-larity among Jews at a time when most European leaders preferred appeasing the anti-Communist dictators of Germany and Italy and the majority of the American people were afraid of new entan-glements overseas. Yet, the balance sheet of his administration's handling of the two main special Jewish concerns with regard to the German problem was not a positive one. Admission of larger numbers of refugees until the war and rescue of Jews from Hitler's

Europe thereafter were not high on the administration's agenda, at least until the belated establishment of the War Refugee Board (WRB) early in 1944.[5] In comparison to what the majority in prepluralistic America and the administration regarded as the national interest, the Jewish case proved the limits of ethnic influence. In a way, these limits remained valid also in various cases in the era of postwar pluralism, with the important exception of the successful Jewish campaign in persuading the U.S. government to recognize and support the new State of Israel.

In the 1930s the large majority of the depression-ridden isolationist-minded public opposed any enlargement of immigration. A strong restrictionist attitude prevailed in both houses of Congress, and the president and his advisers took these factors into account. Only in 1938–39 was the full German and Austrian quota used up for the admission of refugees. At the Evian conference in summer 1938, Roosevelt's main prorefugee initiative after Germany's annexation of Austria, that increase was presented as the American contribution to the refugee problem. The conference concluded with the setting up of the Intergovernmental Committee on Political Refugees (ICR), under a British chairman and an American executive director. However, even though different views prevail about the German motives in launching the Schacht-Wohlthat proposal—financing the emigration of Jews by increasing German exports to the United States and other Western nations—no feasible emergency programs existed to cope with the rapidly growing number of Jewish refugees.[6]

A few months after Evian, in response to the so-called *Kristallnacht* (Night of the Broken Glass) pogrom against German Jews on November 9–10, 1938, FDR recalled from Berlin the last American prewar ambassador, Hugh R. Wilson, who himself happened to be an outspoken supporter of appeasement of Nazi Germany. Yet, in spite of the Jewish community's hearty welcome of the president's action, the recall did not come about because of Jewish pressure, but reflected Roosevelt's desire to use the pogrom's impact on American public opinion to advance a tougher policy against the expansionist Greater German Reich.[7] Contrary to the German propaganda about American and world Jewish power, the Jews' unsuccessful prewar efforts to prevent persecution in Germany and enlarge somewhat the numbers of immigrants from there demonstrated their weakness.

24

In part, American Jewish capability to come to the assistance of German or other European Jews and to pressure the administration in that direction was inhibited by the substantial increase of domestic antisemitism in the late 1930s.[8] Whereas in the early and mid-1930s nativist and pro-Nazi antisemitism had been marginal, the renewed recession and the Coughlinite hate campaign had a major impact in the great cities, where Jews were confronted with hostile Catholic masses, many of them first- and second-generation Americans. In addition to the Christian Fronters, there were the militants and sympathizers of the Nazi German-American Bund, twenty thousand of whom packed New York's Madison Square Garden at a so-called "patriotic" George Washington rally in February 1939. Even when employment and business conditions improved, antisemitism continued to rise, persisting during the war years. At least indirectly, the successes of Nazi Germany before the U.S. entry into the war, too, fostered the anti-Jewish sentiments.

Because of the impact of antisemitism, which did not subside until the end of World War II, Roosevelt preferred to play down the common ground between his policies and the desires of the overwhelming majority of American Jews in the two critical years between the beginning of the war in Europe and Pearl Harbor. Thus, in spite of strong Jewish support for turning the United States into an "arsenal for democracy," the role of Jews in interventionist organizations was usually muffled in order not to complicate the president's task of convincing the American people of the national interest in confronting and defeating Hitler's Reich. After all, a great part of them did not want to go to war against Germany. At one point Rabbi Stephen S. Wise, the leading representative of the American Jewish Congress and the Zionist camp and a loyal FDR supporter, complained to Clark Eichelberger, head of the Committee to Defend America by Aiding the Allies, about the trend of ghettoization, asserting that Jews should not be shut out even at the risk of incurring the charge of warmongering. That exchange took place a few weeks before Pearl Harbor.[9]

Quite naturally, the U.S. entry into the war in December 1941 enjoyed the full support of American Jews, who had long awaited the day when their nation would take the lead to rid the world of the Hitlerite enemy. Subsequently 550,000 Jewish soldiers fought in the armed forces against the German Reich and its Japanese and (until 1943) Italian allies in Europe, the Far East, and North Africa.

In the government's view, the fateful battle against the Axis powers required that all American citizens subordinate any special group interest to the goal of a rapid and full military victory, which would also put an end to the Jewish torment in German-occupied Europe. Even though the Jews were Hitler's chosen victims, the administration wanted to ensure that the war undertaken for America's national interest would in no way be regarded as a "Jewish war," as German propaganda tried to put it. American Jews, whose opposition against the Nazis had now become an all-American endeavor, unequivocally endorsed the nation's war aims, including the demand for unconditional surrender. But as Hitler's Final Solution was revealed, Jewish community leaders desperately searched for some American and Allied intercession to stop the murder and to rescue at least some of their fellow Jews. However, neither the appeal to the president, with whom a high-ranking Jewish delegation met for half an hour in December 1942, nor the efforts to make the American public conscious of the slaughter of European Jewry bore any concrete results. Mass meetings by Jewish organizations to protest Nazi massacres started in July 1942 and continued with a Day of Mourning in December but had no major impact on the non-Jewish majority.[10]

The accumulating news about the murder of hundreds of thousands in the East seldom made headlines in the American press; radio coverage was sparse, and the Hollywood film industry avoided the subject. Because of the exaggerated German atrocity stories of World War I, in January 1943 30 percent of the American population still dismissed the news that two million Jews had already been killed by the Nazis. In March 1943, both the AJ Congress rally "Stop Hitler Now" as well as the pageant "We Never Die," presented by the anti-establishment Committee for a Jewish Army (the predecessor of the Emergency Committee to Save the Jewish People of Europe), gained more publicity than earlier protests. Still, the issue of saving Jews drew support mainly from the liberal section of the public and from a few liberal and left-wing publications. In October 1943, the only Jewish demonstration in the capital, the "Rabbis Pilgrimage for Rescue," was coldshouldered by the president who found no time to see them.[11] The one-sided Jewish love affair with FDR had its shortcomings, but because of the Republicans' policies and preferences in the 1930s and 1940s, that party could not be considered a more promising alternative.

On different occasions, the United States and Great Britain took into consideration the hostile reaction to their rescue of Jews that they expected from Arab Moslem nations from Casablanca to the Persian Gulf region, through which vital supplies were being shipped to the Soviet Union. The British especially were afraid that any large-scale rescue effort might flood Palestine with more Jews and thus undermine the May 1939 White Paper aimed at a permanent Arab majority there, and America's policy was influenced by the growing importance of its Middle Eastern oil interests. No wonder that the Anglo-American conference in Bermuda, which convened in April 1943 as the murder of European Jews reached its climax, was nothing but a diversionary exercise designed to pacify the few who had criticized the indifference of the American and British governments.[12] Most prominent Jewish insiders close to the president, such as Supreme Court Associate Justice Felix Frankfurter, presidential counsel Samuel Rosenman, and Governor Herbert H. Lehman, who after his defeat by Republican Thomas Dewey became executive head of the United Nations Relief and Rehabilitation Administration (UNRRA)—not to mention influential outsiders such as Bernard Baruch—did not attempt to challenge the administration's attitude on what was mainly regarded as a sectarian ethnic concern, just as they had refrained from questioning it before the war.

Henry Feingold, the foremost analyst of the Roosevelt administration's policies and relations with American Jewry during the Holocaust years, was the first to point out that Henry Morgenthau Jr. was the only member of FDR's inner circle who finally dared to confront the State Department with its hostile indifference to the annihilation of the Jews in Europe. Morgenthau was overwhelmed by the Jewish catastrophe and its dimensions; and after the Bermuda conference and the revelation of further procrastination on opportunities of rescue, he challenged the government's policy. Since the beginning of 1943, one of the objectives of the AJ Congress and of the Joint Emergency Committee on European Jewish Affairs had been to gain congressional support for rescue. Stephen Wise and AJC president Joseph M. Proskauer served as co-chairmen of that committee. Subsequently, the effective public relations campaign of the separate Emergency Committee to Save the Jewish People of Europe made its impact. The American Jewish Conference, for its part, espoused the importance of a Zionist solution for Palestine.

With the personal involvement of Randolph Paul, John Pehle, and Josiah DuBois, three committed senior members of the Treasury staff, and the support of an aware portion of the American public, Morgenthau eventually brought about the creation of the War Refugee Board. It was established as a special government agency that became engaged in rescue work early in 1944. Unfortunately, a major part of European Jewry had already been murdered by that time.[13]

In the context of the American Jewish response to the German Final Solution for European Jewry during World War II, two questions that have often been asked still dominate the discussion: Would a more unified Jewish community have been able to achieve better results from the administration in Washington, and would a more articulate emphasis on rescue instead of on the Zionist aim of establishing a Jewish commonwealth in Palestine have resulted in saving many more Jews during the Holocaust?[14] While these questions are legitimate, the answer in both cases is no. Even though the internal divisions and the lack of a powerful American Jewish leadership sometimes made it easier for the Roosevelt administration to evade the refugee and rescue issue until the creation of the WRB at a rather late date, it is not certain that a united community would have been much more successful in the circumstances that prevailed at least until 1944. As for the American Jewish Conference's resolutions in summer 1943, a stronger emphasis on rescue might have been preferable, at least for the record. But it is doubtful whether that actually mattered very much, since no shelters were in sight.

However, postponing the Zionist demand for a Jewish state might have prevented the subsequent mobilization of a major part of American Jewry after the war for achieving the movement's political goal and a safe haven for the survivors. The growing support for the Zionist Biltmore program, its endorsement by a large majority of the American Jewish Conference, as well as the ascendancy of the militant Cleveland Rabbi Abba Hillel Silver over the moderate and accommodating Rabbi Stephen S. Wise, were in part reactions to the helplessness of American Jews who watched the murder of millions of fellow Jews in Europe. The more radical direction caused the withdrawal of the influential AJC from the Conference and brought forth strong opposition from the American Council for Judaism (ACJ), a group of anti-Zionist

Reform rabbis and lay leaders. But despite its negative impact, that split did not substantially change the general trend. Together with the wartime experiences, the massive pro-Zionist drive that peaked a few years later also contributed to a stronger and more self-conscious Jewish community at home. After the end of the war in Europe, this drive would, together with the Jewish Agency for Palestine and later the government of Israel, play a central role in the successful fulfillment of Jewish demands from postwar Germany, contrary to the failure of its efforts in favor of refuge and rescue until the collapse of Nazi Germany.

* * *

With the outbreak of hostilities in Europe in 1939, the major Jewish organizations in America began preparing drafts for the postwar era, after the expected victory over Nazi Germany. The AJ Congress and the World Jewish Congress (WJC), which had been founded upon Stephen Wise's initiative in 1936 to confront the growing Nazi and fascist threat, sponsored the Institute of Jewish Affairs (IJA). With headquarters in New York, established in 1940, the Institute was directed by two eminent lawyers, the brothers Dr. Jacob and Dr. Nehemiah Robinson, both recent immigrants from Lithuania. Initially, the two organizations invited several other major Jewish groups, such as the AJC, the Alliance Israélite Universelle, and the Board of Deputies of British Jews in London, to set up a common institute with the task of preparing a Jewish peace program that would secure international protection of Jewish rights at a future peace conference after the successful conclusion of the war. But the attempt to provide for unified Jewish action failed because of the substantial ideological differences between the pro-Zionist Congress movement supporting Jewish peoplehood and the integrationist AJC opposing Jewish nationalism.[15]

During the war, the WJC diverted much of its energy to immediate rescue activities. However, the IJA, with its staff of trained scholars, continued its research program and published a number of important studies, such as *Starvation Over Europe* (1943), *Hitler's Ten Year War on the Jews* (1943), *The Racial State* (1944), and *The Jewish Catastrophe* (1944). Among other issues, it began to deal with the problems of postwar restitution of Jewish property and compensation for Jewish suffering. The idea that the Jewish people as a whole were entitled to reparations was first raised by Dr. Nahum

Goldmann, who, besides Stephen Wise, was the leading figure of the WJC. Goldmann raised that demand at the organization's Western Hemisphere conference in Baltimore in November 1941, a few weeks before Pearl Harbor.

The IJA and the WJC, its parent body, also became involved in another major topic pertaining to postwar Germany: the punishment of Nazi criminals who had committed crimes against the Jewish people.

In January 1942, the London St. James conference of nine governments-in-exile strongly denounced German crimes and acts of brutality but evaded the special Jewish aspects of the mass killings in the East. The argument was that identifying the suffering of the Jews "might be equivalent to an implicit recognition of the racial theories." In response to that declaration, the WJC appealed to the Allies for an explicit condemnation of German atrocities against the Jews. Roosevelt and Churchill referred to this subject in July 1942; more explicitly it was included in the United Nations declaration of December 1942. However, to the disappointment of American Jewish leaders, it was not mentioned at Allied conferences in Quebec and in Moscow in 1943. Thanks to a demand from the WRB, the topic reappeared in a statement by FDR in March 1944, in spite of adversary advice by counsel Samuel Rosenman that it might stir antisemitic reactions and hurt the "Chief" in an election year.[16]

In 1943 and 1944 the WJC and subsequently the newly established American Jewish Conference continued to call for punitive action against Nazi German criminals and also tried to obtain the help of the exile governments in that aim. Still, Jewish sensitivity prevailed in the advice of Abba Hillel Silver, the stalwart Zionist leader who was not afraid of challenging the White House and the State and War Departments on Palestine, that the American Jewish Conference change the original name of its Statement on Retribution to "Statement on the Punishment of the Nazi Criminals." He warned that the average non-Jewish American would react negatively if the Jews were first to talk about retribution. Although the Jewish tragedy was the greatest of all, Silver thought it preferable that the Jewish statement come second or third after the Czechs or the Poles and suggested that a joint statement might be better.[17]

Eventually, after Washington and London had agreed to the establishment of the United Nations War Crimes Commission

(UNWCC), the WJC demanded that the notion of war crimes be extended both in space (to cover crimes committed against Jews not only in occupied territories but also in Germany and Austria) and in time (to extend them back to Hitler's accession to power in January 1933). This was finally agreed upon only in early 1945, after the administration's long procrastination and the State Department bureaucracy's objections to Herbert Pell, the U.S. representative to UNWCC, an outspoken supporter of Jewish demands.[18] Usually the WJC and the American Jewish Conference, which encompassed the great majority of American Jewish organizations and a large number of local communities, maintained close ties in preparing for the postwar era. The Conference was granted priority in contacts with the administration in Washington, whereas the WJC was the first to make representations to foreign governments and intergovernmental bodies. On such issues the WJC, at that time and for years to come, also spoke for the AJ Congress.[19]

The WJC postwar demands were drafted at its Atlantic City War Emergency Conference in November 1944 when victory in Europe was already in sight. In addition to the Americans, delegates from Europe, Palestine, Latin America, and other nations attended. The conference called for abrogation of all discriminatory measures against Jews, the full restoration of their rights, the granting of international relief for the rehabilitation of the remnants of the Jewish population in Europe, and the establishment of a Jewish commonwealth in Palestine. It endorsed the idea of setting up international and national tribunals to try war criminals, discussed at that time by the Allies, and demanded that all forms of persecution of racial, religious, and political minorities committed since January 30, 1933, be prosecuted. The gathering also requested that in the list of crimes made punishable, the annihilation of the Jewish people in Europe and all acts of violence against Jews in the occupied territories and within the territory of the enemy nations should find their explicit and proper place. The delegates refrained from proclaiming a total all-Jewish boycott of Germany. But the representatives of German Jewish emigrés affiliated with the WJC insisted that no Jew who had escaped from Germany would be compelled to return and that no former Jewish citizen of Germany would ever again have to acquire German citizenship except at his or her own request.

In his keynote address, Nahum Goldmann reiterated the demand that "the Jewish people as a whole should be regarded as the heirs to those of its children who have been murdered." However, difficulties arose in devising a common approach with regard to restitution and indemnification, especially the future use of heirless property outside its original country of location. The resolutions drafted by Jacob Robinson, the IJA's founding director, on which agreement was reached by the delegations, distinguished between restitution of property and compensation for losses suffered by Jewish communities and the claims of individual Jewish victims. The conference suggested that heirless property and rights belonging to organizations and institutions that had ceased to exist be turned over to an international Jewish Reconstruction Commission. That body would use the funds for the rehabilitation of European Jews and their communities, as well as for the development of Palestine through the Jewish Agency. According to Nehemiah Robinson's study *Indemnification and Reparations: Jewish Aspects*, which reflected the views of the WJC, the extent of Nazi Germany's spoliation of Jewish assets amounted to $8 billion, excluding Soviet territory. Robinson's pioneering proposal for a "Jewish Agency for Reconstruction" subsequently served as a basis for the international Jewish successor organizations.[20]

As a matter of fact, comparable proposals—regarding restitution of individual as well as of heirless property and some kind of collective recompense—had been drawn up in Palestine by Dr. Georg Landauer of the Jewish Agency and in detail by Dr. Siegfried Moses, the chairman of the Association of Central European Immigrants there.[21] Moses himself attended the Atlantic City conference as a delegate of the Yishuv (the Jewish community of Palestine). The resolutions passed at the WJC's War Emergency Conference were included in the American Jewish Conference's postwar program and comprised the main Jewish demands from Germany and the victorious Allies: restitution payments for individual claims and claims of Jewish communities and organizations, as well as collective reparations linked with Palestine, which had absorbed a great number of refugees and survivors. These demands were the subject of continuing Jewish efforts until the signing in September 1952 of the Luxembourg Treaty between the Federal Republic of Germany and Israel, as well as the additional protocols with the Conference of Jewish Material Claims Against Germany (Claims Conference).

Because of ideological and organizational differences, the elitist American Jewish Committee refused to cooperate with the WJC in a joint body dealing with postwar reconstruction. Despite its small numbers, at that time and for the next decade or more the AJC was the most prestigious of American Jewish organizations, thanks to the socioeconomic standing of its members and their political connections. Instead, it preferred to set up its own Research Institute on Peace and Postwar Problems as an independent venture. The institute, headed by Dr. Max Gottschalk, brought together a number of prominent Jewish scholars and experts in international law and the social sciences, and was designed to investigate and publish data pertaining to the rehabilitation of European Jewry after the victory over Nazi Germany. In line with AJC's tradition and standards, it cooperated with governmental and nonsectarian peace-planning groups and published a great number of memoranda and pamphlets on the future abolition of discriminatory legislation in Germany and other Axis countries, human rights in general, migration, war crimes, Palestine, restitution, and indemnification. But as Naomi W. Cohen observed in her history of the Committee's first sixty years, the underwriting of the Research Institute's programs already reflected its revised views about Jewish survival and the tempering of its traditional emancipatory philosophy by mid-twentieth-century realities. Its postwar guidelines stressed calling Jewish needs to the attention of statesmen and international councils and, above all, making certain that the catastrophe that befell the Jewish people would never be forgotten.[22]

After the end of the war in Europe, the AJC, which in the past could not overcome its basic disagreements with the pro-Zionist elements in the community, joined forces with the American Jewish Conference, the WJC, the Jewish Agency for Palestine, and the American Jewish Joint Distribution Committee (hereafter JDC or Joint) in the framework of the Five Cooperating Organizations (after the demise of the American Jewish Conference in 1948, only four). That ad hoc group dealt primarily with issues concerning the survivors and other Jewish displaced persons (DPs) in the American occupation zone of Germany and with demands for restitution and compensation. The AJC's new cooperative trend also found expression in the communal field. For a number of years it was an active member of the newly established National Community Relations Advisory Council (NCRAC), in contrast to its withdrawal in 1943 from the American Jewish Conference because of the Conference's endorsement of the Zionist Biltmore program. After a break of more than thirteen years, it rejoined NCRAC in 1966.

In its 1945 statement "To the Counsellors of Peace" that was published before the founding conference of the United Nations in San Francisco, the AJC did not go as far as the WJC, the American Jewish Conference, or the Jewish Agency in demanding collective reparations for the Jewish people, a concept it still did not recognize. It called for the return of individual Jewish property and the use of heirless property for the reconstruction of religious, welfare, educational, and cultural institutions as well as for the rehabilitation of Jewish victims of Nazi persecution. Yet, these differences did not prevent the AJC's future cooperation with other major Jewish organizations on restitution and recompense. In the most critical postwar period the majority of its leadership joined in support of the creation of a Jewish state in a part of Palestine. The AJC also shared the American Jewish consensus with regard to trial and punishment of Nazi criminals. It cited statements issued by the Allies and the governments-in-exile that spoke of vengeance against the guilty. Especially it referred to Acting Secretary of State Joseph Grew promising to punish German leaders and their associates "for the whole broad criminal enterprise, devised and executed with ruthless disregard of the very foundations of law and morality."[23]

The American Jewish Joint Distribution Committee was the main philanthropic agency of American Jewry. With its lay leadership of upper-class German American background, it resembled the AJC in its general outlook. However, during the war and thereafter, the growing influence of the professionals, mainly second-generation East Europeans, contributed to a change of the agency's policy toward more support for the Jewish national home in Palestine and afterwards the State of Israel. Since 1939 it was a part of the United Jewish Appeal, financed together with the United Palestine Appeal by the local Jewish communities, and received 60 percent of the sums allocated for overseas needs. During the war years its professionals and contacts in Europe engaged in desperate efforts to assist persecuted Jews in the Nazi-occupied continent. As soon as victory was in sight, teams were trained in the United States to help the survivors and refugees in the liberated areas. According to its tradition, the JDC refrained from making political statements on Germany. But in addition to its immediate most urgent task of rehabilitating the "Saving Remnant," it came to play an important role in the fight for restitution of Jewish property and afterwards for reparations from Germany, in the framework of the Claims Conference.[24]

Altogether, the impact of statements and demands by American and international Jewish organizations on policymakers in Washington and other Allied capitals in regard to postwar Germany was in the best case short-lived. Even before the final stages of the war, the future of Germany and its interrelationship with the reconstruction of Europe had emerged as the most important problem of American postwar planning, to be decided according to U.S. national interest. The limits of Jewish ethnic pleading became clear after the rapid breakup of the anti-Nazi alliance and the beginning of the Cold War. The initially harsh treatment of occupied Germany, the attempted clean sweep of German elites, and the planned punishment of all Nazi activists, which more or less corresponded with Jewish demands, gave way to more moderate and accommodating policies.

On the other hand, with the wartime changes in American society and the replacement of the former ideal of the melting pot by cultural pluralism, Jews became more self-conscious and influential and they carried more weight in American public opinion than in the 1930s and before 1945. As a keen observer of the postwar American Jewish scene stated in retrospect, never would American Jews feel more physically and psychologically secure than after World War II: "for perhaps the first time in their history" they came to believe "that they had at last become full Americans and that the relationship between the Jewish and American identity was to be one of symbiosis and not of conflict."[25] The future government of the non-Communist part of Germany would take this development into account for many years to come, and it was to play an important role in satisfying at least the other focal Jewish demands with regard to restitution, indemnification, and collective recompense.

2

Morgenthau's Plan, Supporters, and Opponents

As mentioned in the preceding chapter, American Jewish spokesmen called for stern punishment of Nazi war criminals and murderers, and the major organizations drafted proposals for future restitution of Jewish property, individual indemnification, and even collective reparations. However, their impact on postwar American policy with regard to Germany—except the constant reminders of retribution for Nazi crimes—was very limited. The most far-reaching plan to punish Germany and prevent any further recurrence of German aggression did not emerge from any group of the organized community but evolved in the mind of Secretary of the Treasury Henry Morgenthau Jr., the only Jew in Roosevelt's cabinet. Morgenthau's most important adviser, Harry Dexter White, a left-wing economist of East European Jewish origin, played the key role in formulating these proposals. Other high-ranking non-Jewish members of the Treasury staff were involved in preparing the drafts, among them John Pehle and Josiah DuBois. All those who took part resolved to recommend the necessary measures to put an end to the German threat for the next generations.[1]

Nevertheless, many Americans and many more Germans came to regard Morgenthau's recommendations as the clear-cut expression of Jewish vindictiveness. From the beginning, Morgenthau's opponents in the administration decried Jewish vengeance as his motive, and such references reverberated in the 1944 election campaign and thereafter. As for the German side, Morgenthau was the most detested Jew, not only in Nazi propaganda chief Joseph Goebbels's hate campaign during the last months of the war, but also for years to come. The American Jewish attitude toward postwar Germany, especially in the first stages, was linked to the secretary's legacy, although his "plan" soon faded away.[2] Early in 1949 Konrad Adenauer, the leader of the Christian Democratic Union (CDU) and soon to be elected as West Germany's first chancellor, condemned the "Morgenthau plan" as a crime against humanity that could be compared to Nazi wrongdoing and might have caused the death of thirty to forty million people.[3]

Early in his life Henry Morgenthau Jr., whose grandfather Lazarus had immigrated from Mannheim in 1866, inherited anti-German feelings. Henry Morgenthau Sr., his father, served in World War I as American ambassador to the Ottoman Empire, then a German ally, and had been one of the first to alert the world to the deportation and mass killings of the Armenian people by the Turks, with the connivance of German advisers. Hitler's rise to power reaffirmed Morgenthau's dislike of Germany. Even though Morgenthau may have somewhat exaggerated his own part in the 1930s, in his talks with historian John Morton Blum, the compiler of the Morgenthau Diaries, he considered the elimination of Nazism "the first requisite for a peaceful and democratic world." In his capacity as secretary of the Treasury, he invoked countervailing duties on the most important German export commodities as early as 1936. After Munich he participated in the review of American aircraft production, promoted aid to China against Japan, and was in charge of negotiations with France regarding American planes for the French air force.

Afterwards, Morgenthau was prominently involved in promoting military aid to Britain and preparing the U.S. economy for the war. He also tried to interrupt Nazi Germany's continuing economic links with a number of states in Latin America and blocked the American assets of companies such as General Aniline and Film (GAF), a subsidiary of IG Farben. This rather complex operation was to strengthen his resolve to settle, after the war, the account with the German industrial corporations that helped Hitler's ascent to power and supported him loyally during the twelve years of his rule.

Contrary to Morgenthau's dislike of Germany even before the Nazi takeover, he, like many other liberals in the post–World War I era, watched with sympathy the Soviet experience, without taking into account the authoritarian and oppressive nature of their dictatorship. In 1933 he was among the strong supporters of the Roosevelt administration's decision to establish diplomatic relations with Soviet Russia and contributed to achieving that goal.[4] His persistent fight against the German threat he regarded as serving the interests of all liberal peace-loving Americans striving for a better world.

Morgenthau, who resented the Nazi racial doctrines from the first, came from an assimilationist background and, despite generous contributions to Jewish philanthropies, had not been actively involved in Jewish communal activities.[5] However, as a result of the persecution and extermination of the Jews in Europe, he was from time to time contacted by leading spokesmen of the Jewish Agency for Palestine, the World Jewish Congress, the American Jewish Conference, and even the anti-establishment Emergency Committee to Save the Jewish People of Europe concerning rescue and issues related to Palestine. From Rabbi Stephen Wise, who officiated at Morgenthau's wedding in 1916 at New York's Free Synagogue, he learned in September 1942 about the Final Solution. In 1943 the secretary was helpful in foiling the British-American draft statement on the Middle East that denounced Zionist activities as endangering the Allied war effort and called for their suspension until the end of the hostilities when the issue would be dealt with, only with the consent of all sides. Some of these Zionist contacts, as well as increased public criticism and congressional initiatives after the dismal failure of the Bermuda conference, contributed to Morgenthau's decisive role in establishing the War Refugee Board early in 1944. At the same time, his growing involvement in the fate of European Jewry seems also to have radicalized his approach toward the German people and their state, after their expected unconditional surrender. The WRB's insistence upon a tough war crimes policy, in an attempt to deter the Nazis and their allies from murdering the remaining Jews, may have added another dimension to Morgenthau's anti-German stand.[6]

In August 1944, at the time of the successful Allied postinvasion drive into northern France, Morgenthau challenged the concept of a "stern peace with reconciliation" with a defeated postwar

Germany, which was supported by the Departments of State and War. Their reasoning was affected by both the need for quick economic reconstruction of Europe and the growing mistrust of the Soviet Union. This contradicted suggestions about dividing Germany that had been raised at the Moscow foreign ministers conference and the Teheran summit in 1943. In the American public debate, the most important statement in favor of partition had been made by Sumner Welles, a confidant of FDR and undersecretary of state until 1943. In his nonfiction best-seller, *The Time for Decision*, Welles recommended breaking up a demilitarized Germany into three states, but such notions did not sway policy-makers in the State Department. Former Treasury officials, such as Colonel Bernard Bernstein at SHAEF's (Supreme Headquarters, Allied Expeditionary Force) Civil Affairs Division and Colonel L. C. Aarons at the European Advisory Committee in London, provided Morgenthau with information about the Department of War's directives for the occupation of Germany and the State Department's blueprint regarding the economic future of Germany. The blueprint aimed at preventing Germany's renewed industrial hegemony of the continent and endorsed reparations from the current German production. Morgenthau objected to that course because of the post–World War I experience and the generous participation of American financial interests in the relatively quick German recovery after the last war. His response was the Program to Prevent Germany from Starting a World War III, drafted by his staff, mainly by Harry Dexter White.[7] In early September 1944, before the Second Quebec Conference between the United States and Great Britain, the program underwent several adjustments but retained its basic points.

The main elements of the memorandum, which became famous as the "Morgenthau plan," were the complete demilitarization of a partitioned Germany, its industrial disarmament, and the prompt and severe punishment of the main Nazi leaders and criminals. Because of Morgenthau's strong views about the link between German militarism and Nazism, on the one hand, and the German industry, on the other, deindustrialization became the major item in the Treasury's draft. Poland was to receive the main part of Eastern Prussia, except the north, which the Soviet Union would incorporate, and also southern Silesia. France was to annex the Saar region and adjacent areas between the Rhine and the Moselle rivers.

40

A special international zone would encompass the Ruhr area and its surrounding industrial centers. The remaining German territories were to be divided into two independent states—a northern and a southern. According to the draft, the Ruhr and Rhineland were to be stripped of all industrial equipment and plants. Instead of reparations by cash payments or deliveries of goods from current industrial production, the defeated Germans were to be punished by loss of territories and resources, forced labor, and the confiscation of foreign assets outside Germany. German schools and universities were to close until an Allied commission of educators had completed an effective reorganization program; until then all radio stations and newspapers would be discontinued.

According to the memorandum, the responsibility for sustaining the economy and feeding the population would rest with the German people and not with the occupation troops. For at least twenty years after the unconditional surrender, the United Nations (which meant the Allies, not the future international organization) were to retain control over foreign trade and capital imports, prevent the establishment of industries linked to the German military potential, and guarantee the breakup of all large estates and their distribution among the peasants. Finally, while the United States would retain full military and civilian representation on an international commission, American troops would be withdrawn as soon as possible. The primary responsibility for policing Germany and its civil administration would be conferred upon Germany's continental neighbors in Western and Eastern Europe, who, as Morgenthau assumed, would take a much sterner line with the Germans under occupation than would the GIs. In addition to the immediate supreme punishment to be meted out to the top Nazi leadership, Morgenthau insisted on the permanent elimination of the industrial and economic elites, who had supported the aggressive war and the crimes against humanity.[8]

Morgenthau's partial success at the Quebec Conference in September 1944, which he attended together with the president, did not last. The objective of turning Germany into "a country primarily agricultural and pastoral in its character" mentioned in the conference's communiqué was soon dropped. As a matter of fact, it had never been explicitly mentioned in Treasury drafts. Suggestions about partitioning Germany, which at first were broached at the Teheran summit of the Big Three in December 1943, did not come up at Yalta in February 1945 or at Potsdam half a year later. Despite Morgenthau's personal friendship with Roosevelt, it was Henry Stimson, the secretary of war, whose attitude finally prevailed. The State Department, whose chief and his assistants had been upset by Morgenthau's meddling in their affairs and his accusations about the department's handling of rescue, were also victors in this battle. The department favored control of Germany's industry and not its destruction. Edward Stettinius, Welles's successor as undersecretary who replaced Cordell Hull in November 1944, was even more critical of Morgenthau than his ailing predecessor had been.

Stimson, the Republican upper-class Waspish corporation lawyer, dismissed Morgenthau's ideas as an expression of "Jewish vengeance." Having witnessed the dislocation of world and European economy as President Herbert Hoover's secretary of state in the early depression years, Stimson objected to the destruction of Germany's industrial capacity, which he regarded as most important for Europe's postwar recovery. This was basically the approach of the powerful "Eastern establishment" of industrialists, bankers, lawyers, and diplomats whose impact on American foreign policy was much larger than that of the liberal New Dealers and supporters of continuing coexistence with the Soviet Union, among them Morgenthau and his staff. Together with his influential assistant secretary John J. McCloy, Stimson favored as much autonomy as possible for the Army and the military government in the zone to be occupied by American troops but disapproved of Morgenthau's insistence on a permanent partition of Germany. Secretary of the Navy James Forrestal, an early advocate of military preparedness against Russia, shared the same view. Stimson and McCloy also rejected Morgenthau's proposal of immediately putting to death the top Nazi leadership, preferring to try them by an international tribunal.[9]

The secretary of the Treasury, for his part, did not concede defeat and, to a degree, influenced the formulation of JCS 1067, the War Department's punitive directive for the American military government. The directive provided that no steps were to be taken "leading toward the economic rehabilitation of Germany" or designed to maintain or strengthen the German economy. However, it left some room for modifications and improvement of the lot of the German population even before it was superseded in 1947. In this context, Morgenthau was suspicious of appointments of conservative officials regarded as soft on Germany to serve there. In his last talk with Roosevelt, Morgenthau complained about the choice of Robert Murphy as political adviser to the American military governor in Germany. Murphy, a conservative Catholic diplomat, had antagonized American Jewish groups because of his prevarications regarding Jewish rights as U.S. representative in French North Africa before and after its occupation by the Allies. He was known to favor the preservation of a united Germany.[10]

After Roosevelt's death and Truman's accession to the presidency, as well as the growing impact of Allied disunity and the impending Cold War, the demise of the Morgenthau plan became unavoidable. Truman endorsed the views of Morgenthau's opponents in the government and soon made him submit his resignation.[11] Because of deteriorating East-West relations, support for his concept gradually crumbled even in the liberal camp. However, the repercussions of Morgenthau's proposals would continue to affect postwar German attitudes to American and world Jewry.

Influential Jewish insiders in government or close to it were not at all of one mind with regard to Morgenthau's proposals on Germany; there were supporters and critics. Oscar Cox, of the Lend Lease administration and subsequently general counsel at the Foreign Economic Administration (FEA) and its deputy administrator, had been involved with Morgenthau and his staff in promoting the creation of a separate rescue agency in 1943–44. In response to Germany's murderous war, he demanded unequivocally the breakup of Germany's military and industrial power after victory.[12]

At first Morgenthau's ideas drew support from Bernard Baruch, the conservative financier whose views still carried some weight in public opinion. Baruch had no official position in Roosevelt's administration, and personally, he and Morgenthau did not like each other. Baruch, who had most of his public papers drafted by Sam Lubell, a political and economic analyst, shared Morgenthau's views on crushing Germany's industrial power and removing a part of its key plants to other nations. In June 1945 he aroused President Truman's wrath because, at an appearance before the Senate Committee on Military Affairs, he recommended a punitive German settlement when Morgenthau's proposals were already being shunted aside. Yet, in the early 1950s, after the international situation had substantially changed, Baruch resigned himself to accept West Germany as an ally,[13] whereas Morgenthau never changed his mind. Up to the end of his life he regarded Germany as "the single greatest threat to peace in Europe."[14] Similarly, Isador Lubin, a veteran New Dealer who served as assistant American representative on the Allied Reparations Commission in Moscow, in 1945 emotionally favored the "agriculturization" of Germany, as he confessed in an oral history interview thirty years later. However, he felt that one "could not impose such a system in Germany for very long."[15]

Others, like Felix Frankfurter, who had been appointed by Roosevelt in 1939 as a Supreme Court associate justice, privately supported Stimson's approach and encouraged him to oppose Morgenthau's "preposterous idea" of shooting the main Nazi leaders without trial. Unlike Morgenthau and Baruch, cautious Frankfurter preferred not to publicize his advice on what to do with defeated Germany after the war. In an exchange of letters with his old friend Benjamin V. Cohen in August 1945, he expressed his satisfaction that Germany was not being dismembered at the Potsdam summit. Besides, he wondered whether "a true trusteeship of the Rhineland and the Ruhr, for a Europe regarded as an economic organism of which Germany is a part," might not hold more promise for the world than a plan to turn Germany into a pastoral people. In 1946 Frankfurter complained that in the application of the Potsdam agreement Germany was treated as an organic whole and not as a part of Europe. Cohen, who attended the Potsdam conference as an adviser to the American delegation, regarded "the term dismemberment [of Germany] fraught with more emotion than wisdom." During his service with the State Department, he himself contributed his share to the Truman administration's postwar policy on Germany and Europe.[16]

One of the most outspoken opponents of the Morgenthau plan was James P. Warburg, a member of the renowned Jewish family, even though he himself often shunned his Jewish identity. At one point, in 1959, he was to condemn the "chauvinistic nationalism" created by Israel among American Jews and the United Jewish Appeal (UJA) serving Israel's goals. After the war had broken out in Europe, Warburg turned into an active interventionist, worked with both the Committee to Defend America by Aiding the Allies and the Fight for Freedom group, and became the target of intensely xenophobic antisemitic attacks. Nevertheless, when he was for a brief time involved at the Office of War Information in shaping

America's postsurrender plans for Germany, he strongly opposed the concept "of a peace based upon the vengeful application of retributive justice" and all suggestions for partitioning Germany. Having brought home the reality of military defeat to every German, he recommended giving them the chance to reeducate and rehabilitate themselves. After victory in Europe, Warburg soon parted ways with the Truman administration's postwar policies. He disapproved of the trend leading to the establishment of a West German state and to West German rearmament, and repeatedly spoke up in favor of a united neutralized Germany.[17]

Morgenthau's proposals regarding Germany had almost no backing in Congress. However, one of the most consistent supporters of his views was Senator Harley M. Kilgore, a Democratic New Dealer from West Virginia. Upon his return from Europe in 1945, Kilgore chaired the hearings of the Senate Military Preparedness Subcommittee aimed at preventing the German economy from again developing a war potential. Kilgore was to play an important role in the uphill struggle for denazification, decartelization, and control of German heavy industry. He was deeply disturbed by a possible revival of German nationalism. As long as he served on Capitol Hill, the senator was one of the main supporters of Israel, spoke up in the defense of postwar Jewish DPs, and fought the Protocols of the Elders of Zion and other antisemitic propaganda. Following President Truman's reelection, he was instrumental in bringing about the liberalization of the 1948 Displaced Persons Act, which enabled the admission of a larger number of Jewish DPs.[18]

After his departure from the Treasury, Morgenthau stuck to his position portraying Germany as a major threat to peace, contrary to those who hoped to rebuild it as a "bulwark against Bolshevism." In addition to his book, *Germany Is Our Problem*, which was published after he left office, he continued to publicize his views in magazine articles and in the daily press.[19] In the 1948 presidential campaign he abstained from endorsing President Truman's reelection; his rapprochement with the Democratic administration took place later.

In 1946 the former secretary, who was held in high esteem by the Jewish community, accepted the nomination as general chairman of the United Jewish Appeal (1947–50) and raised more money than ever before during these critical years. In 1950 he was appointed chairman of the Board of Governors of the State of Israel Bonds Organization. Morgenthau became an outspoken supporter of the Jewish state and paid several visits to Israel. At one time the former opponent of an East-West confrontation aroused the ire of the Israeli Left by calling for an anti-Communist regional pact to include Israel and the Arab nations. After returning from Israel, he told Secretary of State Dean Acheson that Israel "is definitely on our side in the present East-West conflict" and only refrained from taking a public pro-Western position because of immigration from Eastern Europe. Yet, after resigning from Israel Bonds' chairmanship in 1953, Morgenthau did not understand how Israel's minister of finance, Levi Eshkol, could suggest that he might be helpful to Israel on reparations from Germany, a country where he would never go in his life. Even a senior Israeli minister like Eshkol seemed not to have been aware of Morgenthau's role regarding Germany despite his "German extraction." At their meeting in New York, Morgenthau remarked that "the seeds Goebbels sowed about Roosevelt and [him] are still fresh in the minds of the Germans." He would offer his services to Israel by going anywhere in Europe and perhaps to any Arab country, a suggestion that Eshkol rebuffed.[20]

The change of the political climate and the postwar Red Scare soon brought about the purge—or resignation—of a number of Morgenthau's former close advisers and assistants. The most famous case was that of Harry Dexter White, regarded as Morgenthau's right-hand man. The brilliant economist had joined the Treasury after not having been able to get a teaching job at an elite university and was never involved in Jewish communal life. After the war he was accused of having been a Communist or at least a fellow traveler. He died in 1948 of a heart attack after he resigned from his post as director general of the International Monetary Fund, which he had helped to establish. Despite warnings from FBI director J. Edgar Hoover, Fred Vinson—Morgenthau's successor as secretary of the Treasury—had recommended him to that post. In 1946 White, who opposed the growing anti-Soviet trend, advised Secretary of Commerce and Industry Henry Wallace to withdraw from the administration before he was fired. During the last months before his death White was summoned to testify before the House Un-American Activities Committee (HUAC) in the case of former staff members who were accused of having been members of the Communist party.

In retrospect, Henry Morgenthau III thought that it was Harry Dexter White's anti-German passion that made him particularly attractive to his father, "blinding him to the more complex, sometimes contradictory facets of White's persona." But although the former secretary praised White's contribution in a letter of condolence to his widow after his death, Mrs. White was very bitter that Morgenthau had not spoken out in her husband's defense and did not attend the funeral in Boston. Morgenthau for his part "was never able to resolve the question of White's Communist affiliations" in his own mind.[21]

Bernard Bernstein, another Jewish former high Treasury official, served with the rank of lieutenant-colonel as General Eisenhower's financial adviser at first in Italy, then at SHAEF headquarters in London, and finally in Germany. He was never summoned before HUAC but chose to resign from his post with the military government as early as October 1945. In 1945, Bernstein, like Harry Dexter White of East European parentage, was the most important of the former Treasury people in occupied Germany and distinguished himself in presenting a detailed report on the black record of Germany's giant chemical corporation, IG Farben. Yet, after the reorganization of the military government, he was demoted from the Finance Branch to the Division for Investigation of Cartels and External Assets, with reduced responsibilities. General Lucius D. Clay, General Dwight D. Eisenhower's deputy and head of OMGUS (Office of Military Government for Germany, United States) in Berlin and from 1947 himself commander-in-chief, later recalled in his reminiscences that he never shared Bernstein's philosophy—he must have meant his Morgenthau-like anti-German stand—but did not regard him as being "as doctrinaire, maybe that's the right word, as a number of his associates." Upon Bernstein's return home he served for several years as legal adviser to the American Jewish Conference, and in this capacity he represented it at the Paris peace conference with Germany's allies in 1946. After belated insinuations by Republican Congressman George A. Dondero, both Secretary of War Robert Patterson and John McCloy, at that time president of the World Bank, reaffirmed Bernstein's loyalty.[22]

In the nascent Cold War and Red Scare atmosphere, anti-German liberal Jews were easily suspected by right-wing politicians of serving, directly or indirectly, the Communist cause. They would never forgive or understand that opposition to Hitler in the 1930s before the Ribbentrop-Molotov pact of August 1939 and after the

German invasion in June 1941 fostered sympathy among many American Jews for the Soviet Union, despite the blatant faults of the Communist dictatorship.

The Communist infiltration of the Treasury during Morgenthau's term of office and its probable impact on America's foreign relations was a matter of continuous accusations and revelations by the FBI, right-wing senators, and conservative anti-Communist historians. Communist party membership and pro-Communist activities of several staff members were substantiated, although most of Morgenthau's outspoken critics did not question his own loyalty. A right-wing-dominated special subcommittee of the Senate Judiciary Committee still busied itself with that subject as late as the mid-1960s.[23]

American Jewish organizations, while demanding severe punishment of German Nazi criminals responsible for the murder of millions of Jews, made no formal pronouncements regarding the Morgenthau proposals in 1944–45. At least emotionally, the secretary's ideas about Germany enjoyed much support on the part of the Jewish masses and different groups in the community, from pro-Soviet leftists to the Orthodox. They all had watched from afar the extermination of their coreligionists, without being able to help them. In the words of Ben Halpern, American Jews wanted "all the Germans, as individuals, to atone for the past acts of their rulers." Without discriminating between Nazi and anti-Nazi, "because all of them share some guilt, greater or less in degree, for the past decade," American Jews wished "them to feel responsible for permitting themselves to be ruled by criminals and for becoming accomplices in the slaughter of peoples and despoiling of nations."[24]

Zionist and pro-Zionist organizations, united under the roof of the American Jewish Conference, were perhaps the most sympathetic to Morgenthau because of his support for Zionist positions and requests, as well as for his involvement in rescue and in the WRB. However, neither the American Jewish Conference nor the WJC took a stand on his German plan. Some may have had doubts about the feasibility of his radical recommendations. Others must have taken into account the antisemitic overtones of the 1944 election campaign, during which Republicans pointed out that the Morgenthau plan could damage a quick victorious conclusion of the war in Europe and alluded to left-liberal Lithuanian-born CIO labor leader Sidney Hillman's strong influence with the Roosevelt administration.[25]

On the other hand, groups like the socialist leadership of the Jewish Labor Committee never subscribed to the collective guilt concept relating to all Germans and unequivocally disagreed with Morgenthau's deindustrialization program for both ideological and practical reasons. During the peak of the so-called Final Solution, the JLC reaffirmed that American labor sought no "mass reprisals against the enslaved people of Germany" but appealed to the American administration to warn the Germans "to refuse openly to be identified with the cruelties perpetrated by their leaders."[26] Socialist ideology and solidarity inspired that attitude of most of the JLC leaders, almost all of whom had been first-generation Americans of Eastern European origin.

The non-Zionist AJC, for its part, insisted on strict punishment of war criminals and those involved in crimes against the Jewish people, on denazification and controls by the military government. Yet, whereas different views were voiced among its staff members and its lay leadership in the early postwar years, in the words of Naomi Cohen, the AJC did not find it "feasible or desirable to create a slum country in the heart of Europe." Subsequently it preferred to try and work together with liberal forces in American society for a reformed democratic Germany.[27]

The non-Orthodox religious denominations, for their part, opposed vengeance for spiritual reasons. At the annual convention of the Central Conference of American Rabbis (CCAR) in June 1943, a leading Reform rabbi stated that "in the name of Judaism we could not cherish vengeance towards the misguided people of the world." He was sure "that Jewish spokesmen at the next Peace Conference will be the last ones to demand retribution and reprisals for the misled subjects of tyranny."[28] In a similar vein the Rabbinical Assembly of the Conservative rabbis warned in the summer of 1942 that "a military victory is not, by itself, adequate to secure peace. If we are to achieve peace, we must keep our victory clear of vindictiveness and national self-righteousness. We must understand that the responsibility for the catastrophe which has befallen mankind rests not exclusively on the shoulders of the Axis powers." The primary responsibility for the war rested on abuse of nations; thus a world federation of democratic nations was the alternative.[29] Even after the discovery of the Maidanek death factory by the Russian armies advancing beyond Lublin in August 1944, the editorialist of *Liberal Judaism*, the Reform monthly, commented that "among our emotions, complex and deep as they are, there is no raging, blazing desire for revenge."[30] Rabbi Abraham Cronbach, distinguished scholar at Cincinnati's Hebrew Union College (HUC), pacifist and universalist, and a member of the anti-Zionist ACJ, went even further than the mainstream Reform rabbis. In an exchange of letters with Stephen Wise and with an HUC student of his, Rabbi Eugene J. Lipman, who in 1945 served as a chaplain with the Fourth Armored Division in Germany, Cronbach pleaded for clemency for Nazi war criminals because of his basic opposition "to all wars and to all persecutions and all inflictions of man by man."[31]

In October 1944, historian Koppel S. Pinson, who had spent some time in Germany during the 1930s and was to serve there after the war as educational director for the Jewish DPs in Germany and Austria under the auspices of the JDC, published in the *Menorah Journal* a survey of opinions and proposals regarding the future of Germany. The survey did not deal particularly with Jewish views on that subject. A second essay dedicated to the Jewish position never appeared. Nonetheless, Pinson's comprehensive survey reflected the attitude and expectations of at least a part of moderate liberal elements in the American Jewish community.[32] Pinson rejected extreme anti-German views such as those advocated by groups like the Society for the Prevention of World War III or writers such as Louis Nizer and William Shirer, the noted radio commentator who published his *Berlin Diary* after he returned from the Nazi capital. At the same time, he rebuffed appeasers both from the Right and from the Left. Pinson did not favor the partition of Germany into three states as suggested by Sumner Welles, nor did he regard as feasible any attempt to reduce postwar Germany to a rural and agrarian economy (perhaps he had Morgenthau in mind, but did not mention his name): "German economy's industrial potential and efficiency are needed not merely for the welfare of the German people but also for the welfare of the other peoples of Europe. And the creation of a surplus population of unemployed millions in an agrarian Germany would hardly be helpful to the stability and peaceful security of the European continent." In the long run, the formation of a liberal and democratic Germany depended on its spiritual and intellectual regeneration. Whereas Americans could help in fashioning the mind of a future Germany by selection of politically reliable elements, educational and psychological transformations would have to be carried out by Germans and through Germans. The success of this program was a prerequisite for lasting peace in Europe. Pinson's analysis and recommendations already forecast some of the difficulties and failures of reeducation and denazification that started immediately after occupation and went through different stages.

Similar views were expressed in the AJC's *Contemporary Jewish Record*, the predecessor of *Commentary*, by emigré Princeton historian Erich Kahler, who rejected proposals to break up the national unity of Germany as a guarantee against German nationalism.[33] Instead he endorsed the demand for internal decentralization and organic reshaping of the German provinces. Germany should not be deprived of its industrial potential. Its heavy industry, however, should be nationalized, and a real solution should be linked with a Pan-European economic system. The German problem could only be solved by the creation of a strongly armed supranational organization that would assume the protection of human rights and the maintenance of cooperation, democracy, and social equality. A new Germany, with its old universal, humanitarian ideas, would find its place in such a framework, and this should be the main educational task of the Allies.

The *National Jewish Monthly*, the journal of B'nai B'rith, one of the key partners of the American Jewish Conference, expressed a much sterner attitude toward Hitlerite Germany.[34] Editor Edward E. Grusd opposed "a soft peace . . . [as] an insult to justice" and tried to justify that attitude by quoting from the *New York Herald Tribune*, then the most respectable right-of-center daily in the nation. While dismissing any racialist approach to German blood, he regarded the German people as responsible for the last ten years of murder, rape, theft, torture, and world war.

Most of the Yiddish dailies, which reflected the feelings of the Jewish immigrant masses, usually took a strong anti-German line. However, late in September 1944 one could also find rather skeptical comments regarding the Morgenthau plan, such as by Shlomo Grodzensky, an editor of the Labor Zionist Yiddish weekly, *Yiddisher Kempfer*. Unlike Pinson, he did not believe that after the military defeat of the German empire any group of Germans would be able to establish a really democratic government; he thought that the return to normalcy would take a long time. Nevertheless, he claimed, the victorious powers would have no other alternative than to proceed with Germany's economic reconstruction, and proposals to destroy German industry did not make sense at all.[35]

Hayim Greenberg, the editor in chief both of the *Yiddisher Kempfer* and the *Jewish Frontier*, the Labor Zionist English monthly, did not endorse the collective guilt concept. He could not believe "that the Germans are innately a people of murderers and that they must remain so unto eternity." But the fact of their showing no signs of the wish to be punished had "afflicted the world with a feeling of a dreadful, nightmarish mystery." According to that most prominent Labor Zionist essayist, there could "be only one proof of a general revulsion of feeling in Germany. . . . Let the world punish us."[36] Not surprisingly, no German followed his advice.

More than a year later, after the publication of Morgenthau's *Germany Is Our Problem*, his proposals regarding Germany were reviewed in the *Jewish Frontier* by Nehemiah Robinson, a leading WJC official and one of the founders of its Institute of Jewish Affairs. Robinson expressed doubts about the feasibility of the Ruhr region's deindustrialization and the removal of the German population from there. However, the committed Zionist still subscribed, as many others did under the impact of the Jewish Holocaust in Europe, to Morgenthau's basic thesis that no price was too high to get rid of the constant menace of German aggression and that the settlement of the German problem was the "key to the success of American plans for genuine security in the world."[37] Robinson, one of those most deeply involved in preparing the Jewish case for restitution and compensation, did not seem to have grasped the vital connection between future individual and collective German payments and Germany's economic and financial recovery that would not have been possible under the terms of Morgenthau's policies. But in any case, the plan that had never received an approval of the organized Jewish community had already been shelved. Successively, the community had to get used to the new political constellation that replaced the anti-Nazi grand alliance with a Western bloc which included a major part of Germany, even though for many Jews it was a difficult adjustment.

3

Safeguarding
the Survivors and
Refugees

On May 7, 1945, five years and eight months after the beginning of World War II, Germany unconditionally surrendered to the Allies, who promptly completed the occupation of its territory. The semisovereign Federal Republic of West Germany (FRG) was established four years later—soon to be followed by the Communist-dominated German Democratic Republic in the east. It would take six more years until the FRG regained full sovereignty as an equal member of NATO and the postwar Western alliance, even though the onset of the Cold War had started to affect American policy toward Germany much earlier. According to the Potsdam agreement, occupied Germany was to be ruled by an Allied Control Council and a central administration under its direction. But because of the contradictory interests of the victorious allies, the real power in the four zones of occupation remained in the hands of the occupying armies and the separate military governments.

The jurisdiction of the evolving German provincial authorities was at first very restricted. Therefore, until the end of the decade—and in some cases a few years later—the administration in Washington, the military government in the American zone, and afterwards, the U.S. High Commission there were the main institutions to which American Jews turned for support in dealing with German affairs. These concerns included the fate of the survivors

53

and refugees, the attitude of the U.S. Army and of the local population toward them, restitution of Jewish property, indemnification for the victims of persecution, and denazification and punishment of Nazi criminals responsible for the murder of a major part of European Jewry.

The popular quest for revenge notwithstanding, the most urgent American Jewish concern with regard to defeated Germany was to secure the safety and well-being of tens of thousands of concentration and slave labor camp survivors, as well as of the large number of refugees from Poland, the Soviet Union, and other Eastern European nations who crossed the borders of the American zone. Many were directed there by the underground Zionist Brichah in order to influence American and world public opinion and exert pressure on the British government to open the gates of Palestine. In 1946 the westward movement of refugees increased even more rapidly because of Polish antisemitism, which reached its peak in the Kielce pogrom of July 1946. Although thousands had joined the ranks of the illegal immigrants to Palestine, in 1947 more than 200,000 Jews were living in occupied Germany and Austria. The prolonged stay of a large number of Jews in the American-occupied part of Germany, however, and the lack of immigration havens for them caused serious problems for the Army, which wanted to get rid of such an anti-German element, especially because of the rapidly changing U.S. policy toward the recent enemy. Thus, that precarious situation became a helpful factor in the struggle for the creation of a Jewish state. The Yishuv in Palestine, American Jewry, and the DPs themselves joined in that fateful struggle.[1]

In spring 1945, Jewish survivors in concentration and slave labor camps heartily welcomed the American troops as liberators, in contrast to ambivalent feelings of the great majority of the German population even though they preferred occupation by the Americans and British to the Soviets.[2] For the American commander-in-chief, for officers and men, the catastrophic situation they encountered at the end of the war in the camps they liberated was most shocking. For a long time many Americans had not believed reports about the Nazi atrocities. Now the information proved true, although the camps freed by the Americans and British in the West differed from the extermination camps in the East, which were shut down or, as in the case of Auschwitz, evacuated before they fell into the hands of the Soviet army. Anticipating perhaps future attempts of "Holocaust denial," General Eisenhower paid a visit to Ohrdruf, a subsidiary camp of Buchenwald, "in order to be in position to give first hand evidence . . . if ever . . . there develops the tendency to charge these allegations merely as propaganda."[3]

Upon Eisenhower's suggestion, a delegation of high-ranking American publishers, editors, and journalists was brought over to Europe shortly before the end of the hostilities there. In addition, a congressional delegation was invited to visit occupied Germany. Similarly, visits of delegations from Great Britain took place. The American editors' unanimous conclusion was that the "German people cannot be allowed to escape their share of responsibility" and that "just punishment must be meted out to the outstanding party office holders, to all members of the Gestapo, all members of the SS." Still, as Deborah Lipstadt emphasized, neither the editors nor the members of Congress "were able to admit that though multitudes had been cruelly tortured and murdered, Jews alone had been singled out for total national annihilation."[4] As a result of the extensive news reports, opinion polls showed that a larger number of Americans now favored strict controls, full demilitarization, total elimination of the Nazis, and supervision of German industry.[5] This state of mind reaffirmed the Army's initially stern approach toward the defeated enemy, which called for full segregation between American officers and enlisted men and the German population; however, nonfraternization did not last. At a meeting with Morgenthau in August 1944, General Eisenhower agreed "that the German people should be made to feel a sense of responsibility for the war and that German welfare should take a backseat to the welfare of Germany's victors." The general also approved of free distribution of Henry Morgenthau's *Germany Is Our Problem* in 1945, despite the fact that neither Morgenthau nor his plan were popular with the Truman administration. Two years later, as his biographer Stephen Ambrose pointed out, Eisenhower had softened his attitude toward the Germans and no longer wanted to be connected with the Morgenthau plan.[6]

Contrary to Jewish fears, the attitude of the vanquished German population, except for a few incidents, did not present a physical threat to the survivors and refugees. Although strong antisemitic feelings persisted among many Germans who had remained loyal to the Nazi regime until the bitter end, the Germans submitted to American and other occupying forces without resistance. Thus the main problem posed for the American Jewish community was how to improve the lot of the large numbers of Jews who remained in Germany much longer than expected.

Of major significance for the status of the Jewish DPs in the American zone, and in the long run also for the U.S. involvement in the future of Palestine, was the Harrison report that was sent to President Truman in August 1945. The report was the result of an investigation of the DP situation conducted by Earl G. Harrison, the American representative on the ICR and Dean of the University of Pennsylvania Law school. Harrison was dispatched to Germany by Acting Secretary of State Joseph Grew, upon the urging of Henry Morgenthau, at that point still secretary of the Treasury.

Harrison, along with Dr. Joseph J. Schwartz of the JDC, Patrick Malin of the ICR, and Herbert Katzki of the WRB, who accompanied him, submitted two key proposals:

a) the separation of the Jewish DPs in special assembly centers to be guided by the JDC and the improvement of their living conditions (in fact, the separation had started before the publication of the report);

b) the admission of 100,000 Jews to Palestine. That recommendation in accordance with the Jewish Agency's demand was endorsed by President Truman and reappeared, despite its rejection by British Prime Minister Clement Attlee, in the report of the Anglo-American Committee of Inquiry in 1946.[7]

One of the consequences of the report was that it convinced the War Department and the Army to agree to the appointment of an adviser on Jewish affairs to the American commander-in-chief. For the next four years the persons in charge of this new office were to act both as mediators between the Army and the DPs and as liaisons with the American Jewish establishment. The administration's insistence that the candidates for that position should be acceptable to all the leading Jewish groups expedited the formation of the ad hoc group of the Five Cooperating Organizations, which paid most of the adviser's expenses. As in the past, the administration still objected to covering expenses for special Jewish interests by the American taxpayer. However, that added to the adviser's independent status.

Except for the first appointment of Major Judah Nadich, a chaplain since 1942, all the advisers were civilians with a respectable professional and public record. Judge Simon Hersh Rifkind, a member of the AJC, had served on the federal bench before going to Germany. Rabbi Philip S. Bernstein, a Rochester Reform rabbi, was involved in the WJC; later, in the 1960s, he became the first chairman of the American-Israel Public Affairs Committee (AIPAC). Judge Louis E. Levinthal was the most prominent Zionist among the advisers. The Philadelphia Circuit Court judge went to Frankfurt after he had held high office in the Zionist Organization of America (ZOA), including its presidency. His successor, William Haber, an Ann Arbor professor of economics and a member of AJC's executive committee, chaired the National Refugee Service, the main Jewish agency that dealt with refugees from Germany and Nazi-occupied Europe. The last adviser, Harry Greenstein, was the executive director of the Baltimore Jewish Welfare Fund. During their tour of duty the advisers were awarded the rank of brigadier general, and USFET (United States Forces, European Theater) commanders treated them with respect even when differences of opinion arose. The whole institution was unique for the American zone. Even though in April 1946 a Jewish adviser, Colonel Robert Solomon, was appointed by the British military, his functions did not compare to those of the American advisers. There was no similar setup in the French zone, not to mention the Soviet zone.

A most urgent task for the first advisers was to prevent the closing of the American zone to the ever growing number of new comers from Poland. Due to Jewish pressure in Washington and the advisers' intervention on the spot, the borders remained open in 1946. After General Lucius Clay succeeded General Joseph McNarney as USFET commander in 1947, he tried to enforce stronger measures against further infiltration of refugees. But most of the Jews fleeing Romania and Hungary still succeeded in entering the camps, although the number of newcomers declined significantly in comparison to the preceding year. The continuing migration conflicted with OMGUS's interest in reducing the number of DPs stranded on German territory. During Professor Haber's term of office in 1948, the birth of Israel and the subsequent exodus from the Jewish assembly centers eased tensions with the Army. Others benefited from the 1948 Displaced Persons Immigration

Act even though it discriminated heavily against Jews. In 1949 Harry Greenstein, who served under both General Clay and U.S. high commissioner John J. McCloy, handled the liquidation of most camps and also dedicated much of his time to restitution and indemnification problems. Major Abraham S. Hyman, who assisted all the advisers except Judge Rifkind, filled in as acting adviser during the last ten weeks of 1949.[8]

All the advisers were an important source of information for the American Jewish community about antisemitic occurrences among both the German population and the American forces. The search and seizure operations with the help of German police in Jewish assembly centers, which like all other camps were administered by the UNRRA, often caused tension between the DPs and the Army. After one Jewish DP was killed during an early search action in Stuttgart in March 1946, Judge Rifkind intervened, and General McNarney suspended the authority of German police to enter the DP camps. Nonetheless, raids by GIs continued and even intensified in 1948, when they especially aimed at big Jewish speculators, since black marketeering was a widespread phenomenon before the monetary reform of 1948. William Haber, the Jewish affairs adviser at that time, and Major Hyman, his assistant, were very much concerned about these Jewish black market activities because of their negative impact on both the Army's attitude and the morale of the DPs themselves.[9]

In 1947 the military government, which started transferring more responsibility to local and regional German authorities, was upset by prevailing strong anti-Jewish attitudes among the German population. According to public opinion polls taken in 1946 and 1947, over 61 percent of Germans were still deeply affected by antisemitism. Upon the request of General Clay, Rabbi Philip Bernstein presented a detailed plan to counter German anti-Jewish feelings. Before that he consulted with a visiting AJC delegation and met with a number of DP representatives, individual Germans, and indigenous Jews. The report indicated three main causes for the renascent antisemitism: the economic plight of the German population; its belief that American Jewry was shaping the occupation policy to avenge the murder of millions of fellow Jews; and finally, nostalgic feelings for the Nazi regime "under which they enjoyed gainful employment and the prospect of a dominant position in the world." Others considered the East European Jewish

DP "as a provocative element in the German scene." The DP representatives, for their part, were unanimous in their belief that "the reemergence of anti-Semitism in Germany is, to a considerable extent, conditioned by the interaction between the American troops and the German civilian population." They contrasted the sympathetic attitude of the American troops that had liberated them with the unfriendliness they often encountered among the occupation troops. For the Germans, it was just the opposite.

At one time, Rabbi Bernstein suggested a special education program "to immunize the American soldier against the views of German anti-Semitism," including visits to Jewish camps in order to reduce mutual tension, but as he himself acknowledged, the irritation remained.[10]

American officers, the majority of whom came from conservative small-town and rural America, sometimes suspected left-wing Zionist refugees of pro-Soviet sympathies. High-level intelligence estimates, however, found little evidence of large-scale pro-Soviet infiltration among the camp inhabitants who had fled Eastern Europe on their way to Palestine or the United States.[11] Intimate contacts between American soldiers and German women after the rapid breakdown of the nonfraternization rules also contributed to negative attitudes toward Jews. One of the strongest protests in this context was launched by Julius Klein, then a colonel and later to be awarded the rank of two-star general for serving with the Illinois National Guard. Klein, the national commander of the Jewish War Veterans (JWV) in 1948–49, afterwards became a strong supporter of Chancellor Konrad Adenauer and the Federal Republic and served as lobbyist for German industrial enterprises.[12] Even though antisemitism in the United States declined after the end of the war, American Jews were afraid lest happenings in occupied Germany might cause a backlash at home. Fortunately, these fears proved wrong.

Army chaplains had been the first to meet the "Saving Remnant" in Germany, and a few of them, such as the young Reform rabbi Abraham Klausner in Bavaria and the Orthodox rabbi Robert Marcus in Buchenwald, distinguished themselves helping the survivors after liberation.[13] Zionist activists from the camps took the initiative in conducting public activities and organizing the survivors, and they were soon assisted by Jewish soldiers from Palestine and by emissaries of the Jewish Agency in preparation for aliyah (immigration).[14] Since 1945, periodic visits were made by individuals and delegations of major American Jewish groups. The advisers chosen by the Five Cooperating Organizations usually performed well in their contacts with the Army and the military government. But although it took the JDC longer than expected to bring its staff into Germany, it subsequently played a focal role in the physical rehabilitation of the DPs and refugees until the camps were dismantled. Despite recurrent differences of opinion with the Central Committee of the Liberated Jews, the JDC helped in the rebuilding of the lives of both the camp inmates who left for Israel and the others who preferred to start a new life overseas. Yehuda Bauer, the author of a three-volume history of the JDC's activities from 1929 until 1949, observed that under the impact of postwar experience the JDC changed its course from an anti-Zionist or at most non-Zionist philanthropic organization into an unequivocally pro-Israeli one.[15]

Restitution and indemnification claims from vanquished Germany were perhaps not accorded the same urgency as the efforts in favor of the survivors and the DPs. However, American and other Jewish organizations wasted no time in reminding the victorious allies of the necessity to take up this issue. In October 1945 the American Jewish Conference, the WJC, and the Board of Deputies of British Jews endorsed the Jewish Agency's claim for reparation "due from the enemy states for the infinitude of murder, suffering and destruction which they had inflicted upon the Jewish people."[16] This endorsement followed a note to the Allied governments by Dr. Chaim Weizmann, president of the Jewish Agency and World Zionist Organization, demanding collective payments from Germany to cover the resettlement of Jewish refugees in Palestine, in addition to individual compensation and restitution of Jewish property.[17]

On the diplomatic scene the issue of reparations to Jewish victims was first discussed at the Interallied Conference on Reparations in Paris in December 1945. According to a suggestion by Isador Lubin, the American delegation proposed setting aside for them up to 2 percent of the resources available for reparations. That proposal was not accepted by the other governments; however, the claim of stateless and nonrepatriable victims of Nazism was recognized. Instead of a fixed percentage, the Allies agreed to pay a sum of $25 million derived from German assets in neutral countries and nonmonetary gold found in Germany, with an estimated value of $5 million. Ninety percent of these sums was reserved for Jewish refugees. That agreement established an important precedent, but the sums were insignificant, and the payment took much more time than expected.[18] Moreover, the Paris treaty was badly drafted, and its implementation led to confusion in the allocation of a part of the gold looted by the Germans.

In addition to their efforts for the survivors and refugees, the Five Cooperating Organizations played a significant role in securing the enforcement of the restitution law in the U.S. zone by the American military government. Internal restitution of property was explicitly included in JCS 1067, the directive to the American commander-in-chief that had been drafted with the participation of Morgenthau's Treasury. The appointment in 1946 of a special Internal Restitution Adviser at the OMGUS Legal Division facilitated the advancing of that process. Particularly important was the service in that capacity of Max Lowenthal, an influential liberal lawyer close to President Truman, who would soon be of great help in the struggle for America's recognition of Israel.[19]

Originally, OMGUS preferred that the law should be legislated by the Stuttgart *Länderrat*, the coordinating council of the *Länder* (provincial) governments. Yet, despite the goodwill of several German officials, these efforts foundered because of objections raised by others. Finally, General Clay enacted restitution as Military Law 59 in November 1947. That law also paved the way for a Jewish successor organization to take care of identifiable ownerless and heirless property. The first successor organization—the Jewish Restitution Successor Organization (JRSO) comprised of thirteen agencies—was set up in June 1948 and established its offices in Nuremberg. One of its affiliates, the Jewish Cultural Reconstruction agency, under the presidency of the renowned historian Salo Baron, was charged with locating and salvaging Jewish books, manuscripts, and cultural as well as religious objects looted by the Germans.[20]

Following OMGUS instructions, the German authorities proceeded in legal preparations for individual indemnification. Whereas JCS 1067 expressly dealt only with restitution, the new directive JCS 1779 that replaced it and was more attuned to the changing American attitude toward Germany nevertheless added indemnification as one of the aims of the military government.

Because of German differences of opinion and especially their objections to indemnifying a major part of the DPs, the drafting of the law took more time than expected. Besides, the British military government, as well as some OMGUS officials, thought it unwise to enact such a law only a few weeks after the approval of the new Federal Republic's Basic Law in May 1949 and before its first general elections. Nonetheless, upon the urging of the American Jewish organizations, General Clay's successor John McCloy, who had taken up his office in July 1949, overrode all objections and instructed the *Länderrat* to enact the General Claims Law in August 1949.[21]

To complete the picture, two more organizations became involved at an early date in restitution and indemnification claims. The Axis Victims League, established in 1943 in New York by Bruno Weil, a former leader of the assimilationist German Jewish Central Verein, aimed at satisfying the individual claims of its members, the great majority of whom were Jews. In 1944 Weil was involved in the creation of an additional organization, the American Association of Former European Jurists, which, too, dealt with compensation claims from their former homeland. Because of the nonsectarian self-definition of these groups, there was no basis for their joining the common Jewish effort, and after the establishment of the Claims Conference, even the Germans did not pay much attention to them.[22]

* * *

The policies of the American administration and of the military government, which controlled three *Länder* in the south of Germany as well as two northern enclaves, the city-state of Bremen and a part of the former capital Berlin, underwent far-reaching changes from 1945 until the establishment of the West German Federal Republic in 1949. These changes were brought about by the successive collapse of the Potsdam blueprint for a unified Four Power administration, by French obstruction, and particularly by the East-West antagonism and the impact of the Cold War on the domestic American scene.[23]

However, even during the early punitive stage of JCS 1067, when Germany was still regarded as an enemy, it soon became evident that the directive's immediate implementation depended on the regional and local commanders, who differed in their attitudes toward the vanquished Germans and also toward the Jewish remnants. Jews and American liberals were especially annoyed by the course of the Third Army's battle-proven General George S. Patton, who was in charge of Bavaria, where most of the surviving Jews had been liberated. Patton, of southern heritage and southern California upbringing, was a convinced antisemite. He regarded the Jewish DPs as "lower than animals" and predicted, according to an entry in his diary, that "should the German people ever rise from the state of utter degradation to which they now have been reduced, there will be the greatest pogrom of the Jews in the history of the world," as if the murder of the six million had not been enough. As Judd Teller once remarked, "not since Ulysses S. Grant's notorious order early in the Civil War, expelling Jewish traders from the areas under his command, had an American officer been guilty of such patent anti-Semitism."[24] But Grant was later to apologize for that order until the end of his life.

No wonder that Patton was slow in carrying out the orders to improve the living conditions of the Jewish survivors, as demanded by the Harrison report. In a letter to Secretary Stimson, Patton protested against the pro-Jewish clout in the military government. In his opinion, the early American postwar policies were the result of a conspiracy of international bankers, labor leaders, Jews, and Communists, whereas he regarded the Germans as potential allies against the adversary in the East. Because of Patton's failure to implement denazification, Eisenhower summoned him late in September to his headquarters in Frankfurt, but there was no meeting of the minds between them. Patton stuck to his view "that the Red Army was the real threat and the Germans the real friends." After their futile encounter, Eisenhower relieved Patton from the command of the Third Army and appointed General Lucian Truscott in his place.[25] The turnabout Patton hoped for took place only a few years later; he himself died in December 1945 as the result of an auto accident.

Upon the order of the military government, together with the removal of Patton, Bavaria's conservative provincial government that had been installed in May 1945 was dismissed because of its failure to implement denazification. Fritz Schäffer, until September 1945 Bavaria's prime minister and a leader of the Christian Social Union (CSU), was to emerge later as one of West Germany's most influential politicians. He served as Chancellor Konrad Adenauer's minister of finance (1949–57) and minister of justice (1957–61). In

Adenauer's cabinet he was the main opponent of the 1952 Lux-
embourg reparations treaty between West Germany and Israel.
Schäffer seems never to have forgotten his early trouble with the
American occupation authorities and continued to accuse the mili-
tary government officials who had been involved in his dismissal as
"Morgenthauites."[26]

Liberal and left-wing Jewish newsmen in New York were the
first to protest the happenings in Bavaria and to describe them
as the "American failure in Germany." Among them, the most
prominent was Victor Bernstein of *PM*, who afterwards, before
his appointment as managing editor of the *Nation*, was to serve as
the Jewish Agency's public relations director. In a way, their critical
reports contributed to Patton's removal but at the same time caused
virulent antisemitic reactions on the right.[27] The first round in the
struggle for Bavaria in 1945 was won by the liberals. However,
the portents pointed already in the opposite direction. The Jewish
community and its traditional liberal partners had soon to take
into account that because of the growing rift between the wartime
allies and the fear of further Soviet expansion, American policy
would move more rapidly toward Germany's economic recovery.
As a matter of fact, the shift toward a softer peace had started
before the East-West gap became unbridgeable. But that rift was
an additional reason for American policymakers to rely even more
on conservative anti-socialist political forces in German society and
to look for close cooperation with the qualified German administrative and economic elites, who, until May 1945, had been among
the mainstays of Hitler's Reich.

The change of direction of American policy was reflected in the
successive replacement of anti-Nazi military government officials
from a liberal New Deal background, who were determined to
proceed with Germany's social and economic reorganization, and
by the growing influence of conservative businesspeople there.
William H. Draper, head of the Economics Division of the military
government and one of General Lucius Clay's most influential
advisers, was a leading opponent of the Morgenthau plan and did
all in his power to get rid of its remainders.

During the Weimar Republic the former secretary-treasurer of
the New York investment bank Dillon and Read had traded shares
of German firms and cartels and promoted both investments and
loans to Germany, strengthening the links between American and

German industrial corporations. Other Wall Street investors did the same, supported by law firms that specialized in such transactions. Despite the growing alienation between Washington and Berlin and the differences concerning international trade after Hitler's rise to power, at least a part of these connections were preserved until the war and revived after its end. Upon the conclusion of his service at OMGUS, Draper was appointed undersecretary of the Army and continued to influence American policy in Germany from Washington.

It was no surprise that James Stewart Martin, a left-wing liberal who had served in the Economic Warfare Division of the Department of Justice and been appointed in the winter of 1945–46 as chief of OMGUS Decartelization Branch, was not more successful in advancing decartelization than his predecessors Bernard Bernstein and Russell Nixon, both former Treasury staff members. Martin argued that failure of decartelization was not attributable to the developing tension between the Soviet Union and the United States but mainly to common interests by powerful economic corporations in the United States and Germany.[28] After the factual freezing of decartelization by the military government, a partial deconcentration of German industries had to wait until the 1950s.

A major turning point of postwar American policy toward Germany was Secretary of State James F. Byrnes's Stuttgart address of September 1946. Byrnes's statement meant that despite continuing controls to prevent the revival of Germany's military potential, Germans would no longer be regarded as enemies. He also assured them that U.S. troops would stay in Germany as long as other troops would remain there.[29] Although Byrnes had not yet given up hope of reaching some kind of agreement with the Soviets, the American-British economic joint zone—the Bizonia—was soon established as the nucleus of the future Federal Republic. But even before the Truman administration had taken these steps, the Republican victory in the 1946 congressional elections, after the uninterrupted Democratic hegemony since FDR's accession to power in March 1933, substantially hastened the volte-face.

The most salient expression of the winds of change blowing in the direction of a "soft peace" were the findings of the President's Economic Mission to Germany and Austria under the chairmanship of Herbert Hoover, the last Republican tenant of the White House. In his report published in March 1947, Hoover called for increasing the production of Germany's heavy industry and stopping further dismantlement except some armament plants. He implied that attempts at decartelization and continuing denazification could harm recovery. Hoover's recommendations enjoyed the support of the Republican leadership in both houses of Congress and were publicly endorsed by a broad spectrum of political opinion. A few months later Secretary of State George Marshall, Byrnes's successor, launched the European Recovery Program (ERP). That plan, aimed at dovetailing German economic revival with a general European recovery program, was, in the eyes of Germany's hostile neighbors, preferable to Hoover's unilateral recommendations aimed at improving its lot.[30]

There were some protests and preventive activities of Jewish and other left-liberal and anti-Nazi groups against the pro-German campaign of the opponents of a "harsh peace" and subsequently against the changing American policy toward Germany, but they were rather ineffectual. Early in 1946 representatives of the American Jewish Conference, B'nai B'rith, and even the AJC attended a meeting of the Society for the Prevention of World War III, although that pro–Morgenthau plan society's impact was marginal. The Council of National Youth Organizations affiliated with the Conference followed suit. The Conference also joined a broad coalition of liberal and ethnic groups in endorsing an appeal of the Veterans of Foreign Wars of the United States urging the "quarantining" of the 300,000 soldiers in occupied Germany against fraternization, Nazi ideology, and alarming venereal disease rates. The participating organizations demanded that while policing would be carried out by the young draftees, the governing of the civilian German population should be delegated to mature men, preferably veterans with combat experience. The AJ Congress castigated "the shocking neglect of proper training and education in the principles and ideals of American democracy" in the armed forces in occupied territories. Bernard Bernstein, who, as legal adviser of the American Jewish Conference, represented it at the Paris Peace Conference with Germany's allies, warned Secretary of State James Byrnes after his Stuttgart address that the race with Russia "to make an ally of Germany is the greatest single stimulant for a third world war." The Zionist conflict with the Labor government in London made it easier for him to put a part of the blame for America's changing policy on Great Britain, which was "interested in Germany and German industry in order to solidify a West European bloc of nations."[31]

In March 1947 Henry Morgenthau, who had accepted the UJA general chairmanship, was involved in summoning, together with Eleanor Roosevelt and Edgar Ansel Mowrer, a national conference on the German problem that warned against Germany's revival as a power and the abandonment of the Yalta and Potsdam agreements of the "Big Three." Mowrer, in his *Germany Puts the Clock Back*, written in the early 1930s, described the failure of Weimar democracy and predicted the Nazi takeover and its horrendous implications for the Jews. The meeting, which was attended by Albert Einstein, Sumner Welles, Representative Helen Gahagan Douglas, Fiorello M. LaGuardia, and Erika Mann, Thomas Mann's daughter, called upon the administration to bar John Foster Dulles, the Republican party's main foreign affairs spokesman, from the American delegation to the four-power foreign ministers conference. As head of the prestigious New York law firm, Sullivan and Cromwell, Dulles had been involved in American-German business deals also after Hitler's ascent to power. The critics of the Truman administration's policies demanded that citizens of the United States and other nations who had economic and financial interests in Germany would be barred from all positions in the military government.[32]

AJC staff people, for their part, were privately much upset by former President Herbert Hoover's recommendations to lift controls over German industry. His proposals reminded them of the same "old heavy industry blindness" that brought about World War II.[33] Others were alerted because of the purge of liberal Jewish analysts and information officers, some of whom were suspected of political disloyalty. Earlier, in the first period after the war, hard-nosed Army officers had complained about the "tender-hearted appeal" to the German public by recent German immigrants serving in the military government.[34]

Lucius DuBignon Clay, scion to a southern political family who knew the Washington scene better than most of his fellow generals, was well aware of "the sensitivity of the American Jewish community toward the military government's policies in Germany," which he regarded as "an element of great significance." The problem weighed much less on his counterparts in the Allied Control Council. As head of the military government, Clay intended to make the

U.S. zone a going concern. As early as 1945 he used for that reason the leverage accorded to him in JCS directive 1067 and gradually improved the lot of the Germans under occupation. He reduced day-to-day American supervision and encouraged, as far as possible, German self-government. In 1947 Clay became disturbed by the renewed increase of antisemitism among the German population. Yet talking privately to William Haber, his adviser on Jewish affairs, who mentioned the persistent antisemitism in Germany, he once remarked "that the anti-Germanism among the Jews in Germany is far more bitter than the anti-Semitism among the Germans."[35] His prompt advice to Jewish leaders—which of course they would not follow, then or much later—was "to forget what happened."

Clay repeatedly met with Jewish spokesmen and delegations and was helpful on problems of the DPs and restitution. On political issues he was glad to draw support from prominent Jewish individuals like Bernard Baruch, whose anti-German views mellowed because of the Cold War and the fear of Soviet expansion, and who testified in Congress in favor of the Marshall Plan. In March 1948 Clay denied in a letter to Baruch that he had become "pro-German," an accusation that was made against him mainly because of his "short-range effort to restore the prostrate German economy in order to secure a stable Europe."[36] As he confided to James Warburg, he purposely had not learned German because he wanted "to keep the Krauts at a distance," nor did he have social contact with them.[37] Despite the change of U.S. policy in 1946–47, Clay continued reeducation programs, persisted in denazification proceedings until 1948, and confirmed the execution of more Nazi criminals. But after the final breakdown of East-West efforts to reach agreement about the future status of Germany, he came to regard West Germany as a bulwark against Communist aggression. Thanks to his resolute stand during the Berlin blockade of 1948, he earned much respect from the population of the former enemy.

Altogether, despite differences of opinion and temporary setbacks, the Army's and military government's balance sheet with regard to special American Jewish requests and the Jews assembled in the American zone was a positive one. That included the basic safety of the DPs in their temporary refuge, where they did not want to stay, and Jewish demands for restitution of identifiable property and indemnification of victims of Nazi persecution and their heirs. Whereas the DPs themselves often did not understand the American role and lacked guidance on friendly relations with the Army, organized Jewry appreciated its role. However, there was much less sympathy by American Jews for the rapid turn postwar U.S. policy toward occupied Germany was taking, which sometimes also affected the Army's prompt handling of the situation. In the short run, Jews were worried that the reversal might prevent an effective punishment of the political, military, and economic German elites who had been involved in a most murderous war and in the extermination of the major part of European Jewry. But in the long run, there, too, was the issue of Germany's future in the community of nations. For years to come the Jewish minority would not adjust easily to the policy endorsed by the majority of Americans, even though it would continue to make its point as an influential group in American public opinion.

4

Denazification and
the Major War Crimes Trials

Of the "four Ds"—denazification, democratization, demilitarization, and decartelization, often used to describe the main aims of
early postwar American policy in occupied Germany—denazification together with punishment of the Nazi criminals was the most
important German item on the agenda of American Jewish groups.
Because of the uniqueness of Hitler's war against the Jews, which
had started long before the United States entered World War
II, the American Jewish community attached more urgency and
importance than most other Americans to the severe punishment
of the murderers of their brethren and other victims in Europe. Also
paramount was the cleanup of Nazi party activists from all walks
of German life. After the victorious war, the U.S. government and
a great many Americans soon came to regard the German people
as a crucial factor in Western Europe as well as a potential ally in
the looming confrontation with the Soviet Union. Most American
Jews, for their part, saw Germany as the enemy much longer, and
as a nation that needed more corrective treatment.

However, even before the full impact of the rift between the
members of the wartime anti-Nazi alliance became evident and
before the competition for German favors started, the expectation
that denazification would provide a clean sweep did not materialize.
Eventually, denazification was sacrificed in the process of Western

integration and economic reconstruction, as were other social and structural reforms.

Plans for a large-scale denazification of Germany had been discussed in Washington and London during the last years of the war before the struggle for Europe had entered its ultimate phase. At the Yalta Conference, the Big Three agreed on fundamental denazification objectives such as to "wipe out the Nazi party, Nazi laws, organizations and institutions, and remove all Nazi and militarist influences from public office and from the cultural and economic life of the German people." After the end of the war in Europe, the Potsdam Agreement of August 1945 specified the directions according to which the Allied Control Council (representing the United States, Great Britain, France, and the Soviet Union) would proceed with the arrest and internment of Nazi leaders and influential supporters. All active members of the Nazi party were to be removed from office and positions of responsibility in important private enterprises.

In the American occupation zone alone, 13 million people older than eighteen were required to complete a detailed 130-item questionnaire in order to establish their status in defeated Germany. In a nation that counted approximately 12.5 million members of the National Socialist party and its subdivisions, such a compulsory registration was regarded as a vital condition for immediately relieving the functionaries and their collaborators from all important—and even less important—jobs in the public sector. Besides, the private sector was also affected. Even after Germany's unconditional surrender, these people were considered as a threat to the victors, and getting rid of them was deemed necessary for the personal security of the occupying forces. In the long run, however, the exclusion of the Nazi leaders and active members aimed at securing the democratic character of a reconstructed Germany, the founding or revival of democratic parties, trade unions, and employers' associations. The reasoning was that without establishing a stable German democracy it would be impossible to guarantee the safety of Germany's neighbors and other European states and lay the foundation for constructive economic and political cooperation.

The U.S. administration had been the leading force in the inter-Allied planning for denazification until Potsdam. The implementing of denazification in the American zone followed JCS 1067 and, in principle, had been agreed upon by all the major government departments involved in policy toward Germany. Yet, nuanced differences persisted among the Departments of War and State and Henry Morgenthau's Treasury. Whereas the first two saw denazification as a punitive measure linked with Germany's postwar reconstruction, Morgenthau and left-liberals close to his position hoped to reduce Germany's economic and political power once and for all, and to break up its traditional elites. Left-wing Jewish intellectuals of the Frankfurt School and other anti-Nazi prewar immigrants, who during the war served in the Office of Strategic Services (OSS), shared Morgenthau's opposition against the German economic elites but not his proposals to substantially weaken German industry. They also objected to proposals for the partition of Germany.[1]

Direct denazification handled by American military personnel in 1946 encountered immense technical, administrative, and political difficulties. Quite a number of officers opposed the extensive program; others did not show much interest in its implementation, the most conspicuous case being that of General Patton in Bavaria. Many Germans did not truthfully answer questions about their former involvement in the Nazi regime, nor did they admit to past incriminating activities, despite the threat of heavy penalties. Thus, the whole procedure was not effective. There was a severe shortage of American manpower, and many of those involved lacked a satisfactory knowledge of the German social and political scene. Because of these insurmountable obstacles, the military government conferred the task, early in 1946, upon the civilian German "tribunals" (*Spruchkammern*), which were established by the German *Länder* authorities in coordination with and under control of the OMGUS denazification policy board. These tribunals acted on the basis of the German Law for Liberation from National Socialism and Militarism, the provisions of which were, in part, dictated by American military government officials.

According to the "Law for Liberation," all Germans from the age of eighteen had to file a registration form in order to obtain food stamps or to get employment. Registrants suspected in past Nazi activities were summoned before a local tribunal consisting of representatives of the public who were without Nazi blemishes. The court-like institutions distinguished among five categories in dealing with their cases: major offenders, offenders, lesser offenders, fellow travelers, and noninvolved. The maximum penalty for

major offenders was up to ten years in prison or labor camp internment, loss of their property, and suspension of citizen rights. Lesser
offenders and fellow travelers could get off by paying penalties to
the foundation for compensation of Nazi victims.[2]

The main fault of the "tribunal" system was that it did not take
into account the very limits of the screening, because the great
majority of the German people had supported the Nazi regime
and remained loyal to it until its demise. The whole process soon
met strong objections from different parts of Germany society.
Non-Nazis and sometimes even anti-Nazi members of the tribunals were, in most cases, subjected to strong pressure from fellow
citizens to take a lenient attitude toward the offenders of various
categories. The Protestant and Catholic churches, which American
postwar planners regarded as vital factors for the reconstruction of
German society, were among the strongest and permanent critics of
denazification, as were the right-of-center and right-wing parties.
But denazification was also denounced by the Social Democrats
(SPD), who complained that instead of the real culprits being
targeted, it was mainly lesser evildoers who suffered punishment.[3]

In November 1946 General Clay still criticized the lack of
political will of the German authorities to punish Nazi offenders.
However, with the softening of the American attitude, denazification became successively a process of whitewash and rehabilitation.
Eventually, from among 3.4 million charged in the U.S. zone before
the tribunals, nearly 2.5 million were amnestied without trial, and
three out of ten brought to justice were also amnestied. Only 1,600
persons were classified as major offenders and 22,000 as offenders,
106,000 as lesser offenders and close to half a million as Nazi
fellow travelers; less than 150,000 were declared ineligible to hold
public office and temporarily confined to restricted employment.[4]
Many trials of major offenders were postponed until later when
the political atmosphere had changed because of the Cold War,
which helped them to escape severe punishment. Because a great
part of the German elites had been members of the Nazi party,
pressure was exerted to amnesty them and allow their return to
leading positions in the administration and economy. In 1948 more
than 40 percent of high government officials in Bavaria and the
American part of Baden-Württemberg were former Nazi party
members. Whereas the British and French occupiers followed the
American denazification practice of setting up German tribunals,

they had from the beginning taken a more liberal stand toward former Nazis, the British because of administrative needs and the French because they did not distinguish too much between Nazis and Germans. The radical uprooting of the elites in the Soviet zone was another matter. As Elmer Plischke put it, there denazification played a subordinate role to the destruction of capitalism.[5]

With the establishment of the Federal Republic in 1949, the Americans ceded all control over the remaining denazification cases to the Germans, and with a few exceptions, proceedings were discontinued in 1951. Eventually denazification would end in 1955. Although Adenauer expressly criticized the "injustices" caused by denazification at the presentation of his government's program to the Bundestag in September 1949, the majority of the CDU-led coalition and the Social Democratic opposition still prevented a total repeal of the results of denazification. Instead of a general amnesty favored by the right-wing parties, an amnesty of 800,000 persons was passed by the West German parliament. After 1951, the settlement of the legal status of persons referred to in paragraph 131 of the Federal Republic's Basic Law provided for the return of tens of thousands who had until then been disbarred from jobs in governmental offices.[6]

For a number of years, denazification and its shortcomings were continuously discussed in the Jewish press and in public statements by the American Jewish Conference, the WJC and AJ Congress, the Jewish War Veterans, as well as by Jewish-inspired nonsectarian groups. Although its tone was traditionally more subdued, the AJC also voiced its constant concern about the failures of denazification (see chapters 5 and 6).[7] Protests were submitted by the Jewish organizations to both the executive and legislative branches of government. Sometimes they fulfilled a counterbalancing function against pressure for an immediate halt to denazification from conservative anti-Communist legislators as well as from high government officials in Washington. While these Jewish protests could not put the clock back, they may have been a factor in preventing the administration from scuttling denazification earlier than June 1949. Moreover, at least partly because of Jewish sensitivity, denazification in the American zone until 1948 was relatively the most comprehensive among the western zones. Despite all its shortcomings, denazification still fulfilled a positive function in preventing any substantial Nazi or neo-Nazi revival; and although there was much personal continuity of German elites before and after 1945, there was no continuity of their commitment to Nazi ideology or activity.

Whether the lenient attitude toward millions of Germans who had been active and supportive members of Hitler's party had beneficial or dismal effects on the political and social development of postwar Germany has remained a matter of continuous controversy in German historiography and in German politics. On the one hand, some believe that only a conciliatory approach toward the former Nazis started by the Western allies and pursued even more conspicuously by Adenauer's conservative coalition governments in the 1950s could further a prompt social and economic reconstruction and the gradual growth of democracy in the Federal Republic. On the other hand, critics insist that the faults of denazification and the forgiving attitude of the West German establishment toward Nazi and war criminals were responsible for evading a meaningful confrontation of the German people with their recent past, with all the negative implications for the future.[8] While one has to recognize the rather successful outcome of Adenauer's policies for West Germany's rapid economic recovery and their contribution to the development of its stable postwar parliamentary system, at least from the moral viewpoint of Jewish-German relations an alternative course might have been preferable.

Quite apart from denazification, the handling of the main Nazi war criminals remained in the hands of the Americans and the other allies. The Four Power International Military Tribunal (IMT) that convened in October 1945 and concluded its deliberations in August 1946, not only passed judgment on the twenty-one defendants, twelve of whom were condemned to death, but also convicted collectively three of the indicted criminal groups—the Nazi leadership, the SS, and the Gestapo. Individual members of the cabinet, of the Wehrmacht's High Command and the SA (Sturmabteilung, Storm Troopers), remained subject to trial by the national, military, and occupation courts of the Allied powers. The Truman administration conducted twelve additional war crimes trials at American military tribunals in Nuremberg before which were arraigned 185 defendants from the German High Command, the government, industry, SS, Gestapo, and others. In addition, the U.S. Army prosecuted 1,672 German individuals for violations of the laws of war in military courts. Similar trials took place in the other occupation zones, as well as in countries liberated from the German yoke.

The "Nazi conspiracy of waging an aggressive war" approach on which the IMT proceedings were based did not provide for a really deep insight into all the aspects of the Nazi regime and its ideology, and especially not into the central role that it gave the extermination of European Jewry. The term *genocide*, coined by Raphael Lemkin during the war as a legal definition of Nazi crimes against the Jewish people, appeared only once in IMT's record. The crime against the collective right of the Jewish people to existence would become the central issue only at Adolf Eichmann's trial in Jerusalem fifteen years later.[9] It took even longer until Western and at least a part of German public opinion became fully conscious of the active role played by the German army itself, in addition to the SS, its security service, and a variety of units of the German police under the command of Heinrich Himmler, the SS chief.[10] Nevertheless, despite reservations with regard to certain legal points and despite the fact that Jewish *amici curiae* (Friends of the Court) were not admitted, the court proceedings and the sentences pronounced upon some of the main Nazi criminals revealed at least a part of the magnitude of the Jewish tragedy. In general, the judgment served as a landmark in the history of international law and a warning against premeditated aggression and warfare, though its lessons have not always been heeded.

In contrast to anti-Communist right-wingers and German Americans who could not overcome their hostility to the Roosevelt legacy, including the setting up of the IMT, the Jewish response to the international tribunal's deliberations and judgment was, of course, positive. From the legal viewpoint, Jewish dissenters such as Milton Konvitz, then a promising young judicial expert, rejected the use of ex post facto law and the principle of guilt by association because it might undermine the traditional legal structure.[11] The editorial writer of *Hadassah Newsletter*, representing the large Zionist women's organization, was disappointed by the acquittal of Franz von Papen and Hjalmar Schacht, who had served Hitler's criminal government in various capacities.[12] However, deeper analyses such as by Jacob Robinson, the noted expert in international law, sounded more satisfactory. For Robinson, the founding director of the Institute of Jewish Affairs, the important *novum* was that for the first time in Jewish history, judgment upon the evildoers who had perpetrated crimes against the Jewish people was pronounced by court.[13] Anatole Goldstein, an IJA analyst, commented in *Congress Weekly* that "the Nuremberg trial, with its faithful and dispassionate description of the unlimited sufferings of the Jewish people and the depth of German cruelty, will remain an eternal epitaph on the unknown graves of the six million Jewish victims."[14]

All those who were actively engaged in crimes against humanity were sentenced to death, regardless of whether they participated in other criminal activities. The AJ Congress was very proud of the fact that after the trial, Supreme Court Associate Justice Robert Jackson, who had served as American chief prosecutor at Nuremberg, paid tribute to the IJA for its "prodigious labor and careful research in compiling important evidence." A delegation of the AJ Congress and WJC had met the justice after his appointment to the IMT and discussed in detail the Jewish case.[15]

Some of the first books on the Nuremberg trial were authored by Jewish writers. While Peter de Mendelssohn submitted a rather academic presentation, Victor Bernstein added to his summary of the Nazi crimes and the analysis of their social and political background a critical appraisal of American and British policies in regard to Germany. He included a reminder that some European Jews under Hitler's rule might have been saved if the rest of the world had opened its doors in time. Because of Bernstein's left-wing proclivities and criticism of the Western powers, the AJC preferred not to become identified to any extent with his views by helping the distribution of the book.[16]

As for the German population, the deliberations at Nuremberg failed to obtain the educational and atoning effect that the Allies and especially the Americans hoped to achieve. Despite the extensive coverage and analyses by leading journalists of the new democratic press and radio commentators, there was a big gap between publicized and public opinion. Most Germans remained indifferent if not hostile to the message of Nuremberg, rejected it as an accusation of collective guilt (which it was not) and refused to accept any responsibility for the happenings during the Nazi regime. Only Jewish publications, among them *Der Weg*, which appeared in Berlin, dealt in depth with the Jewish dimension of the trial.[17]

The persecution and extermination of millions of Jews became an important theme in several of the subsequent trials of Nazi criminals and dignitaries before the American tribunals in Nuremberg;

others had a Jewish angle because Jews involved in the prosecution were sharply criticized by conservative judges and politicians at home. Jewish circles were satisfied with the stiff sentences passed in the Einsatzgruppen case, which primarily related to persecution of Jews. Benjamin Ferencz, a young Jewish lawyer who started his career as a war crimes investigator and would soon become executive director of JRSO, was involved in the prosecution of that case. Robert M. W. Kempner, a German Jewish immigrant who later returned to Germany and took up law practice there, assisted Telford Taylor, the chief of counsel for war crimes, in preparing the trial of State Secretary Ernst von Weizsäcker and other high officials of the German Foreign Office. Josiah DuBois, a gentile liberal, had gained much experience during his service at the Treasury on the interaction between American and German corporations and particularly on the role of the huge IG Farben cartel. Thus he was regarded as the most suitable choice for the prosecution of that company's directors and was aided by a group of capable young lawyers, mainly Jews. In Washington Colonel David (Mickey) Marcus, who in 1948 would tragically lose his life in Israel's War of Independence, served in 1946–47 as head of the War Department's War Crimes Branch and was of help. Opponents of these trials often alluded to the strong Jewish presence in the prosecution.[18] On the other hand, the office of the chief of counsel for war crimes found it impossible to schedule a trial dedicated exclusively to crimes committed against Jews, since these had been dealt with in the trials of the Einsatzgruppen and the German Foreign Office.[19]

The Republican victory in the 1946 congressional elections, the deterioration of American-Soviet relations, and the domestic Red Scare—all these cut into the support that the war crimes trials at first enjoyed from the American public. The change in the political climate affected most of the cases dealt with by the Nuremberg tribunals as well as the Army courts. Relatively mild sentences were passed against German industrialists (such as the heads of IG Farben) and high government officials, who were freed after short prison terms. George Kennan, a renowned diplomat who in 1947 had published his famous article on containment in *Foreign Affairs*, was unhappy about the trial of Weizsäcker, whom he had known from his service in Berlin, and called upon McCloy to pardon and release him. In the same vein the noted theologian Reinhold

Niebuhr, a steadfast believer in a "soft peace" with defeated Germany, appealed to McCloy. In contrast to Kennan, Niebuhr was known as a supporter of American Jews in their striving for rescue during the Holocaust and as a co-chairman of the pro-Zionist Christian Council on Palestine since 1942.[20] In the early period of occupation, death sentences passed by military courts were immediately implemented. However, from 1947 on, the review of verdicts of these courts became a continuing challenge for conservative anti-Communist legislators, especially from states with a large German American population.

Critics of Army procedures received strong support from Iowa judge Charles Wennerstrum, who, in an interview in the *Chicago Tribune*, launched an attack against the "vindictiveness of American prosecutors," which mainly meant Jews. The judge had just completed the trial of eleven Germans accused of ordering and executing innocent civilians throughout Europe as reprisals for the shooting or kidnapping of German officers. Post-1933 German Jewish immigrants to the United States, such as Manfred George, the editor of the New York *Aufbau*, were upset by accusations against Robert Kempner in the Swiss weekly *Weltwoche*, which during the war years had taken an anti-Nazi stand. A leading columnist there implied that the "Kempners of Nuremberg" were of the same political ilk as the former secretary of the Treasury Henry Morgenthau and left-wing Czech Social Democrat Zdenek Fierlinger, who in 1948 helped to bring about the Communist takeover in Czechoslovakia.[21]

A particularly long legal struggle took place following the Malmedy Trial before an Army court in 1946, at which all seventy-two arraigned SS soldiers were found guilty of participating in the murder of American POWs. An American lawyer who had been assigned to defend some of the main SS defendants accused War Crimes Group investigators—Jewish refugees who "did not understand the traditional protection afforded to the defense in an American trial"—of exerting illegitimate pressure on the SS POWs. After recurrent appeals for reprieve and delays of execution of those condemned to death, the issue became entangled in internal American politics. Senator Joseph McCarthy, the Republican junior senator from Wisconsin, a state with a large German American population, repeated the accusations against the foreign-born investigators. He argued that they committed "brutalities greater than we have ever accused either the Russians or Hitler's Germany of employing," as a part of his smear campaign against the Democratic administration that invented the war crimes program under Roosevelt.[22] However, the administration in Washington also had second thoughts about the way the program was being implemented. In 1948 Secretary of the Army Kenneth Royall, one of its main critics, dispatched an independent review commission, which recommended the commutation of a number of death sentences. Thereupon, Royall ordered a temporary halt to all executions.

Jewish organizations, for their part, protested General Clay's decision to commute the sentence of Ilse Koch, the wife of the infamous Buchenwald concentration camp commandant, from life to four years' imprisonment. (She was later rearraigned before a German court and again given a life sentence.) For them, it was a step in the wrong direction. In retrospect, Clay justified his decision because Ilse Koch's "crimes were primarily against the German people. They were not war crimes against American prisoners or Allied prisoners." Clay reviewed all the sentences passed by the military courts at Dachau, which handled the defendants more roughly than the Nuremberg tribunals. He set aside 69 convictions, commuted 119 death sentences, and reduced 138 other sentences; however, from October 1948 until the beginning of February 1949, 104 convicted criminals were executed at Landsberg prison. As military governor, he still tried to distinguish between the development of a new democratic West German state that he favored and the punishment of the worst perpetrators of Nazi crimes.[23]

By July 1949, when John McCloy replaced Clay, the United States had tried almost 1,900 Germans for war crimes, imprisoned more than 700, and executed 277. Subsequently, the deteriorating East-West relationship and the establishment of the West German republic caused a definite change, and as the result of a wide-ranging clemency act of the high commissioner, most sentences against the surviving and condemned Nazi criminals were commuted. At that time, as a recent critic of the American war crimes program observed, the "punishment of war criminals, which had been a part of almost every American proposal with regard to the treatment of postwar Germany, ceased to be a priority and became instead a political burden."[24] The Jewish community was disappointed by the reversal. It could not, however, impede the basic change of direction of Washington's policy toward Germany, which was dictated by much more powerful political, economic, and military interests.

Pressure against the sentences passed at Nuremberg as well as against those pronounced by Army courts had built up since the late 1940s, both in the United States and in West Germany. Except for the Communists and a few Social Democrats, all West German political parties, as well as leaders of the Catholic and Protestant churches, had joined the campaign against the sentences. Generals Adolf Heusinger and Hans Speidel, who a few years later were given a leading role in the new Bundeswehr, warned that, if the Landsberg prisoners were hanged, Germany could not be regarded as an armed ally against the East. Despite some objections, Social Democratic members of the Bundestag, among them the Jewish deputy Jakob Altmaier, had joined a delegation to McCloy to urge upon him the abrogation of the last death sentences but were rebuffed.[25] In Washington, recurrent appeals for a reprieve were rejected by the president.[26] Truman still distinguished between the moral duty not to spare the life of the murderers and the need to further political links with West Germany, even though he hesitated for some time over whether the moment for German rearmament had already come.

The high commissioner, for his part, confirmed 5 death sentences out of a total of 15, for commanders of the notorious SS-Einsatzgruppen, who had killed tens of thousands of Jews in Eastern Europe. Together with two defendants sentenced to death by Army courts, they were executed in Landsberg in June 1951, the last executions in West Germany, which had abolished the death penalty. At the same time, McCloy reduced the sentences of 79 Landsberg inmates, allowing for the immediate release of 32 of the prisoners sentenced by American military tribunals in Nuremberg after 1947. Others convicted by American military courts were reprieved by USFET commander General Thomas Handy. No doubt McCloy's far-reaching clemency was motivated by his efforts to strengthen the links with the Federal Republic. The Korean War, which had started in June 1950 and intensified backstage discussions about German participation in Western defense, added even more urgency to that matter.[27]

McCloy's act of clemency aroused strong criticism in all American Jewish organizations. Jewish leaders, including Jacob Blaustein, protested to Secretary of State Dean Acheson, and an NCRAC delegation met with State Department officials and warned that the clemency granted to some of the worst Nazi criminals might weaken the morale of democratic elements in Germany. But their complaints were of no avail.[28] McCloy was encouraged by messages of support from such old acquaintances as Bernard Baruch, even though the veteran financier was not sure whether he "would have been so forgiving in some of the cases."[29] On the other hand, the high commissioner was upset by the ongoing agitation of parts of the German public in favor of the Landsberg prisoners, at a time when many Europeans and Americans regarded his leniency as unjustified and bordering on appeasement. As Thomas Alan Schwartz, the biographer of John McCloy as high commissioner in Germany, put it, the reactions underscored the still prevailing "political difficulties of accepting Germany within the West and the moral compromises and political expediency that were necessary to do so."[30] As for West Germany, McCloy's clemency and the subsequent freeing of the remaining Nazi criminals by the Americans and other Western powers served for a number of years as an excuse for the German prosecution not to arraign Nazi evildoers. A gradual change in confronting the murderous past of many who were regarded as "ordinary citizens" began only in the late 1950s.[31]

PART II

GETTING
INVOLVED
OR
STAYING ALOOF

5

Advocates of Moderation

In general, there was much similarity in the demands of the various major American Jewish organizations: strict punishment of Nazi criminals and officials involved in the persecution of the Jews since 1933; far-reaching denazification, demilitarization, and democratization of Germany and its society; as well as restitution of Jewish property, compensation for the victims, and definite eradication of antisemitism. However, major differences of opinion and emphasis with regard to the Jewish position on postwar Germany were soon to emerge. After all that had happened, should American Jews insist on a punitive policy against the nation that exterminated millions of their brethren in Europe, avoid contact with Germans, and not care too much about their future democracy? Or should they try and take an active role in U.S. efforts to shape another kind of Germany and thus prevent any revival of German threats to the world and to the Jewish people? Contradictory responses to that question caused substantial disagreements in the community for a number of years.

Because of both particular Jewish and general American interests, the prestigious AJC favored an active Jewish involvement in promoting liberal democratic trends in Germany and trying to change its authoritarian political culture. At the end of the war the Committee, originally a small elitist organization, started to gradually broaden its ranks and its appeal to the changing Jewish community by presenting cultural and educational challenges, in addition to its traditional defense activities at home and abroad. Its assumption was that the democratic reeducation of the German people was a basic precondition for fighting antisemitism, which had not disappeared, despite the total defeat of the Nazi state. Renewed antisemitism in Germany would not only endanger the well-being of the surviving Jews and refugees inside and outside the DP camps, but might also have negative repercussions among the soldiers stationed in the U.S. occupation zone and, through them, on the domestic American scene. At the same time, reshaping Germany's political culture was regarded as an essential guarantee for preventing a renewal of the German danger after two bloody global wars in which the United States had become enmeshed. However, another question soon arose: how could these aims be achieved at a time when the Cold War put an end to the wartime anti-Nazi alliance and abruptly changed the international scene?

In the opinion of the AJC, this new development provided an additional important reason for an active and positive Jewish participation in the administration's policy toward Germany. The western part of Germany, which even before the conflict with the Soviets was regarded as a vital asset for the economic reconstruction of Western Europe, soon became a potential ally of the United States and the other Western powers in containing the Communist bloc. Therefore, Jews as American citizens were well advised to insist upon the denazification and democratization of the German people and the strengthening of constructive liberal forces as the only reliable partners in rebuilding a healthy Germany in a Western European framework. Any organized opposition of American Jews against the new foreign policy and strategic approach could isolate them in the eyes of the non-Jewish majority and endanger their postwar achievements on the domestic scene. In this context, the AJC also found it necessary to take issue with Communist attempts to use Jewish anti-German sentiments against Washington's new course, yet that anti-Communist campaign became very controversial and raised strong objections from the liberal forces in the community.[1]

The AJC's emphasis on reeducation and changing Germany's political culture fitted, in a way, its traditional approach to fighting antisemitism and discrimination at home. It was also reinforced by the advice and knowledge of a number of emigré German Jewish social and political scientists, who had come to the United States after Hitler's ascent to power, even though they did not always see eye to eye with the Committee's own professionals. The AJC's wartime association with Professor Max Horkheimer's Institute of Social Research, which had been established in Frankfurt in the last years of the Weimar Republic, enabled the social scientists to conduct a comprehensive interdisciplinary analysis of antisemitism that was summarized in the five-volume series of *Studies in Prejudice*. Theodor Adorno, together with others, authored *The Authoritarian Personality*, the most important of the series.[2] There was a major gap between AJC's basic liberal philosophy and most of the Institute scholars' Marxist approach, even though they aimed to overcome the crisis of Marxist theory with the help of empiric social sciences. However, despite the shortcomings of their sociological and historical attempts to explain the antisemitism of Nazi Germany, their lack of familiarity with American society, and Horkheimer's own pre-Holocaust aloofness from Judaism and Jewishness, the partnership in a way added to AJC's academic standing. It helped its understanding of the social and political forces on the German scene, besides the social scientists' contribution to the Committee's work in education of the public at home. Horkheimer himself served for several years as chief research consultant of the AJC, and in 1944 established its new scientific research department. He continued his connection with the Committee after he and Adorno had returned to Frankfurt, where they rebuilt the Institute of Social Research.[3] Their "Critical Theory," which for many years had a rather limited appeal in the United States, was to play a focal role in the antiauthoritarian upheaval in West Germany in the 1960s.[4]

In the first period of occupation, Arkadi R. L. Gurland, one of the emigré social scientists working for the AJC, submitted a position paper on the fight against antisemitism within the framework of Germany's education for democracy. "If nothing is done to eradicate anti-Semitism during the initial stage of Germany's readjustment to postwar conditions," he warned, "suppression of anti-Semitism under rule of Military Government and its possible resurgence at a time when Germany will be getting on her own feet, will engender a menacing interpretation. Absence of anti-Semitism would stand for ruin, disintegration and chaos; resurgence of anti-Semitism would be synonymous with health, vigor and orderly organization of social life." Without answering the question whether Jews from Germany should again "strike roots amidst the wreckage," the analyst regarded the survival of antisemitism as dangerous to the whole of Europe, not only to Germany.[5] A few years later the same analyst concluded that Germany's main problem was not antisemitism but rather the combination of economic and political conservatism and the entrenched bureaucracy. That view was also endorsed by Franz Neumann, the noted politologist and author of *Behemoth*, who read the memorandum. Neumann, who stayed in the United States until his untimely death in 1954, was known as a strong critic of West Germany's postwar political development. After West Germany's first general elections in 1949, Gurland was critical of Adenauer's victory and of the federalist Basic Law and expressed his sympathy for the Social Democrats and the trade unions.[6]

The inadequacies of the military government's reeducation program soon became evident, and surveys taken by the Information Control Division showed that Germans felt no sense of guilt about having started the war and were inclined to minimize the record of Nazi atrocities. At the same time antisemitism was on the rise again. In 1947 the AJC dispatched several of its leading professionals to discuss corrective steps with OMGUS and also with Jewish and German representatives. In a confidential report, they argued that in spite of denazification, Germans were "still by and large Nazis and that with only minor exceptions they remained as anti-Semitic as they were during the Hitler regime." The change of American policy, which "revealed a disturbing willingness to overlook antidemocratic attitudes on the part of those who are anti-Russian," added, in the opinion of the AJC, even more urgency to revising OMGUS political education practices. Among others, the AJC proposed that the War Department in Washington, which was in charge of the American zone, establish an advisory council on German democracy that would provide information and guidance by American nongovernmental organizations to similar groups in Germany.

Following these contacts, the AJC executive committee pledged full support of a government-sponsored program of German reeducation.[7] One of the results of this renewed emphasis was the visit to Germany by Rev. Everett Clinchy of the National Conference of Christians and Jews (NCCJ) and the subsequent setting up of a number of chapters of Christian-Jewish cooperation. The AJC itself became involved in cooperation with the Lessing Association, a group of liberal-minded Germans dedicated to fighting intolerance and named after the eighteenth-century humanist and playwright Gotthold Ephraim Lessing. Despite endorsement and subsidies from the Frankfurt municipality and a few others, that experiment did not last.[8] However, during the following period a number of American organizations became continuously involved in activities promoting German democratic reorientation. These comprised the American Council on Education, the trade union federations, the churches, the League of Women Voters, as well as the Rockefeller and Ford Foundations. They persisted in their efforts despite the East-West confrontation and its repercussions.

In preparation for the German peace treaty, which was to be discussed at the Moscow conference of the four foreign ministers in April 1947, AJC leaders reiterated that the treaty must establish two basic concepts: "First, German guilt for the unprecedented suffering inflicted upon the Jews from the moment Hitler came to power; second, affirmation of those human rights and fundamental freedoms and guarantees for their maintenance, which would make a resurgence of the Nazi tyranny impossible."[9] The first point, in fact, came close to endorsing the concept of collective guilt without espousing it literally; later on the AJC repeatedly insisted that it was the first Jewish agency to reject the "abortive concept of German collective guilt as a basis for preventing a recurrence of the outrages of Hitlerism." AJC professionals were also afraid that the Marshall Plan, by strengthening Western Germany and rehabilitating its economy, might bolster German contempt for democratic practices. Since it was impossible to challenge that policy, some of the staff people thought it might be advisable that a spokesman for the administration make clear to the German people that the United States did not ignore or condone antidemocratic attitudes among them. However, in the political climate of 1948 such public statements were not made.

As to Germany's political future, in principle the AJC continued to prefer a united country. It was assumed that after the creation of a western state by the Western powers and an eastern state by the Soviet Union, the reestablishment of one united Germany would encounter great difficulties. However, in case all attempts to come to a decent arrangement with the Russians failed, AJC president

Joseph M. Proskauer endorsed the creation—together with France, Britain, Belgium, Luxembourg, and all the others—of a separate West German state as the best possible solution, both economically and politically.[10] Thus, the AJC became the first American Jewish organization to support Washington's major policy decision with regard to Germany. The fact that American forces would stay there made the endorsement easier.

Reviewing the domestic German situation after 1945, AJC analysts and professionals repeatedly stressed the democratic anti-Nazi potential of the Social Democratic party and the trade unions, as opposed to the conservative, if not reactionary, trend of the right wing of the Christian Democratic Union (CDU) and the CSU, its Bavarian sister party.[11] For a while the AJC even considered the possibility of closely cooperating with the Social Democrats. Their leader, Kurt Schumacher, who spent ten years in concentration camps, had been the first German politician to speak publicly of Nazi Germany's responsibility for the murder of six million Jews and of the German duty of recompense. AJC executive vice-president John Slawson first met him during his trip to Germany in August 1947. Paul Jacobs, then with the AJC, somewhat euphorically regarded Schumacher as "the brightest hope we have for any solution in Germany." During Schumacher's visit to the United States in the fall of 1947, he and Fritz Heine, who accompanied him, met with Slawson and other leading members in New York. Schumacher complained about the discriminatory treatment of his party by the military government and inquired whether the AJC could use its influence to change that attitude. Yet, despite mutual expressions of goodwill, proposals for cooperation with the SPD were never institutionalized because of the incompatibility of the partners.

The AJC also feared that such cooperation might antagonize both State Department and military government officials who were inimical to the Social Democrats and might be exploited by right-wing antisemitic forces. In the winter of 1948–49 the Committee tried to obtain Social Democratic support for including a commitment to indemnification and restitution in the West German Basic Law, but with no success. Still, for a number of years to come, SPD functionaries would approach the AJC's European office in Paris and request the supply of educational materials and other publications.[12]

The change in West Germany from military government to a semisovereign political status aggravated the fear of AJC lay leaders and professionals that it might strengthen nationalists and weaken moderates. While recognizing the importance of American–German economic cooperation, the possible repercussions of that change were included in outlines prepared by the AJC staff for an appointment of its president, Jacob Blaustein, with President Truman in the spring of 1949. According to Blaustein, who met Truman in May 1949, the president appeared interested in the suggestion that a commission of outstanding citizens should survey the situation and make recommendations to him.[13] For the next few years the Committee had to grapple with the dilemma of how to pursue its campaign against nationalistic and antisemitic elements in Germany without jeopardizing Washington's basic policy, which it wanted American Jews to support. The balance struck recognized the significance of Western Germany for the United States and its allies, while reiterating warnings against the restoration of reactionary social, political, and economic forces that had been so heavily involved with the Nazi regime. At the same time, the Committee stressed the need to support German liberals and democrats as the only reliable allies against totalitarianism. However, contrary to the AJC, which, despite its endorsement of anti-Communism, continued to favor the left-of-center in Germany, the American administration preferred to rely on right-of-center conservatives and well-qualified technocrats bent on a quick revival of the German economy without striving for far-reaching social reforms and without making a clean break with the past. That made things difficult even for an agency as supportive of the government as the AJC.

In retrospect, the fears of the AJC and of the American Jewish community in general with regard to the postwar situation in Germany were exaggerated. There was still a lot of antisemitism, and the change of German political culture was a rather slow process. However, despite the blatant deficiencies of denazification and the return of former members of the Nazi party to influential public positions, no major neo-Nazi party appeared on the German political scene. A great many former Nazis, while not becoming convinced democrats, did not join neo-Nazi groups but preferred to be integrated, as members or voters, into the legitimate postwar democratic parties. Nationalist forces were kept in bounds by the strong-minded chancellor, whose policy was consistently pro-Western.

In 1949 and in the early 1950s, Germany was a major subject in the deliberations of the AJC staff and lay working groups, as well as in the executive committee. Despite its basic moderate approach and its traditional opposition to public demonstrations and protests, the AJC was not at all of one mind. There were "pro-Germans" like Irving Engel and the extreme anti-Communist Reform rabbi S. Andhil Fineberg, who in the past had distinguished himself in fighting Nazi Germany, or Eric Warburg, who was much more German than American and not representative of the American Jewish community. Edwin Lukas was a committed supporter of reeducation and human relations programs. A permanent skeptic was Lithuanian-born Zachariah Shuster, who observed the German scene from the AJC European office in Paris; another critic was Arthur Mayer, chairman of the committee on Germany in 1950 who authored the pamphlet "The New Threat from Germany." AJC president Jacob Blaustein and Dr. John Slawson, the executive vice-president, could be regarded as critical middle-roaders, with Slawson veering to the skeptics in regard to the new German democracy. Blaustein was the first AJC president of Eastern European parentage; Slawson was born in the Ukraine. Whereas Jews from German origins still dominated the lay executive committee, the number of professionals of Eastern European origin was much larger. Although there was no clear ethnic divide on the German question, differences of opinion were observable among them.

Eventually, the AJC's double strategy, agreed upon by the special committee on Germany, rested on informing the American public, including the Jewish community, of developments in Germany, while at the same time looking for ways of influencing the German people themselves. On the one hand, that meant that the AJC would prepare analyses of the German situation such as "The Recent Growth of Neo-Nazism in Europe" or "Neo-Nazis and Nationalist Movements in West Germany" and distribute them to hundreds of editors, editorial writers, TV and radio commentators, news magazine editors, and other opinion leaders, not to mention the English-Jewish and Yiddish press. Even years later the AJC as well as the Anti-Defamation League of B'nai B'rith (ADL) would be involved in promoting the distribution of anti-Nazi historical studies such as Leon Poliakov's *Harvest of Hate* and Edward Crankshaw's

Gestapo.[14] On the other hand, to broaden the scope of these activities, the Committee looked for suitable allies from the liberal camp and the labor movement. Following its suggestion, NCRAC—the national Jewish communal relations agency in charge of domestic issues—set up the Coordinating Council on Germany with the participation of prominent gentile public figures. Among them were Telford Taylor, the former chief of counsel for war crimes at Nuremberg, Roger Baldwin of the Civil Rights League, Victor Reuther of the United Automobile Workers, and Alfred Bingham, president of the American Association for a Democratic Germany, which counted a number of Jewish intellectuals and professionals in its ranks. In 1950, the Council was reorganized and renamed Citizens Council for a Democratic Germany, but that did not add to its effectiveness, and Jewish sponsors became disillusioned by its lack of impact.[15]

The worsening of East-West relations increased support for Western Germany among anti-Communist liberals, who in the past had been a part of the anti-German consensus on the left, and even more among the American Federation of Labor, which regarded the containment of Communism as much more urgent than the World War II anti-Nazi legacy. This course was especially encouraged by Jay Lovestone, who was International Ladies Garment Workers Union (ILGWU) president David Dubinsky's political and international relations adviser. He was also executive director of the American Federation of Labor's anti-Communist Free Trade Union Committee. Neither the AFL nor Protestant or Catholic church groups ever joined the Citizens Council.

However, the lack of nonsectarian support was only one cause of the Citizens Council's failure. In the opinion of the AJC delegates at NCRAC, which sponsored the Citizens Council and its predecessor, the main blame rested upon the deep split with regard to Germany in the Jewish community itself.[16] Whereas some Jewish organizations, including the AJC, favored cooperation with groups and movements inside Germany aiming at its democratic reconstruction, others maintained that it was not "part of the responsibility of Jewish organizations to ally themselves in any way with any German elements," and felt that their proper role should be to apply pressure upon the American government and upon American public opinion. In fact, as the NCRAC chairman summarized, the

Jewish community as a whole favored some kind of cordon sanitaire between the Germans and the Jewish people.

According to the view of the AJC, that was the wrong approach. Whereas it was necessary to keep alerting American public opinion to dangerous phenomena in Germany, American Jews should not turn their backs on that nation. As Professor Herman A. Gray, himself a historian, put it, Germany was "undoubtedly destined to play an important part not only in the coming history of Europe, but in the history of world developments," a forecast that proved correct four decades later. In expressing only negative attitudes, Jews would not be heard, but charged "with vindictiveness and special pleading." In contrast to Will Maslow of the AJ Congress, who defended the "negative program" and found it quite understandable that "all but a handful" of Jews believed "there should be no traffic with the Germans," AJC executive vice-president John Slawson would not "accept the non-differentiating view of the group guilt of the German people." In particular Jews who suffered from hostile generalizations should beware of such an error.

In May 1951, the AJC's executive committee recapitulated its policy toward West Germany.[17] It rejected two extremes as equally untenable: "the extreme which asserts that all Germans must be permanently rejected and excluded from international society; and the extreme which holds that the fate and future of Germany is a matter on which American Jewish organizations should remain silent." The AJC endorsed a positive stand on the question of Western Germany's place in the free world and called a democratic Germany "the best safeguard against the threat of Communism today and Neo-Nazism in the future." The demands raised by the AJC included a speedy and fair settlement of problems involved with indemnification and restitution; the creation of a prodemocratic social and political climate; adoption of provisions for the protection of human rights and fundamental freedoms, together with international controls of these rights; and intensification of reeducation programs by the United States and the Western allies to democratize German institutions as well as the traditional German concepts of the relations between the individual and the state. They criticized the reemergence and restoration to positions of power of political, industrial, and militaristic elements responsible for World Wars I and II; the reinstatement of former Nazis to influential posts in the government, the civil service, the teaching profession, and the judiciary; and the adoption by the U.S. occupation authorities of the theory that the return of former prominent Nazis to power and influence was essential to the revival of German economy.

The executive committee's statement was preceded by a joint meeting of the AJC European Affairs Committee, its Special Committee on Germany, and its full Foreign Affairs Committee. The minority thought it might be better for the AJC "to refuse to have anything to do with the [German] situation because of the complexity of the problem and the doubts regarding its ability to make a constructive contribution to it." However, the majority concluded that "although Germany has not yet earned the right to take a position in the civilized world, the fact that Western Germany is nevertheless being readmitted to the Western world, is one to which we cannot refuse to react; but to react merely in the spirit of vindictiveness . . . is both futile and self-defeating." Whereas the statement met with much criticism from other Jewish organizations, both High Commissioner John McCloy and the State Department took exception to the AJC's reference to American support for the return of prominent Nazis to positions of power because of its importance for the revival of German economy.[18]

Until the summer of 1950 both President Truman and Secretary of State Dean Acheson had not been enthusiastic about the idea of German rearmament, in contrast to the pressure exerted in that direction by the Pentagon. As a matter of fact, the Labor party government in London had preceded on this issue the antisocialist administration in Washington. However, after the outbreak of the Korean War, German participation in Western defense became an urgent matter for the American government and was supported by a growing part of the American public. Because of the sensitivity of the Jewish community and internal differences of opinion, that delicate issue was not included in the AJC policy statement. In fall 1950, representing the lesser evil in the eyes of the great majority of organized American Jewry, the Citizens Council for a Democratic Germany had publicly opposed as premature all plans for German rearmament. Instead, it had advocated the building up of military strength by the democracies as a precondition to future participation of German troops on a basis that would strengthen German democracy and prevent revival of German militarism.[19]

However, an AJC subcommittee dealing with that subject recommended acceptance of Western Germany's rearmament on the condition that Germany military units would not be placed under German command but would be used only as part of an international Western European or United Nations army, under a unified international leadership. To guard against a nationalistic military threat by German units, a large American military force should remain in Western Europe, and a careful screening of German officers should give preference to proven opponents of Nazism, including participants in the attempted conspiracy against Hitler.[20] Later the AJC, while recognizing American Jewry's anxiety about German rearmament, alerted the communal organizations against engaging in joint activities or even common platforms with Communist groups. These were interested in exploiting Jewish sensitivity for their campaign against West Germany without mentioning the rearming of East Germany.[21]

In accordance with the principles espoused in its statement on Germany in May 1951, the AJC became involved in efforts to establish a German agency for the defense and development of human rights. To that end a German national conference on human rights and group relations was planned. The aim of these efforts was to contribute to the democratization of German society, including the fight against antisemitism and racism, and to promote active voluntary participation of leading German personalities from different walks of life in the planned agency. But despite the initial endorsement of AJC's proposal by McCloy and the invitations extended to anti-Nazi German individuals, "Operation Candle," as the initiative was dubbed by AJC staff member Edwin Lukas, never got off the ground. Because of a reduction of the Office of the U.S. High Commissioner for Germany's (HICOG) staff, it withdrew its financial support, and the Germans were not at all keen to proceed with this venture.[22] Nonetheless, the AJC did persist in its interest in the field of German civic education. From 1959 to 1960 it tried again to help advance democratic trends in Germany through the "German Educators Project."[23] In this aspect it differed from many other American Jewish organizations. After the Luxembourg reparations agreement in 1952 between the Federal Republic and Israel (see chapter 9) had partly mitigated their hostile attitude toward Germany, except for common protests against antisemitic manifestations such as in 1959–60, most American Jewish organizations turned their attention mainly to the Israeli angle in the

German-Jewish relationship and to problems connected with the Claims Conference.

In contrast to the WJC, which in 1944 had proclaimed that no former German Jew should be obliged to retrieve his German citizenship after V-E Day, and had pledged in 1948 that the Jewish people would never set foot again "on the blood-soaked German earth,"[24] the AJC refrained from such statements. After the war it supported the demand for opening the gates of Palestine to the survivors and other refugees willing to go there; and in its statement to the United Nations Special Committee on Palestine in 1947, it came out in favor of the establishment of a Jewish state in a part of Palestine. However, the AJC also joined forces with the anti-Zionist American Council for Judaism in the campaign for liberalizing the admission of DPs to the United States, and was instrumental in securing the 1948 Displaced Persons Act, even though that act discriminated heavily against Jewish candidates for immigration.[25]

In 1948, when General Clay told William Haber, his adviser on Jewish affairs, that "to admit that Jews cannot live in Germany as they do in other countries" was a much too fatalistic and pessimistic view of the situation, he could not convince him, and AJC's John Slawson endorsed Haber's view because of the prevailing antisemitic threat in Germany.[26] Yet, Haber distinguished between the DPs, who he felt should be compelled to leave Germany, and the German Jews living in their communities. They, too, should be encouraged to leave but should not be penalized for the failure to do so, and the main Jewish organizations should work for guaranteeing their rights in the Basic Law of the West German state and their implementation in daily life.[27] As a matter of fact, a majority of the members of the communities in 1949–50 were themselves DPs who preferred to stay there. The percentage of native German Jews declined because of biological reasons, although a few thousand successively returned to Germany, mainly from Israel. In May 1951 the AJC executive committee reiterated its position that the Jews who wished to remain in Germany should be granted full equality of rights and freedom, and conditions should be such as to permit them to live a free and dignified life there.[28] On the whole, for years to come the Jewish communities that remained in Germany played no major role in the framework of American Jewish–German relations. However, their importance grew in the eyes of the West German government, which hoped that its official philosemitic policy would contribute to improving its image in the eyes of Western public opinion.

The Anti-Defamation League of B'nai B'rith (ADL), which emerged in the mid-1950s and 1960s as another relatively open-minded Jewish organization with regard to Germany and approved of contacts and visits there, had in the early postwar period taken a rather critical stand on German developments. As the communal relations arm of B'nai B'rith, for many years the largest American Jewish membership organization, the most important task of ADL was to fight antisemitism, racism, and discrimination on the domestic American scene. After the war it also became active in the field of American Jewish–German relations as well as in supporting and defending Israel. B'nai B'rith itself, whose president Henry Monsky had played a major role in convening the American Jewish Conference in 1943, remained a member of the Conference until its disbandment in 1948. ADL was a founding member of NCRAC until it withdrew from that agency, together with the AJC, in 1952.

In 1949–50 the ADL got involved in the activities of the Coordinating Council on Germany and its successor, the Citizens Council for a Democratic Germany. The League endorsed its call for a presidential inquiry into the shortcomings of American handling of the German situation, as well as its warning against premature German rearmament.[29] The *ADL Bulletin* carried a series of articles very critical of developments in the new West German state, including "Are the Nazis Back in Power?" and "Return of the War Lords."[30] In 1950 the agency drew much publicity by disinviting, at the last moment, Assistant High Commissioner Benjamin Buttenwieser, the scheduled speaker at its annual meeting in Chicago, because of his intended defense of HICOG's policy on Germany. Buttenwieser's thesis was that with many Nazis punished, even though some had escaped, the time had come for leniency so that Germany might start being a democratic and antitotalitarian member of the family of nations.[31] While the ADL's handling of the case was blamed editorially by the *New York Times*, it was praised full-heartedly by the *Reconstructionist, Congress Weekly*, and the Yiddish press.[32]

In a statement published in May 1950, the ADL did not object to the American "goal of reviving a self-sustaining German economy . . . that will operate as a bastion against continued Soviet aggression," but accused the American authorities of having ignored for years the "important qualification of democratic leadership" and neglected their mandate regarding denazification, democratization, and decartelization. The ADL called for a positive program in Germany that would have these effects: it would strengthen the democratic labor movement, the cooperatives, the democratically constituted social welfare agencies, and the municipalities under effective popular control; eliminate all active supporters of the Nazi ideology from policymaking and other positions of authority or responsibility in the administrative, judicial, and educational fields; democratize the economy and curb the concentration of economic power in cartels and trusts; maintain control of the German economy to prevent the country from again becoming an aggressor, and facilitate reeducation of German youth. B'nai B'rith president Frank Goldman spoke in the same vein at the order's triennial convention. The denazification of Germany was an objective to be achieved, he stated, "not so much for the sake of the Jews still remaining in Germany as for the sake of peace itself." By allowing "the enemies of democracy to infiltrate into posts of power," the United States was bankrupting "the very treasure we built up."[33]

Subsequently, after the opening of German-Israeli negotiations on reparations for the Jewish state and the Jewish people, B'nai B'rith and ADL shifted to a moderate position. Frank Goldman became a member of the presidium of the Claims Conference, and under his successor Philip Klutznick (1953–59) B'nai B'rith and ADL supported more contacts and a gradual improvement of relations with the Federal Republic. In 1954 the ADL was the first major Jewish organization to visit West Germany upon an official invitation of the Bonn government. The report weighed positive developments there, especially among German youth, against persisting negative phenomena.[34] This trend of the organization has persisted ever since, despite ups and downs.

The Jewish Labor Committee's attitude toward Germany was another story. Its founding president was Baruch Charney Vladeck, his successor was Adolph Held, and David Dubinsky served as treasurer. The socialist leadership of the JLC had supported German and other European Social Democratic and trade unionist exiles on the eve of and during World War II and disapproved of Morgenthau's ideas and the collective guilt concept, contrary to the much more critical and emotional approach of the members of its constituent organizations. After the war, the JLC leadership continued its links with German Social Democrats and welcomed Social Democratic politicians during their visits to the United States, while their attitude toward the conservative Adenauer government was much cooler.[35] JLC officials tried to convince Jewish circles of the difference and emphasized SPD leader Kurt Schumacher's condemnation of antisemitism and support for restitution and compensation. When Schumacher visited the United States in fall 1947 at the invitation of the AFL, Abraham Cahan, the veteran founding editor of the *Forverts*, greeted him at a reception in his honor as "a new type of socialist." However, JLC executive secretary Jacob Pat, a member of the Jewish Labor Bund, attended the reception with a broken heart. "We sensed that as dangerous as it might be, we have to strip the deep wound—like the physician who cannot refrain from diagnosing the illness," he reported. The SPD traditional fraternal links with the Jewish Labor Bund notwithstanding, after the destruction of East European Jewry among whom he grew up, Pat could not suppress his hostility even toward a "good German," and he continued to express it publicly.[36]

In the summer of 1951 Schumacher welcomed the Bund delegation that attended the reestablishment of the Socialist International in Frankfurt. Mapai, the predecessor of the Israel Labor Party, had opposed the admission of the German Social Democrats to the interim COMISCO (Committee of International Socialist Conferences) and therefore also boycotted the Frankfurt gathering.[37] However, a few months later the few remaining Bund members in New York were very much disappointed by Schumacher's public meeting with former Waffen-SS generals. Schumacher unsuccessfully tried to assuage their anger by pointing to the difference between the Waffen-SS and the original Nazi SS.[38] More than thirty years later, in 1985, the Germans would use a similar excuse before the meeting between Chancellor Helmut Kohl and President Ronald Reagan at Bitburg military cemetery, where a number of SS soldiers rested.

During the negotiations between West Germany, Israel, and the Claims Conference, the JLC kept in close touch with the Social Democratic leadership. In fact, without the full support of the SPD parliamentary group, the Luxembourg reparations treaty would not have been ratified. Yet because of the sensitivity of its grass roots, the JLC preferred holding discussions with the SPD delegation in Paris instead of in Germany. Its president Adolph

Held declared that whatever the outcome of the negotiations on reparations, "Germany will have to do a great deal more before there can be any idea of reconciliation between the Jewish people and Germany."[39]

To the organizations with a moderate attitude regarding postwar Germany, one may add the American Council for Judaism that was set up after the breakaway faction of anti-Zionist Reform rabbis was joined by a number of prominent laymen, such as Lessing J. Rosenwald, the founding president of Sears, Roebuck and Company. Before Pearl Harbor, Rosenwald was involved in the isolationist antiwar American First movement. In 1946–48 he initiated, together with the AJC, the Citizens Committee on Displaced Persons, which conducted a public campaign for admitting a large number of DPs from different Eastern European nations who were still in Germany. Rosenwald's main aim was to bring more Jewish DPs to the United States in order to show that not all of them wanted to go to Palestine.

The Council drew most of its support from members of the older German Jewish group; it was also joined by recent anti-Zionist and patriotic German Jewish newcomers such as Klaus Herrmann. In a way, the ACJ's moderate stand on Germany resulted from its ideological confrontation with the Zionists, most of whom had endorsed a strong anti-German line. In his book *The Jewish Dilemma*, Rabbi Elmer Berger, until 1968 ACJ's executive head, expressed the view that Jewish life in Germany had to be reinstated after the defeat of Hitlerism. Taking into account the failure of emancipation and integration of Jews in Germany in the past, the problem as he saw it was "what shall be done with Germany so that there emerges a nation in which Jews as well as other people will be able to live upon a basis of freedom and equality."[40]

As an "organization of Americans of Jewish Faith" the Council continued to support the integration of Jews into the life of their respective nations, and this included the reestablishment of Jewish communities in Germany, which it regarded as a democratic nation.[41]

Immediately after the end of the war, right-wing nationalist German exiles like Hubertus Prinz zu Loewenstein found it appropriate to approach leading spokesmen of the Council, such as Lessing Rosenwald and Rabbi Morris S. Lazaron of Baltimore, with regard to "an appeal . . . for immediate relief for German people." Loewenstein intimated that such an appeal might counteract the wave of antisemitism created in Germany by "a very unwise policy, connected prominently with the names of Mr. Morgenthau, Mr. Baruch and others." Loewenstein was disappointed by Rabbi Lazaron's vague response and his refusal to take up commitments, although the rabbi emphasized that he was opposed to "any unnecessary suffering in Germany."[42] At first, German observers continued to praise the moderate attitude of the American Council for Judaism. Yet after a few years they grasped the minimal impact of that anti-Zionist group on American Jewry and started to look for more promising ways gradually to conciliate the American Jewish community.[43]

6

Critics and Opponents

The American Jewish Committee was regarded by the American administration and establishment for a number of years as the most influential Jewish group. The Committee was very concerned with the repercussions of Washington's changing German policy on the Jewish community. Since the first years after the war, the AJC had consistently supported democratization and reeducation programs for the German population under OMGUS and later HICOG, with a special emphasis on fighting extreme nationalism, antisemitism, and all racist phenomena. However, the great majority of organized Jewry, represented by such bodies as the American Jewish Conference (until its disbandment in 1948), the WJC and the AJ Congress, most women's organizations, and the various *landsmanshaften*, did not want contact with Germans and did not care much about the future development of Germany and its political culture, even though some of them joined in paying lip service to it.

In addition to their concern for the DPs still on German soil, Zionists and pro-Zionists spent all their energy in gaining political support for the creation of a Jewish state. During Israel's War of Independence and the following critical period, the Zionists and pro-Zionists mobilized vital financial assistance for the new entity. Their attitude toward Germany and the Germans was dominated by the emotional impact of the Jewish tragedy in Europe that they had watched helplessly from afar. As U.S. citizens they did not ignore American national interest, but they were slow to adjust to the substantial change with regard to Germany that was taking place so soon after World War II. This was particularly true at least as long as a part of the material Jewish claims on the defeated enemy nation had not been satisfied. In the meantime, they laid special stress on public statements regarding shortcomings of denazification, antisemitic incidents, and failure of decartelization; on intercessions with the American authorities against appeasement of forces in Germany, which seemed unreliable in their eyes; and on protests against German visitors and German-sponsored events in the United States.

In a way, the outspoken Zionist hostility to Germany resembled the anti-German position of the Yishuv in Palestine and during the very first years of the Jewish state. Only after the signing of the German-Israeli Luxembourg reparations agreement and the additional protocols between the Federal Republic and the Claims Conference (see chapter 9) would their official stand begin to soften. This shift did not affect the Communists who continued to exploit the legitimate post-Holocaust Jewish mistrust of Germany for their campaign against U.S. efforts to rebuild West Germany's economy and bring that country into the Western alliance. During the postwar Red Scare, the facts and myths of Jewish prewar and wartime involvement in Communist party or pro-Soviet activities were an additional obstacle in making the American public sensitive to Jewish qualms about the rapid turnabout of Washington's German policy.

In January 1947 the Interim Committee of the American Jewish Conference, chaired by B'nai B'rith president Henry Monsky, adopted a statement of thirteen principles and proposals to be included in a German peace treaty. During the following years a few changes were introduced to make some of the formulations less emotional, but basically the Conference stuck to the following summary:

1) Germany must acknowledge her shameful guilt for the monstrous crime against the Jews. Without such acknowledgment, a Peace Treaty with Germany would distort the records of history beyond recognition. It would, moreover, prevent that process of atonement which Germany must

undergo before she can again be received into the family of civilized nations.

2) Germany must cleanse her public and private life from the invidious poison of anti-Semitism. . . . Equal rights for all and non-discrimination must be imposed and secured as the guiding principles of her laws and practices.

3) Germany's past conduct has shown that the treatment of Jews within her borders cannot safely be left to her discretion for many years to come. Their status and treatment must therefore be a matter of international concern and supervision.

4) To attest her atonement for her crimes against the Jews, Germany must effectively punish all those who had a hand in the persecution of Jews or benefited from it.

5) Jews who have been deprived of their nationality by discriminatory laws and practices must have the right to reacquire it but shall not be compelled to do so.

6) No Jew should be forced to remain on soil soaked with his brother's blood. Jews in Germany must have the unfettered right to emigrate from Germany and to take their belongings with them.

7) All Jewish displaced persons . . . must have the protection of Allied or other international authorities and must never be allowed to fall under German jurisdiction, but Germany must provide the means for their subsistence.

8) Jews who will remain in Germany must be given freedom of association and the right to pursue their religious, communal and other activities with the same status and privileges they enjoyed before January 30, 1933.

9) The property of which individual Jews have been robbed must be returned to them or their heirs. Heirless Jewish property must be transferred to and applied by a responsible Jewish body to be set up for the purpose of relief and resettlement of Jewish victims of Nazi persecution.

10) Germany must indemnify fully all Jews who have suffered in their person or property from measures and acts of Nazi persecution.

11) To further the process of German education in principles of justice, reparations should be paid by Germany for the damage and suffering she has caused by her persecution of

the Jews. . . . Such reparation should include Jewish cultural property owned by non-Jewish German public institutions.

12) Jews and their property must be exempted from any measures which are applied by the Allies to the property of enemy nationals.

13) The enforcement of all treaty provisions concerning Jews cannot be left to German authorities. The clauses must be supervised by international machinery to which Jewish individuals and their organizations and communities must have access. In addition, the treaty provisions must also be enacted as part of the constitutional law of Germany.[1]

To reinforce its proposals, the AJ Conference presented to the four powers an 850-page volume reviewing "Nazi Germany's War against the Jews," as revealed in the Nuremberg trials.[2] In general, the WJC's claims were similar to those of the AJ Conference, both insisting on the German people's collective admission of the guilt in exterminating European Jewry. In a statement published in March 1947 the WJC demanded that "the preamble to the Peace Treaty should contain an admission by the German Government of the guilt of the Nazi regime and the German people of the conspiracy to destroy European Jewry and of the attempt to poison public opinion through an anti-Semitic propaganda designed to rob Jews of the opportunity of life and labor in other countries."[3]

In 1946 the major Jewish organizations had been disappointed by their very limited impact on the deliberations of the Paris Peace Conference, which drafted the peace treaties with Hungary, Rumania, Bulgaria, Finland, and Italy. Thus they spent much time in preparation for the more important peace settlement with Germany. The breakdown of the four power negotiations and preparations for the establishment of a West German state did not leave much leverage for the realization of punitive demands and caused much disappointment among most Jewish groups. Whereas the AJC approved of the Marshall Plan and later of the setting up of NATO, the American Jewish Conference, for its part, was not prepared to lend support to the plan and to mobilize Jewish public opinion behind it, because of the intended industrial rehabilitation of Germany.[4] Although Morgenthau's anti-German principles were not included in the Conference's public statements, at least some of its representatives clung to them.

In the early postwar period Zionist and pro-Zionist groups in America were regarded as the most hostile toward Germany. This was also registered by semi-official German observers in reports to the Stuttgart Bureau of Peace Problems, the nucleus of the future West German foreign office. Alexander Böker, for instance, who spent the war years in the United States and upon his return to Germany joined the diplomatic service there, distinguished between the hostile "three quarters Nazi like" Zionists and the moderate non-Zionist AJC, the anti-Zionist ACJ, as well as Jewish socialists and trade unionists.[5]

In 1948 the four power negotiations on Germany had already broken down, and no peace treaty was in sight. That did not prevent the WJC's first postwar plenary assembly in Montreux from calling upon the big powers "to include in whichever settlement of the German problem . . . temporary or permanent" the following provisions in favor of the Jewish people and Jews as individuals: recognition of the guilt of Germany for the unprecedented tragedy that befell the Jews after the Nazi accession; payment of reparations by Germany for rehabilitation and resettlement of uprooted Jews, primarily in Palestine; restitution of property or full compensation; assignment of heirless and unclaimed Jewish property to an international Jewish organization; measures to remedy the "failure of denazification and purification of Germany." The WJC, which still counted some Eastern European Communist-dominated communities among its members, expressed its outright opposition to returning to Germany areas that had been detached from it after World War II and to the "reconstitution of the German state as an economic and political and therefore inevitably military power . . . as a threat to Jewish security and peace in the world."[6] The plenary assembly also reiterated "the determination of the Jewish people never again to settle on the blood-stained soil of Germany."

After Montreux, calls for a total Jewish boycott were repeated by Rabbi Mordecai Nurock of the Mizrachi religious Zionist party and other members of the WJC executive in Israel, as well as by the American Labor Zionist leaders Louis Segal and Baruch Zuckerman. The two Labor Zionists did not object to recovering Jewish property from Germany, since "under no circumstances should the murderer be permitted to be our heir." However, they insisted that the Jewish historic account require at least one thing: that "no Jew shall remain on German soil and still maintain his bond with the Jewish people." Their argument was that such an approval "will be an important factor in preventing the terrible period we have lived through from being forgotten and a constant reminder to honorable Germans that they are duty-bound to do something demonstrative that will be accepted first of all by the Jewish world and consequently by all mankind, as a manifestation of sincere regret and thus pave the way for a new attitude." Thus, contrary to the deep-seated ideological opposition of the Zionist Revisionists, they did not exclude the possibility of a future change. Segal and Zuckerman distinguished between Germany and Austria and excluded the latter from a similar boycott. That was characteristic of the lack of knowledge of the Austrians' active participation in the extermination of European Jewry and the wide support of the Austrian people for Nazism.[7]

Nahum Goldmann, WJC acting president after Stephen Wise's death in April 1949, opposed all these calls. He argued that the German situation after World War II could not be compared with that of Spain after the expulsion of the Spanish Jews in 1492 and the subsequent *cherem* (ban) proclaimed against it. Both the Western powers and the Soviet Union were interested in rebuilding Germany, and the Congress movement would not succeed in gaining public support in the United States if it opposed West Germany's becoming self-supporting. Moreover, it would be dishonorable to pronounce such a *cherem* with the foreknowledge that tens of thousands of Jews would not obey it, among them the State of Israel.[8] Statements by Rabbi Robert Marcus, the New York WJC executive director and former head of the Joint Boycott Council in the 1930s, that "the WJC was unequivocally opposed to Jewish businessmen representing German firms abroad," were rebuffed by the moderates in the British section.[9] In fact, a great many Jewish business people had already established close connections with a variety of German counterparts.

In comparison to the Israelis and the Americans, who regarded the WJC not only as a political organization but also as the "conscience of the Jewish people," the British members were the most pragmatic ones. Sidney Silverman, a left-wing Labor MP and an influential spokesman of the European section, warned more than once that Congress would remain isolated if its representatives continued to object to Germany's political independence. He endorsed direct Jewish contacts with both West and East Germany; and Alexander Easterman, the London executive's political director, who favored contacts with democratic forces in Germany to fight antisemitism, predicted rather early that Jewish claims could be satisfied only by German governments. Dr. Noah Barou, the chairman of the London-based European executive, would soon be the first to engage in informal talks with Herbert Blankenhorn, Adenauer's closest adviser on foreign affairs, about a public declaration by West Germany concerning its responsibilities as successor to the Third Reich and the payment of collective reparations to the Jewish people. For all of them, Jewish-German relations were not only a moral problem.[10]

Nonetheless, on the eve of the proclamation of the West German Basic Law and after the first elections to the Bundestag in August 1949, the WJC executive did not regard granting political independence to Germany as justified. It called for continuing occupation of German territory as well as for "closest control of all phases of German public life" until there was "sufficient evidence of a change in the German mentality." In response to Chancellor Konrad Adenauer's offer of a symbolic advance payment to Israel and President Theodor Heuss's statement recognizing German collective shame as opposed to collective guilt, the WJC reaffirmed "that the world generally and the Jewish people in particular will not believe that the German people have begun to realize the enormity of the crisis and to atone for it until they have solemnly and collectively affirmed their guilt through their parliamentary institutions and later through a peace settlement or comparable international instrument unequivocally accepted by the German people." The WJC's attitude toward West Germany mellowed only after the beginning of German-Israeli-Jewish reparations talks and particularly after the Luxembourg agreement in September 1952. In the long run, the shift affected even the WJC's pronounced opposition to German rearmament.[11]

As the only pro-Zionist umbrella organization after the demise of the American Jewish Conference, most of the general statements regarding the Jewish people's attitude toward Germany were handled by the WJC. Conversely, political action on the American scene rested mainly in the hands of its American constituency, the

111

AJ Congress, which itself comprised a great many different groups as well as individual members. Since its inception it had been the politically most liberal of the major Jewish organizations; and in the 1930s, it had taken an activist stand in confronting Nazi Germany. But whereas the leftists or "progressives" in the movement favored mass mobilization, demonstrations, and rallies protesting the rapid change of postwar American policy, the liberal mainstream preferred growing public support by less confrontational tactics.[12]

Thus, despite its strong objections to the New York German Trade Fair in April 1949, Congress leadership shared the other Jewish organizations' decision to stage no protest demonstrations; however, this did not prevent members of its three left-dominated New York divisions from picketing the fair. A few weeks earlier Stephen Wise had censured the "irresponsibility" of the New York Metropolitan Coordinating Committee in setting up an independent Denazification Committee.[13] Yet, even after the purge of pro-Communist groups from its ranks, the AJ Congress continued to oppose the anti-Communist hysteria and rebuffed the Committee's extreme anti-Communist stand.[14]

In 1949–50 the AJ Congress devoted much energy to furthering a congressional investigation of American policy in Germany. Because of its greater public effect it preferred a senatorial to a presidential inquiry, the alternative endorsed by the AJC and the majority of NCRAC member organizations.[15] However, the yearlong effort of the Jewish and supporting non-Jewish groups, such as the American Civil Liberties Union, the American Veterans Committee, the Congress of Industrial Organizations, and Americans for Democratic Action, came to naught, as did the bipartisan resolution introduced by eight senators and eleven congressmen.[16] Even a State Department proposal to assuage protesting members of Congress by dispatching to Germany a group of well-known citizens did not materialize. The international tension caused by the Korean War in the summer of 1950 served as a convenient excuse for High Commissioner McCloy to veto all kinds of investigations into American policy in Western Germany.[17]

In the NCRAC deliberations on Germany in 1949–51 the AJ Congress usually preferred its on-the-spot critique of developments in Germany and American policy there over long-range programs for German democracy. The AJC, for its part, argued that Congress was doing "the Jews of America a great disservice in making it appear that criticism of American policy in Germany was a Jewish issue rather than an American one." The Committee and the majority of NCRAC also made the point that non-Jewish groups taking part in the Coordinating Council and its successor, the Citizens Council for a Democratic Germany, would not agree to cooperate with Jewish groups on a watchdog basis of day-to-day events without promoting democratic and liberal forces in Germany.[18] Because of what most Americans regarded as the danger of Soviet aggression, the NCRAC national coordinator advocated "the admittedly unpopular position that Jewish organizations should, in the interests of the survival of a democratic world society, abandon the attitude of hostility, vengeance and distrust and resume normal and cooperative relationships with the German people in the hope that in this way a democratic Germany will be created which will redeem its sins."[19]

Such a position was not at all acceptable to the AJ Congress. Moreover, besides Congress's own traditional differences with AJC, JLC, and ADL, there was a conflict of interest between its being the American constituency of the WJC and its membership in NCRAC. The Congress, despite Nahum Goldmann's moderate course, comprised a number of extreme anti-German groups, while NCRAC, without much success, endorsed the activities of the Coordinating Council in favor of strengthening German democracy.[20] In September 1952, AJC and ADL withdrew from NCRAC after having been outvoted by a large majority on the recommendations of political scientist Robert MacIver in regard to joint program planning of the Jewish communal organizations. Instead the United Synagogue of America (the Conservative congregations) and the Union of Orthodox Jewish Congregations affiliated. However, under the changing circumstances because of the German-Jewish-Israeli negotiations, the German problem was no longer a critical issue on NCRAC's agenda.

As a watchdog on German developments detrimental to the Jewish interest, the AJ Congress conducted a series of information activities on both the national and local level. Memoranda in regard to disturbing phenomena in German politics were submitted by Rabbi Irving Miller, Stephen Wise's successor as AJ Congress president, to the State Department. At a mass meeting in Brooklyn, the AJ Congress hosted Delbert Clark, former chief correspondent in Germany for the *New York Times*, a strong critic of West

Germany and unequivocal opponent of German rearmament. The organization's Washington representative was involved in drafting a statement by liberal Republican Congressman Jacob Javits against ending the state of war with Germany; Javits was the only member of the House who did not vote for this. The AJ Congress continued to make critical statements regarding Germany also after the signing of the Luxembourg agreement, but the intensity of its drive lessened over the years.[21]

At the Atlantic City War Emergency Conference in 1944, the WJC had passed a resolution that after the war no Jew should be forced to return to Germany. The Montreux postwar plenary assembly reiterated the determination of the Jewish people never again to settle there; this expressed the consensus of the overwhelming majority of Jews in the Diaspora and in the new State of Israel. Nevertheless, while most of the DPs left Germany for Israel, the United States, and other countries in 1948–50, thousands of survivors and refugees decided to stay and thus enlarged the reestablished German Jewish communities. This presented a problem both for the World Zionist Organization and the Jewish Agency, as well as for other major Jewish organizations, which had campaigned for the full exodus of the Saving Remnant since the end of the war. In the first postwar years a number of German Jewish regional organizations in the West and even in the Soviet Zone as well as the central committees of the survivors and DPs affiliated with the WJC; a few of them were invited to attend the WJC plenary assembly at Montreux. The most meaningful affiliation was that of the British zone, where German Jews and DPs had formed a unitary organization. London-based WJC leaders consistently helped them in contacts with the British authorities on the spot and intervened at the Foreign Office and War Office on their behalf.

Nahum Goldmann, for his part, regarded the slogan that no Jew should ever live in Germany as unrealistic. On matters of German-Jewish relations he was more farsighted than many of his colleagues.[22] Goldmann visited Frankfurt in April 1950 and on that occasion introduced Gerhard Jacoby, a former Berlin lawyer who worked for the IJA in New York, as WJC special representative for Germany. In July, Jacoby was instrumental in summoning a national conference of representatives of Jewish communities and thus became involved in setting up the Central Council of the Jews in Germany.[23] That initiative aroused strong objections from the

World Zionist Organization and the WJC's own ranks.[24] However, the pressure from Israeli and American members notwithstanding, the links between the Central Council of the Jews in Germany and the WJC were not cut off. After a number of years they were normalized.

The change of American policy toward Germany—the recent bloody enemy emerging as a potential ally in the confrontation with the Soviet Union—was also a difficult problem for the Jewish War Veterans, one of the smaller but vocal constituents of NCRAC. The organization, whose origins dated back to the post–Civil War era, distinguished itself, as did other veteran groups, in its patriotic appearance. During Israel's War of Independence, it helped in locating well-qualified veterans for the Machal volunteer force. After World War II, its members, who had fought Nazi Germany and its allies, acquiesced to Washington's new anti-Soviet course. Many JWV activities in those years were devoted to Israel, but despite its anti-Communism and qualified acceptance of the Truman and Eisenhower administrations' rapprochement with West Germany, it remained an activist force that watched Germany with suspicion. On several occasions, such as during the German industrial fair in New York sponsored by OMGUS (see next chapter), the major Jewish groups put pressure on the JWV to refrain from anti-German demonstrations in order not to be identified with protests organized by communist groups. JWV branches also protested against visiting German musical performers. General Julius Klein, the organization's national commander in 1948–49 and for a number of years chairman of its international affairs department, changed from a very critical position on Germany and OMGUS leniency to an emphatic pro-German orientation. Eventually the JWV's most prominent postwar spokesman became a lobbyist for the Adenauer government and for German industrial corporations. However, his attitude did not reflect the views of the majority of the organization, which criticized him and caused his temporary departure from its ranks.[25]

From among the religious denominations, Orthodox spokesmen, both Zionist and non-Zionist, usually took the most resolute anti-German stand. Rabbi Joseph B. Soloveitchik, chairman of the National Council of the Mizrachi Organization of America and the most respected intellectual religious figure in American Orthodox Judaism, urged world Jewry "to take revenge against the entire

German people who must be held responsible for the outrageous murder of 6,000,000 Jews." In his opinion, antisemitism was "not related in any way to the political form or the structure of a government . . . [but] to the fascist totalitarian mentality of a people." He could conceive the German people murdering six million Jews even under a democratic regime. Soloveitchik drew a Zionist conclusion from the Holocaust caused by the Germans: "Revenge if performed physically would be only of momentary value. Ours must be an eternal revenge—one which can be had only by rebuilding from the remnants of Dachau, Maidanek and Treblinka a stronger and greater folk in a Jewish national homeland in Palestine."[26]

Orthodox views of Germany, as reflected in the editorials of *Orthodox Jewish Life*, remained very critical also after the establishment of the Federal Republic, which, because of the Cold War, proceeded rapidly toward factual independence: "Civilization can live and mankind remain secure only if the horror that Germany begot shall have been extirpated. The retribution that the world requires of Germany is not the execution of vengeance on its 65 million inhabitants, but the utter eradication of that in German life that Hitler personified." In the opinion of the Orthodox editorialist, not much had been achieved during the six years since the end of the war, and an "uncompromising reeducation" should be regarded as not less important for German identification with the Western cause than political and economic aid. Nonetheless, despite its qualms about the negotiations with Germany on reparations, the periodical published by the Union of Orthodox Jewish Congregations condemned the behavior of Israel's Herut party (the main component of the future Likud) during the Knesset debate in January 1952. It reaffirmed that Israel's policy on German reparations must be determined by democratic means.

The summary of a symposium published in the *Jewish Forum*, a journal edited by Isaac Rosengarten with a great many Orthodox contributing editors, was that "the record of postwar Germany was such as to make it dangerous to allow them, so soon after the commission of their atrocities, when no one shows hardly any signs of moral regeneration, to regain power, sovereignty and independence through remilitarization." Commenting on Chancellor Adenauer's statement of September 27, 1951, the *Jewish Forum*'s editorial writer regarded it as totally inadequate and concluded that Jews should wait "until a more drastic effort be made by Germany both in her daily conduct and in the manner the German people generally, and not just a few government leaders reveal a truly humble and contrite heart."[27]

For the non-Zionist Orthodox of Agudath Israel and the "world of the Yeshiva," the Germans who had committed the greatest crime in human history remained *Amalek* for years to come. According to Orthodox tradition, Jews were commanded to perpetuate their enmity toward *Amalek* because it strove to destroy the Jewish people. The loss of their families, homes, and places of learning in Eastern Europe weighed especially heavy on the Orthodox community. Immediately after the war, the Union of Orthodox Rabbis of the United States and Canada, the rabbinical organization aligned with Agudath Israel, considered convening a world conference on imposing a *cherem* on Germany, but this proposal did not materialize. Despite differences of opinion about whether or not to accept reparation money from Germany, Agudath Israel joined the Claims Conference in 1951. However, it was one of the few dissenting organizations that opposed the opening of negotiations with Chancellor Adenauer, "the evil head of government of a nation of murderers." Rabbi Isaac Lewin, its representative at the Conference's founding meeting, argued that moral amends were not in the gift of the current generation, or of any generation for a thousand years. Germany should be forced to return what had been stolen, but reparation should grant it no measure of moral rehabilitation.[28]

In contrast to the hostility of the great majority of the Orthodox camp, different nuances prevailed among the Conservative and Reform denominations. In an early discussion on the postwar Jewish communities in *Conservative Judaism*, Rabbi Isaac Klein, who spent his leave of absence from his congregation as representative of the Synagogue Council in Germany, attached much importance to the continuing existence of Jewish communities there, which served also as stopover or haven for Jews from Eastern Europe. A prominent Conservative rabbi such as Israel Goldstein, president of the American Jewish Congress and the Western Hemisphere section of the WJC, visited Germany and the Jewish communities there a number of times, despite the critical attitude of the organizations he chaired. A strong supporter of Goldmann's reparations policy, he regarded the Luxembourg treaty as "a historic milestone in international morality."

Rabbi Norman Salit, another noted Conservative rabbi active on the public scene, was invited by the West German government in his capacity as president of the Synagogue Council, together with a delegation of eight religious leaders, to visit that country in 1953. He thus became the first head of a Jewish organization to officially visit Germany. Salit met with Chancellor Adenauer and President Heuss during his visit. However, the Foreign Office in Bonn was disappointed by his critical comments regarding the "piecemeal way in which West Germany was reeducating its people" and his misinterpretation of Adenauer's statement in this context. Later Salit expressed doubts whether Germany had really put an end to antisemitic manifestations.[29] Neither the Rabbinical Assembly nor the United Synagogue were represented on NCRAC during its first years, and none of them particularly dealt with the American Jewish attitude toward postwar Germany in their conferences.

The Union of American Hebrew Congregations (UAHC), on the contrary, was among NCRAC's first members and actively participated in its deliberations on Germany and on the Jewish position regarding developments there. The Central Conference of American Rabbis, the organization of Reform rabbis that discussed the German issue at its annual meeting four months after V-E Day, stated that it would "be moved by no desire for vengeance or retaliation but by imperatives of justice, and the need to avoid future wars. We seek neither a hard nor a soft but a just peace." While it emphasized the German people's guilt, it reaffirmed its conviction that the Germans could be regenerated if they pled guilty to the destruction of large areas of Europe and the cold-blooded murder of almost ten million civilians, rejected the Nazi philosophy, and reeducated their youth. This was a universalist reminder that the Germans killed not only Jews under their control but also many other innocent people. At the same time the CCAR endorsed proposals for either removing heavy industry from Germany or putting it under inter-Allied control. In 1950 the CCAR, together with other NCRAC constituents, called for a presidential commission of inquiry to appraise the accomplishments and failures of the American occupation policy. In 1951 it protested against the American occupation authorities' "veering away from their original policy of seeking to restore the German nation to a worthy position in the family of nations" and being more interested in creating a German buffer-state against an anticipated Russian invasion of

Western Europe than in "ridding the world of the menace of resurgent militaristic chauvinism."[30]

Stephen Wise, a prominent Reform rabbi, founding president of the WJC and for many years head of AJ Congress, had been at the forefront of the struggle against Nazi Germany since Hitler's accession to power in 1933. During the last years of his life, he was troubled by the change of American policy toward Germany; here and there he dispatched protests to members of the administration, as in the case of a German scientist who had been brought to the United States together with his Nazi wife under the "Paperclip" project of securing the services of German weapons specialists and technicians.[31] Wise died in April 1949.

Cleveland rabbi Abba Hillel Silver, Wise's rival in the Zionist leadership, was a most consistent opponent of American postwar policies in the ranks of the Reform movement. In the thirties he had been active in the Non-Sectarian Anti-Nazi League to Champion Human Rights; after the resignation of Samuel Untermyer in 1938, he served as its president. During the crucial 1940s, Silver had a central role in mobilizing American Jewry and public opinion in support for the Jewish state. Silver was very skeptical of the anti-Communist drive to rearm West Germany, contrary to the Potsdam agreement permanently to demilitarize the defeated enemy nation. He thought it would only weaken the democratic forces in Germany that existed despite the failure of denazification and demilitarization. Like James Warburg, he preferred a united, demilitarized Germany that would pacify the whole European continent and enable the German people "to rebuild their life . . . on truly democratic lines and in peaceful ways."[32]

In 1952 the prospective agreement between the Federal Republic of West Germany, Israel, and the Claims Conference with regard to reparations and indemnification encountered some opposition at the CCAR annual meeting, particularly because of the face-to-face negotiations with the Germans. As during earlier annual meetings, differences of opinion were expressed between outspoken supporters, pragmatists, and anti-German skeptics. At the same meeting Silver succeeded in swaying the majority to air its opposition to the remilitarization of Germany, both East and West, and to record its distrust of Germany in the struggle of the free world against all kinds of totalitarianism.[33] Silver, who had launched his attack against Washington's new German course during the Truman administration, stuck to his position after the Republicans entered the White House. However, this did not prevent his invitation to deliver a prayer at President Eisenhower's inauguration. Despite the exacerbating Cold War, Silver continued to endorse diplomacy and negotiations with Soviet Russia and to warn that West German rearmament could cause a third world war. The Communist Yiddish daily *Morgen Freiheit* extensively quoted Silver's Cleveland Temple sermons criticizing U.S. foreign policy, whereas the anti-Communist *Forverts* castigated his statements.[34] In retrospect, despite the upheaval caused by the unification of Germany after the breakdown of the Communist bloc and the end of the Cold War, the great Zionist leader seems to have been wrong on this issue.

For American Jewish Communists and pro-Communists, Jewish opposition to Nazi Germany since the early 1930s and Jewish sensitivity regarding Germany after its defeat by the Grand Alliance were important factors in their approach to individual Jews of different strata and also in obtaining a foothold in the organized community. In 1936 the Jewish People's Fraternal Order (JPFO), a section of the International Workers Order, the large Communist fraternal society, did not gain admission to the AJ Congress and the WJC, because of Communist support for the Arab uprising in Palestine. However, both the JPFO and the pro-Communist American Jewish Labor Council (AJLC) were allowed to join the AJ Congress and the American Jewish Conference in 1944. This was made possible by the wartime anti-Nazi solidarity as well as by an adjustment in the pro-Communist groups' position on a national home for Jews in Palestine; in 1946–47 these groups sometimes favored a more militant line on Palestine than the Zionist majority. Even though most of their members did not belong to the Communist party but had joined for social and cultural purposes, the JPFO and AJLC successfully infiltrated important branches and divisions of the AJ Congress, the most liberal and grassroots Jewish organization.[35] As the pro-Communist *Jewish Life* boasted in retrospect, at the AJ Congress biennial conventions in 1948 the fighting spirit of the radicals still manifested itself in passing resolutions for the abolition of HUAC and for a meeting of Soviet and American leaders to avert the danger of war between the former allies. Together with others, they participated in Henry Wallace's Progressive Party campaign for the presidency, and while Wallace and his party failed dismally, approximately one third of the people who voted for him were Jews, both because of his unequivocal pro-Zionist stand and because of his rejection of the administration's Cold War policies.[36]

Even after the purge of the JPFO and the AJLC from the AJ Congress in the wake of the postwar Red Scare—for the record AJ Congress leaders pretended that the breaking of the organization's discipline and not the ideology was the cause for their expulsion[37]—some Communists and more fellow travelers remained entrenched in local divisions that were dissolved two years later. In April 1951 three large divisions in the New York metropolitan area—Manhattan, Long Island, and the Youth Division—were still able to organize a large protest rally against the rearming of Germany, without permission from the AJ Congress leadership, even though it fully shared the opposition to German rearmament. As a result, the AJ Congress dissolved its Manhattan division. The JPFO and AJLC, for their part, started to set up "United Front" organizations in different parts of the country. Their purpose was to combat German rearmament, to oppose the Korean War, and to promote the peace movement. In New York they were successful in obtaining the cooperation of a few Eastern European *landsmanshaften* and left-wing trade unions. In 1952, they established a special committee against Jewish negotiations with the Adenauer government. Afterwards, although a few protest meetings during such occasions as the 1959–60 swastika epidemic, the German-Israeli arms deal, and the New York encounter between Adenauer and Ben Gurion in March 1960 still attracted substantial audiences, the ranks of Jewish Communists and fellow travelers dwindled.[38]

7

Anti-German Protests at Home

After their immediate postwar involvement in the survivors' and refugees' safety and well-being, American Jews were greatly concerned about the political developments in Germany. Persistent antisemitic and authoritarian phenomena as well as democratic improvements were noted by the American Jewish community. Quite understandably, the community's anxieties were heightened by the growing numbers of official invitations to Germans to visit the United States for industrial, economic, and cultural exchanges. The Jewish community was careful to take note of the impact of these visits upon the American public.

The first Germans brought over to the United States after Germany's unconditional surrender were scientists and technicians in the fields of rocketry and aeronautics, as well as other experts whose knowledge was regarded as vital for the strengthening of postwar American military and industrial capability. Even though many of the participants had been members of the Nazi party, the semisecret "Overcast" project, soon to be renamed "Paperclip," served as immediate intellectual reparations. Despite differences of opinion in the relevant government departments and objections raised mainly by a few Jewish State Department officials and Jewish leaders, the operation did not arouse public protests.[1] Later came chosen visitors from the Protestant and Catholic churches who were considered by Washington's policy planners as most important in the remaking of German society. Also invited were business-men, university lecturers, teachers, journalists, administrators, and professionals—all in the framework of reeducating or reorienting groups of the West German elite, strengthening Western Germany against the Soviet Communist challenge, and restoring German-American cultural and trade relations. In this context, musical performances of famous German artists, and later of orchestras, were also promoted.

The American rapprochement with the former enemy put the Jewish community into a quandary. On the one hand, Jewish orga-nizations favored democratic education of the German public. At least, the organizations paid lip service to it and, in spite of some qualms, the left-of-center groups also adjusted to Washington's anti-Soviet containment policy. On the other hand, they could not overlook the fact that quite a few of the illustrious performers, and even more of the exhibitors invited to take part in the first postwar German industrial exhibition in New York, were tainted by their cooperation with the Hitler regime, if not by their own Nazi pasts. Thus, the question arose of how to deal with the legitimate Jewish sensitivity without isolating the community from the great majority of the American population, which endorsed the outstretched-hand policy toward West Germany because of the Cold War. The test case of the German industrial exhibition, behind which influential political forces and weighty economic interests were aligned, clearly revealed the limits of Jewish ethnic pressure. Nonetheless, Jewish objections in regard to the cultural scene, some of which were more successful, at least in the early period, were registered by the emerging West German political establishment. Bonn would soon start looking for ways to assuage that antagonism, because it recognized American Jewish hostility as an obstacle in the process of narrowing the gap with the American public.

The German industrial exhibition took place in April 1949 at the Museum of Science and Industry in New York's Rockefeller Center. For more than two months it was a matter of great concern to all Jewish communal agencies as well as to NCRAC, the coordi-nating body, characterized by ongoing discussions between working groups of staff people and committees of laymen. The NCRAC deliberations were mainly dominated by the traditional distinction between AJC's cautious attitude and AJ Congress activism, although in principle everybody opposed the exhibition. There were also unsuccessful intercessions by influential individuals. The meager net result was a common statement of protest, while refraining from any demonstrations.[2]

The fair, with the participation of several hundred German firms from all three Western occupation zones, was intended to "strengthen trade relations between the U.S. and Germany which were formerly so extensive and valuable."[3] When General Clay learned of the objections of major Jewish organizations such as the AJC and the WJC, as well as the AJ Congress, he told his adviser on Jewish affairs, Harry Greenstein—who conveyed the message to the Four Cooperating Organizations—that the exhibition would take place on schedule. Clay proclaimed "that he would regard any demonstration as a disservice to the U.S., which is trying to build up the German economy in order to relieve the U.S. taxpayers of its present crushing burden."[4] He appealed directly to prominent American Jews like Judge Joseph Proskauer, past president of the AJC, Bernard Baruch, and *New York Times* publisher Arthur Hays Sulzberger, urging them to use their influence to prevent either picketing or demonstrations by any group. At the same time, he promised that no person previously identified in any way with the Nazi party would be permitted to go to the United States as an exhibitor or as a representative of any exhibitor, and that all the participating firms would be carefully screened, a promise that was only partly fulfilled. Members of Greenstein's staff argued that it was illogical for Jews to oppose the revival of the German economy because they could not otherwise expect to receive indemnification. AJC European representatives looking for a compromise suggested that the German industrialists who would come to New York should formally declare that the victims of Nazi persecution were to be fully indemnified by an economically restored Germany. This proposal was not taken up because of both German unwillingness and Jewish objections.[5]

The American Jewish Committee, while recognizing the necessity of Germany's economic rehabilitation as an important ingredient of American foreign policy, initially voiced strong opposition to the New York fair because the items exhibited were produced by firms dominated by former Nazis. The AJC reiterated its position that only a liberal and democratic Germany could be a reliable ally in the framework of a united and democratic Europe. It also warned that despite temporary economic advantages, support for business and financial corporations that had been heavily involved in the Nazi regime was, in the long run, adverse to American interests.[6] However, the behind-the-scenes efforts undertaken by the AJC, on both the local New York and the governmental level, bore no results. Mayor William O'Dwyer did not intervene; neither could Nelson Rockefeller or the Jewish board members of the museum do anything to cancel the lease for the exhibition. Proskauer's successor as AJC president, Jacob Blaustein, was told by high officials of the Defense and State Departments that the economic rebuilding of Western Germany would proceed. Material presented by Blaustein on Nazi infiltration into the top industrial positions in Germany had no effect on his counterparts.

Moreover, during the controversy over the fair, it became evident to the AJC and to other Jewish organizations that most of their traditional nonsectarian allies were not prepared to share the opposition to the German exhibition. Members of Americans for Democratic Action and other liberal groups were not at all keen to engage in a confrontation with the recently reelected Democratic administration on such a subject, at a time when the Berlin blockade had increased public sympathy for the city and for the West Germans. The trade union federations AFL and CIO preferred that Nazi industrialists be kept out, but on the whole regarded the exhibit as being sound policy in the context of Germany's economic recovery.[7] Besides, the fear of becoming identified with active Communist opposition to the fair also weighed heavily upon the AJC's and NCRAC's strategy. Some were afraid that the failure of Jewish organizations to distance themselves openly from the Morgenthau plan before and after the end of the war contributed to the impression of a link between Jewish and Communist opposition to German recovery. If this view were abetted by the Jewish community through action that appeared to substantiate the belief that American Jews desired to take vengeance upon the German people, their isolation might endanger them.[8]

Such fears seem to have been exaggerated. But without gentile allies and because of the pressure exerted by the administration in Washington and the military government in Germany, the American Jewish Committee acquiesced to the fair taking place as scheduled. Actually, it had objected to public protests and picketing from the beginning. Its consolation was that the agitation had made at least part of the American public conscious of the counterproductive aspects of America's new German policy. But that proved an erroneous assumption. The AJ Congress, on the contrary, still clung to a Grand Alliance–minded and less anti-Communist orientation and objected to the strengthening of West Germany as a bulwark against the Soviet Union. That organization continued to regard the danger to world peace and security from a restored Germany greater than the Soviet threat.

In the opinion of AJ Congress executive director David Petegorsky, the fact that labor and liberal groups "did not understand what was happening" should not have deterred American Jews from making a stand of their own. Petegorsky was one of the leading committed liberal professionals in the Jewish community in the late 1940s and until his untimely death in 1956. A representative of the UAHC added that just because the Communists alleged that they were the sole supporters of liberalism, there was no reason "to abdicate any of the lofty ideals of Judaism." The delegate of the anti-Communist JLC thought it might be preferable to concentrate on the broad aspects of American policy toward Germany, using the fair only as an illustrative point. On the other hand, there were also voices that demanded a resolute stand against the exhibition itself. A spokesman for the Brooklyn Community Council warned that silence would be misunderstood by the Jewish masses. The JWV indicated that while it favored rebuilding the German economy, it fully endorsed Jewish opposition to former Nazis returning to leading posts in German industry.[9]

As a compromise agreed upon by six national Jewish organizations and twenty-seven community councils belonging to NCRAC, a critical and diplomatically worded pronouncement of wishful thinking stated that "the rehabilitation of German economy, but only on a democratic basis, will contribute to world peace security." However, they insisted that Nazis must be screened from German industry, and the German economy must be brought under the control of liberal pro-democratic and trade union elements who were both anti-Nazi and anti-Communist.[10] Because of the restraint of the organized Jewish community, the German exhibit was picketed only by the pro-Communist JPFO, the AJLC, and a few more leftist organizations, such as the Committee of Jewish Writers, Artists and Scientists, the Drug Store Employees Union, and several locals of other unions. Leftist members of AJ Congress's New York divisions also joined in picketing.[11]

The exhibit was arranged very carefully, reminding the visitors that it was set up by the military governments of the three Western zones with no direct political implications. According to a reliable Jewish observer, it was attended by many Americans of German origin, but there were also a lot of Jewish visitors. Despite differences of opinion in the community, American Jewish importers already represented German firms and were interested in using the opportunity to broaden their commercial contacts. In order to attract Jewish buyers, beautiful Chanukah candelabra could be found on one of the silverware stands.[12]

Summing up the Jewish response to the German industrial exhibit, A. S. Lyric, a Jewish writer and journalist, complained that the Jewish organizations, with the exception of the Jewish Agency, which was not involved in the compromise, did not act as free Americans. He maintained that they revealed their inferiority complex when yielding to Washington's demand to refrain from public protests. Lyric ridiculed the congratulatory comment of the *New York World Telegram* for the Jews having "conducted themselves so well." He assumed that the exhibit would have taken place anyway but doubted whether Washington would really have been angered if the Jewish organizations had stated publicly that their conscience did not permit them to sanction the German fair.[13] Lyric and other columnists in the Yiddish press reflected the deep sensitivity and powerful anti-German feelings among the Jewish masses, feelings that were much stronger than the compromise statement reached by NCRAC constituents.

The traditional differences between AJC moderates preferring behind-the-scenes intercessions and activists like the AJ Congress or the JWV again asserted themselves with regard to German visitors brought over to the United States in different exchange programs. AJC professionals and laymen favored, in principle, the invitation of German businessmen, academics, and government officials to the United States and sending American counterparts to Germany. They agreed it was important to tie the former enemy nation closer to the West, stimulate trade, and promote cultural relations as well as tourism. At the same time, they called for effective screening of the growing number of German guests to prevent active and influential Nazis from visiting and for keeping "inadequately informed anti-democratically oriented Americans" from influential positions within Germany. The AJ Congress, for its part, reflected more Jewish grassroots feeling and sometimes did not refrain from unilateral action against the admission of unwanted prominent German guests.

A case that attracted much attention early in 1949 was the cancellation of the admission of world-famous pianist Walter Gieseking, who was scheduled to appear at more than forty performances throughout the United States, starting in New York. Gieseking had been cleared by the denazification court. Although not a card-carrying member of the Nazi party, he had served Hitler's regime well by playing at official events not only in Germany but abroad. In cooperation with the JLC, the AJ Congress had planned to prevent his concert in New York with the help of the Stage Hands' Union, even though all tickets had been sold a month before his scheduled appearance at Carnegie Hall. However, the Immigration and Naturalization Service refused Gieseking's admission after he arrived in New York. Documentary evidence provided by the AJ Congress regarding the pianist's political views and propagandist activities before 1945 convinced the INS not to allow his entry, despite a favorable advisory opinion by the State Department to its consul in France, who authorized the granting of a visa to him.[14] Four years later Gieseking returned to the United States and performed in New York and in other cities. This time the protests of the marginal Non-Sectarian Anti-Nazi League were of no avail, even though New York police patrolled the streets to take care of the demonstrators.[15]

For a dissenting intellectual like David Riesman, the action against Gieseking, while humanly understandable, smacked of racial theory. It was easier for American Jews "to keep Gieseking out of America than [antisemitic congressman John] Rankin out of Congress." No wonder that AJ Congress's handling of the affair was also denounced by S. A. Fineberg, AJC's community service director. In contrast to the Gieseking picketing, he mentioned the widely favorable impact of the Chicago Symphony's retraction of renowned German conductor Wilhelm Furtwängler's appointment as its musical director. As a matter of fact, Furtwängler's case was not exactly similar to Gieseking's. He had damaged his international reputation by remaining in Germany and conducting there during the twelve years of the Third Reich. But he had never shown much sympathy for the Nazis, had quarreled with their leadership, and on several occasions had helped Jewish musicians. After the war Furtwängler was denazified and resumed conducting in Germany and abroad. Nonetheless, a great many American Jewish star performers and conductors like Vladimir Horowitz, Arthur Rubinstein, Nathan Milstein, Gregor Piatigorsky, Isaac Stern, Lily Pons, Andre Kostelanetz, and Eugene Ormandy threatened to boycott the orchestra in case of his appointment. The head of the American Federation of Musicians as well as the board of the Chicago Orchestral Society decided that he was undesirable.[16] Thus Furtwängler remained in Germany, where in 1952 he was reappointed musical director of the Berlin Philharmonic Orchestra, a position he had lost in 1938.[17]

Furtwängler's death in 1954 prevented him from conducting the Berlin Philharmonic during its first postwar visit to the United States in 1955, an act of gratitude to the American people for their assistance during the Berlin blockade of 1948–49. The fact that the orchestra was to perform under the baton of Herbert von Karajan, Furtwängler's successor and a member of the Nazi party since 1933, upset many American Jews. The organized community was shocked that a former Nazi like Karajan was sent by West Germany and admitted by the State Department as an ambassador for forging cultural relations between the two nations. But except for a few demonstrations by the JWV, it refrained from action.

As in the past, the issue was discussed in depth at NCRAC. Differences of opinion among both national and local member agencies precluded publication of a joint statement even though the AJC and ADL had withdrawn from the coordinating body in 1952. The New York CIO council was about to picket the performance but was dissuaded by the JLC and instead joined the JLC in deploring Karajan's choice. The AJ Congress, too, refrained from public condemnations after it had polled its leading members. This time its criticism was limited to a *Congress Weekly* editorial.[18] Heinz Krekeler, West Germany's first ambassador to the United States, regarded it as a great achievement that the successful tour of Germany's leading orchestra had taken place without major disturbances, in spite of the Musicians Union protest in New York.[19] Acts of disapproval in other cities were only marginal. A group of HUC rabbinic students in Cincinnati, while resenting the performance of the Berlin orchestra under the baton of a former active Nazi, nevertheless concluded that the "arbitrary denial of men's rights to a public audience" would harm democracy more than the tour of the orchestra itself.[20]

Irving Engel, Jacob Blaustein's successor as president of the AJC, told Krekeler that in spite of the AJC's displeasure, his organization exerted its influence against public demonstrations.[21] The same advice was given by the ADL to local community councils. It reminded them that attempts to boycott Gieseking's concerts in 1953 had not only been abortive but had aroused the anger of many music-loving liberals. Similarly, the ADL advised against boycotting concert performances by the soprano Elizabeth Schwarzkopf, though she had been a leader of the National Socialist student organization at the Berlin Academy of Music and afterwards joined the Nazi party.[22]

At the next tour of the Berlin Philharmonic Orchestra in 1961, under the baton of Karajan and Karl Böhm, who had also closely cooperated with the Third Reich music and cultural authorities, no public protests were registered. In accordance with the wishes of Jewish circles in Detroit, the original program was changed to enable the orchestra's Jewish concertmaster, Michael Schwalbe, to perform Mendelssohn's violin concerto.[23] At a concert in New York, the soloist was Israeli pianist David Bar-Illan, who after his return to Israel became executive editor of the *Jerusalem Post* and later served as one of Prime Minister Benjamin Netanyahu's policy advisers. Bar-Illan's performance under the baton of Karajan was criticized by the Yiddish press and by Rabbi Jack Cohen, a noted liberal Reconstructionist rabbi and Hillel director. Cohen regarded Bar-Illan's playing with an orchestra sprinkled with Nazi musicians "to be beyond the level of good judgment, to say the least."[24]

It happened that Jewish displeasure added to a more critical reception of prominent German visitors that had been incarcerated by the Nazi regime as political opponents. Such, for instance, was the case of the Protestant pastor Martin Niemöller, who in 1947 was hosted for a few months by the Federal Council of Churches of Christ, which cooperated on many issues with Jewish religious and communal organizations. Niemöller, a nationalistic submarine commander in World War I, had since 1924 consistently voted for the Nazi party, since he favored its program for a national revival "with its denial of all that was meant by individualism, parliamentarianism, pacifism, Marxism and Judaism." However, after Hitler's ascent to power he disagreed with Nazi church policies and became a cofounder of the "Confessional Church." Together with other pastors he rejected the application of the "Aryan paragraph" by the Church and in 1935 refused to endorse the Nuremberg Laws segregating German Jews.

Niemöller spent eight years in concentration camps; after the war he was among the authors of the Stuttgart "Confession of Guilt." That statement was regarded as an important step in the annals of postwar Protestantism, although it did not mention German responsibility for the murder of millions of Jews, which the pastor himself recognized. On the other hand, Niemöller decried American occupation policies, opposed denazification, and, together with many others, believed that the Morgenthau plan was designed as an instrument of American Jews to decimate the German people. Later, in the early 1950s, Niemöller's pacifism led him to endorse pro-Communist and neutralist peace initiatives. The American authorities therefore were concerned about the possible impact of his goodwill visit to Moscow on at least a part of Germany's Protestant clergy.[25]

Several leading American Jewish religious spokesmen ranked high among Niemöller's outspoken critics. Rabbi Stephen Wise deplored his "lamentable past" and questioned why the Federal Council of Churches of Christ had sponsored his speaking tour. Wise charged that Niemöller's talks aimed at selling a "soft peace" for Germany, an assumption that proved correct. Rabbi Barnett Brickner took sharp exception to Niemöller's statement in New York that antisemitism was dead in Germany. Rabbi Abba Hillel Silver, while describing Niemöller as a "good, friendly, well intentioned, courageous man," told the public that he had opposed Hitler and Nazism not because of their humanity-destroying racism but because of their persecution of the German Protestant Confessional Church. Since Niemöller had been taken in by Nazi propaganda in the past, he was "not qualified for the role of a prophet or spiritual leader." Eleanor Roosevelt, too, reminded Americans of Niemöller's ambivalent past.[26] All the goodwill efforts of the Federal Council did not help Niemöller to overcome the lack of confidence on the part of many Americans, particularly since he objected to the emerging Cold War policies.[27]

Another former concentration camp inmate, SPD party chairman Kurt Schumacher, who visited the United States in the same year as Niemöller, was not subjected to a hostile reception from Jewish organizations. As already mentioned, he had friendly discussions with the JLC leadership and AJC professionals.[28] Nevertheless, there were a number of critical comments. Shlomo Grodzensky, essayist and editorial writer of the Labor Zionist weekly *Yiddisher Kempfer*, rejected Schumacher's call for forgiveness and help for suffering Germans, arguing that the will for revenge was not less ethical than forgiveness of all sins.[29] Others complained about his nationalistic confrontation with the Western powers. The ADL refrained from financially supporting Schumacher's lecture before the City Club in Chicago and from arranging a press conference for him because of his unequivocal endorsement of Germany's economic rebuilding.[30] Dr. Samuel Gringauz, the former chairman of the Council of Liberated Jews in the U.S. zone who immigrated to America in 1947, dismissed Schumacher's warning that the danger of antisemitism in Germany would increase because of the decline of the belief in democracy, which depended on Western economic aid. Gringauz demanded German repentance before the survivors could allow the Jews in the Diaspora to engage in a dialogue with the Germans.[31]

During his stay in New York, Schumacher also hoped to meet WJC president Stephen Wise, but such a meeting did not take place.[32]

Ernst Reuter, the Social Democratic mayor of Berlin, who endeared himself to the American public during the Berlin blockade and who often disagreed with Schumacher's criticism of the Western allies, visited the United States a number of times before his untimely death in 1953. Reuter had spent the Nazi period as an exile in Turkey; he returned home in 1946. During his visits to the United States he did not encounter any Jewish protests. But in 1951 his visit to Detroit caused the plenum of the Jewish Community Relations Council to cancel an earlier decision of its executive to join a reception committee in the mayor's honor. The critics tried to justify their refusal because of Reuter's negative attitude toward the demonstrations staged in December 1950 by left-wing Berlin students. They resented his attitude toward members of the Jewish community and students who demonstrated against the performance of actor Werner Krauss. Krauss, the main star of producer Veit Harlan's antisemitic movie "Jud Süss," performed with the visiting Vienna Burgtheater.[33] Gerhard Jacoby, the WJC representative in Germany, praised the stand taken by the German students and by Berlin Jews. However, Ben Zion Hoffman-Tzivyon, a staunch anti-Zionist and a leading columnist in the socialist-oriented *Forverts*, ridiculed the behavior of the Detroit community leaders and regarded it as an insult to a leading Social Democrat who himself had been persecuted by the Hitler regime.[34]

A problem that caused some concern to organized American Jewry in the late 1940s and early 1950s was the admission to the United States of a large number of *Volksdeutsche* (persons of German ethnic origin) who had been expelled after the war from Eastern and Central Europe and found refuge mainly in the Western zones of occupation, two million of them in Bavaria. Their immigration was favored by German Americans who had been in the forefront of the supporters of a "soft peace" with vanquished Germany since 1945—and even before that. All of them, antisemitic nationalists as well as enlightened liberals, decried the Morgenthau legacy, blamed Potsdam, and pressed for the speedy reconstruction of Germany's economy, contrary to a much more reserved and critical attitude of the Jewish community. Even though a large majority of Americans of German descent had already been fully acculturated (in 1950 approximately 14 percent of the U.S. population were of German origin), their sympathy for the old country made an impact on a number of senators and congressmen, especially in the Midwest. Because of FDR's anti-German course, which eventually led to America's entry into the war, most of them had supported the Republicans since the 1930s, and their votes contributed to the Republican victory in the congressional elections of 1946. Under these circumstances, it was no surprise that the postwar immigration of Germans indoctrinated by Nazi rule raised fears among the Jewish community. The original Displaced Persons Immigration Act of 1948 contained a provision that 50 percent of the visas under the German quota were to be allocated to persons of German ethnic origin. Legislation two years later was to provide additional privileges to that group and to raise the number of these prospective immigrants from 27,377 to 54,744.[35]

NCRAC discussions before its participation in a Joint Conference on Alien Legislation together with Catholic and Protestant groups revealed the problem's very special delicacy for American Jews who had since 1946 played a central role in the fight for admitting DPs.[36] Professor William Haber, who had served as

General Clay's Jewish affairs adviser in 1948, remarked that the German refugees had not come into the American zone of their own accord and certainly were not welcomed by the Germans who lived there. However, he was afraid that under the amended DP act the influx into the United States of a large number of antisemites and antidemocratic elements could constitute a serious threat to the safety of the American Jewish community and the American tradition of racial and religious equality. Even among carefully selected Germans who came to Ann Arbor as exchange students, antisemitic sentiments were very strong, and the Germans spread them among the student body.

Irving Engel, an AJC lay leader and Blaustein's successor in 1955, thought that the reaction of Jews to that question was mainly emotional. He stated that Jews had always strongly objected to the principle of guilt by association and that the entry of more anti-semites would be absorbed by American political culture without any serious harm. Moreover, Jewish opposition would be a waste of time because of the great number of Americans of German descent. Shad Polier of the AJ Congress did not accept Engel's judgment that the *Volksdeutsche* were a lesser evil than German citizens, the *Reichsdeutsche*. Throughout the period of Nazi domination, the *Volksdeutsche* were more thoroughly poisoned by the concept of ethnic identification than Germans who lived in Germany proper. He argued that Jews should take a position against an influx of ethnic Germans even at the risk of being called German-haters. Eventually, NCRAC, while supporting the amendment to the DP Immigration Act of 1948, objected to special provisions for the admission of *Volksdeutsche* under the German quota, but its advice was not heeded.

The American Jewish community was often inhibited by the fear of being regarded as serving the interests of the Communist party and its front-organizations against vital American interests in the confrontation with the Soviet Union. This was especially worrisome during the German industrial fair in 1949 and other "German events" described in this chapter as well as in the general context of Jewish protests against the inadequacy of American policy with regard to denazification, democratization, and decarteliza-tion. Morris D. Waldman, John Slawson's predecessor as executive vice-president of the AJC until 1943, thought that the accusations and suspicions regarding Jewish affinity for left-wing causes had contributed to the decline of Jewish influence in Washington, which in 1949, after the last presidential and congressional elections, had become *Judenrein:* "Apart from Ben Cohen, an alternate delegate to the UN, and David Niles, a subordinate in the Executive Department, there is no one left."[37] A New Dealer and active supporter of civil rights, Niles, too, had been accused by right-wingers of Communist ties. Niles, for his part, became involved in fighting the antisemitic canard that Communism was, in fact, a Jewish movement. In that connection he conveyed to FBI director J. Edgar Hoover as early as April 1947 an AJC background memorandum outlining the aims and the strategy for the struggle against Communism as a "subversive conspiratorial movement" in the Jewish community.[38]

During the 1950s the AJC persisted in its efforts to thwart equations of "Jews and Communists." Early in 1951 it analyzed the attempts of American Communists to exploit Jewish sensitivity on the German issue in order to promote united front groups for pro-Communist causes.[39] The AJ Congress considered the AJC document most unfortunate and dangerous; the impression it created was that the bulk of public criticism of developments in Germany and of American policy was Communist-inspired and that virtually all public activity in the United States was organized by Communists. According to the AJ Congress, this contradicted the fact that by far the most important and extensive campaign concerning the German situation was conducted by responsible national and world Jewish organizations. The AJC's cooperation with right-wing anti-Communist groups such as the All-American Conference to Combat Communism was strongly criticized by liberal groups in the Jewish community. In 1952–53 the Committee went as far as actively endorsing the death penalty for Julius and Ethel Rosenberg, who had been found guilty of spying for the Soviet Union. The AJC's hysterical dealing with that case of espionage and its justification of the death sentence passed by a Jewish judge was nothing to be proud of. The AJ Congress, while condemning some of the Soviet actions and supporting the military intervention of the United States and the United Nations in Korea in 1950, still distinguished between the Nazi menace before 1945 and the Communist menace thereafter. It never forgot to mention that the German Nazi regime had been responsible for the murder of six million Jews.[40] However, because of the anti-Jewish and anti-Israel policies of the Soviet Union and its Eastern European satellites, the Congress movement and its constituents successively became much more critical of Communism at home and abroad.

In 1953 the AJ Congress joined a NCRAC resolution that reaffirmed the Jewish organization's "unalterable opposition to Communism as a totalitarian conspiracy which denies the dignity of the individual human soul, a concept basic to Judaism, and those freedoms of religion, the press and assembly . . . which are indispensable attributes of democracy."[41] In the following decades, the struggle for freedom of emigration of Soviet Jews and their religious and cultural rights at home resulted in a much more critical view of Soviet Russia by the whole American Jewish community.

8

Waiting in Vain for a German Change of Heart

Whatever the differences of opinion among the American Jewish organizations and schools of thought regarding the future of Germany and postwar German-Jewish relations, their frustration and disappointment in the lack of individual and collective German soul-searching concerning the crimes committed during the Nazi regime against the Jews of Europe united them. These crimes had been perpetrated by the SS, police reserve battalions of "ordinary Germans," and also many regular soldiers on the Eastern front, without any protest on the part of the German people. The disappointment of American Jewry applied not only to the silence and indifference of the masses but also to the evasion of the unpopular issue by most German politicians and public opinion molders, although there were a few exceptions. Usually they were more occupied with the problems of German refugees from the lost territories in the East and of the returning prisoners of war. Antisemitism had, of course, ceased being part of official German ideology after the nation's unconditional surrender in May 1945. Still, Jewish expectations that the full revelation of Nazi atrocities after Germany's surrender would cause a change of heart in the German population toward the survivors did not materialize nor did it bring about a rapid decline of antisemitism.

After the first shock of the defeat, the antagonistic behavior of the DPs revived, explained, and even justified in German eyes their own anti-Jewish sentiments. Because of a lack of outlets for immediate emigration, the DPs were forced to stay on German soil much longer than expected, most of them in the U.S. occupation zone. Opponents of denazification and decartelization by the American military government pointed to Morgenthau, Roosevelt's secretary of the Treasury, as the man responsible for that policy, with all the implications of Jewish vengeance. The restitution of individual and communal Jewish property that began in the late 1940s encountered bureaucratic obstacles and hostility from the new German "owners," who added another point of friction. The churches, too, including the Protestants who, in 1945, had started to discuss their role and responsibility for what happened during the Third Reich, were late to confront the most ominous German crime against the Jewish people.

Because of the Cold War climate, the impact of American Jewish criticism of the various shortcomings in Germany and the perseverance of antisemitism there were rather limited. Nonetheless, the common interest of the United States and the emerging semisovereign West German state in speeding up Bonn's acceptance by American and Western public opinion soon compelled the Bonn government to pay more attention to the Jewish problem. At home in Germany it contributed to what Frank Stern termed the philosemitic "Whitewashing of the Yellow Badge."[1] Abroad it prepared the way to conciliate American and world Jewry together with the State of Israel.

Reports of chaplains, representatives of Jewish organizations, and journalists in the first months after the end of the war in Europe dealt more with the situation of the surviving Jews than with the German population among whom they were living. One of the first to try to strike a balance in the postwar relationship between Germans and Jews in occupied Germany was Moses Moskowitz, a staff member of the AJC foreign affairs division, who served in OMGUS and dealt with displaced persons. In a much quoted article in *Commentary* that appeared one year after V-E Day, Moskowitz stated that while the number of Germans who admitted having approved of Jewish extermination was nil, the number who would agree that the pogroms were Germany's misfortune was not much larger.[2] In the recital of Nazi crimes at public forums, the six million

Jewish dead did not loom large: except for Heidelberg philosopher Karl Jaspers, married to a Jewish woman, no one had exhorted the German people to repentance and expiation for the mass killings of Jews all over the European continent. According to him, "the failure of the German people to protest against the mass executions of the Jews implicated them in the most hideous of the Nazi crimes." Still, when Jaspers's book *The Question of German Guilt* appeared in 1947 in English, his distinction between four kinds of guilt—criminal, political, moral, and metaphysical, including his justification of the criminal and political penalties imposed by the Allies on the Germans—did not silence Jewish critics who were not satisfied by his treatment of the Jewish problem. "Without gestures of conciliation, without true signs of shame before the Jews . . . we can see in it only a display of empty pride and morbid vanity," Ben Halpern commented.[3]

On the other hand, contrary to more skeptical Jewish observers, Moskowitz concluded that Nazism as a political, social, and cultural philosophy was no permanent part of the makeup of the German masses and that it would never have come to power if Germany had been more mature politically. The behavior of German women, who consorted with both black and Jewish soldiers and officers, was for him a demonstration that Hitler's community of "blood and soil" had dissolved. Moreover, interviews with hundreds of German men and women from all classes of German society proved that while most of them were not free from an anti-Jewish bias, the specific influence of Julius Streicher's propaganda on them had not been much greater. The antagonism toward the Jewish DPs from Eastern Europe was part of the general DP situation in Germany and manifested itself in the resentment of the preferential treatment, food and shelter, and other privileges denied to Germans but given to the DPs. Moskowitz also thought that the great majority of the Jewish survivors felt no particular vindictiveness toward the German people. Although almost no acts of vengeance occurred on the part of the Jews, Moskowitz's argument in this case still sounded somewhat apologetic, since he did not mention the strong hatred of the Germans by East European DPs and survivors.

While some of Moskowitz's conclusions may have been predetermined by his AJC public philosophy, he correctly stated that the most common mechanism by which the German masses avoided a sense of guilt was by convincing themselves that they, too, had been victims of the Nazis. Of course, this was not the truth. To confess a sense of culpability meant to them the acceptance of the collective guilt principle, and this was emphatically rejected by all the churches and the major political parties. At the same time, a new form of antisemitism was rising in Germany: both native and foreign Jewish survivors would haunt the Germans until the many individuals who had personally been involved in the extermination process were brought to justice. This subconscious feeling seems to have lasted in German minds much longer than Moskowitz anticipated. He did not underestimate the impact of twelve years of racialist anti-Jewish indoctrination of Germany's youth. Nevertheless, Moskowitz thought that the total abandonment of Germany by Jews, or its excommunication like that of Spain in the past, would be a "terrible admission of hopelessness of the Jewish position in the heart of Europe." Its implications would be that all efforts to regenerate Germany from within were condemned to total failure; and neither the AJC nor its new intellectual monthly wanted to subscribe to such a pessimistic view.[4]

Thanks to close contacts with the advisers on Jewish affairs, Jewish organizations were usually cognizant of the analyses of antisemitic trends in the German population. These were prepared by the Research Branch, Information Control Division (ICD) of the American military government. Even though they contained no catastrophic predictions (Rabbi Philip S. Bernstein's warning that one day after the withdrawal of American troops there would be pogroms in Germany mainly seems to have been meant to impress the visiting members of the UN Special Committee on Palestine), they still caused much anxiety among American Jews. Discussions and statements of communal agencies as well as articles in the English-Jewish and Yiddish press reflected that concern.

One of the most incisive reports, drafted early in 1947, acknowledged that after being at a low ebb immediately after Nazi Germany's unconditional surrender, antisemitism rebounded and continued to rise. A public opinion poll conducted by ICD in December 1946 revealed that only 2 percent of the German population in the U.S. zone were completely free from racial bias, 20 percent had little bias, and 41 percent were antisemites and intense antisemites. German antisemitism manifested itself in isolated incidents of violence against Jews and administrative sabotage in not allotting to persecuted Jews the privileges to which they were entitled. It also included desecration of Jewish cemeteries, threats, and anonymous letters vilifying Jews sent to newspapers and individuals.

As reasons for reviving antisemitism, the ICD research branch analyst quoted the following: a great decline in German morale, accompanied by an increase in nationalism and antiforeign sentiment; a resentment—mainly unjustified—over the privileges granted to Jews in matters of food rations and dwelling; black market accusations against Polish Jewish DPs though not against the German Jewish survivors; a rationalization by the individual, when confronted with antisemitism, that the Jews deserved the hostility to which they were subjected; and another rationalization that Jews were treated as sternly as they were by the Nazis because they must have been very hostile and pernicious to Germany (the Morgenthau syndrome). Last but not least was the exaggerated influence attributed to the Jews as a pseudomystical evil force in the mental framework of Nazi indoctrination, an opinion that had not basically changed since the collapse of Hitler's Reich. Since Jews were an unpopular subject, leaders in politics, the churches, and education were reluctant to combat antisemitism lest they alienate their followers. Isolated instances of condemnation of antisemitism remained without effect.[5] A similar investigation conducted in the U.S. zone one year later showed a slight decline of overt antisemites but an increase of racist attitudes.[6]

A few months after the establishment of the Federal Republic, HICOG argued that "as a social problem anti-Semitism is of minor significance," although it persisted as an attitude in German life, particularly in the middle and upper classes. According to a public opinion survey carried out in May 1949, about 20 percent were definitely antisemitic, 30 percent were indifferent, and just about one half of the German population could be termed as "non-antisemitic." Another survey taken in December 1949 concluded that despite antisemitic incidents and criticism of the Allied powers in the election campaign there was "no good basis for inferring any recent resurgence of nationalism among the German rank and file."[7] However, a well-informed American Jew such as Professor William Haber was still pessimistic. Haber had served for a year as General Clay's Jewish affairs adviser and drew his conclusions both from OMGUS reports and from his personal experiences. After sounding out Germans of different economic and social strata, trade unionists and professionals, Haber was convinced that it would take generations of reeducation to make headway with the anti-Jewish psychosis embedded in the German mind. A few years after the defeat of Germany, antisemitism had even spread to the working class, which had been relatively less supportive of the Nazis. Haber recommended to the AJC not to invest money and effort in fighting antisemitism in Germany as long as it was not a part of a larger program of democratic education and training.[8] In the long run, the relative containment of antisemitism in the following decade proved Haber's forecast too pessimistic, as were other Jewish forecasts on the eve of the establishment of the West German republic.

Haber obtained his knowledge of the German situation from his service as Jewish affairs adviser. Rabbi Joachim Prinz, a recent immigrant soon to become a leading spokesman for the WJC and the American Jewish Congress, had another kind of experience: until 1937 he had been one of the most notable liberal (Reform) rabbis in Berlin and had gained prominence there in the first years of the Nazi regime. Reporting on his impressions from an information trip in summer 1949, he confirmed that there were no violent outbreaks, no discrimination either in jobs or in schools. Yet there was "subtle anti-Semitism even in the thinking of those people who cannot be suspected of being anti-Semites." After a great many talks with public-opinion molders, politicians, clergymen, and intellectuals, Prinz concluded that "the poison of 12 years of propaganda [had] taken effect in the most well meaning of people." Nonetheless, Prinz shared Goldmann's view that a Jewish community in Germany would continue to exist; he correctly assumed that the majority of those Jews would be former DPs.[9] Reports from observers of the main Jewish organizations such as the WJC representative in Frankfurt and the head of the AJC's European office in Paris amplified the knowledge of organized Jewry with regard to German attitudes toward Jews, shortcomings of denazification, presence of former Nazis in the officialdom, antisemitic and nationalist trends, and other phenomena of the West German state and society. Of especially great importance was the insight provided by the AJC's intelligent and well-versed correspondents, whose reports served as the basis for critical in-depth discussions of the German situation.[10]

Jewish anxiety about the former enemy nation, which since the late forties was regarded as a potential Western ally, was reinforced by skeptical reports of well-known correspondents such as Drew Middleton and Delbert Clark of the *New York Times*. Clark, who summarized his conclusions in *Again the Goose Step*, was an outspoken critic of the administration's Cold War anti-Soviet course and its efforts to pacify the West Germans. Drew Middleton, for his part, warned that if the American army ever withdrew from Germany, a year or two thereafter the United States would encounter a recurrence of nationalism in its worst form. Later, in winter 1952–53, Drew Middleton, who was never liked by the Bonn establishment, informed the American public about the Naumann affair. For some time a group of former influential Nazis led by Goebbels's state secretary Werner Naumann tried to infiltrate the Free Democratic Party until their arrest by the British military government.[11]

Antisemitic and nationalistic outbursts as well as public approval of the return of former Nazis or collaborators to influential positions were reported in the general, the English-Jewish, and the Yiddish press. A few months after the opening of the first Bundestag, Wolfgang Hedler, a member of the right-wing German Party and a junior partner of Chancellor Adenauer's conservative coalition, stated publicly that "Hitler's anti-Jewish laws were all right, maybe gassing was not the right method of enforcing them." Hedler, who had also criticized statements by Schumacher and Paul Löbe, the last Social Democratic president of the Weimar Republic's Reichstag, was dragged out from the chamber by SPD members of parliament. But although Hedler was expelled from the German party's parliamentary group and condemned to nine months' imprisonment, he remained a member of the Bundestag until the end of his term in 1953.

In Hamburg, Veit Harlan, producer of the notorious anti-semitic movie *Jud Süss*, was greeted by public ovations when he was declared innocent of charges of antisemitism. Werner Krauss, star performer in Harlan's antisemitic movie, appeared in Berlin and other cities with the Viennese Burgtheater. He was heartily welcomed by many theatergoers and the city's political and cultural establishment even though the police clashed with demonstrating anti-Nazi leftist students, the first sign of the revulsion of the German young generation from their parents' past. In a way, the confrontation with Veit Harlan in Hamburg, where Erich Lüth, chief press officer of the city-state, called for a boycott of the producer's first postwar movie despite his acquittal, contributed to Lüth's and editor Rudolf Küstermeier's public appeal for "Peace with Israel." That appeal in August 1951 was supported by a number of noted German politicians and public figures. The students' protests against Werner Krauss and their subsequent demonstrations in Freiburg and Göttingen against another movie by Harlan heralded the first positive changes in Germany's political culture at a time of conservative dominance of its politics, but not many of the American Jewish community were aware of them.[12]

The first general elections in the Federal Republic caused much anxiety among American Jews watching the German scene. A clash between Jewish DP demonstrators and Munich police took place in August 1949, following the publication of an antisemitic letter under the fictitious signature "Adolf Bleibtreu, München 22, Palestrinastr. 33" in the Letters to the Editor column of the liberal *Süddeutsche Zeitung*. These letters followed a comment by one of the daily's senior editors on a reference by the incoming American high commissioner John J. McCloy, who defined the postwar German attitude toward the Jews as the most significant test for the new Germany. A crowd of several hundred Jews, who did not exactly distinguish between that letter and the paper's editorial opinion, staged a protest demonstration in the Möhlstrasse, site of various offices of Jewish organizations. Formerly, it had served as a center of black-marketeers and, after the German currency reform, a discount shopping area. At least six Jews were wounded by shots fired by the German police and more Jews were beaten up. According to German police, twenty-six of them were wounded by the demonstrators, who threw stones and wielded sticks against them. Quiet was restored thanks only to the appearance of two companies of American military police and the intervention of a Jewish army chaplain and a JDC executive.

As a matter of fact, the clash with the German police following the letter to the editor had been preceded by a raid of the German police in the Möhlstrasse area authorized by the American military governor. According to Rabbi Prinz, who was visiting Germany at the time, in that special case the German population sided with the Jews because they could buy their merchandise cheaper at the discount shops there.[13]

Norbert Muhlen, a Catholic German refugee of partly Jewish descent, who after the war became a steadfast propagandist for West Germany, tried to convince *Commentary* readers that German postwar antisemitism aimed mainly at foreign Jews, while native German Jews had more or less ceased to be considered Jews by the Germans and had never been attacked on racial or religious grounds.[14] A clear proof that Muhlen was wrong in his distinction between German hatred of foreign Jews and acceptance of their own German Jews was the case of the Jewish gynecologist, Dr. Herbert Lewin. After his liberation from a concentration camp in April 1945, he returned to his practice in Cologne, where the remnants of the local Jewish community were offered assistance by Konrad Adenauer, who for several months served in his former job as mayor of Cologne. In summer 1949 Lewin submitted his candidacy for the position of head physician at Offenbach's Municipal Hospital. Although he received more votes in a secret ballot than his gentile competitors, leading Christian Democratic and Social Democratic members of the city council torpedoed his nomination. The councilmen, including a veteran Social Democrat who had suffered under the Nazi regime, objected to entrusting German women to a Jewish physician who had come back from a concentration camp and whose family had been murdered.

Thanks to the intervention of the American authorities, Lewin was eventually appointed. Both the mayor and the deputy mayor tendered their resignations; most German newspapers and political parties, except the extreme rightists, condemned the handling of the affair by the Offenbach city fathers.[15] But to American Jews, and not only to them, this was another reminder of the prevailing antisemitism on a respectable municipal level.

A cause célèbre in 1951–52 was the arrest, trial, and subsequent suicide of Philipp Auerbach, one of the best-known spokesmen for the Jews in early postwar Germany. After moving from the British to the American zone, Auerbach, a member of the Social Democratic party, became Bavarian state commissioner for the victims of the Hitler regime and was later appointed president of the Bavarian office of indemnification. In addition to these governmental offices, he acquired great influence among the German Jewish survivors and the DPs, served as president of the Association of Jewish Communities in Bavaria, and in 1950 became a member of the newly established Central Council of the Jews in Germany. Complaints that reached the American commissioner in Munich, George Shuster, enabled Auerbach's longtime foe Josef Müller, the Christian Social Bavarian minister of justice, to put him on trial on charges of embezzlement, blackmail, larceny, and fraud, most of which proved incorrect.[16]

Auerbach's handling of the indemnification office's affairs was far from perfect, and he himself confessed to having used the title of doctor of philosophy illegitimately and having obtained his doctorate from Erlangen University on false evidence. However, his own trial revealed strong antisemitic overtones, as did that of Bavarian chief rabbi Aaron Ohrenstein, to which at least a part of the Bavarian CSU establishment contributed. Returning to the hospital after having been sentenced to two years in prison, the forty-three-year-old Auerbach committed suicide. A Committee for Fair Play for Auerbach, set up in New York by Bruno Weil, the president of the Axis Victims League, tried to assist the accused politically, morally, and financially, and to alert American Jews to the antisemitic implications of the case. But the Weil committee did not make a great impact, particularly since Auerbach had never been on good terms with some of the major Jewish organizations. Besides personal animosities, he had quarreled with JRSO because of his attempts to use restituted property for the German Jewish communities instead of transferring their value abroad.[17]

Another cause for American Jewish disappointment with the German public, administrators, and politicians in the early postwar period was their ambivalent attitude toward the restitution of Jewish property, not to mention the opposition of those who had profited from the "Aryanization" of German Jewish property in the 1930s. For General Clay, who enacted Military Law 59 in November 1947, restitution was one of the conditions for a cleanup of the Nazi past and the reconstruction of the German economy, along with denazification, land reform, and dismantlement (which was soon drastically reduced). As it became clear that the new federal government in Bonn would not be able to renege on the principle of restitution and indemnification enforced under direct control of the occupying powers, resistance to restitution among the German population intensified.[18] Warnings were voiced that restitution would cause renewed antisemitism. JRSO was denounced as an agency trying to implement the Morgenthau plan, and the restitution of smaller property encountered many obstacles. Conflicting interests between JRSO representing world Jewry and the German Jewish communities also exacerbated. In meetings with the State Department and the high commissioner, American Jewish leaders repeatedly asked for guarantees regarding the implementation of restitution after the abolition of the occupation status. After protracted negotiations, the three Western powers eventually secured the continuing implementation of restitution and indemnification in the framework of the contractual agreements that they signed with the Federal Republic in May 1952 in Bonn.[19]

In an early confidential report by the Jewish Telegraphic Agency (JTA), the American Jewish leadership was alerted to antisemitic prejudices even among anti-Nazi victims of the persecution. Because of their past, these anti-Nazis felt safe and well enough entrenched to act in accordance with their genuine feelings.[20] While that report sounded exaggerated, there is no doubt that antisemitic reactions, especially concerning the Eastern European DPs, could be observed among them. The foreign Jews from the camps, whom they met in the cities, were accused of being black-marketeers and unwilling to work. The Germans also envied Jews because of the extra food rations and preferential treatment in housing for those living outside the camps. Nonetheless, such generalizations were not characteristic of most of the leading anti-Nazi politicians on the left. The Social Democratic party led by Kurt Schumacher was the only one to assail antisemitism publicly in statements and conferences and to emphasize the German duty to indemnification of the victims on a national level.[21] Antisemitism was much more conspicuous on the right, among the small right-wing parties, and also among parts of the CDU, the backbone of Adenauer's conservative government.

Because of the large number of DPs and Bavaria's own right-wing conservative tradition, antisemitic prejudices were even stronger in the CSU. To repeat an often-quoted story: for one of the leading members of the Munich government who attended the second congress of the liberated Jews in the American zone in Bad Reichenhall, the only pleasing event was the unanimous resolution adopted there: "Let's get out of Germany!" However, that Bavarian politician did not forget to stress the importance of American Jews in renewing Germany's economic relations with the United States.[22]

The Protestant and Catholic churches were the only large social organizations that, thanks to their special status, had survived the collapse of the Nazi Reich. They were regarded by U.S. policy planners as well as by American public opinion as most vital factors in reconstructing German society. In fact, many leading churchmen of both denominations played an ambivalent role in their opposition to denazification and dismantlement, in appeals for clemency for the worst of the Nazi criminals and even in acts of direct or indirect assistance to some of them, most of which did not become known at that time.

As for the Protestants, the October 1945 Stuttgart "Confession of Guilt" recalled the suffering caused by German Christians to other nations but did not mention the murder of the Jews. Its main aim was the rehabilitation of the German church in the eyes of its sister churches in the West and preparing the way for its admission to the World Council of Churches in 1946. However, influential conservative church leaders and most local congregations objected to the Stuttgart manifesto because of its political dimension. The first meaningful and authoritative condemnation of Jewish persecution in the past, as well as of ongoing antisemitic activities, was passed five years later by the German Evangelic Church synod at Weissensee in April 1950.[23]

In contrast to Protestant pastors (including those of the Confessional Church), many of whom were active members of the Nazi party and its subsidiaries, Catholic priests had been prohibited by the Vatican from joining the party. But although many priests had loyally supported Hitler's regime before and during the war, the Catholic bishops at their first postwar gathering at Fulda disposed of the question of guilt, deploring that many Germans—including Catholics—had been deceived by false thoughts of the Nazis and lent support to their crimes. In 1948 the Catholic lay gathering (Katholikentag) in Mainz condemned the crimes committed against Jewish individuals with no opposition from the Germans. Nonetheless, it took much longer for the Catholic church to come to grips with the Holocaust and with the role that anti-Judaic teaching had played in deepening the hatred of Jews in the hearts of millions of believers.[24]

The National Council of Christians and Jews and its president, Reverend Everett Clinchy, with whom the AJC had cooperated in the struggle against antisemitism at home in the 1930s, joined the efforts for advancing democracy in postwar Germany and enjoyed the support of OMGUS and, until 1952, of HICOG. The cooperation with NCCJ was agreed upon by General Clay and Clinchy during the latter's visit to Germany in summer 1947. With financial and logistic help, the Council's emissary, Methodist pastor Carl F. Zietlow of Minnesota, became involved in setting up the first societies for Christian-Jewish cooperation in 1948–49, with the participation of local lay leaders and representatives of all three faiths—Protestants, Catholics, and Jews. In 1950 a coordinating council of all the societies was created, and according to the American model, yearly "Brotherhood Weeks" were launched. While the societies differed in the emphasis of their activities because of the quality and personal views of their members, the future-oriented liberal democratic orientation endorsed by the Americans in the Cold War climate often overshadowed the necessary confrontation with the Nazi past. The societies, including their Jewish members, were mainly instrumental in presenting a more favorable image of the anti-Communist part of Germany. In a modest way they served later as a positive element in West Germany's changing political culture. In the beginning, however, their impact on the fight against antisemitism and anti-Judaic prejudices was rather marginal, not the least so because of the difficulty in applying an American pattern to such a different society as postwar Germany.[25] For American Jews, their small impact was another disappointment.

The end of American direct rule in summer 1949 saw the quickening exodus of Jewish DPs, whose well-being and safety had been a major American Jewish concern since 1945. From the Jewish point of view, despite the satisfaction with the Army's handling of the survivors and refugees, the balance of the military government that lasted more than four years had been mixed: denazification had partly failed; dismantlement had almost been stopped; reeducation encountered difficulties; antisemitism, while not comparable to that of the Third Reich and not presenting an acute danger to Jews on German soil, had survived. On the other hand, important first steps had been taken in the field of indemnification and restitution of Jewish property. However, despite a few individual expressions of good will and remorse, the main problem of German postwar attitudes toward the Jewish people had been left untouched.

Thus, even though American Jews had not made up their minds with regard to the remaining Jewish communities in Germany, they continued to favor the exodus of the DPs. They were also gratified by John J. McCloy's reference, at a gathering of representatives of Jewish communities in Heidelberg in July 1949, to the moral issue involved. General Clay's successor, soon to become the United States' first high commissioner to Germany, expressly emphasized the "world significance of the relationship of the new Germany to the Jews and of the Jews to the new German community." As had his predecessor, McCloy refused to accept the principle that a country like Germany should remain without a substantial Jewish population. In his words, "to admit that Jews cannot live in Germany, as they do in other countries [was] . . . an incongruity itself."

While not minimizing the existing antisemitic manifestations, McCloy expressed the hope that the rather infinitesimal community remaining in Germany would prosper again and that Jews would be restored to positions they occupied in the past. The development of that community would "be one of the real touchstones of Germany's progress toward the light." On this occasion McCloy recalled what he had told a leading German who wanted to forget the past: "The moment that Germany has forgotten the Buchenwalds and the Auschwitzes that [is] the point at which everyone could begin to despair of any progress in Germany."[26]

Characteristic of the patriotic German mentality of the Munich Society of Christians and Jews was the strong protest it voiced against McCloy's reference to persistent antisemitism in Germany.[27] The Society's statement was challenged by Professor Franz Böhm of Frankfurt University, the Catholic chairman of the Frankfurt Society, who a few years later was to lead the West German delegation to the reparation talks in Wassenaar. Böhm saw the main task of the societies in fighting the prevailing antisemitism and not in suppressing responsibility for what happened in the past.[28]

No matter how much McCloy was influenced by his adviser Greenstein, who kept in close touch with the leadership of the major American Jewish organizations, he willingly made his statement on the importance of the mutual German-Jewish relationship. McCloy wanted to forge a close relationship between the United States and the new West German state. The parting Jewish Affairs adviser exhorted the high commissioner that "one thing that has disappointed and disturbed freedom loving people throughout the world has been the failure on the part of any responsible postwar German leader to denounce all that Hitler represented, including the systematic vilification and extermination of the Jewish people . . . unless the leaders of the present government commit themselves in such forthright fashion, the more difficult, if not impossible, will it be to develop the proper attitudes so necessary in a regeneration of the German people."[29]

A few days later McCloy discussed the Jewish problem with the newly elected Chancellor Adenauer; he also agreed to approach the other Western high commissioners in order to persuade Adenauer and President Theodor Heuss to speak up on the Jewish issue.[30] After all, such expressions of goodwill would serve the cause of American policy: to make public opinion more responsive to the acceptance of West Germany as a political ally of the West in the Cold War confrontation. These contacts resulted in the statements of Adenauer and Heuss on the eve of Rosh Hashanah extending greetings to the Jews of the Federal Republic and inviting them "to take part in the intellectual, social and political reconstruction of Germany."[31] McCloy congratulated Adenauer on that message.[32]

However, Adenauer's first address to the Bundestag a few days earlier, which was more important than the Rosh Hashanah greetings, did not satisfy Jewish expectations. The chancellor mentioned the necessity of punishing the "real guilty" for the crimes committed during the Nazi regime and the war but criticized denazification, which had caused much suffering. Balancing right-wing and left-wing extremism, Adenauer pledged to deal with both of them. At the same time, he strongly condemned persisting anti-semitic manifestations and thought it incredible that, after all that had happened, Germans were still persecuting and despising Jews because they were Jews.[33] In his response to Adenauer's outline of his government policies, SPD leader Kurt Schumacher was more explicit. He mentioned the fate of German and European Jews and reminded the German people that the six million murdered Jews would plague them for a long time.[34] But of course Schumacher spoke in the name of the opposition.

In subsequent talks with McCloy, Adenauer confessed that among the German people the National Socialist tradition was still most effective with regard to the "Jewish question." He promised to do all he could and mentioned the possibility of setting up, in the ministry of the interior, a special department for Jewish problems headed by a German Jew. This suggestion was discussed during the next year but rejected by the Jewish community and never implemented. In a new democratic Germany, the Jews did not want to be safeguarded by a special status. With an eye toward Israel and world Jewry, another proposal was made by the chancellor in an interview with Karl Marx, the publisher of the *Allgemeine Wochenzeitung der Juden in Deutschland*. Responding to prearranged questions Adenauer recognized the German duty to economic and moral indemnification and expressed his willingness to supply Israel with goods to the value of DM 10 million as a first step of recompense. However, both Israel and Jewish organizations in the Diaspora did not regard that proposal as a basis for opening meaningful contacts.[35]

More outspoken on the German Jewish post-Holocaust relationship was President Heuss. In his address to the Wiesbaden Society of Christians and Jews, in the presence of McCloy, he spoke of the collective shame that Germans would have to bear as a result of Hitler's persecution of the Jews, which should not be forgotten.[36] Heuss distinguished between collective shame and collective guilt, of which he disapproved. But it would take almost another two years until Adenauer's authoritative statement before the Bundestag on September 27, 1951, and the opening of the reparation talks between Bonn, Israel, and the Claims Conference.

At a meeting of the Society of Christians and Jews in Berlin, during a conference of the Congress of Cultural Freedom in May 1950, Elliot Cohen appealed for German soul-searching as a condition for bridging the gap between the two peoples.[37] Cohen was the founding editor of *Commentary* and the first American Jewish intellectual to address a German forum after the war on the relations of Germans and Jews. He told his listeners that only a few Jews among the five million in America had not lost some friend or relative or a whole family in Hitler's war against the Jews. He complained about the continuing silence on the Jewish tragedy, particularly on the part of German religious and political leaders, scholars, historians, poets, and novelists. Cohen's monthly, which was sponsored by the AJC, had published a number of incisive reports and analyses of the German situation. In a way anticipating Ralph Giordano's definition of "Die Zweite Schuld,"[38] he voiced the warning that "if they [the German people] do not speak out soon, if they do not take measures to show to the world that they are aware of what was done, and that they mean to take steps, steps of correction and self-understanding . . . then indeed all Germans, whether guilty or innocent of past crime, will be implicated. By default, Germany can achieve a collective guilt in the present and future."

In conformity with AJC's basic trend, Cohen favored building "a bridge across the abyss" and starting a German-Jewish dialogue as soon as possible, as a contribution to the new Germany's political culture. He added that taking into account all that had happened, only the Germans—and not the Jews—could take the initiative. Behind the scenes Cohen was approached by West German government representatives who suggested convening a joint German-Jewish conference that would discuss not only the implications of antisemitism for Germany but also concrete questions such as restitution.[39] Nonetheless, neither he nor the AJC regarded such a meeting as desirable at that time. They preferred that the Germans themselves should summon a conference to deal with the Jewish question and the problem of racism as a challenge for German democracy, without linking it at that point with restitution of property or compensation for Nazi crimes. Yet such a conference did not take place. As for the opening of an intellectual German-Jewish dialogue, it was still many years off. The road to overcoming mutual hostile perceptions was a very long one.

PART III

Reparations: Their Impact and Limits

9

The Twisted Road
Toward *Shilumim*

Because of the exacerbation of the Cold War and the hot war in Korea, the role of the Federal Republic of Germany changed more rapidly than expected. In 1950, a year after the military governments of the three Western occupation zones had been replaced, the three high commissioners opened negotiations with Chancellor Konrad Adenauer on reducing the limitations of the occupation status. In 1951 the semisovereign Bonn government's powers were augmented; in 1952 the contractual agreements with the three Western allies prepared the way for West Germany's factual sovereignty and membership in NATO. The implementation of these agreements was delayed because of French rejection of the European Defense Community (EDC) treaty, but the Bonn republic was well on its way to becoming an important ingredient of the Western camp even before it joined NATO as a full-fledged participant in 1955. Thereafter, it emerged as a founding member of the European Economic Community. Thus, postwar American foreign policy and military strategy achieved one of its major aims: West Germany became integrated politically and economically in the Western alliance and was able to contribute substantially to the defense of the West against the Communist East. Adenauer, for his part, preferred the Federal Republic's belonging to the West to uncertain alternatives of a neutral and demilitarized united Germany and consistently stuck to that course, even though he may have hoped that in the long run his policy would lead to reunification.

Whereas most American Jews were at least emotionally reluctant to accept the reemergence of West Germany as an important factor and U.S. ally a few years after the Holocaust, they had no chance to obstruct this process to which the administration attached high priority. Eventually, even organizations that had been more critical of that reversal acquiesced to it. Together with the State of Israel, which began to play a leading role in world Jewish affairs, they intensified their efforts to achieve at least pragmatic goals of immediate Jewish concern, which did not clash with U.S. national interest. Moreover, besides continuing intercessions concerning Jewish demands in Washington, organized American Jewry, as well as the Israeli government, reached the conclusion that they had to approach the Bonn government directly. This was necessary for a satisfactory settlement of collective reparations for the Jewish people, as well as improved indemnification for victims of Nazi persecution. It meant a substantial change of attitude, even though there had been a number of unofficial contacts with German government officials and direct communications with the *Länder* authorities on restitution by JRSO.

The negotiations conducted by Israel together with the Claims Conference and the signing of the Luxembourg Treaty ushered in a new chapter in Jewish-German relations much earlier than expected. The leadership of the Claims Conference was mainly American. Adenauer rightly assumed that his qualified acceptance of German responsibility for crimes against the Jews and West Germany's material amends to Israel and the Jewish people would contribute to an improvement of his nation's moral standing in Western, especially American, public opinion and partly mitigate Jewish hostility, at least on the institutional level.

A few distinguished personalities were to put their imprint on this crucial early chapter of the American Jewish–Israeli–German triangular relationship. The most influential Jewish leader in his contacts with the American administration at that time was Jacob Blaustein, AJC president from 1949 until 1955. While Blaustein did not have his predecessor Joseph Proskauer's intellectual capacities, he now would play a focal role with regard to Jewish demands from Germany. A few years earlier Proskauer, a lifelong opponent of Zionism, had contributed to the rapprochement between the non-Zionist AJC and the Zionists in the common American Jewish effort in favor of a Jewish state.

In 1945 Blaustein attended the preparations for the founding of the United Nations as a consultant of the U.S. delegation. After the end of the war, he took part in the work of the Five Cooperating Organizations dealing with refugees and restitution of Jewish property. He was nominated vice-president of the Jewish Restitution Successor Organization created in 1948 and retained that title until his death in 1970; in October 1951 he also became senior vice-president of the Claims Conference. The public-minded Baltimore multimillionaire, owner of the American Oil Company (Amoco; in 1954 it was to merge with Standard Oil of Indiana and become one of the largest oil companies in the United States) and a major contributor to the Democratic Party's election coffers, had access to the Truman White House. Blaustein also enjoyed good connections with John McCloy, who, as a Wall Street corporation lawyer, had represented Blaustein's oil company for a number of years.[1]

McCloy, a Republican, served during World War II as Henry Stimson's assistant secretary of war. In that position, he rejected in 1944 Jewish pleas for bombing the Auschwitz extermination camp or the railroad tracks leading there, telling his interlocutors that such action was "impracticable" and might "provoke even more vindictive acts by the Germans." Nonetheless, German industrial facilities in the Auschwitz area were bombed by American aircraft in summer and fall of the same year, once even less than five miles from the gas chambers. Later, in the 1960s, McCloy became a supporter of the Arab cause, warning that American support for Israel should be tempered by recognition of the economic importance of the oil-producing countries. In 1973, during the Yom Kippur War, he appealed to the Nixon administration not to increase military assistance to Israel and not to antagonize the moderate Arab states because of the vital access to the oil wells—an attitude then regarded as hostile by American Jews.

However, as President Truman's appointee to the powerful office of high commissioner for Germany, with wide prerogatives that enabled him to act rather independently, McCloy was very helpful to most Jewish requests. He was convinced that their fulfillment might soften American Jewish hostility to Germany and ease the way for West Germany's acceptance by the American public as a trustworthy ally. In a way, the development of a reliable pro-American democratic West German state was also a personal challenge for McCloy, who had been raised in a German American household and had married a prosperous German American woman, a descendant of 1848 immigrants.[2]

Nahum Goldmann, although he never regarded himself as an American Jew, lived in the United States from 1940 until the early 1960s and fulfilled a number of central functions in the community. In 1949, after Stephen Wise's death, he became acting president of the WJC. In addition, he chaired the New York–based American Section of the Jewish Agency executive. Later, he was elected president of both the WJC and the World Zionist Organization. In 1954, he laid the groundwork for the Conference of Presidents of the Major Jewish Organizations in the United States and served as its first chairman. Before the opening of the Israel-Jewish-German negotiations on *shilumim* and during their temporary breakdown in the spring of 1952, he also acted on behalf of the Israeli government, past and future differences of opinion notwithstanding. *Shilumim* was an euphemistic term that was introduced instead of *reparations* in order not to antagonize the Germans and not to cause difficulties with the Western powers.

Goldmann's main contribution was both in coordinating the domestic Jewish scene and in relation to the Germans. On the one hand, he succeeded in swaying the basically anti-German pro-Zionist majority of organized American Jewry and most Diaspora communities, convincing them of the necessity of direct negotiations with the Germans, because of Israel's urgent needs and their own interests. On the other hand, he accomplished the significant task of establishing a relationship of mutual trust with the West German chancellor. This was of great importance not only in paving the way for the Luxembourg Treaty but also for his further successful intercessions as chairman of the Claims Conference. He continued to head the Conference for many years; and whatever Adenauer's motives, his voice and actions were the decisive ones in Bonn.[3]

As for Israel, despite strong public anti-German statements at the UN and other bodies, the ministry of foreign affairs under Moshe Sharett and his director general Walter Eytan were the first to insist that the government revise its policy of ignoring the West German state. Sharett continued to play a leading role in promoting that revision after the signing of the Luxembourg agreement, until

Israel's readiness to establish some kind of diplomatic relationship was rebuffed by West Germany's Foreign Office. The rationale for that rebuttal was the "Hallstein doctrine" and German interests in the Arab world. The doctrine, conceived by Prof. Wilhelm Grewe, a high foreign service official soon to become West Germany's ambassador to Washington, insisted on the Federal Republic's status as the only legitimate representative of the German people. It threatened to break off diplomatic relations with all nations that recognized the German Democratic Republic and tried to prevent a situation where such a development might take place. For David Horowitz, the powerful director general of the ministry of finance, negotiations with the Germans on reparations were the only way to extricate the new nation from its economic and financial straits.[4] Eventually, the historic decision to open direct talks with West Germany was made by Prime Minister and Labor party leader David Ben Gurion, although he personally became involved more deeply in German-Israeli relations only several years later.[5]

At first, the approaching end of American and Allied occupation prompted the major American and international Jewish agencies into coordinated action on safeguarding the restitution of Jewish property, which had been imposed in 1947 by the military government in the U.S. zone and afterwards by the British and the French in their occupation zones. These intercessions started in advance of Israel's official appeal to the United States and the other three occupying powers with regard to the retention of Allied control over restitution, improvement of existing indemnification laws, and speeding up of both restitution and compensation claims. To surmount factual, legal, and bureaucratic obstacles in handing over identifiable heirless property to JRSO, Goldmann, JDC chairman Edward Warburg, and other Jewish leaders in 1950 suggested global settlements with the German *Länder* responsible for the implementation of restitution.[6] McCloy responded positively because satisfactory solutions would contribute to the stabilization of the German economy and also help in improving Germany's image in the United States, particularly since a large part of JRSO claims had been submitted by American citizens. Still, it took a number of years to settle the claims.[7]

A matter of great concern to the Jewish organizations was the composition of the Court of Restitution Appeals on which Jewish claimants often relied. Neither Washington nor London nor Paris accepted Jewish demands to preserve an Allied majority on the mixed board. Eventually, as a compromise with the West German government, a neutral chairman was agreed upon. Nonetheless, the inclusion in the agreement between the three Western allies and the Federal Republic of a German commitment to fulfill all its obligations pertaining to restitution of property and indemnification of the Nazi victims was a significant one. Constant prodding by the American Jewish community had contributed to this end.[8]

A number of McCloy's assistants in HICOG were of Jewish origin. Some of them—for instance, Samuel Reber and Arthur Settel—were regarded by the Jewish organizations as very helpful and cooperative. Shepard Stone, McCloy's public relations and information director, who had fallen in love with Germany during the last years of the Weimar Republic and married into the renowned Hasenclever family, was more interested in German democracy than in Jewish affairs.[9] Assistant High Commissioner Benjamin Buttenwieser, an AJC executive member, preferred to act behind the scenes and not to expose himself; for instance, he became involved in preparations for Adenauer's Bundestag statement in September 1951. In 1950, he angered the ADL leadership that disinvited him from addressing its annual meeting because he played down the threat of Nazi revival. But, on returning home eighteen months later, he complained about the increase of neo-Nazi manifestations. This warning enraged the West German minister of justice Thomas Dehler, a member of the right-of-center Free Democratic Party (FDP, Liberals), who accused him of "Morgenthauism."[10] The nationalistic views of Dehler, a lawyer who survived the Nazi period together with his Jewish wife, were characteristic of at least a part of Adenauer's conservative coalition. However, the crucial decisions relating to Jewish affairs were made by McCloy himself. Sometimes he overrode objections from the State Department and his own staff, for instance, enabling JRSO to transfer monies to the Jewish Agency and the JDC in Israel, despite the still existing freeze on the export of foreign currency. Blaustein was involved in convincing him of the urgency of such matters.[11]

The restitution of communal property in the early 1950s caused conflicts not only with the Germans but also with Jewish groups, particularly with those representing German Jewry. The lingering crisis between the successor organizations and the Council of Jews from Germany was shelved only by a last minute compromise in

1954. But to achieve American and world Jewish consensus on collective reparations from Germany and to obtain a satisfactory settlement for the claims of the State of Israel and the Jewish people was much more difficult than the coordination on restitution through JRSO and the two other successor organizations for the British and French zones. Despite early WJC and Jewish Agency demands of collective reparations, the issue had been stalled because of the lack of a legitimate German government. After its establishment, that government at first hesitated to deal with such claims. There also was strong Jewish opposition to opening direct negotiations with German authorities only a few years after the Holocaust. When reparations for Israel and the Jewish people were finally put on the agenda in 1951 because of Israel's urgent needs and Adenauer's interest in conciliating American Jewry and the Jewish state, the first problem in the American Jewish arena was how to bridge the gap between the many pro-Zionist organizations and the influential non-Zionist AJC, which enjoyed the best contacts with the administration. The next challenge was to bring all of them together under a common roof in expectation of direct talks with the Bonn government in cooperation with Israel.

During a visit to Israel in 1950, Blaustein, as president of the AJC, had reached an agreement with Ben Gurion, whereby Israel would not interfere in internal affairs of Jewish communities abroad.[12] This modus vivendi, however, did not put an end to the ideological differences regarding Zionism and Jewish peoplehood. In 1951, the AJC supported Israel's claim for $1.5 billion in reparations from Germany as compensation for resettling half a million Jewish victims of the German Reich. However, the AJC did not agree with the concept embodied in the original Israeli note "that Israel is entitled to the reparations . . . [and] should be recompensed because of the outrageous annihilation of the tremendous number of Jews." Only Israel's acknowledgment that it would not monopolize the total reparations complex served as a basis for the AJC's participation in the forthcoming conference of Jewish organizations that was to review the whole matter of Jewish claims from Germany.[13] Afterwards, Blaustein used all his influence and especially his personal acquaintanceship with McCloy to persuade the German government to be more responsive to Israel's demands. But, of course, because of his basic strategy of promoting closer American-German relations, McCloy himself was very much interested in a successful outcome of the German-Israeli-Jewish negotiations that were to open in March 1952 in the Dutch town of Wassenaar near The Hague.

While Adenauer's handling of the Jewish problem and his endorsement of reparations for Israel and the Claims Conference may have also been based on a certain moral urge, he did not conceal that, in his view, they matched most important German foreign policy objectives. German interests in the Arab world made their growing impact only somewhat later. Despite his Eurocentric education and background, the septuagenarian, conservative statesman grasped the crucial economic and political role of the American superpower after 1945, and its supreme significance for Germany and Europe. For him, the United States was a bulwark against the expansion of Soviet Communism, which he regarded as the greatest danger to European and Christian values. He was continually afraid of political changes and domestic pressures in the United States that might weaken the American commitment. In his positive appraisal of America, Adenauer differed from some of his contemporaries of the older elite or critics from the Left, who looked disparagingly at the great democracy overseas. This was also true of the middle-aged and younger Germans who in the first years after the defeat were still infected by Goebbels's anti-American propaganda.[14] In his consistent efforts to preserve and strengthen close political relations with the United States, the task of conciliating the American Jewish community, for understandable reasons a hostile factor, came in; and a settlement with the Jewish state became a part of that policy. In a way, Adenauer's successors aimed at the same goal, although the intensity of their efforts varied according to the changing circumstances.

In background talks to editors, in cabinet sessions or meetings of his CDU party executive, the chancellor asserted that without moral as well as legal recognition of Germany's equality by the Western democracies, it would not be able to conduct a successful sovereign foreign policy. An agreement with Israel and the Jewish people was a vital precondition for that. At the same time, such a settlement might have immediate positive repercussions in the United States; sometimes Adenauer also mentioned possible advantages in the economic field. Thus, while the Israel treaty did not result from American governmental pressure, Adenauer's moral decision was linked to political pragmatism. In this context, Adenauer took into account—and sometimes exaggerated—American Jewish influence.[15]

In the past, the anti-Nazi conservative Catholic statesman and former mayor of Cologne had enjoyed good relations with prominent members of the local Jewish community. He was fully conscious of the crimes against the Jews, the concentration camp detainees, and the civilian population in Poland and Russia, crimes committed not only by the SS and Gestapo but also by units of the Wehrmacht itself. In a private letter to Pastor Bernhard Custodis in early 1946, Adenauer referred to the guilt of the German people, including a major part of the Catholic clergy, who had been persuaded by the Nazi propaganda and willingly supported the Nazi regime even when they could see what was taking place openly in Germany during the 1933 (he must have had in mind the anti-Jewish boycott of April 1, 1933) and 1938 pogroms.[16] However, as leader of the conservative Christian Democratic party before and after the establishment of the Federal Republic and as chancellor of an even more right-wing coalition government, he at first moved slowly on the unpopular issue of stretching out a hand to world Jewry. Interviews such as that granted to the *Allgemeine Wochenzeitung der Juden in Deutschland* were trial balloons with a limited impact.[17] He also did not show much interest in the handling of restitution of Jewish property and of indemnification payments by the *Länder* governments, in which the federal government was not directly involved.

Nonetheless, at the beginning of 1951, Adenauer responded to urgings from Jewish circles and from his own advisers and concluded that he must break the deadlock by trying to improve relations with Jews abroad and with Israel. Despite the failure of the first meeting between the chancellor, Israel's ambassador to Paris, Maurice Fischer, and David Horowitz, director general of Israel's ministry of finance, informal contacts regarding the contents of the German declaration continued during the summer. Federal president Theodor Heuss suggested to the chancellor that he address the issue of reparations during the forthcoming Jewish New Year holiday at a plenary session of the Bundestag. In talks with a number of prominent Jews he had observed some softening of their feelings. The president himself returned to the problem of moral compensation for the Jews in a radio talk on the occasion of the "Brotherhood Week" sponsored by the societies for Christian-Jewish cooperation.

Eventually Adenauer made a statement before the Bundestag and expressed his willingness to open negotiations on collective recompense, even though the wording of his declaration acknowledging German responsibility for "the unspeakable crimes committed in the Nazi era in the name of Germany" fell short of fully satisfying Jewish expectations. It also included an apologetic assertion that many Germans had extended help to their Jewish co-citizens. In the name of the Social Democratic opposition, which was not happy with Adenauer's low-key formulation, veteran Paul Löbe, the former president of the Reichstag, addressed the Bundestag. Löbe mentioned the murder of six million Jews by Germany's Nazi rulers for the one reason that they were Jews and expressed the German moral duty to strive for reconciliation with the State of Israel and the Jews world over.[18]

A few weeks after Adenauer's statement, the Conference on Jewish Material Claims against Germany—usually known as Claims Conference—was set up to coordinate the demands and interests of the different organizations. Contrary to the original guidelines from Jerusalem, the meeting of twenty-two major American and world Jewish organizations on October 25–26 in New York became more than a demonstration of support for Israel's claims and established itself as a permanent body.[19] The difference between JRSO and the Claims Conference was that while JRSO had been dealing only with a rather limited problem such as heirless identifiable property, the Claims Conference demanded a global sum for the plundered unidentified Jewish property, as well as indemnification of all the victims of German persecution.

Goldmann, who summoned the meeting upon the request of Israel's government, remained the Claims Conference's undisputed leader for many years to come. He had to work hard to bridge the difference of opinion between "people whose entire past public Jewish record was one of public antagonism." However, after the decision by the Israeli government and the Knesset to open direct negotiations with the Germans, he boasted of having obtained a much larger majority in the executive committee of the Claims Conference than Ben Gurion in Jerusalem. Only Agudath Israel opposed direct talks and, because of Orthodox objections, the Synagogue Council of America abstained, as did the delegate from Australian Jewry.[20] Goldmann tried to convince the opponents of negotiations with Germany that the talks dealt only with reparations for the damage and losses suffered by the Jewish people, and in no way meant reconciliation with those who murdered the six million. Because of the evasive response of the United States and the other Western powers to Israeli and Jewish claims submitted to them, he argued, there remained no alternative other than to try and obtain reparations directly from the resurrected West German state. In January 1952 he secured a majority of twenty out of twenty-six in favor of direct negotiations even in the WJC executive, which usually mistrusted the Germans. In the JDC administration committee, several lay leaders, such as Monroe Goldwater, opposed the agency's participation in negotiations with Germany because of the resentment of a large part of the American Jewish community. The majority, however, favored joining the Claims Conference and taking part in the talks with the Germans.[21]

In one way or another, most of the American Jewish organizations expressed satisfaction with Chancellor Adenauer's declaration of German willingness to make amends for the Nazi crimes and open negotiations with the Jewish people and the State of Israel. The WJC noted, among others, the chancellor's reference to the importance of reeducating the German people, combating the reemergence of antisemitism and indemnifying the Jewish victims. The AJC looked upon Adenauer's statement as a significant first step toward Germany's acceptance "of its moral and legal responsibilities for the unprecedented crimes" committed against the Jews of Europe. There was no surprise in the total rejection of any dealings with the German government by the right-wing Zionist Revisionists of America who followed the Cherut party line in Israel. But to endorse negotiations with Bonn was also not an easy matter for the sister party of the ruling Mapai in Israel, the Labor Zionists, who had been among the outspoken opponents of Goldmann's moderate course in the WJC. After Adenauer's declaration, they approved efforts to safeguard the recovery of Jewish property, but without recognition or rapprochement with Germany. The Yiddish version of the Labor Zionists' arguments was more emotionally anti-German than the English version in its information bulletin.[22]

While most editorials recognized the significance of Adenauer's statement and the forthcoming negotiations with the Germans, comments in English-Jewish publications as well as in the Yiddish papers reflected the community's ambiguity and mixed feelings.

One of the more thoughtful comments appeared in the Labor Zionist monthly *Jewish Frontier* edited by Hayim Greenberg. The author assumed that Adenauer's offer to negotiate restitution for destroyed or looted Jewish property might be accepted "without any qualms that in doing so Germany is being whitewashed of its crimes." But if it was genuine "spiritual purging of unheard-of suffering" that the Germans were seeking, they would be best advised not to link it anyway with material reparations:

> The path for such a purging lies elsewhere, first through an unequivocal realization and admission of guilt, and later through genuine remorse. Atonement and the consequent moral rehabilitation in the eyes of the world are not something to be achieved overnight. The Germans must win these themselves. Even the Jews, who were the victims of the German crimes, cannot grant forgiveness as on a platter. We may have to become reconciled to the thought that at least a generation might pass before relations between Germans and Jews enter upon a "new and healthy basis."[23]

Despite its decline, the Yiddish press still had a large readership in the early 1950s. Strong criticism of the deal with Germany was voiced by famous Yiddish writers and critics. During the ongoing debate, the opponents drew encouragement from fellow writers in Israel. Even before the reparations problem was put on the agenda, poet Hersh Leivick castigated former DPs registering in the United States for indemnification as taking "blood-money from the Germans." In October 1951, he questioned Goldmann's right to assemble the Claims Conference. In the same vein, Isaac Bashevis Singer, the novelist and future Nobel prize laureate, disregarded Adenauer's statement and warned that "from no point of view— whether religious, humane or national—have we the right to accept German money." The Yiddish poet Jacob Glatstein, who served as the AJ Congress public relations officer for the Yiddish press, simply denounced Adenauer's statement as "a lying document," and Aaron Zeitlin questioned the moral basis of the conference summoned by Goldmann.[24] An exception to the hostile reaction of most of the writers was S. Charney-Niger, who welcomed the Bundestag declaration of the chancellor as "a great moral victory" for Jews, together with the rest of the world. Niger also rejected the concept of collective guilt of all Germans.[25] A symposium on the issue of direct negotiations with Germany, published in the *Tog* after the approval of the talks by the Knesset, revealed the ongoing disagreement between cautious pragmatic supporters and rigid moralistic opponents.[26]

After having been involved behind the scenes in the preparations of Adenauer's Bundestag statement, Goldmann met Adenauer at Claridge's Hotel in London in December 1951 in connection with Israel's demand that the chancellor accept, in advance, its claim of $1 billion as the basis for the forthcoming negotiations. That meant West Germany would take upon itself two thirds of the total sum demanded by Israel. In theory, East Germany would have to pay the other third, although that was not in the realm of realistic politics. Adenauer agreed in principle, and the meeting inaugurated a relationship of mutual confidence and goodwill between him and Goldmann, despite their totally different political and personal backgrounds and their incompatible opinions on international affairs, including the East-West conflict. For Adenauer, Goldmann was the ideal partner at the decisive crossroads of the reparation talks. Besides his close links with American Jewry and the Jewish Diaspora, Goldmann had lived in Germany for more than thirty years and had been educated at German universities. He was well versed in German thought and culture; he and Adenauer could talk about more than indemnification and reparations. Thanks to his direct approach to Adenauer, Goldmann could intervene during the negotiations, helping to obtain adequate settlements.[27]

In special cases, other American members of the Claims Conference presidium assisted the common effort. JLC president Adolph Held, for instance, was in touch with the German Social Democrats, although they might have supported the Israeli claims even without the JLC's friendly persuasion. Schumacher appealed to the chancellor from his sickbed to reach a satisfactory agreement with the Jewish side. In October 1952, after the signing of the Luxembourg Treaty, his successor, Erich Ollenhauer, rebuffed objections from a visiting delegation of the Arab League. In March 1953, the SPD parliamentary group provided solid support for the treaty's ratification. Whereas the SPD, too, had absorbed former Nazis into its ranks, 87.5 percent of its members in the first Bundestag had suffered in one way or another from Nazi persecution.[28]

Thanks to his special standing and his close relationship with the chancellor, John McCloy played a significant role during crucial stages of the reparation talks. Neither McCloy, who served as high commissioner until July 1952, nor the administration in

Washington wanted to dictate terms. Still, his friendly persuasion of Adenauer "to get him to adhere to the broad, generous concept was an important factor in arriving at the final results" was how he summarized his part twenty years later. He was also helpful in bringing about a compromise on the separate claim of the Claims Conference, which endangered the conclusion of the agreement in the summer of 1952.[29]

High-ranking and middle-level State Department officials, whom Israeli diplomats and spokesmen for the major American Jewish organizations had regularly approached on reparations since March 1951, at first responded with noncommittal expressions of goodwill and moral support. However, Ambassador Abba Eban thought that his labor had not been in vain; in the spring of 1952, the United States and the other occupying powers, he believed, had become more sympathetic to Israel's demands.[30] At one point in April, Blaustein tried to elicit a statement of support for Israeli and Jewish claims on behalf of President Truman, but on Secretary Acheson's advice, the president refrained from making a public statement.[31] Acheson mentioned the American interest in West Germany's reaching a satisfactory agreement at the talks when he met Adenauer during the signing of the West German–Allied agreement and its annexed protocols in Bonn, but did not promise any American aid for that purpose.[32]

Thus, whereas the Western powers were in no way willing to get involved in the intricacies of Israel's reparation claims, they nonetheless conveyed to Adenauer and his government the urgency of a successful conclusion of the negotiations. A breakdown could have a negative impact on public opinion in their countries. Even the new Republican administration, to which prominent American Jewish spokesmen and supporters of Israel did not have the access they had to its Democratic predecessor, took the same attitude on the eve of the Luxembourg Treaty's ratification.[33] The positive reaction of American public opinion to the signing of the treaty in September 1952 could only reaffirm Adenauer's belief that he was right, even though the public interest there in ratification half a year later was smaller.[34]

The Luxembourg *shilumim* treaty granted Israel $822 million over the next twelve years; most of it was to be covered by the supply of capital goods and up to 30 percent paid to the British Petroleum Company for vital oil deliveries to Israel. The sum included $100 million collective compensation for the Claims Conference, in the Diaspora and in Israel. The importance of the protocol between West Germany and the Claims Conference regarding the improvement, and enlarging the scope of individual indemnification, was not yet fully recognized at that time; in the long run it amounted to much more than all the other payments.[35] Before ratification, Adenauer was confronted with boycott threats by Arab League members, with opposition from financial circles and the export industry. Objections were raised by the coalition parties in the Bundestag and representatives of the *Länder* in the upper house, the Bundesrat. To accommodate the protesting Arabs, Adenauer himself considered accepting UN arbitration for the reparation shipments. However, contrary to Nahum Goldmann's opinion, Ben Gurion unequivocally rejected any control of German supplies by the United Nations or some other international body. Such a control would be interpreted as giving in to Arab pressure and undermine the moral terms of the *shilumim* agreement.[36] Public opinion polls showed that the majority of the West German population was against reparations for Israel, or at least regarded the promised sum as too high.[37] Nonetheless, the treaty was ratified in March 1953, thanks to the solid support of the Social Democratic opposition. Only half the members of the conservative coalition parties voted for ratification; a substantial number abstained, including Minister of Finance Fritz Schäffer, Adenauer's most consistent opponent on the issue of reparations.[38]

Among those who opposed the ratification of the Luxembourg agreement were not only right-wingers but also the Communists who were represented in the first Bundestag. Scholars like Anson Rabinbach tried to explain the Communist vote as a protest against the Adenauer government's "restricting the issue of responsibility to the Jewish crime alone, bracketing out all other claims of reparations" and thus helping the restorative climate and postponing the "mastering of the Nazi past." Whether this was the most important reason for their negative vote at the peak of the anti-Zionist and anti-Israel campaign of the Kremlin and of East Berlin is a matter of conjecture.[39] On the other hand, in his statement before the Bundestag endorsing ratification, Adenauer referred to Soviet anti-semitism that endangered Jews in all Communist-controlled countries in Eastern Europe. At the time that West Germany granted reparations to Israel and improved indemnification payments for

Jews, Adenauer seems to have been interested in establishing a link between these steps and the need for a resolute stand against the Soviet bloc. He hoped that at least some elements of the Jewish community might be of help. Nevertheless, a suggestion that AJC president Jacob Blaustein discuss the danger of Soviet antisemitism at a private audience with the chancellor during his visit to the United States was not followed up.[40]

Adenauer, who for various reasons had been advised to postpone his first visit to the United States, came to Washington in April 1953, a few weeks after the West German ratification of the reparations agreement and of the EDC Treaty (which was later rejected by the French National Assembly). Except for Adenauer's own short reference to the Israel treaty at the National Press Club, the issue was not broached during his talks with the Eisenhower administration. Instead, the chancellor pressed for more leniency with regard to the imprisoned war criminals.[41] Still, some of Adenauer's close assistants, among them Felix von Eckardt, the head of the German Federal Press and Information Office, who accompanied him on the trip throughout the country, thought that such a friendly reception by the American public would not have been possible without the reparation agreement.[42] Besides Goldmann and Blaustein, whom he had met in Bonn in 1952, Adenauer was introduced to other leading members of the Claims Conference and of major Jewish organizations. During Adenauer's next visit in 1954 Goldmann gave a reception in the chancellor's honor at his home in New York. Goldmann's excessive praise of Adenauer sometimes provoked Social Democrats, who reminded him that without their unanimous support the Luxembourg Treaty would not have been ratified.[43] Adenauer also visited the Connecticut home of his good American Jewish friend, Dannie Heineman, who had helped him financially after Hitler's takeover and had been in close touch with him for many years. Heineman was not involved in Jewish communal affairs but seems to have influenced Adenauer's views of the United States.[44]

One of Adenauer's closest political advisers in the late 1940s and early 1950s was Herbert Blankenhorn, a junior diplomat at the German embassy in Washington from 1935 to 1939 and the nephew of the last prewar German ambassador there, Hans Heinrich Dieckhoff. After denazification, the extremely capable former member of the Nazi party moved up and was appointed as CDU executive secretary in the British zone. Since October 1949, he served as Adenauer's adviser for contacts with the high commissioners in the chancellor's office and from 1951 as head of the restored Foreign Office's political department. In that capacity, he was instrumental in securing the reappointment of a number of his former colleague diplomats from the Nazi period.[45] Whatever Blankenhorn's personal interest, he became involved, beginning in the spring of 1950, in behind-the-scenes communications with Noah Barou, chairman of the London branch of the WJC executive. In 1951 he helped draft Adenauer's Bundestag declaration regarding Germany and the Jews.[46] In December 1951, he accompanied Adenauer to his first meeting with Goldmann in London and took part in further crucial meetings and stages of the deliberations in Bonn that paved the way for the *shilumim* agreement. Spokesmen for the Non-Sectarian Anti-Nazi League in the United States continued to complain about Blankenhorn's former Nazi propaganda activities at the embassy in Washington during the 1930s.[47] McCloy tried to soothe these critics, and the State Department rejected demands to bar Blankenhorn's entry into the United States. Blankenhorn came to Washington and conducted diplomatic talks there a few months after Adenauer's visit.[48]

However, the main attacks against Blankenhorn were launched at home in Germany. Right-wingers in the CSU and pro-Arab businessmen and government officials accused him of having sold out to the Jews. Left-wingers argued that by helping the Jewish and Israeli side, he had looked for an alibi for having staffed the reestablished Foreign Office with a large number of former Nazis. Otto Lenz, Hans Globke's short-lived predecessor as state secretary in the chancellor's office, told Blankenhorn frankly that he regarded the agreement with Israel as a major mistake because of the repercussions in the Arab states. People with an anti-Nazi past like Lenz were sometimes less inclined to fulfill Jewish and Israeli demands than former members or supporters of the Nazi party, although one should beware of generalizations. In 1959, Blankenhorn and Walter Hallstein, the former director-general of the Foreign Office and thereafter president of the European Economic Community (EEC) Commission in Brussels, lost a libel case against an official in the Ministry of Economics, an opponent of the reparations treaty who accused them of having promoted the treaty against the best interests of the Federal Republic. Blankenhorn was sentenced to four months' probation but was cleared by the court of appeals and stayed in the foreign service.[49] At his different posts as representative to NATO and ambassador to France, Italy, and Great Britain, he remained an important contact for Goldmann, and their correspondence continued until the late 1970s.[50]

Despite Adenauer's friendly reception in the United States and the positive press comments on his visit, the suspicious attitude of major segments of liberal American public opinion toward the anti-Communist conservative West German government and the post-Nazi German society endured much longer. Newspapers frequently reported the manifestations of neo-Nazism, the triumphal return from prison of notorious SS leaders, and the desecration of Jewish cemeteries. Correspondents and editorialists persisted in equating neo-Nazi activists with ex-Nazis who, in spite of their successful comeback to important administrative and economic positions, did not at all intend to resurrect the Nazi regime. The negative image of the Germans in the media, whether Jews were involved in its presentation or not, continued for many years to strengthen anti-German prejudices; and most Jews in the media did not care for any guidelines by the Jewish establishment.

Moreover, the immediate psychological and emotional impact on American Jewry of the reparation agreement, as well as the restitution and compensation arrangements, does not seem to have been significant. In contrast to many Israelis who depended much more on both collective German assistance and individual compensation payments, American Jews were much less swayed by German deeds and gestures. East European survivors who came to the United States after World War II usually remained hostile, the indemnification money that they started to receive notwithstanding. In the best case, they regarded the money as a very small payment for which they had suffered and not at all as a conciliatory move. At least, that is how the payments were interpreted by the U.S. administration and its allies interested in West Germany's acceptance into the democratic camp. Some of the post-1933 immigrants from Germany who, at first, had been very critical of their former homeland, changed their views—as reflected in the *Aufbau* weekly—and took a more positive attitude, but they were a marginal element on the American Jewish scene.[51] Quite understandably, pro-Communist publications such as *Jewish Life* campaigned against the deal with the Bonn government before and after the signing of the reparations treaty.[52]

All in all, the reparations treaty and its prompt implementation had a softening effect on the attitude of major parts of organized American Jewry, especially the pro-Zionist elements, toward the West German state. Up until 1951, with few exceptions, these had distinguished themselves in their critical attitude toward Germany. In contrast to the AJC, which consistently tried to get involved in proposals and projects concerning the democratization of German education and society, the pro-Zionist camp accorded priority to immediate Jewish interests. From that viewpoint, the reparations treaty was an important achievement. For the editorialist of the *Reconstructionist*, by including payment to Jews of various countries through the Claims Conference, the agreement meant an ideological victory for those who always contended that Jews must be regarded as a people and not merely a religious denomination.[53] Others, like the noted scholar Simon Rawidowicz, objected to depicting the reparations treaty as "a major victory to the Jewish people." In the view of the author of *Babylon and Jerusalem*, there was no recompense for the six million Jewish victims. The negotiations with Germany, to which he did not object, were conducted by the State of Israel and the Jewish organizations but not by the people of Israel.[54]

As a result of the Luxembourg agreement, Jewish pronouncements pertaining to Germany became less hostile. In comparison to the WJC's first postwar plenary assembly in Montreux, the resolutions of the plenary assembly in 1953 in Geneva sounded much more moderate. So did the resolutions of the 1959 plenary assembly in Stockholm. Goldmann even thought of inviting Professor Franz Böhm, the honest German chief negotiator at Wassenaar, to attend the Geneva assembly, but the Bonn government preferred that he stay home.[55] Goldmann, himself a hidden neutralist and early supporter of an East-West detente, vetoed resolutions against German rearmament lest they imperil his relationship with Adenauer. On this issue the majority of the American branch was closer to him than the French and British members who unequivocally opposed German rearmament.[56] Goldmann's personal access to Adenauer and his successors remained very important for gaining further improvements in the scope of indemnification and its procedures. The Federal Indemnification Law of 1953 was amended twice, in

1956 and in 1965, and even though American ambassadors would voice support for improvements of the legislation, it became mainly a domestic German affair.[57] Later the Claims Conference succeeded in obtaining indemnification for groups and cases not included in the original law.

One of the major results of the reparations treaty was the growing impact of Israel and its needs on future American Jewish–German relations. Contrary to Israel's interest in a strong critical stand of the organized community in the early postwar period, it now favored a more pragmatic look at the developments in Germany and the behavior of its government. Adenauer's refusal to bow to American requests and suspend reparation shipments after Israel's invasion of Sinai in November 1956 and its procrastination in withdrawing from the Gaza Strip, as well as the chancellor's meeting with Ben Gurion in 1960 in New York, where he pledged more economic and military assistance to Israel, were to reaffirm that trend. Statements by prominent Jewish leaders took this development into account. Philip Klutznick, B'nai B'rith president in the 1950s, who intermittently continued to serve both the community and the U.S. government in different capacities, explicitly explained his commitment to a well-balanced course with regard to Germany, because of both American national interests and Israel's dependence on German deliveries.[58] Even when protesting in 1953 to Secretary of State John Foster Dulles and High Commissioner James Conant against further clemency or parole for war criminals, Klutznick found it necessary to pay tribute to Adenauer's "striving for democracy and justice . . . [which] is known to us and merits encouragement."[59] Moreover, the triangular link also affected Jewish congressmen who were close to the community, like Jacob Javits and Emanuel Celler.[60] Thus, since the 1950s Israel's influence on the difficult relationship between American Jewry and Germany was basically a moderating one, even though from time to time issues connected with Israel caused strains in those relations.[61]

10

German Diplomats: The Initial Efforts to Soften American Jewish Hostility

Despite the United States' early strategic decision in cooperation with Western Europe to forge a close relationship with the Federal Republic against the Communist threat in the East, and the rapid political rapprochement between the two nations, an important part of the American public remained uneasy about renascent Germany. East Coast quality newspapers and also some popular dailies, critical columnists and commentators, intellectuals and left-leaning liberal groups and publications reflected that uneasiness. As soon as the East-West tension started to decline, the uneasiness became even more conspicuous. American Jews played a significant role in this context, contrary to the limits of their and the organized community's influence on governmental decisions involving the U.S. national interest. Chancellor Konrad Adenauer, West Germany's most prominent statesman, who determined that country's course until the early 1960s, regarded a gradual reconciliation with American and world Jewry as a notable aim in Germany's efforts to gain full acceptance as a morally equal partner of the West. He understood that the formal political alliance that was speeded up by the Cold War would not suffice to achieve that goal. This was the major reason for his concluding in 1952 the Luxembourg reparations treaty with Israel and the Claims Conference. Adenauer accomplished this despite strong opposition in his own cabinet and in German financial and economic institutions. He did not find support from the population either.

Thus, West German diplomats who returned to the United States in the early 1950s, even before the Federal Republic recovered its sovereignty, consistently paid much attention to the American Jewish community and tried to establish contacts with its leadership and public opinion molders. Their aim was to calm Jewish fears of resurgent antisemitism and neo-Nazism and to point to the achievements of the democratic West German state and its assistance to Israel. In spite of the mitigating impact of the German-Israeli-Jewish reparations settlement, relations between organized American Jewry and West Germany in the 1950s and also later remained delicate. In addition, the diplomats had to face the hostile sentiments of Jews in general, many of whom did not want to have anything to do with Germans after the Holocaust.

This chapter deals mainly with the efforts of German diplomats in the United States, their achievements and shortcomings in softening American Jewish hostility in the first decade of their presence there, when that issue seemed most urgent. The importance of their contacts with the Jewish community at critical crossroads in the 1960s, 1970s, and 1980s was to rise again, particularly due to the enormous growth of Holocaust consciousness among American Jewry in the next generation.[1]

Even before the establishment of the Federal Republic in 1949 and the opening in 1950 of the first West German consulate in New York, Germans reporting to the Stuttgart Bureau of Peace Problems were concerned with the hostility of American Jewish groups toward Germany. According to Alexander Böker,[2] a highly intelligent right-wing conservative German who had spent the war years as an exile in the United States and after his return to West Germany joined the staff of Herbert Blankenhorn, moderate American Jewish circles were usually silenced by the Zionists, whose influence in Washington was the greatest. Böker saw secret collusion among organized hate groups, their representatives in Congress, and elements of the Truman administration and its bureaucracy, not to mention some members of the media. His reports evinced no compassion for Jewish suffering during the war, nor did he make any effort to understand the anger and justifiable fears of American Jewry. In the same vein, Georg Federer, a career diplomat who served in the German Foreign Office until 1945, alerted the bureau to the anti-German impact of two unfriendly groups: the Jews and the Communists.[3] He was later appointed counselor at the West German diplomatic mission in Washington and subsequently consul general in New York. However, reviewing the state of American-German relations a few months after the inauguration of the Adenauer government, Böker came to regard reconciliation with American Jewry as one of the most important aims of postwar German foreign policy. He also pointed to the possible impact of Germany's attitude toward the new State of Israel on future American Jewish–German relations.[4]

Böker listed three American Jewish groups he thought would respond to Germany's approach:

1) Conservative anti-Communists such as Bernard Baruch, who in 1945 endorsed Morgenthau's ideas and then changed his mind;

2) The anti-Zionist and assimilationist American Council for Judaism, headed by philanthropist Lessing Rosenwald. Here Böker failed to distinguish between the ACJ and the much more important American Jewish Committee. The AJC, and not the ACJ, published the intellectual monthly *Commentary*, whose objective reports on Germany Böker praised;

3) Jewish social democrats and trade unionists who evinced much sympathy for positive developments in Germany, even though they criticized Bonn's conservative policies.

Böker also focused on the views of the post-1933 German Jewish immigrants in the United States. During the war most were hostile toward Germany, but since then, many were once more becoming friendly. A few changed their views after visits to their old homeland, and some were even prepared to return there, a fact that Böker regarded as being of great propaganda value for Germany.

On the other hand, Böker stressed that a number of American Jewish groups continued their anti-German activities. For instance, he listed the Anti-Defamation League of B'nai B'rith that fought antisemitism in the United States and around the world. He maintained that the ADL—which, according to his sources, was "sometimes called the Jewish Gestapo"—was involved in the activities of the anti-German Society for the Prevention of World War III, which had been established at the end of the war. Even though the ADL sometimes relied on information presented by the Society, it did not subscribe to its program. However, the activity of that marginal group, which continued the Morgenthau legacy, published the magazine *Prevent World War III* and supported anti-German publications such as T. H. Tetens's *Germany Plots with the Kremlin*, caused much concern to the German diplomats in the United States in the 1950s. Tetens, a former contributor to the left-wing journal of opinion *Die Weltbühne*, left Germany in 1933 for political reasons and settled in the United States. In 1961 he published another book very critical of the Federal Republic: *The New Germany and the Old Nazis*.

In addition to Jewish organizations, Böker mentioned four other groups critical of Germany: a section of the Left, especially Communists and left-wing fellow travelers; academics teaching at universities; part of the powerful Eastern establishment; and Poles and Czechs, although their impact was limited. Among the first two groups were, of course, many Jews. Some of Germany's traditional allies—the isolationists and pacifists whom they could count on in the past—were no longer as important for the Federal Republic. In the new political configuration, Bonn had to rely mainly on internationalist-minded forces that had been Germany's traditional enemies for the preceding fifty years. Perhaps that was another reason for conciliating the Jews in that camp.

Despite the shift in Washington's attitude, the hostility toward Germany that prevailed among parts of the American public was also brought to the attention of Bonn's policymakers by visiting German VIPs. For instance, publisher Gerd Bucerius, a CDU member of the Bundestag who until the end of the war had refused to divorce his Jewish wife whom he brought to safety in England, reminded the chancellor's office of the Jews' influence in American politics because of the ruling Democratic Party's dependence on them. Bucerius, who enjoyed Adenauer's personal confidence, understood American Jews' hatred of Germany, although "it came close to self-destruction."[5] He considered Adenauer's statements against antisemitic incidents in Germany as helpful in confronting hostile opinion. Other observers indicated the difference between the hostile climate in New York and the indifferent atmosphere in the Midwest and the West.[6] New York was the home of "the powerful Jewish element, the intellectuals and the rather left-wing metropolitan inhabitants."

West Germany's first postwar consul general in New York was Dr. Heinz Krekeler, a member of the right-of-center FDP, the chancellor's junior coalition partner.[7] In 1951 Krekeler became head of the German diplomatic mission in Washington, later ambassador. Born in 1906, a chemist and industrial manager with family connections to the heads of the powerful IG Farben corporation, Krekeler had never joined the Nazi party or its subsidiary organizations. He presented himself as a strong supporter of German-Jewish reconciliation and his attitude on this issue seems to have satisfied Adenauer, who appointed him. However, Blankenhorn, Adenauer's closest political adviser at that time, thought that the somewhat provincial Krekeler was not a suitable ambassador to Washington and would not succeed in gaining access to the really important people in the field of American foreign policy.[8]

Before Krekeler came to New York—he arrived there three days after the outbreak of the Korean War, which hastened the American-German rapprochement—preparations for opening the consulate general were made by his deputy, Dr. Hans Eduard Riesser.[9] A former diplomat who had started his career as a junior foreign service officer in Washington in the early 1920s, Riesser was forced to quit the service in 1933 because of his "non-Aryan" origin. He had spent most of the Nazi period in France and thereafter lived in Switzerland. Both of his parents had been baptized; his mother was deported to an extermination camp in the East; his grandfather's brother, Gabriel Riesser of Hamburg, had been a fighter for Jewish emancipation in Germany and a member of the Frankfurt parliament in 1848. For several years, Riesser also served as West Germany's diplomatic observer at the UN. His successor as consul general in New York was Adolph Reifferscheidt, an old acquaintance of Adenauer's and an industrial manager who, during the Nazi regime, had been removed from an important job because he refused to join the Nazi party. In response to suspicious public opinion, the consular staff in New York at first included such outspoken anti-Nazis as Hanna Kiep, the widow of the former consul general Dr. Otto Kiep, who had been executed after the failed coup of July 20, 1944, and the Social Democrat Dr. Georg Krauss. But that changed over the years. In 1958 a consul at the New York consulate general was suspended from his post because of antisemitic expressions.

Richard Hertz was the first consul general in Los Angeles, another sensitive spot because of the growing Jewish community and the Hollywood film industry. Hertz, a German Jew who had immigrated to the United States after the Nazi takeover, was conscious of the difference between his personal attachment to the liberal Roosevelt legacy and the prevailing anti-Roosevelt views in the Bonn Foreign Office.[10] Dr. Karl Heinrich Knappstein, a former journalist on the staff of the *Frankfurter Zeitung* (the relatively least Nazified daily closed down by Nazi propaganda chief Joseph Goebbels in 1943), began his long diplomatic career in the United States as consul general in Chicago. From 1954 until 1958, Axel von dem Bussche, a survivor of the anti-Hitler resistance, became counselor at the German embassy in Washington. Rudolf Borchardt, of partly Jewish origin, served in the early 1960s as press attaché. By 1952, however, formal past Nazi party membership was not regarded as an insurmountable obstacle for diplomatic appointments in the United States, as in the case of Georg Federer, who came to Washington as counselor.[11]

The New York consulate was soon flooded by German Jewish immigrants who inquired about indemnification and restitution of their property. As a gesture of goodwill, Krekeler visited Adolf Kober, Cologne's prewar chief rabbi, to whom he conveyed personal greetings from the chancellor, the city's former mayor. By approaching such people, Krekeler and Riesser hoped to improve relations with the German Jewish immigrant community, perhaps as a first step toward winning over American Jewry. But these efforts were not immediately successful; moreover, post-1933 immigrants did not carry much weight in the general American Jewish community.

One of those whom Krekeler approached was Manfred George, the editor of *Aufbau,* a German-language weekly founded in 1934 and widely read by German and Central European Jewish immigrants. Shortly after Adenauer's statement in the Bundestag indicating his readiness to open negotiations with Jewish organizations and with Israel, George sponsored a meeting at Manhattan Town Hall with representatives of a number of Jewish groups. Most of them were German and Central European immigrants. German officials who attended that meeting were struck by the critical tone taken by most of the participants. The speakers expressed doubts about Germany's sincerity regarding restitution and indemnification, mentioned the increasing antisemitism there, and dismissed the possibility of German-Jewish reconciliation.[12] During the war and in the early postwar period, George encountered much enmity on the part of "patriotic" German exiles because of his opposition to a "soft" peace. While *Aufbau* continued to fight German American nationalism and Nazi activities in Germany, he successively took a more benevolent attitude toward the Federal Republic and its government. As he told the German press attaché, he was afraid of moving too fast lest he antagonize a portion of his readers. In 1959, President Heuss proposed to confer upon him the German Great Order of Merit, but George refused to accept it, since that might inhibit his work for Jewish-German rapprochement.[13]

In their attempts to overcome a variety of obstacles, German diplomats enjoyed from the beginning the support of some individual pro-German Jews. Most of them were immigrants who had come to the United States after Hitler's ascent to power. One was Fritz Oppenheimer, a New York lawyer and former OMGUS legal adviser who kept in touch with both the State Department and high German officials and introduced Krekeler to John McCloy.[14] Before Oppenheimer left the military government, the political adviser's office attested that his solutions for Germany's problem had been "American, objective, practical and serene." Afterwards, he supported relaxation of controls in Germany, a commercial treaty between the United States and Germany, and giving to the Federal Republic a voice in European affairs. He did not advise Germany's early rearmament, though, and thought the United States exaggerated the security problem somewhat.

Another Jewish individual most active in promoting friendly relations between America and Germany was banker Eric Warburg. But because of his strong sympathies for Germany, he was not at all characteristic of American Jewry.[15] A son of the German Jewish financier, Max Warburg, who had unsuccessfully negotiated transfer proposals with Reichsbank president Hjalmar Schacht for rescuing a part of German Jewish property, Eric Warburg was naturalized only in 1938 after he had lived in the United States for many years. After Pearl Harbor, he joined the U.S. Army and served in the Intelligence Corps in England, North Africa, Sicily, and France. As an early opponent of the Morgenthau plan, he implored McCloy after his appointment as high commissioner to stop the dismantlement of German industrial plants. He also advocated West German participation in European defense as well as a close scrutiny of war crime judgments obtained by unfair interrogation.

From 1950, Warburg was one of the most active members of the American Council on Germany, which furthered public efforts in favor of American–West German rapprochement. At the same time, he helped to establish the "Atlantik-Brücke," the German counterpart of the Council.[16] In 1956, he returned for good to his native Hamburg. Except for the Nazi period, he had always deeply admired Germany's cultural heritage. He died in Hamburg in 1990 at age ninety. Characteristic for that assimilated American-German-Jewish banker, as Ron Chernow remarked in his chronicle of the Warburg family, was his choice to be buried in the non-Jewish side of the Altona cemetery, near a stone marker that commemorated the baptized Warburgs who had died in concentration camps. His son read aloud prayers and speeches in German and English but not in Hebrew. He wanted to conduct the ceremony in a way that seemed appropriate to his father.[17]

When Krekeler and his staff came to hire an American public relations company to gradually improve postwar Germany's image in the United States and to promote tourism as well as commercial and cultural relations, they chose the Roy Bernard Company, a middle-sized Manhattan agency with twenty years of experience. Its president was L. Roy Blumenthal, who owned the company together with Bernard Gittelson, another Jewish businessman—a fact that probably influenced its selection. In submitting his application to the chancellor's office, Blumenthal expressly referred to Adenauer's "strong statement against anti-Semitism," a phenomenon that was, in his words, one of the main obstacles to the reconciliation of Germany with the American public.[18]

In the mid-1950s General Julius Klein joined the Federal Republic's efforts to present a more attractive image and neutralize negative American Jewish attitudes toward West Germans and their state. Head of a Chicago public relations firm, Klein began his pro-German activities in 1953, when he took on the difficult job of promoting the return of confiscated German assets. He was to remain in the limelight for the next fifteen years. The midwestern conservative Republican, who had been close to Senator Robert Taft in the early 1950s, enjoyed good connections in both houses of Congress. In addition to his business interests, Klein also became actively involved in the triangular relationship between American Jewry, Germany, and Israel. He gained Adenauer's confidence in the early 1950s and continued to praise the achievements of the

186

chancellor and the new Germany for years. In 1954, he conducted a study of American military establishments in Europe as consultant to a Senate appropriations subcommittee. Later, with the help of Krekeler and others, he received well-paying contracts as a registered lobbyist for German industrial interests. In the American Jewish community he remained a controversial figure, but Israeli leaders and diplomats appreciated his help at certain crucial crossroads.[19]

The son of a wealthy fur importer and grandson of a German Jew who immigrated to America in 1848, Klein was born in Chicago in 1901 and for several years attended school in imperial Berlin. In 1917 he volunteered for the United States Army and, after the armistice, served as a low-ranking member of the American military mission in Germany. As a journalist in Chicago in the 1930s, he was involved in intelligence-gathering activities against Nazi and pro-Nazi organizations in the United States. After service in the Pacific during World War II, where he attained the rank of colonel, Klein held office as national commander of the Jewish War Veterans in 1948–49 and remained one of its leading members for many years. Right after the war, he warned against fraternization of the American military with the German population and protested against the reduction of sentences and clemency for war criminals, but later he changed his attitude.

Despite his connections to Robert Taft, "the next president," Klein did not play an important role in convincing Adenauer to come to a satisfactory arrangement with Israel and the Jewish organizations. Israeli diplomats, though, were glad to have found at least one strong supporter in the conservative Republican camp where there were few Jews. With the help of Jewish SPD Bundestag member Jakob Altmaier, Klein exaggerated his own contribution to the reparations settlement and used it to justify his involvement in the campaign to return withheld German property. He soon became engaged in presenting the controversial Friedrich Middelhauve to the American public. Although he had never been a Nazi party member, this right-wing FDP politician had tried to attract former Nazi activists from the Naumann group to North-Rhine-Westphalia's FDP, of which he served as deputy leader. As deputy prime minister of the largest West German state, Middelhauve met prominent Jews during his 1955 visit to the United States, despite some critical voices in the community. During his trips to Bonn,

Klein frequently visited the chancellor's office and was received by Adenauer. There ne also met State Secretary Hans Globke, whose participation in drafting the Nuremberg Laws was often recalled by political adversaries.[20] Klein claimed he helped arrange the New York meeting between Adenauer and Israeli Prime Minister David Ben Gurion in March 1960, at which a military and economic aid package for Israel was agreed upon. In 1965, he earned Israel's gratitude for his part in bringing together Israel's ambassador in Washington, Abraham Harman, and Rainer Barzel, head of the CDU parliamentary group. It was Barzel whose recommendations contributed to convincing Chancellor Ludwig Erhard to establish full diplomatic relations with Israel.[21] In talks with Israeli diplomats, Klein did not conceal his close connections with the CIA but insisted that he did not report on his pro-Israel activities.[22]

The American Jewish community did not like the way Klein conducted his campaign to change the Trading with the Enemy Act in order to allow the return of German assets.[23] Nor were American Jews happy about his promoting the interests of such powerful German industrial corporations as Rheinmetall, which had exploited Jewish slave labor during the war and refused to compensate them. Former president Harry Truman's people also could not stand him and thought little of his rank as a two-star general, conferred upon him by a former Illinois governor for serving with the Illinois National Guard.[24] In the early 1960s, Klein became persona non grata with the Kennedy administration, owing to his involvement in senatorial attacks on Kennedy's new policy aimed at a partial detente with the East, which Adenauer did not like. He was also called before the Senate Committee on Foreign Relations investigating foreign lobbyists. As a result, ambassadors Grewe and Knappstein were more hesitant to support Klein's activities than Krekeler had been in the 1950s.[25]

After the opening of the German diplomatic mission in Washington, Krekeler and other diplomats soon began to establish contacts with senators and congressmen from both parties. There were not many Jewish members of Congress at that time, but their position was a matter of special concern to the Germans. Although the interventions and initiatives of Jewish legislators could not affect the basic course of American foreign policy, they did influence a part of public opinion. Bonn's envoys tried to convince them of the changes in German politics and society.

Krekeler paid special attention to Jacob Javits, the liberal Republican congressman from New York and a member of the House Foreign Affairs Committee. One of the most active Jewish congressmen, Javits represented Manhattan's Washington Heights district, where many German Jewish immigrants had settled. However, his complaints and demands reflected not only the views of his constituents but also those of the many Jewish communal and pro-Israel organizations in which he was involved. The endorsement of American foreign policy, the Cold War, and the interests of the State of Israel gradually changed Javits's position on Germany, as was the case with other Jews in public life.

Javits, who visited Germany first in 1946 and again in 1949, called for a prolonged stay of American forces there in order to secure a peaceful Germany. He unequivocally opposed German rearmament, lest a rearmed and perhaps reunited Germany join forces with Soviet Russia. He also complained about the revival of German nationalism. In July 1951, he was the only member of the House who did not vote in favor of ending the state of war with Germany.[26]

The first meeting between Krekeler and Javits took place on September 27, 1951, the day Adenauer proclaimed his willingness to open negotiations on collective indemnification with Jewish organizations and with Israel. Neither the German diplomat nor the congressman were aware in advance of that timing; however, Javits told Krekeler that, as a Jew, he held Germany responsible for all that had happened to his fellow Jews during the Hitler period. Nevertheless, he had voted in the House of Representatives in favor of assistance to Germany, since he saw no contradiction between these two principles. Krekeler tried to convince Javits that he misunderstood Adenauer when he took a recent statement by the chancellor as proof that West Germany would involve the Western powers in a war in order to regain its lost eastern territories. At the same time he asked Javits to understand the feelings of millions of Germans expelled from the east. Javits, for his part, expressed his deep concern about the latest Soviet proposals regarding the reunification of Germany. It was already evident from his remarks that the Communist challenge to American policy in Europe would eventually bring him closer to a positive appraisal of West Germany.[27]

Following Adenauer's declaration on Israel, Javits commended the German government and people for their readiness to open talks on indemnification. He expressed the wish that the chancellor would use his statement concerning the Jews to set a new moral tone for Germany. Javits also hoped Adenauer would convince the citizens of the Federal Republic they had a role in the unification of Europe and the establishment of a European defense organization. In June 1952, he called upon the House of Representatives to endorse the contractual agreements between the Western allies and the Federal Republic, including the military and economic integration of Germany in the West European community. Javits, who was elected to the Senate in 1956, became a steadfast supporter of the American-German alliance. In 1976 he received the Badge and Star of the German Order of Merit.[28]

As a result of the Luxembourg agreement, another congressman from a district with many Jewish constituents, Emanuel Celler of Brooklyn, also became a supporter of the Federal Republic. In early 1952, he had warned against American haste to admit West Germany as a full partner into NATO because "the fear of the rise of a militaristic Germany [lay] at the heart of the objections of our allies." A few years later he changed his mind and concluded that American policy toward Germany redounded to its benefit. In 1957, he appeared with Krekeler on the Washington television interview program "Between the Lines" and praised West Germany's achievements.[29]

Senator Herbert H. Lehman, the former Democratic governor of New York and Roosevelt's faithful associate, was more reticent. In 1950, Lehman joined with some of his colleagues in calling for a congressional inquiry by a bipartisan commission into the German situation, but the resolution was tabled because of strong opposition on the part of the administration. During the 1952 debate on German rearmament, the senator reluctantly agreed to the rebuilding of West Germany's military strength, but only as an integral part of Western European defense. In the mid-1950s, Lehman opposed efforts of senators from states with a heavy German American population to unfreeze seized German property. In 1955, he complained to Secretary of State John Foster Dulles about the parole granted by the Allied-German Mixed Board to former SS general Sepp Dietrich, a convicted war criminal.[30]

German diplomats, of course, had no contact with expressly anti-German Jewish public figures. The former secretary of the Treasury, Henry Morgenthau Jr., remained a persona non grata in

German eyes, and he would never have talked with them. Albert Einstein, who supported the Morgenthau plan in 1945, persisted in his unequivocal negative attitude to all things German. He had no wish to have dealings with Germans and denounced the Western powers for being hard at work making them strong and dangerous again.[31] On the other hand, German diplomats registered with satisfaction the change of mind of Bernard Baruch, in the past a strong critic, who now expressed his admiration for Adenauer's policies and even endorsed the setting up of German armed forces. Baruch came to be a supporter of the Federal Republic because of its economic and political importance in the confrontation with the Soviet Union.[32]

The ratification of the Luxembourg agreement and its speedy implementation notwithstanding, West Germany was subject to recurrent criticism on the American Jewish communal scene. There were, of course, the leftists who, because of their ideological and political support for the Soviet Union, opposed the Federal Republic. On the right, hostility persisted on the part of the rather marginal Zionist Revisionists and the Orthodox. The liberal pro-Zionist AJ Congress continued for a number of years to oppose German rearmament and to expose black spots in the German political and economic establishment. In contrast to AJ Congress, Nahum Goldmann, the president of the WJC whom Krekeler held in high esteem, steered his pluralist umbrella organization away from its traditional anti-German course. This became evident in the resolutions of the WJC executive meetings and plenary assemblies, and in part it also affected the WJC American section. However, even the critical Jewish groups were not cold-shouldered by the Germans. When AJ Congress president Rabbi Prinz invited the German ambassador Professor Grewe to join him at the public presentation of "The German Dilemma," a pamphlet prepared by his organization, Grewe attended. Two years later, the German consul general in New York, Georg Federer, was invited to attend an official celebration by another activist organization—the Jewish War Veterans.[33]

The first postwar German diplomats were anxious to present themselves and their government's policies to elite groups of the American Jewish community, who were considered more moderate than most of the middle- and lower-class activists. Thus, Krekeler thought it a great honor that in the winter of 1953 he was the first German since World War II to address the elite Manhattan Harmonie Club (established in 1847). The theme of his speech, delivered before two hundred invited guests, was "Today's Germany and World Peace." Historian Saul Padover had served as a psychological warfare officer in the area of Aachen, the first major German city to be occupied by General Eisenhower's forces in fall 1944, and had summarized his experiences in *Experiment in Germany* (1945). He introduced Krekeler and praised West Germany's efforts in strengthening its democratic foundations.[34]

Nonetheless, Krekeler was not successful in establishing close contacts with the AJC, which was still regarded as the most prestigious American Jewish organization. He was impressed by its rather moderate statement recognizing Germany's place in the free world and rejecting the collective guilt accusation of the German people. Yet, he was disappointed by some AJC publications that sounded very critical of renascent neo-Nazism and right-wing nationalism in West Germany. Leading AJC spokesmen, for their part, continued to see high German officials both in Germany and in New York, where they also convened a meeting of Jewish leaders with President Heuss during his 1958 state visit. Irving Engel and Zachariah Shuster met Adenauer in Bonn in the fall of 1959; Blaustein revisited him one year later.[35]

The first major Jewish organization to accept an official invitation from the West German government was the Anti-Defamation League of B'nai B'rith. Krekeler had been irritated by the negative impact of the AJC's studies, especially since these publications reached a much broader public than the Jewish community and presented a serious challenge to German public relations. Thus, he hoped that an on-the-spot survey by another respectable Jewish organization, such as the ADL, which was about to celebrate its fortieth anniversary, might limit the damage. Bonn readily agreed to the ambassador's proposal; eventually the official invitation to ADL was extended by West German state secretary Walter Hallstein early in 1954. The ADL also looked for encouragement from the State Department before making its final decision with regard to the visit. Its delegation, which met with a representative of the department, pointed out that "they could see advantages both in Germany and in the United States to it as it would be a further proof to those Jewish people and organizations who were still doubtful of the good intentions of the Germans in this field that the Federal Republic was doing everything in its power to make up for the cruelties of the Nazi regime. In Germany their experience in such matters might be of real value to the Germans in making progress in eliminating any racial or religious discrimination which might still exist."

The American government, while favoring such a visit, preferred to remain in the background. However, after the visit took place, it thought "its findings might be useful in the execution of the [U.S.] public affairs program in Germany." Philip Klutznick, federal housing commissioner under the Roosevelt and Truman administrations from 1944 until 1946, was involved in convincing the ADL executive committee to accept the German invitation.[36] In 1953, he succeeded Frank Goldman as B'nai B'rith president and emerged as one of the most prominent American Jewish leaders in the postwar era.

Klutznick consistently followed a moderate course with regard to West Germany. In the mid-1950s he became a founding member of the Conference of Presidents of Major Jewish Organizations, which at first was chaired by Nahum Goldmann. During Goldmann's absence from the United States, Klutznick served as its acting chairman. In March 1955 he met Adenauer in Bonn after having discussed his forthcoming visit to the Federal Republic with Krekeler. Klutznick could not endorse Adenauer's proposal that more Jews should return to Germany but assured him of his personal confidence in him and his immediate colleagues.[37]

The three-man delegation, which included ADL's national director, Benjamin R. Epstein, went to Germany in March 1954 as part of a visitors' exchange of twenty-eight Americans from different walks of public life. After the delegation's return, it submitted a detailed report both to Krekeler and to the State Department. An expanded version appeared in pamphlet form, entitled "Germany— Nine Years Later." A few leading ADL officials such as Oscar Cohen, who read the draft before publication, had some critical comments. Cohen thought that while the report dealt with the German people on a realistic basis, there was too much whitewashing of Adenauer and his government. Moreover, there was no "thorough survey or a profound analysis of the situation affecting German Jewry." The report criticized the still existing potential of antisemitism, the "overpowering traditionalism in German life," and the fact that many prominent former Nazis had joined political parties and had returned to high posts in the bureaucracy.

The delegation expressed particular concern over Nazi attempts to infiltrate the FDP, Adenauer's junior coalition partner, and over that party's right-wing nationalist trend. But the report also noted the positive change of mind among young Germans, many of whom were much more liberal than their parents and not at all keen to be drafted into a new army. A press release published in Germany immediately after the conclusion of the delegation's visit stated "that at the present time neo-Nazism and Nazism as organized political movements appear to be at a very low ebb." According to German sources, the hosts were told confidentially that, in order to prevent accusations by other Jewish groups that the delegation had been bribed by the Germans, the final version would be more reserved than the factual position of the organization.[38]

The German consulate general in New York and the diplomatic mission in Washington were established at a time when Israeli diplomats were not yet allowed to engage in any contacts with their German counterparts. Nevertheless, informal talks with Israeli consular officials had already taken place in 1951, even before Adenauer's statement in the Bundestag. After the ratification of the Luxembourg agreement, the Israeli consulate general provided the Roy Bernard Company with advance copies of Consul General Arthur Lourie's address. His German counterpart, Hans Riesser, who had represented his government at the exchange of ratifications of the German-Israeli agreement at United Nations headquarters, paid a visit to the Israeli consulate.[39] In Washington, Israel's ambassador, Abba Eban, accepted Krekeler's invitation to a festive reception in honor of Adenauer during his first visit to the United States in April 1953. Later, restrictions on contacts with German diplomats were relaxed. Krekeler and Eban extended lunch invitations to each other, and before his departure, the German ambassador received an autographed copy of Eban's book, *Voice of Israel*.[40]

Krekeler himself disapproved of Adenauer's support for French and British Suez intervention in 1956, in contradiction to U.S. policy. However, the chancellor's clear-cut refusal to bow to American pressure and threaten Israel with the suspension of reparation deliveries contributed to an improvement in German-Israeli relations, despite Bonn's unwillingness to proceed with the exchange of diplomats. There was a meeting of minds in conversations on a number of subjects between Rolf Pauls, counselor at the German embassy in Washington, and his Israeli counterpart, Yohanan Meroz, subsequently Israel's ambassador to Germany in the 1970s. Pauls was a future ambassador to Israel and the United States who had started his diplomatic career as an assistant to Blankenhorn and State Secretary Walter Hallstein. Adenauer's steadfastness in the face of American pressure was subsequently extolled by German representatives as a proof of German goodwill toward the Jewish people. In fact, it derived not just from sympathy for Israel but from his basic disagreement with American policy at that point. His fear of the repercussions of American-Soviet cooperation at the UN and of the rift between the United States and its West European allies also played a role. He was particularly afraid that it might strengthen the Soviet position in the Middle East. At the same time, Israel's military prowess demonstrated in the short war raised its standing in German eyes. Its importance had decreased temporarily with the advent of the Eisenhower administration. The organized Jewish community, for its part, which did not succumb to the administration's efforts of persuasion and showed full solidarity with Israel during and after the crisis, took notice of the stand taken by the German chancellor.[41]

In the mid-1950s, after the Paris agreements had prepared the way for granting sovereignty to the German Federal Republic, American-German links were put on a new basis. West Germany was admitted as a full-fledged member of NATO, and within its framework, German rearmament and the creation of a new West German army took place. The former enemy nation thus became the mainstay of the Western alliance on the European continent. In general, German diplomats devoted relatively less time to Jewish reaction. However, there were exceptions: during the antisemitic occurrences in the winter of 1959–60, the Eichmann trial two years later, and especially the campaign for abolishing or extending the statute of limitations for Nazi murders, the protests against German experts' contribution to Egypt's armament industry, and Bonn's decision to stop its arms deliveries to Israel.[42]

But although not always a dominant theme, Jewish issues were never dropped from the German agenda. The consul general in San Francisco complained about the damage that public attacks in Germany against indemnification payments caused the German-Jewish rapprochement.[43] For example, he mentioned those by Minister of Justice Fritz Schäffer, former minister of finance and Adenauer's main opponent during the German-Israel negotiations in 1952. Krekeler and his successors summoned representatives of the Claims Conference and other leading individuals to meet with important visiting politicians, who tried to convince their guests of the change that had taken place in Germany. A few of these meetings were especially satisfactory for the German side—for instance, the favorable impact on the Jewish public of talks with Berlin Social Democratic senator Joachim Lipschitz, whose father was Jewish.[44] Nevertheless, German Foreign Minister Heinrich von Brentano found it necessary to remind Grewe, who had succeeded Krekeler early in 1958, that despite Adenauer's personal prestige, Jewish circles and influential American intellectuals did not reveal much understanding for the German position. In principle, though, they recognized the need to cooperate with the Federal Republic.[45]

Albeit not the most important issue, a number of German American organizations and publications sometimes proved embarrassing to early West German diplomats, especially in view of Jewish sensitivity to antisemitism. Members of these groups, not only the Nazi "Bund," had blamed the Jewish boycott and the protests against the Third Reich. They had shown sympathy for the old country at least until the U.S. entry into the war in December 1941.[46] Some of the less acculturated German Americans had not adjusted to the postwar situation wherein a defeated Germany, on its way to becoming an ally of the United States and the West, tried at least in part to atone for its sins against Jews and its European neighbors and to develop a democratic society. They were still nostalgic for the former German Reich and its old boundaries; France remained their traditional enemy, while the black, red, and gold of the West German flag was a symbol of shame and treason. Roosevelt, the wartime president, was the politician they hated most, while Jews in general and American Jews in particular were seen as dangerous opponents who should be fought, not people to whom they should apologize.

Heinrich Knappstein, the first consul general in Chicago and later Germany's observer at the United Nations in New York and ambassador in Washington, was especially aware of these feelings. In Chicago he was in touch with the large German American communities in the Midwest. Krekeler, too, confronted these nostalgic and resentful views when he met German American groups and the local German American press.[47] Krekeler wrote Adenauer that one of the reasons for his guarded attitude toward the nationalistic groups was the chancellor's conciliatory policy in regard to world Jewry.[48] Gradually, the resentment of these German Americans toward the Bonn republic mellowed. Already during Adenauer's first visit to the United States in 1953, he was given a hearty welcome by a major part of the German American community. Consul General Reifferscheidt attended the New York Steuben Parade in 1958, which was to become a yearly event dedicated to the achievements and the legacy of German Americans. Leading politicians from the region were to participate. In 1959, both Consul General Federer and Ambassador Grewe attended the parade.[49] However, the gap between many German Americans and the Jewish community persisted much longer, and anti-Jewish prejudices continued to prevail among them.[50]

11

Antisemitic Manifestations and
Their Abatement

For the Federal Republic of Germany, the Eisenhower years in Washington, which started with Chancellor Adenauer's first visit to the United States, were in the main an era of good feeling. The leading Western power and the former enemy had become friends and close allies. This was true despite the dissension over American policy during the Suez crisis and Adenauer's exaggerated fears of a reduction of American ground forces in Europe because of the Radford Doctrine aimed at replacing them by superior atomic weaponry. After the ratification of the Paris agreements between the United States, Britain, France, and the Bonn government, West Germany was accepted as a full-fledged member of the Western anti-Communist bloc. Its leader, who was reelected in 1953 and 1957 by an increasing majority, enjoyed great prestige among the Republican administration and both houses of Congress. Even though relations between Adenauer and Dean Acheson, who at first had been suspected of unfriendliness by German diplomats, had evolved rather satisfactorily, there was more of a meeting of the minds between him and John Foster Dulles. They shared common anti-Communist ideological rigidity, strong support for West European integration, and emphasis on Christian moral values as opposed to Eastern "atheistic totalitarianism." Their mutual affinity also helped both sides overcome occasional differences of opinion, which became more severe after Dulles's departure from the scene.[1]

Israel was not yet as dominant a force in American Jewish life as it became in the first two decades after the Six Day War. Still, the American Jewish community attached more importance to safeguarding the well-being and security of the Jewish state after its successful Sinai campaign, when it had been forced to withdraw without peace from all territories conquered in November 1956. Thanks to the prompt implementation of the Luxembourg agreement, there was no cause or need for intercessions in Washington with regard to Jewish claims from Germany. At one point, in withstanding American pressure to suspend reparation shipments because of Israel's procrastination in withdrawing from the occupied areas, Bonn revealed more understanding for Jerusalem than did the U.S. administration. In the following years, the Israeli interest overshadowed most other subjects in the American Jewish–Israeli–German triangle, and this affected the attitude toward the West German government of almost all Jewish organizations. On the domestic scene, much of the community's energy was devoted to the civil rights campaign.

Nonetheless, antisemitic occurrences in Germany in the late 1950s, and especially the smear campaign and upsurge of anti-Jewish manifestations in the winter of 1959–60, temporarily revived Jewish worries with renewed intensity. In retrospect, it seems that the importance of these events and also the American Jewish reaction to them were exaggerated. However, that reminder of Jewish sensitivity and Bonn's fear of their negative impact on American and Western public opinion at least partially contributed to a gradual improvement in the field of German education and to a more intensive dealing with the Nazi past. After seven years the most prominent ex-Nazi member retired from Adenauer's cabinet. In a way, steps taken by the Bonn government and, even more, the revulsion of tens of thousands of young Germans who participated in anti-Nazi protest marches in Berlin, Hamburg, Munich, Bonn, and other major cities, revealed positive changes in the Federal Republic's political culture.[2]

On the one hand, the third general election held in the Federal Republic in September 1957 resulted in the ruling moderate conservative CDU's biggest victory. It was the only time it received the absolute majority of seats in the Bundestag. In federal and in state elections, the extreme right-wing groups suffered defeat, losing most of the seats they had gained in the early 1950s. The Sozialistische Reichspartei (SRP), the main neo-Nazi party, had been banned by the Constitutional Court already in 1952. The Deutsche Reichspartei, its successor, was a marginal splinter group, and the larger Nationaldemokratische Partei Deutschlands (NPD) was to make its impact only since 1964. The right-wing voters had, of course, not disappeared but preferred the CDU, the Bavarian CSU, and the German Party, most of whose members were soon to join the Christian Democrats.

On the other hand, there were the first stirrings of the enlightened younger generation. In 1956–57 many German youngsters were moved by the performance of *The Diary of Anne Frank* in the theaters. A much larger number had read the book, which was published in German in 1955. Audiences all over Germany silently watched the tragic story of the young girl caught in Amsterdam in 1944 and deported to Auschwitz and Bergen-Belsen. Each year groups of German high school students visited the mass graves of victims of the Nazi persecution in the concentration camps. In 1958, the first major German war crimes trial against members of an Einsatzkommando who had killed thousands of Lithuanian Jews in 1941 took place in Ulm. The SS defendants were sentenced to much shorter prison terms than requested by the prosecution because of their "complicity in crimes" for which the leaders of the Nazi Reich were mainly held responsible. Still, the revelations and testimonies made a considerable impact on German public opinion molders and had important repercussions. With all its flaws, the trial established in the German mind that "the crimes committed by Germans against the Jewish people were punishable according to sovereign German law, not merely because justice had been imposed by the Allied victory in 1945."[3]

Since the early 1950s, prosecution of Nazi and war criminals by the German courts had declined drastically. A lack of interest that reflected the attitude of both the conservative government and a great majority of the German public was mainly responsible. Difficulties in assembling the evidence also were a factor. Right-wingers in Adenauer's coalition hoped that the time for a general amnesty was approaching. However, after the shocking reminder of the Ulm proceedings, more people became convinced that such trials were necessary for improving the moral standing of the Federal

Republic. According to an Allensbach poll, at that point a majority of 54 percent favored continuing prosecution of Nazi criminals, as opposed to 34 percent who wanted to draw a line over the past. In 1963 and 1965, during the Auschwitz trial in Frankfurt, the proportion changed in the opposite direction.[4] In 1958, the *Länder* governments, with the federal minister of justice, set up the Central Office for Investigation of Nazi Crimes in Ludwigsburg; this new institution helped pave the way for a gradually more intensive prosecution of Nazi criminals.

Still, the number of indictments in the first years after the establishment of the Ludwigsburg Central Office was rather small, both for administrative reasons and because of a lack of contacts with the Eastern European nations that were a vital source of information for the prosecution. Altogether, a total of 105,000 suspects were investigated and approximately 6,500 indicted and sentenced since 1945. However, 70 percent of the convictions resulted from 5,228 indictments brought before the courts during Allied occupation between 1945 and 1949, and most of the sentences did not match the seriousness of the crimes. Erwin Schüle, the state prosecutor at the Ulm trial who became the first head of the Ludwigsburg Central Office, was forced to resign in 1965 because he had been a member in the SA and the Nazi party. Characteristic of the German situation in the first postwar decades was that at least 10 percent of the Nazi criminals involved in the murder of Jews during the Holocaust served as members of the federal police. A measure of continuity existed between the prewar police and security forces under Heinrich Himmler's command and the postwar democratic police force. An outspoken defender of Adenauer's handling of the past, Manfred Kittel, the author of *Die Legende der zweiten Schuld*, conceded as much.[5]

Regardless of West Germany's political stability, rapid economic growth, and the first cautious steps in coming to grips with the nation's Nazi legacy, antisemitic manifestations multiplied in the late 1950s. The Offenburg Nazi teacher, Ludwig Zind, was sentenced to one year's imprisonment because of his anti-Jewish utterances and public support of Hitler's policies. At the time his appeal was rejected, Zind was already on his way to President Gamal Nasser's Egypt, where he joined other Nazis agitating against Israel. West German justice also did not prevent the escape to Egypt of Buchenwald concentration camp criminal physician Hans Eisele, against whom complaints had been launched in 1954 and 1958. Eisele had been set free by the Americans after his death sentence had been commuted to life imprisonment in 1947.

In Hamburg, both the district court and the city state's supreme court rejected the prosecution's demand to put on trial the local merchant Friedrich Nieland, who blamed "international Jewry" for the Holocaust. He argued that no Jew could serve in any responsible position in the Federal Republic. At least one of the Hamburg judges was known to be a veteran supporter of the Nazis, and so were many of West Germany's justices. In Düsseldorf, swastikas appeared on the walls and doors of the new synagogue. All over Germany, a sharp increase in the desecration of Jewish cemeteries was registered. Last but not least, right-wing Bundestag members of the ruling CDU party, such as Jakob Diel, campaigned in an antisemitic vein against the growing burden of the indemnification payments, which had never been popular among the German population. Diel, a former member of the Catholic Center party, had been imprisoned by the Nazis several times. His anti-Jewish hate campaign, including his letters to Adenauer, served as a reminder that German antisemitism was not at all limited to Hitler's movement.[6]

In April 1958, the AJC disclosed the results of disappointing polls and surveys of German public opinion. Of those questioned, about 30 percent "were definitely anti-Semitic" with most of them falling into the post–thirty-five and post-fifty age groups. The highest percentage of antisemitism was found in rural areas. On the basis of the polls, the Committee concluded that a significant proportion of the German population was "still harboring deep prejudices and animosities against Jews." The German authorities were upset by this statement and submitted the results of another poll by the Allensbach Institute to the AJC, which showed that unfriendly attitudes toward Jews in Germany had diminished during the last years. For instance, whereas in 1952 every third person thought it would be best if there were no Jews at all living in Germany, in 1959, only every fifth person held that view. Sociologist Marshall Sklare, at that time a research analyst for the AJC, remained skeptical. He thought that the improvement mentioned in the Allensbach poll was because as time had passed, the possibility of a substantial number of Jews coming back to Germany had receded. Sklare added another possible reason: despite the propaganda against reparations and indemnification, it had become apparent that neither had crippled the German economy and that the Jews were not "despoiling" German resources and rights.[7] The American consulates, the mission in Berlin, and the embassy in Bonn reported back home all the major antisemitic incidents and manifestations but did not attach to them much importance. Complaints by the Jewish organizations did not have a great impact on them.[8]

In 1958, AJC president Irving Engel, his predecessor Jacob Blaustein, B'nai B'rith president Philip Klutznick, JLC president Adolph Held, Rabbi Israel Goldstein of the WJC and AJ Congress, and other distinguished figures in the American Jewish community discussed the recent antisemitic occurrences with West German president Theodor Heuss, who was visiting New York. In line with AJC's viewpoint, Engel rejected the concept of collective guilt and paid tribute to Germany's political leadership's devotion to the principles and objectives of democracy. However, he questioned whether German public life was sufficiently "shielded against the possibility of serious departures from these vital principles and aims." Heuss expressed his interest in further strengthening relations between West Germany and the American Jewish community and agreed that the antisemitic manifestations should be taken seriously. Still, he excluded any possibility of a revival of Nazi totalitarianism. Jacob Blaustein, the Claims Conference's senior vice-president and AJC's elder statesman, remarked that the indemnification program, which had recently been criticized by several German politicians, "must not be viewed merely as a boon to its beneficiaries but also as a fundamental requirement of the revindication of German democracy itself."[9]

AJC lay leaders and professionals continued to broach the problem of German antisemitism in exchanges of views with West German politicians, educators, and social scientists. They placed particular emphasis on the education of the younger German generation and the development of new educational techniques in dealing more effectively with Germany's recent past. After the events of the winter of 1959–60, a German Educators Program was set up, launched by the AJC in cooperation with the Ford Foundation and the Institute of International Education. The program provided for bringing over a number of West German teachers to the United States yearly to study and adopt American democratic methods.[10]

Chancellor Adenauer tried to convince his Jewish interlocutors that antisemitic and antidemocratic phenomena should not be exaggerated. He continued to regard Communism and the Communist dictatorship east of the Federal Republic's border as the main danger and insisted that Communism was involved in deliberate efforts to discredit West Germany abroad. Because of the Soviet diplomatic offensive on Berlin and Adenauer's fear of a reversal of American policy after Dulles's departure, he thought he might gain support for his stand also among American Jews.

The issue of education for democracy was also raised by the AJC delegate to the first German-American conference, held in Bad Godesberg in October 1959. The conference was jointly sponsored by the American Council on Germany and the Atlantik-Brücke, both nonpartisan bodies committed to furthering German-U.S. understanding.[11] Despite good personal relations between certain AJC lay leaders and Christopher Emmet, for many years the Council's executive vice-president and *spiritus movens*, the AJC as an organization often disagreed with the Council's built-in apologetic pro-German policies. Differences of opinion between them were to increase during the Kennedy administration's first steps toward an East-West detente, contrary to the consistent anti-Soviet emphasis of Adenauer and his government.[12]

As in the past, the AJC distinguished between its educational efforts to contain antisemitism in Germany and any boycott threats against West German trade. Stanley Marcus of the Neiman-Marcus department store in Dallas, who inquired about sales promotion in the United States of goods made in Germany, received the unequivocal answer that "since the endorsement by the American Jewish community, with almost complete unanimity of Germany's policy of collective and individual indemnification, no responsible Jewish organization . . . was engaged in any kind or degree of anti-German propaganda." Politically, American Jews had increasingly come to understand the Western security interest in Germany. Thus, it was "unlikely that the less consequential issue of a German merchandising company in the United States would evoke major Jewish protests." AJC's response also mentioned Israel's opposition to any Jewish boycott movement against German goods in the United States because of its dependence on German reparations shipments and payments.[13] In the case of Marcus, a supporter of the anti-Zionist American Council for Judaism, it is doubtful whether the Israeli viewpoint was needed to convince him. Besides, the Israel foreign ministry did not share the concern of American Jewish organizations about the German antisemitic threat. Commenting on a report of the American Jewish leaders' meeting with President Heuss, an official of the ministry's West European division remarked that there was not more antisemitism in Germany than in Britain, France, and the United States itself.[14]

To the AJ Congress, which usually was more suspicious of Germany, the antisemitic manifestations of the late 1950s provided a suitable occasion for the presentation of its critical report "The German Dilemma—An Appraisal of Anti-Semitism, Ultra-Nationalism, and Democracy in Western Germany." The authors of the pamphlet argued that the indifference of large sections of the German people to the problem of antisemitism had emboldened hoodlum elements. They recalled the whitewash and rehabilitation of former Nazis, many of whom had become respectable again and had assumed important roles in the administration and economy, in public and private life. In this context, they referred to the rebuilding of the industrial empire of Alfried Krupp who, after the war, had been imprisoned as a war criminal. Conversely, the pamphlet paid tribute to those forces consciously struggling to induce "a change of heart" in Germany and to create "a more humane and free order." It mentioned the Bonn government's positive record with respect to reparations for Israel and indemnification payments to the victims of the Nazi regime. It also praised the role of certain church groups as well as the contribution of the German media to improving the moral atmosphere in the country.[15]

The AJ Congress pamphlet, the AJC's statements after the American-German Bad Godesberg conference, and the visits and protests of American Jewish organizations during the swastika epidemic in January 1960 caused a major controversy between these organizations and the Central Council of the Jews in Germany. Hendrik George van Dam, for many years the Council's secretary general, insisted that "the Central Council and not publicity-chasing single Americans or American Jewish organizations were the representatives of Jewish interests in the Federal Republic." Van Dam suggested that if Bonn really wanted to listen to Jewish voices outside Germany, it had better heed the opinions of "really competent personalities" such as David Ben Gurion or Nahum Goldmann. Later, during the antisemitic occurrences in January 1960, he argued that the real cause of "criticism of Germany abroad was not German anti-Semitism but foreign anti-Germanism." He recommended that the Adenauer cabinet and its officialdom strengthen its cooperation with German Jewish leadership and be more discriminating in receiving protesting visitors from abroad.[16]

The American Jewish organizations, despite their different strategies, shared the view that an antisemitic upsurge in Germany should not be regarded as a local problem and rebuffed van Dam's "Monroe Doctrine" for German Jews. In their opinion, the postwar Jewish community in Germany—while its safety should be guaranteed—was too weak to cope alone with such a spate of anti-Jewish events.[17] In the short run, van Dam's challenge succeeded in temporarily reducing the flow of interceding Jewish visitors from abroad, which German officials in Bonn resented. But in the long run, the controversy did not change the basic pattern of American Jewry's involvement or its visits and contacts. West Germany remained interested in improving the ambivalent attitude of American Jews toward the German people and their state.

The wave of antisemitic events began with the desecration of the rededicated synagogue in Cologne on Christmas Eve 1959, and extended to swastika daubings of Jewish institutions and defiling of cemeteries. These episodes were perhaps less significant than they appeared to Jewish organizations in the United States and to Western public opinion at that time. There was no connection between that wave and the political or public impact of the extreme Right that had declined since the early 1950s. However, the 470 incidents, which damaged the official German philosemitic image and endangered the process of reconciliation with Jews abroad, came as an unpleasant surprise to the West German government and the whole German establishment. As Ambassador Grewe reported to the West German Foreign Office, the Federal Republic's prestige was badly hurt by the media coverage and the editorial comments on the happenings.[18] Besides the Jewish aspect, Bonn was also afraid that the antisemitic manifestations might undermine its consistent efforts to prove its status as a loyal and legitimate partner of the Western camp. This was especially significant at a time of the deteriorating Berlin crisis and on the eve of a crucial American presidential election.

The AJC was the first American Jewish organization to express its "deep concern" to the West German ambassador in Washington. The Committee demanded an effective investigation, prosecution of those responsible for the last outrages, removal of former

Nazis from official positions, and the outlawing of neo-Nazi parties and foreign fascist groups.[19] Eleonore Sterling, a capable young political scientist and historian reporting from Germany for the Committee, suggested that a strong word from the American president, even though not in public, might be more effective. Such a word, however, was not forthcoming.[20] In the wake of the incidents, certain AJC staff officials even suggested that the time had come for a reappraisal of the agency's moderate stand on Germany. The Jewish community, the officials suggested, should imagine the consequences of the Federal Republic's emerging aggressive role and dismiss the reasoning that criticism of the Bonn government might only play into Communist hands.[21] For Max Horkheimer of the Frankfurt Institute of Social Research, who continued to serve as an AJC consultant, the antisemitic outbreak proved that "there is no democratic tradition in the consciousness of any age groups and the young generation have no feelings about democracy." In his opinion, whatever the causes of the anti-Jewish occurrences might have been, they presented a demonstration of hostility against the West and Western civilization.[22] Commenting on Horkheimer's far-fetched and misleading conclusions, Eleonore Sterling remarked that the famous philosopher and social theorist had embarked on a new kind of pessimism à la Oswald Spengler's *Der Untergang des Abendlandes* (Decline of the West).[23]

Summarizing its view of the "hot winter," the AJC called the explanations offered by the West German White Paper a "dangerous simplification" that did not "take into consideration the social and political forces which made such occurrences possible."[24] The document portrayed the incidents mainly as a result of juvenile antiestablishment delinquency and imitative behavior. Yet, even though there was no meeting of the minds between Jacob Blaustein and Chancellor Adenauer about the urgency of improving West German political education, the crisis in the Committee's relations with Germany soon abated. The Committee continued to engage in promoting and expanding its German Educators Project.[25]

The AJ Congress regarded the antisemitic events as a renewed justification of its critical approach. In its opinion, the desecration of synagogues and cemeteries in Germany emphasized once more the danger of resurgent Nazism and "the inadequacy of the program of the German government in rooting out former and neo-Nazi groups." The statement of seven NCRAC organizations, which included the AJ Congress, was stronger, perhaps because of the participation of the Union of Orthodox Jewish Congregations. It recalled that "Germany remains the breeding ground of anti-Semitism, the manifest source of an infection that can spread swiftly."[26] The usually militant JWV stated that "one must judge the Federal Republic of Germany not on what it inherited from past German regimes . . . but rather on whatever rational steps it has taken and will take to stamp out the current outbreak of anti-Semitism." In contrast to other Jewish groups, it thought Bonn was sincere. At the same time it deplored the United States' failure to deal effectively with the Nazi legacy in the years of occupation, before West Germany regained its sovereignty.[27] The prosocialist JLC reiterated its position that "only with the active assistance of the German democratic labor movement will Germany be able to . . . democratize and reeducate the German nation and to create a climate which will make the existence of neo-Nazism impossible."[28] A two-man delegation of the New York Board of Rabbis who went to Germany a few months later called for supplementing the Federal Republic's economic miracle by a "moral miracle."[29]

The ADL, which was still closely connected with B'nai B'rith, took the most moderate attitude among the competing American Jewish organizations. Its delegation that visited there in January 1960 met with representatives of the major political parties, educators, journalists, and finally with Foreign Minister Heinrich von Brentano. Philip Klutznick, now chairman of B'nai B'rith's International Council, was received by Adenauer. The ADL accepted in part the official German view that the last events were the work of bigots and juvenile delinquents. Still, the organization reminded their German counterparts that the fact that antisemitism could again easily become an export product of Germany "was a frightening thing for Jews and all democracy-loving people in the world."[30]

A few months later, the organization initiated the first American Jewish–West German exchange program, aimed at introducing young German community leaders and officials to the American system of voluntary association.[31] In 1961, one year after the visit of a joint ADL and B'nai B'rith mission to Germany, a team of young Germans from different walks of life came to the United States. The participants were hosted by a number of local communities, although some groups, such as the Atlanta B'nai B'rith women, raised objections. At first they thought the guests would be

German youth of the postwar period, but as it turned out they were mature men who lived and were educated during the Hitler years in Germany. Therefore, they abstained from any participation in the program.[32]

In 1963 a group of ADL civil rights specialists paid a return visit to Germany. At least in public, most of the American Jewish, as well as the German, participants in the exchanges expressed satisfaction with their experiences.[33] Although the ADL members still discovered weak spots and contradictions in West German education for democracy, they found less overt antisemitism there than during the visit of the first ADL mission in 1954. They also took notice of manifestations of philosemitism and support of Israel. The German-born ADL director of foreign research, Jack Baker, formerly Kurt Bachrach, was the first representative of an American Jewish organization to address West German officers at a number of military academies. It seems that his personal background was helpful in the special relationship between the ADL and Germany.[34]

As expected, WJC president Nahum Goldmann was also among the moderates who warned against exaggerating the importance of the incidents and the threat implied to the German Jewish community. Visiting Bonn a few weeks after the desecration of the Cologne synagogue, Goldmann followed a suggestion of Joachim Prinz. He advised the chancellor to demonstrate his goodwill toward Jews in Germany and abroad by joining him and a delegation of the Claims Conference in a commemoration of the Nazi victims at the former Bergen-Belsen concentration camp.[35] Adenauer accepted Goldmann's proposal; it was the only time in his life that he attended a commemoration in a former concentration camp. In November 1952, he had refused a similar invitation and preferred that President Heuss attend the ceremony. However, he did not heed Goldmann's other suggestion that Bonn should assuage Jewish bitterness by establishing diplomatic relations with Israel. The Hallstein doctrine and the Federal Republic's fear of Arab reprisals still prevented such a step. Joachim Fest, then a young promising journalist and member of the ruling Christian Democratic party, implored Goldmann to use the opportunity and press for a purge of former Nazi collaborators from Adenauer's immediate circle. During the *Historikerstreit* in the 1980s, Fest, who authored the best-selling Hitler biography in 1973 and had become one of the publishers of the *Frankfurter Allgemeine Zeitung*, joined Ernst Nolte in the controversy over the uniqueness of the Nazi murder of European Jews.[36]

The Bonn government, no less than Jews in Germany and abroad, had been surprised by the rash of anti-Jewish manifestations after the desecration of the Cologne synagogue, even though there had been a gradual increase of antisemitic occurrences in the preceding two years. This time, the security forces reacted promptly. The Cologne offenders were soon apprehended and sentenced to prison terms, and so were others. Gerhard Schröder, minister of the interior, who presented the government's White Paper to the Bundestag in February, put the emphasis on the imitative behavior of bigots and juvenile delinquents, thus excluding any possibility of a neo-Nazi conspiracy. He also alluded to Communist support of at least a part of the instigators of the incidents, citing their interest in denigrating West Germany. Chancellor Adenauer, and particularly Minister of Defense Franz Josef Strauss, seemed to have preferred stronger language with regard to East German involvement. Relying on secret information of the Defense Ministry, Strauss maintained that the rulers of East Berlin had actively promoted antisemitic activities in the Federal Republic by infiltration and other means.[37] Such activities damaged the image of the Federal Republic, particularly on the eve of the abortive Paris summit meeting of the Big Four. But these suggestions were hard to prove at that time, and the anti-Jewish occurrences were not limited to West Germany. In any case, the American Jewish community continued to put the blame on the faults of the West German regime.

However, as Werner Bergmann emphasized in his analysis of the 1959–60 incidents, the unequivocal condemnation of antisemitic incidents by West German political and cultural elites presented a *novum* in German history and demonstrated the difference from pre-Holocaust reactions.[38] The Bundestag debate on antisemitism that followed the publication of the government's White Paper was one of the most important since the establishment of the Federal Republic. Leading spokesmen of the Social Democratic opposition, such as Carlo Schmid, Adolf Arndt, and the future West German president Gustav Heinemann, pointed to the permanent connection between antisemitism and the weakening of the foundations of German democracy. They castigated the government's failure to deal in a satisfactory way with the Nazi past. CDU Bundestag members, for their part, while condemning the anti-Jewish occurrences, nonetheless reiterated their conviction that the most militant focus of antisemitism after World War II was not in West Germany but in the Communist countries.[39]

The number of antisemitic incidents soon decreased. But even though far-reaching reforms were not yet implemented, the impact of the shocking experience on German political culture was positive. As a result of deliberations of the *Länder* ministers of education, more emphasis was put on teaching contemporary history in high schools; the law against preaching racist hatred was toughened; and the most prominent ex-Nazi in the cabinet, Minister for Refugees Theodor Oberländer, vacated his post. As a youngster Oberländer had participated in the march toward the Feldherrnhalle during Hitler's unsuccessful Munich coup of November 1923; ten years later he joined the Nazi party and rapidly advanced in its ranks. Although he had been accused of having participated in a massacre of Polish intellectuals and Lvov Jews as a lieutenant in the notorious *Nightingale Battalion* during the German invasion of Ukraine, he was cleared by an international committee. Still, many regarded that as a whitewash.

Jerusalem's reaction to the events of the winter of 1959–60 remained low-key. Israel, after all, was dependent on German reparations shipments and the evolving arms deals concerning the export of Israeli military items to Germany and, more important, German deliveries to Israel. The Knesset Foreign Relations and Security Committee pronounced a warning against antisemitic actions, which was transmitted to Bonn. However, during a Knesset debate on a proposal of the Israel Communist Party to cancel an arms export deal, Ben Gurion, who for the last years had stressed the difference between the Nazi state and the "other Germany" of Adenauer and the Social Democrats, again opposed the application of the term "a nation of murderers" to the German people.[40] The 1959 general elections in Israel, precipitated by a government crisis caused by arms deals with Germany, enhanced Ben Gurion's position more than ever.

The possibility of a meeting between Ben Gurion and Adenauer had been broached since the late 1950s. Politically, both had become closer after the Sinai War. Early in November 1956 Ben Gurion dispatched a message to Adenauer explaining Israel's motives. In the following years, more letters were exchanged, and Israeli messengers such as Giora Josephtal, a leading member of the Mapai party, and Ambassador Fischer called on the chancellor's office in futile attempts to establish political and security links with the Western community. Eventually, the visits of Adenauer and Ben Gurion to the United States in March 1960 were chosen as an appropriate occasion for a meeting between the two of them at New York's Waldorf Astoria Hotel. That encounter provided for a further strengthening of the pragmatic relations between Bonn and Jerusalem, even though the subject of diplomatic links was not discussed because of continuing West German objections. It also contributed to improving Germany's image among organized American Jewry after the furor caused by the antisemitic incidents.

The meeting between Ben Gurion and Adenauer on March 14, 1960, the first between the heads of government of Israel and the West German state, took place fifteen years after the end of World War II and seven years after the ratification of the Luxembourg agreement. Ben Gurion used the opportunity to appeal for long-term German credits of approximately $500 million—he had in mind mainly the development of the Negev—as a further step in helping the Jewish state. He also asked for increased and more sophisticated arms shipments to provide for Israel's security. Regardless of their differences in cultural and ideological background and their divergent views on such issues as the future of Asia and Africa, the two statesmen were very favorably impressed by each other. After all, on international affairs, Ben Gurion was relatively closer to Adenauer than was neutralist Goldmann. Israeli sources leaked interpretations that Adenauer had committed himself to development credits of $500 million for the next ten years, while the Germans denied that the chancellor had made any definite pledges. Nonetheless, Adenauer also committed himself to a substantial increase of arms supply for Israel.[41] Goldmann, who was not involved, privately criticized as exaggerated and damaging Ben Gurion's statement that the Germany of today was "a new nation."[42]

One day after his encounter with Ben Gurion, Adenauer met President Eisenhower at the White House. On the eve of the Paris summit and because of Adenauer's fear of the first signs of detente, the State Department advised Eisenhower not to annoy the German guest. The president was counseled to discuss the antisemitic incidents only if Adenauer himself broached them. If he did so, the American side should express its concern about the damage caused to the Federal Republic by those happenings. From the beginning of the year it had become clear that, in contrast to the uproar of American liberal public opinion, the reaction of the administration and also of many legislators on the Hill was rather subdued. This was particularly true when compared to the much more critical view of the British government and the House of Commons. No wonder that the subject did not come up during the talk between Eisenhower and Adenauer. The aging West German leader was mainly concerned with the danger of Communist ideology. But U.S. governmental restraint did not detract from the importance of American publicized and public opinion, which had been much more sensitive to the antisemitic manifestations in Germany.[43]

In a way, the favorable media coverage of the German-Israel summit in New York and its interpretation as a "hopeful sign for the future" helped the Federal Republic and its government improve their standing after the storm of criticism earlier in the year. At a session of the American Council on Germany a few hours after the meeting with Ben Gurion, Adenauer reassured his audience that no Jew in Germany would be hurt by anyone. The German mind, he said, was neither antisemitic nor nationalistic. Rabbi Joachim Prinz, president of the AJ Congress, heaped only praise on the chancellor on that occasion.[44] The AJ Congress's mouthpiece, *Congress Bi-Weekly*, which shared the general verdict about the importance of the German-Israeli summit, nevertheless thought that Ben Gurion's role in that exchange of views was still most difficult: "It was probably tempting not to raise the specter of the past, but he was admirably frank in stating that while 'my people cannot forget the past, we remember it in order that it should not reoccur.' "[45]

Nathan Straus, the liberal left-leaning owner of New York's WMCA, remained unconvinced that a fundamental change had taken place in the Federal Republic. His station counted many listeners among the metropolitan Jewish population who usually were more critical of Germany and the Germans than was the Jewish establishment. He reminded his audience of the former Nazis and Nazi collaborators still in positions of power and concluded, contrary to Ben Gurion, that the "past" was still the present.[46]

Not surprisingly, the increasing number of antisemitic events in West Germany in the late 1950s brought about a temporary renaissance of anti-German public protests. Objections were mounted by "progressive" or pro-Communist Jewish groups, in cooperation with certain *landsmanshaften,* left-wing trade unions or members of the Association of Polish Jews, all of whom reflected the deep hostility of the Jewish masses to Germany. In October 1959, an Israeli consul in New York was surprised by the large number— more than a thousand—of participants at a protest rally against the sale of Israeli arms to West Germany, organized by the Jewish Communist daily, *Morgen Freiheit.* Several of the speakers made it clear that they objected to the arms deal but continued to support Israel. The counselor at the Israeli embassy in Washington confessed that the arms deal with Germany caused uneasiness and confusion in contacts with American Jews, but the remarks of these diplomats had no effect on Israel's policy.[47]

Early in 1960, a number of protest meetings against antisemitism and Nazism in West Germany were staged in New York and other big cities, most of them by left-wing progressives. At a rally sponsored by the Youth Committee against Bigotry, Martin Luther King Jr., the black civil rights leader, and socialist Norman Thomas were among the speakers. The Yiddish *Morgen Freiheit* daily, Morris Schappes's *Jewish Currents,* and also Jack Fishbein in his *Chicago Sentinel* expressed critical views on Ben Gurion's German policy, the sale of Israeli weapons to Germany, as well as the Adenauer–Ben Gurion meeting in New York. This was in contrast to the strong support for Ben Gurion in the American Jewish press. More than once they also cited the criticism encountered by the Israeli prime minister at home, because of both his readiness "to forgive the Germans" and the implied threat that his meeting with the anti-Soviet German chancellor might be considered by Moscow as an anti-Soviet provocation.[48]

In 1961, pro-Communist groups were involved in protest meetings against the West German general Adolf Heusinger, who was appointed and later renominated as chairman of NATO's permanent military committee in Washington. On this occasion, left-wing critics reminded the public of the World War II cooperation between the Wehrmacht and the SS. Because of Heusinger's ambivalent past, the anti-Communist JWV took part in protest actions, whereas AJ Congress did not go further than passing a resolution of disapproval.[49]

The AJ Congress decided that it would not be desirable to pursue the matter by public protests, and disassociated itself from the Communist campaign. Yet despite Rabbi Prinz's hesitation, AJ Congress's leadership passed a resolution in 1962 against extending Heusinger's tour of duty.[50] However, because of the first steps of detente in the early 1960s, the beginning of the American Jewish struggle for Soviet Jewry and the old and new Left's involvement in the growing protest against the Vietnam War, left-wing anti-German activities receded even more to the sidelines.

PART IV

———

HOLOCAUST
CONSCIOUSNESS
AND THE ROLE
OF ISRAEL

———

12

The Eichmann Trial and the Quest for Punishment of Nazi Criminals

The Israeli capture of Adolf Eichmann and his trial in Jerusalem eclipsed American Jews' concern about a new rash of swastikas and other Nazi symbols in Germany in the winter of 1959–60. While the fate of six million murdered Jews was only a secondary item at the trial of the major Nazi leaders in Nuremberg, all its horror was exposed during the deliberations of the court in Jerusalem. In a way, that experience contributed to deepening the links between the American Jewish community and Israel. The trial also reaffirmed Jewish identity in the Diaspora.

In the short run, the affair affected the domestic American Jewish scene perhaps more than the community's attitude toward Germany. The Jewish establishment soon became involved in a confrontation with critics of the trial inside American Jewry. At the same time, it was busy furthering understanding among the American public for Eichmann's seizure and trial. But in the long run, the trial's impact spurred the growth of Holocaust consciousness, reaching its peak in the following decades. It also impeded for a number of years any major improvement in American Jewry's perceptions of Germany.

From the very moment Eichmann was kidnapped, Israeli diplomats tried to obtain maximum support from American Jewish organizations for Israel's actions and its decision to put the Nazi criminal on trial in Jerusalem. American Jewish solidarity with Israel was important as such, but it was also a precondition for a successful information drive among the vast non-Jewish majority. Despite the unease among liberals and trepidation engendered by Eichmann's capture and forceful removal from Argentina, the great majority of committed American Jews soon became convinced that Israel's handling of the case was justified and joined forces in trying to influence the American government and public.

Full support of Israel was expressed by the Yiddish and English Jewish press; rabbis of all the major denominations dedicated their weekly sermons to the affair. Jewish groups and individuals appealed to Vice-President Richard Nixon, Secretary of State Christian Herter, senators and congressmen; letters were dispatched to the country's leading newspapers.[1] *Commentary*, the most prestigious Jewish periodical, published an article by Jacob Robinson, the distinguished veteran legal expert, strongly backing Israel's claim of jurisdiction.[2] A second round of intense public and community relations activity followed early in 1961, before the opening of the trial; another followed after the passing of the death sentence.

Nonetheless, despite the solid backing of the majority, there was no full unanimity. Rabbi Dr. Louis Finkelstein, the renowned scholar and chancellor of the Jewish Theological Seminary in New York, at first hesitated over whether in his nonpolitical position he could take a stand on such an issue as Eichmann's capture. Eventually he promised the Israeli consul general that Conservative rabbis would support Israel's case.[3] In contrast to the close cooperation on the Luxembourg reparations agreement, divergent views were also expressed by Nahum Goldmann, the WJC and World Zionist Organization president. At first Goldmann suggested that Israel turn Eichmann over to an international tribunal; subsequently he proposed that the court in Jerusalem at least be supplemented by non-Jewish judges. Ben Gurion angrily rejected such alternatives, which contradicted Israeli and Zionist consensus.[4]

Joseph M. Proskauer, past president of the AJC and himself a retired judge, was afraid that the trial in Israel might increase antisemitism in the United States. He felt it was important to create a sympathetic climate in American public opinion that would "permit America to furnish Israel with defensive weapons to meet the Russian threat."[5] Proskauer referred to the *Washington Post*'s critical editorial that the government of Israel was not entitled to speak and act on the Eichmann issue in the name of an "imaginary Jewish ethnic unit." He also detected antisemitism in some of the last statements of Senator William Fulbright (D, Arkansas), a persistent critic of Israel and Zionism. Because of such negative repercussions he thought that some way might be found "to turn the man over to West Germany or some international tribunal for trial." Ben Gurion took his time for a detailed reply to the respected American Jewish leader, the former anti-Zionist who had become a strong supporter of the State of Israel. Ben Gurion did not exaggerate the importance of the *Washington Post's* editorial although it reflected a section of American public opinion that was critical of Israel's kidnapping of Eichmann and putting him on trial in Israel. While there were antisemitic manifestations in the United States, he did not regard the American people as antisemitic and did not believe that because of the trial in Jerusalem America would change its policy on the vital question of Israel's security.[6] In any case, for Ben Gurion, Eichmann's trial in Israel, which he regarded as the heir of the six million murdered Jews, was first of all a matter of historic justice.

Not surprisingly, the main objections in the Jewish community to the trial were raised by the anti-Zionist American Council for Judaism. This body hoped to use the case to regain some of its earlier standing after its decline in influence since the establishment of Israel and the gradual improvement of U.S.-Israel relations. The ACJ served as a platform for Harvard historian Oscar Handlin's attack on Israel's leaders for exploiting the Holocaust to legitimize the Jewish state, thus anticipating similar accusations by Israel's revisionist "new historians" in the post-Zionist climate of the 1990s. In 1950, Handlin, a noted scholar of American ethnicity and immigration, had rejected the anti-Zionist implication of Dorothy Thompson's insistence that "America demands a single loyalty." He emphasized just the opposite, that America did not take the traditional tack of denying that Jews had such loyalties. Now, a decade later, Handlin expressly refused to recognize Israel's claim that it alone was competent to represent the Jewish people as a national entity. He also recalled that Jews were not the only victims of Hitler's savagery and accused Israel of setting "national, almost tribal interests . . . above the more general, universal ones," not to mention the breach of the right of refuge by its violent act of kidnapping.[7]

Handlin was challenged not only by Zionists such as Marie Syrkin, a professor of Brandeis University, but also by Irving Howe, a socialist intellectual and *Dissent* editor. However, contrary to massive grassroots support for Israel's position, Handlin's reasoning was shared in part by other members of the liberal scholarly and intellectual community, both Jewish and gentile. They expressed concern about the role of Israel, the fairness of the trial, and even the ethics of Judaism "because of Israel's desire for vengeance rather than for justice." From Mexico City, Erich Fromm, author of *The Sane Society*, wrote to the *New York Times* that "the kidnapping of Eichmann is an act of lawlessness of exactly the type of which the Nazis themselves . . . have been guilty."[8] The ACJ, for its part, revived in that context accusations about the collaboration of Zionists and Nazi officials prior to 1939 as well as during the Holocaust years. It rehashed the slander that a great part of Nazi racial theory about Jews was based upon an active understanding and support of the Zionist doctrine that all Jews should leave Germany and settle in Palestine.[9]

A much more significant controversy was caused by Hannah Arendt's report on the Eichmann trial for the *New Yorker*, which in 1963 appeared in book form.[10] After the publication in 1951 of *The Origins of Totalitarianism*, her first major opus, the Jewish German-born public philosopher, political thinker, and essayist had established herself as a prominent voice among America's leading intellectuals. As a young undergraduate, she studied at Marburg under Martin Heidegger, with whom she had an affair and who had a long-lasting impact on her. But despite the famous existentialist philosopher's support for national socialism, which he never publicly recanted, their personal contact was restored after the war, upon Hannah Arendt's urging, and lasted until the end of their lives. At the same time, she developed a lifelong friendship with her doctoral guide and revered teacher Karl Jaspers, who had been removed by the Nazis from his teaching job in Heidelberg. Jaspers, who before the Nazi takeover was close to the right-wing intellectual critics of the Weimar Republic known as supporters of the "Konservative Revolution," moved after the war to Basel. From there he repeatedly voiced his criticism of the West German government's security policies and its insistence on German reunification.

Arendt's position moved from sympathy for the Jewish pioneers in Palestine in her first years of exile in Europe to fierce criticism of

Zionist nationalism during the war, which she spent in the United States. In an essay, "Zionism Reconsidered," which appeared in 1945 in the *Menorah Journal* after it had been rejected by *Commentary*, she argued that the promising social revolutionary Jewish national movement had failed. She maintained that Zionism had developed to the detriment of Palestinian Arabs, the Diaspora, and international understanding. In 1948, she joined Hebrew University president Judah Magnes's opposition to the Jewish state. In an article in *Commentary*, "To Save the Jewish Homeland: There Is Still Time," she cited the American proposal of an interim United Nations trusteeship as the only hope to forestall a Jewish state, to prevent partition, and to halt the ascendancy of Jewish and Arab terrorists to power.[11]

The trial in Jerusalem, which Arendt covered thirteen years later, served as an opportunity for her to express anew her dislike of Zionist nationalism and its militaristic trend. She strongly criticized the conduct of the trial, and especially the nationalistic particularist purposes it served. While obviously showing no sympathy for Eichmann, she noted that he was less the evil incarnate and the initiator of the liquidation of European Jewry, as Israeli chief prosecutor Gideon Hausner tried to portray him, than a cog in the murder machine. Arendt accused Israel's prime minister, David Ben Gurion, of conducting a show trial for educational purposes and objected to efforts to link the Holocaust with an "eternal antisemitism" to legitimize and strengthen the Jewish state. In her view, the genocide was not just a problem of relations between Jews and non-Jews but a crime against the human race, committed against but not limited to the Jewish people. Even though her analysis of Ben Gurion's motivation was partly correct, she distinguished between Hausner, who served Ben Gurion and the state, and the three German-born judges who handled the case in a rather fair way.

However, more than on all other issues, the author annoyed the Jewish community, and not only supporters of Zionism, by her contention that the Jewish communal leadership in Germany and Europe shared responsibility for the destruction of the Jewish people. Without this cooperation, she wrote, the Holocaust might not have reached the dimensions it did.[12] In his 1961 study, *The Destruction of the European Jews*, historian Raul Hilberg had expressed similar views on the failure of European Jewry to engage in active resistance and its self-deception about the German extermination program.[13] For many years, Hilberg's thesis encountered much disapproval by Jewish historians in Israel and the Diaspora. But his profound though controversial scholarly work did not evoke the immediate response elicited by Arendt's volume among the American Jewish public.

Hannah Arendt's treatment of the Eichmann trial aroused a storm of criticism from different people in Israel and in the American Jewish community, which raged for a number of years. Gershom Scholem's disgust with Arendt's "lack of love for the Jewish people" was so deep that he broke off their longtime friendship. Kurt Blumenfeld, the liberal German Zionist leader who in the 1930s had provided her with a job at Youth Aliyah in Paris, was deeply angered. Siegfried Moses, on behalf of the Council of Jews from Germany, made a "declaration of war" against the author and her book.

At home in the United States, she was debunked by Norman Podhoretz, then still a liberal, in his *Commentary* summary of objections to her volume raised by Lionel Abel, Marie Syrkin, Walter Laqueur, and others. In the forefront of the communal assault on Arendt was the ADL, which inspired hostile book reviews in the English-Jewish press. Nahum Goldmann also joined the chorus of her critics, telling a meeting of the Bergen-Belsen Survivor Organization in New York that Arendt had accused European Jews of letting themselves be slaughtered by the Nazis and of displaying "cowardice and lack of will to resist." Jacob Robinson's *And the Crooked Shall be Made Straight*, the most comprehensive rebuttal of Arendt's *Eichmann in Jerusalem*, appeared in 1965.

While Arendt complained that the Zionists and organized Jewry in the United States were resorting to any means to destroy her reputation, she drew support from gentile intellectual friends such as Mary McCarthy and Dwight MacDonald. A few young Jewish new leftists, too, were content that her critical analysis had stirred up a generational conflict in the Jewish community. Yet, despite her disagreements with the Zionists and the Jewish establishment, she refused offers of protection and support from anti-Zionist ACJ.[14] Overseas, she also found consolation in the private correspondence with philosopher Karl Jaspers, who hailed her essay as "an act of aggression against life-sustaining lies." He predicted that a time would come when Jews would erect a monument to her in Israel. At least until now, that prediction has not come true, although as a result of generational and ideological changes she has recently enjoyed a much better reputation in Israel's academia.[15]

For the record, it must be mentioned that in 1967 Hannah Arendt was elated by Israel's victory in the Six Day War. Arendt expressly distinguished between aggressive and defensive military involvements, and she regarded the 1967 war, unlike the 1956 Sinai Campaign, as legitimate. According to her biographer, Elizabeth Young-Bruehl, several months after that war she confessed to her good friend Mary McCarthy that "any real catastrophe in Israel would affect [her] more deeply than almost anything else." At the beginning of the Yom Kippur War in October 1973, she feared Israel might be destroyed, and attended an emergency meeting at Columbia University's Law School, where various suggestions for aiding Israel were considered. She even made a contribution to the right-wing Jewish Defense League, as she did in 1967, perhaps unaware of the League's extremist program.[16] Nonetheless, such an emotional display of sympathy toward Israel in times of stress did not detract from the sum total of her legacy, which was profoundly critical of Zionism and Jewish nationalism and of the link between American Jewry and Israel as an obstacle to a settlement with the Palestinian Arabs. In all, that rather long controversy contributed to the Jewish community's growing interest in the Holocaust, in addition to the trial itself. Arendt, for her part, came to be regarded as a pioneer both of the universalist interpretation of the Holocaust and of the functionalist—as distinguished from the intentionalist— approach, stressing the impersonal bureaucratic process of mass murder in a totalitarian state.[17]

Of course, there were also radical American Jews who had often been critical of Israel and its political tendencies. As a result of the Eichmann trial, some of them came to better understand the reasons for "Jewish parochialism, chauvinism and distrust." For Paul Jacobs, for instance, attendance in the courtroom in Jerusalem was an experience that forced him to confront his admitted ignorance and insensitivity in the past to the Jewish problem. He had opposed the trial in Israel's capital before it started. Yet, it strengthened his Jewish identity, which had been marginal to him in comparison to the radical movement and the case of the Spanish Republicans struggling against the Fascists before World War II. As he confessed in *Midstream*, the moment he saw Eichmann walk into his cage on the day the trial opened, he could not rid himself of the guilt that he "did not do enough for Israel, not even for Jews as such, but for six million human beings."[18]

According to summaries of the *American Jewish Year Book*, gentile America's response to Eichmann's capture and trial ranged from approval or condoning of Israel's role to condemnation. There was no consistent correlation between the political orientation of newspapers and their comments and reports on the Eichmann case; approval and opposition were expressed in both conservative and liberal papers in different regions of the country. Skepticism toward Germany in general was much rarer than the distinction between Adenauer's Federal Republic and the former Nazi Reich. ADL, surveying more than a thousand editorials, found that whereas comments at the time of Eichmann's capture had run 7 to 3 against Israel, one year later it ran 10 to 3 in Israel's favor. Opinion polls showed that 50 percent of the public felt that Israel was the proper place to try Eichmann, in comparison to 36 percent who preferred handing him over to an international court; 71 percent thought it was a good thing, and 21 percent a bad thing, for the world to be reminded of the Nazi concentration camp horrors; approximately the same majority regarded the trial in Jerusalem as fair. An analysis of these polls by the AJC found that educated respondents with at least some college training were less ready to credit Israel with sufficient objectivity to conduct the trial than the less educated.[19]

The verdict pronounced upon Eichmann in December 1961 came as no surprise to the American public, but the issue of his execution became the subject of an intense public debate and continued even after his hanging. To hang Eichmann seemed absurd to some papers; not to hang him seemed absurd to others. The *New York Times* and several other dailies echoed Martin Buber's suggestion that Eichmann be imprisoned and condemned to hard labor to the end of his days.[20] Buber's objection to the death sentence was shared in Jerusalem by other noted scholars such as Gershom Scholem and Samuel Hugo Bergmann. According to the recollections of Myer Feldman, President John F. Kennedy's Jewish affairs adviser, the president thought the Israelis would probably come out better if they commuted the death sentence, but he refrained from any official intercession in the affair, nor did he offer advice through private channels.[21] It was common knowledge that Kennedy was regarded as more friendly to Jews than President Eisenhower had been. Jews usually expected more support from a Democratic president than from a Republican.

Opposition to applying the ultimate punishment to Eichmann was also preponderant in the Jewish community. According to a NCRAC analyst, this attitude was not motivated by a profound sense of revulsion against capital punishment but by growing fears that Israel, and with her the Jews, could not afford to be accused of vengeance.[22] However, after the execution, spokesmen of organized Jewry did their best to defend the ultimate penalty confirmed by Israel's Supreme Court.

During the Eichmann trial in 1961, NCRAC commissioned a survey to measure the public's image of the German people. In a similar study twenty years earlier, the five most frequent adjectives were warlike, cruel, treacherous but hard-working, and intelligent. All adjectives in the current study were positive: hard-working, intelligent, progressive, practical, and brave. By and large, America's image of the Germans sixteen years after World War II was favorable. This did not alleviate the Jewish organizations' task of raising public opinion against negative outbursts. In general, during the Eichmann trial, the strongest anti-German sentiment still came from the South and the East, the least from the West and Midwest.[23]

Another poll conducted in July 1961 showed that the trial had not substantially affected the feelings of Americans toward the German people. Seven percent reported that they had become more sympathetic to the Germans as a result of the trial. Seventeen percent had become less sympathetic, 55 percent reported no change, and 21 percent expressed no opinion.[24] As for Israel, the NCRAC survey concluded that there was not much hostile reaction against it as a result of the trial in Jerusalem. If the trial sparked any reaction to Jewish people in America, the positive reactions undoubtedly outweighed the negative ones.[25]

Despite such polls, indicating a rather moderate decline in sympathy, leading politicians in Bonn as well as German diplomats in the United States were very much concerned about the possible unfavorable repercussions of the proceedings in Jerusalem on the Federal Republic's standing in American public opinion and their impact on American–West German relations. The German consul general in New York broached the subject in talks with representatives of the ADL, the American Jewish organization that had the best contacts with the German diplomats since the mid-1950s. Benjamin Epstein, ADL national executive director, thought that a public German statement recognizing Israel's right to put Eichmann on trial, as well as a summary of Germany's own legal actions against Nazi criminals, might help to stress the difference between the Nazi regime and the liberal democratic character of postwar West Germany.[26] The day the trial opened, the acting German consul general summoned a meeting with representatives of all the major Jewish organizations who expressed similar views. Israeli diplomats, too, were approached by their German counterparts in regard to the Eichmann trial. Wilhelm Grewe, the ambassador in Washington, discussed it with Israel's ambassador, Abraham Harman, and in New York the German consul general met members of Israel's consulate general in the presence of ADL.[27]

Adenauer himself, who at first had been concerned about possible negative repercussions for the German people, declared on the eve of his visit to the United States that from the moral viewpoint, Israel had the right to put on trial the man whom it regarded as one of the worst mass murderers. His main worry was that State Secretary Hans Globke, his closest adviser, should not become involved and be called to testify at the trial in Jerusalem. Whatever the doubts about Globke's service during the Nazi regime, as interpreter of the Nuremberg racial laws and elsewhere, Bonn's wish with regard to Globke was honored by the Israeli side. Moreover, all efforts by the GDR to incriminate Globke with the help of the observer it dispatched to the trial were of no avail.[28]

In contrast to its unwillingness to get involved in the American Jewish–German confrontation over the antisemitic occurrences of the winter of 1959–60, Israel played an active role in the Jewish community's actions on the Eichmann affair. It was interested in preserving the support of American public opinion while not endangering continuous West German material assistance. The Germans, for their part, reminded the American Jewish organizations of the prompt implementation of the reparations agreement. They also discreetly referred to the unofficial agreement on further aid for Israel reached between Adenauer and Ben Gurion in March 1960. They could not grasp, though, that despite the conciliatory summit meeting between the two leaders, Ben Gurion's putting Eichmann on trial in Jerusalem affected American Jewry in just the opposite direction.

West German public opinion polls and surveys did not show any upsurge of antisemitism there as a result of Eichmann's trial and death sentence. These polls were conducted upon the initiative of the AJC by the Institute of Social Research in Frankfurt in April–May 1961 and in January–February 1962. On the contrary, they confirmed a continuing small improvement in comparison to polls taken over the last decade. Hundreds of editorials that appeared all over Germany expressed much soul-searching. In the opinion of one of the AJC staff people, the reaction of the West German press to the Eichmann case constituted one of the most important and promising developments since the end of Nazism.[29]

The Eichmann trial took place at a very inconvenient time for West Germany. Its relations with the new Democratic administration were less close than they had been with its Republican predecessor, especially as long as John Foster Dulles served as secretary of state. In the winter of 1960–61, both the outgoing and incoming administrations in Washington were at odds with the Federal Republic over the balance of payments and the costs of keeping American forces on German soil. But even before the Berlin Wall definitively divided the former German capital for the next twenty-eight years, Adenauer became afraid of the new preferences and the winds of change blowing from President John Fitzgerald Kennedy's brain trusters in Washington.

Afterwards, the chancellor was irritated by the relatively mild American response to the wall built by the Ulbricht regime in coordination with the Soviet Union, by the new NATO strategy of flexible response, and by the friendly reception in Washington of Social Democratic opposition spokesmen. This included Berlin mayor Willy Brandt, who showed more understanding for the JFK administration's new emphases. After the building of the Berlin Wall, Adenauer dispatched Kurt Birrenbach, a CDU member of the Bundestag well versed in international affairs, on a special mission to the United States to find out why Washington and the other Western allies remained indifferent to the new Soviet and East German challenge. The chancellor advised him to meet with influential Jews in addition to leading members of the American foreign and security policy establishment. Birrenbach saw, among others, Nahum Goldmann, the lawyer David Ginsburg, Adenauer's friend Dannie Heineman, and Abraham Feinberg, president of the Mayser Corporation and one of Israel's main supporters. In these talks he tried to impress upon them the similarity between divided Berlin and Jerusalem. Some revealed understanding for the German point of view, whereas others were noncommittal. As Erhard's emissary after Adenauer's retirement, Birrenbach was to take part in the 1965 West German–Israeli negotiations about a settlement with regard to the suspended arms shipments and the establishment of full diplomatic relations between the two countries.[30]

In 1962, Adenauer had to replace Ambassador Grewe, whom Kennedy and his advisers could not stand. In 1963, the gap between Bonn and Washington widened even more because of the atomic test ban agreement between the United States, Great Britain, and the Soviet Union and the new Elysée Treaty between Adenauer and French president Charles de Gaulle. Only after Adenauer's departure in October 1963 did his pro-American successor, Ludwig Erhard, together with other "Atlanticist" ministers from the CDU and FDP, attempt to restore mutual confidence with the hegemonic power overseas on which the Federal Republic's security still relied.

German VIPs visiting the United States and diplomats serving there usually credited much of the anti-German sentiment to the fact that many influential Americans in television, radio, book publishing, and the film industry were Jews who did not forget and did not want others to forget what happened to European Jewry during the Holocaust. Even before the Eichmann trial and its impact on the American media, the Germans were upset by the record-breaking sales of William Shirer's 1959 best-seller *The Rise and Fall of the Third Reich*. Shirer, himself a non-Jewish left-liberal who served as CBS Berlin correspondent until 1941, treated the Nazi movement as a representative product of Germany's political culture. His book shaped the view of many Americans more than evenhanded scholarly publications.[31] Well-done TV productions, later screened as films, such as Stanley Kramer's *Judgment at Nuremberg*, were regarded by progovernment German observers as much more damaging to Germany's image than the old anti-German propaganda films of World War II. Anti-Nazi Social Democratic mayor Willy Brandt in December 1961 sponsored the film's premiere in West Berlin, with General Lucius Clay as Kennedy's special representative in the audience. Still, Christopher Emmet, executive head of the lobbylike American Council on Germany, found it necessary to remind the public of producer Kramer's Communist-front record, complaining that nobody was mentioning it since it smacked of McCarthyism.[32]

As a retaliatory action to protect German interests in the early 1960s, German diplomats discreetly approved of local protests by German Americans against anti-German productions in the media;[33] they would not have considered such means in the 1950s. However, the consul general in New York warned his superiors in Bonn against exaggerating the impact of the anti-German manifestations. He stressed the fact that leaders of the Jewish community such as Nahum Goldmann, Irving Engel of the AJC, and Benjamin Epstein of the ADL promised cooperation in containing the "anti-German wave." On an earlier occasion, the consulate general in New York engaged the help of the ADL to prevent the screening of Leni Riefenstahl's Nazi production *Triumph des Willens.*

On the other hand, Ambassador Harman was told by his superiors in Jerusalem to see to it that important Germans understood the damage caused to them by Bonn's ambiguous attitude to Israel. The refusal to establish diplomatic relations, Germany's hesitation on Israel's request for closer links with the EEC, and the insistence of full secrecy regarding the assistance agreed upon at the Adenauer–Ben Gurion meeting in 1960 contributed to Jerusalem's concern. Chaim Yachil, the director general of the Israel foreign ministry at that time, shared the view of Harvard professor Henry Kissinger that Germans were still sensitive to American Jewish opinion.[34]

The influence of organized American Jewry on people of Jewish origin in the media and in the film industry was admittedly limited. The American Council on Germany, however, which counted a number of Jewish Americans not representative of the community in its ranks, was very much interested in gaining some kind of support from the major Jewish organizations for its activities and publications. Emmet repeatedly heaped much praise upon them, but mostly his efforts were in vain. For instance, in 1960, after the swastika daubings and antisemitic manifestations of the winter of 1959–60, both the AJC and ADL regarded the Council's pamphlet, "The Vanishing Swastika," as one-sided and apologetic. The AJC refused Emmet's request that it buy and distribute a thousand or more copies, even without the Committee's endorsement. Benjamin Epstein, ADL's national director who had known Emmet since his anti-Nazi activities in the 1930s, thought that the pamphlet was even more far-reaching in its whitewash of the significance of former Nazis in government than the attitude of many officials in Bonn. Nonetheless, Jewish criticism did not prevent the publication of the booklet by the traditional pro-German Henry Regnery publishing house in Chicago and its wide distribution in the United States and Canada.[35]

A few years later, the AJC also took issue with another apologetic statement circulated by the American Council on Germany. It glossed over the problems presented by the election successes of the extreme right-wing NPD in the fall of 1966, at a time when Kurt Georg Kiesinger, himself a former member of the Nazi party, was appointed federal chancellor as Erhard's successor.[36] That statement was signed by twenty-nine American experts on Germany, including not only the regular pro-German public and academic figures but also political scientist Hans Morgenthau and Henry Kissinger, who a few years later would become President Richard M. Nixon's main adviser on security and foreign affairs.[37]

Two years after the Eichmann trial, the American Jewish community became deeply involved in the campaign for extension of the German statute of limitations in cases of murder that was to go into effect in May 1965. After a long pause, which lasted until the late 1950s because of the Cold War and the conservative political climate at home, West Germany had finally started to look for Nazi criminals and to bring them to court. Authorities were helped by incriminating material gathered by the Ludwigsburg Central Office for Investigation of Nazi Crimes. The World Jewish Congress, particularly its New York office, made a substantial contribution to the preparation of a number of trials through an intense search for witnesses in America, Israel, and other nations. Until his death in 1964, IJA director Nehemiah Robinson, who had been involved in reparations and uncovering of Nazi crimes since the 1940s, was successful in establishing good working relations with German judges and state prosecutors.[38]

However, according to the German penal code of 1871, under which Nazi criminals were prosecuted and punished, the statute of limitations applied to all crimes. Thus, since the Bundestag's conservative majority had rejected the extension of the statute in 1960 in cases of manslaughter,[39] it was likely that after May 1965, Nazi criminals who had successfully evaded detection and indictment would be able to survive in safety without further prosecution. Israel, American Jews, and other Diaspora communities joined forces against such a possibility and, with pressure exerted by various nations, eventually prevailed. The improved atmosphere in East-West relations made the Jewish community more resolute in its efforts than it had been in opposing the amnesty and commutation of sentences of Nazi criminals by the American authorities in the heyday of the Cold War.

In a way, the belated Nazi trials in West Germany added to the urgency of the campaign for extending the statute of limitations in cases of murder. Fritz Bauer, the state prosecutor in Hessen, himself a former Jewish exile who had helped Israel find Eichmann in Argentina, meticulously prepared the Frankfurt trial of twenty-two former Auschwitz guards and medical personnel. Yet, his expectation that the biggest mass trial of Nazi murderers since Nuremberg would shock the German public and contribute to its self-cleansing did not materialize. Despite the German media's detailed reporting of the case, the number of Germans who favored an end to further prosecution of Nazi criminals grew during the proceedings. Whereas 53 percent of those interviewed in mid-1964 considered it proper to continue such trials, at the end of the year 63 percent of all German men and 76 percent of German women wanted to put an end to them. Six life sentences were passed at the Auschwitz trial in Frankfurt, four at the Treblinka trial in Düsseldorf, and a few more at other trials. However, a great many defendants accused of murder received shorter sentences.[40]

In the early 1960s, a partial purge in the West German judiciary system took place. Approximately 150 judges and state prosecutors who had been involved in illegitimate severe sentences during the Nazi dictatorship voluntarily retired. However, many judges who remained in office continued to rely on the excuse that defendants of lower ranks had only fulfilled the orders of their superiors. There also was a growing tendency of the assize courts, comprised of three professional judges and six lay jurors, to hand down verdicts of complicity in murder rather than murder itself, a fact sharply criticized by most of the serious media. Altogether, the first major trials in the mid-1960s showed how little had been done until then to cope with many thousands implicated in the Nazi murder machine.[41]

Skepticism prevailed, therefore, over Bonn's argument that the putting into effect of the statute of limitations would not mean the cessation of all the outstanding Nazi crime trials. Under the existing law, the suspects needed only to be formally charged before the statute's expiration to secure their prosecution. The long-delayed search for incriminating material against suspected Nazi criminals in Russian, Polish, and Czechoslovakian archives revealed many unknown testimonies and added further proof of the necessity of at least extending the statute, if not for its abolition.

In the last months of his chancellorship, Adenauer told Ambassador Eliezer Shinnar, the head of the Israeli mission in Cologne, that he was very much concerned about the damage caused to the Federal Republic by the continuing trials of Nazi criminals eighteen years after the end of World War II. He suggested a dubious quid pro quo: putting an end to all the trials, together with the establishment of full diplomatic relations with Israel.[42] Adenauer left office without establishing such relations, and as a result of Ben Gurion's resignation and domestic pressure, Israel became an active participant in 1964 in the fight against the implementation of the statute. Because of Israel's dependence on German financial as well as military aid, Ben Gurion was careful not to raise the issue of Bonn's handling of Nazi criminals after the Eichmann trial in Jerusalem, and he refrained from exposing the blemished record of several high West German officials. His successor Levi Eshkol's attitude in regard to Germany was more critical,[43] and Foreign Minister Golda Meir's even more so. However, because of the importance of the American-German alliance and West Germany's vital interest in preserving the goodwill of American public opinion, the brunt of the world Jewish campaign was borne by organized American Jewry.

At the end of 1964, the West German government declared that it would not extend the statute of limitations on Nazi war crimes, which was to go into effect in mid-1965. Upon the suggestion of Israeli diplomats in Washington and New York, the Conference of Presidents of Major American Jewish Organizations, whose importance and range of activities grew in the 1960s, called for a change of that attitude in an appeal to West German foreign minister Gerhard Schröder. But the minister, no friend of Israel and a persistent opponent of Jewish pressure, refused to meet with a Jewish delegation during his visit to the United States in December 1964.[44] Schröder himself, a member of the Nazi party, had been expelled from its ranks because of his marriage to a woman of Jewish descent.

Ambassador Knappstein, who was familiar with the Jewish community from long years of service as consul general in Chicago and as observer to the United Nations in New York before his appointment to Washington, was more forthcoming. He did not share his government's initial insistence that the statute should not be extended for constitutional reasons. He hinted to the Jewish leaders, whom he asked to call off public protests, that the cabinet's negative decision would not remain the final one. As a matter of fact, contrary to the German ministry of justice, high officials in the Foreign Office favored postponement in order to relieve pressure, and Chancellor Erhard himself was known to support the extension of the statute.[45] Jewish community leaders also appealed to legislators on Capitol Hill to use their good offices for the statute's extension. Subsequently, Senators Jacob Javits and Abraham Ribicoff introduced a sense-of-Congress resolution asking the president to formally make this a request from the West German government.[46]

Although all American Jewish organizations were of one mind about the urgency of extending the German statute, in the final stage the traditional differences of opinion reappeared regarding the steps necessary to achieve the common aim. As in the past, the AJC opposed public protests. Morris Abram, its president at that time, met the West German minister of justice Ewald Bucher in Bonn and tried to convince him of the necessity to postpone the implementation of the statute for at least five years. Abram wanted to start the twenty-year period in 1949, when the Federal Republic was established, and not in 1945.[47] Jacob Blaustein, the AJC's elder statesman, told Knappstein "that Germany would make a grievous mistake if it acted under the erroneous impression that U.S. public opinion—either non-Jewish or Jewish—was no longer sensitive as to what Germany does, or does not, from here on."[48]

The member organizations of the Presidents Conference preferred direct action and endorsed picketing in fifteen key cities where West German consulates were located. The JWV played a leading role in organizing the protests. A partner that cooperated with the JWV was the Orthodox Young Israel, which hence became a permanent participant in anti-German demonstrations.[49] NCRAC encouraged public statements by nonsectarian civic, professional, and civil rights groups, and particularly by Christian clergymen. The ADL appealed to public opinion in states and cities that were not targeted by the Presidents Conference.[50] However, an extremely critical advertisement of the JWV in the national press that recalled German brutality and arrogance in World Wars I and II incurred much criticism not only from Julius Klein, who submitted his resignation from the organization, but also from the Jewish establishment. Philip Klutznick, for instance, regarded it as detrimental from the American, the Jewish, and the Israeli viewpoints.[51]

Though not the only factor, the American Jewish campaign and Israel's demands undoubtedly contributed to the change of attitude of West Germany's government, which finally extended the statute until 1969. Pressure had constantly mounted not only from Jewish circles but also from foreign governments whom Bonn could not afford to ignore, especially because of the incriminating material supplied by Eastern European archives. The four-and-a-half-year extension was the minimal period demanded by the AJC; others thought it was too short. According to German public opinion polls, the majority of the Germans felt otherwise: 57 percent of them wanted to put an end to the trials of Nazi criminals altogether, 11 percent had no opinion on that issue, and, despite the evidence produced at the trials of the Nazi murderers in Auschwitz and other extermination camps, only 32 percent favored the lifting of the statute.[52]

Nonetheless, the Bundestag debate of March 10, 1965, on the postponement of the statute of limitations saw more German soul-searching than had most of its earlier deliberations.[53] The House was split between those who recognized the priority of historical responsibility and those who refused to budge from existing legal principles, some of them bona fide and others for political reasons. The Social Democratic legal expert, Adolf Arndt, himself partly of Jewish origin, reminded his fellow parliamentarians that "everybody in Germany knew that Jews were being murdered, possibly not all the details, but there was no one who today would not be lying if he claimed that he was ignorant."

Arndt asked forgiveness for not having protested when German Jews were deported to the East. Ernst Benda, a prominent Christian Democrat of the party's liberal wing, who later served as president of the Federal Republic's Constitutional Court, refuted all comparisons between Nazi crimes and indiscriminate Allied bombings in their war against Nazi Germany. In principle, the majority of the Social Democrats favored total abolition of the statute by a constitutional amendment, mainly for reasons of Germany's democratic regime, not because of foreign pressure. But since they found no partners who would support abolition, they agreed to the rather limited extension by regular legislation. This compromise was also endorsed by former chancellor Adenauer and confirmed in the Bundestag by a majority of 344 to 96, and 4 abstentions.[54] The experience of the following years showed that the postponement until 1969 was not enough. Thus, in 1969, the statute was extended for another ten years until its final abolition in 1979.

13

Changing Circumstances and Futile Dialogues

Late in March 1965, the West German government and parliament bowed to pressure from abroad and decided to postpone the application of the statute of limitations, thus providing for further prosecution of Nazi criminals accused of murder. But even more crucial for the American Jewish–Israeli–German triangular relationship was Chancellor Ludwig Erhard's decision, taken in the same month, to establish full diplomatic relations between Bonn and Jerusalem. After agreement between both nations had been reached in May, ambassadors were exchanged in August. The American Jewish community, which was very much involved in the campaign for postponing the statute of limitations, also contributed to Bonn's rather belated decision on normalizing relations with the Jewish state.

Both the establishment of diplomatic relations with Israel and the postponement of the statute of limitations were regarded by some American Jewish leaders as paving the way for an improvement of American Jewry's attitude toward Germany. There were deliberations on the subject in communal agencies, exchanges of views at symposia, and more visits to the Federal Republic by rabbis and secular intellectuals, but without concrete results. The only outcome was that for organized Jewry the interest in the German problem that had increased again during the swastika rash and the

Eichmann trial lost its urgency. The exception was issues connected with Israel, support for which had become the common denominator in American Jewish life. On the political level, the German issue reemerged forcefully only twenty years later, as a part of the conservative trend of the 1980s. To great dismay and despite strong Jewish protests, West German chancellor Helmut Kohl insisted on a common visit with President Ronald Reagan to Bitburg military cemetery where a number of veteran SS soldiers were interred.

American Jewry's growing Holocaust consciousness and its impact on communal priorities would soon add another dimension to the complex American Jewish–German relationship and reinforce the grass roots' negative perception of the German people. The Germans, for their part, regardless of their persisting interest in conciliating American Jews, directed their main efforts in those years toward Israel and its Jewish society. There they succeeded in lifting a great many barriers in a remarkably short period. Mutual ties between German and Israeli groups and institutions became even stronger in the 1970s, the growing political difficulties between both governments notwithstanding.[1]

The long delay in establishing diplomatic relations between the Federal Republic of Germany and Israel was caused by Bonn's insistence on the so-called Hallstein doctrine, as well as by German economic and political interests in the Arab nations hostile to Israel. Israel had been ready for such links since the late 1950s but did not find it suitable to force the issue. In the 1960s, it would agree only to full-fledged relations and not to any halfway alternative, which some West Germans had in mind. According to the Hallstein doctrine, West Germany regarded itself as the only legitimate representative of the German nation, and the Foreign Office in Bonn continued to argue that diplomatic relations with Israel might cause Arab nations to retaliate by establishing relations with the East German government. Thus the issue of formalizing relations with Israel was put on ice for close to a decade.

Instead, the pragmatic West German–Israeli relationship that began with the ratification of the reparations agreement in 1953 was augmented by arms deliveries and additional credits for Israel's development. Israel had become interested in obtaining quasi-military equipment from Germany even before the Sinai campaign, but that successful war provided the opportunity for the first deals based on mutual benefit. Franz Josef Strauss, West Germany's defense minister, and Shimon Peres, the director general of Israel's ministry of defense, initiated the sale of Israel's Uzi submachine guns to Germany and the first deliveries of German weapons to Israel. Israel needed the German weapons, and Strauss favored strengthening Israel's military capacity as a de facto ally against Soviet expansion in the Middle East.[2] Ben Gurion's meeting with Adenauer in 1960 in New York paved the way for a substantial increase of German arms supplies in the early 1960s. At the same time, West German foreign-policymakers, some of whom regarded Israel as a "nuisance factor," presented their refusal to establish diplomatic relations with Israel also as a service to the Western alliance, as well as to Germany's own political and economic interests. They argued that both the European allies and the United States, who themselves had such relations for many years, were interested in preserving the traditional German-Arab friendship and not endangering it because of Israel.

Quite understandably, German ambassadors to the Arab capitals such as Cairo, Baghdad, and Damascus were in the forefront against any shift of Bonn's policy in favor of diplomatic relations with Israel. However, most of the foreign affairs establishment shared the same views, as shown in the memoranda and correspondence of the recently published volumes on German foreign policy since 1963.[3] Even after the establishment of diplomatic relations, Asher Ben-Nathan, Israel's first full-fledged ambassador to Bonn, was greeted with distinct coolness by German diplomats in charge of contacts with him.[4] At the discussions of the CDU/CSU parliamentary group, too, the opponents of establishing diplomatic relations with Israel had prevailed, pointing to both Germany's political and its economic interests. Those who warned that Bonn's procrastination might sooner or later endanger the achievement of the Luxembourg Treaty in "assuaging the aggressive polemic of world Jewry against Germany" remained in the minority.[5]

Before leaving office in October 1963, Adenauer explained to former president Theodor Heuss that he had failed to establish diplomatic relations with Israel because of Washington's advice against it.[6] As a matter of fact, the Americans never pressured Bonn to proceed with the establishment of relations with Israel and refused to promise the Germans preventive steps against retaliatory measures of Egypt and other Arab nations. However, the U.S. position was never as clear-cut as German spokesmen repeatedly tried to interpret it, even though their view was shared in part also by Israel's envoy Eliezer Shinnar.[7] The main reason for Adenauer's retreat was that he could not obtain a majority in the CDU parliamentary group and in the cabinet for such a decision. Foreign Minister Schröder led the opposition and enjoyed the full support of the FDP ministers, the coalition's junior partner, in addition to most Christian Democrats. The FDP objected to normalization of relations with Israel just as it had opposed the extension of the statute of limitations.

After Schröder had consistently opposed Adenauer's attempts to conclude his chancellorship by exchanging ambassadors with Israel, he recommended to Adenauer's successor, Erhard, in 1964 that he stop military cooperation with Israel. He also suggested that Erhard invite Egypt's President Nasser to pay an official visit to Bonn.[8]

Before the triangular German-Israeli-Egyptian crisis reached its peak in the winter of 1964–65, German-Israeli relations in 1963–64 had been marred by Egypt's employment of West German scientists and military experts for its rocket research and armaments industry. In fact, Israel's leadership was divided in its evaluation of this threat to its security, which Ben Gurion himself did not exaggerate. Nevertheless, even before Ben Gurion's resignation, in June 1963, which in part was caused by that issue, the foreign ministry decided to mobilize American Jewish support in the campaign against the German experts, both in contacts with the administration and congressmen and in talks with German diplomats and politicians. Leading spokesmen of the AJC and B'nai B'rith broached the problem with German ambassador Knappstein; Philip Klutznick tried to engage Myer Feldman, President Kennedy's and his successor Lyndon Johnson's Jewish affairs adviser, as well as Jacob Arvey, still an influential voice among the Democrats.[9] All these intercessions did not bear quick results. The West German government did not wish to antagonize Egypt, since 1958 a main recipient of German development aid and rated as a central factor in Germany's Middle East policy. At least some of its policy molders regarded the scientists' employment as a balancing factor at a time when Israel enjoyed a growing amount of German military assistance. Averell Harriman, at that point undersecretary of state for political affairs, expressed understanding for Egypt's interest in establishing its own aircraft production by using Western sources. If the German experts returned home, "they might well be replaced by Soviet Bloc personnel, again forcing the UAR [United Arab Republic, as Egypt was called during its ephemeral union with Syria] into greater reliance on the USSR."[10]

Nonetheless, American Jewish pressure persisted. In Chicago, for instance, fifteen local rabbis picketed the German consulate half a year before the nationwide protest action in January 1965.[11] Thus, the issue of the German scientists became one of the central themes of what the Israeli diplomats in the United States dubbed "Operation Germany." The others were the fight for extension of the statute of limitations, the suspension of German arms deliveries, as well as the establishment of full diplomatic relations between Bonn and Jerusalem.

The normalization of diplomatic relations finally took place during Chancellor Erhard's relatively short term of office, as a result of the crisis caused by the curtailment of German arms shipments to Israel. It was the irony of history that these relations were established by a political leader whose accession to power in October 1963 had been greeted by the Arab nations because he was regarded by them as more forthcoming than Adenauer. In 1964, Erhard had unwillingly bowed to demands of the Johnson administration to supply Israel with secondhand American M-48 tanks and other military equipment via third countries, a rather complex transaction that did not remain secret. Before that Israel's prime minister Levi Eshkol had paid the first official visit of an Israeli head of government to Washington. Although the Johnson administration was more sympathetic to Israel than its predecessors, it still preferred the indirect arming of Israel. In October 1964, the Egyptian daily *Al-Gumuria* published a news report on German-Israeli scientific cooperation falsely implying that atomic research for military purposes at the Weizmann Institute in Rehoboth was involved. Following that story, which among others also aimed at fending off the Israeli campaign against the German scientists and experts in Egypt, details of the German-Israeli arms deal were leaked to the German press. These revelations played into the hands of German politicians and officials who wanted to put an end to the military supplies.[12] Subsequently, the Bonn government hinted that no additional agreements on military aid to Israel would be concluded. Nevertheless, Egyptian president Nasser, encouraged by the Soviet Union, exploited the critical juncture and extended an official invitation to the East German leader, Walter Ulbricht, to visit Cairo. Even before that visit took place, West Germany had officially renounced further arms shipments to Israel. Although it left the door open for financial compensation to Israel for the undelivered shipments, the Federal Republic's public giving in to Arab blackmail and abandoning its commitments to Israel raised a storm of protest both in Israel and in the American Jewish community, as well as in some other major communities of the Western Diaspora. Whereas a number of American Jewish leaders had been privy to the importance of the supply of the German weapons, only its suspension made the broader community conscious of the loss.

The cancellation of the West German arms shipments to Israel, which had been preceded several months earlier by a decision not to take up any further commitments, was supported by the overwhelming majority of Germany's public opinion and of its three political parties. It immediately prompted spontaneous trade boycotts of German goods by major Jewish business firms. The organized American Jewish community refrained from nationwide action to curtail imports from Germany as long as there was hope for some satisfactory settlement with Israel.[13] It assumed that at least some influential West German representatives might become concerned about the damage caused to the Federal Republic's standing at a time when it was trying to cooperate as closely as possible with the Johnson administration on NATO strategy and European affairs. AJC president Morris Abram protested bitterly to German state secretary for foreign affairs Karl Carstens, the future federal president who never revealed much sympathy for the Jewish state. The AJC, Abram asserted, had never manifested such a "widespread, deep and spontaneous reaction" as that triggered by Bonn's refusal to fulfill its defense commitments to Israel. The same German government that had cited concern for the impact upon the younger generation as one of the reasons against extending the statute of limitations, lest it be interpreted as yielding to expediency, now returned to a "discredited Realpolitik based on opportunism and disregard of principle." Carstens emerged as one of the strongest opponents of Israel among the makers of Bonn's foreign policy. In a circular letter to German diplomatic missions abroad in November 1964 he had unequivocally come out against the future supply of weapons to Israel, the establishment of an embassy there, and against legislative steps to halt the employment of scientists in

Egypt. After Erhard's decision to offer Israel the establishment of diplomatic relations, Carstens continued to oppose any notion of a special German moral commitment to Israel.[14]

As in the past, Bonn tried to use the Communist threat in Europe and the Middle East when appealing to Secretary of State Dean Rusk against possible Jewish boycotts of German exports to the United States. The Israeli embassy instructed the Presidents Conference to tell Knappstein that it would be able to prevent a "grassroots explosion" only in case of a meaningful German action, and not by his appeals to the Department of State.[15] For the Conference, the handling of the German crisis was an important achievement; it overshadowed the special status that the AJC enjoyed in the past in the eyes of the American government. Early in March 1965, its leaders discussed the situation with Rainer Barzel, chairman of the CDU parliamentary group after Brentano's untimely death, who visited the United States at that time and was received by President Johnson and high officials of the administration. Barzel also met separately with a representative of the AJC. The Christian Democratic politician was upset by the negative impact of his government's handling of the affair both on Jews and on the American public in general. Following the suggestion of General Julius Klein, he discussed ways to dissolve the crisis with Israeli ambassador Abraham Harman and immediately upon his return to Bonn reported to the chancellor.[16] For many years Barzel was held in high esteem by American Jewish leaders, thanks to the role he played during that critical period.

It seems that Barzel's impressions and recommendations were a major factor in Erhard's unilateral decision to compensate Israel and American Jewry by proposing the establishment of full diplomatic relations, a political choice that comprised a moral element. That step was also supported by several other prominent CDU/CSU politicians who wanted to teach Nasser a lesson, and by Heinrich Lübke, the president of the Federal Republic. Erhard finally made up his mind, relying on his special powers as chancellor. He could not obtain a majority in the cabinet, as many of the ministers still preferred the lesser evil of establishing a consulate general in Israel that would later be raised to ambassadorial status. But Israel explicitly rejected such a compromise formula.[17] The Social Democratic opposition criticized the government's handling of the case. However, in spite of its friendly attitude toward Israel and especially Israel's labor movement, it preferred the formulation of a common Middle East policy by the three parties represented in the Bundestag. Helmut Schmidt, the future chancellor who visited the United States at the same time as Barzel, complained about the exaggerations introduced by certain Jewish organizations into the debate, but was sure that the crisis would not affect the American commitment to preserve its position in Europe.[18] The Knesset expressed its willingness to establish relations with West Germany even before all the details had been worked out.

After Erhard's decision, it still took two months of tough bargaining with regard to compensating Israel financially for the canceled arms shipments before the agreement establishing full diplomatic relations was signed. Kurt Birrenbach, an influential CDU member of the Bundestag who enjoyed excellent contacts with the American foreign policy establishment and powerful economic circles, was chosen by the chancellor to conduct the talks with the Israelis in Jerusalem.

Following Birrenbach's marriage to a woman of partly Jewish descent, he left Germany in 1939 for Argentina where he was employed by American and German corporations. Returning home ten years later he became a leading board member of the Thyssen corporation and, besides, gained much experience in the field of international relations. Before taking up his mission to Israel he revisited the United States and met Secretary of State Dean Rusk, Undersecretary George Ball, as well as Dean Acheson and John McCloy. He hoped to convince them of the necessity of replacing the Federal Republic in providing arms for Israel and at the same time of reaffirming support for Bonn's balanced course as a moderating factor in the Middle East. Birrenbach also tried to explain the German position to Jewish community leaders such as Rabbi Joachim Prinz of the Presidents Conference and Morris Abram of the AJC. He warned them that the immediate establishment of full diplomatic links with Israel might cause a breakdown of West German Mideastern policy and have negative repercussions on the whole German-Jewish relationship. Birrenbach himself belonged to those German politicians and diplomats who preferred opening a consulate general in Tel Aviv as a temporary solution leading to the establishment of diplomatic relations. But when he arrived in Israel with proposals which the Israelis would not consider acceptable, the die had already been cast by the chancellor's solitary decision.[19]

After protracted and difficult negotiations concerning the financial compensation for the curtailed arms shipments and continuing economic aid, diplomatic relations were established on May 12, 1965, and ambassadors exchanged three months later. The United States, which had been instrumental in the triangular arms deal in 1964 and helped to settle the crisis, subsequently became a major supplier of arms for Israel. In addition to 40 tanks from Germany, Israel was to receive 210 tanks directly from the United States. The Germans, for their part, also took it upon themselves to pay the bill (DM 140 million) for Israel's purchase of missile boats, a submarine, and various kinds of military equipment in other countries. As a matter of fact, the settlement did not put an end to continuing West German–Israeli cooperation in the fields of security, intelligence, transfer of knowledge, and common measures against terrorism. As for the German military experts and scientists in Egypt, in 1965 most of them had left and obtained employment at home or in other places.

In response to President Nasser's demonstrative hosting of East German leader Walter Ulbricht and his intention to open a consulate general in East Berlin, West Germany suspended its economic assistance to Egypt. Upon the urging of the Western allies, however, it refrained from breaking off relations.[20] That was done by Egypt and most of the other Arab nations in retaliation for Germany's establishing relations with Israel. The three exceptions were Morocco, Tunisia, and prerevolutionary Libya. Nevertheless, even the countries that broke off relations did not extend diplomatic recognition to the GDR, as West German opponents of relations with Israel had warned for years.

At this point 56 percent of the West German public favored the establishment of relations with Israel, 10 percent opposed, 22 percent had no clear view, and 12 percent of those polled abstained. But when confronted with a choice between relations with Israel and the Arab nations, only 35 percent preferred Israel, 29 percent preferred the Arabs, 24 percent would not state their preference, and the rest abstained.[21] Twenty years after the Holocaust a great many Germans still had their difficulties with the Jewish state.

The overwhelming majority of American Jewish organizations welcomed the establishment of German-Israeli relations, the few exceptions being the Communists and the ultra-Orthodox groups.[22]

After the statute of limitations had been extended and even before the agreement on full diplomatic relations between West Germany and Israel was finalized, attempts to evaluate the repercussions of those events and their implications for the attitude of American Jewry toward Germany were made at NCRAC's executive committee.[23] The main question posed, as defined by NCRAC's chairman, Aaron Goldman, was whether there was evidence "of genuine democratic sentiment among the masses of the German people and whether there were elements and forces at work in Germany that merited a positive attitude and perhaps support of American Jews; in short, whether a change in the posture of American Jews was required or justified by recent developments."

For Benjamin Epstein, ADL's veteran national director, the time had come to transcend mere criticism, censure, or condemnation of German anti-democratic or anti-Jewish hostility. He recalled that even as good a friend as Berlin's mayor Willy Brandt, the chairman of the Social Democratic party, had pointed out that constant repetition of accusations against Germans as a collective would bring diminishing results. Others who had been combating neo-Nazism and promoting goodwill said the same. It would particularly cause resentment among Germany's youth, who were unwilling to bear any longer the burden of moral responsibility for the crimes of their fathers. This forecast by Brandt proved wrong, since the young generation would soon start to question their parents' deeds and behavior during the Nazi regime. Epstein's advice was to pay more attention in the future to positive factors in Germany, such as the prodemocratic mass media, labor unions, youth and student groups, as well as to genuine democratic politicians from the major parties. The relationship with all those of goodwill in Germany would be even more fruitful if, on occasion, American Jews did not hesitate to praise their accomplishments, thus encouraging them and dispelling allegations that German goodwill was not being reciprocated.

Will Maslow, a leading official of the AJ Congress, acknowledged the importance of the linkage between West Germany's relations with Israel and its relationship with the Jewish people as a whole. He took into account that continuing financial, scientific, political, and indirect military German assistance to Israel would undoubtedly affect the attitude of Jews throughout the world toward the Federal Republic. While buying a Volkswagen car, using the Lufthansa airline, and drinking German wine were issues for each individual to decide, he excluded future organized boycotts of German goods. He admitted, though, that during the last crisis, the impact of pickets and the threat of boycott were more efficient than Rabbi Prinz's meeting with Barzel and Ambassador Knappstein's talks with the Presidents Conference. There were, however, positions on which American Jews should reserve the right of independent judgment, such as opposition to German nuclear development and to reunification of East and West Germany. The debate in which different opinions were expressed was concluded without seeking or reaching a common stand. But questions about American Jewish response to developments in Germany would reverberate over the next decades, when circumstances changed for both better and worse.

The future of German-Israeli relations, the need for a further extension of the statute of limitations in cases of murder, the extension of material indemnification for Nazi victims from Eastern Europe, as well as the importance of civic education, particularly because of the revival of right-wing nationalism and recurring antisemitic manifestations, were the main topics in meetings between the American Jewish leadership and Chancellor Erhard. Erhard thus continued the established pattern of exchanges of views with American Jewish spokesmen both in Bonn and in the United States.[24]

In his youth Erhard was a student of Franz Oppenheimer, the renowned German Jewish Zionist scholar. In the early 1950s he had been one of the strongest supporters of German reparations to Israel and had rebuffed contentions that they might harm the German economy. Talking to American Jewish spokesmen, he reiterated his belief in the "irrevocable links" between German and Jewish history, as he had done on various occasions before being elected Adenauer's successor. The Jewish interlocutors emphasized Germany's special obligations to Jews the world over, stemming from the tragic events of the Hitler period.

While acknowledging Erhard's historic contribution in establishing full diplomatic links with Israel, American Jews were nevertheless concerned about the new concept of "normalization" of relations. This was discussed in a number of leading German newspapers and reflected the thoughts of influential German circles. American Jews were afraid that it meant considering the effects of the Nazi era as past history.[25] In regard to Nazi war criminals, Erhard complained that the issue continued to be exploited by the Communist bloc for political reasons. He himself would appreciate it if Jewish organizations explicitly condemned Soviet and East German reluctance to release pertinent documents that were needed to bring Nazi criminals to justice.[26]

A new development in the contacts between the American Jewish establishment and West German representatives were attempts to conduct public dialogues, the contents of which were published in the Jewish press. Early in 1966, German ambassador Knappstein participated together with Joachim Prinz, chairman of the Presidents Conference and a prominent member of the AJ Congress and WJC, in the first public dialogue of its kind at Brandeis University.[27] Knappstein was held in high regard by the Jewish leadership thanks to his goodwill during the critical period of the winter of 1964–65.

In 1963, with the endorsement of Nahum Goldmann, Prinz had approached Willy Brandt with regard to a proposal by young German Social Democrats and left-wing Catholics to organize a dialogue between them and American Jews. At that time, the idea was dropped because of strong resistance from the AJ Congress executive committee.[28] Three years later, the Knappstein-Prinz encounter raised no objections. Brandeis University was chosen as host of that dialogue because of its early contacts with the Federal Republic. Since 1958, German students had attended courses there; later, a West German student served as the first president of the Brandeis International Student Association.[29] When Ambassador Rolf Pauls succeeded Knappstein in 1969, he chose to make his first public address regarding Jewish affairs at the same place.

At the Brandeis dialogue, Knappstein reminded the audience of West Germany's impressive record on personal and collective indemnification, its consistent support of Israel, and the ongoing prosecution of Nazi criminals. In regard to the perseverance of many former members of the Nazi party in high office, the ambassador asked his listeners to distinguish between active promoters of Nazism and opportunistic fellow travelers. He also called upon the American Jewish community to acknowledge the changes that had taken place in postwar Germany and to provide encouragement for further constructive efforts. On other occasions, Knappstein praised Jewish contributions to German culture and science before Hitler. During the following years German spokesmen would continue to espouse the achievements of that ambiguous symbiosis, but their words often fell on the deaf ears of the public they hoped to convince.

Joachim Prinz, for his part, tried to illustrate the great difficulties of improving mutual relations by two recent cases. As chairman of the committee planning to build a New York memorial for the six million Jewish victims, he had received a design that utilized the tale of Cain and Abel. That design was expressly rejected by the ghetto fighters and the former inmates of concentration camps, who objected to applying the example of the two brothers to Jews and the Germans who had murdered them. As for the continuing private boycott of German goods by many American Jews, Prinz quoted a recent letter to the AJ Congress by a noted Jewish writer who indicated why he himself persisted in that boycott: "I bear no hate—not for Germans, nor for anyone, and if a German were dying, even a Nazi, and any act of mine could save his life, I would prefer that act regardless of the cost. But I will not sail in his ships, fly their airlines, ride in a car Adolf Hitler specified and designed. I will not bend to him and I will not take his hand, and most of all, I will not forget. Future generations will and must. That is for them. But I saw a whole people turn executioner, and I cannot forget it."

In any case, while many Jews were reluctant to forgive and forget, Prinz regarded the further strengthening of German democracy and the continuing support of Israel as preconditions for an improvement—not yet normalization—of relations between Germans and Jews. It should be noted that Prinz did not share the disapproval of German reunification that was shared by most Jews. On the contrary, he was afraid that if German unification were not achieved in this generation, "the collective disappointment [of the Germans] will turn into a sense of national humiliation, which was often the cause of German nationalism and therefore anti-Semitism."[30]

Prinz also participated in the high-level German-Jewish dialogue convened by Nahum Goldmann during the WJC's fifth plenary assembly in Brussels in August 1966. In contrast to skeptic Gershom Scholem, who stated that "after the horrible past, new relations between Jews and Germans must be prepared with great care," Salo Baron, the dean of Jewish historians living in the United States and himself a witness at the Eichmann trial, sounded rather euphoric. He expressed the hope that a modus vivendi between the

German nation and world Jewry, including Israel, would prove to be of great importance, not only for both peoples but for all humanity. Despite the boycott by right-wing and left-wing Zionist parties, Goldmann regarded that symposium as a step toward creating a basis for coexistence between the two peoples.[31] However, it made no major impact in Europe or in the United States, where the WJC did not carry much weight anyway.

As in the past, the Orthodox community remained the most critical among the Jewish rabbinical and congregational organizations. Activist Young Israel shared pickets and other protest actions with the Jewish War Veterans; in deliberations of the WJC's American section, Hillel Seidman, representing Poale Agudath Israel of America, protested against having any relations with Germans "since there could be no relationship between the murderers and their victims." Rabbi Zalman Shneur Schneerson, the Lubavitcher rebbe, unequivocally opposed any common meetings or dialogues between Germans and Jews, arguing the Germans should not be trusted.[32] As for the Conservatives, at the yearly meetings of their Rabbinical Assembly there was usually no discussion of German problems. Dr. Louis Finkelstein, the chancellor of the Jewish Theological Seminary, did not get involved publicly in such issues; and a number of Conservative rabbis, such as Israel Goldstein, made their views known in their communal, not rabbinical, capacities.

Only once, in the winter of 1962–63, did *Conservative Judaism,* the Conservative movement's journal, dedicate its pages to an in-depth debate of the German-Jewish problem.[33] The platform was shared by Rabbi Richard L. Rubenstein, a religious thinker and Hillel director, who had visited Germany twice in the early 1960s and returned with ambivalent impressions, and Dr. Jacob Neusner, then a young Judaic studies scholar, who was to earn great fame in the 1970s and 1980s. Neusner did not request that those few who had survived should forgive, but he criticized the indiscriminate hatred for Germany on the part of others, both Jews and non-Jews. There was no rational ground for continuing to look for the blood on the hands of every German, whatever his age or station in life. In Neusner's opinion, it was a great iniquity to continue to hate all Germans, including children not even born when Hitler died, or men and women who themselves suffered under Hitler. Moreover, many individuals of other nations, not least of them Jews, did not do all that might have been done to save the lives of those condemned to die.

Rubenstein could not accept Neusner's reference to the six million dead as "martyrs against their own will for the sanctification of God's name." He found it impossible to believe in any way, actually or metaphorically, that God had used Adolf Hitler and his criminal band as a rod of his anger. The real Jewish problem for him was how to cease being the victim, not how to forgive the murderers. Even if the entire German nation were to ask for forgiveness—and that did not happen—such a relationship with them should be opposed. On the other hand, bitter hatred of all things German should also be disapproved of, not because the hatred was necessarily undeserved but because by doing so, Jews perpetuated their victimhood. The Jewish task was to cease being the victim: "Germans and Jews must relate to each other not as murderer and victim, but as human beings struggling as best they can with an indecent past which has by no means lost its poison." Only on this basis were fruitful relations between Jews and Germans possible and even desirable, though the Jews should never again be dependents or clients of the Germans.

More supporters of a cautious rapprochement with postwar Germany could be found among Reform rabbis than among other Jewish religious groups. This was partly because the Reform movement had absorbed a relatively large number of refugees from Germany in its ranks who served as rabbis in the United States or were ordained at Hebrew Union College after the war. However, different views were voiced there too. Rabbi Maurice Eisendrath, UAHC president for many years and involved in NCRAC deliberations on American Jewish–German relations since the late 1940s, remained uneasy about Germany despite its democratic achievements and close relationship with Israel. He did not believe that postwar Germany should have been dismembered or permanently quarantined. Instead, he viewed with disquiet its growing influence in the Atlantic alliance and the deference accorded to Germany by American foreign-policymakers because of what he regarded as an illusion that only Germany provided America with a safe buffer against the Soviet Union.[34] Rabbi Alexander Schindler, his deputy and successor, put more emphasis on West Germany's attitude toward Israel.

There also were individual bona fide initiatives, such as Rabbi Joseph Asher's proposal that a team of German-speaking American rabbis be sent to Germany to teach German youth and teachers about Jews and Judaism. Asher, a German-born rabbi who served in the Australian army and after the war was ordained at HUC, had for a number of years opposed any ties with the West German republic. After his visit to his former homeland in 1955, however, he called for "a reorientation of the Jewish relationship with Germany" and for reaffirming the lost promise of the German-Jewish symbiosis. Such an attitude was welcomed by the Germans but was not at all characteristic of the great majority of American rabbis. Following the publication of his article in *Look* magazine, Asher and the magazine received about two hundred letters, the majority favorable, although some were "vitriolic and hyper-emotional." The UAHC Commission on Interfaith Activities endorsed the proposal, and in the summer of 1966, a group of Reform rabbis spent two weeks in Germany at the invitation of the *Länder* ministries of education. Quite a few Reform rabbis had, of course, visited Germany before that; some had served in communities and others had been there as members of bilateral exchange programs. But this was the first time that the study and teaching took place in the framework of a special pilot project for non-Jews.[35]

Commentary, the intellectual monthly published by the AJC and at first edited by Elliot Cohen, devoted for a number of years a substantial quantity of essays and incisive articles to the post-1945 German-Jewish complex. In 1950, Cohen was the first American Jewish intellectual to address a German audience after the war and to appeal for German soul-searching as a condition for a new dialogue.[36] Norman Podhoretz, Cohen's successor, visited Germany seventeen years later, early in 1967, together with a group of twelve American intellectuals, most of them Jews, whose trip was sponsored by the Ford Foundation and the German Atlantik-Brücke. The group met with politicians, including the new chancellor Kurt Georg Kiesinger, who in December 1966 had been installed as the head of a "grand coalition" with the Social Democrats. They also met with businessmen and bankers and conducted informal talks with writers and students. Podhoretz's overwhelming impression was that, in one way or another, the Nazi past was being buried, either intellectually by rationalizing it as an "excess of nationalism" or symbolically by destroying it as evidenced by "sanitizing" the environment of Dachau concentration camp. The German students he met, most of them in their twenties, he found to be almost neurotically obsessed with the question of Nazism. Their chronic state of anxiety and irresolution on the subject was mirrored in their confused attitudes toward words like *liberal* and *democracy*. His conclusion was that as long as the fundamental idea of civil liberties for all was not grasped and exercised, no progress toward true democracy could be made in Germany. As a nation the Germans still suffered from what could be termed a vast inferiority complex. For reasons buried in their history, they conveyed a sense of alienation from Western civilization even while stressing their devotion and contribution to its culture.[37]

Other members of that group of intellectuals and writers, while not being able to overcome their prejudices and not forgetting that they were in the country that had devised and implemented Nazism, were more optimistic about the young German generation.[38] Diana Trilling took heart for the German future from her meetings with students of various universities. The new generation was enormously attractive also to Harvey Swados, author and professor of literature, even though he was made uneasy by the guilty generation that had not yet passed from the face of the earth. Midge Decter, Norman Podhoretz's wife and a noted essayist in her own right, remained critical. She was upset to hear sincere and responsible Germans maintaining that the elevation of a former member of the Nazi party to the office of chancellor in effect constituted a proof of Germany's repudiation of Nazism because people did not take Nazism seriously. If Nazi Germany was, as people used to say, the land of Wagner, Fichte, and Nietzsche, it meant that present-day Germany was the land of Hegel-turned-sour.[39]

The visit of the intellectuals, who summarized their impressions in *Atlantic Monthly*, took place before the psychological, cultural, and social upheaval caused by the students' movement a few months later. Some of the group and others who preceded them had already noticed the gradual change in West Germany's political climate and political culture, even before the end of the right-of-center hegemony in Bonn and the students' riots and protests of 1967–68. In the 1950s, the Cold War's heat and the requirements of West German economic reconstruction had deliberately prevented a confrontation over the Nazi period. Many former members of the

Nazi party, including the economic and social elites who served the Third Reich, were integrated into the democratic Federal Republic and contributed to its "economic miracle."

Since the early 1960s, however, at least a part of the motivated young generation began to look into their nation's past and to question their parents. This process was speeded up by the impact of the swastika rash of 1959–60 and especially by the lessons of the Eichmann trial in Israel and the major trials of the Nazi criminals at extermination camps in Germany. After the success of *The Diary of Anne Frank* many German theatergoers were moved by Max Frisch's *Andorra* and Ralph Hochhuth's *The Deputy* in the early 1960s. Hochhuth's play decrying Pope Pius XII's reluctance to intervene in favor of the Jews made a great impact in many European countries as well as in the United States, where it contributed to Holocaust consciousness. In 1961, Hamburg historian Fritz Fischer blamed German nationalism and imperialism for World War I as well as for World War II. A few years later, the German psychologists and authors Alexander and Margarethe Mitscherlich were to castigate the German people for their inability to mourn the victims of the Holocaust they had caused, and the Frankfurt School's "Critical Theory" was to supply the philosophical superstructure for the "mastering of the past," if only the past could really be mastered.[40]

Writing in *Commentary* in April 1964, Norman Birnbaum, who had been a frequent visitor to Western Germany, observed that German society had become increasingly opaque, German culture more agonized, the German populace more profoundly restive, German life more cosmopolitan. A most encouraging recent development, in his opinion, was a renewal of the country's intellectual and literary life. He particularly pinned hopes on the Social Democrats and trade unions as indispensable background forces for a democratic German ethos.[41]

These positive changes in German political culture starting in the 1960s, the intellectual distancing from the Nazi and nationalist legacy and the endorsement of Western democratic norms, although registered by a few clear-eyed observers, did not receive much attention among American Jews, most of whom continued to be more concerned about the reappearance of extreme rightists.

At the AJC's sixty-first annual meeting in May 1967, Marvin Kalb, the renowned TV commentator who addressed the plenary session, sounded moderately optimistic about the future of German democracy, in spite of the recent successes of the extreme right-wing NPD at elections to several legislatures of West Germany's federal states. He expressed the view that although not all Germans had changed, Germany as a nation had. AJC's veteran executive vice-president, John Slawson, disagreed with the speaker, mainly in regard to what he himself thought of as the fundamental authoritarian streak penetrating German culture and education.[42] Only a few months earlier, all the organizations and community councils comprising NCRAC had publicly voiced their concern about the growth of the NPD as well as about the fact that CDU could not find a leader other than Kiesinger, a former Nazi.[43] In Germany, Max Horkheimer, who personally respected Kiesinger as an honest man and a good democrat, called his appointment "the termination of confession of guilt."[44] An AJC delegation also raised the NPD problem in talks with Eugene Rostow, undersecretary of state for political affairs. The delegation was told that it was essentially a German issue and that any U.S. government intervention could be counterproductive, in contrast to statements by private American organizations. Rostow disagreed with suggestions made by the AJC interlocutors that the United States take a stand against German reunification, the Hallstein doctrine, and Bonn's unwillingness to recognize the Oder-Neisse border.[45]

Most American Jewish leaders subsequently met with Kiesinger as they met with Erhard, his predecessor, and with his Social Democratic successors after 1969. Representatives of the Claims Conference demanded further improvements of restitution payments; others discussed Israel's needs, the impact of the EEC on its trade, and a further extension of the statute of limitations. The Germans, for their part, recalled their assistance to the Jewish community in the Federal Republic, the yearly events of Brotherhood Week, the rebuilding of synagogues and community centers, as well as the protection of cemeteries. However, despite more or less satisfactory results on concrete issues, there was no meeting of the minds in the sporadic encounters between American Jewish organizations and German representatives, and their impact on the German scene was minimal. Except for right-wing conservative Caspar Schrenck-Notzing's vitriolic *Charakterwäsche*,[46] there was less talk in West Germany about the hostile "Morgenthau legacy" than in the 1940s and 1950s. Yet, here and there German observers and journalists continued to explain American uneasiness about Germany by citing the influence of Jews on American public opinion.

As a matter of fact, relations with Israel too were strained in the first period after the exchange of ambassadors. The Germans complained about the hostile demonstrations against their first ambassador Rolf Pauls, when he submitted his credentials to President Zalman Shazar and the German national anthem was played. Israeli diplomats in the United States had a hard time explaining to American Jews why Israel had to agree to the appointment of the former Wehrmacht officer. A conflict with Bonn caused by Israel's refusal to accept him would be a victory for the Arabs just after they had suffered a defeat by the establishment of West German–Israeli diplomatic relations.[47] In 1966, Pauls's criticism of Israel's official support for Poland's western Oder-Neisse border caused an uproar in Israel's public.[48] A few weeks earlier former chancellor Adenauer's private goodwill visit to Israel was marred by a quarrel with Prime Minister Eshkol because of the critical tone of the host's dinner speech.[49] Much tension was also caused by the protracted talks on German economic aid to Israel. The Germans definitely rejected Israel's claim for continuing financial aid, according to the 1960 understanding between Adenauer and Ben Gurion, in addition to regular development aid. They did not bow to any further pressure from Israel and the American Jewish community on this issue. Eventually the Federal Republic pledged yearly development loans for Israel up to DM 140 million (DM 160 million in the first year).[50]

In his recollections, Israel's first ambassador Ben-Nathan pointed to the difference between the friendly and understanding publicized opinion, such as the quality newspapers and periodicals, TV, and radio, and the ambiguous public opinion he encountered in Germany. For instance, he quoted the question put to him in 1966 by West German president Heinrich Lübke: Why did Israelis continue to rebuke the Germans after all they had done for them by paying compensation for many years? Ben-Nathan thought that the rather unsophisticated president was characteristic of the German "silent majority."[51] Nevertheless, the expanding flow of visiting German youngsters, high school and university students, trade unionists, church groups, Social Democrats, and others to Israel contributed to establishing mutual links that were reciprocated by the Israelis in increasing numbers in the following decade. Scientific cooperation between the Max Planck Society and the Weizmann

Institute in Rehoboth started already in the early 1960s; in 1960 Israeli firms began to participate in the main German trade fairs; and despite the uproar in the Knesset caused by a visiting German teacher addressing Israeli high school students in winter 1961, the directives established by the Israeli government for controlling the different kinds of cultural activities did not prevent their gradual expansion. Germans soon discovered that in attempting to conciliate world Jewry, it was easier for them to make progress in Israel than in relations with the American Jewish community. This was particularly true after the show of solidarity during the Six Day War and despite the political differences that were soon to emerge as a result of Israel's military victory.[52]

Henry M. Morgenthau Jr. (1891–1967), secretary of the
treasury, 1934–1945.
Courtesy: American Jewish Archives, Cincinnati.

Stephen S. Wise (1874–1949), Zionist leader, president
of the American Jewish Congress, and founding president
of the World Jewish Congress in 1936.
Courtesy: American Jewish Archives, Cincinnati.

Abba Hillel Silver (1893–1963), rabbi, Zionist leader, author, critical of postwar American policy toward Germany.
Courtesy: American Jewish Archives, Cincinnati.

Abraham Cahan (1860–1951), America's most eminent Yiddish journalist, editor of the *Forward.* Welcomed Kurt Schumacher during his visit to the United States in 1947.
Courtesy: American Jewish Archives, Cincinnati.

Dr. Kurt Schumacher (1895–1952), chairman of the
Social Democratic Party of Germany, 1945–1952.
*Courtesy: Press and Information Office of the Federal
Government, Bonn—Federal Photographic Service.*

Dr. William Haber (1899–1989), adviser on Jewish affairs
to the American commander-in-chief in Germany, 1948.
Courtesy: American Jewish Archives, Cincinnati.

Rabbi Philip S. Bernstein (1901–1985), adviser on Jewish affairs to the American commander-in-chief in Germany, 1946–1947.
Courtesy: American Jewish Archives, Cincinnati.

Elliot Cohen (1899–1959), founding editor of *Commentary*.
Courtesy: American Jewish Committee, New York.

Herbert Blankenhorn (1904–1991), Chancellor
Adenauer's foreign policy adviser in the early 1950s,
afterwards ambassador to NATO, France, Great Britain,
and Italy.
*Courtesy: Press and Information Office of the Federal
Government, Bonn—Federal Photographic Service.*

Jacob Blaustein (1892–1970), American Jewish
Committee leader, senior vice-president of the Claims
Conference.
Courtesy: American Jewish Committee, New York.

John J. McCloy (1895–1989), U.S. high commissioner
for Germany, 1949–1952, and the leadership of the
American Jewish Committee at their annual meeting in
1953. From left, Irving Engel, AJC president after Jacob
Blaustein; John J. McCloy; Jacob Blaustein, president of
the AJC 1949–1955, Benjamin B. Buttenwieser, assistant
high commissioner, 1949–1951.
Courtesy: American Jewish Committee Library/Archives.

Jacob K. Javits (1904–1986), elected to the House of
Representatives in 1946 (R, New York), and to the Senate
in 1956.
Courtesy: American Jewish Archives, Cincinnati.

President Theodor Heuss (1884–1963), president of the Federal Republic of Germany 1949–1959, engaged in efforts to improve German-Jewish relations after the Holocaust, 1949–1959.
Courtesy: Press and Information Office of the Federal Government, Bonn—Federal Photographic Service.

Konrad Adenauer (1876–1967) and David Ben Gurion (1886–1973) meet at New York's Waldorf Astoria, March 14, 1960.
Photo: INP/dpa.

Philip M. Klutznick (b. 1907), B'nai B'rith president, 1953–1959; president of the World Jewish Congress, 1977–1979; secretary of commerce and industry, 1979–1981.
Courtesy: American Jewish Archives, Cincinnati.

General Julius Klein (1901–1984) with President Dwight D. Eisenhower (1890–1969).
Courtesy: American Jewish Archives, Cincinnati.

Hannah Arendt (1906–1975), public philosopher,
essayist, and author of, among others, *Eichmann in
Jerusalem*.
Courtesy: American Jewish Archives, Cincinnati.

Nahum Goldmann (1895–1982), cofounder of the World
Jewish Congress, WJC president 1949–1977, here
together with Chancellor Konrad Adenauer and David
Ben Gurion during Adenauer's visit to Israel in 1966.
*Courtesy: Press and Information Office of the Federal
Government, Bonn—Federal Photographic Service.*

Dr. Joachim Prinz (1902–1988), a leader of the American Jewish Congress and the World Jewish Congress, former Liberal rabbi in Berlin.
Courtesy: American Jewish Archives, Cincinnati.

Karl-Heinrich Knappstein (1906–1989), West Germany's consul general in Chicago 1950–1956, observer at the UN in New York, 1960–1962, and, finally, ambassador in Washington, 1962–1968.
Courtesy: Press and Information Office of the Federal Government, Bonn—Federal Photographic Service.

Dr. Rainer Barzel, born 1924, chairman of the
parliamentary group of the Christian Democratic Union
in the 1960s. His meetings with American Jewish
representatives contributed to Chancellor Ludwig
Erhard's decision to establish full diplomatic relations
with Israel.
*Courtesy: Press and Information Office of the Federal
Government, Bonn—Federal Photographic Service.*

Morris B. Abram, born 1918, community leader,
president of the American Jewish Committee and head
of different Jewish organizations.
Courtesy: American Jewish Committee, New York.

Willy Brandt (1913–1992), chancellor of the Federal
Republic of Germany 1969–1974, meets with Rabbi
Dr. Max Nussbaum (1910–1974) of the World Jewish
Congress during his visit to the United States, February 1,
1972.
*Courtesy: Press and Information Office of the Federal
Government, Bonn—Federal Photographic Service.*

Rolf F. Pauls, born 1915, the Federal Republic's first
ambassador to Israel, 1965–1968, thereafter ambassador
to the United States, 1969–1973.
*Courtesy: Press and Information Office of the Federal
Government, Bonn—Federal Photographic Service.*

Chancellor Helmut Schmidt, born 1918, talks with
Richard Maass, past president of the American Jewish
Committee, September 10, 1981.
*Courtesy: Press and Information Office of the Federal
Government, Bonn—Federal Photographic Service.*

Cynthia Ozick, born 1928, writer and critic, reflects
Jewish doubts about today's Germany.
Courtesy: American Jewish Archives, Cincinnati.

Dr. Niels Hansen, born 1924, West Germany's ambassador to Israel, 1981–1985, thereafter ambassador to NATO. Before coming to Israel, he served in different capacities in New York and Washington.
Courtesy: Press and Information Office of the Federal Government, Bonn—Federal Photographic Service.

Chancellor Helmut Kohl, born 1930, and President Ronald Reagan, born 1911, at Bitburg military cemetery, May 5, 1985.
Courtesy: Press and Information Office of the Federal Government, Bonn—Federal Photographic Service.

Chancellor Helmut Kohl and President Ronald Reagan
at the Belsen memorial, May 5, 1985.
*Courtesy: Press and Information Office of the Federal
Government, Bonn—Federal Photographic Service.*

Chancellor Helmut Kohl meets Howard Friedman,
president of the American Jewish Committee, and other
leading members of the organization, July 25, 1986.
*Courtesy: Press and Information Office of the Federal
Government, Bonn—Federal Photographic Service.*

Lothar de Maizière, born 1940, the only democratically elected prime minister of East Germany, 1990. Photo taken during his service as member of the Bundestag after reunification.
Courtesy: Press and Information Office of the Federal Government, Bonn—Federal Photographic Service.

Edgar M. Bronfman, born 1929, president of the World Jewish Congress since 1981.
Courtesy: WJC Israel Office.

Abraham Foxman, born 1940, national director of the Anti-Defamation League of B'nai B'rith, Holocaust survivor.
Courtesy: American Jewish Archives, Cincinnati.

14

Disappointment with the Social Democrats

In the fall of 1966, three years after the departure of West Germany's founding chancellor Konrad Adenauer, Ludwig Erhard's resignation ended the long hegemony of right-of-center governments led by the CDU. After a short interlude of difficult partnership between the Christian Democrats and the Social Democrats, the Bundestag elections in September 1969 enabled the Social Democrats to set up, with the Free Democrats as junior partners, an alternative left-of-center coalition that was to rule the Federal Republic for the next thirteen years. Although a few cautious steps had already been taken by his predecessor, Willy Brandt's Social-Liberal government initiated major changes in West Germany's relations with its Eastern neighbors—the Soviet Union, Poland, Czechoslovakia, and also the Communist-controlled German Democratic Republic. On the domestic scene, the Brandt government undertook substantial social, legal, administrative, and educational reforms that liberalized German society. Thanks to both the rapprochement with Eastern Europe and the reformist breakthrough at home, Brandt came to be regarded as one of the most important statesmen in the history of the Federal Republic, second only to Adenauer. As chairman of the Social Democratic party, he continued to influence the German political scene after he was replaced as chancellor by Helmut Schmidt, who held office until October 1982.

There were ups and downs in the relations between American administrations and West Germany's left-of-center governments in the 1970s. President Nixon's Republican administration, with Henry Kissinger as its national security adviser and since 1973 as secretary of state, eventually acquiesced to Brandt's *Ostpolitik*. It conformed with the overall trend of the East-West detente in the early 1970s, despite American suspicions about long-term implications of the new German policy and dislike of Brandt's personal style. The consolidation of Bonn's course toward East and West under the pragmatic Helmut Schmidt provided for a much better atmosphere between him and Kissinger, who remained in charge of American foreign policy during the administration of President Gerald Ford.

In the late 1970s, Schmidt was disappointed by the effects of President Jimmy Carter's vacillations on the state of the general East-West detente. Kissinger's own German Jewish origin did not influence his attitude toward West Germany and its government in any special way. He judged leading German politicians according to the national interest of the United States, which continued to attach much importance to the alliance with the Federal Republic in the changing political and strategic circumstances of the 1970s. As far as the Jewish community tried to exert pressure on Washington in these years, its agenda included support for Israel in the Middle East conflict and Soviet Jewish emigration.

Nonetheless, it was mainly the Israeli angle that caused strain and misunderstandings between West Germany in the Social-Liberal era and most American Jewish organizations, their liberal proclivities and the Social Democrats' cleaner past notwithstanding. There were a number of reasons for that. The quest for strong U.S. support made Israeli governments before and after the Yom Kippur War afraid of the repercussions of the Federal Republic's accommodating new course regarding Eastern Europe. In German public opinion, the Left that had heartily supported Israel in the 1950s and early 1960s switched allegiance after the Six Day War and joined in its majority the critics, if not opponents, of the Jewish state. Soon the change of heart affected the younger generation of the Social Democrats as well. After the Knesset elections in May 1977, the replacement of Labor by the Likud-led government headed by anti-German right-winger Menachem Begin deepened the divide. But it was just that growing disillusionment with Israel that encouraged the West German government to look for new ways to improve its relations with American Jewry.

In November 1966, a number of American Jewish leaders and organizations were disappointed by the CDU choice of Kurt Georg Kiesinger as Erhard's successor for the chancellorship because of his former Nazi party membership and service in the Third Reich's foreign office.[1] At the same time, they were pleased with the appointment of Willy Brandt, as vice-chancellor and foreign minister, one of the few German political leaders with an unequivocal anti-Nazi record. Their acquaintanceship reached back to meetings when Brandt served as mayor of Berlin. In 1961, he had delivered a pro-Zionist address at the New York Herzl Institute shortly after his first visit to Israel; during his visit, B'nai B'rith president Label A. Katz expressed appreciation for what Brandt had done in the period of swastika daubings.[2] Even though in his youth Brandt had shared the doubts of most Socialist comrades about the Zionist venture, the Jewish catastrophe in Europe, as he later recalled in his memoirs, had convinced him to endorse a more favorable approach to the practical accomplishments of Zionism in Palestine.[3]

However, Brandt's appreciation of Israel's achievements did not prevent him from taking a sympathetic attitude to Egypt's president Gamal Abdel Nasser and his nationalist revolution, as part of the liberation movements of the Third World. No wonder that Brandt's view of Nasser and his visit to Cairo in 1963 caused concern among Israelis even before the former mayor and chairman of the Social Democratic party became foreign minister and thereafter chancellor.[4]

In 1965, Brandt met with an AJC delegation and discussed with its members the situation in the Middle East and other issues of special American Jewish interest. He expressed his opinion that West Germany had waited too long in developing a well-integrated Middle East policy. He himself would have preferred a multilateral arms agreement instead of the semisecret one with Israel that had been unilaterally canceled, but he doubted whether the remaining German scientists in Egypt could be compelled to leave. On this he was wrong because most of them soon left. Brandt's reference to the German educators program, in which the AJC had been involved for a number of years, did not satisfy his Jewish counterparts. Like most other Germans, he thought that education toward democracy should be primarily a German concern and give Germans a sense of pride. Expert advice and recommendations would be welcome, but no sense of outside domination should be conveyed. That would only endanger the chances of permanently altering outmoded traditions and concepts.[5]

Brandt paid his first visit to the United States in his new ministerial capacity in February 1967. On that occasion, he had a short meeting with a small group of the top American Jewish leadership. The subjects discussed were the rise of the extreme right-wing NPD, the state of German-Israeli relations, and the statute of limitations that was to expire in 1969. Brandt's concise analysis of the NPD as a mixture of "poujadists" (a short-lived populist, mainly lower-middle-class movement in France in the 1950s), genuine nationalists (whose views were not restricted to that group alone), far rightists, and a sprinkling of would-be Nazis, most of whom were over forty-five, did not fully satisfy the Jewish spokesmen. The next elections, however, would prove that their fears were exaggerated.

At the meeting with Brandt, AJC president Morris Abram renewed the demand for extension or abolition of the statute of limitations. Joachim Prinz, still chairman of the Presidents Conference of Major Jewish Organizations, hoped that thanks to the renewed diplomatic relations between West Germany and a number of Arab governments, Bonn would use its influence to bring peace to the Middle East. Prinz was also concerned about the attitudes of socialist students in Berlin, whom he had met during his last visit there, with regard to Germany's past and their historic responsibility. For instance, he complained, "they considered the concentration camps and the bombing of [German] cities by the Allies of equal significance." Furthermore, they regarded criticism of Germany from other countries as "unwanted interference."[6] After the Six Day War, organized Jewry in the United States would become even more concerned about the expressly anti-Israel, anti-Zionist, and pro-Arab trend of student radicals and other leftists in Germany, which was reinforced by their anti-Americanism.[7]

In 1967, half a year after the setting up of the Kiesinger-Brandt coalition in Bonn, American Jewish organizations took notice of the massive West German support for Israel during the Six Day War. At that point the Federal Republic was also one of the few European states that allowed American weapons to be shipped to Israel through their territory and airspace. This was the first time since the creation of the Jewish state that the majority of the German population came out in its support. The wide sympathy from Social Democrats, trade unionists, and a major part of anti-Communist conservatives contributed to lowering the postwar barriers between Germans and Israelis and ushered in an era of manifold contacts and exchanges. However, Israel's changing image from a beleaguered underdog David to an oppressor Goliath keeping hold of the conquered territories soon caused a reversal of sympathy for Israel among the German Left. A far-sighted observer such as Eleonore Sterling, who until her untimely death in 1968 surveyed the developments in Germany for the AJC, was uneasy about the exaggerated enthusiasm of the right-wing popular Springer press, which dominated a great part of the West German media.[8] That support only reinforced the hostility to Israel of students and other young leftists, although it was not caused by it.

Brandt's distinction between the Federal Republic's official policy of nonintervention and neutrality and an attitude of moral indifference that he ruled out was, of course, welcomed in Israel and in the Diaspora.[9] Helmut Schmidt, then head of the party's parliamentary group and usually regarded as more reserved on Israel, made the strongest pro-Israel statement during the Bundestag debate in June 1967.[10] Yet regardless of the broad public backing of Israel and the SPD's sympathies for it and especially for the Israeli labor movement, motives of realpolitik affected Social Democratic policymakers not less than those of the other main parties. At a meeting of NATO's foreign ministers just after the conclusion of the June war, Brandt mentioned the legitimate interests of the Arab nations, most of whom had broken off diplomatic relations with West Germany after its decision to establish such relations with Israel in 1965. At subsequent meetings, Brandt expressed the hope that Israel's success would enable it to proceed toward a secure and stable peace, because a military victory itself would not solve the problems.[11]

In spite of their understandable personal preference for Brandt because of his anti-Nazi credentials, the records of the American Jewish organizations reveal that Jewish leaders met in the years 1967–69 more often with Kiesinger, the CDU chancellor, than with the Social Democratic foreign minister. The same was true during the Brandt chancellorship and at least the first years of Helmut Schmidt's term of office, if compared with Helmut Kohl, who took over in 1982. Because of both the Social Democratic anti-Nazi past and the more independent West German policy in the framework of the Atlantic alliance, Social Democratic chancellors seemingly cared less for frequent personal meetings with spokesmen of organized American Jewry. Still, they satisfied most of the latter's essential demands no less than had Adenauer's conservative successors.

In 1967, Kiesinger's past Nazi party membership did not prevent Jacob Blaustein, senior vice-president of the Claims Conference and one of the Jewish community's elder statesmen, from striving to establish a kind of "personal relationship" with him regarding further improvement of the indemnification payments. Goldmann, who was the first to meet the new chancellor, discussed with him matters pertaining to the Claims Conference.[12] Philip Klutznick tried to convince Kiesinger to process restitution payments more rapidly, as the administrative technicality arising from the *Länder* responsibility was of little import to the outside world, which judged the program as a responsibility of the whole German nation.[13] On another occasion, Jewish leaders broached the issue of abolishing the statute of limitations, a demand that was fulfilled only in 1979.[14] In 1969, the statute was extended for another ten years by a majority of 280 to 127, with four abstentions. In contrast to 1965, when the cabinet left the initiative to the Bundestag, the legislation to extend the statute was this time introduced by the Social Democratic minister of justice in the grand coalition headed by Kiesinger. But contrary to Kiesinger's personal view, the majority of the CDU parliamentary group still prevented the final abolition of the statute.[15]

In 1969, Kiesinger told an AJC delegation that Asher Ben-Nathan, Israel's ambassador in Bonn, had asked him to discuss the situation in the Middle East with President Nixon. The chancellor indicated his willingness to assist Israel but preferred a "non-spectacular support" that would minimize Arab reprisals. He also promised to help Israel improve its links with the EEC, French objections notwithstanding. At the same meeting, AJC executive vice-president Bertram Gold, who in 1967 had succeeded John Slawson, did not forget to raise the issue of the Oberammergau passion play production. The AJC and other Jewish groups regarded the revision of its text as important in their fight against church antisemitism.[16]

On another occasion Kiesinger indicated to B'nai B'rith president William Wexler his concern about the deepening Soviet infiltration into the Middle East. In his estimate, which Brandt and the Social Democrats did not share, the Soviet tactic transcended the Arab-Israeli conflict and was threatening to escalate into an East-West confrontation. Middle East leaders whom he met, such as the shah of Iran, Pakistan's ruler General Ayub Khan, and Turkey's president General Cevdet Sunay, had expressed doubts whether the United States could be relied upon to frustrate a Russian drive for dominance in the region.[17] Like his predecessors, Kiesinger hoped to enlist Jewish influence on American public opinion in favor of a more resolute anti-Soviet policy. That would serve as a reward for West Germany's spontaneous support for Israel during the Six Day War and its continuous economic and political backing of the Jewish state, which some German conservatives regarded as an important anti-Communist ally. In fact, Soviet antisemitism and the drive for opening the gates for Soviet Jews to immigrate to Israel or other places had at that time already become an item of great urgency on the American Jewish agenda, setting aside the historical and emotional problem of Jewish-German relations.[18]

In the summer of 1969, on the eve of the West German federal elections, which were to put an end to the three-year interregnum of the coalition between the two large parties and open a new era in the country's postwar history, Philip Klutznick paid another visit to Germany. He met many politicians and officials and discussed the remaining difficulties regarding restitution and indemnification, the development of German-Israeli relations, and the changes taking place in the Jewish community in the Federal Republic as well as its relationship with the non-Jewish population. Klutznick remarked that as an American Jew it was not easy for him to accept, as he had done long ago, the necessity for an intimate relationship between the United States and the West German republic. Yet he had done so because, first, he was by nature a universalist, and second, he thought he was a realist. In his opinion, Washington's policy since 1945 had vindicated itself: "A defeated and broken Germany could not help rebuild a shattered Europe [he must have thought of the Morgenthau plan], nor could a [whole] Germany influenced by Eastern Communist policies be helpful to the Western hopes for a better world."

As for the relations between American and world Jewry and West Germany, Klutznick came to the conclusion that "there will continue to be a cautious alert on the part of organized Jewry outside Germany as well as by those Allied interests who poignantly remember the violent bestial Nazi period—but it is especially evident that a new plateau has been reached in which the tones are more normal and the postures somewhat more relaxed."[19]

Klutznick at that time served in no major Jewish official capacity, but was still regarded as one of the most important American Jewish leaders. His voice was authoritative and remained so during the 1970s. In 1977, Nahum Goldmann, whose dovish views on the Arab-Israel conflict he shared, secured his election to the presidency of the WJC, a position he held for only two years because of his appointment as secretary of commerce and industry by President Carter. But as Klutznick himself confessed, even on the Jewish leadership level few would go as far with regard to Germany as he did on the basis of what he regarded as American national interest, the interest of the Jewish people, and the well-being of the State of Israel.

Incidentally, Klutznick and Jacob Blaustein, another consistent pragmatic supporter of improving relations with Germany, were both second-generation Americans of East European parentage. In postwar American Jewish demography, the attitude of the leadership toward Germany was not determined by ethnic descent. The overwhelming majority of American Jews were of East European origin; there were pragmatists as well as strong opponents of any contact with Germany in their ranks. The most resolute anti-German, Henry Morgenthau Jr., happened to be a grandson of a nineteenth-century immigrant from southwest Germany.

The first left-of-center West German government, headed by Willy Brandt and dominated by the Social Democratic party, acceded to power in October 1969, more than two years after Israel's military victory in the Six Day War. During its long opposition years, the SPD had been in the forefront of improving relations with Israel and the Jewish people. Besides a moral commitment to Jews after the Holocaust, that attitude was based on Social Democratic values shared with the Israeli labor movement, on the appreciation of Israel as the only democracy in the Middle East, on its economic and social achievements, and on the assumption that Israeli experience in economic and technological development might serve as a bridge between Germany and Third World nations.

Admittedly, from time to time differences of opinion popped up that strained the friendly relations between both sides. The SPD condemned Israel's intervention in Sinai in collusion with France and Britain and did not like its support for French colonialist policies in Algeria. In the early 1960s, the party was not at all happy about the secret West German–Israeli arms deal engineered by Franz Josef Strauss, its bitter enemy; and Social Democratic politicians preparing for an active role in their country's leadership moved from one-sided friendship for Israel to a more evenhanded attitude toward the Middle East and Arab nationalism.[20]

Nevertheless, the balance sheet of Social Democratic–Israeli relations until 1967 was positive. Yet, because of Israel's holding on to the conquered territories after the war, the emergence of the PLO, and the Palestinian quest for self-determination, the gap widened. Moreover, from the early 1970s, the Social-Liberal government's policy was also affected by the European Political Cooperation (EPC) of the six and afterwards the nine members of the European Community (EC), where France and several other nations took a much more critical view of Israel.[21] As for the Free Democrats (the Liberals), the junior partner in Brandt's and Schmidt's cabinets in charge of the Foreign Office, most of them never revealed much sympathy for Israel's position.

In addition, the integration of many 1968ers into the reform-oriented SPD enhanced the criticism of Israel in its ranks, first of all among the younger membership. Besides strong objections to Israel's policies regarding the Palestinians and the Arab nations, their attitude was also affected negatively by the strengthening of Israel's anti-Communist strategic relationship with the Nixon administration. Left-wingers outside the party were even more hostile to Israel, and some of the radicals went as far as joining the Palestinian struggle against the Jewish state.[22] Younger American Jewish intellectuals were often disappointed by the German leftists' approach. Some of them had come to Germany in the 1970s to do research on the Frankfurt School's Critical Theory, which influenced both them and their German counterparts. They concluded that the anti-Vietnam/anti-American sentiment among young German leftists and their identification with the Third World revolutionary movement were much more a constitutive aspect of their consciousness than the revolt against their fathers and Germany's Nazi past.[23]

In July 1973, Brandt became the first German chancellor to pay an official visit to the Jewish state. His anti-Nazi past, his demonstrative kneeling before the Warsaw Ghetto memorial during his visit to Poland in 1970, and the fact that in his government and in high administrative posts were people with an untainted past, encouraged him to try to follow a new, more balanced course in relations with Israel, the basic moral commitment and continuing economic and political assistance notwithstanding.

Thus, in spite of Brandt's glowing reception in Israel, there was no common ground between him and Israel's prime minister Golda Meir, with whom he had clashed at meetings of the Socialist International regarding the occupied territories and the stalled diplomatic process. The Brandt government's attempt to dilute special relations with Israel into a formula of "normal relations with a special background" failed to satisfy Israel, which was also afraid of the implications of Brandt's conciliatory policy toward the Soviet Union and other Eastern European states.[24]

Oil and commercial links had already begun to influence the EC's and West Germany's Middle East policies in the early 1970s, but the impact of the oil weapon increased because of the first global oil crisis after the Yom Kippur War. At the end of that war, Brandt vowed his government's support for efforts to end the hostilities and achieve peace on the basis of Security Council Resolution 242. According to the European interpretation, this meant withdrawal from all occupied territories. When the West German government refused late in October 1973 to allow the use of Bremerhaven port for further American military supplies for Israel, Bonn explained that it did so as a "demonstration of neutrality," even though Brandt repeated that there can be "no neutrality of the heart and conscience" toward Israel.[25]

In the wake of the Yom Kippur War, West Germany and the other members of the European Nine added to their demand for an end of occupation the recognition of the legitimate rights of the Palestinians. In November 1974, Rüdiger von Wechmar, the German representative to the UN, which the Federal Republic together with the GDR and other nations had joined one year earlier, endorsed the request of self-determination for the Palestinians, including their right to an "independent authority."[26]

The reaction of organized Jewry in the United States to the new West German cabinet reflected its own concerns as well as the attitude and feelings of the Israeli government. At a private luncheon with German ambassador Rolf Pauls, former ambassador to Tel Aviv, representatives of leading American Jewish organizations noted with satisfaction the defeat of the extreme right-wing NPD, which did not gain the necessary 5 percent of the total vote to qualify for any seats in the Bundestag. An ADL memorandum emphasized that the Brandt government was composed of men with a clean past, with the only exception of Minister of the Economy Karl Schiller, who had worked in an economic institute during the war. It expressed the hope that any changes in the new government's foreign policy would be of "nuance" and not fundamental. Nevertheless, doubts regarding the new coalition's impact on Israel were also voiced. Brandt's desire for a rapprochement with the East might have some "softening effect" on Germany's overall policies, including the Middle East. As a resistance fighter he would be less solicitous in regard to Israel than Kiesinger, the former Nazi, who was always attempting to live down his past.[27] Then again, one of Brandt's close political advisers was Hans-Jürgen Wischnewski, who was well known for his pro-Arab sympathies.[28]

Since its inception in October 1969, the SPD-led West German government maintained casual contacts with the leadership of the American Jewish organizations, some of whom were concerned that the Federal Republic's pro-Israel attitude was being supplanted by a new pragmatic, more pro-Arab policy. In fall 1970, Professor Horst Ehmke, a member of Brandt's cabinet, tried to dispel these fears in talks with Jewish leaders in New York.[29] Another goodwill messenger was trade union banker Walter Hesselbach, chairman of the board of the Bank für Gemeinwirtschaft and one of Israel's best and most committed friends in the German labor movement.[30] On this occasion the German emissaries were asked whether in view of its new relationship with Eastern Europe and especially with Moscow, Bonn might be helpful regarding Soviet Jews and their struggle for emigration. Later Brandt himself was approached on the same issue by American Jewish leaders who tried to convince him that just because of Germany's guilt and his own anti-Nazi record, he should mention the subject in his talks with Soviet leaders.[31] Indeed, he proved helpful.

In December 1970, Brandt's kneeling before the Warsaw Ghetto fighters memorial during his visit to Poland had a great impact on Jews throughout the world. But the growing gap between Israel's and West Germany's policies, as well as the European Community's position in regard to the Middle East conflict, made it difficult for Ambassador Pauls and his successor Berndt von Staden to calm American Jewish fears and satisfy their demands. Remarks of the ambassador that the Brandt government believed it was time to normalize relationships with Israel and the Jewish world caused anxiety among the Jewish interlocutors lest "normalizing" meant lessening of German historic responsibility after the Holocaust. At one point, on the eve of the Yom Kippur War, Joachim Prinz complained to von Staden that some of the former German diplomats in the United States, because of their Nazi connection, had been easier to deal with since they were troubled by problems of conscience concerning Jews.[32]

The Brandt government's cessation of the supply of American arms to Israel in the last week of the October war caused much disappointment among organized American Jewry. Even a good friend of the Federal Republic such as Hans Steinitz, Manfred George's successor as editor of *Aufbau*, strongly criticized at an official German reception the withholding of arms from the Israeli ships and rhetorically asked whether Social Democrats were pro-Israel only when in opposition. Kurt Mattick and Paul Corterier, two Social Democratic members of the Bundestag Foreign Affairs Committee, told American Jewish friends in January 1974 that Israel would find it easy to come to terms with President Anwar Sadat concerning the Sinai. Yet, they were adamant that Israel give up its claim to Jerusalem, which should become a "free city" to be governed by the United Nations or placed under the supervision of some other international authority. The Jewish hosts unequivocally rejected that advice of their German guests, who also warned them that Israel's religious fanaticism would find no sympathy among the Europeans and the Social Democratic parties.[33]

There was not much love lost between Brandt, the former exile and active anti-Nazi resister, and Henry Kissinger, the German-born Jew who had managed to leave Nazi Germany in good time. But this lack of sympathy had nothing to do with the attitude of organized American Jewry and Germany. Brandt, the Social Democrat, tried to follow an independent course in his rapprochement with Eastern Europe. He could not accept Kissinger's insistence that the Great Power detente must be designed and implemented first of all by Washington. As Brandt stated in his memoirs, he never belonged to Kissinger's admirers. In his opinion, Kissinger's policy was too old-fashioned and adopted the balance of power categories of the nineteenth-century "Concert of Europe."

Kissinger, for his part, was in no way anti-German. Even as head of a U.S. Army counterintelligence detachment in Bensheim immediately after the war, he avoided any expression of hatred of Germans and chided other Jewish GIs for doing so.[34] But he harbored doubts about the political maturity of the Germans and especially the Social Democrats. Though he did not dislike Brandt personally as much as Nixon did, he regarded him as a political romantic. In retrospect, however, Kissinger recognized Brandt's historic achievement: "to find a way to live with the partition of Germany which for the entire postwar period his predecessors in Bonn had refused to accept . . . to recognize the division of his country was a courageous recognition of reality. For German unification was not achievable without a collapse of Soviet power, something that Bonn was in no position to promote."[35]

Nonetheless, during the Yom Kippur War the relationship between Kissinger and Brandt reached another low point, since Kissinger regarded the West German government's behavior as a stab in the United States' back at a critical moment when it faced great difficulties. On October 23, after the cease-fire had come under stress, the American ambassador in Bonn, Martin Hillenbrand, was abruptly informed—as Kissinger recounted in his *Years of Upheaval*[36]—that the Federal Republic would no longer approve shipment of American material to Israel from German ports; a second strong German demand was made one day later. The American response was "that for the West to display weakness and disunity in the face of a Soviet-supported military action against Israel, would have disastrous consequences." This disaccord and the deepening gap between the U.S. and the European Community policies in view of the oil crisis strained American-German relations in the last months of Brandt's chancellorship.

But although President Nixon's and Secretary Kissinger's handling of the situation was of great importance for the restoration of Israel's strength and morale after the traumatic war, American strategy in October 1973 and thereafter was determined by U.S. national interest in the superpower confrontation over the Middle East much more than by any domestic pressures. European pressure for Israel's rapid return to the 1967 borders was mainly oil-motivated.

After Brandt's departure and the appointment of Helmut Schmidt as chancellor, Kissinger's personal trust in Schmidt and his subsequent friendship with Hans-Dietrich Genscher, who succeeded Scheel as foreign minister, contributed to a substantial improvement in Washington-Bonn relations.[37] Yet, differing interests and viewpoints would continue to put their mark on a number of important policy issues, including the Middle East.

Under Schmidt's chancellorship (1974–82), the discord between the SPD-led coalition and Israel with regard to a Middle East settlement deepened, although their expanding bilateral cooperation encompassed a growing number of governmental and nongovernmental fields. In 1975, Schmidt reiterated West Germany's support for Israel's right to exist in secure and recognized borders, and also its respect of the legitimate rights of other nations and peoples in the area.[38] Yitzhak Rabin, the first Israeli prime minister to visit Germany, demanded from Bonn more understanding for Israel's position in the face of the EC's political attitude, though the Federal Republic was very helpful in confirmation of the first major trade agreement between the EC and Israel.[39] Schmidt himself never paid an official return visit and came to Israel only in 1985 and 1991 as a private citizen.

West Germany's growing capacity as a world economic power, the steady increase of its political influence in Europe and the Western alliance, as well as the lack of Schmidt's own emotional involvement in Israel made him a much more difficult partner for Israel than Brandt had been. Still, Schmidt publicly recognized Germany's historic responsibility and emphatically expressed this at a ceremony marking the fortieth anniversary of the *Kristallnacht* pogrom. As former Israeli ambassador Yohanan Meroz recalled in his memoirs, Schmidt disliked Israel's behavior as a superpower and thought it should adopt other mores.[40] The chancellor managed to reduce his nation's dependence on Middle East oil supplies, but he highly valued the importance of Arab markets to German exports in a time of reduced economic growth. These dwarfed economic relations with Israel regardless of the fact that the Federal Republic had already become Israel's second largest trade partner.[41]

The end of Labor's long-lasting hegemony in Israel and Menachem Begin's and his Likud party's rise to power after the Knesset elections in May 1977 caused a substantial deterioration in Israel's relations with the Schmidt government. Despite the Egyptian-

Israeli peace treaty of March 1979, which provided for the complete withdrawal of Israel's forces from the Sinai three years later, Bonn became upset by Israel's refusal to deal seriously with the Palestinians and its establishment of further new settlements in the occupied areas. In 1980, West Germany coauthored the EC's Venice resolution calling for the withdrawal of Israeli troops from all occupied territories, the recognition of the Palestinian right to self-determination, and the participation of the PLO in the peace process. During Schmidt's visit to Saudi Arabia in April 1981, no arms deal was struck. However, Schmidt upset Israel with his references to the equal moral rights of the Palestinians and Germany's commitment to them. His emphasis on the traditional German-Arab friendship, which reminded many Israelis of the Jerusalem Mufti's collaboration with Nazi Germany during World War II, plus Begin's personal accusations against Schmidt as a former loyal officer in Hitler's Wehrmacht, all added more strain to the relationship.[42] The wave of criticism that swept West Germany during Israel's invasion of Lebanon in summer 1982 caused a further deterioration in the bilateral political climate.

As in the past, American Jewish organizations both praised and criticized various steps and decisions of the Schmidt government. The chancellor usually devoted most of his time during visits to the United States to bankers, captains of industry, and the American Council on Germany. At the bicentennial celebrations in 1976 no meeting between him and the American Jewish leadership took place. Ambassador von Staden recommended such a meeting, but was rebuffed by Genscher's Foreign Office. A talk with State Secretary Maria Schlei, who accompanied Schmidt, was regarded as an alternative. She herself was instructed not to devote much time to the Zionism-racism UN resolution, although the ADL delegation came to thank the West German government for its stand during the General Assembly debate.[43]

A few years later the ADL found it necessary to voice a protest against Willy Brandt's meeting with Austrian chancellor Bruno Kreisky and PLO chairman Yassir Arafat in Vienna. The ADL national leadership adjusted to the new Likud rulers in Jerusalem much more easily than the AJC and AJ Congress, although Labor too was not yet friends with the PLO. At a meeting with Hans-Jürgen Wischnewski, an influential member of the last Social Democratic government, the ADL leadership argued that "the good will of the American Jewish community toward the Federal Republic, developed miraculously in view of the history of the German and Jewish peoples, was dissolving." The reason quoted was the surfacing of German corporations "to sell advanced weaponry to those who would again kill Jews."[44] Brandt, who in 1976 had been elected president of the Socialist International, continued to serve as chairman of the West German Social Democratic party, and in both capacities was interested in promoting the rights of the Palestinians. However, when asked to sign a statement describing Zionism as a "symbol of Jewish self-determination" and as the Jewish people's "reply to centuries of persecution which culminated in the Holocaust," he refused. While reaffirming solidarity with Israel and its labor movement, he stated that it could not be his task to engage himself in "a Jewish discussion on Zionism and its various brands of self-expression."[45]

More important was organized Jewry's renewed campaign for full abolition of the statute of limitations in cases of murder. A *novum* in a delegation meeting early in 1979 with Ambassador von Staden was the inclusion of three survivors of the Holocaust: Abraham H. Foxman, associate director of ADL who was saved from the Nazis in Poland by a Catholic nursemaid; Ernest W. Michel, executive vice-president of the United Jewish Appeal of Greater New York, who was imprisoned in Auschwitz and Buchenwald; and John Fox, vice-president of the Philadelphia Jewish Community Relations Council, who survived Buchenwald and Dachau. Their participation was an indication of the growing weight of the Holocaust survivor generation in American Jewish communal affairs. Members of an NJCRAC subcommittee also approached Congresswoman Elizabeth Holtzman, who entered a resolution with almost one hundred cosponsors in the House of Representatives expressing the "sense of Congress that the government of West Germany abolish or extend the statute of limitations."[46]

In June 1979, leading members of the AJC met with Chancellor Schmidt in New York after they had heaped much praise on him at an earlier appointment in Bonn for the leadership he had provided in the effort to eliminate the statute of limitations on war crimes and murder. The abolition of the statute by the Bundestag a few weeks later ended the prolonged struggle in which the American Jewish community had been involved since 1964. However, the exchange of views with Schmidt demonstrated to them the depth of the crisis in German-Israeli relations, in spite of the signing of the Egyptian-Israeli peace treaty. Schmidt argued that because of Israeli prime minister Begin's provocative policies, the Saudis would not withstand pressure to use their oil power in ways damaging to Western interests. As a result, Western nations would sooner or later turn on Israel, which might find itself completely alone. The chancellor's advice was that "the friends of Israel should help Israel to understand that by her actions she is preparing the road to her future isolation."

On the human rights issue and the forthcoming Madrid conference (a continuation of the earlier meetings at Helsinki and Belgrade), which interested American Jewry, particularly in connection with freedom of immigration for Soviet Jews, Schmidt made it clear that he opposed a "frontal attack" against the Soviet Union. The most important thing, in his opinion, was a successful conclusion of SALT II. In his view, the change of Soviet policy with regard to Jews and other emigrants was not fundamental but rather an act of expedience relating to Moscow's desire for SALT; otherwise all efforts to increase immigration would be meaningless.[47]

Robert Goldmann, who was often on the defensive among his colleagues for being "too understanding" of the new Germany and who admired Schmidt's leadership, thought that the chancellor's criticism of Israel's prime minister went "beyond the limits of propriety." He also disapproved of Schmidt's and President Carter's attempts to engage American Jews on the SALT II side by linking the problem of Soviet Jewish emigration with the U.S. Senate's confirmation of the treaty. Al Moses, on the contrary, criticized the AJC for becoming "a lackey of whomever the Prime Minister of Israel is at the moment."[48] The top leaders of the moderately liberal AJC, who had not been surprised by Schmidt's blatant statements in view of the shifting patterns of both European and Middle East politics, found themselves in a quandary. On the one hand, they dared not come out openly against the Israeli government and its policies. On the other hand, they refrained from personal and public attacks on the West German chancellor, who had been so frank with them at a private meeting.

A few weeks after Schmidt's visit to Saudi Arabia, in May 1981 a sharp confrontation between him and a delegation of the Presidents Conference took place in Washington. Howard Squadron, president of the AJ Congress and at that time chairman of the Presidents

Conference, recalled the recent events that demonstrated the deterioration of Israel's position: its growing isolation on the international scene because of West Germany's participation in the EEC; the 1980 Venice declaration; and particularly the chancellor's public references upon the conclusion of his visit to Riad. Schmidt was also taken to account for refusing to pay a visit to Israel in spite of the invitation extended to him. The chancellor rebuffed the criticism and reiterated his support for "Israel's right to live in safe and recognized borders." He stressed Saudi Arabia's realistic attitude to Israel and the Middle East situation, the calls for Jihad notwithstanding. Schmidt was accompanied by Eric Warburg, who had become a close friend of his and who tried to convince the participants of Schmidt's favorable record. Flattering his interlocutors, Schmidt remarked that as representatives of American Jewry, they enjoyed more influence in Jerusalem and Tel Aviv than they themselves believed and that they should make use of it.[49] In fact, the opposite was true: the members of the Presidents Conference acted according to Israel's instructions. Even before that meeting, the ADL had urged all its officials in places where German consulates were located to express to them "sentiments of outrage" over Schmidt's statements on his way back home from Riad. An exception was the position by Edgar Bronfman, Philip Klutznick's heir as head of the WJC. Bronfman, who would soon emerge as a strong critic of Chancellor Kohl because of his insistence on meeting President Reagan at Bitburg military cemetery, found it necessary to apologize to Schmidt for Begin's accusations against him because of his World War II service as an officer in the Wehrmacht.[50]

Altogether, the deteriorating political climate between the Federal Republic and Israel adversely affected relations between organized American Jewry and Germany, although a major Jewish demand such as the abolition of the statute of limitations was finally fulfilled in 1979.[51] Also, additional requests of the Claims Conference for indemnification and hardship payments for latecomers from Eastern Europe were satisfied in 1980 by the last Social Democratic government. In contrast to most Diaspora leaders, Nahum Goldmann, the Conference's aging chairman, had forged close links with both Brandt and Schmidt, thanks in part to their common criticism of Israel's policies.[52] For more than a decade after the establishment of German-Israeli diplomatic relations and because of the stalemate in American Jewish–German relations,

Bonn had directed its main efforts in conciliating world Jewry to the expanding partnership with Israel. Now, in the late 1970s and early 1980s, there was a reversal. Because of West Germany's growing disappointment with the Jewish state and its government, it turned the tables and redirected its efforts to American Jewry, which continued to be a force in American public opinion. Except for Israel, this was the leading factor in the Jewish world.

In the eyes of German diplomats observing the Jewish scene in the United States, the persistent negative attitude toward Germany among the younger generation of American Jews added urgency to these efforts. American Jewry still continued to be regarded by policymakers in Bonn as a major stumbling block for a more assertive role of the Federal Republic in the world. That new German emphasis depended on willing partners from the American Jewish side who were soon found. Particularly for the AJC, which had lost its paramount position of earlier years and was superseded in different fields by the Presidents Conference, AIPAC, and the National American Jewish Conference on Soviet Jewry, the new kind of mutual American Jewish–German links became an important challenge. Afterwards B'nai B'rith and ADL would follow suit. Thus a new chapter in American Jewish–German institutional relations began, despite the difficulties caused for such a rapprochement by the growing impact of Holocaust consciousness among American Jewry and German disapproval of Israel's policies.

The turning point was the presentation to Chancellor Schmidt in June 1979[53] of an AJC draft concerning an exchange program for future leaders in the Federal Republic and the American Jewish community. In order to provide young American Jewish leaders with a more objective view of democratic Germany, groups from a variety of professional fields, as well as those active in the community, were invited to visit there. Upon their return, they were to transmit their knowledge and experience to others in the Jewish community as well as to the broader American society. Conversely, Germans of similar age groups and professional backgrounds—younger members of the Bundestag and regional legislators, educators, journalists, and representatives of the Protestant and Catholic churches—would come to the United States to study the American Jewish community, the largest in the world, and its contribution to the social and political life of America, its history and future. Seminars for the German guests, which would deal with religious, cultural, and educational institutions, community relations, and philanthropic and social welfare activities, would be held in New York. The participants would also visit other major communities such as Los Angeles, Chicago, and Philadelphia and meet with American Jewish legislators in Washington.

The memorandum to the German chancellor was preceded by informal contacts between West German diplomats serving in the United States and some influential AJC executives. William S. Trosten, bilingual and married to a German woman, and often critical of the Israel-centered trend of organized Jewry, played an important role in forging the new relationship. Because of his personal commitment, he had maintained close contacts with a variety of officials of the Foreign Office in Bonn over the years and cooperated closely with Rabbi Marc Tanenbaum, AJC director of interreligious affairs and afterwards head of its international affairs department. Among their counterparts in the German consulate general in New York was Dr. Wolf Calebow, who later served in the same capacity at the embassy in Washington. After Trosten's retirement from the Committee in 1989 he established, with Theodor Ellenoff, an AJC past president, the pro-German Armonk Institute for furthering friendly relations between American Jews and Americans in general and Germany. That private institute has enjoyed the strong backing of the Bonn government. For the last few years it has been instrumental in bringing over American high school and college teachers, not only Jews, to Germany, to get acquainted with its politics and society.

Upon his return from the United States, Schmidt submitted the AJC draft to the Konrad Adenauer Foundation, related to the Christian Democrats, then still in opposition. In 1980 the Foundation established its first visitors exchange program with the AJC.[54] The new direct American Jewish–German relationship expanded gradually during the next decade. There was, of course, no contradiction between the new ethnic venture and American national interest. On the contrary, the Republican administrations in the 1980s were very much interested in strengthening the American-German alliance and in lessening criticism and furthering understanding for Germany also among the Jewish community.

15

The Growth of
Holocaust Consciousness
and Its Impact on
American Jewish–German Relations

For thirteen years, from October 1969 until September 1982, the left-of-center coalition led by the Social Democrats held power in West Germany, even though its reformist zeal was blocked by a renascent conservative trend in German society in the late 1970s. In 1982, Chancellor Schmidt's last cabinet was replaced by the right-of-center coalition of CDU leader Helmut Kohl, who in fall 1996 already had remained in power longer than any other German head of government since Otto von Bismarck. In Israel, the Labor party's long hegemony since its creation in 1948 was interrupted between 1977 and 1992 by either Likud-led or national unity governments dependent on the Likud. In 1996, after an interval of four years, Labor was again relegated by the voters into opposition.

There were ups and downs in American Jewish–German relations during these two decades. But in addition to German and Israeli political changes, the growth of Holocaust consciousness in American Jewish life added another polarizing dimension to that already complex relationship. Still, it did not prevent the establishment and broadening of a variety of American Jewish and German exchange programs from the early 1980s. At least until the Bitburg imbroglio in 1985, the increasing Holocaust consciousness was not connected to any major happening on the West German scene. Instead, that awareness resulted from the accumulating impact of the Eichmann trial, the struggle against the enactment of the statute of limitations, American Jewish concern for Israel's safety during the wars of 1967 and 1973, and the generational change in the community. It also coincided, after the optimism of the halcyon days up to the mid-1960s, with the reappearance of antisemitic manifestations at home as well as abroad, which made American Jews temporarily more conscious not only of the similarity but also of the differences between themselves and other Americans.

After V-E Day and the liberation of the concentration and slave labor camps, the safety and well-being of the few survivors and of the larger number of refugees who assembled in the American occupation zones of Germany and Austria had become American Jewry's most urgent concern. Even though the latter welcomed the exposure of Nazi atrocities and the sentences passed upon their perpetrators by the Nuremberg IMT, the destruction of European Jewry had not been central to the deliberations of that court. Because of the Cold War and the American national interest in incorporating the only perfunctorily denazified West German state in the Western camp, the Jewish community had to adjust to the new situation. While Jews did not forget, they at least took advantage of Adenauer Germany's interest in gaining acceptance by American public opinion in their efforts to obtain restitution and indemnification for the victims, and *shilumim* for Israel and the Claims Conference. In 1957, in an often quoted remark, sociologist Nathan Glazer wondered why American Jews were not interested in the two main events in recent Jewish history: the Holocaust and the creation of the State of Israel. The formulation of this rhetorical question was, of course, exaggerated, but it contained a kernel of truth.[1]

Interest in the Holocaust revived as a result of the Eichmann trial in Jerusalem that focused attention on Nazi Germany's crimes against the Jewish people. The controversy caused by Hannah Arendt's reports from the courtroom in Jerusalem, and especially by her accusations against the Jewish leadership during the years of Nazi persecution and mass murder, increased the awareness of the problems Jews faced during the tragic period. In 1963, the major concentration camp trials in Germany began, and the community became involved in a continuing struggle to extend the German statute of limitations, which threatened to put an end to the prosecution of Nazi criminals.

Holocaust consciousness became even stronger during the Six Day War and the Yom Kippur War. After the latter, Irving Greenberg called Israel "the response of the Jewish people to the Holocaust, its dialectical contradiction." At the same time, the domestic crisis of the civil rights movement, to which American Jews had contributed much financial and organizational assistance as well as intellectual energy, and the subsequent rise of black nationalism redirected Jewish concern to the community's own problems and revived fears of antisemitism.[2] Besides, interest in the Holocaust period also increased because of the failure of the Roosevelt administration to try to rescue at least a part of European Jewry, exposed first in Arthur D. Morse's *While Six Million Died.* The historical monographs of Henry L. Feingold, David S. Wyman, Saul Friedman, and others added to this awakening. These books revived the debate on organized American Jewry's response in those fateful years.[3]

In part, Holocaust consciousness among American Jews and its commemoration grew because of the emergence of Holocaust survivors in the United States—the second largest group in size after those who immigrated to Israel—and their children as an important force in the community. After a period of acculturation and economic progress, as Eva Fogelman and William Helmreich have pointed out, the survivors became active on the local and national Jewish scene. The children of the second generation, whose identity had been strengthened by the flowering of Jewish causes during the late 1960s and early 1970s, soon followed suit.[4] Quite a few rose to leadership of major communal organizations; others were important contributors to new types of agencies such as the Holocaust-centered Simon Wiesenthal Center, which sprang up on the campus of the Los Angeles branch of Yeshiva University. Elie Wiesel, a survivor of Auschwitz, whose novels, *Night, Dawn,* and *The Accident,* made him one of the foremost molders of Holocaust consciousness in the 1960s, was already regarded in the 1970s as one of the most respectable figures of American Jewry and attracted worldwide attention that would later secure him the Nobel Peace Prize.

Even though a substantial number of survivors had preferred to come to the United States after the war, they felt closer to Israel than most other American Jews and visited there more often. The affiliation of many survivors and their families with Orthodox synagogues and day schools gradually enlarged the Orthodox presence in several organizations, in comparison to the almost total non-Orthodox hegemony of Reform and Conservative lay representatives and officials in earlier times. Over the years, this contributed to an ideological, cultural, and political shift to the right, even more so with regard to Israel's policies, when in 1977 the Likud replaced Labor as the leading political force. Quite understandably, a large segment of the survivors took a negative attitude toward Germany and Germans, although there were exceptions.[5]

The rise of Holocaust consciousness, the politicization of the survivors in the 1970s, the changing East-West relations, as well as continuing Jewish concern with neo-Nazi activities abroad, also furthered the American administration's new look into the admission or infiltration of former perpetrators of crimes against Jews during the peak of the Cold War. Some of those infiltrators were regarded then as helpful tools in the confrontation with Communist regimes in Eastern Europe. On the one hand, Democratic Jewish members of the House such as Elizabeth Holtzman from Brooklyn and Joshua Eilberg from Philadelphia were instrumental in arranging the first public hearings on this matter. Afterwards, a law was passed making racial, religious, or political persecution a ground for deportation. An appropriation of $2.3 million granted to the Department of Justice to investigate and prosecute Nazi and fascist criminals living in the United States enabled the attorney general to establish the Office of Special Investigations (OSI) in 1979, and this agency has been prosecuting Nazi suspects ever since.[6] On the other hand, these Jewish-sponsored initiatives triggered more intense antisemitic, anti-Holocaust activities. With the support of Willis Carto's Liberty Lobby, an Institute for Historical Review opened on the West Coast and published the quasi-respectable *Journal of Historical Review*, which tried to convince university students and faculty members of the legitimacy of Holocaust revisionism. No wonder that nationalistic German-American groups shared anti-Holocaust measures on the local and state level, especially in opposing the introduction of the Holocaust into the public school system's history curriculum.

The first American memorial to the victims of the Holocaust, which was to be built at a site in New York's Riverside Park between 83rd and 84th Streets and dedicated by Mayor William O'Dwyer in October 1947, was never erected. Neither in the late 1940s nor in the early 1950s did the main Jewish organizations support the building of such a monument. They had other priorities, and the Cold War climate was not favorable for such an undertaking. In the mid-1960s the atmosphere had changed; more organizations endorsed the idea, and for several years the Memorial Committee originally sponsored by the Warsaw Ghetto Resistance Organization was chaired by Joachim Prinz, a leader of the AJ Congress and the Presidents Conference. However, it was more than thirty years until the New York Holocaust memorial in Lower Manhattan across from Ellis Island and the Statue of Liberty was completed.[7]

In the meantime, since the 1970s, monuments and memorials have been dedicated and sponsored by survivors and other American Jews in nearly all major American (and Canadian) cities. In 1978, President Jimmy Carter, following the advice of Jewish White House assistants, decided to establish the U.S. Holocaust Memorial Commission, later renamed the Holocaust Memorial Council. Partly this was intended to placate American Jewish leaders upset by his sale of F-15 fighter planes to Saudi Arabia and by his reference to a Palestinian homeland. Carter's decision, however, opened a new chapter by introducing the Holocaust into America's civic culture, the "Americanization of the Holocaust."

In his founding statement, Carter mentioned three reasons for the commission: first, it was American troops who liberated many of the Nazi camps and the United States became a homeland for many survivors; second, the nation must share the responsibility "for not being willing to acknowledge forty years ago that this horrible event was occurring"; and finally, only by study of the systematic destruction of the Jews could Americans as humane people learn how to prevent such enormities in the future. The main result of Carter's initiative was the U.S. Holocaust Memorial Museum, near the Washington Monument and the Jefferson Memorial in the nation's capital, which caused much concern in the ranks of the West German establishment (see chapter 18). The museum was inaugurated in April 1993, fifteen years later, by another Democratic president, Bill Clinton. In 1992, another large museum on the West Coast opened its doors: the Simon Wiesenthal Center's "Museum of Tolerance—Beit Hashoah," built upon the initiative of Rabbi Marvin Hier, the head of that new agency.

By the 1970s, Yom Hashoah (Holocaust Day), which originated in Israel in the early 1950s, had become an annual day of remembrance in the American Jewish calendar, years before it was authorized as an established ecumenic event. Groups of Jewish youngsters began to visit Auschwitz and other sites of the Final Solution in Poland, and in 1983, many thousands of Holocaust survivors attended their first convocation in Washington. In the 1980s, university courses on the Holocaust were widely taught in the Judaica curriculum.[8]

Gradually, Holocaust consciousness and its recognition as a major component of Jewish identity also pervaded at least a part of American Jewish intellectuals. During World War II and for a number of years thereafter, many of them had been uninclined to deal with that disastrous event and preferred to maintain their cosmopolitan position. The so-called "other intellectuals," committed Labor Zionists such as Hayim Greenberg, Marie Syrkin, and Ben Halpern, whose contributions appeared mainly in the *Jewish Frontier*, or Ludwig Lewisohn and Maurice Samuel, were a different case. As Stephen Whitfield recalled in 1979 in his essay "The Holocaust and the Intellectuals,"[9] participants in the 1944 *Contemporary Jewish Record* symposium had felt no obligation to incorporate in the depiction of human actuality experiences of the mass murder which was then taking place. In *Commentary*'s 1961 discussion of Jewishness and the younger intellectuals, only two out of thirty-one mentioned the impact of the Holocaust; there was no reference to the Holocaust in the *Judaism* symposium of the same year.

However, in the August 1966 issue of *Commentary* dedicated to the condition of Jewish belief, Seymour Siegel, a leading scholar and professor at the JTS, already came to the conclusion that "Jewish thought must try to fathom the meaning of the European Holocaust . . . For all Jews (and non-Jews as well) it remains the most agonizing question of our age." By now, both writer Alfred Kazin and psychiatrist Robert Jay Lifton had become more conscious of the implications of the Holocaust than before. In another *Judaism* symposium in 1974, after the Yom Kippur War, the Holocaust and Nazi atrocities were recognized by a third of twenty-six academics, writers, artists, and scientists as crucial to their awareness of themselves. That symposium of affiliated and nonaffiliated intellectuals also showed a much higher degree of Jewish self-identification and of Israel's significance for them. In 1970, Saul Bellow, who in *Herzog* had only marginally touched the Jewish tragedy in Europe, published his *Mr. Sammler's Planet*. Dealing with the world of a survivor, he argued that the Holocaust's main truth was that the Enlightenment's conception of man as a rational being was moribund.[10] Bellow's visit to Auschwitz in 1959 had a long-lasting impact on him.

The subject that permeated major parts of the community was picked up by popular novelists, magazines, and the mass media. The telecasting in 1978 of Gerald Green's *Holocaust* series attracted wide attention not only among Jews but also among the general American public. Renowned critics such as Robert Alter warned that the Holocaust should not be made the ultimate touchstone of Jewish values and emphatically opposed any comparisons between the Arab threat and Nazism, which were popular in pro-Likud circles.[11] Historian Ismar Schorsch was against imparting new life to the "lachrymose conception of Jewish history" (a concept against which Salo Baron fought all his life) and cautioned that if the Holocaust alone sustained American Jewish consciousness, it would grant a posthumous victory to Adolf Hitler.[12] However, the critique of Holocaust distortion by commercialization, politicization, and theologization, though an important intellectual corrective, did not change the basic state of mind of American Jewry. The continuous preoccupation with the Holocaust for which the German people and the Nazi regime had been responsible reaffirmed the negative perception of the Germans in the eyes of many Jews.

It must be mentioned that in intellectual debates on Jewish-German relations, here and there moderate views were expressed, particularly by former German Jews who had immigrated to the United States after 1933 or after the war. Leo Trepp, a rabbi and religious thinker, rhetorically asked in *Sh'ma* whether Jews, living under God's commandment, could reject all Germans and their children without destroying themselves in hate. Werner Cahn-mann, a former official of the Central Verein in Bavaria who had been engaged in efforts to improve American Jewish–German re-lations since the 1950s, went further and complained about Jewish lack of response to all German goodwill gestures: "[While] the monstrosity of genocide cannot be erased from our memories, . . . the ritualistic genuflections we have become addicted to will not help us solve the problems of the present period in history."

Herbert Strauss, who as a young man had escaped from Ger-many to Switzerland in 1943 and was to serve in the 1980s as the founding director of the Berlin Center for Research of Antisemitism, did not deny that there was also a negative side to contemporary Germany: "survival of yesterday's attitudes and of people who had been part of the Nazi machine at one level or another; belief in titles, class, dogmas; forgetfulness, rationalization, even die-hard nationalism and provincialism; appeals to hatred or fears, authoritarianism or anti-Semitism." Nonetheless, postwar German democracy had functioned longer and better than the Weimar Republic; West Germany had paid (until 1973) DM 50 billion in restitution and indemnification to Nazi victims; and the story of postwar German-Israeli and German-Jewish relations had revealed "on the German side, people of high moral stature," some of whom he called his friends. Strauss concluded that no one of his age could have a simple relationship with Germany and nobody could avoid having a relationship with it, since he needed to come to grips with the experiences that formed his generation and its Jewish existence.[13]

However, it seems that the views of other participants in the *Sh'ma* debate such as Cynthia Ozick and Harry Gersh were more representative of the mood of the American Jewish community. Gersh, although his family had left his native Bessarabia after the Kishinev pogrom many years before Auschwitz, was not ready for friendship with Germans after what had happened from 1933 to 1945. He opposed making any personal contribution to their economy and wondered whether he could bring himself to buy a German car. Only after the generation of Germans who knew and accepted Hitler had perished would he "be ready to accept their children and their children's children." Cynthia Ozick, when asked by Harper and Row for a favorable comment for advertising a new German book by Dieter Wellershoff, who at seventeen had been sent to serve in the German army on the Eastern front where he was wounded, replied:

> a book by a German is not for me . . . it's a complex and transcendent thing, not simply a matter of perpetuating hatred . . . the point is that I, in my generation, will not perpetuate the connectedness of speaking to, for, or about a German. . . . It so happens that in the roads of that 'Eastern Front' (how much the cool geography of war terminology covers up!—on that Front lay a civilization now decimated, a language now extirpated) my great-aunt Feyge-Etel perished fleeing from Dieter Wellershoff.[14]

In 1976, the German Carl Duisberg Society and Common Cause, an American organization concerned with improving U.S.-German relations, were involved in the visit of a group of young German intellectuals to the United States. They were mostly leftist writers, poets, and playwrights, and they met with, among others, American Jewish counterparts. At a session at the ADL national headquarters, most of the Jews said that while they approved of the encounter intellectually, they had to overcome emotional obstacles to participate. At a "frank and freewheeling dialogue" of twelve Germans and twelve Jews, the Germans disapproved of the popular American Jewish opinion that all German leftists were anti-Zionists. Fred Viebahn, a twenty-eight-year-old poet and member of the board of the Association of German Writers, could not grasp why young Jews like Abraham Foxman, then still a junior ADL executive, disliked all Germans, as at least some of them, including his own family, had been persecuted because they were Socialists and Communists. For Heike Doutine, daughter of a Nazi party member who served as a soldier in the Wehrmacht and herself the author of the *German Requiem*, about growing up in postwar Germany, meeting with Jews face-to-face was difficult. Her advice was that "Germans should remember more [of the Holocaust], while Jews should perhaps forget a little."

Of course, the Jewish partners would not agree that guilt was limited only to contemporaries of the Nazi period. Lawrence Leshnik of the ADL staff, an anthropologist who came to the United States from Germany when he was six years old, confessed that he could not maintain feelings of ill will against young Germans but demanded that they remember their responsibility to face up to their past. He also recalled his shocking experience during Middle East "teach-ins" after the Six Day War when young Germans—not "visceral anti-Semites" but "intellectual anti-Semites"—castigated Israel as "the new imperialistic power of the world." Foxman admonished them that "it wasn't only the Holocaust that must not be forgotten, but that Israel must not be abandoned." Despite the difficulties that had arisen during the debate, ADL officials recommended that the concept of such dialogues should be implemented as one of their program activities.[15]

In talks with the AJC, which also hosted the German visitors, the representative of the Carl Duisberg Society suggested that *Commentary* conduct, either alone or in conjunction with some

German cultural institution, a symposium on the Jewish-German relationship. The symposium should counteract to some extent the anti-Israel position of many of the critical German intellectuals. Podhoretz, now a leading neoconservative dedicated mainly to the fight against Communism and leftism abroad and at home, did not regard such a symposium as a "dramatic and exciting enough subject" for publication. As an alternative, he proposed holding such a conference in Israel or in Germany, preferably at Nuremberg, "with the focus on the isolation of Israel and its being made into a pariah of the nations, in much the same way as Jews found themselves isolated in a growing environment of hatred in the 1930s."[16] But such a conference did not take place.

A *Midstream* symposium a few years later demonstrated a similar ambiguous state of mind among committed Jewish intellectuals in regard to Jewish-German relations. Warnings were voiced that to indict young Germans and their future generations because of the sins of their fathers was incompatible with Judaism's moral imperatives. However, most of the participants, including such eminent scholars as historian Michael A. Meyer, stated that in spite of the right of the younger German generation to begin with a clear slate, the "Jewish attitude toward Germany . . . must be characterized by a sense of balance" and the West German Federal Republic could not be disconnected from the German Reich that preceded it. The time for a dialogue had come, but it was much too early to speak about normalization. Encounters between Germans and Jews would be strained for generations, even though rationally Jews recognized the fact of a new Germany.[17]

Beginning in the mid-1970s a group of younger Jewish intellectuals and social scientists challenged Gershom Scholem's negative verdict on the German Jewish symbiosis as "one-sided and nonreciprocative" and refused to accept his repudiation of the German-Jewish intellectual synthesis. Conversely, they argued that such a symbiosis continued to exist, if not yet at the level of a German Jewish presence in contemporary Germany, then at the level of an intellectual and cultural tradition that resonated and bloomed beyond the historic borders of 1945, mainly in the English-speaking world. A sense of identification with that culture remained essential for their self-definition, as Anson Rabinbach admitted. That link was reinforced by the impact of the Frankfurt School on themselves as well as on their counterparts in Germany. But while their contribution to historical and sociological analyses of post-Holocaust German-Jewish relations was respectable, and some of them established themselves at American elite universities, they did not yet affect the larger Jewish community in the United States.[18]

In 1978, German diplomats in the United States, who had been concerned about the possible negative impact of the NBC *Holocaust* series on American-German relations, were pleased that the telecast did not cause an outbreak of anti-German feelings. Following the controversial and commercially successful American showing, the WDR (Westdeutscher Rundfunk), the largest of West Germany's regional television networks, immediately obtained broadcasting rights for Germany. But because of the refusal of four other regional networks to show the film on the highly watched First Program, the telecast was postponed until January 1979. Through their contacts with the German Information Center and consulate general in New York, organizations such as the ADL prodded the German authorities to proceed with the screening of the series.[19] It was finally telecast during four consecutive days on the Third Program, which usually drew a much smaller though intelligent audience. Yet according to reliable surveys, 40 percent of all West German TV viewers—approximately fifteen million people—watched the program every night; more than 35,000 telephone calls (four times the number reported by NBC during the film's American showing) were received by the stations, and an equal amount of telegrams and letters were sent.[20] Many East Germans in regions adjacent to the Federal Republic also watched the film, although their own TV network did not broadcast it for political reasons.

The major debate that preceded the screening revealed again the split in German society with regard to its historic responsibility for the murder of millions of European Jews. The film showing also highlighted the difficulty faced by many Germans in coming to grips with their past, forty years after the *Kristallnacht* pogrom and thirty-four years after the end of World War II. Many leading members of the ruling Social Democratic party, including Chancellor Schmidt and Willy Brandt, regarded the event as "a healthy and necessary part of the Federal Republic's political development."[21] The deterioration of West German relations with Israel after Begin's accession to power did not affect the Social Democrats' commitment not to blur the lessons of the past. The CDU, again the largest single party after the 1976 Bundestag elections, exerted pressure on TV officials at least not to telecast the series on channels that normally reached mass audiences. Franz Josef Strauss, prime minister of Bavaria and unsuccessful CDU/CSU candidate for chancellor in the 1980 federal elections, thought the film was not balanced because it gave the "false impression" that brutalities were committed only by the German people.[22] Violent neo-Nazi groups on the extreme right even bombed two television transmitters during the showing of a preparatory documentary.

As Jerry Herf pointed out, opposition to the screening also came from various groups of leftist radicals. In their opinion, *Holocaust* served the interests of the United States and Israel.[23] On the other hand, the DGB (Germany's Trade Union Federation) and its constituent unions voiced strong support. Most columnists and critics of the liberal dailies and periodicals argued in favor of the telecast; they were joined by the *feuilleton* section of the conservative *Frankfurter Allgemeine Zeitung*, which at first had been critical of the series when it was screened in the United States. *Der Spiegel*, too, heaped praise on it after the performance, although it had opposed the program before it was shown to the German public.

There is no doubt that the screening of *Holocaust* in Germany—despite its debatable quality—was a significant event, shocking the German public and making more Germans conscious of Hitler's Final Solution than all the preceding efforts and explanations by their own media. The "pedagogy of the Holocaust" was especially important for the younger generation born in the Federal Republic after the war. But although the immediate post-*Holocaust* climate may have advanced the final abolition by the Bundestag in July 1979 of the statute of limitations for murder, its long range political impact seems to have been limited. It did not affect the election of the conservative CDU politician Karl Carstens, a former member of the Nazi party, as federal president in the spring of 1979. The program also did not arrest the renewed conservative trend in German politics that in October 1982 was complemented by the replacement of Schmidt's social-liberal coalition with Kohl's right-of-center government.

In February 1979, a few weeks after the shocking experience of *Holocaust*, one poll indicated that in contrast to past opinions, 51 percent of West German viewers wanted prosecution of Nazi criminals to be continued as opposed to 45 percent who insisted it should be ended. One year later, after the statute of limitations had been abolished, support for Nazi crimes trials evaporated; the number of opponents of further prosecution rose to 57 percent, while those in favor fell to 34 percent.[24] Another survey conducted by the ADL showed that while the telecast of *Holocaust* stimulated education about the Nazi era and encouraged controversy between parents and children, 59 percent of those interviewed believed Germany could no longer be held responsible for the crimes committed under the Nazi regime. The same percentage argued that those who talk about the wrongs done to the Jews should also talk about the wrongs done to Germans, such as the bombardments of the cities and the expulsion from the east.[25]

Characteristic of the winds of change blowing in the early 1980s was the much-quoted address of Hermann Lübbe, a leading neoconservative political philosopher and professor at Zurich University. At a symposium held in January 1983 in Berlin on the fiftieth anniversary of Hitler's rise to power, the first of the many anniversaries that would continue until 1995,[26] Lübbe strongly criticized the intense post-1968 cultural and political preoccupation of the younger left-wing generation with the Nazi past. In his view, this threatened the stability of the Federal Republic. Conversely, he extolled the reticence and discretion with which the Germans dealt with that past in the postwar years, thus making possible their country's reconstruction and consolidation. Lübbe's attitude was contrary to the Mitscherlich couple's complaint about the German "inability to mourn."[27]

American Jewish consciousness of the Holocaust and the ongoing German difficulties with that subject quite naturally affected the new direct dialogue between organized American Jewry and the Federal Republic, which began in the early 1980s. However, the "Americanization of the Holocaust" added even more urgency to German efforts to improve relations with the Jewish community. In 1980, the Konrad Adenauer Foundation established a visitors exchange program that has continued ever since.[28] The program, financed by both partners, brought mainly young German academicians, civil servants, and businesspeople to the United States and Jewish counterparts to Germany. For a number of years these exchanges were complemented by AJC chapter missions. Three years later, the Friedrich Ebert Foundation, connected with the Social Democratic party,[29] followed suit and initiated a different sort of exchange, based on mutual visits of Social Democratic politicians and officials and select AJC officers. In 1988, both sponsored a conference on including material about American Jewish life in West German high school textbooks. In the early 1990s, the Friedrich Naumann Foundation, close to the liberal Free Democratic Party, also became involved in several projects together with the AJC.

Subsequently, as a result of the rivalry between American Jewish organizations, contacts that had started in the mid-1950s between the West Germans and the ADL, as well as B'nai B'rith, were reinvigorated,[30] and additional programs with German political foundations were set up. Still, the Adenauer Foundation remained the leading one in the American Jewish–German exchange programs before and after Germany's reunification.

Quite separately, representatives of the major Jewish organizations met with German diplomats in Washington and New York, as well as with officials in Bonn. At personal meetings and in their correspondence, Israel's security, the sale of German weapons to Arab nations, neo-Nazi activities, manifestations of antisemitism, and the situation of Soviet Jewry came up. On a higher level, most of these issues were discussed by the Jewish leadership with Chancellor Kohl and members of his government. Besides, the rotation of German diplomats between Washington, New York, and Tel Aviv, which had begun in the late 1960s, added to a better understanding of matters of triangular concern. Rolf Pauls, the first German ambassador to Israel, had been stationed in the 1950s as counselor at the German embassy in Washington, where he returned in 1969 as ambassador. Niels Hansen became ambassador to Israel in 1981 after he had served in different capacities in Washington and New York; similarly a number of lower-rank diplomats rotated between the United States and Israel.

Helmut Kohl had first met with representatives of the Presidents Conference and other Jewish groups as chairman of the CDU, when that party was still in opposition. In 1978, he had addressed the American Federation of Jews from Central Europe at the Leo Baeck Institute in New York and thanked them for their support of U.S. efforts to rebuild Germany after the war, as well as for their "critical observation" of its development as friends.[31] At the first meeting with the American Jewish leadership six weeks after his appointment as chancellor, Kohl impressed them favorably. He reiterated that he was the "political grandson" of Adenauer and wished to continue the tradition of friendship with Israel that extended back to Adenauer's meeting with Ben Gurion. He told them that his parents had not been Nazis and that as first chancellor of the postwar generation, he could speak and act free of any prewar liability. As for Israel's prime minister, Kohl thought that some remarks made by Menachem Begin were "not good," but he favored reconciliation and felt "that we should let bygones be bygones."

Kohl expressed his strong support for the Israeli-Egyptian peace treaty (Schmidt had been more reserved with regard to it because of the lack of progress toward a comprehensive peace) and promised to strengthen the Federal Republic's ties of friendship with Israel. In response to a question, he remarked that there would be no German recognition of the PLO without a fundamental change in its position.[32] However, other contacts with Kohl were less harmonious. In 1984, for instance, American Jewish leaders bombarded him with protests against the sale of sophisticated West German weapons to Saudi Arabia. In this context, representatives of the American Gathering of Jewish Holocaust Survivors visited the German ambassador.[33] Despite all the expressions of goodwill, the pro-Arab orientation of Germany's business circles influenced the Kohl government perhaps even more than its predecessors.

Alois Mertes, minister of state in the German Foreign Office (deputy foreign minister), devoted special attention to American Jewry on behalf of the Kohl government until his untimely death in June 1985. In his last address to a Jewish audience, Mertes tried to convince his critical listeners that German patriotism forty years after World War II was no different in essence from the principles of human rights and democracy sponsored by the AJC. But despite mutual manifestations of well-disposedness, the deep gap between the two sides—a function of their national memories—persisted, as was shown during Reagan's and Kohl's visit at Bitburg military cemetery, which happened to belong to Mertes's own constituency.[34]

The German objective in the manifold exchange programs was to show the new generation of American Jewish communal leaders and professionals the achievements of postwar German democracy and the changes their society had gone through since the Nazi period. Some also expected that better contacts with American Jews might serve as reassurance for German-Jewish reconciliation. This interaction, of course, would take into account the difficulties with Israel's right-wing government, the demographic and cultural changes in Israel, and last but not least, the widening gap between Bonn and Jerusalem caused by Germany's support for Palestinian self-determination and its political and economic interest in the Arab world.[35] Speaking before a B'nai B'rith audience in Washington in 1985, the German ambassador Günther van Well flattered American Jews as "the main torch bearers of Ashkenazi heritage," presumably having in mind the majority of Israel's citizens who lacked the traditional ties with Europe and the United States.[36]

The aims of the Jewish participants were more limited. They tried to explain to their German counterparts the functioning of the American Jewish community and its impact on the American public by cooperation and coalition-building with other groups, and by its contribution to the labor movement, to civil rights, and to other important issues.[37] But they also reminded the Germans of the consistent American Jewish concern with Israel's security and well-being. Thus Howard Friedman, an AJC lay leader who in 1991 delivered the annual Alois Mertes Lecture (named in Mertes's honor after his death), went as far as defining "steadfast German support for Israel . . . [as] an earmark of the vitality of the commitment of Germany and its people to free institutions," to free societies.[38] In 1984 Friedman, at that time president of the AJC, participated in the Berlin ceremonies marking the fortieth anniversary of the German opposition's attempt to assassinate Hitler. It was the first time that a representative of American Jewry attended such a commemoration.[39]

No quick rapprochement was achieved at the early American Jewish–German encounters that began in 1980, mutual courtesies notwithstanding. The youngish and not so young German visitors repeated their willingness to accept at least a measure of historical responsibility for what had happened to Jews in Europe during the war, although they rejected any kind of collective guilt. To grasp the uniqueness of the American Jewish community and its workings in the midst of pluralistic American society was a hard task for them, after lack of any meaningful contacts for forty years. Some of the members of the AJC mission, such as David Gordis, at that time vice-president of the University of Judaism in Los Angeles, were struck by the ambivalence of their own feelings toward the Germans, "awestruck by the abilities and talents of the culture as well as terrorized by their capacity for murder." Gordis was not impressed by the German sense of emotional confrontation in coming to terms with the Holocaust. The fact that the screening of the *Holocaust* series had such an immense impact, he felt, proved that there had not been much teaching about the event beforehand.

Mark Spiegel, a Los Angeles attorney, complained that the feeling of "collective shame" for the Holocaust related more to the shame of the Germans than to the suffering of the Jews. But others argued that the Holocaust was, after all, "both a human and a German undertaking and that to hone in only on its German characteristics would limit its usefulness as a lesson to all people." Moreover, West Germany "was not only the author of the Holocaust but also a modern nation of 61 million people" and was a co-leader of the Western world, together with the United States.[40] Besides the Israeli angle, that recognition was an important reason for organized American Jewry to engage in the mutual exchange programs that aimed at some kind of rapprochement. Gradually, despite continuing differences of opinion, the network of mutual acquaintanceships and organizational links widened and became stronger. In 1985, it withstood the shock of the major U.S.-Jewish-German crisis caused by the Bitburg event.

16

Bitburg and
Its Repercussions

The new series of American Jewish–German programs was established at a time when West German politics tilted back to the conservative side. Moderate conservatives such as Chancellor Kohl, who, because of the "grace of his late birth" was saved from becoming involved with the Nazi regime or serving in Hitler's army, continued to pledge assistance to Israel, here and there mentioning Nazi wrongdoings and crimes against the Jewish people. At the same time, the Germans tried to base German-Jewish relations more on the present and future than on the past. This was part and parcel of the Federal Republic's overall effort to assert its status as a leading European ally of the United States forty years after World War II and to dissociate itself as much as possible from its predecessor.

However, the 1985 Bitburg affair, intended as a symbol of normalcy along the above lines, served, in fact, as a reminder of the persevering impact of that past. President Reagan's compliance with Chancellor Kohl's insistence that they together visit the German military cemetery, where, among others, a number of SS soldiers were buried, came as a major shock to the organized Jewish community, even more so since many other Americans supported their president's stand against his critics. For Jews, it demonstrated the wide gap between their Holocaust consciousness and the attitude of the Gentile majority, the "Americanization" of the Holocaust notwithstanding; whereas the relationship between their organizations and the German counterparts continued, old wounds reopened. The Jewish confrontation with the administration over Bitburg also served as a reminder of the limits to ethnic pressures. In the last stages of the Cold War, Washington rightly or wrongly regarded this visit as a matter of crucial national interest; for American Jewry, opposing it had mainly great moral value.

The Bitburg episode that shook American Jewish confidence both in Reagan and in Kohl occurred during an era of good feeling between the conservative governments of the two Western allies, despite lingering German doubts about the U.S. Strategic Defense Initiative. It originated from the German leader's request that President Reagan accompany him to a German military cemetery during his planned visit to the Federal Republic in spring 1985. Kohl also asked Reagan to join him in placing a wreath there, as a symbolic act of reconciliation forty years after the end of the war in Europe. Kohl had not been invited by the former allies to commemorate the fortieth anniversary of the landing at Normandy but as a conciliatory gesture had been asked by French president François Mitterand to join him in a wreath-laying ceremony at the World War I cemetery of Verdun. Accordingly, he wanted the American president to share in a similar demonstrative act during his European visit commemorating the fortieth anniversary of V-E Day, even though many Germans still regarded it as a date not of liberation from the Nazi dictatorship but of their nation's defeat.[1]

The trouble started when, in order not to annoy his German hosts, Reagan decided not to include in his itinerary Dachau concentration camp, which had been liberated on April 29, 1945, by the U.S. Army. The controversy grew heated when it became known that at Bitburg military cemetery, where both chief executives were to visit, close to fifty soldiers of the Waffen SS had been interred, some of them veteran members of the criminal Nazi "elite" organization. This contradicted Reagan's own gullible description of the SS men buried there as "victims of Nazism . . . drafted into service to carry out the hateful wishes of the Nazis." Even the White House's belated decision to add a visit to the Bergen-Belsen memorial did not calm the storm of protest of Jewish organizations, nor did it satisfy legislators of both houses of Congress, church leaders, and some prominent individuals. Newt Gingrich, the future leader of the Republican majority in the House of Representatives, was among the conservative Republican opponents of the president's appearance at Bitburg. Gingrich of Georgia and Vin Weber of Minnesota called Bitburg the "Watergate of symbolism," and expressed concern about its potential unfavorable effect on the Republican party. During the White House ceremony at which Reagan awarded author Elie Wiesel the Congressional Gold Medal for Achievement, Wiesel, then still chairman of the U.S. Holocaust Memorial Council, appealed to the president that his place was not with the SS but with the victims of the SS.[2] Reagan, who was told by Kohl that a cancellation of the Bitburg visit "would have a serious psychological effect on the friendly sentiments of the German people for the United States of America and the Reagan administration" and might even topple his government, decided to stick to the original plan and not to disappoint his friend and ally.

The confrontational course of some of the White House advisers involved in Kohl's visit, such as antisemitic right-wing Republican Patrick Buchanan, made things even more difficult. But as Reagan's Secretary of State George Shultz recalled in *Turmoil and Triumph*, the person most responsible for preventing any compromise on the controversial visit was the German chancellor. Shultz, who accompanied Reagan even though he and the State Department had not played any major role in the preparation of the visit, felt that Kohl exaggerated the threat to his government: "His unbending iron will did seem to demonstrate a massive insensitivity, on the one hand, to the troubles he was causing Ronald Reagan, and on the other hand, to the trauma this episode caused to the Jewish community around the world, and beyond the Jewish community, to all who remembered the Holocaust and its horrors."

While Shultz remained critical of the Bitburg affair, he nevertheless paid tribute in his memoirs to Ronald Reagan's "stubborn determination and willingness to do what he considered to be right, regardless of the apparent political fall-out."[3] A few years later, Shultz complained again about Kohl's lack of sensitivity when the chancellor was reminded at high-level talks of the involvement of German companies in setting up a poison gas factory in Libya. That involvement of German industrial enterprises in the development of nonconventional weapons by Libya as well as by Iraq triggered protests by a number of American Jewish organizations. In March 1989, Seymour Reich, B'nai B'rith president who also served as chairman of the Presidents Conference, discussed the matter with Kohl, warning that it might affect the Jewish-German relationship throughout the world.[4]

In his confrontation with American Jewry over Bitburg, Reagan drew unequivocal support from former secretary of state Henry Kissinger, who had never been particularly sensitive to Jewish complaints regarding Germany. Later, Kissinger opposed the siting of the Holocaust Memorial Museum in Washington, preferring New York. Arthur Burns, the American ambassador in Bonn, on the contrary, regarded the Bitburg decision as ill-conceived and, as a Jew, understood the feelings of moral outrage voiced by the visit's opponents. Because he did not wish to hurt Kohl, whom he regarded as one of the staunchest friends of the United States, and also because of fear of reawakening antisemitism if American-German relations were to be seriously damaged, he advised President Reagan to stick to his planned route. However, Burns concluded from the affair that the reconciliation between the German public and other peoples of the world was less complete than generally supposed and that the German nation could not escape the historical burden of the responsibility for the Holocaust.[5]

For a number of years, American Jewish–German relations had centered on exchanges of views between the Jewish leadership and West German government officials, on Jewish complaints about neo-Nazism and demands regarding the statute of limitations, on intercession in favor of Israeli interests, and, since 1980, on the mutual visitors programs. Now, because of President Reagan's controversial visit to Bitburg and its implications, the focus temporarily shifted back to the relationship between the American Jewish community and Washington. All attempts to intercede on Bitburg with the Federal Republic's government were unsuccessful, and Israel remained on the sidelines. In fact, its dependence on the friendship and financial assistance of the Reagan administration and the support of West Germany continued to be a mitigating factor in the response of the major Jewish organizations to the challenge.

In principle, the entire Jewish community was united in its opposition to the demonstrative visit of the American and German leaders to the Bitburg cemetery, albeit there remained the traditional differences regarding the organizations' emphases and actions. As soon as the definite schedule of Reagan's trip to Europe had been officially announced, the AJC protested discreetly to the

White House and tried to obtain nonsectarian support from different religious denominations, black and white ethnic organizations, and other groups. Behind the scenes, in talks with Reverend Billy Graham, the president's close friend, and Michael Deaver, who was organizing Reagan's trip, AJC officials proposed to reconceptualize it: instead of Bitburg, dramatize American-German reconciliation by a visit to the grave of Konrad Adenauer or the Remagen Rhine Bridge. But although Reagan and Kohl went to the Adenauer grave, Bitburg was not canceled. The only achievement of the AJC intermediaries was that the president agreed to reduce the visit to the Bitburg cemetery to a perfunctory ceremony, without making any statement there.[6] Former associate Supreme Court justice Arthur Goldberg, a past president of the AJC, was disappointed by the Committee's (and everyone else's) "under reaction" to the events,[7] but the majority of the organization favored the moderate course. This was because of both AJC contacts with the administration and its interest in not damaging its relations and programs with its German counterparts.

In Washington, D.C., on the day Reagan visited Bitburg, the Committee was instrumental in organizing a memorial ceremony at Arlington National Cemetery instead of a public demonstration at Lafayette Park across from the White House. Since shouting and placards were not permitted at Arlington, it made sure that the anti-Reagan component would be minimized.[8] Having been in the forefront of the new mutual relationship with West German political foundations, AJC leaders also tried to change the mind of the Kohl government, but their intercession in Bonn bore no results. This did not prevent them from hosting West German deputy foreign minister Alois Mertes, who fully supported Kohl's point of view, as guest of honor at their annual meeting in New York during the same week as Kohl's and Reagan's visit to Bitburg.[9]

Before the wreath-laying ceremony in Bitburg, disapproving statements condemning the visit were made by all the main American Jewish organizations—B'nai B'rith, ADL, JWV, AJ Congress, the Union of American Hebrew Congregations, different Zionist and Orthodox groups, and others. Among the first to speak out against Reagan was Menahem Rosensaft, founding chairman of the International Network of Children of Jewish Holocaust Survivors, who later staged a protest demonstration at the site of the Jewish memorial at Bergen-Belsen.[10] The liberal AJ Congress vented its protest in a wreath-laying ceremony at the Munich graves of Hans and Sophie Scholl, young students executed by the Nazis in 1943 for their resistance activities as part of the White Rose group, but the White Rose Foundation set up by the AJ Congress soon folded.[11] Israel Singer, chief executive of the WJC, accused key leaders of the community of engaging in "whitewash" and acting as defenders of the Reagan administration. For the New York–based international umbrella organization chaired by Edgar Bronfman, the controversy served as an opportunity to reemerge as a more militant factor, particularly with regard to Germany. Bronfman went so far as to suggest that the leaders of Jewish communities in seventy countries contact the U.S. ambassador and demand that President Reagan not visit Bitburg.[12] This was a major change from the moderate accommodating course of Nahum Goldmann and his successor Philip Klutznick, and complemented the WJC's turn toward an activist position in the campaign for Soviet Jewry. In the long run the WJC would translate its activism into spearheading the campaign for the restitution of Jewish property in Eastern Europe and the recovery of Jewish assets from the neutral countries, most of which helped the German economy in World War II.

However, not only the AJC but also several other major agencies concluded immediately after the Bitburg event that continuing the confrontation with the administration would be self-defeating. Despite their disappointment with Kohl, they also applied the same conclusion to the Federal Republic. Abraham Foxman, associate national director of ADL, recalled President Reagan's support of Israel, his use of the Air Force to rescue Ethiopian Jews, and his help for Soviet Jewry.[13] Morris Abram, chairman of the National Conference on Soviet Jewry and a past president of the AJC, stated in the *New York Times* that "Bitburg was the mistake of a friend—not of an enemy."[14] In a similar vein, Kenneth J. Bialkin, chairman of the Presidents Conference, mentioned Reagan's consistent support for Israel and world Jewish affairs and praised his speeches at Bergen-Belsen and the U.S. airbase in Bitburg, which confirmed Jewish "confidence in his compassion and understanding."[15]

Presumably, the American Jewish establishment took into account that the reaction of Israel's leadership to Bitburg was rather subdued. Shimon Peres, Israel's prime minister at that time, expressed "deep pain" at the American president's visit to Bitburg, while reaffirming his belief that Reagan was "a true friend of the

Jewish people and the State of Israel," and so did President Chaim Herzog. Israel's ambassador Yitzhak Ben-Ari attended the wreath-laying ceremony at Bergen-Belsen that was boycotted by the Jewish community. A few prominent individuals, including former prime minister Menachem Begin, reacted angrily, but Israel's concern was mainly confined to press comments.[16]

President Reagan's decision to attend the wreath-laying at Bitburg encountered bipartisan opposition in both houses of Congress and was criticized in editorials in some of the major dailies, news magazines, and journals. Leading conservative columnists, however, including consistent friends of Israel like George Will, endorsed Reagan's perseverance in going through with the planned visit. On the church level, public support for the Jewish position in the confrontation over Bitburg came mainly from mainstream Protestant denominations, whereas most of the evangelical groups (except for controversial Jerry Falwell of the Moral Majority), who usually showed more understanding for Israel's policies, remained silent. Reverend Billy Graham, a friend of both Reagan and the Jews, preferred to intervene privately.

Among the conservatives, only the American Legion and other veterans organizations stood up to the president, because they were incensed by the choice of Bitburg. Some of the SS soldiers interred there had committed crimes against American servicemen during the Battle of the Bulge.[17] Contrary to the unprecedented 82 to 0 resolution against the visit adopted by the U.S. Senate and the letter signed by the majority of the House, a *Washington Post–ABC News* public opinion poll taken in April showed that only a slim majority of Americans disapproved of Reagan's going to Bitburg (52 percent against, 44 percent in favor, the rest offered no opinion). According to that poll, 51 percent thought that by laying a wreath at Bitburg cemetery, Reagan would not dishonor Holocaust victims, compared with 33 percent in disagreement and 16 percent who were not sure. A *USA Today* poll published ten days before Bitburg reported a 52 percent disapproval rate, compared with an 88 percent disapproval of American Jews. Another *Washington Post–ABC News* poll published ten days after the event found that 60 percent of Americans felt that "Jews were making too big a deal over Reagan's visit."[18]

A more detailed analysis prepared by Roper several months later showed that there was no linkage between approval or disapproval and antisemitism in this case. On the contrary, young people born after the end of World War II and the better educated, who were less antisemitic, approved of Bitburg more than the average because they saw Reagan's visit as a contribution to international amity and the healing of old wounds. The elderly and less educated approved less than the average, although they tended to be more antisemitic. The higher disapproval ratio of blacks reflected their general disapproval of the president. But contrary to Jewish expectations, the disapproval ratio of liberals was a little lower than that of conservatives, presumably because of their support of reconciliation with the former enemy.[19] Political analyst William Schneider, writing in October 1985 in the *National Journal,* pointed out that thanks to his standing up to the critics of his visit to Bitburg, Reagan reversed his approval rating, which had begun to fall after his second inauguration.[20]

In contrast to the fluctuating American response, Kohl's insistence on Bitburg enjoyed the solid support of West German public opinion. Sixty-four percent regarded Reagan's visit there as a sign of American-German reconciliation; in the eyes of 79 percent, all the interred at Bitburg were German soldiers and not Nazis, and 90 percent of those polled argued that the young German generation must not feel guilty of the crimes of the Holocaust.[21] The confrontation also provoked antisemitic outbursts in major West German publications. Reviving traditional antisemitic canards such as Jewish money power, cleverness, and conspiracy, the popular weekly magazine *Quick,* based in Munich, reminded its readers that American Jews were doing everything they could to sabotage an honorable German-American reconciliation and reopen German wounds. The respectable conservative *Frankfurter Allgemeine Zeitung* argued in an editorial that Jews should be careful not to overstrain relations because the consequences could be negative for them and for Israel.[22]

According to George Shultz, even such a high German official as Helmut Teltschik, for many years Chancellor Kohl's foreign policy and national security adviser, found it necessary to mention— in a talk with Assistant Secretary of State Richard Burt—that in view of American Jewish influence, as demonstrated before Reagan's visit, young Germans were saying "they now understood the problem Germany faced prior to World War II."[23] In an open letter addressed by Alfred Dregger, the right-wing chairman of the CDU parliamentary group, to Senator Howard Metzenbaum and other cosigners of an appeal to the president to reconsider his visit to Bitburg, he described their action as an insult to his brother and his comrades who had been killed on the eastern front in defense of their homeland. Dregger used the apologetic version that the German people "was subjugated by a brown dictatorship for twelve years," but there was no word about the Nazi guilt for murdering the Jews.[24] The Social Democrats' motion accusing Kohl of injuring U.S.-German relations was rejected by a small margin, but a more meaningful motion of the Greens to condemn the visit to Bitburg received only the party's own twenty-four votes.[25]

Nevertheless, more important than the perfunctory challenge of the opposition parties in the Bundestag were the dissenting voices of prominent individuals who rejected the chancellor's course; while they could not reverse his policy, they still carried some moral weight. Jürgen Habermas, West Germany's foremost left-liberal social philosopher, challenged the chancellor's "defusing the past," as he would rebuff one year later Ernst Nolte's attempt to "relativize" the Holocaust at the start of the Historians' Debate.[26] President Richard von Weizsäcker's address a few days after Bitburg, on the fortieth anniversary of Nazi Germany's unconditional surrender on May 8, 1945, had an especially great impact.[27] Relying on the Baal Shem Tov that "the secret of redemption lies in remembrance," Weizsäcker told the German people that the only way to come to terms with the shame and horror of their past was by continuing to remember it. While Weizsäcker rejected collective guilt, as his predecessors had done, he advised all those who directly experienced the Holocaust years to quietly ask themselves about their involvement then. Although the German president had no executive power, the moral weight of his speech helped to limit the damage caused by Bitburg to American Jewish–German relations since 1985.

In the same week of Weizsäcker's address, SPD chairman Willy Brandt called upon his countrymen to dispose of the false euphemism regarding what happened "in the name of the German people," which had been used since the early days of the Federal Republic. He asked them to recognize that dreadful deeds had happened in their country and were performed by Germany itself.[28]

At a post-Bitburg analysis, the main questions posed by the AJC staff to a national advisory panel of prominent participants related to the possible backlash in the United States over Jewish reaction to the trip, and the effect of the episode on U.S.–West German as well as on Jewish-German relations. The comments noted that antisemitism was permanent in the United States, "like the disease, herpes, it never goes away forever, flares up occasionally, but is not fatal." There should be no overreaction to what had happened; in the short run, efforts should be made to cultivate relationships with key administration officials. Helmut Sonnenfeldt, a former member of the NSC staff and the State Department's planning council, approached the issue mainly from the viewpoint of America's national interest. Like his mentor Kissinger, he thought the administration would have been better served if it had done more to explain the political background of the Bitburg visit. The greatest danger was that Bitburg might have aroused antisemitic and anti-American feelings among the German Right, which had been quiescent; whereas anti-American attitudes had existed on the left, now Left and Right together might destabilize the German political process. The consensus of the entire panel was that the AJC should not dwell upon the Bitburg affair any longer. Whether the anti-Jewish feeling generated by the controversy was episodic or more symptomatic of a larger problem, the Bitburg visit itself was not a continuing event. Keeping it alive would only bring about the backlash the community wanted to avoid.[29]

Stuart Eizenstat, chief domestic adviser to former president Jimmy Carter, drew other conclusions. He thought that Bitburg would always remain a major incident from the Jewish community's standpoint, whereas for the non-Jewish community it was a footnote. In terms of how the Holocaust would be remembered, perhaps there was a silver lining: "The whole debate that was engendered by the Bitburg incident tended to elevate the historical significance of the Holocaust to a level that it would not have had in terms of general consciousness were it not for the incident. . . . To that extent, it could even have led to a greater sensitivity by a greater number of people to the tragedy of the Holocaust."[30]

Differing appraisals could also be found among Jewish authors and intellectuals. To quote a few views, for Mark Krupnick, professor of English at the University of Wisconsin, writing in the *Christian Century*, the effect of President Reagan's and Chancellor Kohl's decision to sacrifice the Jews to political expedience had been mainly positive: "The Bitburg fiasco has awakened a whole new generation of American-born Jews to the isolation and vulnerability of the Jewish condition." This was very important because "Jewish piety toward the past cannot depend solely on those who experienced the Nazi terror at firsthand."[31]

In the context of the emerging controversy over the uniqueness of Jewish lessons of the Holocaust, Michael Walzer's message in *Congress Monthly*, the liberal mouthpiece of the American Jewish Congress, was universalistic: "Nazism was evil set loose in the world, and the protest against Reagan's Bitburg visit was an insistence that the evil not be forgotten or forgiven. In the 1930s and 40s, the evil stench ran with terrible force, but we are not the only actual or potential victims. Nazi-like regimes pose a general threat to all that is decent in human life. We are, perhaps, uniquely ready to recognize that threat, and that is the only uniqueness we should claim in the modern world."[32]

Indiana University scholar Alvin Rosenfeld held an opposite view. Referring to the tension between the "universal" and the "unique," he thought that memory placed primary historical demands upon the Jewish people: Jews should "remember what happened not, in the first place, to prevent a given ever from happening again, but because it already has happened—and has happened to them." They should know the truth about the world they live in and also see to it that the dead of the Holocaust are not overtaken by oblivion.[33]

Charles Silberman, author of *A Certain People*, was reassured in his optimistic view of the Jewish future in America: "Nothing could be more significant than the absence of any significant upturn in anti-Semitism . . . a large majority supported [the Jews'] right to protest, and roughly half the population opposed the President's visit. For all the pain it brought, therefore, the Bitburg incident demonstrated that for American Jews, the United States is now home as well as haven; once characterized as 'eternal strangers,' Jews are now natives, free to assert their pain and anger—able and willing to 'speak truth to power.'"[34]

Midge Decter in *Commentary* was mainly critical of the German chancellor: "To insist upon hallowing the earth that contains SS bodies is not an act that in any way serves to relieve one of penitence. Rather, it is an act that retroactively denies the need to have repented in the first place. As for American Jews, forgiving the Germans is not and has not for a very long time now been much of a problem. It is the forgetting—their own as well as others'—that troubles them."[35]

Lucy Dawidowicz, a veteran contributor to the same journal and a historian who dedicated her most important work, *The War Against the Jews, 1933–1945*, to the memory of the murdered European Jews, revisited Berlin a few months after Bitburg. She was impressed by the Federal Republic's stable and successful democracy and was struck by the desire of many Germans to learn more about Jews and Jewish civilization as "a form of moral education." In her opinion, the curse wherewith any Jew was entitled to curse the German nation to eternal hell was "finally inadequate."[36] But, as developments in Germany were soon to prove, her conclusion that "with the virtual disappearance of neo-Nazi parties, the era of anti-Semitism in German political history has come to an end" was overly optimistic. Even in 1985, she overlooked the fact that legislation against the denial of the Holocaust (the so-called Auschwitz-Lüge) was passed by the Bundestag only after the right-of-center coalition linked it with putting on trial those who disregarded atrocities committed against the German people at the end of World War II.

Bitburg had reopened Jewish wounds and caused disappointment with Kohl's government. However, the crisis of the spring of 1985 did not interrupt the American Jewish–German relationship that had been institutionalized since the beginning of the decade. The reasons that had motivated Jewish groups to enter that relationship persisted despite Bitburg, whereas the Germans, regardless of their political victory, multiplied their efforts in order to limit the damage of the affair in the American Jewish community.

In an address to the Board of Governors of B'nai B'rith in May 1985, two weeks after Bitburg, the West German ambassador urged Jewish-German reconciliation and called for a "solid, long-term basis" of that relationship.[37] The youth exchange with ADL and B'nai B'rith, which had been planned for some time, was now finally implemented. Another group of youngsters chosen by the ADL participated together with several hundred American youth leaders in Berlin's 750th anniversary celebration in 1987. A delegation of the AJC that visited West Germany in October 1985 felt that "the Federal Republic now is truly a democracy" and that its political structure was "fairly close to that of the U.S." Jews appeared to be fully accepted, and there was but a modicum of antisemitism and neo-Nazism left in Germany. Yet, the future of the Jewish community there was viewed as being dim: not enough Jews were left, and their number was below the "critical mass" necessary to have an impact on the social, cultural, or economic life of Germany.[38]

President Weizsäcker, who earned much praise in the Jewish community for speaking up against forgetting the Nazi past, was awarded the Burton Joseph humanitarian prize by the ADL;[39] the same award had been conferred upon Willy Brandt in the 1970s. In November 1988, Weizsäcker welcomed a delegation of one hundred New Yorkers, major contributors to the city's UJA Federation, led by former Auschwitz and Buchenwald inmate Ernest Michel, who came to Germany to commemorate the fiftieth anniversary of *Kristallnacht*.[40] Weizsäcker's daughter and two speechwriters of the chancellor were among the young Germans who visited the United States in the exchange program between the AJC and the Adenauer Foundation.[41] In cooperation with the JLC, the American Federation of Teachers, and the ADL, German educators observed the teaching of Jewish history and the Holocaust at American schools;[42] in 1990 the Friedrich Ebert Foundation published a first study of the American Jewish community, which was to be used by German educators and public opinion molders.[43] There were also pilot projects such as "Bridge of Understanding," coordinated in Germany by Professor Hans-Adolf Jacobsen, a noted political scientist at Bonn University. Jacobsen hosted Jewish students on behalf of the Foreign Office and the German Academic Exchange (DAAD, Deutscher Akademischer Austauschdienst), in cooperation with the B'nai B'rith Hillel Foundation.[44]

In 1988, the ADL participated in a major survey of the Center for Research of Antisemitism in Berlin. The Allensbach poll, which was commissioned in that context by the ADL and carried out among 2,500 Germans over the age of sixteen in September and October 1987, showed that 8 percent of all West Germans were still "vehemently" antisemitic and an additional 15 percent had a "definite anti-Jewish prejudice." But among Germans below the age of thirty, the part of those with anti-Jewish prejudices fell to 9 percent compared to 27 percent for persons over sixty. As for the future, 67 percent thought that forty years after the war the Germans "should stop talking so much about persecution of Jews." According to that poll, most antisemites were also anti-Arab, anti-Turkish, and generally anti-foreign, whereas those who supported Israel's security also tended to support the Palestinian cause. That last finding contradicted American Jewish assumptions. Thus, the ADL representative maintained there was a link between antisemitism and anti-Zionism and argued against the "futility and artificiality of trying to separate these attitudes into airtight compartments," which was a widespread notion in parts of European and American public opinion.[45]

In 1987, another prestigious program aimed at furthering mutual understanding between American Jews and postwar Germany was inaugurated. Recognizing "that the American Jewish community plays an important role in shaping American attitudes toward Germany," the Atlantik-Brücke, the German partner of the American Council on Germany, initiated, together with the AJC, yearly conferences that rotated between the United States and Germany. Since the 1950s, Atlantik-Brücke had devoted itself to improving German-American relations; its membership comprised leading representatives of German political, academic, financial, and other elite groups. Because of the triangular link, in 1994 Israel was added. As one of the participants summarized the first conference, the results were still disappointing and confirmed the existence of a vacuum in both communication and understanding: "The Germans are unclear about who American Jews are, do not fully understand, and sometimes misunderstand, their sensitivities regarding Germany. American Jews, on the other hand, see Germany as locked in a time warp of twelve years, 1933–1945, and do not fully appreciate the development of a democratic Germany since 1945."[46]

In the words of Alvin Rosenfeld, bridging the gap of mutual perceptions remained a major obstacle. Any German attempt to reinterpret the past in more "normal" terms directly challenged Jewish historical memory; conversely, Jewish memories impeded "German desires for a reconciliation with their past." Even German efforts to establish and maintain good relations with Israel had not received much attention among the broader strata of American Jews. Nonetheless, the importance of this issue was constantly stressed by most Jewish delegates at the AJC–Atlantik-Brücke meetings.

Summarizing the first conference, the American participants stated that both as Americans and as Jews, their feelings regarding West Germany were negative. The basic reason for this was the immense power of the memory of the Holocaust: "To overcome this negative attitude, American Jews must feel that Germans are not denying the past, and then they would be willing to learn more about Germany today." Both Americans and Germans were of one mind about the shortcomings of the media in their coverage of American Jews and Germans. Too often, American reporters in Germany focused exclusively on the negative, whereas the German media reinforced the stereotype of the hostile "Jewish lobby" instead of dealing with the deeper causes of American concern.[47]

Besides Bitburg and German resentment caused by the WJC's campaign against Austrian president and former UN secretary general Kurt Waldheim, who served in the German army in the Balkans, the projected Holocaust Memorial Museum in Washington became the subject of another bitter American Jewish–German confrontation. Since the early 1980s, Chancellor Kohl's strong opposition to that project had been no secret. German participants in the annual encounters of the AJC and Atlantik-Brücke repeatedly pointed to the damage that such a museum would inflict upon the image of the West German republic, whose liberal democratic system and contribution to the defense of the Western free world would not be reflected there.[48] However, in spite of some differences of opinion in the Jewish community with regard to the museum's location near the hallowed memorials of George Washington and Thomas Jefferson, the resolve of the committed individuals and donors to complete the museum as soon as possible was only reaffirmed by the Bitburg incident. Moreover, contrary to Bitburg, in the Jewish endeavor of building the museum no conflict of interest with American foreign policy was involved.

Well-versed American Jews watching the German scene were also worried by the repercussions of the *Historikerstreit*, during which conservative and revisionist historians attempted to relativize Nazi Germany's guilt for the murder of the Jews. In the 1986–87 controversy, however, the liberal historians' insistence on the uniqueness of the Holocaust had the upper hand.[49] Before that, American Jewish organizations had registered the resurfacing of anti-Jewish sentiments with the staging of Rainer Werner Fassbinder's controversial play, *Garbage, the City, and Death*, at Frankfurt's municipal theater. In this case, anti-Jewish prejudices were indirectly defended, mainly by leftists and liberals, on the principle of free speech. The performance was finally canceled after members of the local Jewish community—among them Ignatz

Bubis, who would soon emerge as the influential leader of the Jews in Germany—had occupied the stage on the first night and persisted in their protests. In contrast to the Bitburg affair, this time the Jewish community was supported by conservative politicians and critics.[50]

For understandable reasons, the sector of the American public that most enthusiastically welcomed the American-German reconciliation over the graves at Bitburg were nationalistic-minded German Americans. Although their views and attitudes had no major impact on the relations between American Jewry and West Germany, and united Germany after 1990, their actions were, of course, harmful. In 1977, plans to introduce Holocaust studies in New York high schools drew fire from the German American Committee of Greater New York headed by George Pape, who happened to be a relative of Karl Carstens, the Federal Republic's fifth president. That experimental curriculum was also opposed by Arab-American spokesmen. Pape at first stated that there was no real proof that the Holocaust happened. Later he tried to relativize its horrors by equating the killing of the Jews with "the countless civilians . . . slaughtered for political purposes during the last half century."[51]

Efforts of the German consulate general in New York to help improve strained relations between Jewish and German-American organizations by denouncing the distribution of inflammatory material on the part of irresponsible groups were not effective because of the deep chasm dividing the communities. Proposals to have the *Aufbau*, the German Jewish immigrants' weekly, participate in the annual German American Steuben parade did not materialize.[52] The German American National Political Action Committee (GANPAC), a radical right-wing group founded in 1982 by Hans Schmidt to fight anti-German sentiment in the media and promote Holocaust revisionism, cooperated with the anti-Holocaust Institute for Historical Review in Santa Monica, California.[53] At the peak of the Bitburg crisis, Elsbeth M. Seewald, president of the German American National Congress (DANK), who enjoyed good contacts with the West German government and received some financial support from Bonn, appealed to members of the House of Representatives in favor of the planned visit by President Reagan and against dishonoring German war dead. Two years later she published an open letter to members of the Senate protesting the blacklisting of Austrian president Waldheim by the OSI, which prevented him from revisiting the United States.[54]

In the early postwar period, German American nationalistic groups were relatively isolated and only gradually earned the confidence of the diplomatic representatives of the Federal Republic. In the 1980s they enjoyed a measure of respectability with both German and American authorities. In October 1987, President Reagan proclaimed an annual German-American Day and thus acceded to the request of DANK and other German American organizations. All these groups had a clear preference for the conservative government in Bonn, as well as for the Republicans in American politics. In 1988, a flier paid for by GANPAC warned German Americans and other citizens not to vote for Democratic presidential candidate Michael Dukakis unless they wanted more Holocaust studies in their schools. The *Steuben News,* the official publication of the Steuben Society of America, "a patriotic organization comprised of American citizens of German ancestry," usually was in the forefront of the fight against deportation of "loyal German Americans" because of alleged Nazi war crimes.[55]

In all, events in the 1980s were a reminder of the fragility of the complex American Jewish–German relationship. On the strictly political level, Bitburg was a victory for both Reagan and Kohl over Jewish pressure. But the depth of Jewish opposition resulting from Holocaust consciousness robbed the German chancellor of some of the fruits of his victory. It also threw a shadow on the staged reconciliation ceremonies, revived Jewish suspicions of postwar Germany, and damaged German efforts to improve relations with American Jewry, the least friendly sector of American public opinion toward the Federal Republic. To find ways to bridge the gap between the Jewish historical memory of the Holocaust and the German quest for more normalcy and a new sense of national identity, regardless of the events of the past, remained the difficult task of the American Jewish–German exchanges that continued despite Bitburg. However, doubts persisted as to how much these institutionalized relations reflected the true feelings of the majority of American Jews toward Germany. Probably they remained more hostile.

PART V

AMERICAN JEWS
and
EAST GERMANY

17

From Grotewohl to de Maizière

On April 12, 1990, after the demise of the Communist regime, the German Democratic Republic accepted German historic responsibility for the murder of the Jewish people during World War II. At least for the record, that declaration of the first freely elected East German parliament—the *Volkskammer* (People's Chamber)—went much further than Chancellor Adenauer's statement of September 27, 1951, before the Bundestag. However, it was made only a few months before unification of Germany was agreed upon, and the outstanding issues of restitution and indemnification were transferred to the government of the enlarged Federal Republic in Bonn.

Thus, the unhappy chapter of American Jewry's relationship with East Germany, even though it had played only a marginal role in Jewish perceptions of postwar Germany, came to an end. Early denazification in the East had been much more stringent than in the Western zones, and there had never been a statute of limitations. However, the Cold War climate, the persistent anti-Israel stance of the Communist regime since the early 1950s, its unwillingness to recognize German responsibility for the Holocaust, as well as its refusal to satisfy Jewish demands for restitution of property, indemnification, and compensation—these factors had stiffened the negative attitude of the American Jewish community toward the GDR for many years.

In the first years after the war, as mentioned in an earlier chapter of this study, the most urgent American Jewish concern with regard to defeated and occupied Germany was to secure the well-being of concentration and slave labor camp survivors and of the growing number of refugees from Poland, Soviet Russia, and other East European nations that swelled the population of the assembly centers in the U.S. zone in southern Germany and western Austria.[1] Even though thousands of these refugees crossed the territory of the Soviet occupation zone on their way, they did not settle there. In contrast to the Jewish communities outside the DP camps in the Western zones, which comprised growing numbers of East European survivors and refugees, the small communities in the Soviet zone consisted mainly of surviving German Jews. Subsequently, exiles returned, among them active Communists as well as renowned pro-Communist and leftist intellectuals, authors, and artists. For a number of years they were to play an important role in the cultural and political life there, although with a few exceptions they did not join the communities. In the early period, East Berlin Jews enjoyed substantial philanthropic help from the JDC, as did the western part of the still united community. Later East German Jewish spokesmen were urged to denounce the JDC operatives as agents of American imperialism.[2]

In its first pronouncements after the war, the German Communist Party, soon to merge with the East German Social Democrats into the Socialist Unity Party (Sozialistische Einheitspartei Deutschlands, SED), reminded fellow Germans of their guilt and responsibility for the war and the murderous deeds. Its leaders recalled the memory of the victims of the Nazi terror but with no special emphasis on the Jewish catastrophe. In the first years after the war, the suppression of the Third Reich elites and of Nazi party activists by the Soviet military government and the East German authorities was far more radical than the measures taken by the American, British, and French in their zones. As already stressed in the first part of this study, the Western powers favored the integration of most of the German elites and their participation in the revival of the West German economy and the development of a stable democratic and anti-Soviet West German state. Yet, except for marginal Communist and pro-Communist groups, in the deteriorating climate of East-West relations, mainstream American Jewish organizations would never point to East German handling of the former economic and social elites as an example that should be followed. Moreover, denazification in the Soviet zone ended formally sooner than in the West because of the regime's simplistic antifascist legitimation. For the record, Thuringia, one of the East German provinces, had in 1945 been the first in all Germany to enact a law of restitution. This exceptional process, however, did not last longer than two years because of the change of East Germany's indemnification policy and the abolition of the status of the provinces. The preferential pensions and social benefits granted to Jews as "victims of Fascism" were somewhat lower than those of anti-Nazi (mainly Communist) resistance fighters, but still very much above the average. They were supposed to satisfy the needs of East German Jews, instead of indemnification or restitution of property as discussed and legislated in the West.[3]

East Germany's hostility toward Zionism and the State of Israel gradually increased after the early 1950s. In 1948, before the establishment of Israel and during its War of Independence, the Jewish community there enjoyed short-lived sympathy from the leaders of the ruling Socialist Unity Party. That attitude was in line with Soviet support for the emerging Jewish state, which they hoped would help to evict the British from the Middle East and perhaps also encourage at least a part of American Jewry to oppose the anti-Soviet course of the Truman administration. Early in 1948, the party's central committee welcomed the UN decision to divide Palestine into Jewish and Arab states and called the creation of the Jewish state an important contribution to enabling Hitler's victims to build new lives for themselves. In May the party daily *Das Neue Deutschland* condemned Arab air attacks on the new nation, which had just declared its independence.[4]

Chaim Yachil (Hoffmann), who represented the Jewish Agency for Palestine in occupied Germany and afterwards became Israel's first consul in Munich accredited to the American military government, and Eliyahu Livneh, who succeeded him a year later, met in April 1948 with Otto Grotewohl, co-chairman of the SED and from October 1949 the GDR's first prime minister. As part of indemnities, they discussed the possibility of East German help for the emigration of Jews from the DP camps in the American zone to the emerging Jewish state. But Grotewohl's suggestions with regard to East German ships and a global payment did not prove to be realistic at a time of the Berlin blockade and growing East-West tension in Germany.[5]

Nonetheless, expressions of goodwill from East Berlin in the summer of 1948 continued. Wilhelm Pieck, the Communist chairman of the SED and after the establishment of the GDR its first president, congratulated Jews in Palestine and in Germany on the proclamation of Israel's independence, and the rejoicing small Jewish communities in the Soviet zone hoisted the blue and white flag. In an article in the East Berlin journal *Die Weltbühne*, Leo Zuckermann, Pieck's assistant, acknowledged the Jewish right to restitution and compensation. On this issue he followed in the footsteps of another former Mexican exile, the veteran gentile Communist Paul Merker, who had dealt with the uniqueness of the Jewish catastrophe in his writings during the war years and continued to support financial indemnification for all surviving German Jews after his return to East Germany in 1946. In 1948, Merker emphatically expressed his solidarity with the Jewish people and his support for Israel. In 1952, he was imprisoned and condemned as an American and "imperialist agent," and even after the revision of his verdict in 1956, he was never fully rehabilitated.[6]

As the late East German historian Olaf Groehler pointed out in his analysis of the GDR's treatment of the Holocaust and the Jewish problem, a number of Communist exiles in the West such as Merker distinguished themselves both from the Moscow exiles and from those incarcerated in Germany during the Third Reich. Whereas the two latter groups regarded the Jewish question and therefore also the Holocaust as part of the class struggle and totally subordinated the racial antisemitism of the Nazi regime to its anti-Communism, those who found refuge during that period in the West—whether Jews or gentiles—revealed more understanding for the central role of antisemitism in Nazi ideology and politics.[7]

The friendly welcome by the East German SED and the Soviet Union, as well as Israel's insistence on a policy of nonalignment with both the two rival blocs, explained in part the cool reception of the new Jewish state by West Germany's Social Democrats. The party was also angered by Mapai's hostility toward them in COMISCO, the predecessor of the revived Socialist International. The Social Democrats' attitude improved after Israel's Labor-led government proceeded gradually toward a more pro-Western foreign policy.[8]

Because of their growing support for the U.S. anti-Soviet course as a result of the Cold War, American Jews, too, were interested in a clearly pro-Western orientation of the Israeli government. Leading in that direction was the AJC, but other groups and influential individuals, including Henry Morgenthau Jr., also tried to influence Israel in the same way.[9]

Several events soon caused a change in the Soviet Union's policies toward the Jewish state and the Middle East. The victory of the pro-Western Mapai in Israel's first Knesset elections in January 1949, the exclusion of the (then) pro-Soviet Mapam from Ben Gurion's coalition government, the volatile anti-Zionist Soviet reaction to the enthusiastic welcome of Golda Meir, Israel's first minister plenipotentiary, by thousands of Moscow Jews, and the Kremlin's growing disappointment with Israel's stand on international affairs contributed to this change. The hostility that replaced the short-lived friendship was further exacerbated when anti-Zionism and antisemitism became important elements in Stalin's domestic policies in the last years of his life, reaching their climax during the Doctors' Plot.[10]

Despite Israel's official stance of nonalignment, it was regarded by the Communist bloc as an ally of the "imperialist camp." Israel had, after all, politically supported the United States during the Korean War. The reversal of Moscow's attitude as well as its anti-Zionist campaign affected all East European countries as well as the GDR. Except for the prosecution of Paul Merker, who was not Jewish, no anti-Zionist show trials took place in East Germany. However, some Jews, who after the war had returned to East Germany and joined the GDR elite, were purged in the early 1950s, and a few others were arrested. Steven S. Schwarzschild, an American Reform rabbi, officiated in 1948–50 in the still united Berlin Jewish community. In June 1950, he broached with President Pieck and Otto Nuschke, the minister in charge of church affairs, the possibility of religious care for members of the Jewish faith who had been detained by the East German authorities or interned by the Russian military administration. On the same occasion, the setting up of a government office for Jewish affairs was discussed.[11] But these proposals were not implemented, and the "imperialist, fascist, plutocratic, capitalist and reactionary" rabbinate was soon condemned by a number of East German Jews in letters of resignation to their communities.

Israel's decision to open direct talks with the West German Federal Republic regarding reparations and the conclusion of the Luxembourg *shilumim* treaty added another dimension to East Germany's anti-Zionism, which aroused great fears among the members of the Jewish community. From November 1952 to March 1953, a few hundred Jews, including some of its leading members, fled from East Berlin to the West, altogether 550 from the entire GDR. Rabbi Nathan Peter Levinson, who served as rabbi in Berlin from 1950 to 1953, encouraged the exodus. The escapees included Julius Meyer, the Communist head of the Federation of East Germany's Jewish communities, Leo Zuckermann, and Albert Hirsch.[12] Jewish party members were interrogated about past and present connections with Jewish organizations or with relatives in the West. Quite a few prominent Communists who happened to be Jews were purged from their positions in the party and in East Germany's cultural life, although some of them made a comeback several years later.[13] Alexander Abusch, for instance, executive secretary of the Cultural League until 1953, served as deputy prime minister in the 1970s. Other Communists of Jewish origin such as Albert Norden and Hermann Axen were not affected by the purge and served in influential positions during the next decades.

The restitution laws based on the Potsdam Agreement of 1945 were abolished in the GDR in August 1952, shortly before the signing of the Israeli–Jewish–West German reparations treaty. However, these laws had never been of practical importance to survivors or heirs of the Jewish property owners. In general, "Aryanized" property had been taken over by the custodians and where possible nationalized but not handed back to the former "capitalist" owners.[14]

Reports about the anti-Zionist campaign in East Germany and the flight of hundreds of Jews from East to West caused much concern in the American Jewish community, even though it affected a relatively small group. Relying on information obtained by one of the leading ex-Communist refugees, the AJC alerted the American public about an alleged order by the East German Ministry of State Security to put under supervision persons who were regarded as non-Aryans or of mixed parentage. It interpreted that order as an attempt to attract neo-Nazi elements for the anti-American hate campaign. Although there was no lack of reliable and incontestable material about the difficulties encountered by Jews in

East Germany, this particular item proved incorrect.[15] But the issue served the AJC well in its campaign to educate the American Jewish community on the necessity of supporting the administration's anti-Communist policy, which was not popular among leftist groups and left-liberal individuals.

During the crisis of the winter of 1952–53, the WJC empowered Rabbi Israel Goldstein, chairman of its American executive, to check with the West Berlin Jewish community whether the WJC should appoint a field representative there, whose task would be to organize emigration of the remaining Jews from the GDR. The WJC usually took a more moderate stand with regard to the Communist regimes than the AJC and the ADL. Heinz Galinski, chairman of the West Berlin community, agreed on the condition that the emigration work would be carried out in full cooperation with the Western allies and especially the American authorities.[16] However, there was no more need for such an emergency action. The East Berlin government showed signs of being embarrassed by the exodus of a great number of Jews and its negative publicity. Thus, it decided to support the remaining communities while stressing the difference between "meritorious anti-Zionism" and "reprehensible antisemitism." In the following years sentences by East German courts for antisemitic insults were widely publicized, and more synagogues were consecrated or rededicated, including the East Berlin synagogue in the Rykestrasse, regardless of the small numbers of congregants and the lack of rabbis. From the economic viewpoint, Jews, many of whom were engaged in academic and intellectual professions, enjoyed a better life than many other citizens.

Since the early 1960s, the GDR party and state authorities tried to utilize the Jewish communities in their confrontation with the West German Federal Republic, as witnesses to East Germany's mastering the Nazi past. Eichmann's trial in Jerusalem served as an opportunity to publish in East Germany a few historical works dealing with the Holocaust without, however, infringing on the basic Communist doctrine. Here and there the Jewish communities voiced complaints regarding the population's lack of knowledge about the Nazi persecution of the Jews and occasional antisemitic manifestations. In 1978, its fortieth anniversary, the first major East German governmental commemoration of *Kristallnacht* took place, not at least because of the growing attention paid to these commemorations in West Germany. That was already a few years after East Germany had been admitted to the United Nations and established diplomatic relations with the United States. For both economic and political reasons, East Berlin gradually took the first steps to improve relations with the capitalistic West and particularly the American superpower.[17]

In all, since the crisis of the early 1950s, the small Jewish communities in East Germany enjoyed relative stability, although on different occasions their leading representatives were asked to participate in statements critical of Israel, the Federal Republic, and the United States. These efforts were not always successful. Among the signatories of an anti-Israel manifesto during the Six Day War, no members registered with the communities could be found, only the regime's devoted supporters of "Jewish origin" such as Albert Norden, Alexander Abusch, and Gerhart Eisler, the brother of the composer Hanns Eisler. With all their loyalty to the East German state, the organized Jewish communities refused to condemn Israel, and despite pressure applied by the Communist rulers, defended it on a number of issues. Even during the Lebanon war of 1982, Helmut Aris, chairman of the Association of East German Jewish communities and a SED party member, rejected all comparisons between Israel's offensive war of which he disapproved and the imperialist aggression of fascist Germany.[18]

In 1956, the fruitless East German–Israeli contacts in various East European capitals regarding Israel's demands for reparations were discontinued. The GDR's anti-Zionist and anti-Israel policy became more emphatic after the Sinai Campaign, as did all the Communist states who preferred solidarity with President Nasser's Egypt. Economic, technological, and military support of Arab nations became an important element of East Berlin's Middle East policy and also served its ongoing competition with West Germany for international recognition. Although the GDR recognized the existence of Israel and the right of self-determination of its people, from 1967 the chasm between Israel and East Germany deepened even more, and this also affected American Jewry. The PLO, which expanded its struggle against Israel and conducted terrorist activities both inside Israel and abroad, was granted military supplies, instruction, and training facilities by the GDR as well as medical treatment for the wounded. During Yassir Arafat's visit to East Berlin in 1973, the establishment of an official PLO representation was agreed upon one year before such an office opened in Moscow. In 1979, the East German regime condemned the signing of the Egyptian-Israeli peace treaty and supported the Arab rejectionist front. Anti-Israeli outbursts reached another peak during the Lebanese invasion by Israel's army in 1982. East Berlin's attitude toward Israel began to mellow only in the latter 1980s, mainly as part of its efforts to gain respectability among American Jews and advance a rapprochement with the United States.

American Jews, who at first had insisted on the full demilitarization of defeated Germany together with its thorough denazification and democratization, had to overcome great psychological difficulties in adjusting to West German rearmament in the mid-1950s. They did so because of the American national interest in strengthening the Western alliance, and also taking into account the interests of Israel, which was dependent on the *shilumim* deliveries and other kinds of German assistance. However, it was easy for them to condemn the Soviet Union's arming of East Germany's National People's Army as well as the Communist regime's laxity toward a number of former Nazis who advanced in several of its institutions and organizations.

During the 1956–57 Sinai-Suez crisis, the American Jewish community acknowledged Chancellor Adenauer's support for Israel in refusing to suspend *shilumim* shipments. This benevolent stand was diametrically opposed to that of East Germany, whose prime minister, Otto Grotewohl, called upon the Bonn government to stop the "so-called reparations" that made it possible for the "aggressive circles" of Israel to finance its struggle against the "national liberation movement of the peoples of the Middle East."[19] The Eichmann trial in 1961 did not affect the GDR's hostile attitude toward Israel, even though it dispatched to Jerusalem an observer, the lawyer Friedrich Karl Kaul, who was received by both the minister of justice and the chief prosecutor. In the context of that trial, East Berlin's main aim was to blame Adenauer and the Ben Gurion government for a secret deal according to which State Secretary Hans Globke, who had participated in drafting the Nuremberg racial laws in 1935, would not be called to testify as a witness.[20] Nonetheless, despite the continuing anti-Israel course, historian Herbert Strauss, who visited the GDR in 1963, did not find much antisemitism there. He concluded that the East Berlin propaganda machine was grateful for its small but valuable Jewish population, used it to harass the Bonn government, and rewarded it by subsidizing the existing communities.[21]

There was a further upsurge in American Jewish criticism of Communist East Germany in the mid-1960s, after East German leader Walter Ulbricht's visit to Cairo in February 1965, where he endorsed President Nasser's confrontational policies. Rabbi Joachim Prinz, chairman of the Presidents Conference, noted that whereas the Bonn regime, responding to Jewish reminders, had at least "begun the great task of moral redemption," East Germany had rebuffed every Jewish approach, rejected every appeal, ignored every demand, and at the same time encouraged "Arab adventurism" aimed against Israel. On this occasion, Prinz enumerated a list of veteran Hitler supporters who were serving in official positions in East Germany, including twenty-nine former Nazi party members in the Volkskammer.[22]

Despite the GDR's longstanding refusal to enter negotiations on restitution and collective compensation, neither Israel nor the American Jewish community had given up hope for a change of that country's attitude. Israel renewed its efforts in that direction when the admission of the two German states to the UN became imminent in 1973. It started a campaign to convince other countries to take the position that if East Germany was to be considered as a "member of the international community in good standing," it should take action on restitution and indemnification.[23] Both the American Jewish Committee and Nahum Goldmann, the WJC president, were critical of Israel's raising the issue in public. Goldmann talked about the problem with West German chancellor Willy Brandt and Egon Bahr, one of his closest advisers, and hoped he would be able to meet Erich Honecker, who in 1971 had succeeded Walter Ulbricht as the GDR's leader. But despite "friendly greetings" conveyed to Goldmann from Honecker through historian Josef Wulf, such a meeting never took place.[24]

Because of the Claims Conference's continuous involvement with West Germany, Goldmann thought the GDR might prefer to deal with another body such as the WJC, but the consensus of the major Jewish organizations was that negotiations with the East Germans about restitution and indemnification must remain in the hands of the Claims Conference.[25]

Representatives of the Jewish organizations discussed the matter with State Department officials, reminding them of American support for West German payments of restitution and compensation in the early 1950s. However, it became evident that regardless of moral support for Jewish claims, no preconditions would be made for the admission of the GDR to the UN, which took place in 1973.[26]

American Jewish expectations that things would change for the better with the establishment of diplomatic relations between Washington and East Berlin too did not materialize. Arthur Hartman, assistant secretary of state for European affairs, disappointed his Jewish interlocutors, telling them that it would not be possible to make the issue of reparations a part of the formal agreement regarding diplomatic relations with East Germany. Instead, he promised to press the GDR for a settlement of claims by victims of the Nazi persecution and by Americans whose property had been seized, as soon as diplomatic relations were established.[27] Objections by Senator Jacob Javits that a satisfactory settlement of the claims should be made a condition for normalizing relations with East Berlin were of no avail.[28] Nineteen seventy four was not 1951–52, and Henry Kissinger as secretary of state was even less supportive of Jewish demands regarding reparations than Dean Acheson had been in 1952. Moreover, for the Jewish community, which was deeply involved in its campaign for advancing free emigration of Soviet Jewry, compensation from East Germany was basically a marginal issue. All that was agreed upon was the GDR's commitment to enter into talks about unsolved property questions, which included claims of American (former German) citizens who had suffered from Nazi persecution, and that did not mean much. Again, a decade later, long after diplomatic relations between Washington and East Berlin had been established, Jewish pressure failed to move the State Department on alleviating trade with the GDR in the hope it might further an agreement about compensation.

Whereas the East German government refused to enter direct negotiations with the Claims Conference because of its status as a "private organization," it agreed that the Conference should discuss American Jewish claims with the Anti-Fascist Resistance Fighters Committee (AFC), one of its front organizations. For the next two years, Benjamin Ferencz kept in touch with the AFC on behalf of the Claims Conference, and its representatives repeatedly contacted the State Department but did not manage to obtain an appointment with the East German ambassador in Washington. Nor were they successful in promoting the idea of settling restitution claims by increased East German exports to America.[29] As a gesture of goodwill, in 1976, the AFC transferred "for humanitarian reasons" to the Claims Conference's account a symbolic sum of $1 million for U.S. citizens of Jewish faith who were victims of Nazi persecution, without implying recognition of any legal or moral claims of Nazi victims in general. Upon the advice of Nahum Goldmann, the check was returned to the East German committee.[30]

However, this was not the end of the story. During the next decade, the Claims Conference persisted in its attempts to try and make progress both by involving U.S. officials and friendly legislators as well as by directly approaching the GDR government and its Communist party leadership. A sum of $100 million as an appropriate basis for settlement of Jewish claims at first cropped up in 1977 at a meeting of representatives of the Claims Conference with David Bolen, the American ambassador to Berlin. That was, of course, much less than the third of the original reparations sum which Israel had demanded from East Germany in 1952. Rabbi Israel Miller, one of the few prominent Orthodox leaders continuously involved in negotiations with the Germans, who, after Goldmann's death in 1982, became chairman of the Claims Conference, met East German foreign minister Oskar Fischer in 1978. On that occasion, as well as during further meetings with Fischer and GDR ambassador Horst Grunert, the sum of $100 million was mentioned. Aging Nahum Goldmann, who had retired from the WJC presidency, met Grunert in 1979, but the contacts with the East Germans rested mainly in the hands of Miller and Saul Kagan, the Claims Conference's executive director. Both also told their interlocutors that a compensation payment for the Jews could be made in goods as West Germany had done in the framework of the Luxembourg agreement.[31]

A subject of special interest for East Germany was obtaining the full or at least partial Most Favored Nation (MFN) status for its exports to the United States in order to improve its negative trade balance. This became even more important because of the GDR's growing economic difficulties in the 1980s. Representatives of the Claims Conference indicated to the East Germans that they might be of help on the trade issue if at least a part of the increased GDR exports would serve to satisfy Jewish compensation demands. That idea of a package deal between compensation for Jews as well as American property claims and trade concessions to East Germany was discussed for a number of years on different levels in Washington and East Berlin.[32] Jewish congressmen such as William M. Lehman tried to be of help, and the matter of Jewish compensation claims also came up during a visit of a congressional delegation to East Berlin headed by Representative Thomas P. Lantos. Lantos, a California Democrat and Holocaust survivor from Budapest, reminded his host Honecker of their common background in fighting Nazi tyranny.[33]

At one point, Assistant Secretary of State for European Affairs Lawrence Eagleburger, who in 1992 would conclude his long diplomatic career as President Bush's last secretary of state, considered asking the Reagan White House's support for a limited MFN status for the GDR. Nonetheless, it soon became evident that the basic differences were too great for an agreement to be reached. The Reagan administration, not at all interested in helping East Germany's economy, objected to any linking of Jewish and other claims with trade concessions;[34] it insisted that, first of all, American and Jewish claims had to be settled. Conversely, the East Berlin politburo did not budge from its standpoint that the GDR had fulfilled its reparation requirements according to the 1945 Potsdam agreement and had no obligations regarding Jewish claims.[35] High-level meetings such as those between Rabbi Miller and Honecker in June 1987 in Berlin and between Hermann Axen, a politburo member and himself a survivor of Auschwitz, and American counterparts in Washington were inconclusive.[36] A frank though private confession of foreign minister Oskar Fischer, who was involved in contacts with Jewish organizations for a number of years, that both German states shared historic responsibility for what happened to the Jews, was an exception to the rule.[37] A far-reaching revision of the GDR's policy toward Jews and Israel was to take place only after the collapse of the Berlin Wall and on the verge of the GDR's disappearance from the international arena.

The meetings with the Claims Conference were only one part of East German–American Jewish contacts in the 1980s. Other groups that became involved were the AJC and the WJC. B'nai B'rith president David Blumberg was the first head of a major Jewish organization to visit East Germany in 1983, but neither B'nai B'rith nor ADL showed much interest.

Howard Friedman, president of the AJC, went there in 1984. He had been preceded in 1983 by another delegation of the AJC which met with Klaus Gysi, the East German state secretary for church affairs, and three representatives of the Jewish community. Gysi, himself partly Jewish, found the question regarding anti-semitism "insulting" and insisted upon the distinction between antisemitism and anti-Zionism.[38] At a subsequent meeting with Gysi the possibility of bringing over an American rabbi to East Berlin was broached. The AJC had been encouraged by the positive experience of another former German rabbi, Ernst Lorge, who conducted Rosh Hashanah and Yom Kippur services there in 1984. Lorge was favorably impressed by the cooperative attitude of the East German authorities and their "frank admission of all the details of the Holocaust." The gullible rabbi also sounded convinced that the majority of the young people in East Germany had accepted Communism and friendship with Russia.[39]

Gysi, who was in charge of Jewish affairs in the East German government, appreciated the contacts with the AJC because of both its important standing and its definition as a non-Zionist organization. He must not have known that in the 1980s the Committee cooperated on most things with the pro-Zionists in the Presidents Conference, which it was soon to join. In 1987, the AJC was instrumental in installing in East Berlin, after long and protracted negotiations, Rabbi Isaac Neuman of Urbana, Illinois, as the first resident rabbi since the death of Dr. Martin Riesenburger in 1965. Yet, Neuman resigned after only eight months.[40] Despite the lack of a permanent rabbi, quite a number of acculturated nonidentifying Jews joined the activities of the community in the capital, among them Communists and pro-Communists, another sign of changing times.

East Germany's contacts with the WJC, which, since Bitburg, had taken a very critical view of Kohl's conservative government, became politically even more important. In 1986, the WJC opened a worldwide campaign against Kurt Waldheim, the former UN secretary general and successful conservative candidate for the presidency of Austria, because of his wartime activities while serving with the German army in the Balkans. Although East Berlin's anti-Israel propaganda and support for the Arab cause did not yet cease, in 1986 a delegation of the East German Jewish community was allowed to attend the WJC plenary assembly in Jerusalem as observers.[41]

The Bitburg affair had revealed the chasm between American Jewish and West German attitudes regarding the Holocaust. However, despite the strong disapproval of Reagan's and Kohl's wreath-laying at Bitburg military cemetery by the East German media, the gap between American Jewry and the GDR was still deep. For many years the persecution and murder of Jews during the Nazi regime, though not played down, had been explained there mainly as a result of fascist ideology and politics. The GDR did not deal with the special background and causes of Nazi racial antisemitism and the particular historic responsibility of the German people for what had happened. Jewish peoplehood was not acknowledged; Jews were recognized only as a religious denomination; and the long-term anti-Zionist and anti-Israel hate campaign had made Israel and Zionism synonyms of aggression and expansionism.

In order to reduce that gap, East German moves to conciliate American Jewry—not for moral reasons but because of its influence on American public opinion and in Congress—were intensified in the second part of the decade. This also brought about a gradual mellowing of the hostility toward Israel. Because of its growing economic difficulties, the GDR was quite obviously interested in increasing its exports to the United States. In addition, warming up relations with Washington was important for improving the GDR's international standing. Last but not least, after his official visits to Bonn and Paris, Honecker hoped to crown his diplomatic achievements by a state visit to the United States.

In 1988, the fiftieth anniversary of the November pogrom served as a prime opportunity for the Communist East German regime to demonstrate its new approach toward Jews in both parts of Germany, in Europe, in the United States, and even in Israel. At an international press conference, the establishment of "Neue Synagoge Berlin-Centrum Judaicum," a foundation for the restoration of Berlin's largest and most famous synagogue at the Oranienburger Strasse, was proclaimed. In the anniversary week of *Kristallnacht*, many public commemorations, including a special session of the Volkskammer, took place, with invited guests from many countries, including Israel.[42] The event helped to upgrade the image of Honecker and his government, and a number of Jewish organizations were impressed by the GDR's preservation of Jewish culture. Moreover, early in 1989 upon the invitation of Yad Vashem and the WJC, whose leaders were interested in the advancement of Israeli–East German relations, an official East German delegation visited Israel. It was headed by Kurt Löffler, Klaus Gysi's successor as secretary of state for church affairs.[43] For the sake of evenhandedness, the visit was preceded by the recognition of Palestinian statehood and the granting of an embassy status to the PLO office in East Berlin. In spring of the same year, the Jewish communities in the GDR, in the past captives of the government's anti-Zionist and anti-Israel policies, were for the first time allowed to commemorate Holocaust Day and celebrate Israel's Independence Day. Characteristic of the changing attitude was also the admission of the East Berlin authorities (during the trials of skinheads who had committed acts of vandalism against Jewish objects) that fascist antisemitic occurrences could happen even in a socialist nation.

The East Berlin leadership attached special importance to the October 1988 visit of WJC president Edgar Bronfman and the delegates accompanying him. Because of Bronfman's commercial interests in Seagram's and DuPont, his personal contacts in Washington, as well as the WJC's critical view of Chancellor Kohl's policies, he was regarded as a person who might help East Germany's tottering economy and advance its political rapprochement with the United States. At the meeting with Bronfman, Honecker praised WJC's support of the tiny Jewish community in East Germany and espoused his country's antifascist legacy. Bronfman, for his part, paid tribute to the fact that the GDR had taken upon itself the responsibility for the past. With regard to Israel, two weeks before its elections, both Bronfman and Honecker agreed on their preference for Labor party leader Shimon Peres over Likud prime minister Yitzhak Shamir. At the conclusion of the meeting, Honecker conferred upon Bronfman the GDR's highest award for foreign citizens. The same award was also conferred upon Gerhart Riegner, the former secretary general of the WJC, who had visited the GDR several times and lectured on ecumenic affairs, and upon Heinz Galinski, the head of the West Berlin Jewish community.[44]

According to *Das Neue Deutschland*, Bronfman told his host that from the Jewish viewpoint he had no objection to the United States granting the GDR the MFN status and extending an invitation to its president.[45] However, the Reagan and Bush administrations were much more interested in their close relationship with the Federal Republic and made no move regarding an invitation to Honecker. Nor was any breakthrough achieved on East German reparations for Jews. In a letter to Honecker six months after their meeting in Berlin, Bronfman expressed his disappointment about the lack of any progress. In May 1989 Avi Beker, the executive director of the WJC office in Jerusalem, reminded his hosts of the urgency of fighting Palestinian terrorism and the still lacking recognition of German responsibility for the Nazi past. WJC emissary Maram Stern, for a number of years president of the Union of European Jewish Students, and WJC secretary general Israel Singer tried in vain to obtain at least a symbolic commitment from East Berlin that would help the WJC to continue its accommodating policy toward the GDR and also serve that state's interest. In July 1989, the East German embassy in Washington was told by the State Department that "an arrangement regarding the Jewish claims would decisively improve readiness and chances for a further development of the bilateral relations" but that neither at present nor in the near future was the granting of trade alleviations probable.[46]

The last chapter in the relationship between American Jewry and East Germany began after the fall of the Berlin Wall and the replacement of Honecker that preceded it. The breakdown of the Communist regime, which was already in full swing during the short term of office of Hans Modrow, the last Communist head of government, brought about a rapid change in East Berlin's attitude toward Israel and the Jewish people. In the winter of 1989–90, the Modrow government, which included in its ranks former opponents of the regime, still hoped that an international Jewish organization like the WJC might use its influence in Western capitals to prevent the unification of Germany and save the GDR's survival as a separate independent state. After all, in the first weeks after the fall of the Wall, that was the preference of France, Britain, and of other European neighbors of Germany. Gregor Gysi, Klaus Gysi's son and leader of the Partei des demokratischen Sozialismus (PDS), the successor party of the SED, came out in favor of the immediate establishment of diplomatic relations between the GDR and Israel. Two months later, he appealed to the worldwide Jewish community for global financial assistance for the GDR, because German unification would be bad for the whole world, and particularly for Jews.[47] But that appeal was of no avail.

In a letter to Bronfman in February 1990, Modrow recognized East Germany's coresponsibility for the crimes committed against the Jewish people during the Nazi period and reiterated his country's pledge to oppose racism, Nazism, and antisemitism. Modrow also was prepared to provide material support for former Jewish victims of the Nazi regime as a "humanitarian pledge,"[48] even though collective compensation was not mentioned. In Copenhagen a GDR delegation conducted talks with Israeli diplomats about establishing diplomatic relations, but they were inconclusive because of the outstanding issue of reparations. Nonetheless, in March the Modrow government conveyed to Israel's prime minister Yitzhak Shamir the same statement it had presented to the WJC president one month earlier.

In principle, the April 1990 declaration of East Germany's Volkskammer, its freely elected parliament, with regard to the German people's historic responsibility and the pledge to material recompense, fully satisfied world Jewish and Israel's demands. In July 1990, the Volkskammer also went on record as retracting the GDR's support for the UN resolution of November 1975 denouncing Zionism as a kind of racism; only the PDS members abstained.[49] Another step of the first and only democratic East German government under Lothar de Maizière was the opening of East Germany's doors to a large number of immigrants from the Soviet Union. But despite its goodwill there was no more time for a comprehensive reparations agreement (except for an understanding relating to immovable property) or for establishing diplomatic relations between East Berlin and Jerusalem. The changes of 1989–90 had come too late. With regard to the Jewish people and Israel, the sum total of East Germany, despite its emphasis on its antifascist character, remained negative from both the moral and material viewpoint. In July 1990, the die had already been cast, and on October 3, 1990, the separate East German state ceased to exist.

Thus, the issue of reparations and the implementation of restitution was handed over to united Germany. Under an agreement between both German states pertaining to the implementation of the Unification Agreement of September 1990, the Federal Republic committed itself to enter into negotiations with the Claims

Conference about additional payments for Nazi victims who had received no compensation or only a minimal one. Simultaneously, a property restitution law was drafted that applied to all confiscated property, including that from the Nazi period that preceded Communist confiscation. However, Jewish hopes that the preamble to the Unification Treaty would include an explicit reference to Germany's historic responsibility for the Holocaust were not fulfilled, mainly because of objections from the West German political establishment.

PART VI

UNIFICATION AND BEYOND

18

Expectations and Question Marks

In 1989 both West and East Germany celebrated their fortieth anniversary. Before the end of that year, however, the breakdown of the Berlin Wall and the collapse of the Communist regime in the GDR paved the way for the reunification of Germany in October 1990.[1] Since then, momentous changes have taken place on the international scene. The Eastern bloc fell apart; the Soviet Union disintegrated; all Communist dictatorships in Europe were replaced by democratic or semidemocratic forms of government, although in some of these countries reformed Communists who defined themselves as Social Democrats returned to power as a result of free elections; and united Germany with close to eighty million inhabitants reemerged as Europe's strongest nation and the leading member of the European Community.

For a great many American Jews, the unforeseen rapid unification was an emotionally painful experience. Together with others, they had come to regard the partition of Germany as a kind of historic punishment for Hitler's war of aggression and genocide, although in fact that partition was the result of the Cold War and not of the Morgenthau plan or any other preplanned agreement between the victorious allies. The unification was even more upsetting because of the growth of Holocaust consciousness since the 1970s, which had reinforced the negative perceptions of the

341

Germans held by a great number of American Jews. However, the organized Jewish community acquiesced to the fait accompli that the American administration helped to bring about and that was supported by the majority of American public opinion. In part, East Germany's dismal record on reparations and restitution and its long-term hostility to Israel, which prevailed almost until the end of the Communist regime, helped the community to overcome its qualms. Despite recurrent differences of opinion, the relatively new though ambivalent relationship between Jewish organizations and German institutions has continued to expand since then, although it is difficult to gauge whether the cooperative attitude of the Jewish partners reflects the feelings of their constituents, many of whom continue to hold stereotyped ideas about contemporary Germany. Perhaps characteristic of the anti-German prejudices persisting among the wider strata of American Jewry is an episode mentioned in the recollections of Marc Fisher, the *Washington Post*'s correspondent to Germany until 1993. Even though his family had not been directly affected by the Holocaust, Fisher recalls that his father regarded his son's taking up the post in Germany as "an incomprehensible act of aggression."[2]

In a way, Jewish opposition to Germany's unification in 1990 was even likely to be less effective than attempts by several Jewish groups to slow down the establishment (and afterwards the rearmament) of the West German Federal Republic in the early 1950s. Then, too, national interest considerations prevailed over ethnic pressures. In the late 1940s and early 1950s, the Truman administration had decided that to contain the perhaps exaggerated threat of Soviet power and consolidate Western Europe, there was no alternative but to establish in the three Western occupation zones a pro-Western anti-Communist German state and link it to the Western alliance by a policy of double containment. That meant preventing both the expansion of the Soviet Union and the revival of German nationalism. Still, President Truman, Secretary of State Dean Acheson, Secretary of Defense General George Marshall, and many others were not enamored of the Germans after the bloody war, their working relationship with Chancellor Konrad Adenauer notwithstanding. The reservations of the Jewish community, for its part, contributed to securing West Germany's commitments on collective reparations, personal indemnification, and restitution of

Jewish property. These pledges helped West Germany's gradual acceptance as an ally by Western public opinion.

During the forty years of the Federal Republic's separate existence, there were ups and downs in its relationship with the United States. In all, however, the Federal Republic distinguished itself as a stable, democratic state and trusted ally. In the 1980s, Chancellor Kohl, who brought the Christian Democrats back to power in 1982, and the Republican administrations of Presidents Reagan and Bush enjoyed a close relationship. Thus, when the occasion for German unification arose after the breakdown of the Berlin Wall, it received unequivocal support from Washington, contrary to the hesitations of Britain and France as well as other European nations.[3]

In the summer of 1990, the Kremlin finally accepted the main American condition—which the Bonn government also favored—that a united Germany would stay in NATO. Other issues were agreed upon in multilateral and bilateral diplomatic talks without causing major difficulties. These issues were the reduction of Germany's Bundeswehr to 370,000 soldiers, the recognition of the Oder-Neisse border with Poland, the prohibition of production of ABC weapons, the large German compensation payments for the evacuation of Soviet troops, and economic assistance to the Soviet Union.

The administration's clear-cut policy in favor of German unification enjoyed much support in both houses of Congress and in the media. According to polls taken in November 1989 after the breakdown of the Berlin Wall, 67 percent of the American public supported unification (72 percent of high school graduates and 57 percent of university graduates). In March–April 1990 the support grew to 76–77 percent, whereas 42 percent of American Jews opposed unification. In May 1990 the majority of supporters reached 84 percent.[4]

It did not come as a surprise that the concern voiced among American Jews regarding German unification was greater than among other groups of the population, although a substantial percentage endorsed it. At the time of German unification in 1990, the American Jewish community was politically much stronger than during the establishment of the West German republic in 1949; Jewish individuals and organizations were not inhibited from expressing their views as during the anti-Communist hysteria of the late 1940s and early 1950s. Besides their domestic agenda, most of their energy was devoted to the support of Israel, which remained a mitigating factor with regard to Germany. In spite of the persistent Jewish grassroots dislike of Germany and the German people, the majority of the organized community soon concluded that it made no sense to engage in a futile confrontation on the German issue.

After short-lived protests by leading politicians, among them Prime Minister Yitzhak Shamir, Israel itself adjusted to the new situation in order not to antagonize the Bonn government, which remained an important source of assistance to the Jewish state.[5] Moreover, the intensive contacts with German diplomats stationed in the United States and exchange programs between American Jewish organizations and German political foundations that had been established in the 1980s also contributed to a smoother acceptance of united Germany by organized Jewry.

As in the past, the traditional cleavage between American Jewish moderates and organizations more critical of Germany reemerged on the eve of unification. AJC,[6] B'nai B'rith,[7] and ADL, despite Abraham Foxman's personal difficulties "to share the joy of the German people,"[8] endorsed unification on the basis of West Germany's record and Jewish concerns such as antisemitism, reparations, Israel, and Holocaust education. Yet, ADL leaders were angered by comments of the deputy chief of mission in the West German embassy in Washington that Germany "should be entitled to a lunatic fringe" and that German history should be treated the same as American history.[9] Naturally, such arguments by German diplomats reflecting the conservative "epochal tide" sounded blasphemous to Jewish ears. The JLC, which continued its fraternal links with the German Social Democrats, expressed support for German unity in a European framework, conditional on its preserving its special responsibility to the Jewish people.[10] The German-born UAHC president, Rabbi Alexander Schindler, one of the most prominent figures in the organized community, resigned himself to unification but "without enthusiasm"; the Union's Social Action Committee in Washington refrained from taking a stand on the issue.[11] The State Department outlined to interested Jewish groups the favorable effects of a united Germany.[12]

For the WJC, which acted as an umbrella organization for many Diaspora communities and a number of American Jewish groups, the road to endorsing German unification was more twisted. The Modrow government in East Berlin had hoped to obtain Jewish support for the continuing existence of the GDR, but there was no way the WJC could help it to achieve that goal.[13] At a meeting in Berlin summoned in May 1990 by the WJC, the European Jewish Congress, and the Central Council of the Jews in Germany Congress unenthusiastically acquiesced to German unification on the condition that united Germany would stick to its close relationship with Israel, pledge not to produce ABC weapons, and honor international human rights.[14] It was the first time after World War II that a major international Jewish body convened on German soil. However, the WJC as well as other Jewish organizations were disappointed by the Bonn government's framing of the preamble of the unification treaty. Rather than acknowledge the Nazi horrors, it merely made an oblique reference to the German people's responsibility "before history." Jewish protests to the State Department with regard to that omission were of no avail.[15]

Misgivings with regard to the rapid unification were voiced by the Simon Wiesenthal Center, various *landsmanshaften*, and spokesmen for Holocaust survivor organizations, such as Benjamin Meed, chairman of the World Gathering of Holocaust Survivors. Other Holocaust remembrance activists, such as Menahem Rosensaft, did not see a divided Germany as a safeguard for German democracy or a viable European community. In the view of Henry Siegman, a left-liberal and at that time executive director of the AJ Congress, there existed no serious danger that united Germany would "slide back to the pathological forms of nationalism that have had such catastrophic consequences for the world, and particularly for Jews." However, in comparison to Weizsäcker's emphasis on a "painfully honest reflection" on the German past, Siegman complained that Chancellor Kohl aimed "at a denial of the singularity of what happened" and sought to minimize it by putting it "into perspective."[16] As in the past, different Orthodox rabbinical groups and individuals were the most outspoken opponents of German unification. For instance, the president of the Rabbinical Association of Greater Miami told German ambassador Jürgen Ruhfus "that maybe in 500 years or so it might be a good time for [German unification] to happen."[17]

Jewish publications and columns or statements by Jewish authors seem to have reflected grassroots emotions in the community more closely than some of the mainstream organizations that stuck to a moderate line. Elie Wiesel, a pioneer in promoting Holocaust consciousness, was happy when the Berlin Wall came down and freedom prevailed among the East Germans, but he was troubled that the memory of what had happened to the Jews might suffer as a result of unification, particularly since Germany "fell prey to perilous temptations of ultranationalism" whenever it became too powerful. In his view, Germany needed "to come to terms with its past before we can accept in good faith all it says about its own future."[18] For Cynthia Ozick, the cavorting of young Germans in Berlin streets in November 1989 recalled their cavorting fifty-one years earlier at the *Kristallnacht* pogrom. To the writer who would never set foot in Germany there was no longer a Jewish problem in Germany but a German problem. She thought that contrary to German expectations, they would have "to deal with their ancestors' extermination of the six million the same way Americans will always have to wrestle with the demons of slavery."[19]

Opponents of German unification could be found on both the right and the left. A. M. Rosenthal, a consistent neo-Conservative and opponent of Germany, complained in the *New York Times* that neither in the endless newspaper columns nor in the statements of so many leaders of nations could he find such words as: "Jew, Auschwitz, Rotterdam, Polish *Untermenschen*, Leningrad, slave labor, crematorium, Holocaust, Nazi."[20] Michael Lerner, editor of the left-liberal journal *Tikkun*, resisted the idea that "Germany deserved reunification, that they've served their time and now can forget the past." In retrospect Lerner, a graduate of the American New Left, blamed the United States for sacrificing morals for political expediency when it enlisted Germans on the American side of the Cold War and did not insist upon a serious denazification of West Germany. He was also sorry that the post-Holocaust urgent demand of the refugees in the DP camps for a Jewish state made it impossible "to take the years, perhaps the decades, it might have needed to work out a relationship with the Palestinians that would not have resulted in the replacement of hundreds of thousands of them."[21] Alan M. Dershowitz, law professor, lawyer, enfant terrible on the American Jewish scene, and author of *Chutzpah*, regarded "the reunification of the Germans and the establishment of the most powerful nation in Europe less than half a century after the destruction of Nazism . . . simply the natural consequence of refusing to recognize the responsibility of the German nation for the incalculable evil it wrought." The right way to treat the Germans after World War II would have been "not to apply to them the Marshall Plan but the Morgenthau Plan."[22]

Among those who revealed more understanding for the momentous change in Germany was Michael Wyschogrod, scholar and one of the moderate Orthodox intellectuals. He did not regret the nonimposition of the Morgenthau Plan on Germany and said that "to resist reunification today would be to serve the Morgenthau Plan a resurrection it does not deserve." Instead, the duty of the Jews should be to prevent the forgetting of Auschwitz.[23] Similarly, for Harvard historian Charles Maier, author of *The Unmasterable Past*, the task for Germans was "to remember Auschwitz and insure that it does not happen again anywhere." However, he did not agree with the opponents of unification that Auschwitz should forever deprive Germany of a unified nation state.[24] Almost all the participants in a symposium published in May 1990 in B'nai B'rith's *Jewish Monthly* also supported German unification.[25]

The main setbacks in American Jewish–German relations in the first years after unification were caused by the Federal Republic's reaction to the 1991 Gulf War, the racialist antiforeign outbreaks in Germany that peaked in 1992–93, the renewed manifestations of antisemitism, and last but not least, the controversy over the Holocaust Museum in Washington. Even though the German government contributed heavily to the financing of the military operation against Iraq, and Washington took into account the legal restraints that prevented the Federal Republic from active participation in the international force, the United States was upset by the hostile anti-American attitude evinced by a part of the German public. Germany's pacifist peace movement denounced the war as an unjustified imperialist assault on a weak Third World nation. In the view of the German-Israeli historian Dan Diner, the behavior of major parts of the German Left during the Gulf War was but another expression of German anti-Americanism and a reminder of Germany's fragile link to the West and its political culture.[26]

For the American Jewish community, which in its overwhelming majority supported the military action of the United States and its allies against the Iraqi threat, Israel's security added a further dimension. Jewish organizations protested the assistance German firms had provided to Iraq's chemical weaponry and armaments industry, although they were not the only Western nation to do so. German diplomats, who tried to refute accusations that the Bonn government approved or knowingly tolerated such deals, reminded the critics of its emergency allocation of DM 250 million to Israel as "humanitarian aid" during the missile attacks. Germany also pointed to the dispatch of Patriot missiles, the supply of chemical-weapons-detecting equipment, and the construction of two submarines, which amounted to close to DM 1.4 billion.[27] Nonetheless, both the Israeli public and the American Jewish community were disappointed by the hostile attitude of most German "Greens" and the lack of sympathy for Israel from antiwar Social Democrats and trade union representatives. The hysterical reactions of the German peace movement were regarded as unpalatable, as even a friendly American Jewish observer of the German left-wing scene like Andrei Markovits remarked.[28]

The anger at Germany's behavior during the Gulf War reflected both American Jewish and Israeli complaints. However, the avalanche of xenophobic, extreme right-wing, and antisemitic incidents that started in both the eastern and western parts of reunited Germany and subsided only in 1994 was of primary concern to American Jews. It affected Israel much less, where the peace process and the differences of opinion regarding the future of the occupied territories dominated the political stage. Through 1992, more than 2,500 assaults—mainly against Turkish guest-workers, Third World asylum seekers, and refugees from the former Communist countries—were carried out by neo-Nazis and other radical rightists, causing 17 deaths, 600 injuries, and damage to many refugee shelters. More than one-third involved arson and fire bombings. In 1993, while the total number of attacks of neo-Nazi and skinhead violence decreased slightly to 2,232, the number of antisemitic incidents rose, including 72 violent acts against Jews. The torching of the Lübeck synagogue compound—the most overt of the anti-Jewish occurrences—happened in March 1994 when the number of incidents was already declining. In 1992, memorials were devastated in the former concentration camps of Sachsenhausen and Ravensbrück. Between October 1990 and the summer of 1992, 367 Jewish cemeteries were vandalized; there were more desecrations of Jewish cemeteries than on the eve of the Nazi takeover in 1933.[29]

For American Jews well conscious of the link between xenophobia, racism, and antisemitism, fighting these evils was a must. Although the safety of the gradually expanding German Jewish community played a relatively larger role than during the wave of antisemitic incidents in the winter of 1959–60, the broader implications for the Jewish situation in Europe and the whole Jewish-German relationship were always taken into account. Jewish communal agencies in the United States were encouraged to act cooperatively in scheduling meetings with American officials and German consular representatives and in the planning of educational forums. The AJC also advised the German Jewish community to increase its part in the struggle against antisemitism and racism by seeking coalitions with liberal progressive forces and the churches; although such cooperation took place in reaction to special events, it was not institutionalized.[30]

The antisemitic and racialist events as well as the repercussions of the Gulf War probably speeded up the signing of an agreement between the German government and the Claims Conference regarding the payment of another $670 million over seven years in Jewish post-unification claims. Similarly, arrangements were made regarding restitution for Jewish property in East Germany that had been seized by the Nazis. In July 1992, the German government introduced anti-boycott measures regarding trade with Israel, thus settling a problem that for many years had been of great concern to Israel and the American Jewish community.[31]

Following their experience at home, the American Jewish organizations most involved in relations with Germany commissioned periodical public opinion polls there that served as a basis for survey research on German antisemitism and other attitudes of the German population. The Allensbach poll commissioned by the ADL in the fall of 1987 (see chapter 16) showed that 8 percent of the West Germans were still vehemently antisemitic and that an additional 15 percent shared a definite anti-Jewish prejudice. Sixty-seven percent thought that, forty years having passed since World War II, Germany should stop talking so much about persecution of the Jews. The first AJC survey in cooperation with the German Emnid Institute was undertaken in October 1990, at the time of German unification, in both parts of Germany. According to that survey, 58 percent of Germans either strongly (30 percent) or somewhat (28 percent) wanted to put the memory of the Holocaust behind them, 39 percent endorsed the view that "Jews are exploiting the Holocaust for their own purposes," 52 percent believed that Israel had no special claim on Germany and was "a state like any other," 38 percent thought that Jews exert too much influence on world affairs, and 38 percent subscribed to the view that "Zionism is racism." While 79 percent supported a ban on antisemitic groups, only 22 percent favored payment of reparations to Jews after unification. The findings did not come as a surprise but again demonstrated the big gap between the German public and the political leadership, which on all items evinced attitudes far more favorable toward Jews.

A later AJC/Emnid study based on a poll conducted in January 1994 concluded that more than one in five Germans harbored a negative attitude toward Jews. Twenty percent and 31 percent believed that Jews exerted too much influence in German society and world events, respectively; 22 percent would prefer not to have a Jewish neighbor; 37 percent thought the Holocaust was not relevant because it happened fifty years ago; and 52 percent argued that in the aftermath of German unification they "should not talk so much about the Holocaust, but should rather draw a line under the past." Nevertheless, German attitudes towards other minorities such as Gypsies, Turks, Vietnamese, Africans, Poles, and Arabs tended to be more negative than toward Jews.[32]

In fact, the data regarding German public opinion revealed in the 1994 survey did not differ substantially from the results of earlier polls in the last decades. Expectations that antisemitism, which had been a key ingredient of Nazi ideology, would disappear after the Third Reich's demise and the occupation of Germany by the victorious powers had proved wrong long ago. In all, the years since the end of World War II antisemitism had been not only fought by the state authorities but also tabooed by society. However, there were signs that the taboo was breaking down in the 1990s.[33] This presented a serious problem to German Jewry and, if not contained, could in the long run affect the whole post-Holocaust relationship between Germans and Jews.

The breakdown of the social taboo on antisemitism could become even more threatening in the event of a rightward shift of German political culture. During the Historians' Debate in the mid-1980s with the liberals, the right-of-center and conservative historians had been in the minority. Yet, after the unification of Germany, at least some of them thought the time had come to try and redefine the German people's national identity.[34] Furthermore, in the post–Cold War climate, a new generation of revisionist historians and "New Right" intellectuals, in addition to relativizing the Holocaust, came to challenge Adenauer's unequivocal pro-Western foreign policy legacy. They also criticized some of the liberal and pluralistic foundations of German postwar society. In the 1970s and 1980s the main assault on American and Western policies had come from German leftists and a part of the Social Democratic opposition. Now the threat emerged that at least on the intellectual level a reversal of roles would take place. Any weakening of American influence in Germany could have a negative impact on Jewish-German relations.[35]

It must be noted here that on the eve of and immediately after unification, American Jewish organizations (as well as Israelis) assumed that the momentous change would serve as an opportunity for educating the sixteen million new citizens from the East about the German historic responsibility for the destruction of European Jewry. Until then the topic had been sidelined by the simplistic antifascist explanation of Hitler's regime and the conception of the GDR as a "new and clean" antifascist state. Reality proved to be more complex. The inclusion of the East Germans in the visitor and exchange programs indeed exposed them to more information about the Jewish people and a more truthful and balanced picture of Israel than that supplied by the GDR and its media. But as far as antisemitism was concerned, all the polls confirmed that East Germans harbored fewer antisemitic prejudices than Germans in the West. In contrast to 24 percent of West Germans, only 8 percent of Germans in the East felt that Jews have too much influence in German society; compared to 44 percent of Germans in the West, only 19 percent of the population in the East thought that "Jews are exploiting the Holocaust for their own purposes"; 22 percent (as compared to 40 percent in the West) maintained that "the Holocaust is not relevant today because it happened about 50 years ago." For whatever reason, despite the GDR's consistent anti-Israel policy, the population showed more sympathy for Jews than in the West. Maybe the antifascist indoctrination, though it evaded the special Jewish issue, had some positive effects after all.[36] In retrospect, with all the faults and the oppressive character of the East German Communist dictatorship that lasted much longer than the Third Reich, there could be no comparison between the GDR and the genocidal Nazi regime, not only from the Jewish viewpoint.[37]

For a number of years, the U.S. Holocaust Memorial Museum in Washington, which opened its doors in April 1993, was another source of friction between American Jewry and Germany. The Holocaust Memorial Council, appointed and reappointed by the American president, comprised over the years a number of representatives and spokesmen of Jewish organizations and institutions, Holocaust survivors, intellectuals, rabbis, and historians. In addition, a few distinguished members of non-Jewish communities served on the Council. Despite its officially nondenominational nonsectarian character, the Holocaust Memorial Museum became a most impressive symbol and demonstration of the power of the American Jewish community. The Federal Republic of Germany, both before and after unification, regarded the museum's depicting Nazi Germany's horrendous crimes as a threat to its close postwar relationship with the United States and the American people. No wonder that the controversy's repercussions were felt continuously in the Jewish-German debate. Yet in contrast to Bitburg, where President Reagan was afraid to retract his promise to Chancellor Kohl lest it damage the American-German alliance, the Holocaust Museum was a domestic American affair, and its completion would not be hindered by any outside factor.[38]

Since the project had been launched in the early 1980s, the Kohl government had hoped to add to the museum an exhibition that would at least partially improve Germany's image by demonstrating its post-1945 achievements and reliability, its assistance to the State of Israel, and its indemnification and restitution payments to Jewish survivors of the Holocaust and their heirs.[39] Eventually all these efforts, which went on for a number of years, failed. Even the proposal of including in the exhibition a photograph of the former German chancellor Willy Brandt kneeling at the Warsaw Ghetto Memorial in 1970—as Edward Linenthal recalled in *Preserving Memory*—was dropped because of strong emotional opposition. The survivors in the Memorial Council refused to accept any financial contributions from German government sources; most of the $167 million for the museum aiming at the "Americanization" of the catastrophe of European Jewry were raised by American Jews.[40]

Recurrent suggestions of German individuals—in informal discussions and in articles in leading German newspapers—that American Jews should "rid themselves of their obsession with the Holocaust" and focus on their religious and cultural sources received perhaps the most cogent reply from Howard Friedman, a past AJC president who had been engaged for many years in promoting contacts between the American Jewish community and German institutions:

> The Jewish soul will forever be seared by the experience of the Holocaust. One-third of the Jewish people were its mortal victims. A thousand years of German-Jewish history came to an end, and an entire infrastructure of Jewish institutions was destroyed. There is simply no way to diminish the monumental significance of these events to modern Jewish life. Nor is there any way to attenuate the unprecedented horror which these events represent to the vitality of the human spirit itself. It is an historic event which must forever be at the forefront of the consciousness not only of the Jewish people, but of the German people themselves in whose name those terrible events were perpetrated. Nor can the events be isolated from their roots in German history which ultimately permitted the events to transpire.[41]

All these setbacks and disappointments notwithstanding, the bilateral relationship between organized American Jewry and its German counterparts continued and even expanded. The Jewish organizations involved in the dialogue pointed to Germany's significance as a centrally placed country in Europe, its vital importance to Jewish and Israeli interests, as well as their own role as an active force in the American community. Although the Germans became conscious of the limits of Jewish ethnic power at Bitburg and during the unification year, they persisted in their efforts at conciliating American Jewry because of its ongoing impact on parts of publicized and liberal public opinion. The assaults against foreigners, including permanent residents, and anti-Jewish occurrences, which revived anti-German prejudices in the American public, made these contacts ever more urgent for the German side. Besides, the Germans also took into account that in the printed and electronic media, publishing and academia, Jews were relatively more involved with German issues than other Americans.

As a result of the common interest, the number of American Jewish–German encounters—exchange visits, symposia, VIP delegations, and "summit meetings" with Chancellor Kohl, President Weizsäcker, and lately his successor Roman Herzog—increased after unification.[42] During his visit to Israel in December 1994, Herzog was hosted by Israel's Council on Foreign Relations, which operates under the auspices of the WJC. The AJC and the Atlantik-Brücke conducted yearly conferences, according to their schedule.[43]

In 1994, under the impact of the Clinton administration's reaffirmation of the close American-German alliance and Germany's place as "a partner in leadership," the AJC endorsed the granting of permanent membership to Germany as a part of the enlargement of the UN Security Council, a proposal that other Jewish organizations would not yet share.[44] In 1998 the AJC opened its Lawrence Ramer Center in Berlin, united Germany's capital. The German Jewish community, Germany's impact in Europe, the further immigration of Jews from the former Soviet Union, and the interests of Israel were mentioned as reasons for that step.

B'nai B'rith, for its part, started bringing over to Germany young Jewish legislators and officials on the federal as well as on the state level and hosted a similar German group at home. It also organized a business leaders' trip, and the ADL offered programs, such as its own "A World of Difference," to combat extremism and promote pluralism and democratic values.[45] In 1993, a large delegation of 320 UJA contributors—in the words of Ambassador Richard C. Holbrooke probably the largest group of American Jews since the crossing of the Rhine by the American Army in March 1945—visited united Germany on its way to Eastern Europe and to Israel. The American embassy in Bonn was satisfied that the steady flow of Jewish delegations balanced the decline of other American political guests in Germany, in comparison to the much larger number of German visitors to the United States.[46] American Jewish delegations included East German cities in their itinerary in order to increase Jewish exposure there. East Germans also participated in the visitor groups that came over to the United States.

A *novum* in the exchange programs and visits of American Jewish leaders to Germany was the growing attention paid to the German Jewish community, which for many years had remained on the sidelines of the American Jewish–German–Israeli triangle. Since the late 1980s, its numbers had increased to at least 60,000 members, thanks to the admission of thousands of Jews from the former Soviet Union, despite protests and objections from Israel. In the mid-1990s the Jewish community in Germany was the third largest in Western Europe. Together with non-Jewish partners it numbered more than 80,000 persons. As a result of the large immigration from the former Soviet Union, the community was plagued by difficult problems of social adjustment; even so, there were signs of its renascent cultural creativity.[47] Because of sociological and generational changes, the so-called Jews in Germany were successively becoming German Jews.

The German Jewish community leadership, too, became more self-conscious and self-assured, and while it spoke up forcefully in Germany, it also attached importance to strengthening its links with American and international Jewish organizations.[48] This was a major change from its attitude thirty years earlier when the Central Council's secretary general advised the Adenauer government against American Jewish interference.[49] In contrast to all his predecessors, Ignatz Bubis, the chairman of the Central Council of the Jews in Germany, managed to establish himself as an important public figure. For a number of years, Bubis had been serving on the central committee of the FDP. For a short period Michel Friedman, another leader of the Frankfurt community, became a member of the CDU central committee but was not reelected in the fall of 1996.

In July 1994, an official delegation of the New York Board of Rabbis, which included Orthodox members, accepted an invitation to visit Germany. The rabbis, who attended the inauguration of President Roman Herzog, were impressed by many positive developments in Germany and realized that "perhaps there has been a significant enough change so that the Germany of 1994 need not be treated like the Germany of 1944." Nevertheless, they added that as Jews they would not and dared not forget what happened and recalled the words of the late Rabbi Abraham Yehoshua Heschel that "we are also unable to forgive, since only the victims and the Almighty God can do that for the perpetrators."[50]

For Ismar Schorsch, chancellor of the Jewish Theological Seminary, a historian of German Jewry and one of the leading minds of the Conservative movement, to remember was not enough. In a 1994 symposium in *Sh'ma* dedicated to the question of whether it was time to forgive Germany, he stated that while Jews were obliged "to remember the Holocaust in all its horrendous brutality," they were also obliged to do whatever they could to prevent its recurrence, and that required more "than acts of memory and cries of alarm at the excesses of every skinhead and neo-Nazi." In his view:

Given the importance of a reunited, democratic Germany to the welfare of Europe and the world, Jews need to muster the good judgment and moral courage to reinforce the vast majority of Germans who share our loathing of the Nazis and who accept the burden of their history and who have done so much to atone for it. . . . The future is too precarious to allow us the comfort of focusing exclusively on the past or seeing the present only through its constricted lens.[51]

Arthur Hertzberg, historian, rabbi, and one of the American Jewish community's most prominent intellectuals, never brought himself to visit Germany, despite a number of invitations from German academic institutions. He could not contemplate walking down the street, or into a lecture hall, or into a café to wonder, as he looked at people of his own generation, who among them took part in the murder of his family. Nonetheless, in the fall of 1995 he wrote: "The next generation will—[he] would even add must—make peace. Those who made the horrors of the past are beyond forgiveness, but Jews must make friends with those who will, together with our children and grandchildren, be part of the next century."[52]

In all, at the end of 1995, five years after Germany's reunification and after the fiftieth anniversary of the end of the Holocaust and World War II, it seemed that some of the Jewish fears with regard to developments in Germany were exaggerated. The antiforeigner and right-wing extremist manifestations lessened somewhat, though they did not disappear. Neither was there a further increase of antisemitism that might endanger the German Jewish community. One year earlier, in March 1994 and in the following months, American Jews were impressed by the outpouring emotions of hundreds of thousands of young Germans watching Steven Spielberg's *Schindler's List*, which recalled the experience of the *Holocaust* telecast in Germany in 1979.[53] In a way, it was a consolation for them after the disappointing involvement of other parts of the younger German generation in the antiforeigner and antisemitic happenings.

The assumption that the exhaustive dealing with the more recent past of the Communist GDR would make the "mastering" of the Nazi period much more difficult also did not materialize. Despite the continuing search in Stasi (the Ministry of State Security) files, the need to advance a rapprochement with East Germany put limits to that confrontation. On the other hand, the most obstinate

German critics of the Holocaust Memorial Museum in Washington had to confess that, even with all the millions of visitors, the museum did not endanger the solid American-German political alliance, which continued under President Clinton as it had under his Republican predecessors.

As for Israel, Chancellor Kohl's second visit to Jerusalem in June 1995 was the most successful of any leading German statesman to that time.[54] Similarly, much praise was heaped on President Ezer Weizman's address to the Bundestag during his state visit to Germany in January 1996[55] even though it was marred by basic differences of opinion with regard to the legitimacy of the expanding Jewish community in Germany, a fact that Israel's establishment has refused to internalize. In a way, President Roman Herzog's simultaneous proclamation of the day of the liberation of Auschwitz as Holocaust Remembrance Day in Germany closed the circle of symbolic gestures. But there would not yet be any drawing of a line under Nazi Germany's extermination of six million European Jews; it will continue to affect world Jewish-German relations for years to come.

19

An Ambiguous Balance

More than fifty years after the end of World War II and the greatest catastrophe in the history of the Jewish Diaspora, the relationship between the American Jewish community and postwar Germany remains an ambiguous one. Despite the great strides recently made in relations with a number of German political foundations on bilateral issues, an ambivalence toward Germany persists even among members of organizations engaged in mutual exchanges and dialogues. In the broader Jewish community a more negative attitude seems to prevail.[1]

After all, one must realize that Jewish organizations of all kinds exist on a voluntary basis, and they and their leaders do not automatically reflect grassroots thoughts and feelings on Germany. Conversely, even German individuals and groups of goodwill, too, share great difficulties in understanding the special character, behavior, and motivation of the large Jewish community, which they regard as a continuing stumbling block in forging the American-German friendship. The legacy of the Holocaust, which affects both sides in different ways, makes that relationship even more complex.

A summary of American Jewish postwar positions and actions on Germany in the context of U.S. foreign-policymaking reaffirms the limits of ethnic pressure and moral motivations as compared to national interest and realpolitik, although the German issue so central for Washington was not the foremost of Jewish concerns. This was made apparent by the ineffectiveness of Jewish opposition to the rapid change of America's attitude toward the former enemy. Only five years after the war, that same country was welcomed as a potential ally against the Communist threat, disregarding at least some of America's original postwar aims. One generation later, in 1985, concerted Jewish pressure could not change President Ronald Reagan's decision to demonstrate American-German friendship by a meeting with German chancellor Helmut Kohl at Bitburg military cemetery, where a number of SS soldiers were interred. Yet again any Jewish attempt to oppose Germany's unification five years later was doomed in advance. Still, Jewish intercessions in the first postwar decade were more successful with regard to such issues as restitution, indemnification, and German reparations. In this case, the fulfillment of such demands was helpful in promoting West Germany's acceptance as a friend and ally of the United States against the Soviet Union and its satellites, including Communist-controlled East Germany.

On the other hand, despite the fact that the makers of Germany's foreign policy grasped the limits of Jewish ethnic power, they nevertheless did not underestimate—and sometimes overestimated—American Jewish influence on the American public. After the bloody war, they understood that Germany's acceptance by U.S. public and publicized public remained an important condition for a real conciliation between the former enemies. The American Jewish community, for its part, knew how to make use of this factor in furthering American and world Jewish interests, at the same time, at least indirectly, also contributing to the evolution of a better Germany. Helmut Schmidt, the former chancellor and now one of the publishers of Germany's most respectable weekly, *Die Zeit*, referred to this subject in one of his incisive articles on Japan; he quoted a noted Japanese journalist:

> You Germans were lucky that members of the people overtaken by you—especially the Jews in the United States—forced you to confront your recent history and tell the next generations the truth about it. We Japanese had the misfortune that no Chinese, Korean or Indonesian aroused the world and forced us to seek the truth—we ourselves have not been motivated to do it.[2]

While not the result of any planned efforts of the organized Jewish community, such productions as the *Holocaust* series in 1978–79, and Spielberg's *Schindler's List* in 1994, as well as Daniel J. Goldhagen's 1996 academic best-seller *Hitler's Willing Executioners*, played a significant role in making new German generations more conscious of the heinous crimes committed by many of their predecessors.

In spite of diverging political, social, and organizational traditions, a number of issues relating to postwar Germany encouraged successful cooperation between the main Jewish groups. At first, they concentrated on the safety and well-being of the camp survivors and East European refugees in the DP assembly centers in the American zone. Afterwards, they joined forces in securing restitution of Jewish property and individual compensation. In 1951–52, they brought about—together with the State of Israel—the reparation settlement with the German Federal Republic. In the following decade, organized American Jewry's efforts contributed to the postponement of the German statute of limitations, making further prosecution of Nazi criminals possible, and to the belated establishment of diplomatic relations between West Germany and Israel. Despite these common causes, however, the traditional differences between organizations endorsing public action and others preferring backyard intercession reasserted themselves.

The main cleavage among organized Jewry with regard to Germany centered on two questions: Should the Jewish community persevere in its punitive approach and focus its attention only on direct Jewish demands, or should it join liberal forces in the United States and in Germany to further the progress of a peaceful and democratic German state and society? In contrast to the critical and skeptical AJ Congress and WJC (with the exception of Nahum Goldmann, its president), the AJC and subsequently the ADL and B'nai B'rith rationalized their emphasis on German democracy on the basis of both American and broader Jewish interests. They considered Germany's position in Europe and how it might affect the future of Jews there and in the Middle East. The ADL was the first American Jewish agency to pay an official visit to West Germany in the mid-1950s and also to initiate a few exchanges in the early 1960s. The AJC, however, pioneered in the establishment of lasting new forms of cooperation with German political foundations in the 1980s, in part thanks to West Germany's disappointment with Israel's right-wing government after the priority accorded by Bonn to Jerusalem since the Six Day War.

As for the Luxembourg reparations treaty, which was signed in 1952 and ratified in 1953, its impact on American Jewry at large was rather limited. Nonetheless, it softened the hostility of the organized pro-Zionist camp toward Germany and also affected the attitude of committed Jewish legislators on Capitol Hill. Only the Revisionist Zionists and most Orthodox on the right and Communists and pro-Communists on the left persisted, though for different reasons, in opposing any contacts with the Federal Republic. The JLC leadership, though not all of its members and affiliates, took a moderate line from the beginning. On the other hand, most of the survivors were hostile to Germany. In the following decades the growing Holocaust consciousness made the American Jewish-German relationship even more complex.

Since the establishment of the West German state in 1949, the right-of-center Christian Democrats under Adenauer, Erhard, and Kiesinger and since 1982 under Kohl were the leading political party there, always in cooperation with the Bavarian CSU and mostly joining in a coalition with the FDP as its junior partner. The Social Democrats under Willy Brandt and Helmut Schmidt headed the government for thirteen years, and for a three-year period served in a "grand coalition" under Christian Democratic leadership. Konrad Adenauer, the founding father of the Federal Republic, was highly esteemed by American Jewish organizations, although his efforts to conciliate American and world Jewry originated not just from moral persuasion but from Germany's political aims as well. In addition to signing and implementing the Luxembourg agreement, against the wish of major parts of the German public and members of his own conservative coalition, Adenauer withstood American pressure to threaten Israel with the suspension of the reparation shipments during the Sinai-Suez conflict. In 1960, at his meeting with Ben Gurion at New York's Waldorf Astoria, he promised more economic and military aid. At the same time, he evaded the issue of diplomatic relations with Israel because of the Hallstein doctrine and the fear of retaliation by the Arab states in recognizing East Germany. That step was eventually taken by Chancellor Erhard, Adenauer's successor.

Contrary to the parties of the right-of-center, who after the war insisted on quickly reintegrating all of the former elites except for conspicuous Nazi activists, the Social Democrats pointed to the party's anti-Nazi and antiauthoritarian ethos when they took power in 1969. Almost all of the leading members of the Social Democrats could boast of their clean past. Because of that difference, however, they often felt less obliged to satisfy American Jewish (and Israeli) requests or pay attention to their complaints. Thus, despite Brandt's genuflection at the Warsaw Ghetto fighters memorial, American Jews were disappointed by his government's Mideastern policy before and during the Yom Kippur War, especially by its interference with further supply of American arms to Israel from Bremerhaven. American Jews were even more dissatisfied with Helmut Schmidt, who openly criticized Israel's behavior, especially after Likud leader Menachem Begin's accession to the prime ministership. Schmidt, unlike Brandt, had no anti-Nazi past.

After the return of the CDU to power in 1982, Chancellor Kohl paid more attention to American Jewish leadership and the Jewish organizations. Despite Bitburg and the controversies with the WJC, his record was regarded in general as a positive one. Because of American Jewry's permanent concern with racist and antisemitic manifestations, it usually focused on the German right wing, albeit since the aftermath of the Six Day War and the students' upheaval of 1968, there was no lack of extreme anti-Zionist as well as anti-Judaic expressions among the leftists. Because of the East-West conflict, the anti-Israel stand of the Communist East Berlin government, and its refusal to take upon itself any material, or at least moral responsibility, as one of Nazi Germany's successor states, American Jewry did not begin to deal with the East German regime until the last decade of its existence. But despite East Germany's desire to improve relations with American Jewry because of its economic needs and its leader Erich Honecker's wish to pay an official visit to Washington, their mutual contacts remained ineffective and soon became irrelevant because of the breakup of the GDR. In any case, Jewish pressure on the Reagan administration to link East German compensation payment for Jews with trade concessions for the GDR was not successful. Thus, the limits of Jewish ethnic power in the making of U.S. policy were again made clear.

Even before American Jewish solidarity with Israel reached its apogee during the Six Day and Yom Kippur Wars, Israel was an important factor of the American Jewish agenda, overshadowing American Jewry's German problem. Thus, Israel's direct and indirect interests were broached in most American Jewish talks with German politicians and diplomats as well as in the community's contacts with the U.S. administration. After the successful outcome of the *shilumim* negotiations, American Jewish protests and appeals followed the lines drawn by Israel's diplomats and policymakers in Jerusalem. This was particularly true on such issues as preserving U.S. public support during the Eichmann trial, opposing the employment of German scientists and military experts by Egypt, the suspension of German arms supplies to Israel in 1965, and afterwards the involvement of German industrial enterprises in the production of unconventional weapons in Libya and Iraq. In contrast to the American Jewish community, Israel was for many years less concerned about recurrent antisemitic phenomena. Because of its dependence on both American and German assistance, it also took a low-key stand on the Bitburg affair that shook American Jewry. In all, while Israel sometimes advised moderate positions and on other occasions endorsed pickets and public protests, its practical needs generally served as a moderating influence on American Jewry's moralistic posture.

The Jewish community in Germany, which was often pampered by German governments in the West and for the last decade of the GDR's existence also in the East, until recently only tangentially affected American Jewish relations with postwar Germany. Its significance, however, may increase in the future. The Germans, for their part, consistently try to gain sympathy by pointing to the German-Jewish heritage as a "way of the future."

Five years after the reunification of Germany and its return—even without nuclear weapons—to the rank of Europe's leading power, the course and pace of American Jewish–German relations are hard to predict. While there are several important Jewish organizations striving for steady improvement, there remains much opposition, particularly among survivors, Orthodox, and other skeptical components of the community. As mentioned earlier, the grassroots feeling is much less sympathetic, and a great many American Jews continue to refrain from buying German products or visiting Germany.

A number of factors affect relations between organized Jewry and Germany, both in a positive and a negative way. One of the most important is the future of the American-German alliance. In the late 1940s and early 1950s, only a few years after the traumatic shock of the murder of a great part of European Jewry, most American Jews watched the American-German rapprochement with ambivalent feelings. Today, the safeguarding of the close American-German relationship and Germany's link to NATO have become a pre-condition for American Jewish ability to have some impact on the German scene, though to a lesser extent than in the past. Only if that relationship is preserved will it proceed to serve as a watchdog while distinguishing between the German realities of today and the horrors of the past.

As for Israel, whatever the fate of the peace process with its Arab neighbors, whether it proceeds or breaks down, it may lessen the probability of further open or backdoor Jewish intercessions on such issues as German-Israeli relations. Moreover, developments inside the American Jewish community such as the problems of Jewish identity, the growing rate of intermarriage, and the Jewish state's decline as a unifying factor for American Jews because of political and religious reasons, may gradually weaken the close links between Israel and the largest Jewish diaspora.[3] Nonetheless, even though Israel has progressed much more rapidly on the path of normalization with Germany than most of Diaspora Jewry because of its economic, political, and military needs (as demonstrated during Chancellor Kohl's second visit to Jerusalem in June 1995), it will continue to play some role in the American Jewish–German relationship for a number of years. Finally, the attitude of American Jewry may also be affected more than in the past by the position of the German Jewish community itself.

Very much depends, of course, on the developments in Germany. Will the united nation, whose borders have moved eastward and which will soon transfer its government from the banks of the Rhine to the banks of the Spree, preserve its free democratic society and stick to the unequivocal Western commitment of the Federal Republic? With the help of the Western powers, and particularly of the United States, the postwar republic has become the most successful political creation in modern German history.[4] On the one hand, a steadfast commitment to promote further European cooperation and preserve the partnership with the United States is shared by the major German political parties; and there is also the growing impact of globalization in the fields of economics, communication, and scientific work. Fortunately, Kohl's and his party's defeat and the victory of the Social Democrats in the general elections of September 1998 do not seem to endanger the continuity of German foreign policy. On the other hand, already in the decade preceding unification at least a part of the conservative right-wing camp strove to strengthen German national consciousness. In the long run, the danger exists that such a trend might revert to a nationalism challenging Western values and orientation, attempting to reduce Germany's responsibility for the last great war, and weighing Nazi crimes against the destruction of German cities and the suffering of millions of expellees from the East. Especially worrying were the right-wing manifestations in the Bundeswehr, Germany's democratic army, and the growing strength of right-wing extremism among the younger generation, particularly in former East Germany.[5] At the 1998 Frankfurt Book Fair, prize-winning German author Martin Walser's implied call for containing the continuous public commemoration of the Holocaust for the sake of normalization as well as the protracted controversy over the erection of a central Holocaust memorial in Berlin also caused concern in Jewish circles.

Still, at least for the time being, challenges from the Right, in the political and intellectual debate in Germany, have not erased the impact of Auschwitz as a moralizing and restraining force. Despite the ongoing debate among Germans whether to regard May 8, 1945, as a day of liberation or defeat, no nationalistic deviations were apparent during the commemoration of its fiftieth anniversary. Most German leaders said all the right things on that occasion.[6] The yearly celebrations of Germany's unification remain subdued, in part because of the psychological and sociological gap still dividing Germans in the West and the East.

Another positive sign in German political culture was the sympathetic reaction of younger Germans who filled auditoriums during the recent public discussion of Goldhagen's *Hitler's Willing Executioners*. Whatever the faults of Goldhagen's basic concept and his attempt to explain the Holocaust only by a special kind of German eliminationist and exterminationist antisemitism, the listeners seem to have been shocked at least by the young American Jewish scholar's findings, which challenged the nonpersonal emphasis on "industrial extermination" and the "banality of evil." In his book, Goldhagen drew attention to "ordinary Germans'" mass killings of Jews in Polish towns and villages and their atrocities in the slave labor camps and during the death marches before the collapse of Hitler's Reich.[7]

Because of the gap between American Jewry and Germany, which will presumably persist for a few more generations, Germans of goodwill striving for conciliation should be wary of two pitfalls: exerting pressure to close the chapter of the Holocaust, as some conservatives and right-wingers advise; and attempting to obfuscate the particular fate of the Jews as victims of the murderous Nazi policies by stressing mainly the universal lessons of the Holocaust, as some Western and German liberals and leftists would prefer, though its lessons affect of course not only the Jews. While these views are shared by their liberal and radical Jewish confrères in Israel and Diaspora countries, they are rejected and perceived as counterproductive by the mainstream communities.

Earlier in this study, John McCloy, who as U.S. high commissioner contributed greatly to the successful launching of the postwar Federal Republic, was quoted as saying that the attitude toward the Jewish community was one of the real touchstones of Germany's progress toward the light. He added the warning that the moment Germany had forgotten the Buchenwalds and the Auschwitzes, that was the point at which everyone could begin to despair of any progress in Germany.[8] Despite the two generations that have passed since, and the manifold changes Germany has experienced, it seems that the essence of this statement is still valid today.

ABBREVIATIONS

AAPBD	Akten zur Auswärtigen Politik der Bundesrepublik Deutschland
ACDP	Archiv für Christlich-Demokratische Politik
ACJ	American Council for Judaism
ADL	Anti-Defamation League of B'nai B'rith
AdsD	Archiv der sozialen Demokratie
AFL	American Federation of Labor
AIPAC	American-Israel Public Affairs Committee
AJA	American Jewish Archives
AJA	*American Jewish Archives*, periodical
AJC	American Jewish Committee
AJ Conference	American Jewish Conference
AJ Congress	American Jewish Congress
AJHSA	American Jewish Historical Society Archives
AJJDC (also **JDC** or **Joint**)	American Jewish Joint Distribution Committee
AJLC	American Jewish Labor Council
AJW	*Allgemeine Jüdische Wochenzeitung*, weekly
AJYB	*American Jewish Year Book*, annual
BA	Bundesarchiv Koblenz
BBA	B'nai B'rith Archives
BGA	Ben-Gurion Archive
BGD	Ben-Gurion Diaries
CCAR	Central Conference of American Rabbis
CCRC	Cincinnati Jewish Community Relations Committee/Council
CDU	Christian Democratic Union
CIO	Congress of Industrial Organizations

COHC	Columbia University Oral History Collection
COMISCO	Committee of International Socialist Conferences
CSU	Christian Social Union
CZA	Central Zionist Archives
DANK	German American National Congress
DGB	Germany's Trade Union Federation
DRP	Deutsche Reichspartei
EC	European Community
EDC	European Defense Community
EEC	European Economic Community
EPC	European Political Cooperation
ERP	European Recovery Program
FAZ	*Frankfurter Allgemeine Zeitung*
FDR	Franklin Delano Roosevelt
FDRL	Franklin Delano Roosevelt Library
FDP	Free Democratic Party
FEA	Foreign Economic Administration
FES	Friedrich-Ebert-Stiftung
FRG	Federal Republic of (West) Germany
FRUS	*Foreign Relations of the United States*, series
GAF	General Aniline and Film
GDR	(East) German Democratic Republic
Gestapo	Geheime Staatspolizei, since 1936 part of the Sicherheitspolizei (Security Police)
HICOG	Office of the U.S. High Commissioner for Germany
HSTL	Harry S. Truman Library
HUAC	House Un-American Activities Committee
HUC	Hebrew Union College
ICD	Information Control Division
ICR	Intergovernmental Committee on Political Refugees
IfZ	Institut für Zeitgeschichte
IJA	Institute of Jewish Affairs
ILGWU	International Ladies Garment Workers Union
IMT	Four Power International Military Tribunal
INS	Immigration and Naturalization Service
ISA	Israel State Archives
JFK	John Fitzgerald Kennedy
JFKL	John Fitzgerald Kennedy Library
JLC	Jewish Labor Committee
JPFO	Jewish People's Fraternal Order
JRSO	Jewish Restitution Successor Organization
JTA	Jewish Telegraphic Agency
JTS	Jewish Theological Seminary
JWV	Jewish War Veterans
JWVA	Jewish War Veterans Archives
KAS	Konrad-Adenauer-Stiftung
LBI	Leo Baeck Institute
LC	Library of Congress

LZOA	Labor Zionist Organization of America
MD	*Morgenthau Diary* (the two published volumes on Germany)
MFN	Most Favored Nation
NA	United States National Archives
NATO	North Atlantic Treaty Organization
NCCJ	National Conference of Christians and Jews
NCRAC	National Community Relations Advisory Council (afterwards NJCRAC; since 1997 Jewish Council for Public Affairs)
NGC	*New German Critique*
NJM	*National Jewish Monthly*, afterwards *Jewish Monthly*
NPD	Nationaldemokratische Partei Deutschlands
NYR	*New York Review of Books*
NYT	*New York Times*
OMGUS	Office of Military Government for Germany, United States
OSI	Office of Special Investigations
OSS	Office of Strategic Services
PA/AA	Politisches Archiv des Auswärtigen Amtes
PDS	Partei des demokratischen Sozialismus
PLO	Palestine Liberation Organization
R&A	Research and Analysis Branch
SA	Sturmabteilung (Storm Troopers)
SAPMO	Stiftung Archiv der politischen Parteien und Massenorganisationen im Bundesarchiv
SD	Sicnerheitsdienst (Security Service of the SS)
SED	Sozialistische Einheitspartei Deutschlands (East Germany)
SHAEF	Supreme Headquarters, Allied Expeditionary Forces
SPD	Social Democratic Party of Germany
SRP	Sozialistiche Reichspartei
SS	Schutzstaffel
Stasi	State Security (East German) SWC Simon Wiesenthal Center
SWCA	*Simon Wiesenthal Center Annual*
UAHC	Union of American Hebrew Congregations
UJA	United Jewish Appeal
UNRRA	United Nations Relief and Rehabilitation Administration
UNWCC	United Nations War Crimes Commission
USFET	United States Forces, European Theater
VfZ	*Vierteljahrshefte für Zeitgeschichte*
WJC	World Jewish Congress
WJCC	World Jewish Congress Collection
WNRC	Washington National Record Center
WRB	War Refugee Board
WZO	World Zionist Organization
YIVO	Yiddisher Vissenshaftlicher Institut (Jewish Scientific Institute)
YVS	*Yad Vashem Studies*
ZOA	Zionist Organization of America

NOTES

CHAPTER 1

1. Howard M. Sachar, *A History of the Jews in America* (New York, 1992), 229–34, 239–41; Naomi W. Cohen, *Not Free to Desist: The American Jewish Committee, 1906–1966* (Philadelphia, 1972), 87–90. Naomi Cohen recalls the division in the AJC executive where Jacob Schiff at first represented strong pro-German sentiments and Oscar Straus espoused the cause of the Triple Entente. On the dissolution of the German-Jewish nexus in the United States since the 1870s, see Naomi W. Cohen, *Encounter with Emancipation: The German Jews in the U.S., 1830–1914* (Philadelphia, 1983), 62–63, and Avraham Barkai, *Branching Out: German-Jewish Immigration to the United States, 1820–1914* (New York, 1994), 178–89. For different views of the German-Jewish legacy, see Abraham J. Peck, ed., *The German-Jewish Legacy in America, 1938–1988: From Bildung to the Bill of Rights* (Detroit, 1989).

2. Shlomo Shafir, "American Jewish Leaders and the Emerging Nazi Threat (1928–January 1933)," *American Jewish Archives* 31 (Nov. 1979): 150–83.

3. Henry L. Feingold, "Courage First and Intelligence Second: The American Jewish Secular Elite, Roosevelt, and the Failure to Rescue," in *FDR and the Holocaust,* edited by Verne W. Newton (New York, 1996), 51–87, here p. 54. Feingold's article appeared at first in *American Jewish History* 72 (June 1983): 424–60. For the whole period see Feingold's *A Time for Searching: Entering the Mainstream, 1920–1945,* vol. 4 of *The Jewish People in America,* a series sponsored by the American Jewish Historical Society (Baltimore, 1992), ch. 8: "The American Jewish Response to the Holocaust"; also the collection of his essays published during the last two decades: *Bearing Witness: How America and Its Jews Responded to the Holocaust* (Syracuse, 1995). For the Jewish anti-Nazi boycott movement see Moshe R. Gottlieb, *American Anti-Nazi Resistance, 1933–1941*

(New York, 1982). I have also relied here and there on my own unpublished doctoral dissertation, "The Impact of the Jewish Crisis on American-German Relations, 1933–1939" (Georgetown University, 1971).

4. For Jewish electoral support of FDR and the Democratic party, see Lawrence H. Fuchs, *The Political Behavior of American Jews* (Glencoe, Ill., 1956), 71–79, 99–101. Cp. also Werner Cohn, "The Politics of American Jews," in *The Jews: The Social Patterns of an American Group*, edited by Marshall Sklare (New York, 1958), 614–26. Characteristic of the idolizing attitude toward Roosevelt that prevailed among American Jews in the 1940s is Edward N. Saveth's article, "FDR and the Jewish Crisis, 1933–1945," in the *American Jewish Year Book* (hereafter *AJYB*) 1945/46, vol. 47, pp. 37–50. For Morgenthau's involvement in Germany, see chap. 2.

5. The restrictionist American policy with regard to the refugees has been the subject of David S. Wyman's meticulous *Paper Walls: America and the Refugee Crisis, 1938–1941* (Amherst, 1968). Barbara Stewart dealt with the problem from the first stages of the Nazi ascent to power until 1940 in her volume, *United States Government Policy on Refugees from Nazism, 1933–1940* (New York, 1982). A later study by Richard Breitman and Alan M. Kraut covered the whole period: *American Refugee Policy and European Jewry, 1933–1945* (Bloomington and Indianapolis, 1987). Breitman rendered a harsher judgment on the Roosevelt administration's refugee policy in his contribution, "The Failure to Provide a Safe Haven for European Jewry," in Newton, *FDR*, 129–43. In his view, the Western powers "should have conducted refugee negotiations with Germany in 1938–1939 more aggressively, if only because there was some chance of saving substantial numbers of lives."

6. Henry L. Feingold, *The Politics of Rescue: The Roosevelt Administration and the Holocaust, 1938–1945* (New Brunswick, N.J., 1970), 22–44; Wyman, *Paper Walls*, 43–63. S. Adler-Rudel who himself participated at the Evian Conference published his reflections thirty years later: "The Evian Conference on the Refugee Question," *Leo Baeck Institute Yearbook 1968*, vol. 13 (London, 1968), 235–73. My lecture on the Evian Conference at the Seventh Yad Vashem International Historical Conference in March 1989 was published in *Yalkut Moreshet:* "Veidat Evian" (The Evian Conference) 55 (Oct. 1993): 147–66. See also Yehuda Bauer's recent study, *Jews for Sale: Nazi-Jewish Negotiations, 1933–1945* (New Haven and London, 1994), ch. 2: "Failure of a Last-Minute Rescue Attempt," 30–43.

7. In contrast to his unequivocally anti-Nazi predecessor William E. Dodd, Ambassador Hugh R. Wilson consistently hoped for an improvement of bilateral American-German relations despite the territorial expansion of Germany and the increasing persecution of the Jews. For his views see his *A Career Diplomat: The Third Chapter: The Third Reich* (New York, 1960) edited by his son Hugh R. Wilson Jr. On FDR's motives in recalling Wilson from Berlin, see Joseph Alsop and Robert Kintner, *American White Paper: The Story of American Diplomacy and the Second World War* (New York, 1940), 24–25. A faction in the State Department which hoped to limit the protest to a mere written expression of disapproval was overruled by FDR in a long final discussion at the White House. Nonetheless, at least until the German occupation of

Czechoslovakia in March 1939, the possibility of sending back an American ambassador to Berlin was not definitely discarded.

8. Charles Herbert Stember's *Jews in the Mind of America* (New York, 1966) contains a large number of tables based on relevant polls taken since 1938 as well as careful interpretations and analyses of the data. See pp. 53–139. See also Edward Shapiro, "The Approach of War: Congressional Isolationism and Anti-Semitism, 1939–1941," *American Jewish History* 74 (Sept. 1984): 45–64.

9. Stephen S. Wise to Clark M. Eichelberger, Nov. 17, 1941, and Eichelberger to Wise, Nov. 19, 1941, American Jewish Historical Society Archives (hereafter AJHSA), Waltham, Mass., Stephen S. Wise Papers, P-134, box 85. See also Mark Lincoln Chadwick, *The Hawks of World War II* (Chapel Hill, N.C., 1968), 79–71, 178, 189. According to Chadwick, the New York Jewish ethnic allegiance, along with the international organizations in Manhattan, helped in making that city the center of pro-Allied sentiment, just as German-American reactions contributed to Chicago's isolationism (20).

10. The high-ranking Jewish delegation that met the president on December 8, 1942, included Rabbi Stephen Wise (American Jewish Congress), Henry Monsky (B'nai B'rith), Rabbi Israel Rosenberg (Union of Orthodox Rabbis of the United States and Canada), Maurice Wertheim (American Jewish Committee), and Adolph Held (Jewish Labor Committee). Roosevelt agreed to include the war crimes warning in the United Nations declaration ten days later, but it bore no concrete results. Reports on the murder of the Jews in the East reached the American Jewish press through *JTA* (Jewish Telegraphic Agency) *Daily News Bulletin* as early as July 1941, but the mass killings only seldom received extensive coverage in American dailies. David S. Wyman, *The Abandonment of the Jews: America and the Holocaust, 1941–1945* (New York, 1984), 19–30, 61–78. For a critical view of the Jewish establishment cp. Haskel Lookstein, *Were We Our Brothers' Keepers? The Public Response of American Jews to the Holocaust, 1938–1944* (New York, 1985), 105–14.

11. Deborah E. Lipstadt, *Beyond Belief: The American Press and the Coming of the Holocaust* (New York, 1986), 240–41. In addition to 30 percent who dismissed the extermination news, another 24 percent had no opinion on that issue. Wyman, *Abandonment of the Jews*, 85–95, 152–53.

12. Monty N. Penkower, "The 1943 Joint Anglo-American Statement on Palestine," in *Essays in American Zionism: Herzl Yearbook*, vol. 8, edited by Melvin J. Urofsky (New York, 1978), 212–41. On the Bermuda Conference see Feingold, *Politics of Rescue*, 167–207; Wyman, *Abandonment of the Jews*, 104–23.

13. Feingold, "Courage First and Intelligence Second," 65–68. On the creation of the War Refugee Board, see Wyman, *Abandonment of the Jews*, 193–206; Breitman and Kraut, *American Refugee Policy and European Jewry*, 187–90; Monty N. Penkower, "Jewish Organizations and the Creation of the War Refugee Board," in *The Annals of the American Academy of Political and Social Science* 450 (July 1980): 122–39; Monty N. Penkower, "The Bergson Boys," *American Jewish History* 70 (Mar. 1981): 281–309; Judith Tydor Baumel, "The IZL Delegation in the USA, 1939–1948: Anatomy of an Ethnic Interest/Protest Group," *Jewish History* 9 (Spring 1995): 79–89. The first to call attention to the Roosevelt administration's failure with regard to rescue until the

establishment of the WRB was Arthur D. Morse, *While Six Million Died: A Chronicle of American Apathy* (New York, 1967), esp. pp. 3–99. The Emergency Committee to Save the Jewish People of Europe was led by Hillel Kook alias Peter Bergson, the IZL (Irgun Zvai Leumi) emissary to the United States.

14. For a summary of the different views and approaches, see Deborah E. Lipstadt, "America and the Holocaust," *Modern Judaism* 10 (Oct. 1990): 283–96. Cp. also Frank W. Brecher's afterword in his *Reluctant Ally: United States Policy Toward the Jews from Wilson to Roosevelt* (New York, 1991), 95–117. Henry L. Feingold discussed the record of the American Jewish community in his B.G. Rudolph Lecture in Judaic Studies *Did American Jewry Do Enough During the Holocaust?* (Syracuse, N.Y., 1985), and in "Was There Communal Failure? Some Thoughts on the American Jewish Response to the Holocaust," in Newton, *FDR*, 89–107, reprinted from *American Jewish History* 81 (Autumn 1993): 60–80. In contrast to outspoken critics of the "abandonment of the Jews" such as Wyman, Feingold takes a more balanced attitude toward the American government and also refrains from accusations of American Jewish leaders, with all their shortcomings. The impact of antisemitism in limiting FDR's policy choices with regard to refugees and rescue is emphasized by Leonard Dinnerstein, "Franklin D. Roosevelt and the Jews: Another Look," *Dimensions* 10, no. 1 (1996): 3–8. For a recent defense of Roosevelt's stand, Arthur Schlesinger Jr., "Did FDR Betray the Jews?" *Newsweek*, Apr. 18, 1994, p. 43. Melvin J. Urofsky dealt with the Zionist ascendancy in the first chapters of his *We Are One!: American Jewry and Israel* (Garden City, N.Y., 1978), 1–93. Cp. also David H. Shpiro, *From Philanthropy to Action: The Political Transformation of American Zionism in the Holocaust Years* (Oxford, 1993).

15. A. Leon Kubowitzki, *Unity in Dispersion: A History of the World Jewish Congress* (New York, 1948), 134–48; Naomi W. Cohen, *Not Free to Desist: The American Jewish Committee, 1906–1966* (Philadelphia, 1972), 265–66.

16. Kubowitzki, *Unity in Dispersion*, 148–96; on the reparations demand at the Baltimore Conference, Nahum Goldmann, *Mein Leben als deutscher Jude* (Munich, 1980), 372. Sam Rosenman's adversary advice quoted by Wyman, *Abandonment of the Jews*, 256.

17. American Jewish Conference, Statement on Punishment of War Criminals, Aug. 28, 1944, and Abba Hillel Silver to Louis Lipsky, Aug. 18, 1944, Central Zionist Archives (hereafter CZA), Jerusalem, American Jewish Conference Collection, C7/450. A statement on the punishment of war criminals by the WJC preceded that of the conference.

18. In the winter of 1944–45, Herbert C. Pell was forced to resign because no funds had been appropriated for his continued participation in the commission's work. Pell, who was welcomed by the American Jewish Conference and other Jewish groups, was not reappointed to his job, but Congress allocated the necessary funds for his successor, who did not antagonize the State Department.

19. The American Jewish Conference never affiliated with the WJC, but both reached a working agreement on postwar cooperation. Interim Committee of the AJ Conference, Mar. 21, 1944, AJHSA, AJ Conference Papers, I-67, Waltham, Mass.

20. Kubowitzki, *Unity in Dispersion*, 221–35; Nehemiah Robinson, *Indemnification and Reparations: Jewish Aspects* (New York, 1944), 83, 248–56; Nahum Goldmann's

keynote address, Nov. 26, 1944, American Jewish Archives (AJA), Cincinnati, Ohio, World Jewish Congress Collection, Manuscript Collection 361 (hereafter WJCC), A67/8. Since I saw most of the WJC correspondence in the late 1980s, I have mainly used the old registration numbers.

21. Georg Landauer, for many years director of the Jewish Agency's Central Bureau for the Settlement of German Jews, stressed the great importance of a collective claim of the Jewish people against Germany in a memorandum to the Jewish Agency executive in September 1943. Siegfried Moses, another former prominent German Zionist, summed up his ideas about individual compensation and a collective claim for reparations to the Jewish people in a pamphlet, *Jewish Postwar Claims*, which was published in September 1944 by the Association of Immigrants from Central Europe. Nana Sagi, *German Reparations: A History of the Negotiations* (Jerusalem, 1980), 17–27.

22. Cohen, *Not Free to Desist*, 265–66. For AJC's subsequent support for the partition of Palestine and the creation of a Jewish state, see Menahem Kaufman, *An Ambiguous Partnership: Non-Zionists and Zionists in America, 1939–1948* (Jerusalem and Detroit, 1991), 224–41, 275–311. For the postwar changes of the AJC, see also Henry L. Feingold, "The Continued Vitality of the American Jewish Committee at 80," *AJYB*, *1987*, vol. 87, pp. 341–53. The Jewish Labor Committee also had a separate Research Institute for Jewish Postwar Problems.

23. *To the Counsellors of Peace: Recommendations of the American Jewish Committee* (New York, March 1945). Recommendations, pp. 1–9, 101–8. Cp. with the memorandum of the American Jewish Conference's Interim Committee submitted to Secretary of State Edward R. Stettinius Jr., Apr. 2, 1945. CZA, Israel Goldstein Papers, A364/1956.

24. Yehuda Bauer, *Out of the Ashes: The Impact of American Jews on Post-Holocaust European Jewry* (Oxford, 1989), xi–xxv. Edward M. M. Warburg, the Joint's postwar general chairman, became the first president of the Jewish Restitution Successor Organization, and Moses A. Leavitt, the organization's vice-chairman, headed the delegation of the Claims Conference at the Wassenaar negotiations with the Federal Republic of Germany in 1952.

25. Edward S. Shapiro, "World War II and American Jewish Identity," *Modern Judaism* 10 (Feb. 1990): 65–84, quote from p. 65. For the postwar changes on the American Jewish scene, see his *A Time for Healing: American Jewry Since World War II*, vol. 5 of *The Jewish People in America*, a series sponsored by the American Jewish Historical Society (Baltimore, 1992).

CHAPTER 2

1. The main sources on Henry Morgenthau Jr., whose policies with regard to Germany are being dealt with in this chapter, are the Morgenthau Diaries, a collection of protocols, memoranda, and correspondence for the years of Morgenthau's service as secretary of the Treasury, and in addition, Morgenthau's Presidential Diaries, both deposited at the Franklin Delano Roosevelt Library (FDRL) at Hyde Park, N.Y. Two volumes of the Diaries, *Morgenthau Diary (Germany)*, were published for a subcommittee of the U.S. Senate Committee on the Judiciary and prefaced by Anthony Kubek (Washington, D.C., 1967), hereafter MD. The Diaries and his talks with the former secretary also served as the basis for John Morton Blum's three

volumes *From the Morgenthau Diaries* (Boston, 1967). An abridged and updated version appeared three years later: John Morton Blum, *Roosevelt and Morgenthau: A Review and Condensation of "From the Morgenthau Diaries"* (Boston, 1970). While some of Morgenthau's recollections have to be used with care, the Blum volumes remain a most important source. For additional insights see Henry Morgenthau III, *Mostly Morgenthaus: A Family History* (New York, 1991), 297–427.

On the occasion of Morgenthau's one hundredth birthday, an article I wrote on Morgenthau's involvement in rescue, Germany, and Palestine appeared in the Hebrew periodical *Yalkut Moreshet:* "Henry Morgenthau umeoravuto behatzala, be-Germania ube-Eretz Israel" (Henry Morgenthau Jr. and his involvement in rescue, Germany, and Palestine) 51 (Nov. 1991): 35–49.

2. Characteristic of the continuing right-wing German exposure of the "Morgenthau legacy" twenty years after the end of World War II was Caspar Schrenck-Notzing's *Charakterwäsche: Die amerikanische Besatzung in Deutschland und ihre Folgen* (Stuttgart, 1965). Schrenck-Notzing has served for many years as editor of the right-wing intellectual monthly *Criticon,* and his book was reprinted in 1981 and appeared in paperback in 1993. By contrast, Morgenthau's proposals on Germany and the futile efforts of the American left-liberals to influence postwar U.S. policies were recently accorded a sympathetic treatment by the left-wing German author Bernd Greiner, *Die Morgenthau Legende: Zur Geschichte eines umstrittenen Plans* (Hamburg, 1995). Greiner puts much of the blame for the failure of the Morgenthau plan on the common interests of American and German industrial corporations, which favored rapid postwar reconstruction instead of industrial reorganization and decartelization. Because of the looming confrontation with the Soviet Union, the United States soon discarded Morgenthau's proposals for Germany's industrial disarmament and for punishing the German economic elites who helped Hitler's rise to power and supported his war of aggression. For Joseph Goebbels's propagandistic use of the Morgenthau proposals, see Office of War Information Special Report on Enemy Handling of Morgenthau Plan for Germany, quoted by Greiner, *Die Morgenthau Legende,* 15. A review of anti-Morgenthau writings can be found in the same monograph, pp. 17–27. Warren F. Kimball, one of the few American defenders of Morgenthau's motives, regarded the "plan" as an attempt at internationalizing the agrarian myth and rejected the accusation that the secretary's intention was to starve the German people. *Swords to Ploughshares: The Morgenthau Plan for Defeated Nazi Germany* (Philadelphia, 1976), esp. pp. 25–27, 59–62.

3. Konrad Adenauer, *Reden, 1917–1967,* edited by Hans-Peter Schwarz (Stuttgart, 1975), 125. Quoted in Henning Köhler, *Adenauer: Eine politische Biographie* (Berlin, 1994), 18. As late as 1967 Adenauer described the Nuclear Non-Proliferation Treaty, which he strongly opposed, as a "Morgenthau Plan in Quadrat." *Der Spiegel,* Feb. 27, 1967, p. 21. There were also critics on the left such as Victor Agartz, the trade union economist, who condemned Morgenthau's attempt to reduce German civilization into primitivity. Greiner, *Die Morgenthau Legende,* 17.

4. Blum, *From the Morgenthau Diaries, Vol 1: Years of Crisis,* 149–54, 161–67, 181,

452–53, 458, 466–67, 508, 515–17, 521–28. On Morgenthau's positive view of the Soviet Union, Morgenthau, *Mostly Morgenthaus*, 270–71, 313.

5. Besides other sources, I have relied on an interview with Henry Morgenthau III, Cambridge, Mass., Sept. 23, 1990. Despite his aloofness toward communal activities, on September 14, 1933 Henry Morgenthau Jr. accompanied Judge Irving Lehman, a member of the AJC executive committee, to a meeting with FDR at the White House at which the German Jewish situation was broached. Nonetheless, that meeting as well as following consultations bore no results. Breitman and Kraut, *American Refugee Policy and European Jewry*, 18–19. Earlier, on April 6, 1933, Morgenthau attended a meeting of leading AJC members who convened to review the response to the Nazi anti-Jewish boycott of April 1. Yehuda Bauer, *My Brother's Keeper: A History of the American Jewish Joint Distribution Committee, 1929–1939* (Philadelphia, 1974), 107.

6. David Ben Gurion saw Morgenthau in the winter of 1941–42 and was impressed by his optimism regarding the future of Zionism. Shabtai Tevet, *Kin'at David: The Life of David Ben Gurion* (in Hebrew), vol. 3 (Jerusalem, 1987), 399. During his stay in the United States in 1942–43, Chaim Weizmann, president of the World Zionist Organization (hereafter WZO), met with Morgenthau several times and continued to be in touch with him mainly on Zionist affairs. E.g. Michael Cohen, ed., *The Letters and Papers of Chaim Weizmann*, vol. 21, Series A (Jerusalem, 1979), 39.

A most helpful conduit for Stephen Wise, Chaim Weizmann, and other Jewish leaders was Henrietta Klotz, for many years Morgenthau's secretary, a convinced Zionist from Orthodox background. For Morgenthau's part in foiling the anti-Zionist British-American draft statement of summer 1943, see Penkower, "The 1943 Joint Anglo-American Statement on Palestine"; chap. 1, note 12, above. For the creation of the WRB, chap. 1, note 13, above, especially Wyman, *Abandonment of the Jews*, 193–206.

7. The basic documents on the proposals of Morgenthau and his opponents regarding postsurrender Germany in September 1944 are reprinted in U.S. Department of State, *Foreign Relations of the United States* (hereafter *FRUS*), *The Conference at Quebec 1944* (Washington, D.C., 1972), 86–89, 93–97, 98–100, 101–8, 123–26, 128–43. For the most detailed draft of the so-called Morgenthau plan see Morgenthau to Roosevelt, Sept. 5, 1944, Suggested Post-Surrender Program for Germany, pp. 101–8; for Henry L. Stimson's objections see his memorandum to FDR, Sept. 5, 1944, as well as his memo of Sept. 9, 1944, pp. 123–26. For Stimson's views see also the entry in his diary, Sept. 5, 1944, Yale University, Sterling Library, H. L. Stimson Diaries. Some of the relevant entries have also been quoted in Henry L. Stimson and McGeorge Bundy, *On Active Service in Peace and War* (New York, 1947), 568–83, 584–91. For Hull's views, Cordell Hull, *Memoirs*, 2 vols. (New York, 1948), 207–8, 1605–15. A memorandum on the development of American postwar policy for Germany, drafted on September 4, 1946, shortly before Secretary of State James F. Byrnes's Stuttgart address, contended that Morgenthau prepared his so-called plan in conjunction "with his friends among the more extreme Jewish elements" in the United States. U.S. National Archives, Department of State Decimal Files, Record Group 59, 862.00/9–446 (hereafter NA, RG59 and file number).

8. Whereas the first Treasury drafts stressed the importance of Germany's partition into three separate entities, Morgenthau's subsequent proposals for the Second

Quebec Conference focused on the deindustrialization of the Ruhr and an early withdrawal of American troops to be replaced by soldiers from Eastern and Western Europe. The Quebec memorandum, initialed by Roosevelt and British Prime Minister Winston Churchill, did not mention the suggested division of Germany into several states or the annexation of the Saar region to France, but it placed the latter together with the Ruhr region under international supervision. It also mentioned the aim of making Germany "a country primarily agricultural and pastoral in its character." Sept. 15, *FRUS, The Conference at Quebec 1944*, 466–67. Some of Morgenthau's proposals in 1944 sprang from the recommendations that Robert McDonnell, an oil manager who was put in control of American assets of German companies after the U.S. entry into the war against Germany, submitted to the secretary in 1943. MD, vol. 1, 354–57. In his recent monograph Wilfried Mausbach saw the main importance of Morgenthau's recommendations in the linkage between retribution and deindustrialization and American security policy. *Zwischen Morgenthau und Marshall. Das wirtschaftliche Deutschlandkonzept der USA 1944–1947* (Düsseldorf, 1996), summary pp. 368–75.

9. For the development of the War Department's alternative conspiracy-criminal organization approach, which prevailed over Morgenthau's suggestions and paved the way for the trial of the Nazi criminals before an international military tribunal, see Bradley F. Smith, *The Road to Nuremberg* (New York, 1981), particularly his conclusions, pp. 247–61. See also Michael R. Marrus, "The Prelude to the Nuremberg Trial," *Dimensions* 10, no. 1 (1996): 23–27.

10. FDRL, Henry Morgenthau Jr. Presidential Diaries, vol. 7, p. 1501, April 11, 1945. In addition to his disfavor of Robert Murphy, whose memoirs *Diplomat Among Warriors* (Garden City, N.Y., 1964) prove the consistent conservative line of this experienced diplomat, Morgenthau opposed the candidacy of James Dunn, another conservative diplomat, and preferred the anti-German Charles Bowers as political adviser to General Dwight D. Eisenhower, but Murphy was appointed.

A bête noir in the eyes of Morgenthau was also James W. Riddleberger, a State Department official with prewar experience in Berlin. Riddleberger, who attended the presentation of the Morgenthau plan at Harry Hopkins's office, thought it was "silly and superficial." Characteristic of Riddleberger's attitude to defeated Germany was his objection to a proposal that all monuments of German militarism must be destroyed. Harry S. Truman Library (hereafter HSTL), Independence, Mo., James W. Riddleberger, Oral History interview, 1972.

11. On the demise of the Morgenthau plan and Truman's accession to the presidency, Blum, *From the Morgenthau Diaries*, vol. 3, *Years of War*, 421–76. Upon Morgenthau's resignation, Stephen Wise dispatched to him a letter of appreciation extolling the honor he "brought to the record of American Jews." July 13, 1945, AJHSA, Stephen Wise Papers, P-134, box 117.

12. Wyman, *Abandonment of the Jews*, 183, 186–87, 202–3. See also FDRL, Oscar S. Cox Papers, box 85. The FEA recommended changing Germany's economic structure from heavy to light industries. For its attitude see Mausbach, *Zwischen Morgenthau und Marshall*, 102–9, 153–57.

13. Samuel Lubell, memorandum on German control, Mar. 18, 1945, and memorandum to Baruch, Apr. 1, 1945, Princeton University, Bernard M. Baruch Papers,

vol. 3, pp. 37–45 and box 39. In 1943 Lubell submitted to Baruch several memoranda on continuing pro-German activities in the U.S., e.g., May 26, 1943, box 39. See also Baruch's appearance before the Senate, U.S. Senate, 79th Congress, First Session, Hearings, Committee on Military Affairs, June 22, 1945. Successively he changed his view, Bernard M. Baruch, *Baruch: The Public Years* (New York, 1960), 406–9, and Jordan A. Schwarz, *The Speculator: Bernard M. Baruch in Washington, 1917–1965* (Chapel Hill, N.C. 1981), 475–80. On Baruch's conversation with the West German Consul General Hans Eduard Riesser, see Riesser to the Foreign Office in Bonn, May 20, 1952, Politisches Archiv des Auswärtigen Amtes (hereafter PA/AA), III 210.07/80. See also Riesser's memoirs *Von Versailles zur Uno-Aus der Erinnerung eines Diplomaten* (Bonn, 1962), 254. Baruch strongly opposed slowing down the rearming of Western Europe and opening negotiations over Germany with Moscow.

14. Blum, *Roosevelt and Morgenthau*, xiii. William H. Draper Jr., a Republican who served under the Roosevelt and Truman administrations and a consistent opponent of the Morgenthau plan, recalls a conversation with Morgenthau before his death during which he "did not give any ground." HSTL, Oral History interview, 1972.

15. Isador Lubin's Oral History interview, 1974, HSTL. Because of Lubin's support for the deindustrialization of Germany, in 1945 President Truman appointed Edwin W. Pauley instead of Lubin as chief representative on the Allied Reparations Commission. Lubin was demoted to the second spot.

16. Stimson Diaries, Sept. 20, 1944, Yale University; Felix Frankfurter to Benjamin V. Cohen, Aug. 9, 1945, Manuscript Division, Library of Congress (hereafter LC), Benjamin V. Cohen Papers, box 8; Entry of Nov. 4, 1946, *From the Diaries of Felix Frankfurter*, edited by Joseph P. Lash (New York, 1974), 286–87; Cohen to Frankfurter, Aug. 13, 1945, Benjamin V. Cohen Papers, box 8. In 1947 Cohen, then a counselor at the State Department, objected to former president Herbert Hoover's recommendation that there should be no further dismantlement from Germany other than direct arms plants. However, he recommended that the United States should be careful not to give the impression that it was bent upon restricting Germany's legitimate peace industries and obstructing its efforts to improve the standard of living of the German population. Draft of a letter to President Truman, May 9, 1947, LC, Benjamin V. Cohen Papers, box 15.

17. James P. Warburg, *The Long Road Home: The Autobiography of a Maverick* (Garden City, N.Y., 1964), xvii–xviii, 223–25, 233, 254–58; also *Germany: Key to Peace* (Cambridge, Mass., 1953), 2–7. An article by James Warburg in favor of a "soft peace" (*New York Times Magazine*, Aug. 20, 1944) aroused critical comments in the Jewish community, e.g., Arthur Meyerovitz of the New York Federation of Reform Synagogues to Warburg, Aug. 22, 1944, John Fitzgerald Kennedy Library, Boston, James F. Warburg Papers, box 27. James Warburg's smear of the UJA was criticized in an editorial of *Congress Biweekly*, Dec. 14, 1959. See also Ron Chernow, *The Warburgs: The Twentieth Century Odyssey of a Remarkable Jewish Family* (New York, 1993), 479–93, 581–82.

18. See various clippings and notes, FDRL, Harvey M. Kilgore Papers, boxes 35, 38, 92.

19. *Germany Is Our Problem* (New York and London, 1945), a major part of which

was prepared with the help of the Treasury staff before the secretary resigned in July 1945, was the first project of the Elinor and Henry Morgenthau Jr. Foundation of Peace, chaired by Eleanor Roosevelt, Harold K. Hochschild, and Morris L. Ernst. "Our Policy Toward Germany," a series of articles by Henry Morgenthau Jr., appeared in the *New York Post*, Nov. 24–29, 1947; another series based on the Morgenthau Diaries appeared in *Collier's*, Sept.–Nov. 1947.

20. Morgenthau's statement quoted in Ernest Stock, *Chosen Instrument: The Jewish Agency in the First Decade of the State of Israel* (New York, 1988), 40. For the regional pact controversy, see State of Israel, Israel State Archives (hereafter ISA), *Documents on the Foreign Policy of Israel*, vol. 5, edited by Yehoshua Freundlich (Jerusalem, 1988), Companion Volume (CV): E. Eilat to M. Sharett, Jan. 26–27, 1950, Doc. 48, pp. 30–32. In response to questions by Mapam and the Communist Party, Ben Gurion argued that Morgenthau's was only a private view of an individual. On his talk with Secretary of State Acheson, see HSTL, Dean Acheson Papers, Memos of Conversations, 64b, Feb. 15, 1950. On Eshkol's remarks, FDRL, Henry Morgenthau Jr., Presidential Diaries, vol. 8, pp. 1814–1817, Dec. 9, 1953.

21. *Mostly Morgenthaus*, 310–14, 423–27. David Rees's biography *Harry Dexter White: A Study in Paradox* (New York, 1973) also does not provide any conclusive answer regarding White's pro-Communist past. His advice to Henry Wallace is mentioned in Robert Donovan, *Conflict and Crisis: The Presidency of Harry S. Truman, 1945–1948* (New York, 1977), 116.

22. Bernard Bernstein, Oral History interview, 1975, HSTL; Lucius D. Clay, interview, 1971, p. 544, Columbia University Oral History Collection, New York. Cp. also James Wechsler, *The Age of Suspicion* (New York, 1953), 190–98. For Robert Patterson's and John McCloy's letters of July 16 and 22, 1947, respectively, CZA, Goldstein Papers, A364/1959.

23. A most critical review of Communist infiltration in the Treasury was published by Anthony Kubek, a rightist Dallas University historian, as introduction to two volumes of the *Morgenthau Diary (Germany)* for the use of a subcommittee of the Senate Committee on the Judiciary (Washington, D.C. 1967), 1–81. Kubek implied that White, "the actual architect, as well as the master-builder, of the Morgenthau Plan," served the interests of the Soviet Union. Gabriel Kolko, one of the leading New Left historians in the 1960s, argued just the opposite. According to his view, Morgenthau's plan was contrary to the interests of the Soviet Union, which expected large-scale reparations from Germany. The Treasury Department's proposals would have made such reparations impossible. *The Policy of War: The World and U.S. Foreign Policy* (New York, 1968), 320–33, esp. p. 324.

24. Ben Halpern, "The Nuremberg Trial," *Jewish Frontier* 13 (Jan. 1946): 30–32. He expressed the same view in an interview with the author, Brookline, Mass., June 24, 1988.

25. Blum, *From the Morgenthau Diaries*, vol. 3, *Years of War*, 378–79. For Jewish concern with the Republicans' antisemitic references to Sidney Hillman's role in the Roosevelt administration and in the 1944 presidential campaign, see Manifestations of Antisemitism in the 1944 Campaign, report to the Plenary Session of NCRAC, Jan. 14, 1945. AJHSA, NCRAC Papers, I-172, box 2.

26. JLC to Cordell Hull, Sept. 24, 1943, signed by Philip Murray, William Gillespie, Adolph Held, and David Dubinsky, FDRL, Sam Rosenman Papers, box 2. Also my written interview with Emanuel Muravchik, a former leading official of the JLC, New York, June 19, 1988. For the JLC and the Holocaust, see Gail Malmgren, "Labor and the Holocaust: The Jewish Labor Committee and the Anti–Nazi Struggle," *Jewish Spectator* 57 (Summer 1992): 31–36. For its help to refugees from German-speaking countries, Jack Jacobs, "A Friend in Need: The Jewish Labor Committee, and Refugees from the German-Speaking Lands, 1933–1945," *YIVO Annual* 23 (1996): 391–417.

27. Cohen, *Not Free to Desist*, 480.

28. Julius Gordon, "A Light to the Nations," in *Central Conference of American Rabbis* (hereafter *CCAR*), vol. 53, edited by Isaac E. Marcuson (Philadelphia, 1943); Fifty-Fourth Annual Convention, June 22–27, 1943, New York, pp. 204–16. Five years earlier, the majority report presented to the forty-ninth annual convention of Reform rabbis at Atlantic City, N.J., gave an "unequivocal negative answer" to the question of whether the United States should go to war to stop Fascist expansion in Europe, Asia, and Africa, *CCAR*, vol. 48 (Philadelphia, 1943), 133–42. In 1939–40 the CCAR started to differentiate between aggressive states and those being attacked. See also Ofer Shiff, "Coping with the Holocaust from a Standpoint of Inner Dissonance: The American Jewish Reform Movement in the 1930s and 1940s," in *OT*, edited by Daniel Carpi, et al. (Ramat Gan, forthcoming.)

29. Forty-Second Annual Convention, June 29–July 1, 1942, New York. *The Rabbinical Assembly of America*, Proceedings 1941–1944, vol. 8 (New York, 1946), 120–28.

30. "Vengeance Is Mine," *Liberal Judaism* 12 (Oct. 1944): 1–3.

31. See my article, "The View of a Maverick Pacifist and Universalist: Rabbi Abraham Cronbach's Plea for Clemency for Nazi Criminals in 1945," *American Jewish Archives* 42 (Fall–Winter 1990): 147–54.

32. Koppel S. Pinson, "On the Future of Germany: A Survey of Opinions and Proposals," *Menorah Journal* 32 (Oct.–Dec. 1944): 125–60. A follow-up article by the same author dedicated to the question of the Jews in the settlement with Germany never appeared.

33. Erich Kahler, "The German Problem, II, Solution?" *Contemporary Jewish Record* 7 (Dec. 1944): 608–15. Prague-born Erich von Kahler, in the past one of the few Jewish members of the elitist anti-democratic Stefan George circle in Germany, espoused in his exile years liberal universalist views.

34. "A Soft Peace . . . An Insult to Justice," *National Jewish Monthly* (*NJM*) 59 (Oct. 1944): 33. The editorial of the next issue stated: "We do not think there is anything in their 'blood' that makes Germans the way they are. They can be taught civilization, as other savages have been taught. But the time to do it is before they launch World War III." *NJM* 59 (Nov. 1944): 81.

35. "The German Question," *Yiddisher Kempfer*, Sept. 29, 1949, pp. 3–4. Grodzensky used the pseudonym G. Salomon.

36. "Crime and Punishment," *Jewish Frontier* 11 (Dec. 1944): 12–14.

37. "The Morgenthau Plan," *Jewish Frontier* 13 (Jan. 1946): 32–36.

CHAPTER 3

1. According to UNRRA statistics, in September 1945 there were 53,322 Jews among 1,488,077 DPs in Germany, Austria, and Italy. The estimates of Jewish survivors at the end of the war in Europe vary from 50,000 to 70,000. Thousands died after liberation and many others returned to their countries of origin to look for their families. In 1946–47 approximately 185,000 Jewish DPs lived in camps in Germany and 45,000 in Austria, the overwhelming majority of them in the American zones of occupation. On UNRRA data, Malcolm J. Proudfoot, *European Refugees: A Study in Forced Population Movement* (Evanston, Ill., 1956), 238–39, 339–41. For other estimates, Yehuda Bauer, *Flight and Rescue: Brichah* (New York, 1970), 319–21. In addition to this early monograph, Bauer dealt with the survivors and DPs in West Germany, Austria, and Italy in the third volume of his history of the American Jewish Joint Distribution Committee, *Out of the Ashes: The Impact of American Jews on Post-Holocaust European Jewry* (Oxford, 1989), esp. pp. 23–70, 193–236. Cp. also Abraham S. Hyman's belated recollections *The Undefeated* (Jerusalem, 1993). I have relied in some of the following pages on Leonard Dinnerstein's pioneering study *America and the Survivors of the Holocaust* (New York, 1982). See also Haim Genizi, *America's Fair Share: The Admission and Resettlement of Displaced Persons, 1945–1952* (Detroit, 1996).

2. Klaus-Dietmar Henke, the author of a detailed monograph on the American occupation of Germany in 1945, contends that in the early days of occupation the great majority of the German population felt closer to the pragmatic American military government than to the National Socialist regime they had served for twelve years: *Die amerikanische Besetzung Deutschlands* (Munich, 1995), 31. Still, whatever their attitude really was, one should not compare it with the joy felt by the liberated.

On the occasion of the fiftieth anniversary of the end of the war in Europe, five years after Germany's reunification, the German federal president, chancellor, and other leading politicians portrayed May 8, 1945, as a day of liberation. This view was also stressed by a great many liberal and left-of-center historians, political scientists, and journalists who partook in the debate. Nevertheless, the belated reappraisal, though positive from the viewpoint of German political culture at the end of the twentieth century, did not reflect the feelings of most Germans two generations ago. On the other hand, there is no doubt that they preferred the American (and British) occupiers in the West to the Russians. For the debate, see Kurt Sontheimer, "Selbstverständlich war dies nicht: Ein Rückblick auf den Streit um die Bewertung des 8. Mai," *Süddeutsche Zeitung*, July 21, 1995; Hans Mommsen, "Der 8. Mai 1945: Endpunkt einer Hybris: Es war ein beispielloser säkularer Zusammenbruch," *Das Parlament*, Apr. 28, 1995, p. 1; Bernd Faulenbach, "Das Ende, das ein Anfang war," *Vorwärts*, May 1995, pp. 32–33; Klaus Harpprecht, "Der Tag der Rettung," *Die Zeit*, May 5, 1995, p. 26. Horst Möller, Martin Broszat's heir as director of the Munich Institut für Zeitgeschichte, remained more critical of the reinterpretation of May 8 as a day of liberation: "Die Relativität historischer Epochen: Das Jahr 1945 in der Perspektive des Jahres 1989," *Aus Politik und Zeitgeschichte*, B18–19/95, Apr. 28, 1995, pp. 3–9. See also the review essay by Enrico Syring, "Der noch immer umstrittene Jahrestag," *Das Parlament*, Aug. 25, 1995, p. 13.

3. John S. D. Eisenhower, ed., *Dwight D. Eisenhower: Letters to Mamie* (Garden City, N.Y., 1978), 248.

4. Deborah E. Lipstadt, *Beyond Belief*, 254–57. See also Norbert Frei's critical account, "'Wir Waren Blind, Ungläubig und Langsam': Buchenwald, Dachau und die amerikanischen Medien in Frühjahr 1945," *Vierteljahrshefte für Zeitgeschichte* 35 (1987): 385–401.

5. *The Gallup Poll: Public Opinion, 1935–1971*, vol. 1, *1935–1948* (New York, 1972), the poll of May 1945 (p. 506) as compared to the preceding October poll, published Nov. 20, 1944 (p. 470). According to a National Opinion Research Center poll of the University of Denver early in 1945, most Americans made a fundamental distinction between the German people and their Nazi leaders, recommended a lenient postwar treatment stressing reeducation and reconstruction of German industries, and opposed long-term occupation of Germany or drastic dismemberment. FDRL, Isador Lubin Papers, box 113.

6. Stephen E. Ambrose, *Eisenhower*, vol. 1, *Soldier, General of the Army, President-Elect, 1890–1952* (New York, 1983), 420–23; David Eisenhower, *Eisenhower at War* (New York, 1986), 402–3. See also Stephen E. Ambrose's contribution, "Eisenhower and the Germans," in *Eisenhower and the German POWs: Facts against Falsehood*, edited by Günter Bischof and Stephen E. Ambrose (Baton Rouge and London, 1992), 29–38.

Bruno Bettelheim's first paper on his concentration camp experiences in 1938, published by the *Journal of Abnormal and Social Psychology* in 1943, was distributed in 1945, upon General Eisenhower's personal request, to the traumatized American troops who opened up Buchenwald. See Rosemary Dinnage's review of Nina Sutton, *Bettelheim: A Life and a Legacy*, "The Survivor," *New York Review of Books* (hereafter *NYR*), June 20, 1996, pp. 10–14, here p. 11.

7. The full text of the Harrison Report is reprinted as Appendix B in Dinnerstein, *America and the Survivors of the Holocaust*, 291–305. See also ch. 2 of his study, pp. 39–71. On the Harrison Report, cp. interview with Dr. Joseph Schwartz, Aug. 14, 1962, Hebrew University Institute of Contemporary Jewry, Oral History Division, Jerusalem. Much of Schwartz's language was included in Harrison's final draft.

At first Henry Morgenthau had suggested to President Truman that a Cabinet-level committee deal with the problem of the DPs, but the president objected. Eventually he agreed to the State Department's dispatch of Earl Harrison. The preference of the Zionists for that nomination was James McDonald, who was known as a supporter of some of the major Zionist demands. Mayer W. Weisgal to Henrietta Klotz, June 14, 1945, CZA, Z5/1046.

8. Haim Genizi has discussed the importance of this new office in his monograph: *Yoetz Umekim: hayoetz latzava haamerikai vesheerith hapleita* (The Adviser on Jewish Affairs to the American Army and the Displaced Persons, 1945–1949) (in Hebrew) (Tel Aviv, 1987). See also his article on Rabbi Philip Bernstein, "Philip S. Bernstein: Adviser on Jewish Affairs, 1946–1947," *Simon Wiesenthal Center Annual* 3 (1986): 139–76. Acting adviser Abraham S. Hyman's final report on Jewish affairs in Germany and Austria was released by the Army on March 12, 1950. HSTL, Harry N. Rosenfield

Papers, box 16. Hyman served as the last adviser until December 31, 1949, when the office was closed. Attempts of the Four Cooperating Organizations to convince High Commissioner John McCloy of the necessity to continue the office despite the end of the military government were not successful, Zachariah Shuster to John Slawson, Sept. 30, 1949. Records of the AJC, YIVO New York, RG347, FAD-1 (Germany), box 23 (hereafter YIVO, AJC Records, FAD and box number). For the British adviser, see Hagit Lavsky, "British Jewry and the Jews in Post-Holocaust Germany: The Jewish Relief Unit, 1945–1950," *Journal of Holocaust Education* 4 (Summer 1995): 29–40.

9. Bauer, *Out of the Ashes*, 204–5, 268–69; Leonard Dinnerstein, "German Attitudes Toward the Jewish Displaced Persons (1945–50)," in *Germany and America* edited by Hans Trefousse (New York, 1980), 241–46.

10. Philip Bernstein to Commander-in-Chief, European Command, July 16, 1947, OMGUS Papers, Institut für Zeitgeschichte, Munich (hereafter IfZ), MF260, AG1947/2/1.

11. E.g., in the summer of 1947 General Clarence R. Huebner complained to Judge Louis E. Levinthal that, contrary to his assurances, intelligence officers had discovered that more than half of the three thousand inhabitants of one of the Jewish assembly centers were Communists. As a "proof," Huebner provided Levinthal with a pin that had on it a hammer and sickle and at the bottom the inscribed name of Ber Borochov, the noted Labor Zionist leader. Interview with Louis E. Levinthal, June 29, 1962, HU Institute of Contemporary Jewry, Oral History Division. However, the deputy director of Intelligence, Headquarters European Command, found little evidence to indicate large-scale pro-Soviet infiltration among the Jewish DPs. Report to Director of Intelligence, OMGUS, Mar. 5, 1948. OMGUS Papers, IfZ, MF260, POLAD 34/17.

Joel Wolfsohn, AJC European director (1947–49), found it advisable to remind the military government that shortly after the end of the war almost all Polish Jews living in Russia decided to quit their place of refuge and returned to Poland. Besides, in the local elections in the DP camps, left-wing candidates were the least successful. Wolfsohn to John Slawson, AJC executive vice-president, May 21, 1948, HSTL, Joel Wolfsohn Papers, box 18.

12. Julius Klein, "Germans Still Subvert the Yanks, *NJM* 62 (Sept. 1947): 1. For the immediate pro-German impact of the end of nonfraternization, see Richard Joseph with Waverley Root, "Why So Many GIs Like the Germans Best," *Readers Digest*, Mar. 1946.

13. Alex Grobman, *Rekindling the Flame: American Jewish Chaplains and the Survivors of European Jewry, 1944–1948* (Detroit, 1993), 36–61, 65–88, 192–97. See also Louis Barish, ed., *Rabbis in Uniform: The Story of the American Jewish Military Chaplains* (New York, 1962); Abraham J. Klausner, "First Days at Dachau," *Journal of Modern Judaism* 5 (Spring 1985): 26–32; Interview with Abraham S. Hyman, n.d., HU Institute of Contemporary Jewry, Oral History Division.

14. Ze'ev Mankowitz, "The Formation of She'erith Hapleita: November 1944–July 1945," *Yad Vashem Studies* 20 (1990): 337–70; Abraham J. Peck, "'Our Eyes Have Seen Eternity': Memory and Self-Identity Among the She'erith Hapletah," *Modern Judaism* 17 (Feb. 1997): 57–74; Juliane Wetzel, "'Mir szeinen doh': München

und Umgebung als Zuflucht von Überlebenden des Holocausts, 1945–1948," in *Von Stalingrad zur Währungsreform: Zur Sozialgeschichte des Umbruchs in Deutschland*, edited by Martin Broszat, et al. (Munich, 1988), 327–64; Chaim Yachil, "Peulot hamishlachat haeretzisraelit besheerith hapleita, 1945–1948," *Yalkut Moreshet* 30 (Nov. 1980): 7–40; and 31 (Apr. 1981): 133–76. Dr. Zalman Grinberg, the first chairman of the Central Committee of the Liberated Jews for the U.S. Zone, played an important role in the formation of the She'erith Hapleita in the first year after liberation. In the British Zone the mantle of leadership of the survivors fell upon Joseph (Yossele) Rosensaft.

15. Bauer, *Out from the Ashes*, xx–xxv, 261–99. Abraham J. Peck, in his review in *Holocaust and Genocide Studies* 5 (1990): 345–48, regarded Bauer's appraisal of the JDC as too positive. See also Dalia Ofer, "Defining Relationship: The Joint Distribution Committee and Israel, 1948–1950," in S. Ilan Troen and Noah Lucas, eds., *Israel: The First Decade of Independence* (Albany, 1995), 713–31. On the support of the JDC for the illegal aliyah, see Idit Zertal, *Zehavam shel hayehudim: Hahagira hayehudit hamachtartit leeretz Israel, 1945–1948. From Catastrophe to Power: The Jewish Illegal Immigration to Palestine* (in Hebrew) (Tel Aviv, 1996), esp. pp. 372–411.

16. American Jewish Conference, Report to the Third Plenary Meeting, CZA, Goldstein Papers, A364/1958; Sagi, *German Reparations*, 31–33.

17. Chaim Weizmann to the Secretary of State, Sept. 20, 1945, *FRUS*, 1945, vol. 3 (Washington, D.C., 1968), 1302–5; Department of State, Memorandum of conversation between Goldmann, Maurice Perlzweig, Dean Acheson, and others, Oct. 19, 1945, USNA, RG59, 740.00119 EW/9–2045; Jacob Blaustein to Secretary of State James Byrnes, Oct. 17, 1946, YIVO, AJC Records, GEN-10, box 281.

18. Sagi, *German Reparations*, 33–38. Memorandum of the American delegation, July 18 and 21, 1945, FDRL, Isador Lubin Papers, box 109, quoted in Ronald Zweig, "Reparations from Germany and Israel-Diaspora Relations" (in Hebrew), *Zionism* 14 (1989): 231–39. See also Jonathan Boyd and Stephen Ward, *Nazi Gold: The British and Allied attempt to deal with loot from the Second World War and the Implications for the Tripartite Gold Commission* (London, 1997), 17–19.

19. Michael J. Cohen, *Truman and Israel* (Berkeley, 1990), 77–82. Lowenthal's papers, which also contain his correspondence regarding his rather short service as OMGUS internal restitution adviser, are deposited at Wilson Library, University of Minnesota, Minneapolis. He too was suspected by the FBI as being sympathetic to communism because of his membership in various leftist groups such as the National Lawyers Guild and his connections in the past with "numerous organizations of doubtful background." Edgar Hoover to Rear Admiral Sidney W. Souers, July 20, 1950, HSTL, President's Secretary's Files.

20. Sagi, *German Reparations*, 39–42. JRSO comprised the following thirteen Jewish organizations: Jewish Agency for Palestine; JDC; WJC; AJC; Agudath Israel; Board of Deputies of British Jews; Central British Fund; Council for the Protection of the Rights and Interests of the Jews from Germany; Central Committee of the Liberated Jews in Germany; Conseil representatif des juifs en France (CRIF); Jewish Cultural Reconstruction; Anglo-Jewish Association; Interessenvertretung israelischer Kultusgemeinden in der US-Zone.

21. For a detailed treatment of the origins of restitution and indemnification

see Constantin Goschler, *Wiedergutmachung und die Verfolgten des Nationalsozialismus, 1945–1954* (Munich, 1992), 23–148, esp. pp. 144–48. Goschler acknowledges that material compensation for the Nazi victims resulted not only from moral motives but also served West Germany's rehabilitation, pp. 59–60. For the protracted deliberations of the *Länderrat* on restitution, see Günter Plum, ed., *Akten zur Vorgeschichte der Bundesrepublik Deutschland, 1945–1949*, vol. 3 (Munich, 1982), 556–59, 743–58, 781–83, 785–89. For Greenstein's intervention, Greenstein to McCloy, July 19, 1949, CZA, Goldstein Papers A364/2527; discussion of the General Claims Law, July 20, 1949, ibid.

22. The papers of Bruno Weil, an important source for the Axis Victims League, and the Axis Victims League Collection are deposited at the Leo Baeck Institute archives in New York.

23. In addition to John Gimbel's pioneering study on American policy in occupied Germany, *The American Occupation of Germany: Politics and the Military, 1945–1949* (Stanford, Calif., 1968), a few others should be mentioned here: Edward N. Peterson, *The American Occupation of Germany: Retreat to Victory* (Detroit, 1977); John H. Backer, *Winds of History: The German Years of Lucius DuBignon Clay* (New York, 1983); Robert Wolfe, ed., *Americans as Proconsuls: The United States Military Government in Germany and Japan* (Carbondale, Ill., 1984); Donald R. McCoy and Benedict K. Zobrist, eds., *Conference of Scholars on the Administration of Occupied Areas, 1943–1955* (Independence, Mo., 1970). The most detailed treatment in German is by Wolfgang Krieger, *General Lucius D. Clay und die amerikanische Deutschlandpolitik* (Stuttgart, 1987).

24. Diary, Oct. 1, 1945, Martin Blumenson, *The Patton Papers* (Boston, 1974), 787–89. See Judd Teller's review of "Eisenhower and the Jews" by Judah Nadich, "The U.S. Army and the DPs," *Commentary* 17 (Mar. 1954): 302–5.

25. Blumenson, *Patton Papers*, 735, 745. Many antisemitic entries are found in Patton's diary, usually linking Jews with communism. On the meeting between Eisenhower and Patton, see Ambrose, *Eisenhower*, 423–25.

26. The American decision to replace the conservative Schäffer government was made upon the advice of Walter Dorn, a liberal midwestern history professor of German American origin. After his service with the Office of Strategic Services (OSS), Dorn joined the staff of General Clarence Lionel Adcock, head of the Army's G-5 and subsequently head of OMGUS Frankfurt until its merger with OMGUS Berlin under General Lucius Clay. Later, Dorn was appointed Clay's adviser on denazification. In contrast to Robert Murphy, who supported Bavarian conservatives because of their traditional strength there, Dorn preferred the Social Democratic former exile Wilhelm Hoegner, who he hoped would promote American reform policies and denazification that had been stalled by Schäffer and his right-wing colleagues. German historian Lutz Niethammer discussed the affair in his detailed survey of denazification in Bavaria, *Entnazifizierung in Bayern: Säuberung und Rehabilitierung unter amerikanischer Besatzung* (Frankfurt, 1972), 229–36. For a critical view of the American intervention against the Bavarian conservatives, Edward N. Peterson, *The American Occupation of Germany: Retreat to Victory* (Detroit, 1977), 214–25. Schäffer continued to complain about the military government officials who dismissed him and nominated Wilhelm Hoegner instead. For instance, "Erinnerungen an den bayerischen Dschungel-Krieg 1945,"

Tages-Anzeiger (Regensburg), Mar. 12–13, 1955. According to an investigation by the Special Branch of the Office of Military Government for Bavaria, Schäffer was considered (falsely, I would add) as a Nazi sympathizer and collaborator and declared ineligible as officer of a political party and candidate for public office. Peter Vacca, Branch Chief of Intelligence, to Schäffer, Apr. 24, 1946, Bundesarchiv Koblenz (BA), Nachlass (NL) Schäffer, 168/9.

27. In his column of October 3, 1945, in the *New York Daily News*, which also appeared in the *Washington Times Herald*, John O'Donnell accused Felix Frankfurter, White House counsel David Niles (alias Neyhus), and labor leader Sidney Hillman of involvement in the removal of General Patton from Bavaria. On October 13, an editorial in the *Daily News* defended O'Donnell on the basis of his right to freedom of speech even though representatives of the Jewish community had informed the paper about the true facts of the case. On October 19, O'Donnell retracted his accusation that Patton's removal was the result of a "Jewish plot" because of the alleged Jewish origin of a soldier slapped by Patton. As a matter of fact, the soldier slapped by Patton in 1944 was not of Jewish descent but of German origin, and his family belonged to the First Nazarene Church. *Congress Weekly*, Oct. 12 and 26, 1945, both p. 1; *ADL Bulletin* 2 (Nov. 1945): 1.

28. James Stewart Martin, *All Honorable Men* (Boston, 1950), 176–240; also Drew Middleton, *The Struggle for Germany* (Indianapolis, 1949), 37f. Draper's connection with Wall Street was often exploited by Soviet propaganda. On Draper's record see also Christopher Simpson, *The Splendid Blond Beast: Money, Law, and Genocide in the Twentieth Century* (New York, 1993), 246–50.

29. Byrnes's Stuttgart speech is reprinted in U.S. Department of State, Office of Public Affairs, *Germany, 1947–1949: The Story in Documents* (Washington, D.C., 1950), 2–8. An analysis and evaluation of that address by John Gimbel, "Byrnes Stuttgarter Rede und die amerikanische Nachkriegspolitik in Deutschland," appeared in *Vierteljahrshefte für Zeitgeschichte* 20 (1972): 39–62.

30. For the Marshall plan, see John Gimbel, *The Origins of the Marshall Plan* (Stanford, Calif., 1976), here p. 4.; also Charles S. Maier and Günter Bischof, eds., *The Marshall Plan and Germany: West German Development within the Framework of the European Recovery Program* (New York, 1991). For JCS 1779 see Hermann-Josef Rupieper: *Der besetzte Verbündete: Die amerikanische Deutschlandpolitik, 1949–1955* (Opladen, 1991), 36–39.

31. Miriam Stuart, Society for the Prevention of World War III, to I. L. Kenen, American Jewish Conference, Feb. 5, 1946; Miriam Stuart to Dr. Frank Barth, AJ Conference, Feb. 18 and Mar. 13, 1946; Frank Barth to Miriam Stuart, May 16, 1946, CZA, AJ Conference Collection C7/1266; Veterans of Foreign Wars of the United States, Press Release, Mar. 22, 1946, YIVO, AJC Records, FAD-1, box 23A; Resolution at American Jewish Congress Convention, New York, June 2, 1946, AJHSA, AJ Congress Papers, I-77, box 51; Bernard Bernstein, Nov. 7, 1946 broadcast of "America's Town Meeting," CZA, AJ Conference Collection, C7/1250; AJ Conference Bulletin, Feb. 20, 1946, AJHSA, AJ Conference Papers, I-67, box 9.

32. FDRL, Henry Morgenthau Papers, box 387; *NYT*, Mar. 7, 1947. At a meeting of the Progressive Americans in September 1946, Morgenthau warned against the offen-

sive of conservative reactionary forces but did not join Henry Wallace's left-dominated Progressive Party. For John Foster Dulles's connections with prewar Germany, see the biography of his brother Allan: Peter Grose, *Gentleman Spy: The Life of Allan Dulles* (Boston, 1994), e.g., pp. 132–33. As late as spring 1939 John Foster Dulles thought the dispatch "of a huge American army to Europe at the cost of one or two million lives" would be worse than the defeat of the Western powers. A German victory in such a war would be "deplorable" but not necessarily "catastrophic."

33. H. J. Seligman to John Slawson, Mar. 24, 1947, YIVO, AJC Records, FAD-1, box 23A. A few weeks earlier Seligman alerted Slawson to the danger for Jews from the rapid change of American policy. Zachariah Shuster questioned whether it might be advisable for the AJC to contact the initiators of the conference on Germany planned for March 1947. Seligman to Slawson and Shuster to Slawson, Feb. 6, 1947, ibid.

34. E.g., Paul W. Freedman's complaint to Joel Wolfsohn, AJC Paris, June 29, 1948, YIVO, AJC Records, FAD-41 (European Office), box 20. Hans Habe, the first editor of the *Neue Zeitung* published by the American authorities, did not accept the view that Jews and other recent immigrants to the United States could not continue to serve in occupied Germany because they were not able to forget the past. The reason for the difficulties they encountered was their disagreement with the changing policies of the military government. "Emigranten in Deutschland," *Aufbau*, Aug. 6, 1948, pp. 5–6. See also Guy Stern, "The Jewish Exiles in the Service of U.S. Intelligence: The Post-War Years," *Leo Baeck Institute Year Book 1995*, vol. 40, pp. 51–62.

It should be noted that even before the unfolding of the anticosmopolitan campaign in the Soviet Union in 1948, the Soviet Military Administration in East Germany took care to reduce the relatively large number of Jewish officers there. Norman M. Naimark, *The Russians in Germany: A History of the Soviet Zone of Occupation* (Cambridge, Mass., 1995), 31, 338.

35. John H. Backer, *Winds of History: The German Years of Lucius DuBignon Clay* (New York, 1983), 53–54. For Haber's recollection of his talks with Clay, see NCRAC Seventh Plenary Session, Apr. 28–May 1, 1949, Atlantic City, N.J., transcript, p. 398, AJHSA, NCRAC Papers, I-172, box 3. Cp. also the biography by Jean Edward Smith, *Lucius D. Clay: An American Life* (New York, 1990).

36. Clay to Baruch, Mar. 2, 1948, Princeton University Library, Baruch Papers, box 78.

37. Warburg, *Long Road Home*, 232.

CHAPTER 4

1. On denazification see Elmer Plischke, "Denazification in Germany: A Policy Analysis," in Wolfe, *Americans as Proconsuls*, 198–225; Gimbel, *American Occupation of Germany*, 101–10, 158–62, 171–74; Tom Bower, *The Pledge Betrayed: America and Britain and the Denazification of Postwar Germany* (Garden City, N.Y., 1982), 134–50; also Clemens Vollnhals, ed., *Entnazifizierung: Politische Säuberung und Rehabilitierung in den vier Besatzungszonen* (Frankfurt, 1990), 55–64. For an early negative appraisal, see John H. Herz, "The Fiasco of Denazification in Germany," *Political Science Quarterly* 63 (1948): 569–94.

2. For the German exiles' contribution to the Research and Analysis Branch

(R&A) in the OSS, see Petra Marquardt-Bigman, *Amerikanische Geheimdienstanalysen über Deutschland, 1942–1949* (Munich, 1995), 146–68, here pp. 152–53, 158. See also Alfons Söllner, ed., *Zur Archäologie der Demokratie in Deutschland*, 2 vols. (Frankfurt, 1986).

3. Frank M. Buscher, "Kurt Schumacher, German Social Democracy and the Punishment of Nazi Crimes," *Holocaust and Genocide Studies* 5 (1990): 261–73.

4. Gimbel, *American Occupation of Germany*, 106; Plischke, "Denazification in Germany," data quoted on p. 216.

5. Niethammer, *Entnazifizierung in Bayern*, 531; Vollnhals, *Entnazifizierung*, 62; Plischke, "Denazification in Germany," 218–19.

6. Udo Wengst, *Beamtentum zwischen Reform und Tradition: Beamtengesetzgebung in der Gründungsphase der Bundesrepublik Deutschland* (Düsseldorf, 1988), 252.

7. E.g., "At the Grave of Denazification," News Release from the Office of Jewish Information, AJ Congress, Apr. 5, 1949, AJHSA, AJ Congress Papers, I-77, box 51; Supplementary Memorandum on Denazification, 1949, ibid.

8. For negative repercussions of the failure of denazification for German political culture, see Niethammer, *Entnazifizierung in Bayern*, conclusion (653–66), and recently Greiner, *Die Morgenthau Legende*, 348–52. The most influential defender of the conciliatory approach is Hermann Lübbe, who in his address on the fiftieth anniversary of Hitler's ascent to power praised Adenauer's postwar course in contrast to the critique of the sixty-eighters. For a cogent critical appraisal see Norbert Frei, *Vergangenheitspolitik: Die Anfänge der Bundesrepublik und die NS-Vergangenheit* (Munich, 1996). See also his essay, "'Vergangenheitsbewältigung' or 'Renazification'? The American Perspective on Germany's Confrontation with the Nazi Past in the Early Years of the Adenauer Era," in: *America and the Shaping of German Society*, 1945–1955, edited by Michael Ermarth (New York and Oxford), pp. 47–59.

9. Jacob Robinson, "The International Military Tribunal and the Holocaust: Some Legal Reflections," *Israel Law Review* 7 (Jan. 1972): 1–13. For the concept of genocide coined by Raphael Lemkin, see his *Axis Rule in Occupied Europe: Laws of Occupation: Analysis of Government Records for Redress* (Washington, D.C., 1944).

10. Helmut Krausnick and Hans-Heinrich Wilhelm were the first German historians who referred to the criminal involvement of the German army in the extermination of the Jews, *Die Truppe des Weltanschauungskrieges: Die Einsatzgruppen der Sicherheitspolizei und des SD, 1938–1942* (Stuttgart, 1981). The first full-sized critical analysis of the role of the Wehrmacht in the war against the Soviet Union was authored by Jörg Friedrich, *Das Gesetz des Krieges: Das deutsche Heer in Russland 1941 bis 1945* (Munich, 1993). See also the Omer Bartov's monograph, *Hitler's Army: Soldiers, Nazis and War in the Third Reich* (New York, 1991).

In connection with the 1995 exhibition on the crimes of the Wehrmacht sponsored by the Hamburg Institute for Social Research, Hannes Heer and Klaus Naumann edited a special volume dedicated to the subject: *Vernichtungskrieg: Verbrechen der Wehrmacht, 1941 bis 1944* (Hamburg, 1995). Daniel Jonah Goldhagen in his *Hitler's Willing Executioners: Ordinary Germans and the Holocaust* (New York, 1996) also mentions the Wehrmacht's part in the killing of the Jews even though he concentrates on reserve police units.

11. Milton P. Konvitz, "Will Nuremberg Serve Justice?" *Commentary* 1 (Jan. 1946): 9–15.

12. *Hadassah Newsletter* 26 (Oct. 1946): 2 (editorial).

13. Jacob Robinson, "The Jewish Tragedy at Nuremberg," *Hadassah Newsletter* 26 (Dec. 1946): 9–11, 30.

14. Anatole Goldstein, "Nuremberg: A Fair Trial," *Congress Weekly*, Nov. 1, 1946, pp. 5–7. In the same vein, Gerhard Jacoby, "The Verdict of Nuremberg," *Jewish Frontier* 13 (Nov. 1946): 32–35.

15. AJC press release, Nov. 12, 1946, AJHSA, AJ Congress Papers, I-77, box 51; Minutes of meeting with Justice Robert H. Jackson, New York, June 12, 1945, ibid. Despite the interest of organized Jewry to be represented at the IMT deliberation, representatives of the American Jewish Conference like Frank Barth thought that nonappearance might be preferable in order to avoid charges that "the Jews sought vengeance and achieved it." Barth to Meir Grossman, July 26, 1945, CZA, AJ Conference Collection, C7/448.

16. Peter de Mendelssohn, *The Nuremberg Documents: Some Aspects of German War Policy, 1939–1945* (London, 1946); Victor Heine Bernstein, *Final Judgment: The Story of Nuremberg* (New York, 1947); Note by Eugene Hevesi, Mar. 14, 1947, YIVO, AJC Records, FAD-1, box 23A. An important addition to the books on the Nuremberg trials is Telford Taylor's *The Anatomy of the Nuremberg Trials* (New York, 1992). Taylor's volume, more than other works on the trial, focuses on the evidence of the Holocaust, in particular on its part in the case of the Soviet prosecution. For a critical view of the trial, see István Deák's review essay "Misjudgment at Nuremberg," *NYR*, Oct. 7, 1993, pp. 46–52. Bradley F. Smith in his *Reaching Judgment at Nuremberg* (New York, 1977) praises the Court's achievement in remedying the most dangerous defects of Allied war crimes policy as well as its restraint in contrast to the "sweeping and often inaccurate charges made by the prosecution," pp. 304–5.

17. Anneke de Rudder, "Verpasste Chance: Das Urteil von Nürnberg und die Deutschen," *Die Zeit*, Aug. 16, 1996, p. 10. Whereas the controversy about the Nuremberg trial's judicial aspects continues, on the fiftieth anniversary of the opening of the trial Alfred Streim, the head of the Ludwigsburg Central Office for Investigation of Nazi Crimes who died in 1996, expressed his positive attitude to the trial. "Gut, dass der Prozess zustande kam," *Tribüne* 34, no. 3 (1995): 134–39.

18. Robert S. Marcus, "Greatest Murder Trial in History," *Congress Weekly*, May 14, 1948, pp. 5–7; Robert M. W. Kempner, *Ankläger einer Epoche* (Frankfurt, 1986), 310–23. Josiah E. DuBois Jr., *The Devil's Chemists: Twenty-four Conspirators of the International Farben Cartel Who Manufacture Wars* (Boston, 1952), describes the preparations and the atmosphere of the IG Farben trial in Nuremberg, at which none of the defendants was found guilty of war crimes! For a critical view of the persecution's strategy during the IG Farben trial, see Peter Hayes, "IG Farben und der IG Farben Prozess: Zur Verwicklung eines Grosskonzerns in die nationalsozialistischen Verbrechen," in Fritz Bauer Institut, *Auschwitz, Rezeption und Wirkung. Jahrbuch zur Geschichte und Wirkung des Holocausts* (Frankfurt, 1996), 99–121.

19. Office of Chief of Counsel for War Crimes to Rezzo Kastner, Sept. 17, 1947, CZA, WJC British Section Collection, C2/1825.

20. Robert S. Marcus, "Why Nazis Go Free," *Congress Weekly*, Nov. 8, 1948, pp. 5–7; Bower, *Pledge Betrayed*, 248–71; George Kennan, memorandum for McCloy, June 2, 1949, and Reinhold Niebuhr to McCloy, June 15, 1949, Amherst College Archives, McCloy Papers, box HC4/19. For Kennan's views of Germany, see David Allan Mayers, *George Kennan and the Dilemmas of U.S. Foreign Policy* (New York and Oxford, 1988), 64–85, 145–52.

21. Manfred George, "Ein infamer Angriff," *Aufbau*, Oct. 1, 1948, pp. 1–2.

22. Bower, *Pledge Betrayed*, 269. On McCarthy's "investigation" of the Malmedy affair see Richard A. Rovere, *Senator Joe McCarthy* (New York, 1959), 111–18.

23. "The Real Crisis in Germany," *Congress Weekly*, Oct. 1, 1948, pp. 3–4; Lucius D. Clay, Columbia University Oral History Collection, New York, 1971, pp. 571–72; Smith, *Lucius D. Clay*, 296–308. Arthur L. Smith Jr. attempted to portray a less criminal profile of Ilse Koch, justified General Clay's reduction of her sentence, and criticized the life sentence passed on her by an Augsburg German court. Arthur L. Smith Jr., *Die Hexe von Buchenwald: Der Fall Ilse Koch* (Weimar, 1994).

24. Frank M. Buscher, *The U.S. War Crimes Trials in Germany* (New York, 1989), 150. Buscher's well-balanced monograph is the most detailed study of the subject.

25. Arthur Settel, "Seven Nazis Were Hanged: The Diary of a Witness," *Commentary* 29 (May 1960): 369–79. On the warnings of Generals Heusinger and Speidel, Adenauer's advisers on defense, see Kai Bird, *The Chairman: John J. McCloy, the Making of the American Establishment* (New York, 1992), 364.

26. E.g., William D. Hasselt, Secretary to the President, to Warren S. Magee, May 19, 1951, HSTL, OF 325.

27. Thomas Alan Schwartz, "John J. McCloy and the Landsberg Cases" in *American Policy and the Reconstruction of Western Germany, 1945–1955*, edited by Jeffry M. Diefendorf, Axel Frohn, and Hermann-Josef Rupieper (Washington and Cambridge, 1993), 433–54; Buscher, *U.S. War Crimes Trials in Germany*, esp. pp. 59–71.

28. Jacob Blaustein, Irving Miller, Frank Goldman, Adolph Held, Henry Albert, Maurice N. Eisendrath to Acheson, Feb. 20, 1951, YIVO, AJC Records, FAD-1, box 24; Summary of meeting of Jewish organizations with the Department of State, Mar. 13, 1951, ibid., box 24; NCRAC meeting, Mar. 20, 1951, AJA, Manuscript Collection 202, Cincinnati Jewish Community Relations Committee/Council (hereafter CCRC Papers), box 50/9. In Tel Aviv, Israel's foreign minister Moshe Sharett presented an aide memoire to the American ambassador, Mar. 12, 1951, ISA, FM Records, 344/15.

29. Baruch to McCloy, Mar. 12, 1951, Princeton University, Baruch Papers, box 100.

30. Schwartz, "John J. McCloy and the Landsberg Cases," 450. For a very critical view of McCloy's clemency decision see Kai Bird, *The Chairman*, 359–75.

31. See chap. 11.

CHAPTER 5

1. Reform rabbi Solomon Andhil Fineberg played a major role in AJC's dealing with Communist influence in the American Jewish community and for several years was involved in that campaign as program coordinator. See his introduction to the files on Communism in his papers deposited at the AJA, Manuscript Collection 149, box 1/1.

An AJC memorandum, "The Communist Propaganda on Germany," was published in April 1951, YIVO, AJC Records, FAD-1, box 33. The first to protest against that memorandum was the AJ Congress. Rabbi Irving Miller to Irving Kane, NCRAC, June 1, 1951, AJHSA, NCRAC Papers, I-172, box 55.

2. *The Authoritarian Personality* (New York, 1950) was authored by T. W. Adorno, Else Frankel-Brunswick, Daniel J. Levinson, and R. Nevitt Sanford; a preceding volume of the series was edited by Max Horkheimer and Samuel H. Flowerman.

3. In contrast to more orthodox Marxists linked with the Frankfurt School, who continued to stress the centrality of monopoly capitalism in their analyses of Nazism, Horkheimer himself came to see Nazism as the most extreme example of a general trend toward total domination in the West. Thus he regarded as the ultimate source of antisemitism the rage against the nonidentical that characterized the totalistic dominating impulse of Western civilization. On Horkheimer's connection with the AJC, see his letter to Slawson, Jan. 10, 1948, Max Horkheimer Papers, Frankfurt Municipal and University Library, II 14. Back in Germany, in addition to his professorial duties, he served as consultant to the AJC, and the Frankfurt Institute of Social Research administered the German Educators Project.

4. For the most comprehensive study of the Frankfurt School, see Rolf Wiggershaus, *Die Frankfurter Schule: Geschichte, theoretische Entwicklung, politische Bedeutung* (Munich, 1986). Here the English translation by Michael Robertson has been used: *The Frankfurt School: Its History, Theories, and Political Significance* (Cambridge, Mass., 1994). For its connection with the AJC, pp. 274–76, 351, 357, 363–67. See also Martin Jay's essay "The Jews and the Frankfurt School: Critical Theory's Analysis of Antisemitism," in his *Permanent Exiles: Essays on the Intellectual Migration from Germany to America* (New York, 1985), 90–100. Martin Jay's earlier monograph, *The Dialectical Imagination: A History of the Frankfurt School and the Institute of Social Research* (New York, 1973), deals only with the period that preceded the Institute's return to Frankfurt after the war.

5. Draft of an early postwar program "Fight Against Antisemitism within the Framework of Germany's Education for Democracy," submitted by Arkadi R. L. Gurland, n.d., YIVO, AJC Records, FAD-1, box 20.

6. Morris Fine to Fineberg, Eugene Hevesi, and Simon Segal, Oct. 27, 1950, YIVO, AJC Records, FAD-1, box 22. Gurland repeatedly criticized the reports of the AJC European office in Paris because he thought they exaggerated the dimensions of antisemitism and neo-Nazism. See also his analysis after the first Bundestag elections, "Why Democracy Is Losing in Germany?" *Commentary* 8 (Sept. 1949): 227–37.

7. Memorandum by Zachariah Shuster and David Bernstein to Slawson, May 10, 1947; D. Bernstein to Slawson, May 26, 1947, and Dec. 11, 1947, YIVO, AJC Records, FAD-1, box 23A; John Slawson, Joel D. Wolfsohn, Zachariah Shuster, European Survey, July 10–Aug. 9, 1947, HSTL, Joel Wolfsohn Papers, box 18. See also Cohen, *Encounter with Emancipation*, 480–89.

8. On the Lessing Association, Horkheimer to Shuster, Mar. 16, 1948, Horkheimer Papers, Frankfurt, II 13.

9. Proskauer, Blaustein, Slawson to Secretary of State George Marshall, 1947, YIVO, AJC Records, FAD-1, box 23A. See also Eugene Hevesi, AJC, Committee on

Peace Problems, Third Session, Jan. 23–24, 1947, memorandum on the peace treaty with Germany, CZA, AJ Conference Collection, C7/390/2.

10. D. Bernstein (AJC Washington Office) to Slawson, Dec. 11, 1947, YIVO, AJC Records, FAD-1, box 23A; Department of State, Policy Planning Staff, Special Counseling Group on German Policy, Questions, Sept. 15–16, 1948, AJC Archives, New York, Joseph M. Proskauer Papers, RG1, EXO16, Steering and Foreign Affairs Committees 1945–1948.

11. The AJC's positive attitude to the SPD seems to have been influenced by Gurland, who prepared analyses for it on the German situation until his return to Germany in the winter of 1949–50. E.g., A. R. L. Gurland memorandum, Oct. 1947, YIVO, AJC Records, FAD-1, 42. Sociologist Hans Speier and political scientist Franz Neumann endorsed that view, letters to Samuel H. Flowerman, Nov. 21, 1947, ibid. However, Max Horkheimer remained skeptical because of the SPD's policies before and after Hitler's ascent to power. Horkheimer to Slawson, Jan. 10, 1948, Horkheimer Papers, Frankfurt, II 14. Slawson met Schumacher first during his visit to Germany in summer 1947.

12. I have treated this relationship in an article "Eine ausgestreckte Hand: Frühe amerikanisch-jüdische Kontakte zu deutschen Sozialdemokraten in der Nachkriegs-zeit," *Internationale wissenschaftliche Korrespondenz zur Geschichte der deutschen Arbeiterbewegung* 25 (June 1989): 174–87. Paul Jacobs summarized the talks between the AJC executives and Schumacher, Jacobs to Slawson, Oct. 29, 1947, YIVO, AJC Records, FAD-1, box 34. For the contacts in winter 1948–49 see Max Isenbergh to Hevesi, Jan. 28, 1949, YIVO, AJC Records, GEN-10, box 280, quoted in Goschler, *Wiedergutmachung*, 204–5.

13. Hevesi to Blaustein, Mar. 1, 1949, YIVO, AJC Records, FAD-1, box 25. The meeting with President Truman took place only on May 18, 1949. HSTL, PSF, President's Appointments File, Daily Sheets, box 92. Summary of AJC activities in West Germany, Dec. 5, 1949, YIVO, AJC Records, FAD-1, box 23.

14. AJC Staff Committee on Germany, May 10, 1950, YIVO, AJC Records, FAD-1, box 26. See also other minutes of the staff committee, Apr. 27 and May 31, 1950, ibid., and of the lay committee, Apr. 4, Apr. 20, May 23, and Dec. 12, 1950, ibid. The AJC executive committee met on Apr. 30, 1950, ibid., box 23.

15. For the disappointment with the Citizens Council, AJC Staff Committee on Germany, Dec. 11, 1950, and discussion of the German program, June 6, 1951, YIVO, AJC Records, FAD-1, box 26. Even AJCs own specially appointed committee on Germany had a few non-Jewish members. Cohen, *Not Free to Desist*, 486. One of them was Telford Taylor, who was held in high esteem by the Jewish community thanks to his role as chief of counsel for war crimes at the Nuremberg trials.

16. NCRAC plenary session, May 22, 1951, AJA, CCRC Papers, box 50/9, and NCRAC Committee on Germany, Mar. 16, 1951, YIVO, AJC Records, FAD-1, box 22.

17. *Committee Reporter* 8 (May–June 1951): 1, 7; transcript of the AJC executive committee meeting of May 5–6, 1951, New York, AJC Blaustein Library, New York; S. Andhil Fineberg, William E. Wiener Oral History Library, AJC, New York, pp. 156–58. The collection is now deposited at the New York Public Library, Jewish Division.

18. E.g., Henry Byroade, Director, Bureau of German Affairs, to Blaustein, July 2, 1951, YIVO, AJC Records, FAD-1, box 21.

19. Alfred Bingham, Telford Taylor, and Victor Reuther to President Truman, Oct. 7, 1950, AJA, CCRC Papers, box 56/10; Alfred M. Bingham and Telford Taylor, "Do We Need a New German Army?" *ADL Bulletin* 7 (Oct. 1950): 3–4, 8; and "Beware of German Rearmament," *Congress Weekly*, Oct. 23, 1950, pp. 12–13.

20. AJC Staff Committee on Germany, Dec. 28, 1950, YIVO, AJC Records, FAD-1, box 26, and Draft Statement on the Rearmament of Germany, Jan. 15, 1951, ibid., box 22.

21. The first AJC memorandum on "Communist Propaganda on Germany" was published in April 1951, note 1 above. See also AJC, Memorandum on Communist Propaganda Plan to Exploit the Issue of Rearming West Germany, Feb. 28, 1955, ibid., box 25.

22. Blaustein to McCloy, July 12, 1951, and McCloy to Blaustein, Aug. 29, 1951, Washington National Record Center (hereafter WNRC), RG466, Records of the U.S. High Commissioner for Germany, U.S. High Commissioner John J. McCloy, box 30; A Proposal for Cooperation with McCloy, Hevesi to Slawson, Simon Segal and Edwin Lukas, Dec. 9, 1952; Lukas to Blaustein, Feb. 2, 1953; Shuster to Lukas, April 15, 1953; Lukas to Shuster, May 28, 1953; all YIVO, AJC Records, FAD-1, box 34. Summary, Lukas to Slawson, June 7, 1955, ibid., box 25. Cp. Cohen, *Not Free to Desist*, 487–89.

23. See chap. 10. Summary of the German Educators Project, prepared in 1979, in AJC Archives, BGX 79, Germany/West.

24. Resolution of the WJC Second Plenary Assembly, Montreux, July 5, 1948. AJA, WJCC, A46/5.

25. Cohen, *Not Free to Desist*, 288–92, 299–309; Kaufman, *Ambiguous Partnership*, 224–40.

26. William Haber to Slawson, Jan. 11, 1949 and Slawson to Haber, Feb. 7, 1949, YIVO, AJC Records, FAD-1, box 23A.

27. William Haber, Final Report to the Five Cooperating Organizations, Dec. 20, 1948, ibid. After the dispersal of the American Jewish Conference in 1948, only Four Cooperating Organizations remained.

28. AJC executive committee, statement on Germany, May 5–6, 1951, see note 17 above; "Western Germany: Democratization and the Prospects of Jewish Communal Life," a report from the Paris Office, received Aug. 28, 1955, YIVO, AJC Records, FAD-1, box 22. The report recommended that AJC should become more active in Germany on a communal level and, as a first step, bring about close cooperation with the newly established organization of the Jews in Germany.

29. ADL, Foreign Language Department, Report #2 covering the period between Nov. 1949 and Feb. 1950, AJA, CCRC Papers, box 56/10. For the postwar transformation of ADL into an activist agency and its subsequent strong support for Israel, see Deborah Dash Moore, *B'nai B'rith and the Challenge of Ethnic Leadership* (Albany, NY, 1981), 123–24.

30. "Are the Nazis Back in Power?" *ADL Bulletin* 7 (May 1950): 1, 6–7; "Return of the War Lords," *ADL Bulletin* (July 1950): 5–6.

31. On Buttenwieser's canceled address, May 14, 1950, see AJA, Records of Coor-

dinating Body of Jewish Organizations 1949–1953, Manuscript Collection 76, box 1. ADL press release, May 21, 1950, ibid.; Buttenwieser's address, May 14, 1950, ibid.

32. "Justification of the ADL," editorial, *Reconstructionist*, June 16, 1950, p. 1; "Mr. Buttenwieser's Speech," editorial, *Congress Weekly*, May 23, 1950, p. 3; *Morgen Freiheit* and *Morgen Journal*, quoted in *Yiddish News Digest*, May 16, 1950, and Alexander Bickel in *Forverts* and Jacob Glatstein in *Morgen Journal*, *Yiddish News Digest*, May 19, 1950, Blaustein Library, New York.

33. ADL, "Why We Are Losing in Germany? A Report on the Failure of Denazification, Decartelization and Democratization of Western Germany," May 1950, YIVO, AJC Records, FAD-1, box 32; Frank Goldman, "The Failure of Denazification," *NJM* 64 (July–Aug. 1950): 394–97. Text of Goldman's message at the Triennial Convention, Mar. 18, 1950, AJA, B'nai B'rith, District Grand Lodge #2, Manuscript Collection 36, box A/25.

34. See chap. 10. After a visit to Germany in 1954, the ADL's complete report appeared in a brochure, "Germany—Nine Years Later."

35. See chap. 2, note 25.

36. Report on Kurt Schumacher's meeting with Jewish labor leaders in New York, "Schumacher und die jüdischen Arbeiterführer," *Aufbau*, Oct. 3, 1947, p. 17f. Fritz Heine, one of Schumacher's close associates who had returned from exile in Britain, accompanied Schumacher on his visit to the United States. For the next decade he continued to serve as a liaison with the Jewish labor movement.

37. Schumacher's address in Frankfurt, July 1, 1951, in *Kurt Schumacher: Reden, Schriften, Korrespondenzen, 1945–1952* edited by Willy Albrecht (Berlin, 1985), 895–98.

38. Emanuel Novogrudsky to Schumacher, Nov. 16, 1951, Jewish Labor Bund Archives, now deposited at YIVO, Files Bund in America, Coordinating Committee, cooperation with Bundists in Germany; Schumacher to Liebman Hersch, Oct. 30, 1951, *Schumacher: Reden, Schriften, Korrespondenzen*, 895–98.

39. "The Role of the Jewish Labor Committee in Negotiations on Jewish Material Claims," JLC Silver Jubilee Convention, Atlantic City, N.J., Mar. 1960. I am indebted to Fritz Heine for providing me a copy of that publication.

40. Elmer Berger, *The Jewish Dilemma* (New York, 1945), 24. For the early history of the AJC, see Thomas Abraham Kolsky, *Jews Against Zionism: The American Council for Judaism, 1942–1948* (Philadelphia, 1987).

41. I have relied on the information furnished by Professor Klaus Herrmann of Concordia University in Montreal, a vice-president of the ACJ, Mar. 3, 1995.

42. Hubertus Prinz zu Loewenstein to Rabbi Morris S. Lazaron and Lessing J. Rosenwald, both Nov. 2, 1945, IfZ, Loewenstein Papers, ED 206, 30 and 30A. For Lazaron's response, see Loewenstein's letter to one of his correspondents, Nov. 19, 1945, ED 206/30A.

43. Alexander Böker, report to the Bureau for Peace Problems (Büro für Friedensfragen), Feb. 1949, BA, Collection Büro für Friedensfragen, 457; report on the American position in Germany, Jan. 15, 1950, PA/AA, II 210–01/80.

CHAPTER 6

1. AJ Conference, Bulletin of Activities and Digest of the Press, Jan. 27, 1947, CZA, AJ Conference Collection, C7/390/2.

2. Ibid., Mar. 1, 1947.

3. Statement by the WJC on a peace settlement with Germany, published in *Congress Weekly*, Mar. 21, 1947, pp. 14–15.

4. A. C. A. Liverhant (AJ Conference) to W. Borah, Jan. 26, 1948, CZA, AJ Conference Collection, C7/3.

5. A. Böker, report to the Bureau of Peace Problems, Feb. 1949, BA, Collection Büro für Friedensfragen, 457.

6. Resolution of the WJC Second Plenary Assembly, Montreux, July 5, 1948, AJA, WJCC, box A46/5.

7. Zuckerman-Segal memorandum, July 3, 1950, AJA, WJCC, box 80/1; Minutes of the WJC executive (American branch), Oct. 1, 1950, ibid., box 3A/3.

8. Goldmann against *cherem*, Minutes of the WJC executive (American branch), Oct. 1, 1950, box 3A/3. See also WJC, minutes of the Israel executive, Tel Aviv, May 18, 1949, CZA, Nahum Goldmann Archive, Z6/243.

9. Minutes of the London members of the WJC executive, Jan. 6, 1949, AJA, WJCC, box 3A/1.

10. Minutes of the WJC European branch, Apr. 18–19, 1949, AJA, WJCC, box 3A/1; Minutes, London members of the WJC executive, Oct. 13, 1949, ibid. Easterman to Marcus, Oct. 21, 1949, ibid., box 80/2. For Blankenhorn see chap. 9.

11. WJC, Statement on Germany, Paris, Apr. 19, 1949, and New York, Apr. 25, 1949, AJA, WJCC, box 3A/4; Minutes of enlarged meeting of the European members of the WJC executive, Paris, Aug. 25–28, 1949, ibid., box 3A/3; WJC, Statement on Germany, Dec. 20, 1949, box 80/1; Minutes of the WJC executive (American branch), Oct. 1, 1950, ibid., box 3A/3. For the changing attitude of the WJC after the Luxembourg agreements, see chap. 9. E.g., Proceedings of the Third Plenary Assembly, Aug. 4–11, 1953, Geneva, box 248/4.

12. See chap. 7.

13. Stephen Wise to Nathan M. Padgug, Feb. 23, 1949, AJHSA, AJ Congress Papers, I-77, box 6. The leftist committee was soon dissolved. Minutes of the executive committee, Feb. 28, 1949. The AJLC and JPFO were disaffiliated three months later. Irving Miller to all councils, divisions, chapters, and members of the administrative committee, ibid., box 51.

14. See, for instance, Dr. David Petegorsky's references to Rabbi Irving Miller's letter to Irving Kane concerning the AJC memorandum "Communist Propaganda on Germany," NCRAC Committee on Germany, June 22, 1951, AJA, CCRC Papers, box 57/1.

15. NCRAC executive committee, June 16, 1949, AJHSA, NCRAC Papers, I-172, box 32; Summary of American Jewish Congress Activities in Regard to Postwar Germany and Neo-Nazism, 1951, AJHSA, AJ Congress Papers, I-77, box 51.

16. Jules Cohen to NCRAC membership, Mar. 29, 1950, Coordinating Council on German Democracy Statement, AJA, CCRC Papers, box 56/10.

17. SR260 calling for a presidential investigation of American policy in Germany was supported by the following eight senators: Guy Gillette (D, Iowa); Irving M. Ives (R, New York); Claude Pepper (D, Florida); Herbert H. Lehman (D, New York); Robert C. Hendrickson (R, New Jersey); Harley M. Kilgore (D, West Virginia); Paul H. Douglas (D, Illinois); and Dennis Chavez (D, New Mexico).

H.R.578 to 586, identical with SR260, was sponsored by the following members of the House: Jacob K. Javits of New York and Walt Horan of Washington, Republicans; John A. Blatnik of Minnesota, Emanuel Celler of New York, Herman P. Eberharter of Pennsylvania, Foster Furcolo of Massachusetts, Henry Jackson of Washington, Hugh B. Mitchell of Washington, Barrett O'Hara of Illinois, Franklin D. Roosevelt Jr. of New York, and Mrs. Chase Going Woodhouse of Connecticut, Democrats. On the State Department proposal to send a private group of well-known citizens, see Kimball to Nicholson, Aug. 1, 1950, NA, RG59, 762A.00/8–150; Byroade to Acheson, Aug. 24, 1950, ibid., 762A.00/8, 1650; McCloy to Acheson, Aug, 4, 1950, ibid., 762A.00/8–450; Byroade to McCloy, Aug. 4, 1950, ibid.

18. NCRAC executive committee, June 16, 1949, AJHSA, NCRAC Papers, I-172, box 32; also NCRAC Committee on Germany, June 22, 1951, AJA, CCRC Papers, box 57/1.

19. NCRAC Committee on Germany, Mar. 16, 1951, AJHSA, NCRAC Papers, I-172, box 54; Statement by Irving Kane, NCRAC chairman, May 22, 1951, YIVO, AJC Records, FAD-1, box 22. NCRAC Committee on Germany, June 22, 1951, AJA, CCRC Papers, box 57/1.

20. Marcus to Goldmann, Petegorsky and others, Sept. 14, 1949, AJA, WJCC, 200/2.

21. See Summary of American Jewish Congress Activities in Regard to Post-war Germany and Neo-Nazism, 1951, AJHSA, AJ Congress Papers, I-77, box 5; AJ Congress press release, Rabbi Miller warns of democracy's "Waterloo," McCloy called "arch-appeaser," Jan. 30, 1950, ibid., box 51; Miller to Dean Acheson, May 17, 1951, and Perry Laukhuff, Dept. of State, to Miller, June 11, 1951, ibid.; AJ Congress press release on Delbert Clark's appearance at Brooklyn meeting, June 5, 1951, AJA, WJCC, box 173/3; Nehemiah Robinson, IJA, to Javits, July 17, 1951, concerning his statement against terminating the state of war with Germany, AJA, WJCC, box C20/2; AJ Congress administrative committee, June 23, 1952, AJHSA, AJ Congress Papers, I-77, box 5, and Nov. 28, 1954, ibid., box 7; AJ Congress executive committee, Mar. 21, 1955, ibid.; draft resolution prepared for AJ Congress convention, Apr. 12–15, 1956, Washington, D.C., ibid.

22. Minutes of enlarged meeting of the European members of the WJC executive, Paris, Aug. 25–28, 1949, AJA, WJCC, box 3A/3.

23. Summary of the Heidelberg Conference, Mar. 13–14, 1949, and Apr. 4, 1949, ibid., box 1-A/1; Gerhard Jacoby to the executives of the WJC—London, New York, Tel Aviv, July 18, 1950, report on the Frankfurt conference with representatives of the Jewish communities, CZA, Goldstein Papers, A364/1034b. For the early communal organization of postwar German Jewry see also Michael Brenner, *Nach dem Holocaust: Juden in Deutschland, 1945–1950* (Munich, 1995), 111–16.

24. Marcus to Easterman, July 20, 1950, CZA, WJC British Section Collection,

C2. (I saw this correspondence at the IJA in London before the papers were transferred to the CZA.) Jacoby to Goldmann, Oct. 31, 1950, CZA, Goldmann Archive, Z6/386; Minutes of the WJC executive (American branch), New York, Oct. 1, 1950, AJA, WJCC, box 3A/3. Because of its pro-Zionist orientation and the anti-German resolutions passed before and after the establishment of the Federal Republic, the WJC connection encountered opposition on the part of assimilated "patriotic" German Jews such as Sigmund Weltlinger. Weltlinger, a prominent figure in the postwar Berlin Jewish community and the Berlin municipality's official in charge of Jewish affairs, played a leading role in the local society for Christian-Jewish cooperation.

25. Jewish War Veterans (JWV), minutes of meeting held at Waldorf Astoria Hotel, Mar. 6, 1949; JWV Policy on Germany, Sept. 17–18, 1949, JWV Archives, Washington, D.C., Germany file; Joseph F. Barr to members of the JWV policy committee, June 10, 1955, IfZ, Heinz Krekeler Papers, ED135/94. Ambassador Heinz Krekeler Papers (ED 135), which are deposited at the archives of the Munich Institute für Zeitgeschichte, contain important documentation on his service in the United States. For JWV protest activities see chap. 7; for Julius Klein, chap. 10. For the history of the organization, see Gloria R. Mosesson, *The Jewish War Veterans Story* (Washington, 1971).

26. *Jewish Advocate*, May 23, 1949, p. 11.

27. "Rehabilitation of Germany," *Orthodox Jewish Life* 18 (Apr.–May 1951): 3–4; "Reparations," *Orthodox Jewish Life* 19 (Jan.–Feb. 1952): 3–4; "Remilitarizing Germany (A Symposium)," *Jewish Forum* 34 (Oct. 1951): 167–75, 199–200; "Should Jews Deal with Germany Now?" *Jewish Forum* 34 (Nov. 1951): 201, 214. The journal continued to take a very critical view of German developments in the following years.

28. Dov Ber Warshawsky, *A Shpigl fun Undzer Tsayt* (A Mirror of Our Time) (New York, 1986), 189–92; for Rabbi Isaac Lewin's position, Protocol of the Waldorf Astoria meeting, Oct. 25–26, 1951, CC16600, quoted in Ronald W. Zweig, *German Reparations and the Jewish World: A History of the Claims Conference* (Boulder, Colo., 1987), 17. On the ultra-Orthodox view of Germany see also Rabbi Yoel Schwartz and Rabbi Yitzchak Goldstein, *SHOAH: A Jewish Perspective on Tragedy in the Context of the Holocaust* (Jerusalem, 1990), 23–25, 149, 290–91.

29. Isaac Klein, "Jewish Communities in Germany," *Conservative Judaism* 6 (Oct. 1949): 74–79; Israel Goldstein, *My World as a Jew: The Memoirs of Israel Goldstein* (New York, 1984), 278–92, see p. 284; von Heyden, note on conversation between Rabbi Norman Salit and West German president Theodor Heuss, Nov. 12, 1953, PA/AA, II 210/01–35, vol. 252; A. Frowein to Heinz Trützschler, Mar. 15, 1954, PA/AA, II 211–06, vol. 311.

30. Isaac E. Marcuson, ed., *CCAR Yearbook*, vol. 55 (Philadelphia, 1946), Fifty-sixth Annual Convention, June 25–27, 1945, Atlantic City, N.J., Report of Commission on Justice and Peace/The Peace with Germany, pp. 114–15; *CCAR Yearbook*, vol. 60 (Philadelphia, 1950), Sixty-first Annual Convention, June 7–12, 1950, Cincinnati, pp. 187–88; *CCAR Yearbook*, vol. 61 (New York, 1951), Sixty-second Annual Convention, June 19–24, 1951, New London, Conn., pp. 102–3.

31. Stephen Wise to Secretary of War Robert Patterson, and to Secretary of the Army Kenneth Royall, quoted in Tom Bower, *The Paperclip Conspiracy: The Hunt for the*

Nazi Scientists (Boston, 1987), 206–8. See also Melvin J. Urofsky's biography of Wise, *A Voice that Spoke for Justice: The Life and Times of Stephen S. Wise* (Albany, N.Y., 1982), 260–75, and Gottlieb, *American Anti-Nazi Resistance*, 65–70, 86–96, 125–52, 176–90, 210–12, 274–75.

32. "Shall We Re-Arm Germany?" Address delivered by Rabbi Abba Hillel Silver at The Temple, Mar. 4, 1951, Cleveland, Ohio, pp. 9–10; also his address "American Stake in Human Freedom," Dec. 12, 1953, quoted in *In Time of Harvest: Essays in Honor of Abba Hillel Silver on the Occasion of his Seventieth Birthday* edited by Daniel Jeremy Silver (New York, 1963), 89–90. Like Wise, Silver had been active in the anti-Nazi boycott movement in the 1930s. After the resignation of Samuel Untermyer in 1938, Silver became president of the Non-Sectarian Anti-Nazi League to Champion Human Rights.

33. Proceedings of the Sixty-third Annual Convention of the CCAR, Buffalo, N.Y., June 10–15, 1952, AJA; *CCAR Records*, Manuscript Collection 34, box 40, pp. 120–27, 196–97; Bertram W. Korn, ed., *CCAR Yearbook*, vol. 62 (Philadelphia, 1953), 178–79.

34. E.g., *Morgen Freiheit*, Mar. 7, 1951; *Yiddish News Digest*, Mar. 10 and Dec. 7, 1951; *Yiddish News Digest*, Dec. 1, 1951; *Forverts*, Mar. 15, 1951; *Yiddish News Digest*, Mar. 16, 1951, Blaustein Library.

35. Stephen Wise himself changed his attitude several times. In 1936, he thought it "bad Zionist politics" not admitting the pro-Communist group to the WJC; like many others, he and the AJ Congress were upset by the Molotov-Ribbentrop agreement of August 1939, but after the German invasion in June 1941, he again avoided criticism of Soviet Russia and the Soviet sympathizers in the United States. On Communist infiltration of the AJ Congress see Nathan Glazer, *The Social Basis of American Communism* (New York, 1961), 154–57, and Paul Lyons, "Philadelphia Jews and Radicalism: The AJ Congress Cleans House," in *Philadelphia Jewish Life, 1940–1985*, edited by Murray Friedman (Ardmore, Pa., 1986), 107–23. An important document on Communist infiltration of AJ Congress is a memorandum of Justice Wise Polier, 1949 (n.d.) AJHSA, AJ Congress Papers, I-77, box 51. Horace M. Kallen expressed his misgivings about the role of Communist and party line groups in the AJ Congress and their functioning as officials, and above all, as paid employees. His own experience with all of them was "that they cannot be trusted to serve the ends of liberty to which they declare allegiance, that their intention is jesuitical, and that whatever they do is for the greater glory of the Communist fatherland." Kallen to Petegorsky, June 3, 1947, YIVO, Horace M. Kallen Papers, box 30/533.

36. Arthur Liebman, *Jews and the Left* (New York, 1979), 504–14; Louis Harap, "American Jewish Congress Veers Right," *Jewish Life* 3 (July 1949): 9–12.

37. Irving Miller to all councils, divisions, chapters, and members of the administrative committee, May 31, 1949, AJHSA, AJ Congress Papers, I-77, box 51.

38. Continuations Committee of the Conference Against Jewish Negotiations with the Adenauer Government in Germany, resolution adopted Mar. 26, 1952, CZA, Goldmann Archive, Z6/1812.

CHAPTER 7

1. Bower, *Paperclip Conspiracy*, 124, 140, 162–65, 170–81, 187–89, 196–97. For the most detailed treatment of the subject, see John Gimbel, *Science, Technology, and Reparations: Exploitation and Plunder in Postwar Germany* (Stanford, Calif., 1990), esp. pp. 37–59. A draft press release regarding Paperclip of Mar. 11, 1946, was never published "because such publicity may lead to erroneous interpretations on the part of Scientific, Labor, Zionist or Left Wing political elements which might exert sufficient pressure upon Congress and the Departments concerned in evolving the policies, to defeat the ultimate objectives derived in long range exploitation" (44). A few years later the American public was shocked by the revelation that the Air Force employed a German physician, Dr. Walter Schreiber, who had been implicated in the brutal experiments performed by Nazi doctors on concentration camp victims. For the protests see HSTL, Gf2168, e.g., Nov. 14, 1951, Mar. 5, Apr. 24 and 29, 1952.

2. See the continuing discussions of the AJC Staff Policy Committee on Germany, and the NCRAC Committee on Overt Anti-Semitism from February until the opening of the exhibition early in April 1949. YIVO, AJC Records, FAD-1, box 23A.

3. *Monthly Bulletin of the United States–German Chamber of Commerce*, Jan. 15, 1949, cited in AJC confidential note, Feb. 11, 1949, ibid.

4. Harry Greenstein to AJC, AJJDC, Jewish Agency, WJC, Mar. 21, 1949, ibid.; also deliberations mentioned in note 2 above.

5. Easterman to Marcus, Mar. 10, 1949, CZA, WJC British Section Collection, C-2; Isenbergh to Slawson, Mar. 12, 1949, YIVO, AJC Records, FAD-1, box 23A.

6. Resolution of the AJC administrative committee, Mar. 8, 1949, quoted in letter from David Danzig to Matthew Brown, Mar. 11, 1949, YIVO, AJC Records, FAD-1, box 23A.

7. Slawson to Shuster and Isenbergh, Mar. 21, 1949, YIVO, AJC Records, FAD-1, box 23A.

8. NCRAC, Committee on Overt Antisemitism, Apr. 6, 1949, YIVO, AJC Records, FAD-1, box 23A.

9. NCRAC executive committee, Mar. 21, 1949, AJHSA, NCRAC Papers, I-172, box 32.

10. News from NCRAC, for release Apr. 8, 1949, YIVO, AJC Records, FAD-1, box 23A; also AJC memorandum, Apr. 11, 1949, ibid.

11. NCRAC statement regarding the picketing of the fair by leftist groups (according to *Daily Worker* of Apr. 6, 1949), Apr. 7, 1949, YIVO, AJC Records, FAD-1, box 23A; Louis Harap, "American Jewish Congress Veers Right," *Jewish Life* 3 (July 1949): 9–12. Before the fair opened NCRAC called a meeting of the Yiddish press, which had published extremely critical comments, to explain to them the position of the Jewish organizations.

12. Kurt Grossmann to Marcus, Apr. 25, 1949, AJA, WJCC, box 129, German fair folder.

13. A. S. Lyric, "American Jews and the New Germany," *Yiddish News Digest*, May 12, 1949, Blaustein Library.

14. Petegorsky to Congress and chapter officers, Jan. 26, 1949, AJHSA, AJ Congress Papers, I-77, box 72.

15. See the apologetic interview of Richard Dyck, "Der Fall Gieseking: Versuch einer Klärung durch persönliche Aussprache," *Aufbau*, May 1, 1953, pp. 5–6.

16. David Riesman addressed the NCRAC convention on freedom of expression, Atlantic City, Apr. 27–May 1, 1949, AJHSA, NCRAC Papers, I-172, box 3. S. Andhil Fineberg, "In the Wake of the Gieseking Case," *Committee Reporter* 6 (Apr. 1949): 3; "Wir wollen Furtwängler nicht," *Aufbau*, Jan. 14, 1949, p. 13.

17. On Furtwängler's record see Samuel Lipman, "Furtwängler and the Nazis," *Commentary* 95 (Mar. 1993): 44–49, and Robert Craft, "The Furtwängler Enigma," *NYR*, Oct. 7, 1993, pp. 10–14.

18. NCRAC executive committee, Mar. 27, 1955, AJHSA, NCRAC Papers, I-172, box 33; Arnold Forster (ADL) to Charles Posner, Cincinnati Jewish Community Council, Feb. 23, 1955, AJA, CCRC Papers, box 67/8.

19. IfZ, Krekeler Papers, ED 135/173, pp. 176–78. Vols. 173 and 174 contain his unpublished MSS.

20. Stanley Chyet, et al., to the editor of *Cincinnati Times Star*, Mar. 4, 1955, AJA, CCRC Papers, box 67/8.

21. Irving Engel to Krekeler, Mar. 21, 1955, and Krekeler to Engel, May 10, 1955, IfZ, Krekeler Papers, ED 135/75.

22. Forster to Posner, Feb. 23, 1955, AJA, CCRC Papers, box 67/8.

23. German consulate in Detroit to Foreign Office, Bonn, Nov. 14, 1961, PA/AA, 305 82.60/91.36, vol. 184.

24. An exchange of letters, Rabbi Jack J. Cohen to David Bar-Illan (at that time he spelled his name Bar-Ilan) Nov. 7, 1961, and Bar-Illan to Cohen, *Reconstructionist*, Dec. 29, 1961, pp. 29–31. A critical comment on that exchange by Ruth Levin appeared in the *Reconstructionist*, Jan. 26, 1962, pp. 29–30. Abraham Harman, Israel's ambassador to the United States, did not attend Bar-Illan's performance with the Berlin Philharmonic because "of a previous engagement."

25. For an early contemporary appraisal, see Alfred Werner, "The Case of Pastor Niemöller," *Congress Weekly*, May 2, 1947, pp. 12–14. For an analysis of Niemöller's attitude to the Jewish question see Leonore Siegele-Wenschkewitz, "Auseinandersetzung mit einem Stereotyp: Die Judenfrage im Leben Martin Niemöllers," in *Die Deutschen und die Judenverfolgung im Dritten Reich*, edited by Ursula Büttner (Hamburg, 1992), 295–319.

26. *Cincinnati Times Star*, Feb. 3, 1947. See also Niemöller's interview with Kurt Kersten in *Aufbau*, Jan. 31, 1947, pp. 1–4.

27. Niemöller stuck to his favorite theme, criticism of German rearmament supported by the United States, also during later visits. In 1960 he elaborated his attitude at a lecture at New York's Herzl Institute, expressing his understanding for "the attitude of Jews toward Germans which no amount of atonement could overcome." Morris Kertzer to David Danzig, Mar. 8, 1960, YIVO, AJC Records, FAD-1, box 25.

28. See chap. 5.

29. "Crime without Punishment?" *Yiddisher Kempfer*, Oct. 17, 1947, pp. 3–5, 8; Ruth Karpf, Letters to the Editor, *Aufbau*, Oct. 17, 1947, p. 4.

30. ADL, Joseph Lichten to Ben Goldman, Sept. 27, 1947, ADL Archives, New York, ADL Correspondence Files, Foreign Countries, Germany (hereafter ADL FC Germany).

31. Dr. Samuel Gringauz in a talk with Manfred George, "Chancen des neuen deutschen Antisemitismus," *Aufbau*, Oct. 31, 1947, pp. 7, 11.

32. Schumacher to Hamburger, Dec. 27, 1947, and Hamburger to Schumacher, Feb. 18, 1948, Archiv der sozialen Demokratie (hereafter AdsD), Friedrich-Ebert-Stiftung (FES) Bonn, Schumacher Collection, Q23.

33. B. M. Joffe, Jewish Community Council of Detroit to CRCs, Feb. 16, 1951, AJA, CCRC Papers, 57/1; Report of the *Forverts* correspondent in Detroit, Feb. 7, 1951, *Yiddish News Digest*, Feb. 8, 1951, Blaustein Library.

34. B. Z. Hoffman-Tzivyon, "Jewish Interests," *Yiddish News Digest*, Feb. 20, 1951; Jacoby to WJC executive, Jan. 11, 1951, CZA, Goldstein Papers, A364/1034a. In Cincinnati the Jewish Community Relations Council opposed the decision of the City Council to enter a "Sister-City Plan" with the City of Munich and instead recommended a less committal affiliation program of Cincinnati citizens. Jacob Marcus to Louis Schwab, Mar. 26, 1951, AJHSA, NCRAC Papers, Overt Antisemitism, I-172, box 55. See also minutes of the Cincinnati CRC, Mar. 16, 1951, and Shuster to Slawson, Mar. 20, 1951, ibid.

35. Minutes of NCRAC executive committee, Feb. 28, 1950, AJHSA, NCRAC Papers, I-172, box 32.

36. Dinnerstein, *America and the Survivors of the Holocaust*, 117–82; Cohen, *Not Free to Desist*, 286–92.

37. M. D. Waldman to Jacob Blaustein, Dec. 10, 1949, YIVO, AJC Records, Morris D. Waldman Files, box 639/B.

38. Accusation on Communist ties, e.g, Charles R. Hill, Aug. 17 and 23, 1940, HSTL, David Niles Papers, boxes 29, 30; Edgar Hoover to David Niles, Apr. 1947, ibid., box 35, Hoover file. See also Alfred Steinberg, "Mr. Truman's Mystery Man," *Saturday Evening Post*, Dec. 24, 1949.

39. AJC memorandum "The Communist Propaganda on Germany," Apr. 1951, YIVO, AJC Records, FAD-1, box 33. See also the subsequent memo by Elliot E. Cohen, editor of *Commentary*, to Slawson, Dec. 12, 1952, AJA, S. Andhil Fineberg Papers, box 1/7.

40. Irving Miller to Irving Kane, NCRAC, June 1, 1951, AJHSA, NCRAC Papers, I-172, box 55; also NCRAC, Minutes of the executive committee, Oct. 10, 1950, AJHSA, NCRAC Papers, I-172, box 32; David Petegorsky's elaboration on that subject, NCRAC Committee on Germany, June 22, 1951, AJA, CCRC Papers, box 57/1; NCRAC executive committee, Oct. 10, 1950, AJHSA, NCRAC Papers, I-172, box 32.

41. NCRAC, 11th Plenary Session, Chicago, Oct. 10–12, 1953, AJA, CCRC Papers, box 51/3.

CHAPTER 8

1. Frank Stern, *The Whitewashing of the Yellow Badge: Antisemitism and Philosemitism in West Germany, 1945–1952* (Oxford and New York, 1992).

2. Moses Moskowitz, "The Germans and the Jews: Postwar Report: The Enigma of German Irresponsibility," *Commentary* 2 (July 1946): 7–14.

3. Ben Halpern, "Guilty, But Not Answerable," *Jewish Frontier* 15 (Apr. 1948): 41–60. Jaspers's book *The Question of German Guilt* (New York, 1947) appeared in English one year after his Heidelberg lectures *Schuldfrage* had been published in German. In the late 1940s and early 1950s there were almost no reverberations of the Jewish catastrophe in German historical research and philosophical thought.

4. For the differences of opinion between William Haber and General Lucius Clay regarding that subject, and the treatment of the postwar Jewish community in Germany see chap. 3.

5. Causes of Anti-Semitism (prepared by Research Branch, ICD, OMGUS), draft, quoted in D. Bernstein to Slawson, May 26, 1947, YIVO, AJC Records, FAD-1, box 23A; Report #49 (Mar. 3, 1947), in *Public Opinion in Occupied Germany: The OMGUS Surveys, 1945–1949,* edited by Anna J. Merritt and Richard L. Merritt (Urbana, Ill., 1970), part 1. Political Perspectives in Occupied Germany, pp. 146–48 (survey conducted in Dec. 1946). For Rabbi Bernstein's statement, see Thomas P. Liebschütz, Rabbi Philip S. Bernstein and the Jewish Displaced Persons, Rabbinical Thesis, HUC Cincinnati, AJA, p. 105. For the strained relations between the Jewish survivors and refugees and the Germans cp. Brenner, *Nach dem Holocaust,* 77–87.

6. Report #122 (May 22, 1948), Merritt and Merritt, *Public Opinion in Occupied Germany,* 239–40 (survey conducted in Apr. 1948).

7. HICOG, Report on Nationalism in Western Germany, Feb. 1950, NA, RG59, 762A.00/3–350; HICOG, Reactions Analysis Branch, Public Affairs Office, Report #1, Series #2, Dec. 30, 1949, RG59, FW 762A.00/5–1050.

8. William Haber, Final Report to the Five Cooperating Organizations, Dec. 20, 1948, YIVO, AJC Records, FAD-1, box 23A.

9. Joachim Prinz, memorandum on a trip to Germany, July 22, 1949, AJHSA, AJ Congress Papers, I-77, box 72.

10. For the IJA, see Gerhard Jacoby, "The German Mind Today," *Congress Weekly,* May 21, 1951, pp. 10–12, and Nehemiah Robinson, Danger Points in Western Germany, Aug. 1951, AJA, WJCC, box 80/2. The study "Anti-Democratic Trends in Western Germany" was compiled by Jacoby upon his return from Germany to New York. Zachariah Shuster, in charge of the AJC Paris European office, received for many years extensive reports and analyses from correspondents in Germany, the most important of whom were Samuel Wahrhaftig, Paul W. Freedman, and Eleonore Sterling. The critical survey "The New Threat from Germany" (1950) was authored by Arthur Mayer, who at that time chaired AJC's Committee on German Affairs. Distribution of AJC pamphlets "Neo-Nazi Strength and Strategy in Western Europe" mentioned in Leo J. Margolin to Slawson, Aug. 10, 1953, YIVO, AJC Records, FAD-1, box 21. Hannah Arendt spent several months in Germany in 1949–50 and summed up her impressions in an essay "The Aftermath of Nazi Rule: Report from Germany," in *Commentary* 10 (Oct. 1950): 342–53. She saw the most significant symptom of German intelligentsia's unwillingness to shoulder the burden of responsibility bequested to it by the Hitler

regime in the fact that not only the active Nazis but the convinced anti-Nazis were excluded from positions of power and influence in postwar Germany.

11. Delbert Clark's recollections, *Again the Goose Step* (Indianapolis, 1949), quoted in Louis L. Snyder, "Nazism Resurgent: What Should Be Done About It?" *Menorah Journal* 60 (Spring 1952): 37–54. Clark, a persona non grata in German eyes, was hosted by the American Jewish Congress. Drew Middleton summed up his experience in Germany in *The Struggle for Germany* (Indianapolis, 1949). For Middleton's reports on the Nazi penetration of the FDP see *NYT*, Nov. 16, 1952; Nov. 29, 1952; Jan. 18, 1953.

12. Three of the judges who declared rightist MP Wolfgang Hedler not guilty of charges of slander and incitement of racial hatred were former Nazis, *NYT*, Feb. 16, 1950; Norbert Muhlen, "The Return of Goebbels' Film Makers," *Commentary* 11 (Mar. 1951): 245–50; and Hilde Walter, "German Students Seek Peace with the Jews: Behind the Fight Against Nazi Movie-Makers," *Commentary* 14 (Aug. 1952): 124–30. The Lüth initiative was welcomed by Herman Gray, chairman of the AJC foreign affairs committee, Aug. 31, 1951, CZA, Goldmann Archive, Z6/529. See also memorandum by Kurt Grossmann, Movement in Germany: We Beg Israel for Peace, Dec. 26, 1951, CZA, Z6, 595/5. A number of leading Social Democrats joined Erich Lüth's and Rudolf Küstermeier's appeal. Erich Lüth himself summed up his initiative in a book, *Die Friedensbitte an Israel: Eine Hamburger Initiative* (Hamburg, 1976). Marian Gide, the *Forverts* roving correspondent based in Germany, was one of the few who paid attention to the students' anti-Nazi protest movement. E.g., *Forverts*, Feb. 14, 1952.

13. Norbert Muhlen, "The Shooting on the Moehlstrasse: Is It Nazi Anti-Semitism All Over Again?" *Commentary* 8 (Oct. 1949): 355–60; Frank Goldman to John McCloy, Aug. 12, 1949, OMGUS Papers, IfZ, MF260, 3/160–3/14 CAD; McCloy to Goldman, Aug. 1949, ADL Archives, ADL FC 1949–52, German Campaign.

14. Paul W. Freedman to Shuster, "The Norbert Muhlen Article in *Commentary*," 1949, YIVO, AJC Records, FAD-41, box 20. See also Norbert Muhlen, "In the Backwash of the Great Crime: Today's Barriers Between Jews and Germans," *Commentary* 13 (Feb. 1952): 107–14, esp. p. 114.

15. Alfred Werner, "Dreyfus in Offenbach," *Jewish Frontier* 17 (Mar. 1950): 14–17.

16. The most detailed treatment by Constantin Goschler, "Der Fall Philipp Auerbach: Wiedergutmachung in Bayern," appeared in a volume edited by Ludolf Herbst and Constantin Goschler, *Wiedergutmachung in der Bundesrepublik Deutschland* (Munich, 1989), 77–98. For a sympathetic appraisal see Wolfgang Kraushaar, "Die Affäre Auerbach: Zur Virulenz des Antisemitismus in den Gründerjahren der Bundesrepublik," *Menora* 6 (1995): 319–43. See also Erich Lüth's contribution "Mein Freund Philipp Auerbach," in *Vergangene Tage: Jüdische Kultur in München*, edited by Hans Lamm (Munich, 1982), 490–94. Norbert Muhlen's comment after the trial was rather apologetic and excused the Bavarian politicians from antisemitic overtones, "In the Backwash of the Great Crime," *Commentary* 13 (Feb. 1952): 107–14, esp. pp 111–14.

17. Bruno Weil appealed in vain to the State Department, which regarded the Auerbach case as an internal German matter to be dealt with by the German courts and authorities. Weil to Riddleberger, May 12, 1952, and George Baker to Weil, May 22,

1952, NA, RG59, 262.0041/5–1252. The AJC also thought that "a definite antisemitic undercurrent" characterized the proceedings against Auerbach. For Hoegner's remark, see Wilhelm Hoegner, *Der schwierige Aussenseiter* (Munich, 1959), 271–72.

18. Harry Greenstein, the last adviser on Jewish affairs, voiced his concern about the German organizations' campaign against restitution in his address to the JDC annual meeting in New York. AJJDC, Thirty-fifth Annual Meeting, New York, Jan. 8, 1950, AJJDC Archives, New York, 3353.

19. Rainer Erb, "Die Rückerstattung: ein Kristallisationspunkt für Antisemitismus," in *Antisemitismus in der politischen Kultur nach 1945*, edited by Werner Bergmann and Rainer Erb (Opladen, 1990), 238–52; Goschler, *Wiedergutmachung*, 172–83, 241–57.

20. "The Jewish Problem of the American Administration in Germany," JTA, Feb. 15, 1947. Gerhard Seger, a Social Democratic exile who preferred to remain in the United States, told Kurt Grossmann in 1948 that at seventy-five Social Democratic meetings which he had addressed the responsibility for the war and the atrocities was admitted. Kurt R. Grossmann, "Germany Revisited," *Congress Weekly*, Sept. 17, 1948, pp. 6–8.

21. See my essay "Die SPD und die Wiedergutmachung gegenüber Israel," in Herbst and Goschler, *Wiedergutmachung*, 191–213.

22. Josef Baumgartner on Mar. 4, 1947, quoted in *Lehrjahre der CSU: Eine Nachkriegspartei im Spiegel vertraulicher Berichte an die amerikanische Militärregierung*, edited by Klaus-Dietmar Henke and Hans Woller (Stuttgart, 1984), 122.

23. Clemens Vollnhals, *Evangelische Kirche und Entnazifizierung: Die Last der nationalsozialistischen Vergangenheit* (Munich, 1989), esp. pp. 34–37, summary pp. 281–88; Siegfried Hermle, "Die Auseinandersetzung mit der nationalsozialistischen Judenverfolgung in der Evangelischen Kirche nach 1945," in Büttner, *Die Deutschen und die Judenverfolgung*, 321–37; Rolf Rendtorff and Hermann Henrix, eds., *Die Kirchen und das Judentum: Dokumente von 1945–1985* (Paderborn, 1988), 540f.

24. Bernd Nellessen, "Die schweigende Kirche. Katholiken und Judenverfolgung," in Büttner, *Die Deutschen und die Judenverfolgung*, 259–71, esp. p. 268; Klemens Richter, ed., *Die Katholische Kirche und das Judentum: Dokumente von 1945–1982* (Freiburg, 1982), 63–65, 66, 122–50; Frederic Spotts, *The Churches and Politics in Germany* (Middletown, Conn., 1973), 89–116; also the recent article by Michael Phayer, "The German Catholic Church After the Holocaust," *Holocaust and Genocide Studies* 10 (Fall 1996): 151–67.

25. For the most comprehensive treatment of the first years of the Christian-Jewish societies in Germany see Josef Foschepoth, *Im Schatten der Vergangenheit: Die Anfänge der Gesellschaften für Christlich-Jüdische Zusammenarbeit* (Göttingen, 1993). A synopsis of his study appeared in *Zwischen Antisemitismus und Philosemitismus: Juden in der Bundesrepublik*, edited by Wolfgang Benz (Berlin, 1991), 63–70. Cp. Frank Stern, "Philosemitism—The Whitewashing of the Yellow Badge in West Germany, 1945–1952," *Holocaust and Genocide Studies* 4 (1989): 463–77, esp. pp. 472–76.

26. Remarks by John J. McCloy at the Conference on the Future of Jews in Germany, Heidelberg, July 31, 1949, HSTL, Harry N. Rosenfield Papers, box 16.

27. Foschepoth, *Im Schatten der Vergangenheit*, 82–83.

28. Ibid., 101–5.

29. Greenstein to McCloy, Sept. 19, 1949, AJA, WJCC, box 131, folder: German attitudes to Jews 1949.

30. Ibid. See also Blankenhorn's entry in his diary, Sept. 25, 1949, BA, Herbert Blankenhorn Papers, NL351/1B.

31. Harry Greenstein's final report to Secretary of the Army Gordon Gray, Dec. 10, 1949, HSTL, Harry N. Rosenfield Papers, box 16; Abraham S. Hyman's final report, Jan. 30, 1950, CZA, Goldmann Archive, Z6/72.

32. McCloy to Adenauer, Sept. 28, 1949, Allied High Commissioners, Conversations with Adenauer, PA/AA, II 212–6, 1949–51, vol. 1.

33. *Verhandlungen des Deutschen Bundestages*, 1. leg. period, 5. session, Sept. 20, 1949, pp. 22–30, here p. 27.

34. *Verhandlungen des Deutschen Bundestages*, 1. leg. period, 6. session, Sept. 21, 1949, pp. 36–37.

35. Hans-Peter Schwarz et al., eds., *Akten zur Auswärtigen Politik der Bundesrepublik Deutschland* (hereafter *AAPBD*), *Adenauer und die Hohen Kommissare, 1949–1951* vol. 1 (Munich, 1989), 25–26. The full text of Adenauer's interview with Karl Marx, Nov. 11, 1949, is reprinted in Rolf Vogel, ed., *Deutschlands Weg nach Israel: Eine Dokumentation* (Stuttgart, 1967), 17–19. The interview appeared in the *Allgemeine Wochenzeitung der Juden in Deutschland* (today *Allgemeine Jüdische Wochenzeitung*, hereafter *AJW*), Nov. 25, 1949.

36. Address to the Society for Christian-Jewish Cooperation, Wiesbaden, Dec. 7, 1949. Theodor Heuss, *An und über Juden: Aus Schriften und Reden, 1906–1963* (Düsseldorf, 1964), 121–27.

37. "What Do the Germans Propose to Do," *Commentary* 10 (Sept. 1950): 225–28.

38. Ralph Giordano, *Die Zweite Schuld oder von der Last Deutscher zu sein* (Hamburg, 1987). In his book the German Jewish author exposed the German failure, mainly in the 1950s, to deal with the consequences of the Holocaust.

39. AJC, Minutes of the meeting of the AJC Staff Committee on Germany, Nov. 9, 1950, YIVO, AJC Records, FAD-1, box 26.

Chapter 9

1. The most comprehensive source on Blaustein is Remembering Jacob Blaustein: An Oral History Collection, comprising fifty-seven oral history interviews, which was deposited at the William E. Wiener Oral History Library of the American Jewish Committee, now at the New York Public Library, Jewish Division. Blaustein's important contribution in mobilizing American support for *shilumim* has been described by Yeshayahu A. Jelinek in his article "John J. McCloy, Jacob Blaustein, and the Shilumim: A Chapter in American Foreign Affairs," in *Holocaust and Shilumim: The Policy of Wiedergutmachung in the Early 1950s*, edited by Alex Frohn (Washington, 1991), 29–46.

2. For John J. McCloy, see Kai Bird's critical biography *The Chairman: John J. McCloy, the Making of the American Establishment*; for his relations with Jews and Jewish problems, pp. 201–27, 314–15, 334–36, 479–82. The best treatment of McCloy's decisive role in Germany is by Thomas Alan Schwartz, *America's Germany: John J.*

McCloy and the Federal Republic of Germany (Cambridge, Mass., 1991), on Wiedergut-machung, pp. 175–84. McCloy's role in the American Establishment, together with Dean Acheson, Charles Bohlen, Averell Harriman, George Kennan, and Robert Lovett, has been described by Walter Isaacson and Evan Thomas, *The Wise Men: Six Friends and the World They Made* (New York, 1986). McCloy's pro-Arab attitude during the Nixon presidency has been discussed, among others, by Alan Brinkley in his article "Minister Without Portfolio," *Harper's*, Feb. 1983, pp. 31–46, esp. 45–46. For a very critical view, see Steve Whitfield, "The Real (John J.) McCloy?" ("A partial view of the man who advocated incarceration of Japanese Americans, counseled clemency for Nazi war criminals, and has been called 'the most influential private citizen in America' "), *Moment* 8 (Sept. 1983): 45–52. McCloy's appointment as high commissioner in spring 1949 was welcomed by Eric Warburg and David Ginsburg, an influential Washington lawyer who often advised Israel's diplomats there. The American Association for a Democratic Germany, which counted a number of Jewish intellectuals and public men in its ranks, promised cooperation. The pro-German National Council for Prevention of War at first opposed his nomination but changed its mind. Warburg to McCloy, Apr. 21, 1949; Ginsburg to McCloy, June 20, 1949; Bingham to McCloy, May 19, 1949; Frederick J. Libby to McCloy, Apr. 25, 1949, May 17, 1949, and June 17, 1949, Amherst College Archives, McCloy Papers, box HC1/54.

3. A scholarly biography of Nahum Goldmann has not yet been written. He himself authored several autobiographies, which, despite their importance, have to be used with caution. The last and most comprehensive appeared in German: Nahum Goldmann, *Mein Leben als deutscher Jude*, vol.1, and *Mein Leben: USA-Europa-Israel*, vol. 2 (Munich, 1980–81). See also Raphael Patai, *Nahum Goldmann: His Mission to the Gentiles* (Tuscaloosa, Ala., 1987), 169–201.

4. See, for instance, the documentation in Yehoshua Freundlich, ed., State of Israel. Israel State Archives. *Documents on the Foreign Policy of Israel*, vol. 5, 1950 (Jerusalem, 1988), CV, P. Naphtali to M. Sharett, Jan. 24, 1950, Doc. 43, pp. 25–26; G. Landauer to Sharett, Mar. 17, 1950, Doc. 141, pp. 96–97; Memorandum by B. Guriel, June 12, 1950, Doc. 276, p. 148; Consultation at the Ministry of Foreign Affairs, Aug. 1, 1950, Doc. 328, pp. 169–71; P. Naphtali to Sharett and E. Kaplan, Sept. 1, 1950, Doc. 366, pp. 192–93; M. Amir to West European Division, Jerusalem, Nov. 13, 1950, Doc. 460, p. 237; E. Lionel to West European Division, Nov. 22, 1950, Doc. 476, pp. 243–44; also vol. 6, 1951, ed. by Yemima Rosenthal (Jerusalem, 1991), CV, Ed. Note, Cabinet Debate on Israel Restitution Claim from Germany, Jan. 3, 1951, p. 6; Y. Tekoah to W. Eytan, Jan. 4, 1951, Doc. 3, p. 1. For the important role of Foreign Minister Moshe Sharett in preparing the way for negotiations with the West German government in regard to reparations, see Gabriel Sheffer, *Moshe Sharett: Biography of a Political Moderate* (Oxford, 1996), 524–64, 606–7, 637–39. See also David Horowitz, *In the Heart of Events* (Jerusalem, 1980), 223–25. A great many references to Israeli-German relations may be found in Sharett's diary *Yoman Ishi* (Personal Diary), in Hebrew (Tel-Aviv, 1978), 8 vols.

5. Yehudit Auerbach, "Ben Gurion and Reparations from Germany," in *David Ben-Gurion: Politics and Leadership in Israel*, edited by Ronald Zweig (London, 1991), 274–92; cp. also Moshe Pearlman, *Ben Gurion Looks Back* (London, 1965), 162–70.

Ailing President Chaim Weizmann favored reparations but only as a token gesture; in his view, nothing could exonerate Germany from the heinous crimes committed against the Jewish people. Norman Rose, *Chaim Weizmann: A Biography* (New York, 1986), 451.

6. Warburg and Goldmann to McCloy, Mar. 20, 1950, WNRC, RG466, McCloy Papers, box 7; McCloy's meeting with Goldmann, Maurice Boukstein, Joseph Schwartz and Benjamin Ferencz, Apr. 10, 1950, ibid., box 12. The Israeli note regarding restitution and indemnification was dispatched to the four powers on Jan. 16, 1951. Israel Foreign Office, *Documents Relating to the Agreements between the Government of Israel and the Government of the Federal Republic of Germany* (Jerusalem, 1953), 13–15.

7. McCloy repeatedly told the West German minister-presidents that they should work with JRSO to arrange "some sort of global settlement" that would provide a speedy solution to many of the claims and would also make a good impression abroad. E.g., McCloy to the minister-presidents of the *Länder* in the U.S. zones, May 8, 1950, and Aug. 22, 1950, WNRC, RG466, McCloy Papers, boxes 12 and 18. Still, despite McCloy's prodding, it took the various *Länder* two years to reach bulk settlements with JRSO. Cp. Schwartz, *America's Germany*, 176–78.

8. For the Jewish demands to preserve the Allied Restitution Court of Appeals or at least an Allied majority on the new Court of Restitution Appeals, see Department of State memorandum of a conversation, Sept. 18, 1951, NA, RG59, 262.0041/9–1851, and Sept. 27, 1951, ibid., 262.0041/9–275. Blaustein appealed in vain on this issue to President Truman, Aug. 25, 1951, WNRC, RG466, McCloy Papers, box 30. The compromise between the Allies and the Germans in regard to a mixed court with a neutral chairman was reached in March 1952. Note of Mar. 25, 1952, PA/AA, II 241–27g, vol. 3, quoted in Goschler, *Wiedergutmachung*, 255. For the differences of opinion about stipulation of human rights guarantees in the contractual agreement see Blaustein to McCloy, Feb. 18, 1952, and McCloy to Blaustein, Jan. 15, 1952, YIVO, AJC Records, FAD-1, box 34. For a succinct treatment of the linkage between continuing restitution and indemnification and West German sovereignty, cp. Goschler, *Wiedergutmachung*, 241–47.

9. For Shepard Stone, see Thomas Kielinger, "Shepard Stone, 80, untiring intermediary and promoter of German-America ties," *German Tribune*, Apr. 17, 1988 (translated from *Rheinischer Merkur/Christ und Welt*, Mar. 25, 1988); Marion Gräfin Dönhoff, "Grosses Herz, souveräner Sinn," *Die Zeit*, May 11, 1990, p. 20. For Stone's own appraisal of the American role in Germany see his essay "The Founding of the Federal Republic—An Assessment of the Role of the U.S.A., 1945–1949 and Beyond," in *America and the Shaping of German Society*, edited by Michael Ermarth, pp. 203–210.

10. Jack Raymond, "Buttenwieser Says Germans Show Little Remorse for Nazi Wrongs," *NYT*, Dec. 1, 1951; *NJM* 66 (Jan. 1952): 1. For the full text of Thomas Dehler's address to a meeting of German Jewish lawyers in Düsseldorf, Dec. 15, 1951, see his papers at the Archiv des Deutschen Liberalismus, Friedrich-Naumann-Stiftung, Gummersbach, N1–774.

11. Blaustein to Abba Eban, June 28, 1951, ISA, FM Records, box 344/18.

12. Cohen, *Not Free to Desist*, 309–15, esp. pp. 312–13.

13. Blaustein to Acheson, June 5, 1951, ISA, FM Records, 344/18; Blaustein to

Eban, July 23, 1951, ibid., 344/21. For AJCs acceptance to attend the Claims Conference, Blaustein to Goldmann, Oct. 18, 1951, CZA, Goldmann Archive, Z6/1621. The Israeli note regarding reparations from Germany that was sent to the four occupying powers is reprinted in Israel Foreign Office, *Documents Relating to the Agreement between the Government of Israel and the Government of the Federal Republic of Germany* (Jerusalem, 1953), 34–41. Jacob Robinson was unhappy about addressing the request to the occupying powers and not to the Germans. "From the politico-psychological viewpoint we are behaving à la Arabe," he complained to Walter Eytan. "We do not want to recognize Germany, but we want to get from them compensation. The Arab states refuse to recognize the existence of Israel, but want us to pay compensation to their co-nationals [in the ethnical sense]." Robinson to Eytan, Feb. 6, 1951, ISA, FM Records, 2413/2.

14. For America's image in the eyes of Adenauer, see Hans-Jürgen Grabbe, "Das Amerikabild Konrad Adenauers," in *Amerikastudien* (American Studies) 31 (1986): 315–23, and Hans Peter Mensing, "Amerika-Eindrücke Konrad Adenauers und Adenauer-Bilder in den USA," in *Adenauer und die USA. Rhöndorfer Gespräche*, vol. 14, edited by Klaus Schwabe (Bonn, 1994), 241–63. The same volume includes a few more relevant lectures on Adenauer and the United States. See also Hans-Jürgen Schröder, "Kanzler der Alliierten? Die Bedeutung der USA für die Aussenpolitik Adenauers," in *Adenauer und die deutsche Frage*, edited by Josef Foschepoth (Göttingen, 1988), 118–42.

15. Adenauer to Hermann J. Abs, Apr. 8, 1952, *Adenauer, Briefe, 1951–1953*, edited by Hans Peter Mensing (Berlin, 1987), 198–99; Adenauer at the CDU federal executive committee, Sept. 5, 1952, Günter Buchstab, ed., *Adenauer: "Es musste alles neu gemacht werden," Die Protokolle des CDU-Bundesvorstandes, 1950–1953* (Stuttgart, 1986), 140–41; May 28, 1952, *Adenauer: Teegespräche, 1950–1954*, edited by Hanns Jürgen Küsters (Berlin, 1984), 284–85. See also Walter Hallstein on the importance of the Israel treaty, Mar. 20, 1953, ibid., pp. 422–34, esp. pp. 424–25, 433–34. Cp. Yeshayahu A. Jelinek's balanced appraisal: "Political Acumen, Altruism, Foreign Pressure or Moral Debt—Konrad Adenauer and the 'Shilumim,'" in *Tel Aviver Jahrbuch für deutsche Geschichte*, vol. 19, edited by Shulamit Volkov and Frank Stern (Tel Aviv, 1990), 77–102. In contrast to Michael Wolffsohn, "Die Wiedergutmachung und der Westen-Tatsachen und Legende," *Aus Politik und Zeitgeschichte* 16–17 (1987): 19–25, Norbert Frei is convinced that Adenauer's reparation agreement with Israel eased the way for the acceptance of Germany's integration in the Western camp by its impact on the American media. Norbert Frei, "Die deutsche Wiedergutmachungspolitik gegenüber Israel im Urteil der öffentlichen Meinung der USA," in Herbst and Goschler, *Wiedergutmachung*, 215–30.

16. Adenauer to Pastor Custodis, Feb. 23, 1946, *Konrad Adenauer: Briefe, 1945–1947*, edited by Hans Peter Mensing (Berlin, 1983), 172–73.

17. See chap. 8, note 35. The interview, which took place November 11, was published November 25, 1949.

18. *Verhandlungen des Deutschen Bundestages*, 1. leg. period, 165. session, Sept. 27, 1951, pp. 6697–6700. The German mission in Washington summarized the impact of Adenauer's statement on the American media as very positive. The press attaché quoted in particular from the friendly editorials in the *Washington Post* and the *NYT*,

both Sept. 30, 1951. The *New York Herald Tribune* and the *Louisville Courier Journal* were more reserved. Oct. 2, 1951, PA/AA, III 210–01/35. On Altmaier's role in 1951 and 1952 see Willy Albrecht's article "Ein Wegbereiter: Jakob Altmaier und das Luxemburger Abkommen," in Herbst and Goschler, *Wiedergutmachung*, 205–13. Altmaier's own recollections must be used with caution. On President Heuss's involvement see *Adenauer-Heuss. Unter Vier Augen. Gespräche aus den Gründerjahren 1949–1959*, edited by Hans Peter Mensing (Berlin, 1997), 68–70, 81.

19. Statement issued by the Conference on Jewish Claims Against Germany, Oct. 25–26, 1951, *Documents on the Foreign Policy of Israel*, vol. 6, edited by Yemima Rosenthal (Jerusalem, 1991), 733–34; detailed report by Esther Herlitz, Nov. 1, 1951, ISA 130.10/2543/7. For the history of the Claims Conference see Ronald Zweig, *German Reparations and the Jewish World: A History of the Claims Conference* (Boulder, Colo., 1987). For Israel's initial lack of confidence in the Diaspora-dominated Claims Conference, see Gershon Avner, Oral History interview, Sept. 30, 1971, HU Institute of Contemporary Jewry, Oral History Division.

20. WJC, Minutes of the WJC executive (American branch), Jan. 22, 1952, AJA, WJCC, box 34/4. The quote is from Saul Kagan's interview, Blaustein Oral History Collection. See also Nahum Goldmann's Oral History interview, Nov. 14 and 20, 1961, HU Institute of Contemporary Jewry, Oral History Division. For a critical view of Goldmann and differences of opinion between him and the Israeli side, see Felix Eliezer Shinnar, Oral History interview, Nov. 18, 1970, ibid.

21. Minutes of the WJC executive (American branch), Jan. 22, 1952, AJA, WJCC, box 3A/4. For Goldmann's arguments in favor of direct negotiations with Germany see his article "Direct Israel-Germany Negotiations? Yes," *Zionist Quarterly* 1 (Winter 1952): 9–13. For the JDC deliberations see Minutes of the Administration Committee of the JDC, Jan. 24, 1952, AJJDC Archives, #3370.

22. *Jewish Chronicle Feature and News Service*, London, Sept. 30, 1951, CZA, Goldmann Archive, Z6/1597; WJC executive (American branch), Sept. 27, 1951, AJA, WJCC, box 3A/3; AJC, Oct. 12, 1951, YIVO, AJC Records, FAD-1, box 21; David Bukspan, Harry Levi, Joseph B. Schechtman to N. Goldmann, Oct. 25, 1951, CZA, Goldmann Archive,Z6/1597; Joseph B. Schechtman, "Against Dealing with Germany," *Congress Weekly*, Feb. 11, 1952, pp. 5–7; LZOA, correspondence and miscellaneous items, Information bulletin, Jan. 10, 1952, AJA, MF1584, O 3, 1951-JE 3, 1954. Cp. Baruch Zuckerman's articles in *Yiddisher Kempfer*, Nov. 2, 1951, pp. 1–2, and Jan. 18, 1952, pp. 1–2.

23. Samuel Gringauz, "How Sincere Is Germany," *ADL Bulletin* 8 (Oct. 1951): 1, 6, 8; "The Basis of German-Jewish Relations," *Jewish Frontier* 18 (Oct. 1951): 5–7.

24. Hersh Leivick, "Blood-Money from Germans," *Jewish Frontier* 17 (May 1950): 14–15, and Samuel Gringauz's reply to Leivick, "Germans Should Pay," ibid., 16–19. Leivick repeated his opposition after Adenauer's statement, *Yiddish News Digest*, Oct. 18, 1951; in the same vein, I. Bashevis Singer (Isaac Warshowsky, his pen name as a journalist), "Why Jews Must Not Accept Germany's Offer of Restitution," *Yiddish News Digest*, Oct. 8, 1951; Jacob Glatstein, *Yiddish News Digest*, Oct. 8, 1951; Aaron Zeitlin, *Yiddish News Digest*, Nov. 9, 1951, AJC, Blaustein Library. Ben Gurion told a delegation of Israeli writers who came to protest negotiations with Germany that he

did not believe in Adenauer's moral urges but rejected their plea to refrain from direct talks with the Germans (as demanded in the writers' resolution of Oct. 13, 1951). For Ben Gurion, as he told them, the criterion was the German readiness to do "serious things from a pragmatic (not moral) aspect." Ben-Gurion Archive, Ben-Gurion Diary, Oct. 30, 1951, hereafter BGA, BGD respectively.

25. S. Niger (Shmuel Charney-Niger), "Miracle vs. Vaudeville?" *Yiddish News Digest*, Oct. 8, 1951; Ben Zion Hoffman-Tzivyon, "Jewish Interests," *Yiddish News Digest*, Oct. 16, 1951. On another issue, essayist Hoffman-Tzivyon expressed his support for an agreement by the Jewish Agency to import prefabricated houses from Germany for homeless refugees in Israel. However, the Bundist writer took the opportunity to expose "the system of double book-keeping" used by the ruling Mapai regarding Germany. On the one hand, it refused to participate in the international Socialist conference in Frankfurt because it took place in a German city, and censured the Jewish Socialist Bundists for attending that meeting. On the other hand, it made agreements with the German government.

26. Salomon Dingol, the *Tog* editor, Shmuel Charney-Niger, Samuel Margoshes, and Aaron Alperin were among the supporters of negotiations; Hersh Leivick, Shlomo Bickel, and Mordecai Danzis opposed them and regarded the Knesset's decision as an error. *Der Tog* (The Day), Jan. 20, 1952, quoted in *Yiddish News Digest*, Jan. 21, 1952, AJC, Blaustein Library.

27. For Nahum Goldmann's appraisal of this relationship, see Nahum Goldmann, *Mein Leben als deutscher Jude* (Munich, 1980), 382–425; idem, "Adenauer und das jüdische Volk," in *Konrad Adenauer und seine Zeit: Politik und Persönlichkeit des ersten Bundeskanzlers*, edited by Dieter Blumenwitz (Stuttgart, 1976), 427–36. Adenauer devoted to the negotiations with Israel one chapter in his memoirs: Konrad Adenauer, *Erinnerungen*, vol. 2 (1953–1955) (Stuttgart, 1966), 132–62. See also the chapters devoted to Israel, Goldmann, and the Jews in the two main biographies: Hans-Peter Schwarz, *Adenauer: Der Aufstieg, 1916–1952*, vol. 1 (Stuttgart, 1986), 897–906, and Henning Köhler, *Adenauer: Eine politische Biographie* (Berlin, 1994), 698–722. Cp. Günther Gillessen, "Konrad Adenauer und der Israel-Vertrag," in *Politik, Philosophie, Praxis: Festschrift für Wilhelm Hennis zum 65ten Geburtstag*, edited by Hans Maier et al. (Stuttgart, 1988), 556–68. My article "Goldmann and Adenauer" appeared in the Hebrew journal *Gesher* 40 (Summer 1994): 59–83.

28. Held to Heine, Mar. 31, 1952; Heine to Held, May 24, 1952; Held to Heine, July 29, 1952; Heine to Held, Aug. 7, 1952; Held to Heine, Jan. 29, 1953, AdsD, FES, Bonn, Fritz Heine Papers, box 20; Schumacher to Adenauer, May 10, 1952; Albrecht, *Kurt Schumacher: Reden—Schriften—Korrespondenzen*, 1005–6; SPD Pressedienst P/VII/258, Nov. 7, 1952; P/VII/264, Nov. 14, 1952 AdsD, Bonn. For the high percentage of persecuted Social Democrats in the first Bundestag see Susanne Miller, "Zwischen Konfrontation und Anpassung: Die SPD Bundestagsfraktion, 1949–1957," *Die Neue Gesellschaft/Frankfurter Hefte* 42 (Jan. 1995): 94–95.

29. John J. McCloy, Jacob Blaustein Oral History Collection, AJC, New York; McCloy to Adenauer, letter presented to the chancellor July 15, 1952, BA, Blankenhorn Papers, 351/16. Very positive on McCloy's role with regard to Jewish requests is Ben-

jamin B. Ferencz, Oral History interview, Apr. 1971, HU Institute of Contemporary Jewry, Oral History Division, Jerusalem. Cp. also Schwartz, *America's Germany*, 175–84.

30. E.g., Moshe Keren to Foreign Ministry, July 3, 1951, on meeting between Eban and Henry Byroade, ISA, FM Records, 344/15; memorandum of conversation between Eban and Byroade, Oct. 30, 1951, NA, RG59, FW 262.84A41/10–3051; memorandum of conversation between Jewish leaders (Blaustein, Held, Goldmann, Goldman, Goldstein, Moses Leavitt, Seymour Rubin, and Secretary Acheson, May 2, 1952, HSTL, Acheson Papers, box 67; Eban to Keren, June 6, 1952, ISA, FM Records, 358/20.

31. Blaustein to Truman, Apr. 11 and 18, 1952, YIVO, AJC Records, GEN-10, box 276; Acheson to Truman, Apr. 22, 1952, *FRUS*, 1952–54, vol. 9, part 1 (Washington, 1986), no. 423, pp. 917–19; Acheson to McCloy, Apr. 22, 1952, ibid., no. 424, pp. 919–20.

32. Sharett to Acheson, May 22, 1952, *FRUS*, 1952–1954, vol. 9, part 1, no. 439, pp. 936–38; McCloy, from Acheson, May 25, 1952, ibid., no. 440, p. 938; Acheson to Sharett, June 3, 1952, ibid., no. 442, p. 939. For the crisis of the Shilumim negotiations, see Yeshayahu A. Jelinek, "Die Krise der Shilumim/Wiedergutmachungs-Verhandlungen im Sommer 1952," *Vierteljahrshefte für Zeitgeschichte* 38 (1990): 113–39; cp. Kai von Jena, "Versöhnung mit Israel? Die Deutsch-Israelischen Verhandlungen bis zum Wiedergutmachungsabkommen von 1952," *Vierteljahrshefte für Zeitgeschichte* 34 (1986): 457–79. See also additional relevant articles in Herbst and Goschler, *Wiedergutmachung.*

33. John Foster Dulles and Harold Stassen disscused the Israel treaty during their visit to Bonn early in February 1953. *Die Kabinettsprotokolle der Bundesregierung 1953*, vol. 6 (Boppard, 1993), 171–75. They met with Adenauer February 5, 1953. See also Adenauer to Schäffer, Feb. 12, 1953, *Adenauer: Briefe, 1951–1953* (Berlin, 1987), 342. For American-Israeli relations during the Republican administration see Isaac Alteras, *Eisenhower and Israel: U.S.-Israeli Relations, 1953–1960* (Gainesville, Fla., 1993).

34. E.g., *Washington Post* editorial "German Gesture," Sept. 11, 1952; *New York Times*, "Germany's Atonement," Sept. 16, 1952; *Christian Science Monitor,* "An Act of Restitution," Sept. 15, 1952, PA/AA, II 244–13/52. Dean Acheson expressed his satisfaction with the agreement and his hope for its ratification without delay. Sept. 10, 1952, BA, Blankenhorn Papers, 351/14.

35. Israel Foreign Office, *Documents Relating to the Agreement between the Government of Israel and the Government of the Federal Republic of Germany,* 94–123. According to data of the German ministry of finance, the sum total of all German indemnification payments, including the Shilumim Treaty and restitution, as well as compensation of former public employees and pledges to other nations amounted to DM 93 billion until January 1994. Most of the individual indemnification payments went to Jews in Israel and in the Diaspora. See Karl Brozik, "Einmalig und voller Lücken: Entschädigung und Rückerstattung," *Tribüne* 34 (June 1995): 176–85. For a critical discussion of Israeli policy and politics with regard to reparations and indemnification see Tom Segev, *The Seventh Million: The Israelis and the Holocaust* (New York, 1993), 189–226.

36. Adenauer to Heinrich von Brentano, Dec. 23, 1952, *Adenauer: Briefe, 1951–1953*, 308–11; BGA, BGD, Nov. 10, 1952.

37. Michael Wolffsohn, "Das Wiedergutmachungsabkommen mit Israel: Eine Untersuchung bundesdeutscher und ausländischer Umfragen," in *Westdeutschland, 1945–1955*, edited by Ludolf Herbst (Munich, 1986), 203–18, here pp. 207–8. See also an AJC analysis of an American-sponsored public opinion survey conducted one month after Adenauer's statement to the Bundestag, Apr. 22, 1952. *Archives of the Holocaust*, vol. 17, edited by Frederick D. Bogen (New York and London, 1993), Doc. 179, pp. 383–401.

38. The vote was 238 in favor, 34 against, and 86 abstained. The great majority of the CSU, the Bavarian sister party of Adenauer's CDU, abstained, among them Franz Josef Strauss, who was to play an important role in West Germany's military assistance to Israel. Communists, right-wingers, one-third of the FDP, and five members of the CDU voted against. *Verhandlungen des Deutschen Bundestages*, 1. leg. period, 254. session, Mar. 18, 1953, pp. 12273–82, and 255. session, Mar. 18, 1953, pp. 12362–66.

39. Anson Rabinbach, "The Jewish Question in the German Question," *New German Critique* 44 (Spring–Summer 1988): 159–92, here p. 166.

40. Eugene Hevesi to Simon Segal, Mar. 26, 1953, YIVO, AJC Records, FAD-1, box 34.

41. Reference to Adenauer-Dulles talks, Apr. 7–8, 1953, BA, Blankenhorn Papers, 351/19A. The records of the Department of State Policy Planning Staff show no mention of broaching the restitution problem during Adenauer's visit, Apr. 7 and 17, 1953. U.S.-German political talks, Washington, D.C., NA, RG59, Records of the Policy Planning Staff 1947–1953, box 16. The Israel agreement was shortly mentioned in Adenauer's NPC address, Apr. 8, 1953. Archiv für Christlich-Demokratische Politik (ACDP), Konrad Adenauer Stiftung, St. Augustin, Felix von Eckardt Papers, I-010–004/1.

42. Felix von Eckardt, *Ein unordentliches Leben: Lebenserinnerungen* (Düsseldorf, 1967), 213, 234; E.g., Harry Levin to Karl E. Allen, editor, *Sun and Arizona Sentinel*, Mar. 20, 1953, ACDP, Eckardt Papers, I-010–004/1; Krekeler to Foreign Office, March 20, 1953, PA/AA, III 210–01E.

43. Altmaier to Barou, Apr. 5, 1953, CZA, Goldmann Archive, Z6/3680; Putzrath to Grossmann, Apr. 29, 1953, and Grossmann to Putzrath, May 5, 1953, ibid., Z6/761. On Goldmann's efforts in 1954, see Abraham Harman to Israel Foreign Ministry, Nov. 2, 1954, ISA, FM Records, 597/8 I.

44. Mensing, "Amerika-Eindrücke," esp. pp. 258–62. Before World War II Heineman (1872–1960), who as president of the SOFINA electrical corporation had known Hjalmar Schacht since 1933, became involved in the preparations for the Schacht-Rublee negotiations concerning an emigration plan for German Jews. He met Schacht incognito December 12, 1938. See also a letter by Sigmund Warburg to Heineman, Dec. 12, 1938. Daniel N. Heineman Correspondence (copy of the James Heineman Collection, New York), Archiv Stiftung Bundeskanzler-Adenauer-Haus, Rhöndorf.

45. For a critical appraisal of Blankenhorn's role in the early fifties, see Hans-Jürgen Döscher, *Verschworene Gesellschaft: Das Auswärtige Amt unter Adenauer zwischen Neubeginn und Kontinuität* (Berlin, 1995), esp. pp. 77–84, 107–8. A contemporary profile

by Walker Henkels appeared in the *Frankfurter Allgemeine Zeitung* (hereafter *FAZ*), June 2, 1955, ISA, FM Records, 597/8 I.

46. The contact between Blankenhorn and Noah Barou was established in April 1950, with the help of German Jewish businessman Günther Lewy, who fled to Britain from the Nazis. Entry of Apr. 28, 1950, BA, Blankenhorn Diary, Blankenhorn Papers 351/5. His drafting of Adenauer's statement is mentioned in *Die Kabinettsprotokolle der Bundesregierung*, vol. 4, 1951, edited by Hans Booms (Boppard, 1988), 662. The different drafts are in PA/AA, Bureau of the State Secretary, vol. 1. Representatives of the WJC and of the Allied High Commission participated in preparing the final draft. Benjamin Buttenwieser, former assistant high commissioner for Germany, later recalled Blankenhorn's part in Adenauer's statement and praised his ability and trustworthiness. The Reminiscences of Benjamin J. Buttenwieser (1975), Oral History Research Office, Columbia University, New York, 1981, pp. 164–66. Herbert Blankenhorn's memoirs, *Verständnis und Verständigung: Blätter eines politischen Tagebuchs von 1949 bis 1973* (Frankfurt, 1980), are an important source for the early German-Israeli relations. More details are available in his large collection deposited at the Bundesarchiv in Koblenz, NL351.

47. James Sheldon to Dean Acheson, Mar. 10, 1952, and Perry Laukhuff to Sheldon, Mar. 17, 1952, NA, RG59, 762A.00/3–1052. An early warning regarding Blankenhorn by Secretary of State Edward Stettinius to Robert Murphy is quoted in Bower, *Pledge Betrayed*, 357.

48. John McCloy to Sheldon, Mar. 25, 1952, WNRC, RG466, McCloy Papers, box 39; Office memorandum, M. J. Meketon to Margaret C. Christman, July 8, 1953, NA, RG59, 761A.00/7–853; Entry of July 19, 1953, James Bryant Conant Papers, Harvard University Archives, UAI 15898–13, box 7, JBC Journal, Germany. According to James Bryant Conant, who became high commissioner for Germany in 1953, Blankenhorn's visit on the eve of the foreign ministers conference of the three Western powers was regarded as "effective but not well received."

49. Aiming, among others, at Blankenhorn, Franz Josef Strauss was among those who early in 1953 demanded an inquiry into the origins of the reparations treaty. He pointed to the loss of sympathy for Germany among the Arab nations and refuted the argument that the treaty would improve West Germany's position in the Western world. Deliberations of the parliamentary group of the CDU/CSU, Feb. 24, 1953, ACDP. For the left-wing accusations, see memorandum presented to Goldmann June 27, 1953, CZA, Goldmann Archive, Z6/1019. For State Secretary Otto Lenz's opposition, see the entry in his diary of March 2, 1953, *Im Zentrum der Macht: Das Tagebuch von Staatssekretär Lenz 1951–1953*, edited by Klaus Gotto, Hans-Otto Kleinmann and Reinhard Schreiner (Düsseldorf, 1989), 570–72. The trial of Blankenhorn and Hallstein in 1959 was reported in *Der Spiegel*, Mar. 11, 1959, pp. 18–20; Apr. 1, 1959, p. 16; Apr. 22, 1959, pp. 19–20; Apr. 29, 1959, pp. 17–20. Walter Hallstein was acquitted because of lack of evidence. See also *Der Spiegel*, Apr. 15, 1959, pp. 8–9. Henning Köhler, the author of a recent Adenauer biography, wondered why Blankenhorn never challenged in court those who accused him of having been bribed in 1953 for his part in bringing about the German-Israel agreement. Köhler, *Adenauer*, 720.

50. Goldmann often mentioned Blankenhorn's helpfulness in the cause of repara-

tions. E.g. *Mein Leben als deutscher Jude*, 378–79, 411. Blankenhorn, for his part, praised Goldmann, *Verständnis und Verständigung*, 359.

51. *Aufbau*'s editorial on the occasion of Adenauer's visit dealt with the importance of the Israel treaty and of indemnification for Germany's regaining the moral right to equal cooperation with the nations, "Adenauer in USA," Apr. 10, 1953, p. 4. An improvement of *Aufbau*'s attitude toward postwar Germany took place successively since 1951. For the history of the weekly and its impact on Jewish-German relations see Susanne Bauer-Hack, *Die jüdische Wochenzeitung Aufbau und die Wiedergutmachung* (Düsseldorf, 1994), 135–92.

52. Louis Harap, "The Adenauer Deal and Peace," *Jewish Life* 5 (Mar. 1952): 3–5; Leonard Piper, "Behind the Reparations Pact," *Jewish Life* 6 (Nov. 1952): 9–10.

53. "The Bonn Agreement," *Reconstructionist*, Oct. 3, 1952, pp. 5–6.

54. Simon Rawidowicz, *Bavel viyerushalaim (Babylon and Jerusalem: Toward a Philosophy of Israel's Wholeness)*, 2 vols. in Hebrew (Waltham, Mass., 1957), vol. 1, pp. 472–505, here p. 501.

55. Goldmann to German Foreign Office, June 17, 1953, and Hallstein to Goldmann, July 3, 1953, PA/AA, II 212–6, vol. 2; Blankenhorn to Hallstein, June 30, 1953, and Blankenhorn to Böhm, July 30, 1953, PA/AA, II 212.06, vol. 3/4. Later Böhm received the 1954 Stephen Wise Award for his efforts to combat antisemitism in Germany and for his role in negotiating the Jewish material claims against Germany.

56. WJC, minutes of the executive (American branch), Apr. 29, 1954, and Dec. 18, 1954, AJA, WJCC, 3A/4; minutes of the London executive, May 24, 1954, ibid., 3A/1; minutes of the plenary session of the executive, Paris, Jan. 27–30, 1955, ibid., 3A/2.

57. James Conant to Goldmann, July 27, 1954, CZA, Goldstein Papers, A364/2507; Blaustein to George C. McGhee, July 6, 1963, and Aug. 19, 1963, CZA, Goldmann Archive, Z6/1163; McGhee to Blaustein, Aug. 13, 1963, and May 28, 1965, ibid.

58. Written interview with the author June 15, 1988. For Klutznick's attitude see also chaps. 10, 11, and 13.

59. B'nai B'rith, Washington, To members of the Board of Governors, Maurice Bisgyer, July 22, 1953, message by Klutznick to Dulles and Conant, ADL Archives, ADL FC Germany.

60. See chap. 10.

61. I do not share Michael Wolffsohn's opinion of "Israel as an irritant in German-American relations." From the viewpoint of American Jewish public opinion and particularly organized Jewry, except for some critical phases, Israel, as shown throughout this study, was a mitigating factor. America's policy toward Germany reflected, of course, U.S. national interests and demonstrated the limits of ethnic pressure. Nevertheless, because of American pluralism and the interrelationship between public opinion and foreign policy it is mistaken to dismiss the role of American Jews in the German-American-Israeli triangle, and contrary to Wolffsohn, most German governments since Adenauer took this into account. Cp. Michael Wolffsohn, *Eternal Guilt? Forty Years of German-Jewish-Israel Relations* (New York, 1993) e.g., pp. 12–15, 154–57.

CHAPTER 10

1. See the following chapters, particularly chaps. 11, 12, 13, 15, and 16.

2. Report to the Friedensbüro, Feb. 1949, BA, Collection Büro für Friedensfragen, vol. 457.

3. Letter by Georg Federer to colleagues in Germany, May 7, 1950, BA, Blankenhorn Papers, 351/1a. Federer visited the United States at the invitation of the Lutheran World Relief. His diaries during his wartime service in Berlin nevertheless ascertain that despite party membership he was very critical of the Nazi warfare against the Jews. His Tagebuchaufzeichnungen 1939–1943 are deposited at the IfZ Archives in Munich.

4. A. Böker, Report on American policy toward Germany, Feb. 2, 1950, BA, Blankenhorn Papers, 351/3. Report on the American position on Germany, PA/AA, II 210–01/80, vol. 262. For the German diplomatic mission's concern with the Society for the Prevention of World War III, e.g., Jan. 12, 1954, ibid., III 205–01/75. The New York Jewish lawyer Isidore Lipschutz, the Society's treasurer, was regarded as its moving spirit in the 1950s.

5. Gerd Bucerius to the Chancellor's office, May 10, 1950, PA/AA, II 210–01/80, vol. 262.

6. Private letter to Theo Kordt, Aug. 10, 1950, PA/AA, II 205–00/80.

7. I relied here and in the following pages on Krekeler's MS, ED 135/173, and on my interview with him, Bad Salzuflen, Sept. 1, 1989. For Krekeler's general political views, see also his contribution to Rudolf Birkl and Günter Olzog, eds., *Erwartungen: Kritische Rückblicke der Kriegsgeneration* (Munich, 1980), 133–38. According to Krekeler, his prewar Jewish friend George Gregory was of great help to him in the first days in New York.

8. Blankenhorn, entry of Aug. 22, 1952, BA, Blankenhorn Papers, 351/13. Adenauer's first choice for the post in New York was the conservative CDU politician Hans Schlange-Schöningen, but because an American journalist discovered antisemitic references in his prewar record, he was sent to London instead.

9. See his *Von Versailles zur Uno: Aus der Erinnerung eines Diplomaten* (Bonn, 1962), particularly pp. 225–48, 255ff. For Consul Hans von Saucken's suspension, see *Frankfurter Rundschau*, Sept. 22, 1958. According to the reminiscences of another German diplomat, the "non-Aryan" Riesser, who "whispered and talked too much with his untidy hands," served during his exile in Paris as a liaison for the German counterintelligence (Abwehr). Werner Otto von Hentig Papers, 1fZ, Aufzeichnungen 1945–1968, Entry of Dec. 31, 1964.

10. Hertz confessed to Krekeler his admiration for Roosevelt's policies. Hertz to Krekeler, July 7, 1952, IfZ, Krekeler Papers, ED 135/58. Krekeler himself was denounced by right-wing Germans for placing a wreath on Roosevelt's grave in Hyde Park, New York, although he did it as a private person and not as a diplomatic representative of the Federal Republic, ibid., ED 135/173, p. 83.

11. In 1952 Krekeler did not predict any difficulties for Georg Federer, a former Nazi party member who would soon take up office in Washington, D.C., but advised him to avoid publicity upon his arrival in New York. Krekeler to Federer, Oct. 28, 1952, ibid., ED 135/42. Since many former members of the Nazi party found their

way back into the Foreign Office, gradually their number also grew at various West German consulates in the United States.

12. Krekeler to Adenauer, Apr. 8, 1951, ibid., ED 135/39; Manfred George to Krekeler, Oct. 8, 1951, ibid., ED 135/76; Report by Consul Georg Krauss on the *Aufbau* Town Hall meeting, Oct. 25, 1951, Krekeler to Foreign Office, Bonn, Oct. 26, 1951, PA/AA, III 212–6, vol. 1.

13. Conversation between Walter Gong and George, Nov. 5, 1951, Krekeler to Foreign Office, Bonn, Nov. 14, 1951, PA/AA, III 212–06, vol. 1. George to Heuss, Sept. 1, 1959, AdsD, Jakob Altmaier Papers, box 3.

14. Donald R. Heath to James R. Riddleberger, May 22, 1946, USNA, RG 59, Records of the Office of West European Affairs 1941–1954, Misc. German files, box 2, LOT 55D371; Note Lucius D. Battle, May 3, 1950, NA, RG59, 762.00/5 350; Oppenheimer to Krekeler, Sept. 21, 1950, and Oppenheimer to Riesser, Dec. 19, 1950, IfZ, Krekeler Papers, ED 135/102; ibid., ED 135/173, p. 24.

15. On Warburg see Ron Chernow, *Warburgs*, 493–536, 565–95, 655–721; David Farrer, *The Warburgs: The Story of a Family* (New York, 1975), 186–95.

16. On the American Council on Germany, see Henri Jacob Hempel, "Deutsch-Amerikanische Dialoge: Geschichte und Leistung des American Council on Germany," *Das Parlament*, Sept. 23, 1988, p. 20. Jewish members of the Council—such as Eric Warburg, Fritz Oppenheimer, the historian Hans Kohn, and Adenauer's old friend Dannie Heineman—were not at all representative of the Jewish community, which was sometimes very critical of the Council's position.

17. On Eric Warburg's burial site, see Chernow, *Warburgs*, 721.

18. L. Roy Blumenthal to Adenauer, June 8, 1950, PA/AA, III 210–01/80, vol. 1.

19. The main collection of the Julius Klein Papers has been deposited at the JWV Archives in Washington, D.C. Many of the memoranda and statements should be used with care because of Klein's inclination to exaggerate his achievements. See also Krekeler to Foreign Office, Bonn, Dec. 5, 1957, IfZ, Krekeler Papers, ED 135/48.

20. Shepard Stone to McCloy, May 21, 1952, WNRC, John McCloy Papers, box 42. After the signing of the Luxembourg agreement, Klein expressed his deep gratitude to Adenauer, Oct. 7, 1952, PA/AA, II 244–13/13, vol. 9. Altmaier exaggerated Klein's part in breaking the 1952 deadlock. See memo, Oct. 31, 1953, conversation with Klein, Dec. 19, 1953, and memo, May 5, 1959, AdsD, Altmaier Papers, box 1. For Klein's good contacts in Bonn, see "Gemeinsame Arbeit," *Der Spiegel*, Apr. 10, 1963, pp. 72–73; also "Häufig beim Kanzler," *Der Spiegel*, Sept. 12, 1962, pp. 45–51. Among others, Klein was instrumental in arranging a meeting between Middelhauve and Philip Klutznick on May 13, 1955 (Cp. note 37). Middelhauve also met Eugene Hevesi, the secretary of AJC's Foreign Affairs Committee, despite AJC's skepticism because of Middelhauve's role in West German policies. Memo for General Klein, May 24, 1955, IfZ, Krekeler Papers, ED 135/94.

21. Secret memorandum by Julius Klein, Mar. 3, 1965 (transcribed Oct. 25, 1965), BBA, Washington, D.C. On Klein's part in Ben Gurion's meeting with Adenauer in 1960, Kurt Birrenbach to Klein, June 25, 1965, IfZ, Krekeler Papers, ED 135/94. Yohanan Meroz, the deputy head of the Israeli mission in Cologne, was rather skeptical about Klein's mediation between Adenauer and Ben Gurion. In August 1959 Klein told

him about an informal high-ranking meeting in Germany at which a great many foreign dignitaries would participate together with Adenauer and Ben Gurion, and which would pave the way for the subsequent establishment of diplomatic relations between West Germany and Israel. Meroz to Foreign Ministry and to Eliezer Shinnar, Aug. 6, 1959, ISA, FM Records, 3099/24. On Klein's part in 1965, Shinnar to Klein, May 28, 1965, and David Ben Gurion to Klein, Aug. 4, 1965, IfZ, Krekeler Papers, ED 135/94.

22. Consul General Yaacov Barmor, Chicago, to Foreign Ministry, Jan. 15, 1965, ISA, FM Records 3505/13.

23. Memo on German assets, Feb. 1958, JWV Archives, Germany file.

24. Harry H. Vaughan, memo for the president, June 11, 1952, HSTL, confidential file Julius Klein, and Oct. 2, 1962, HSTL, presidential files, box 2.

25. Brentano to Knappstein, Feb. 15, 1963, and Knappstein to Brentano, Feb. 15, 1963, BA, Brentano Papers, NL 239/111. Klein testified at a hearing of the Senate Foreign Relations Committee early in 1963. News Release, JWV Archives, IB18; "Gemeinsame Arbeit," *Der Spiegel*, Apr. 10, 1963, pp. 72–73.

26. Memo of conversation at the Department of State, Jan. 18, 1950, NA, RG59, 762a 00/1–1850; Manfred George, "Lange Besetzung Deutschlands nötig," interview with Jacob Javits, *Aufbau*, Dec. 30, 1949, pp. 3–4. In addition to Javits's official correspondence, I also relied in the following pages on his autobiography, written with the assistance of Rafael Steinberg, *Javits: The Autobiography of a Public Man* (Boston, 1982), 183–88.

27. Krekeler to George, Oct. 4, 1951, Deutsches Literatur-Archiv Marbach, 75.3059; Krekeler to Foreign Office, Bonn, Oct. 1, 1951, PA/AA, III 210–01/80, vol. 2.

28. Javits to Adenauer, Oct. 1951, PA/AA, II 244–10, vol 1; Manfred George, "Deutsche Sphinx?—Keine Sphinx," interview with Jacob Javits, *Aufbau*, Dec. 21, 1951, pp. 1–2; memo of conversation at the State Department, Jan. 10, 1952, NA, RG59, FW762A.0221/1–952; Riesser to Foreign Office, Bonn, Feb. 25, 1951, PA/AA, III 210–01/80, vol. 3; Javits to Adenauer, Oct. 27, 1959, NA, RG59, FW762.00/10–2759; Javits, *Autobiography*, 188. The German award was conferred upon Javits by Niels Hansen, who served at that time at the embassy in Washington. In 1981 Hansen was appointed ambassador of the Federal Republic to Israel.

29. Emanuel Celler, One Minute Speech, Mar. 11, 1952, LC, Emanuel Celler Papers, box 40; Emanuel Celler's "Random Thoughts on Germany," *Congressional Record*, 85th Cong., 1st Session, July 13, 1957, Appendix, A 5790–91; television interview, "Between the Lines," Washington, Oct. 1957, IfZ, Krekeler Papers, ED 135/71.

30. Senator Lehman's radio statement on Germany, Apr. 24, 1950, Herbert H. Lehman Papers, Columbia University, New York, Speeches; Julius Edelstein to Seymour Rubinstein, Aug. 19, 1952, ibid.; Edelstein, political statements, C78–40 I (Mar. 1951–Jan. 1953); Lehman to Louis Elkan, May 17, 1954, ibid., Restitution of alien property (German), C78–39; Lehman to Dulles, Nov. 2, 1955, and Dec. 3, 1955, ibid., box 237. See also The Reminiscences of Herbert H. Lehman, Columbia University Oral History Collection, New York, 1961, p. 556.

31. On Albert Einstein's views, Sept. 13, 1952, *New York Telegram and Sun*. Although Einstein was a supporter of Israel, the Luxembourg agreement did not affect his attitude toward Germany. See also Ronald W. Clark, *Einstein: The Life and Times, An Illustrated*

Biography (New York, 1971), 329–31. Einstein rebuffed unequivocally advances by Riesser, Krekeler's deputy.

32. Riesser to Foreign Office, Bonn, May 20, 1951, PA/AA, III 210–07/80, vol. 3; Riesser, *Von Versailles zur Uno*, 254.

33. Krekeler recalled his admiration for Goldmann in an interview, Sept. 1, 1989, Bad Salzuflen. For AJ Congress–WJC differences of opinion see Maurice L. Perlzweig to Isaac Toubin, Mar. 1, 1957, AJA, WJCC, H142/58; Perlzweig to Prinz, June 30, 1959, and Alexander Easterman to Perlzweig, Nov. 10, 1959, CZA, WJC British Section Collection, C2 (before that at IJA, London); Grewe to Foreign Office, Bonn, Nov. 13, 1959, PA/AA, 305 81.12/1–91.36, vol. 118. Federer addressed the JWV in 1961, Federer to Foreign Office, Bonn, PA/AA, B32 305, II, A6, vol. 164.

34. Krekeler to Foreign Office, Bonn, Dec. 18, 1952, PA/AA, III 210–02/80, vol. 3; IfZ, Krekeler Papers, ED 135/173, pp. 137–38.

35. Krekeler to Foreign Office, Bonn, May 15, 1951, PA/AA, III 210–01/80, vol. 1; Nov. 27, 1952, PA/AA, III 212–06. On the AJC meeting with Heuss, see Simcha Pratt to Foreign Ministry, June 23, 1958, ISA, FM Records, 3100/16; on the meeting of Irving Engel and Zachariah Shuster with Adenauer, see Shuster to John Slawson, Oct. 17, 1959, YIVO, AJC Records, FAD-1, box 27.

36. Krekeler to Foreign Office, Bonn, Nov. 27, 1953, PA/AA, III 212–06, vol. 311; Hallstein to Henry E. Schultz (ADL), Feb. 17, 1954, ADL Archives, FC Germany, 1953–58, Exchange; Dulles to HICOG, Oct. 23, 1953, NA, RG59, 862A.411/10–1353; Edelsberg to Geoffrey Lewis, Mar. 8, 1954, ibid., 762.00/3–854; State Department to U.S. Information Agency, July 15, 1954, ibid., 762.00/7–1554.

37. Philip Klutznick responded to the author's questions in a written interview, June 15, 1988. See also Klutznick's conversation with Friedrich Middelhauve (a right-wing FDP politician, at that time deputy prime minister of North Rhine–Westphalia), May 13, 1955, IfZ, Krekeler Papers, ED 135/93; and his report to the Board of Governors, May 25, 1955, BBA; Klutznick to Adenauer, Mar. 21, 1955, PA/AA, Bureau of the State Secretary, 210–01/347. Cp. Philip M. Klutznick, with Sidney Hyman, *Angles of Vision: A Memoir of My Lives* (Chicago, 1991), 182–83.

38. Von Kessel (German embassy in Washington) to Foreign Office, Bonn, July 15, 1954, PA/AA, III 212–06, vol. 3; von Lilienfeld to Foreign Office, Bonn, Apr. 14, 1954, PA/AA, III 212–06, vol. 311. Klutznick to N. C. Belth, July 15, 1954, and Oscar Cohen to Belth, June 14, 1954, ADL Archives, ADL FC Germany, 1953–58, Exchange.

39. Summary added to report from Washington, Aug. 6, 1951, PA/AA, III 210–01/35, vol. 13; also IfZ, Krekeler Papers, ED 135/173, p. 79; Arthur Lourie to Foreign Ministry, Apr. 27, 1953, ISA, FM Records, 3028/8.

40. IfZ, Krekeler Papers, ED 135/173, p. 123; Y. Ilsar to E. Shinnar, Mar. 7, 1956, ISA, FM Records, 587/811; Continuation of Krekeler MS, IfZ, Krekeler Papers, ED 135/174, p. 251.

41. IfZ, Krekeler Papers, ED 135/174, p. 299; Yohanan Meroz, memo of conversation with Rolf F. Pauls, Nov. 30, 1956, and Feb. 25, 1957, ISA, FM Records, 3054/10. Pauls, a former assistant to Blankenhorn, had been introduced to Reuven Shiloah, the Israeli minister in Washington, by Nahum Goldmann. During Erich Ollenhauer's visit to Washington, Krekeler met John Foster Dulles who called upon

the German government to exert pressure on Israel. Krekeler told Dulles again that the Federal Republic would not suspend reparations. BA, Blankenhorn Papers, 351/74b. Adenauer himself recalled his deep concern with regard to the rift between the United States and its European allies during the Suez conflict in his reminiscences. Konrad Adenauer, *Erinnerungen*, vol. 3 (Stuttgart, 1967), 226–27. See also Adenauer, meeting with journalists, Nov. 5, 1956, *Adenauer: Teegespräche, 1955–1958*, edited by Hanns Jürgen Küsters (Berlin, 1986), 156–67, and Arnulf Baring, ed., *Sehr geehrter Herr Bundeskanzler!: Heinrich von Brentano im Briefwechsel mit Konrad Adenauer, 1949–1964* (Hamburg, 1974), 199–203.

42. In Krekeler's summary of his American experience, upon the conclusion of his tour of duty in the United States, he failed to mention the Jewish problem. Feb. 1958, IfZ, Krekeler Papers, ED 135/48.

43. Kessel to Foreign Office, Bonn, Oct. 4, 1957, PA/AA, III 305–81.34/91.36, vol. 3; Kempff, consul in San Francisco, to Foreign Office, Bonn, Jan. 14, 1958, PA/AA, III 82.04–92.19.

44. E.g., Fritz Schmidt, consul in Philadelphia, to Joachim Lipschitz, June 3, 1958, Landesarchiv Berlin, Rep. 4, Issues/2140/188.

45. Brentano to Grewe, Apr. 10, 1958, PA/AA, 305 82.01/91.36, vol. 125.

46. See Gerhard Falk, "The Reaction of the German-American Press to Nazi Persecutions, 1933–41," *Journal of Reform Judaism* 32 (Spring 1985): 12–23.

47. There is no better evidence for the attitude of those German American organizations than the correspondence of the German diplomats, e.g., Knappstein to Krekeler, Apr. 3 and 22, 1952, IfZ, Krekeler Papers, ED 135/57; also Krekeler to Hallstein, Nov. 23, 1951, PA/AA, III 210–02/80, vol. 1; Krekeler to Foreign Office, Bonn, May 27, 1952, PA/AA, III 210–01/80, vol. 3; Krekeler to Foreign Office, Bonn, Oct. 14, 1952, ibid.

48. Krekeler to Adenauer, Aug. 20, 1952, IfZ, Krekeler Papers, ED 135/39. In his report on Adenauer's visit to the United States in April 1953, the Israeli counselor Yaacov Shimoni mentioned that at one of his meetings with German Americans, Adenauer pointed to the example of American Jewish solidarity with Israel through the UJA and the Bonds Drive. Adenauer hoped to secure from them financial help for the integration of refugees from the lost territories in the East on the same basis. Shimoni to Foreign Ministry, May 5, 1953, ISA, FM Records, 357/21.

49. New York Consul General Reifferscheidt to Foreign Office, Bonn, Sept. 25, 1958, PA/AA, 305 81.16/91.36, vol. 226; Federer to Foreign Office, Bonn, Sept. 22, 1959, ibid., 305 81.16/91.36, vol. 1064.

50. See also chap. 16.

CHAPTER 11

1. For the most detailed analysis of John Foster Dulles's German policy in the context of its integration in the Western bloc, see Detlef Felken, *Dulles und Deutschland: Die amerikanische Deutschlandpolitik, 1953–1959* (Bonn and Berlin, 1993), 507–16. Despite his rollback and German reunification rhetoric, "a strong united European community, including Germany" was Dulles's preference. In the late 1950s, he also came to prefer a more flexible approach on the part of Adenauer with regard to West

Germany's policy. For Dulles's prewar sympathy for Germany see Townsend Hoopes, *The Devil and John Foster Dulles* (Boston, 1973), 46–48, and Michael A. Guhin, *John Foster Dulles: A Statesman and His Times* (New York, 1972), 45–47, also Grose, *Gentleman Spy*, 132–33.

2. For a rather balanced appraisal of the changes on the German scene see Clement Vollnhals, "Zwischen Verdrängung und Aufklärung: Die Auseinandersetzung mit dem Holocaust in der frühen Bundesrepublik," in Büttner, *Die Deutschen und die Judenverfolgung*, 357–91. Eleonore Sterling summarized and analyzed the reaction to the antisemitic manifestations in her report on West Germany, Jan. 1960, to Shuster, Jan. 26, 1960, YIVO, AJC Records, FAD-1, box 31. There were a few Jewish observers who called attention to the postwar changes in the younger German generation in the late 1950s, e.g., Leon Fram, "There Is a New Germany," *Congress Weekly*, Oct. 7, 1957, pp. 10–13, and Alfred Werner, "It Can't Happen There," *NJM* 79 (May 1958): 4–5, 26–27.

3. The establishment of the Central Office for Investigation of Nazi Crimes was at first broached by Stuttgart attorney general Erich Nellmann whose department had been in charge of the preparations of the Ulm trial. See Eleonore Sterling's detailed report to Shuster on the trial, Apr. 28–Aug. 29, 1958, YIVO, AJC Records, FAD-1, box 31.

4. Elisabeth Noelle-Neumann, *Jahrbuch der öffentlichen Meinung, 1958–1964* (Allensbach, 1965), 221. Idem, *Jahrbuch der öffentlichen Meinung, 1965–1967* (Allensbach, 1967), 165.

5. These data were quoted by Alfred Streim, head of the Ludwigsburg Central Office for Investigation of Nazi Crimes, in a *Spiegel* interview, Feb. 13, 1995, pp. 30–34. Writing in 1988, Tom Bower remained skeptical about the achievements of the Ludwigsburg Central Office, *Pledge Betrayed*, 361–68. Even a neoconservative defender of the West German dealing with the Nazi past in the 1950s such as Manfred Kittel noted the black record of many members of the police: *Die Legende von der "Zweiten Schuld": Vergangenheitsbewältigung in der Ära Adenauer* (Berlin, 1993), 175–76.

6. Jakob Diel, a former member of the Catholic Center Party, never joined the Nazis but conducted an anti-Jewish hate campaign, including his letters to Adenauer. See, for instance, Jakob Diel to Adenauer, Dec. 28, 1957, and Jan. 8, 1960, ACDP, Jakob Diel Papers, I-139.

7. "Germany—Is The Past Forgotten?" *Committee Reporter* 12 (Aug. 1959): 1–8, here p. 1; Marshall Sklare to Slawson (including the Allensbach statement "Anti-Jewish Attitudes in Germany on the Decline," June 29, 1959), Aug. 25, 1959, YIVO, AJC Records, FAD-1, box 38.

8. E.g., American consulate general, Hamburg, to State Department, Jan. 23, 1959, NA, RG59, 862A.411/1–2359; Jan. 28, 1959, ibid., 862A.412/1–2859; U.S. Embassy Bonn to State Department, Jan. 22, 1959, ibid., 862A.411/1–2259; U.S. Mission Berlin to State Department, June 4, 1959, ibid., 762A.00/6–459; AJC delegation at the State Department, June 4, 1959, ibid., 762A.00/6–459.

9. AJC, meeting with President Heuss, June 22, 1958, Waldorf Astoria, New York, June 25, 1958, and Oct. 1, 1958, YIVO, AJC Records, FAD-1, box 34; Consul General Simcha Pratt to Foreign Ministry, June 23, 1958, ISA, FM Records, 3100/16.

A separate meeting suggested by Goldmann did not take place because of Heuss's full schedule.

10. The German Educators Project continued throughout the 1960s. Summary in BGX 79, Germany/West, received Apr. 9, 1979, AJC Records, New York; Adenauer's letter to the AJC, Mar. 6, 1959, AJC news release, YIVO, AJC Records, FAD-1, box 34; Adenauer to Shuster for Engel, Oct. 28, 1959, ibid., box 34; Theodor Heuss, statement to the AJC annual meeting, news release, Apr. 16, 1959, ibid.; Shuster to Slawson, July 27, 1959, ibid., box 21.

11. Shuster to Slawson, report on the Godesberg Conference (Oct. 1–4), Oct. 17, 1959, ibid., box 27. Statement on Democratic Education in West Germany, AJC executive board meeting after the Godesberg Conference, Oct. 31, 1959, ibid., box 40.

12. See chap. 12.

13. Hevesi to Slawson, Oct. 6, 1959, YIVO, AJC Records, FAD-1, box 21.

14. Remark of a Western European division official on a dispatch from Simcha Pratt to Foreign Ministry, June 23, 1958, ISA, FM Records, 3100/16.

15. The pamphlet was prepared by the AJ Congress Commission on International Affairs and edited by Philip Baum and Herbert Poster. Joachim Prinz wrote the foreword.

16. H. G. van Dam, "Pawns in the Quest for Publicity," A World Jewish Affairs Feature, Nov. 5, 1959, YIVO, AJC Records, FAD-1, box 21; Timmermann, note about a conversation with van Dam, Feb. 25, 1960, PA/AA, 305 81.12/1–91.36, vol. 118.

17. "Missbrauch der Publizität," *Allgemeine Wochenzeitung der Juden in Deutschland*, Nov. 13, 1959; "German Jew Scares a U.S. Jewish Group," *NYT*, Nov. 11, 1959; Shuster to Hevesi, Nov. 17, 1959, YIVO, AJC Records, FAD-1, box 21; E. Sterling to Shuster, Nov. 22, 1959, ibid., box 30.

18. Press and Information Office, Bonn, Jan. 5, 1960, PA/AA, 305 81.12–91.36, vol. 61; Brentano to Adenauer, Jan. 8, 1960, BA, Heinrich von Brentano Papers, 239/158. Brentano preferred a statement by the chancellor to be subsequently endorsed by parliament.

19. Jan. 5, 1960, administrative committee minutes, AJC Archives, New York; Report from Shuster, Bonn, Jan. 10, 1960, YIVO, AJC Records, FAD-1, box 25.

20. E. Sterling to Shuster, Jan. 26, 1960, YIVO, AJC Records, FAD-1, box 31.

21. David Danzig to Slawson, Mar. 4, 1960, YIVO, AJC Records, FAD-1, box 25.

22. Horkheimer, Summary of Analysis of German Situation, Mar. 17, 1960, YIVO, AJC Records, FAD-1, box 27.

23. E. Sterling to Shuster, Apr. 11, 1960, YIVO, AJC Records, FAD-1, box 30.

24. AJC, 53rd Annual Meeting, Apr. 22–24, 1960, Statement on Recent Developments in Germany, ibid., box 37; Incidents in Germany, report by Shuster, Apr. 24, 1960, ibid., box 20.

25. Memo, Adenauer-Blaustein-Shuster conference in Bonn, June 29, 1960, YIVO, AJC Records, FAD-1, Series 1963–1970, box 24; also Shuster to Slawson, July 5, 1960, ibid., box 26; Grewe to Herbert B. Ehrman, June 28, 1960, ibid.

26. AJ Congress, round robin letter by Joachim Prinz, Jan. 7, 1960, AJHSA, AJ Congress Papers, I-77, box 52; AJ Congress executive committee, Jan. 14, 1960, ibid., box 7. Statement of seven national Jewish organizations released by NCRAC, Jan. 5,

1960, ibid., box 52. For a negative German response regarding an official invitation to Prinz, see Joseph Thomas, May 31, 1960, PA/AA, B32, 305 II A6, vol. 108.

27. JWV Headquarters Letter, vol. 2, no. 1, Jan. 1960, JWV Archives.

28. JLC, Silver Jubilee Convention, Mar. 25–27, 1960, Resolution on Germany and Resurgent Antisemitism, Mar. 27, 1960, Robert Wagner Labor Archives, New York University, JLC Collection.

29. German Consul General Georg Federer, Oct. 21, 1960, Report on visit of two members of the New York Board of Rabbis to Germany, PA/AA, B32, 305 II A6, vol. 107.

30. Benjamin R. Epstein, Report to B'nai B'rith International Council, Jan. 26, 1960, ADL Archives, ADL FC Germany; Letter to ADL Board Members, Feb. 8, 1960, ibid.; Philip M. Klutznick to Label Katz, Henry Schultz, Maurice Bisgyer, Ben Epstein, Saul Joftes, Feb. 12, 1960, BBA, Germany file.

31. Ben Epstein to Federer, May 26, 1960, ADL Archives, ADL FC Germany Exchange Program 1960–1961; ADL news release, June 6, 1960, ADL Archives, ADL FC Germany; Mission to Germany in summer 1960 by ten B'nai B'rith representatives, ibid., Exchange Program 1960–1961; also "Mission to Germany," *NJM* 75 (April 1961): 10, 30–31.

32. "The ADL Exchange: Exposure to American Democracy," *ADL Bulletin* 18 (Nov. 1961): 4, 5, 8; Mrs. Bernard Facher, Atlanta, to Benjamin Epstein, Oct. 24, 1961, ADL Archives, ADL FC Germany Exchange Program 1960–1961.

33. Bonn, Sept. 25, 1963, Statement of the ADL Study Group, ADL Archives, ADL FC Germany. Oscar Cohen, the ADL program officer who at first expressed doubts about the exchange project with Germany, met with German political leaders, educators, and scientists and was instrumental in formulating study programs at meetings in Frankfurt and Unesco conferences he attended. Sept. 6, 1963, ibid. See also Morton J. Sobel, "West German Schools: Is Democracy Taking Root?" *ADL Bulletin* 21 (Jan. 1964): 6–7.

34. ADL news release, Aug. 24, 1962, and Baker to Forster, Oct. 30, 1962, ADL Archives, ADL FC Germany; Jack Baker, "The German Army: How New? How Different?" *ADL Bulletin* 17 (Dec. 1960): 1–2, 8; Bachrach-Baker to Thomas, Jan. 21, 1959, and Schweinitz to Foreign Office, Bonn, Sept. 30, 1960, PA/AA, B32, 305 II A6, vol. 108.

35. Goldmann's first statement in Jerusalem, Jan. 3, 1960, as reported by the JTA Bulletin of Jan. 4, 1960, CZA, Goldmann Archive, Z6/1757; "Nahum Goldmann zur Hakenkreuzepidemie," Jan. 21, 1960, *Neue Zürcher Zeitung*, Jan. 23, 1960; Entry of Jan. 18, 1960, Blankenhorn, *Verständnis und Verständigung*, 357–58; "Adenauer und Goldmann gedenken der Opfer von Bergen-Belsen," Feb. 2, 1960, *FAZ*, Feb. 3, 1960, BA, Blankenhorn Papers, 351/99, pp. 104, 138.

36. Goldmann to Adenauer, Feb. 13, 1960, CZA, Goldmann Archive, Z6/2034. Joachim Fest to Goldmann, Jan. 16, 1960, ibid., Z6/1530.

37. Ulrich Brochhagen, *Nach Nürnberg: Vergangenheitsbewältigung und Westintegration in der Ära Adenauer* (Hamburg, 1994), 289–97.

38. Werner Bergmann, "Antisemitismus als politisches Ereignis. Die antisemitis-

che Welle im Winter 1959/1960," in *Antisemitismus in der politischen Kultur nach 1945*, edited by Werner Bergmann and Rainer Erb (Opladen, 1990), 253–75.

39. *Verhandlungen des Deutschen Bundestages*, 3. leg. period, 103. session, Feb. 18, 1960, pp. 5581–613.

40. On Ben Gurion and Germany in those years see Pearlman, *Ben Gurion Looks Back*, 162–70; his statement in Jan. 1960 in the Knesset, *Divrei Haknesset* (Protocols of the Knesset), 28, The Fourth Knesset, 23rd Session, Jan. 5, 1960, pp. 247–48. Ben Gurion was usually less troubled by antisemitic manifestations in Germany than the Jewish organizations in the Diaspora. E.g., in August 1959 he was told by Shinnar not to be concerned about antisemitism in Germany; moreover, the young generation there was free of antisemitism. BGA, BGD, Aug. 13, 1959.

41. Ben Gurion's first letter to Adenauer was dispatched on November 1, 1956. BGA, Correspondence. The next letter he dispatched on September 18, 1957 in connection with Israel's attempt to establish a framework of cooperation with NATO. Giora Josephthal came to discuss the matter with Adenauer a few months later. On Fischer's mission to Germany, BGA, BGD, June 17, 1958. For Ben Gurion German investments in Israel and scientific cooperation, including military equipment and particularly guided missiles, were more urgent than diplomatic relations. On Fischer's and Shinnar's talk with Adenauer, see BGA, BGD, July 19, 1958. Minutes of Adenauer–Ben Gurion meeting, Mar. 14, 1960, ISA, FM Records, 3294/4 in English. For the full text including military assistance, see "Document: David Ben-Gurion and Chancellor Adenauer at the Waldorf Astoria," March 14, 1960, introduced by Zaki Shalom, in *Israel Studies*, vol. 2 (Spring 1997), pp. 56–71. Cp. also Yeshayahu A. Jelinek and Rainer A. Blasius, "Ben Gurion und Adenauer im Waldorf Astoria. Gesprächsaufzeichnungen vom israelisch-deutschen Gipfeltreffen in New York am 14. März 1960," *Vierteljahrshefte für Zeitgeschichte* 45 (1997): 30–43. For the German view of the differences of opinion that popped up, see Blasius's introduction, 309–29. General Julius Klein, who met Adenauer on the eve of his meeting with Ben Gurion, reassured the Israelis of Adenauer's goodwill. Ya'acov Herzog to Chaim Yachil, Mar. 18, 1960, ibid. Cp. Konrad Adenauer, *Erinnerungen, 1959–1963*, vol. 4. Fragmente (Stuttgart, 1968), 32–39. Although the development of the Negev was not explicitly discussed at the Waldorf Astoria meeting between Ben Gurion and Adenauer, Ben Gurion stressed it in his correspondence with Adenauer after their encounter. E.g., Ben Gurion to Adenauer, Oct. 2, 1960, and Ben Gurion to Adenauer on the occasion of the chancellor's 85th birthday, Jan. 1, 1961, BGA, Correspondence.

42. Goldmann to Shinnar, Mar. 31, 1960, CZA, Goldmann Archive, Z6/2017.

43. Position Paper, Visit 14–17, 1960, Mar. 9, 1960, Eisenhower Library, Abilene, Kans., White House Central Files, Confidential File, 1953–1961, box 80, quoted in Brochhagen, *Nach Nürnberg*, 305–6, p. 436, note 33. The press summary of the German embassy in Washington emphasized the contribution of the Adenauer–Ben Gurion meeting to neutralizing hostile reactions caused by the antisemitic manifestations. Press survey for Mar. 1960, Apr. 12, 1960, PA/AA, 305 81.39–91.36/554, vol. 121.

44. Hans-Peter Schwarz, *Adenauer: Der Staatsmann, 1952–1967*, vol. 2 (Stuttgart, 1994), 541–45.

45. "Maker of Peace," *Congress Bi-Weekly*, Mar. 21, 1960, p. 3. *Congress Weekly* changed successively into *Congress Bi-Weekly* and into *Congress Monthly*.

46. "Watch on the Rhine," editorial broadcast over WMCA, New York, Apr. 1, 1960, YIVO, AJC Records, FAD-1, box 37.

47. David Rivlin to A. Yaffe, New York, Oct. 13, 1959, and Moshe Erel, Washington, D.C., to Pinchas Eliav, Jerusalem, Nov. 25, 1959, ISA, FM Records, 3099/24.

48. E.g., Morris U. Schappes, "The Month's Issues and Events," *Jewish Currents* 14 (Apr. 1960): 5–6, 38; see also an earlier editorial by Schappes in *Jewish Currents* 14 (Feb. 1960): 3–7, 40.

49. Report by Hasso von Etzdorf about the anti-Heusinger demonstration in New York, Feb. 3, 1961, PA/AA, 305 81.12/1–91.36/157/61, vol. 164. Such demonstrations also took place in Chicago and San Francisco. Charles R. Allen Jr. regarded Heusinger as responsible for executions during the war, "Heusinger and the Einsatzgruppen," *Jewish Currents* 15 (Oct. 1961): 7–11, 38.

50. AJ Congress executive committee, Mar. 16 and May 2, 1961, AJHSA, AJ Congress Papers, I-77, box 7; AJC governing council, Nov. 10–11, 1962, ibid., box 9.

CHAPTER 12

1. Israeli diplomats' involvement in effort to convince American as well as Jewish public opinion of the soundness of Eichmann's capture and his forthcoming trial in Israel is widely documented in the Israel Foreign Ministry Records, 3059/1–4, ISA, Jerusalem. See, for instance, Consul General Benjamin Eliav in New York to Ambassador A. Harman in Washington, D.C., June 13, 1960; Consul general in Los Angeles Yaacov Avnon to Michael Arnon, Washington, D.C., June 13, 1960; David Rivlin, consulate general New York, to Harman, June 22, 1960, all ISA, FM Records, 3059/1.

2. Jacob Robinson, "Eichmann and the Question of Jurisdiction," *Commentary* 30 (July 1960): 1–5.

3. Eliav to Harman, June 13, 1960, ISA, FM Records, 3059/1.

4. Goldmann at first expressed his reservations in the Tel Aviv daily *Haboker*, May 31, 1960. Ben Gurion to Goldmann, June 2, 1960, and Goldmann to Ben Gurion, June 2, 1960, BGA, Correspondence.

5. Joseph M. Proskauer to Ben Gurion, May 31, 1960, BGA, Correspondence.

6. Ben Gurion to Proskauer, July 7, 1960, ibid. The *Washington Post*'s critical editorial appeared on May 27, 1960. Later Telford Taylor, the former chief of counsel for war crimes, joined the opponents of the trial in Israel because Eichmann was not an Israeli citizen and Israel did not yet exist when he committed the crimes. *New York Times Magazine*, Jan. 22, 1961.

7. Oscar Handlin, "The Ethics of the Eichmann Case," reprinted from *Issues* 15 (Winter 1961): 1–8.

8. Marie Syrkin, "Eichmann and American Jewry" (A Reply to Oscar Handlin) *Jewish Frontier* 28 (May 1961): 7–12; Oscar Handlin to Arnold Forster, ADL, Mar. 20, 1961, and Forster to Handlin, Mar. 23, 1961, ISA, FM Records, 3059/4. Handlin argued that the publication of his article in *Issues* did not mean that he was endorsing the ACJ. New England Zionist Council to Aviad Yafeh, Israel Consulate General New

York, Feb. 13, 1961, ibid. Erich Fromm's letter to the *NYT* of June 17, 1960, quoted in Shlomo Katz, "Thoughts on the Eichmann Case," *Midstream* 6 (Summer 1960): 83–87.

9. ACJ, Leonard R. Sussman, memorandum, Dec. 12, 1960, AJA, American Council for Judaism Papers, Manuscript Collection 17, box 4/6; News from the ACJ, June 24, 1961, ISA, FM Records, 3295/9.

10. Hannah Arendt, *Eichmann in Jerusalem: A Report on the Banality of Evil* (New York, 1963).

11. Elisabeth Young-Bruehl, *Hannah Arendt: For Love of the World* (New Haven and London, 1982), 223–31.

12. Arendt, *Eichmann in Jerusalem*, esp. pp. 6–17, 104–11, 232–56; Young-Bruehl, *Hannah Arendt*, 332–47.

13. Raul Hilberg, *The Destruction of the European Jews* (Chicago, 1961), 662–69.

14. Young-Bruehl, *Hannah Arendt*, 347–60. Before the publication of Jacob Robinson's detailed response *And the Crooked Shall Be Made Straight: The Eichmann Trial, the Jewish Catastrophe, and Hannah Arendt's Narrative* (New York, 1965), his July 1963 Report on the Evil of Banality was used by a number of Arendt's critics. Gideon Hausner, the chief prosecutor, published his *Justice in Jerusalem* in 1966. On the Arendt controversy see also Sachar, *History of the Jews in America*, 839–41.

15. The *Hannah Arendt/Karl Jaspers Correspondence, 1926–1969* (New York, 1992) is an important testimony of German Jewish intellectual history, though some of the letters exceed in mutual flattery. The German original version edited by Lotte Köhler and Hans Sauer appeared in 1985 in Munich. Arendt's relationship with Martin Heidegger has recently been the subject of a rather superficial short monograph by Elzbieta Ettinger, *Hannah Arendt/Martin Heidegger* (New Haven, 1995). For the growing interest in Hannah Arendt in Israel, see *History and Memory* 8 (Fall-Winter 1996), Special Issue: Hannah Arendt and the Past.

16. Young-Bruehl, *Hannah Arendt*, 455–56.

17. For a mainly sympathetic view of Hannah Arendt's book on the Eichmann trial, see the introduction to a recent edition of *Eichmann in Jerusalem* (Munich, 1986) by Hans Mommsen, one of Germany's foremost historians of the Nazi period, "Hannah Arendt und der Prozess gegen Adolf Eichmann," i–xxxvii. See also Klaus Naumann, "Sympathy for the Devil?" *Mittelweg* 36, no. 3 (Feb.–Mar. 1994): 65–79, and Dan Diner, "Hannah Arendt Reconsidered: On the Banal and Evil in Her Holocaust Narrative," *New German Critique* 71 (Spring/Summer 1997): 177–90.

18. Paul Jacobs, "Eichmann and Jewish Identity," *Midstream* 7 (Summer 1961): 33–38.

19. George Salomon, "America's Response," *AJYB* 1962, vol. 63, pp. 85–103.

20. George Salomon, "The End of Eichmann: America's Response," *AJYB* 1963, vol. 64, pp. 247–59.

21. Myer Feldman, Oral History Interview, July 29, 1967, JFK Presidential Library, Boston, Mass.

22. Impact on American Public Opinion of the Eichmann Trial: Thelma Richards, The Jewish Response, NCRAC Plenary Session, June 22–25, 1961, Washington, D.C., AJA, NCRAC Nearprint, box Special Topics. Israeli diplomat Michael Arnon, too,

reported on Jewish concern, Arnon to Harman, Mar. 21, 1961, ISA, FM Records, 3059/4.

23. Impact on American Public Opinion of the Eichmann Trial, John Fenton, General Public Reaction, pp. 85–98.

24. George Salomon, "America's Response," *AJYB* 1962, vol. 63, pp. 85–103, here p. 102.

25. John Fenton, General Public Reaction, p. 98.

26. Federer, Feb. 3, 1961, PA/AA, VII 708.82/70–92.19, vol. 1037.

27. German consulate general, Apr. 13, 1961, PA/AA, 305 82–91.36, 510, v. 168; Arnon to Foreign Ministry, Feb. 10, 1961, ISA, FM Records, 3059/4.

28. Brochhagen, *Nach Nürnberg*, 336–41. Inge Deutschkron dealt with Eichmann and the repercussions of the affair in West Germany in her *Israel und die Deutschen* (Cologne, 1983), 119–41. On Globke and the Eichmann trial see also *Der deutsch-israelische Dialog. Dokumentation eines erregenden Kapitels deutscher Aussenpolitik*, edited by Rolf Vogel, Pt. 1, vol. 1 (Munich, 1987), 175–90. Ben Gurion recorded in his diary Shinnar's information that although Globke had written commentaries on the Nuremberg race laws, "he behaved well." BGA, BGD, Dec. 5, 1960. In contrast to criticism and accusations from different sides, see for a more sympathetic appraisal of Globke, Robert M. W. Kempner, "Begegnungen mit Hans Globke: Berlin-Nürnberg-Bonn," in *Der Staatssekretär Adenauers; Persönlichkeit und politisches Wirken Hans Globkes*, edited by Klaus Gotto (Stuttgart, 1980), 213–19. On Globke and the United States see Klaus Dohrn, "Globkes Verhältnis zu den Vereinigten Staaten," in *Der Staatssekretär Adenauers*, 172–83.

29. Max Horkheimer, Effects of Eichmann Trial on West German Public Opinion, Frankfurt Municipal and University Library, Horkheimer Papers, V, 13. Hevesi to Slawson, May 29, 1961, YIVO, AJC Records, FAD-1, box 25.

30. Frank A. Mayer, "Adenauer and Kennedy: An Era of Distrust in German-American Relations?" *German Studies Review* 17 (Feb. 1994): 83–104; Wolfram E. Hanrieder, *Germany, America, Europe: Forty Years of German Foreign Policy* (New Haven and London, 1989), 170–94; Manfred Görtemaker, "Adenauer und die amerikanische Deutschlandpolitik," in Schwabe, *Adenauer und die USA*, 75–101. See also Wilhelm Grewe's memoirs, *Rückblenden, 1976–1951: Aufzeichnungen eines Augenzeugen deutscher Aussenpolitik von Adenauer bis Schmidt* (Frankfurt, 1979), 502, 546–53. The latest monograph on this period is Frank A. Mayer's *Adenauer and Kennedy: A Study in German-American Relations* (New York, 1996). On Birrenbach's mission to Washington in October 1961, see Kurt Birrenbach, *Meine Sondermissionen. Rückblick auf zwei Jahrzehnte bundesdeutscher Aussenpolitik* (Düsseldorf, 1984), 16, 36, 63.

31. Federer to Foreign Office, Bonn, Jan. 19, 1962, PA/AA, B32 305 II A6, vol. 164. Klaus Mehnert, report on visit to the U.S., Mar. 18, 1961, PA/AA, M305, Mar. 1961, vol. 69; Rainer Brockmann, responding to Marguerite Higgins, *Die Welt*, Apr. 18, 1962. Her article "Die antideutsche Welle in Amerika" appeared in *Die Welt* of Apr. 6, 1962.

32. *Judgment at Nuremberg* had already met strong German objections when it was screened on TV in 1959. German embassy, Krapf, to Foreign Office, Bonn, Apr. 21, 1959, PA/AA 305 82.60/91.36, 384, vol. 86. By chance, the premiere in Berlin

coincided with the sentencing of Eichmann on Dec. 14, 1961. Judith E. Doneson, *The Holocaust in American Film* (Philadelphia, 1987), 104–5. For Emmet's remark, see his memorandum "A New Threat to Unity of Berlin," Jan. 1962, YIVO, AJC Records, FAD-1, 1963–1970, box 23.

33. German embassy to Foreign Office, Bonn, May 3, 1961, PA/AA 305 82.60/ 91.36, vol. 137.

34. New York consulate general, von Rhamm, Aug. 5, 1960, PA/AA 305 82.60/ 91.36, v. 137. Yachil to Harman, Feb. 8, 1962, ISA, FM Records, 3399/7, and to Consul General Shlomo Argov, Sept. 3, 1962, 6526/19.

35. Simon Segal to Slawson, Apr. 27, 1960; Engel to Emmet, Apr. 28, 1960; Emmet to Engel, Apr. 29, 1960, all YIVO, AJC Records, FAD-1, box 25; Memorandum on "The Vanishing Swastika," by Horkheimer, 1960, Horkheimer Papers, V 13; Epstein to Schultz, Mar. 8, 1960, and Emmet to Epstein, May 5, 1960, ADL Archives, ADL FC Germany.

36. AJC, Some observations on the statement of the American Council on Germany, Nov. 30, 1966, YIVO, AJC Records, FAD-1, 1963–1970, box 25.

37. American Council on Germany, The Meaning of the German Elections, Nov. 1966; Release Dec. 30, 1966, Experts on Germany Deny Neo-Nazi Revival, ibid.

38. Nehemiah Robinson, Documentation of persecution of war criminals, Mar. 1961, AJA, WJCC, C25/14; Memorandum by Oskar Karbach, Apr. 22, 1963, ibid., H145/95; Further memoranda by Karbach, Jan. 28, 1965, and Apr. 22, 1964, CZA, Goldmann Archive, Z6/1166; Report of the International Affairs Department, London, to the meeting of the WJC world executive, Jerusalem, July 1964, WJC Israel Executive Office, Jerusalem. After Karbach's death the West German government stopped its cooperation with the WJC on prosecution and trials of Nazi criminals. Walter Scheel to Goldmann, Feb. 4, 1974, CZA, Goldmann Archive, Z6/2466.

39. *Verhandlungen des Deutschen Bundestages*, 3. leg. period, 117. session, May 24, 1960, pp. 6679–95.

40. War Crimes and Nazi Crimes, *AJYB* 1965, vol. 66, pp. 409–12; Trials of Nazi Crimes, *AJYB* 1966, vol. 67, pp. 347–50. *Congress Bi-Weekly*, Jan. 13, 1964, p. 3, complained about the apathy of the American press at the start of the Auschwitz trial. For a recent roundup of the trial thirty years after its conclusion, see Peter Jochen Winters, "Das Unfassbare vor Gericht," *FAZ*, Aug. 19, 1995.

41. On the German public discussion regarding the treatment of Nazi crimes after 1945 see Peter Steinbach, *Nationalsozialistische Gewaltverbrechen: Die Diskussion der deutschen Öffentlichkeit nach 1945* (Berlin, 1981). Much more critical of Adenauer's conservative government's treatment of the issue as part and parcel of its anti-Communist policy is Gotthard Jasper, "Wiedergutmachung und Westintegration," in *Westdeutschland*, edited by Ludolf Herbst, 183–202. For a recent critique of American and West German handling of the Nazi criminals and former Nazi elites, see John Weiss, *Ideology of Death: Why the Holocaust Happened in Germany* (Chicago, 1996), 380–96.

42. Rainer A. Blasius, et al., eds., *AAPBD, 1963*, vol. 1 (Munich, 1994), May 28, 1963, Doc. 182, pp. 593–96. Blasius edited the first collections of the *Akten zur Auswärtigen Politik der Bundesrepublik Deutschland*, 3 vols. (1963); 2 vols. (1964); and 3 vols. (1965) (Munich 1994/1996).

43. Despite Eshkol's statement at his first press conference that he would continue Ben Gurion's German policy, he sounded much more critical in an interview for the West German television, particularly in regard to the German scientists in Egypt, an issue that contributed to Ben Gurion's resignation. Eshkol's statement in his press conference was brought to the attention of Foreign Minister Gerhard Schröder, July 29, 1963, PA/AA, I B4, vol. 42. Interview with Peter von Zahn, Aug. 16, 1963, *FAZ*, Aug. 17, 1963, quoted in *Von Adenauer zu Erhard: Studien zur auswärtigen Politik der Bundesrepublik Deutschland*, edited by Rainer A. Blasius (Munich, 1994), 182.

44. Presidents Conference to Schröder, Nov. 20, 1964, quoted in Maurice Bisgyer, *Challenge and Encounter: Behind the Scenes in the Struggle for Jewish Survival* (New York, 1967), 110–12; Conference of Presidents, release, Dec. 23, 1964, AJHSA, AJ Congress Papers, I-77, box 52 (Schröder had responded negatively to the Conference's first protest on Nov. 24, 1964).

45. NCRAC memo, Feb. 3, 1965, on the Presidents Conference meeting with Knappstein, Jan. 27, 1965, AJA, Lou H. Silberman Papers, Manuscript Collection 103, box 2/1.

46. Feb. 1, 1965, Release, Javits, Ribicoff Introduce Nazi War Crimes Resolution, Javits to Morris Abram, Feb. 4, 1965, YIVO, AJC Records, FAD-1, 1963–1970, box 27.

47. Jerry Goodman to area directors, Jan. 7, 1965, YIVO, AJC Records, FAD-1, 1963–1970, box 22; AJC release on Abram's meeting with Minister of Justice Ewald Bucher, Jan. 18, 1965, ibid., box 27. Levy Eshkol and Golda Meir thanked Abram for his efforts, ibid.

48. Blaustein to Goldmann, Jan. 22, 1965. He met with Knappstein on Jan. 8, 1965. YIVO, AJC Records, FAD-1, 1963–1970, box 24.

49. JWV, Morton Sobel to regional commanders, Jan. 6, 1965, JWV Archives, Germany file; Henry Siegman, NCRAC, Report of Jan. 14, 1965, Nationwide Protest, Jan. 26, 1965, Lewis H. Weinstein Papers, P-641, AJHSA, box 14.

50. NCRAC memo, Feb. 3, 1965, see note 57 above; Alexander Miller (ADL) to ADL regional offices, Feb. 17, 1965, ADL Archives, ADL FC Germany. See also statement by Richard Cardinal Cushing against the going into effect of the statute of limitations. Cardinal Cushing to Lewis H. Weinstein, Feb. 11, 1965, Lewis Weinstein Papers, P-641, AJHSA, box 14.

51. JWV, Statement of the National Policy Committee of the JWV, Feb. 13, 1965, published as a full-page advertisement, "A Message for the Conscience of the World from the Jewish War Veterans of the USA," in the *New York Times* and *Washington Post*, Feb. 18, 1965, quoted in Mosesson, *Jewish War Veterans Story*, 127. Ralph Plofsky, the JWV national commander, regarded the advertisement as one of the greatest achievements of the JWVs recent history. Report to the executive committee, Apr. 10, 1965, JWV Archives, Germany file. Klutznick protested against the advertisement's content to Monroe R. Steinberg, JWV national executive director, Feb. 22, 1965, ADL Archives, ADL FC Germany; also Julius Klein to Ralph Plofsky, Feb. 19, 1965, ibid.

52. Poll quoted in "Germany's Action on the Statute of Limitations," editorial in *Reconstructionist*, Apr. 16, 1965, pp. 4–5.

53. *Verhandlungen des Deutschen Bundestages*. 4. leg. period, 170. session, Mar. 10, 1965, pp. 8520–71. Eleonore Sterling reported on the debate, which made a great

impact on her. Sterling to Shuster, Mar. 1965, YIVO, AJC Records, FAD-1, 1963–1970, box 30.

54. *Verhandlungen des Deutschen Bundestages.* 4. leg. period, 175. session, Mar. 25, 1965, pp. 8761–89. For the preceding discussion in the SPD parliamentary group, see Heinrich Potthoff, ed., *Die SPD-Fraktion im Deutschen Bundestag, Sitzungsprotokolle 1961–1966* (Düsseldorf, 1993), 597–609. According to his biographer Rudolf Morsey, President Heinrich Lübke favored the extension of the statute of limitations from 20 to 30 years. *Heinrich Lübke. Eine politische Biographie* (Paderborn, 1996), 425.

Chapter 13

1. I have dealt with these ties in my contribution to a volume edited by Moshe Zimmermann and Oded Heilbronner, *"Normal" Relations: Israeli-German Relations,* in Hebrew (Jerusalem, 1993), 129–54. See also different articles in Otto R. Romberg and Georg Schwinghammer, eds., *Twenty Years of Diplomatic Relations between the Federal Republic of Germany and Israel* (Frankfurt, 1985), and Otto R. Romberg and Heiner Lichtenstein, eds., *Thirty Years of Diplomatic Relations between the Federal Republic of Germany and Israel* (Frankfurt, 1995).

2. Lily Gardner Feldman, *The Special Relationship between West Germany and Israel* (Boston, 1984), 122–38. See also Rolf Vogel's interviews with Franz Josef Strauss and Shimon Peres, *Deutschlands Weg nach Israel,* 137–44; Schwarz, *Adenauer: Der Staatsmann, 1952–1967,* 541–45; Franz Josef Strauss, *Erinnerungen* (Berlin, 1990), 341–51; Shimon Peres, *Kela David* (David's Sling), in Hebrew (Jerusalem, 1970), pp. 49–68.

3. For the best summary from the German viewpoint see Rainer A. Blasius, "Geschäftsfreundschaft statt diplomatischer Beziehungen," in his *Von Adenauer zu Erhard: Studien zur auswärtigen Politik der Bundesrepublik Deutschland 1963* (Munich, 1994), 154–210.

4. Interview with Asher Ben-Nathan, Tel Aviv, Dec. 8, 1994. Ben-Nathan also referred to the initial difficulties he encountered in Bonn in his reminiscences, which appeared in the publications mentioned in note 1 above.

5. The Franz Böhm Papers contain a number of letters and minutes documenting the differences of opinion in the CDU-CSU parliamentary group on establishing diplomatic relations with Israel. E.g., Böhm to Schröder, Mar. 21, 1963; Böhm to Gerstenmaier, Jan. 21, 1963; Böhm to Hallstein, Jan. 23, 1963; Gerstenmaier to Böhm, Jan. 24, 1963; Birrenbach to Böhm, Mar. 2, 1963; minutes of the working group for foreign policy, Dec. 10, 1963, all at the ACDP, St. Augustin, I-200–006. The two members dispatched by the Foreign Office on a goodwill mission to the Middle East were Ernst Majonica, the head of the working group for foreign policy, and Berthold Martin. Both opposed diplomatic relations with Israel.

6. Heuss to Adenauer, Sept. 28, 1963, and Adenauer to Heuss, Oct. 8, 1963, Theodor Heuss Papers, NL 221/63. In contrast to his achievements in relations with Europe and the United States, Adenauer did not mention his efforts in conciliating the Jewish people in his good-bye address to the Bundestag. *Verhandlungen des Deutschen Bundestages,* 4. leg. period, 86. session, Oct. 15, 1963, pp. 4165–69. Israel and the Jewish people were also not mentioned at the official funeral ceremonies in April 1967,

attended by Israel's foreign minister Abba Eban and former prime minister David Ben Gurion.

7. Conversation between Schröder and Dean Rusk, Paris, Apr. 10, 1963, *AAPBD*, 1965, vol. 1, no. 45, pp. 477–79; Conversation between Schröder and George Ball, Middlebury, Tex., Sept. 22, 1963, ibid., vol. 3, no. 358, pp. 1210–11. George Ball referred to the American position in his talk with Israeli ambassador Abraham Harman and Minister Mordecai Gazit on January 5, 1965. ISA, FM Records, 6541/30. See also Zeev Shek, FM West European Division, to Mordecai Gazit, Nov. 5 and 15, 1964, ISA, FM Records, 3528/28. For Shinnar's viewpoint, Shinnar to Yachil, Oct. 15, 1963, and Shinnar to Uri Lubrani, Prime Minister's office, Nov. 19, 1964, ibid. In March 1965 the rumors that the U.S. government did not support the establishment of diplomatic relations between West Germany and Israel caused much consternation among American Jewry. Consul General Katriel Katz to Shlomo Argov, Mar. 24, 1965, ISA, FM Records, 3534/5.

8. Schröder to Adenauer, Mar. 13, 1963, *AAPBD*, 1963, vol. 1, no. 121, pp. 404–5; Aug. 27, 1963, ibid., vol. 2, no. 318, pp. 1063–65. Schröder to Erhard, Nov. 9, 1964, *AAPBD*, 1964, vol. 2, no. 315, pp. 1244–48.

9. Jerry Goodman to Simon Segal, June 14, 1963, YIVO, AJC Records, FAD-1, 1963–1970, box 22. Maurice Bisgyer and Bernard Simon (B'nai B'rith), meeting with Ambassador Heinz Knappstein in March 1963, quoted in Bisgyer, *Challenge and Encounter*, 109–10; Epstein to Brentano, Mar. 27, 1963, and Brentano to Epstein, Apr. 26, 1963, ADL Archives, FC Germany; Yaacov Barmor, Consul General in Chicago, to Ambassador Harman and Foreign Ministry, Apr. 5, 1963, ISA, FM Records 6526/18.

10. Harriman to Senators Scott, Javits, Dott, Prouty, Keating, and Kuchel (who protested to President Kennedy on Apr. 5, 1963), Apr. 12, 1963, PA/AA, I B 4, vol. 18, transmitted to Bonn by Ambassador Knappstein, Apr. 18, 1963.

11. "Rabbis Picket, Then Meet with German Consul," *Chicago Sun Times*, July 2, 1964. For the Jewish written protests, e.g., German consulate general Chicago to Foreign Office, Bonn, June 24, 1964, PA/AA, II 6 84.03/91.36. "Operation Germany" in 1964–65 was mainly directed by Mordecai Gazit, the minister in Washington. E.g., memo of Zeev Sufot to Harman, Dec. 12, 1964, ISA, FM Records, 6541/29.

12. Zeev Shek to heads of diplomatic missions, Nov. 1, 1964, ISA, FM Records, 3533/1. Later Ambassador Knappstein stated that the U.S. administration may have leaked the German-Israeli arms deal in order to improve Germany's image in American public opinion. Barmor to Gazit, Jan. 26, 1965, ISA, FM Records, 6541/34. However, when asked by Dean Rusk who leaked the arms deal, Knappstein pointed to the Egyptians because they wanted to justify the invitation to Ulbricht. Knappstein to Foreign Office, Feb. 18, 1965, *AAPBD*, 1965, vol. 1, no. 85, pp. 351–55.

13. The West German government announced its decision to cancel arms shipments to Israel on Feb. 12, 1965. For Jewish reactions see NCRAC, Siegman to member agency executives and committees on community relations, Feb. 19, 1965, AJA, Lou H. Silberman Papers, box 2/1; Statement by Prinz in the name of the Presidents Conference, Feb. 1965, no exact date, AJHSA, AJ Congress Papers, I-77, box 52, Germany; Isaiah Terman to area directors and executive assistants, Mar. 4, 1965, YIVO, AJC Records, FAD-1, 1963–1970, box 23.

14. Morris B. Abram to Carstens, Feb. 19, 1965, ibid. Quite understandably, Nahum Goldmann, too, advised against boycotts. Goldmann to Eshkol, Feb. 12, 1965, CZA, Goldmann Archive, Z6/1141. Carstens's critical attitude toward Israel is well documented in German diplomatic papers. E.g., his circular letter to German diplomatic missions of Nov. 3, 1964, *AAPBD*, 1964, vol. 2, no. 308, pp. 1227–29; Carstens to Birrenbach, Apr. 8, 1965, *AAPBD*, 1965, vol. 2, no. 173, p. 689. Carstens's views of Israel mellowed during his later capacity as president of the Bundestag. See, e.g., his chapter on his visit to Israel in May 1478. Karl Carstens, *Erinnerungen und Erfahrungen* (Boppard, 1993).

15. Knappstein to Foreign Office, Feb. 18, 1965, *AAPBD*, 1965, vol. 1, no. 85, pp. 351–55; Harman to Foreign Ministry, Feb. 22, 1965, ISA, FM Records, 3533/4.

16. Rainer Barzel recalled his role at a symposium on German-Israeli relations at Hebrew University, Jerusalem, Nov. 8–9, 1990. See his essay "The Road to Diplomatic Relations" in Zimmermann and Heilbronner, *"Normal" Relations*, 12–23. See also Julius Klein's memorandum of Mar. 3, 1965, transcribed Oct. 25, 1965, BBA, Germany file, and Israel's New York consulate general to Foreign Ministry, Mar. 5, 1965, ISA, FM Records, 3532/9.

17. For a detailed description of the crisis leading to Erhard's decision, see the reminiscences of Horst Osterheld, *Aussenpolitik unter Bundeskanzler Ludwig Erhard, 1963–1966: Ein dokumentarischer Bericht aus dem Kanzleramt* (Düsseldorf, 1993), 149–73. Osterheld was a high official in the chancellor's office under both Adenauer and Erhard. See also Ludwig Hentschel's biography, *Ludwig Erhard: Ein Politikerleben* (Munich and Landsberg), 550–58. Cp. Erich Mende, *Von Wende zu Wende, 1962–1982* (Munich and Berlin, 1986), 173–75.

18. Minutes of the SPD parliamentary group, Feb. 16, 1965, and of the party council, Mar. 13, 1965, AdsD/Bonn, Protocols of the SPD parliamentary group/protocols of the party leadership, ibid., vol. 22. The Knesset expressed its willingness to establish diplomatic relations with Germany on March 16, 1965, by a majority of 66 against 29 and 10 abstaining. The left-wing Socialist Mapam, the Communists, and Menachem Begin's Cherut voted against.

19. Birrenbach, *Meine Sondermissionen*, 83–117. An earlier report on his mission to Israel is included in *Ludwig Erhard: Beiträge zu seiner politischen Biographie. Festschrift zum fünfundsiebzigsten Geburtstag*. Edited by Gerhard Schröder a.o. (Frankfurt, 1972), 363–82.

20. Osterheld to Erhard, Mar. 5, 1965, regarding U.S. ambassador George McGhee's recommendation not to break off diplomatic relations with Egypt. Ludwig Erhard Archives, Bonn, NE 285. On the United States becoming a major arms supplier to Israel see Steven L. Spiegel, *The Other Arab-Israeli Conflict: Making America's Middle East Policy from Truman to Reagan* (Chicago and London, 1985), pp. 130–35.

21. Infas poll of May 1965, quoted in Deutschkron, *Israel und die Deutschen*, 311.

22. Ch. Zohar, New York consulate general to Foreign Ministry, Mar. 30, 1965, ISA, FM Records, 3532/9; Yaakov Jacobs, "The Heart and the Mind," *Jewish Observer* 2 (Mar. 1965): 4–6.

23. NCRAC executive committee, minutes, May 2, 1965, AJA, Lou H. Silberman Papers, box 2/1. In accordance with the Jewish organizations, most of the national

Jewish publications welcomed the breakthrough in German-Israeli relations. E.g., "Toward Reconciliation," *Congress Bi-Weekly*, Mar. 29, 1965, pp. 3–4; "Germany Takes Step Towards Its Rehabilitation," *NJM* 79 (Mar. 1965): 11; "Reasons to Hope for a Better Future," *Reconstructionist*, Apr. 2, 1965, pp. 3–4; "Bonn and Jerusalem: Mutual Recognition," *Reconstructionist*, May 28, 1965, pp. 3–4.

24. AJC, meeting of a delegation headed by Morris Abram and Chancellor Erhard, June 2, 1965, New York, and memorandum for Erhard, June 2, 1965, YIVO, AJC Records, FAD-1, 1963–1970, box 24; Joachim Prinz, chairman of the Presidents Conference, met Erhard in Düsseldorf late in Mar. 1965, News AJ Congress, Apr. 2, 1965, AJHSA, AJ Congress Papers, I-77, box 52; B'nai B'rith, Office of the President, Dec. 30, 1965 on meeting with Erhard, Dec. 20, 1965, in Washington, D.C. BBA, Germany file.

25. Ibid.; also meeting between AJC leadership and Knappstein, Nov. 30, 1965, YIVO, AJC Records, FAD-1, 1963–1970, box 24.

26. AJC, meeting with Erhard, June 2, 1965, ibid.

27. Joachim Prinz, "The Germans and the Jews: The Truths That Must be Faced," and Heinrich Knappstein, "Our Steps Toward Reconciliation," *Congress Bi-Weekly*, Mar. 7, 1966, pp. 6–10.

28. AJ Congress, minutes of the executive committee, June 13, 1963, AJHSA, AJ Congress Papers, I-77, box 7.

29. Marvin Bernstein, Brandeis University president, in *Sh'ma*, Dec. 14, 1973, p. 16.

30. Joachim Prinz, "Germans and Jews," based on an address to the WJC executive meeting in Strassbourg, July 11, 1965, *Congress Bi-Weekly*, Sept. 20, 1965, pp. 5–6.

31. WJC, Fifth Plenary Assembly, Brussels, Session on Germans and Jews, Aug. 4, 1966. For a detailed report of their deliberations see Vogel, *Deutschlands Weg nach Israel*, 212–75. "Jews and Germans," an essay by Gershom Scholem, adapted from his address, was published in *Commentary* 42 (Nov. 1966): 31–38.

32. Minutes of the American Section of the WJC, Sept. 16, 1965, AJA, WJCC, A85/109; Zohar to Foreign Ministry, Apr. 27, 1965, ISA, FM Records, 3534/6.

33. Jacob Neusner and Richard L. Rubenstein, "Germany and the Jews: Two Views," *Conservative Judaism* 17 (Fall–Winter 1962–63): 31–47. Rubenstein dealt with Germany and the Jews also in articles in other publications. E.g., "The Nazi Revival and the West," *Jewish Frontier* 27 (Mar. 1960): 7–13, and "A Rabbi Visits Germany," *Reconstructionist*, Feb. 24, 1961, pp. 6–13.

34. Maurice Eisendrath, *Can Faith Survive? The Thought and Afterthoughts of an American Rabbi* (New York, 1964), 81–83.

35. Jerry Goodman to Simon Segal, Aug. 31, 1965, Frankfurt Municipal and University Library, Horkheimer Papers, V, 8. See also Joseph Asher, "Our Attitude to the Germans—A Time for Reappraisal?" *Pointer* (Summer 1966), AJC, Blaustein Library, New York, and Moses Rischin's introduction "The German Imperative and the Jewish Response," in *The Jewish Legacy and the German Conscience*, edited by Moses Rischin and Raphael Asher (Berkeley, Calif., 1991).

36. See chap. 8.

37. Norman Podhoretz, Impressions on recent visit to Germany, AJC, staff advi-

sory committee minutes, Feb. 15, 1967, YIVO, AJC Records, FAD-1, 1963–1970, box 21.

38. "Germany 1967" ("American writers and editors, back from a visit to Berlin and major West German cities, give their personal impressions of Germans today"), *Atlantic Monthly*, May 1967, pp. 43–56.

39. Ibid., 51.

40. Alexander Mitscherlich and Margarethe Mitscherlich, *Die Unfähigkeit zu Trauern* (Munich, 1967); the English translation appeared eight years later: *The Inability to Mourn: Principles of Collective Behavior* (New York, 1975). For the Frankfurt School's Critical Theory and the events of 1967–68, see Wiggershaus, *The Frankfurt School*, 609–36. Theodor Adorno published his essay "What Does Coming to Terms with the Past Mean," first delivered as a lecture to the Frankfurt Society for Christian-Jewish Cooperation, already in 1959.

41. Norman Birnbaum, "Stirrings in West Germany," *Commentary* 37 (Apr. 1964): 53–58.

42. AJC Sixty-first Annual Meeting, May 18–21, 1967, New York, transcript, Blaustein Library, New York.

43. NCRAC, Julian Freeman to membership, Dec. 8, 1966, YIVO, AJC Records, FAD-1, 1963–1970, box 25; Letter by Aaron Goldman, NCRAC to Dean Rusk, Dec. 8, 1966, ADL Archives, ADL FC Germany; ADL national director Benjamin Epstein had protested Kiesinger's appointment as leader of the CDU even before he became prime minister, Nov. 11, 1966, ibid.

44. Horkheimer to Slawson, Dec. 31, 1966, YIVO, AJC Records, FAD-1, 1963–1970, box 25.

45. Sandy Bolz to Slawson, Mar. 29, 1967, notes on meetings with Undersecretary of State Eugene Rostow and Deputy Undersecretary Fay D. Kohler, Mar. 10, 1967. The AJC delegation was led by Irving Engel. YIVO, AJC Records, FAD-1, 1963–1970, box 26.

46. Caspar Schrenck-Notzing, *Charakterwäsche: Die amerikanische Besatzung in Deutschland und ihre Folgen* (Stuttgart, 1965). Schrenck-Notzing, the editor of *Criticon*, continues to play a prominent role in the post-unification right-wing German intellectual scene.

47. Ambassador G. Avner, Ottawa, to Foreign Ministry, Sept. 7, 1965, ISA, FM Records, 3528/28.

48. Even before Pauls's controversial address in May 1966 regarding the Polish border, he was critical of Prime Minister Levi Eshkol's lenient attitude toward the Soviet Union. Pauls to Foreign Office, Jan. 18, 1966, copy in SPD, PV Akten 4328, AdsD. The Social Democratic *Vorwärts*, May 18, 1966, showed more understanding of Israel's position.

49. On Adenauer's visit to Israel in May 1966, see Goldmann, *Mein Leben*, 420–21; Schwarz, *Adenauer: Der Staatsmann, 1952–1967*, 965–70. According to Schwarz, Adenauer was not optimistic about Israel's future but thought that the West must continue to help it.

50. Deutschkron, *Israel und die Deutschen*, 324–35.

51. Asher Ben-Nathan, "The Road to Establishing Relations— The Israeli View,"

in Zimmermann and Heilbronner, *"Normal" Relations*, 24–31. See also his article "Brücken über viele Kluften: 30 Jahre des Gebens und Nehmens," *Tribüne* 34 (Mar. 1995), 79–103. Inge Deutschkron's report on Lübke's criticism of Israel in a talk with Ben-Nathan was denied by the German government's spokesman. Morsey, *Heinrich Lübke*, p. 424.

52. I have discussed several aspects of the growing informal German-Israeli relationship in my monograph *Yad Mushetet, Hasocial demokratim hagermanim veyachasam liyehudim uleIsrael bashanim 1945–1967* (An Outstretched Hand: German Social Democrats, Jews and Israel, 1945–1967), in Hebrew (Tel Aviv, 1986), 128–41, 142–55. See also Deutschkron, *Israel und die Deutschen*, 142–57. Two pioneering memoranda dealt with the political tourism of young Germans to Israel: Heinz Westphal, Mar. 28, 1961 (in my possession) and Jürgen Weichert, Mar. 25, 1963, AdsD, Carlo Schmid Papers, 42 (general correspondence). The development of these relations is well documented in the relevant files of the Israel Labor Party Archives in Beit Berl and the Labor Archives-Lavon Institute, Tel Aviv.

Chapter 14

1. Benjamin Epstein, Nov. 11, 1966, ADL Archives, ADL FC Germany; Philip Baum, round robin letter, Jan. 11, 1967, including report by Joachim Prinz and his questioning the German ambassador as to why Kiesinger was chosen. AJHSA, AJ Congress Papers, I-77, box 52.

2. The speech is reprinted in Willy Brandt, *Deutschland, Israel, und die Juden* (Berlin, 1961). Meeting between Brandt, Label Katz, and Maurice Bisgyer, New York, Mar. 19, 1961, BBA, Germany file.

3. Willy Brandt, *In Exile: Essays, Reflections, and Letters* (London, 1971), 219–20.

4. I have dealt with Israel's suspicions of Brandt's sympathies for the Arab national liberation movement in *Yad Mushetet*, 184–85. See also AdsD, Brandt-Depositum, Publications, Nov. 1963, vol. 167, Press Clippings, Cairo, Nov. 8, 1963; SPD, PV, Bureau of the president, file 3. Reuven Barkatt, at that time secretary general of Mapai, raised questions about Brandt's statements concerning German weapon exports and Arab refugees, at a meeting with Herbert Wehner and Hans-Eberhard Dingels in London, Nov. 22, 1963.

5. AJC, Morris Abram, et al., Meeting with Brandt, Apr. 19, 1965, New York, YIVO, AJC Records, FAD-1, 1963–1970, box 25.

6. Report on meeting with Brandt, Feb. 9, 1967, New York, YIVO, AJC records, FAD-1, 1963–1970, box 25; Forster to Epstein, Feb. 10, 1967, ADL Archives, ADL FC Germany.

7. E.g., Shuster to Goodman, June 12, 1969, AJC Archives, BGX 69–71, Germany/West; at a later date David Geller to Bernard Resnikoff, Oct. 1, 1975, BGX 75.

8. E. Sterling, reports to Shuster, July 17, 1967, and Oct. 13, 1967, YIVO, AJC Records, FAD-1, 1963–1970. The author saw these two reports in 1982 before they were transferred to YIVO.

9. *Verhandlungen des Deutschen Bundestages*, 5. leg. period, 111. session, June 7, 1967, pp. 5267–88, 5303.

10. Ibid. See also Rolf Vogel, *Der deutsch-israelische Dialog*, vol. 1, pt. 1, pp.349–56, and for German public support, 360–73.

11. Minutes of the SPD central committee and the party council, June 9 and July 1, 1967, respectively, AdsD, Bonn, Minutes of the SPD central committee, 1967.

12. Blaustein to Goldmann, Aug. 29, 1967, and Blaustein to Kiesinger, Aug. 31, 1967, AJC Archives, BGX 67–68, Germany/West. Goldmann met Kiesinger on Dec. 17, 1966, AJA, WJCC, I 8/2.

13. Philip M. Klutznick, "West Germany Revisited," *NJM* 83 (Sept. 1969): 18–19.

14. Rabbi Israel Miller and Morris Abram met Kiesinger, Aug. 17, 1967, AJA, WJCC, A45/3 17 (144).

15. Cp. Deutschkron, *Israel und die Deutschen*, 244–47.

16. News from the Committee, Aug. 8, 1969, and Goodman to Shuster, Aug. 21, 1969, AJC Archives, BGX 69–71, Germany/West.

17. B'nai B'rith, Office of the President (William Wexler), A Visit to Germany, Mar. 1968. BBA, Germany file.

18. News from the Committee, Sept. 6, 1968, AJC Archives, BGX 67–68, Germany/West.

19. Some observations by Philip M. Klutznick based on visit to the Federal Republic of Germany and Berlin, June 30 to July 5, 1969, ADL Archives, ADL FC Germany.

20. Shlomo Shafir, "The Attitude of the German Social Democratic Party towards Israel," in Zimmermann and Heilbronner, *"Normal" Relations*, 129–54.

21. Amnon Neustadt, *Die deutsch-israelischen Beziehungen im Schatten der EG-Nahostpolitik* (Frankfurt, 1983), 154–75, 216–39, 276–87.

22. Martin Kloke, *Israel und die deutsche Linke: Zur Geschichte eines schwierigen Verhältnisses* (Frankfurt, 1990), 65–111; Anson Rabinbach, "The Jewish Question in the German Question," *New German Critique* 44 (Spring–Summer 1988): 159–92, esp. 175–78.

23. Ibid.; also Jack Zipes, "The Vicissitudes of Being Jewish in West Germany," in *Germans and Jews since the Holocaust: The Changing Situation in West Germany*, edited by Anson Rabinbach and Jack Zipes (New York, 1986), 27–49.

24. Brandt's statements before and after his visit to Israel, *Bulletin des Presse-und Informationsamtes der Bundesregierung*, June 5, 6, and 13, 1973. See also Rolf Vogel, *Der deutsch-israelische Dialog*, vol. 1, pt. 1, pp. 453–57; Willy Brandt, *Erinnerungen* (Frankfurt, 1989), 446–47.

25. *Verhandlungen des Deutschen Bundestages*, 7. leg. period, 62. session, Oct. 26, 1963, p. 3630; *Bulletin des Presse-und Informationsamtes der Bundesregierung*, Oct. 30, 1973, p. 1389ff.

26. United Nations General Assembly Official Records, A/Pv2291, quoted in Neustadt, *Die deutsch-israelischen Beziehungen im Schatten der EG-Nahostpolitik*, 276–87.

27. ADL, Owen S. Rachleff and Arnold Foster, to regional offices, Oct. 3, 1969, ADL Archives, ADL FC Germany; Jack Baker and Owen S. Rachleff, Nov. 20, 1969, ibid.; News from the Committee, Sept. 30, 1969, YIVO, AJC Records, FAD-1, 1963–1970, box 20.

28. For Hans-Jürgen Wischnewski's sympathy for the Arab nations and their na-

tional liberation movements, see his political memoirs: *Mit Leidenschaft und Augenmass: In Mogadishu und anderswo* (Munich, 1989), 105–74.

29. Goodman to Gold, Sept. 28, 1970, YIVO, AJC Records, FAD-1, 1963–1970, box 25; A. S. Karlikow to Goodman, Nov. 10, 1970, AJ Archives, BGX (69–71) Germany/West.

30. Philip Klutznick was asked to chair a luncheon meeting with Hesselbach, Nov. 23, 1970, Klutznick to Gold, Nov. 6, 1970, AJC Archives, BGX 69–71, Germany/West; Epstein to Wexler, Nov. 25, 1970, ADL Archives, ADL FC Germany. Klaus Harpprecht, a renowned journalist and one of Brandt's close advisers, had suggested before Brandt's visit to Poland that he make a public gesture to balance Jewish complaints about Ben Wisch's (Hans-Jürgen Wischnewski's) advances toward the Arab world. Harpprecht, who was married to a Jewish survivor of the Holocaust and had a good knowledge of the American scene, proposed that the chancellor address a Jewish gathering or dispatch an emissary to assuage Jewish fears and also amend the term "normalization." Brandt responded that Ehmke tried during his visit to the United States to right the misconception and that there were no acute problems with Israel. Harpprecht to Brandt, Oct. 2, 1970, and Brandt to Harpprecht, Nov. 3, 1970, Brandt-Depositum, Brandt's correspondence as chancellor, BK, 8.

31. B'nai B'rith delegation, led by President David M. Blumberg, met Brandt early in 1972, BBA, BBIC Briefs, Mar. 20, 1972.

32. Owen S. Rachleff to Epstein, May 26, 1971, leadership meeting with West German Ambassador Rolf Pauls, ADL Archives, AdL FC Germany; meeting with his successor, Ambassador Berndt von Staden, Sept. 11, 1973, ibid.

33. Goodman to Gold, Jan. 9, 1974, AJC Archives, BGX 74, Germany/West.

34. Walter Isaacson, *Kissinger: A Biography* (New York, 1992), 53–55.

35. On Kissinger and Brandt, see Henry Kissinger, *The White House Years* (Boston, 1979), 405–12, 529–34; idem, *Years of Upheaval* (Boston, 1982), 143–46, quote p. 145; Brandt, *Erinnerungen*, 185–95.

36. Kissinger, *Years of Upheaval*, 711–17.

37. Ibid., 908–9, 1194–96.

38. SPD conference on foreign affairs, Jan. 17–19, 1975, AdsD, Bonn.

39. *Bulletin des Presse-und Informationsamtes der Bundesregierung*, July 15, 1975, p. 863.

40. Yohanan Meroz, *In schwieriger Mission: Als Botschafter Israels in Bonn* (Frankfurt, 1986), 61–68. Despite Schmidt's critical attitude, Meroz preferred him to Willy Brandt.

41. Suzan Hattis Rolef, *The Middle East Policy of the Federal Republic of Germany* (Jerusalem, 1985), 20, 38.

42. *Bulletin des Presse-und Informationsamtes der Bundesregierung*, May 6, 1981, pp. 341–47. At an election speech one year earlier Schmidt had linked his support for Palestinian self-determination with the insistence on self-determination of the German people. SPD Service Funk, TV, Apr. 15, 1980, 228/80, AdsD. For the debate in Israel, see Nachum Orland, *Das Deutschlandbild der israelischen Presse* (Frankfurt, 1984), 43–60.

43. Lawrence S. Leshnik to A. Forster, July 19, 1976, meeting of ADL delegation with Maria Schlei, July 15, 1976, New York, ADL Archives, ADL FC Germany. See also note of June 11, 1976, AdsD, Bonn, Helmut Schmidt Depositum, 6680.

44. Burton Joseph, ADL past national chairman to Ambassador von Staden, Oct. 19, 1977; Maxwell Greenberg, ADL national chairman, to Brandt, July 9, 1977, ADL Archives, ADL FC Germany. JLC president Jacob Sheinkman protested against the Vienna meeting, JLC News, July 16, 1979 (copy of the release received from the JLC). On the meeting with Wischnewski, Nathan Perlmutter, May 14, 1982, ADL Archives, ADL FC Germany.

45. Eli Eyal, WZO to Brandt, Sept. 5, 1980, and Brandt to Eyal, Sept. 18, 1980, AdsD, Brandt-Depositum, P.V., P.K., vol. 111. For Brandt's attitude toward Israel, see also my interview with him, Nov. 15, 1982, Bonn. The major part was published in *Davar*, Nov. 26, 1982. The tape is deposited at the Israel Labor Party Archive in Beit Berl.

46. NJCRAC (the adjusted acronym of the National Jewish Community Relations Advisory Council instead of NCRAC), Jacqueline K. Levine to NJCRAC and Council of Jewish Federations member agencies, report on meetings with West German ambassador and government officials re: Unprosecuted Nazis in the USA, Feb. 9, 1979; also Geller to Karlikow, Feb. 8, 1979, AJC Archives, BGX 79, Germany/West.

47. AJC delegation led by Richard Maass, meeting with Helmut Schmidt in New York, June 8, 1979, AJC Archives, BGX 79, Germany/West. An AJC leadership group met with Schmidt in Germany in March; William Trosten was instrumental in arranging an appointment with the chancellor despite a very unpleasant confrontation between him and a delegation of the Simon Wiesenthal Center earlier the same week. Statement presented by Maass to Schmidt, Mar. 29, 1979, AJC Archives, BGX 79, Germany/West. The AJC leadership group visiting Germany in the spring of 1979 also took up the issue of the Oberammergau passion play because of the townspeople's opposition to change its traditional antisemitic performance to conform with the teachings of the Second Vatican Council. Joseph Cardinal Ratzinger, the head of the Bavarian church, did not agree that the play was a litmus test regarding antisemitism. He distinguished between Hitler's genocidal antisemitism and the folk culture expressions of antisemitism which were grounded on an old tradition of worship. Bert Gold, account of the trip to Germany in Mar. 1979, Apr. 17, 1979, AJC Archives, BGX 79, Germany/West.

48. Robert Goldmann to Richard Maass, June 15, 1979, and Maass to Goldmann, June 30, 1979, AJC Archives, BGX 79, Germany/West; Maass to Gerald S. Jeremias, Oct. 15, 1980, AJC Archives, BGX 80, Germany/West.

49. Report on the meeting between Schmidt and nine representatives of the Presidents Conference, May 21, 1981, AdsD, Schmidt Depositum, 6770.

50. ADL, Forster memorandum to regional offices, May 18, 1981, ADL Archives, ADL FC Germany. For Edgar Bronfman's attitude toward Germany see his *The Making of a Jew* (New York, 1996), 97–106, here pp. 99–101. For the German reaction cp. Rolf Vogel, *Der deutsch-israelische Dialog*, vol. 1, pt. 2, pp. 797–805.

51. The statute of limitations for all cases of murder was abolished in the Bundestag on July 3, 1979, by a small majority of 253 against 228.

52. Goldmann, *Mein Leben als deutscher Jude*, 426–48. Goldmann suggested to Brandt a meeting of Jewish, Israeli, and Palestinian intellectuals in Vienna in January 1978, but it was postponed because of Sadat's visit to Jerusalem. CZA, Goldmann

Archive, Z6/2740. At a meeting of the WJC governing board in 1980 in Amsterdam, the Nahum Goldmann Medal was conferred upon Helmut Schmidt, and Bronfman made the presentation. Bronfman, *Making of a Jew*, 46–47. In 1980 the CDU agreed to support the "last payment" of an additional DM 440 million for indemnification of hardship cases only on the condition that pension rights were restored to Hitler era civil servants who had never been cleared by the denazification courts. *JTA Daily News Bulletin*, Jan. 3, 1980, AJC Records, FAD, Germany/West, 1980.

53. Exchange Program for Future Leaders in the Federal Republic of Germany and of the American Jewish Community, AJC, German Jewish Relations File, Blaustein Library, New York.

54. See chap. 15.

CHAPTER 15

1. Nathan Glazer, *American Judaism* (Chicago, 1957), introduction, quoted by Judith Miller, *One, by One, by One: Facing the Holocaust* (New York, 1990), 221.

2. Irving Greenberg, "The Interaction of Israel and the Diaspora after the Holocaust," in *World Jewry and the State of Israel*, edited by Moshe Davis (New York, 1977), 259–82; also his letter to the editor, *Commentary* 76 (June 1981): 405.

3. For the bibliographical data of the books by Arthur D. Morse, Henry L. Feingold, David S. Wyman, and others see chap. 1, notes 3, 5, 6, and 13, above. In the early 1980s, Arthur Goldberg, following a suggestion of Holocaust survivor Jack Eisner, contacted historians and community leaders to deal with the role of the American Jewish leadership during World War II. A volume edited by Seymour Maxwell Finger, who directed the commission, comprises the findings: *American Jewry During the Holocaust* (New York, 1984). On the controversy caused by the inquiry see Lucy Dawidowicz, "Indicting American Jews," *Commentary* 75 (June 1983): 36–44 and the subsequent exchange of views, *Commentary* 76 (Sept. 1983): 4–28.

4. Eva Fogelman, "From Mourning to Creativity: The Second Generation of Survivors in Israel and the United States," *Midstream* 37 (Apr. 1991): 31–33; William B. Helmreich, *Against All Odds: Holocaust Survivors and the Successful Lives They Made in America* (New York, 1992), 109–11, 184–97, 264–65.

5. Cp. Edward S. Shapiro's review essay, "The Holocaust and American Jewish Consciousness," *Congress Monthly* 57 (Nov.–Dec. 1990): 18–19. For a comparison with the impact of the Holocaust on Israeli consciousness and political culture, see Charles S. Liebman and Eliezer Don-Yehiya, *Civil Religion in Israel: Traditional Judaism and Political Culture in the Jewish State* (Berkeley, Calif., 1983), 100–7, 137–48, 151–53.

6. Allan A. Ryan Jr., "Attitudes Toward the Prosecution of Nazi War Criminals in the United States," in *Contemporary Views on the Holocaust*, edited by Randolph L. Braham (Boston, 1983), 201–6. See also Allan Ryan's account *Quiet Neighbors: Prosecuting Nazi War Criminals in America* (San Diego, 1984). Ryan was the first chief of OSI, 1979–1983.

7. Rochelle G. Saidel, *Never Too Late to Remember: The Politics Behind New York City's Holocaust Museum* (New York and London, 1996), 43–67, 230–46.

8. Cp. Sachar, *History of the Jews in America*, 845–47; Miller, *One, by One, by One*, 221–31, 256–57; Saidel, *Never Too Late to Remember*, 93–108; James E. Young,

"Holocaust Memorials in America: The Politics of Identity," in *Survey of Jewish Affairs*, edited by William Frankel (London, 1991), 161–73; Michael Berenbaum, *After the Tragedy and Triumph: Essays in Modern Jewish Thought and Experience* (Oxford and New York, 1991), 3–20. See also Alvin H. Rosenfeld, "The Holocaust in American Popular Culture," *Midstream* 29 (June–July 1983): 53–59.

9. Stephen Whitfield, "The Holocaust and the American Jewish Intellectual," *Judaism* 28 (Fall 1979): 391–401; "Under Forty: A Symposium on American Literature and the Younger Generation of American Jews," *Contemporary Jewish Record* 7 (Feb. 1944): 3–36; "Jewishness and the Younger Intellectuals," *Commentary* 31 (Apr. 1961): 308–35; "Conditions of Jewish Belief," *Commentary* 42 (Aug. 1966): 71–160; "Where Do I Stand Now?" *Judaism* 23 (Fall 1974): 389–466. In an earlier Judaism symposium, "My Jewish Affirmation," twenty-one Jewish intellectuals ignored the subject of the Holocaust, *Judaism* 10 (Fall 1961): 291–352. On the "committed" Jewish intellectuals, see Carole S. Kessner, ed., *The "Other" New York Jewish Intellectuals* (New York, 1994), 1–22.

10. Quoted in Sachar, *History of the Jews in America*, 848.

11. Robert Alter, "The Deformations of the Holocaust," *Commentary* 71 (Feb. 1981): 48–54. See also the responses in Letters from Readers, *Commentary* 71 (June 1981): 2–12. Cp. Leon A. Jick, "The Holocaust: Its Use and Abuse in the American Public," *Yad Vashem Studies* 14 (1981): 308–18.

12. Ismar Schorsch, "The Holocaust and Jewish Survival," *Midstream* 27 (Jan. 1981): 38–42.

13. Leo Trepp, "What Shall We Do About Germany"; Werner Cahnmann, "Germany: The Time Has Come for Friendship"; Herbert A. Strauss, "My Germany—and Yours?" *Sh'ma*, Apr. 13, 1973, pp. 89–94.

14. Harry Gersh, "The Germans, A Time for Etiquette," *Sh'ma*, Sept. 7, 1973, pp. 122–23; Cynthia Ozick, "Germany, Even Without Munich," *Sh'ma*, Oct. 13, 1972, pp. 150–52. As a matter of fact, Wellershoff volunteered in 1943 for service in an elite unit (Panzergrenadierdivision Hermann Göring) but was sent to the eastern front at a time when almost all Jews in the western part of the Soviet Union occupied by the German army had already been killed and the territory liberated by the Soviet Army. His autobiographic memoirs of the war years appeared fifty years later, *Der Ernstfall: Innenansichten des Krieges* (Cologne, 1995). Wellershoff, a prominent German writer, confessed that during his service he considered volunteering for an execution unit, in order to sense together with others how one feels killing people. See Michael Wild's review of his book "Die Welt, ein Stolperfeld," *Süddeutsche Zeitung*, Apr. 18, 1995.

15. "The Holocaust: Young Germans and Jews Speak Their Minds," *ADL Bulletin* 33 (Mar. 1976): 1–6. "Young Jews, Germans Talk It Over," *New York Post*, Feb. 14, 1976; Leshnik to Ted Freedman, Mar. 25, 1976, ADL Archives, ADL FC Germany.

16. Ralph Bass to Wolfgang Sannwald, Feb. 12, 1976, AJC Archives, AJC Records, International meetings, Feb. 11, 1976, Germany, FAD-E, 76; David Geller to Morris Fine, June 14, 1976, ibid., BGX 76, Germany/West.

17. Symposium: "Germans and Jews Today," *Midstream* 27 (Oct. 1981): 26–40.

18. Anson Rabinbach, "Reflections on Germans and Jews Since Auschwitz," in Rabinbach and Zipes, *Germans and Jews since the Holocaust*, 3–22.

19. Klaus Wippermann, "Holocaust?—Das Gespräch einer Nation und sich selbst," *Tribüne* 18 (Sept. 1978): 22–45.

20. Andrei S. Markovits and Christopher S. Allen, "The German Conscience: 'Holocaust' on German TV: A Special Report," *Jewish Frontier* 46 (Apr. 1979): 13–17.

21. For a detailed critical analysis see Jeffrey Herf, "The 'Holocaust' Reception in West Germany: Right, Center, and Left," in Rabinbach and Zipes, *Germans and Jews since the Holocaust*, 208–33. See also note 20 above.

22. Wippermann, "Holocaust?" 22–45.

23. Jeffrey Herf, "'Holocaust' Reception." Cp. also Jean-Paul Bier, "The Holocaust and West Germany: Strategies of Oblivion," *New German Critique* 19 (Winter 1980): 9–29.

24. "Impact of 'Holocaust' Series not Lasting," David Kanter, JTA, Bonn, Mar. 25, 1979, AJC Records, FAD, Germany/West, 1980.

25. "German Survey of Holocaust Response," *ADL Bulletin* 36 (Nov. 1979): 10.

26. Hermann Lübbe, "Der Nationalsozialismus im deutschen Nachkriegsbewusstsein," *Historische Zeitschrift* 236 (1983): 579–99.

27. See ch. 13, note 40, above.

28. Exchange Program for Future Leaders in the Federal Republic of Germany and of the American Jewish Community, Dec. 1980 and Mar. 1982, German-Jewish Relations file, Blaustein Library; *The American Jewish Committee: Germany, A Summary of Programs, 1945–1991* (New York, 1991). See also Theodore Ellenoff, AJC Oral History Collection, Third part of interview, Dec. 10, 1988.

29. William S. Trosten to Robert S. Jacobs, Apr. 8, 1983, and Trosten to Heinz Kühn, chairman of the FES, Dec. 20, 1984, AJC Archives. Hans-Jochen Vogel, chairman of the SPD parliamentary group, promised AJC president Howard Friedman full support in implementing exchange programs, May 15, 1984, ibid., German Exchange Programs, WTX, 84–83-82. For the Naumann Foundation dialogue of Poles, Israelis, and American Jews, see AJC Office of European Affairs, Summary of Programs, Jan. 1993–Mar. 1994.

30. Frank Reiss to Abraham Foxman, Mar. 7, 1985, on ADL leadership meeting with German ambassador Günther van Well, Mar. 4, 1985, ADL Archives, ADL FC Germany.

31. June 26, 1978. First speech by Helmut Kohl at the Leo Baeck Institute in New York, in *Chancellor Helmut Kohl on the German-Jewish Question in Connection with the Role of the Leo Baeck Institute*. A publication in the Deutschland-Berichte series, pp. 13–15.

32. Kenneth J. Bialkin to Nathan Perlmutter, Nov. 16, 1982, ADL Archives, ADL FC Germany. In March 1984 Kohl met again with a group of American Jewish leaders upon an invitation of WJC president Edgar Bronfman. Note of A. Foxman, Mar. 8, 1984, ibid.

33. E.g., Julius Berman, Presidents Conference, to Kohl, Jan. 16, 1984; Kohl to Berman, Feb. 22, 1984; Howard Friedman, AJC to Kohl, Jan. 16, 1984, AJC Records, Germany WTX 83–84, Arms Sales to Saudi Arabia; Kenneth Bialkin (ADL) protested to Kohl, Jan. 3, 1984, Teltschik to Bialkin, Jan. 9, 1984, ADL Archives, ADL FC

Germany. Meeting with representatives of Jewish Holocaust survivors, Feb. 10, 1984, reported Feb. 13, 1984, ibid.

34. See chap. 16.

35. Andrew Baker, "Reconciliation: Linked by the Holocaust, Germans and American Jews Seek to Heal the Wounds," *Jewish Monthly* (replaced *National Jewish Monthly [NJM]*) 102 (Jan. 1988): 18–19.

36. Address of van Well to B'nai B'rith Board of Governors, "German Jewish Relationship after Bitburg," May 21, 1985, ADL Archives, ADL FC Germany, May 22, 1985.

37. See note 35, above.

38. Howard Friedman, Alois Mertes Memorial Lecture, Bonn, Oct. 29, 1991, AJC Archives.

39. Remarks by Howard Friedman, July 20, 1984, Berlin, ibid.

40. Neil Kramer to Aaron Eshman, Aug. 20, 1980, AJC Records, FAD, Germany/West, 1980. Cp. also impressions of German visitors to the United States, "18 West Germans, Seeking Amity, Visit U.S. Jews," *NYT*, Apr. 5, 1981, and "18 Visitors from Germany Learn About Jews on Trip," *Newsday*, Apr. 3, 1981, AJC Archives, FAD-D, Germany/West, 1981.

CHAPTER 16

1. Two volumes contain a wealth of material about the Bitburg controversy: Geoffrey Hartman, ed., *Bitburg in Moral and Political Perspective* (Bloomington, 1986), and Ilya Levkov, ed., *Bitburg and Beyond* (New York, 1986). For a summary see Deborah E. Lipstadt, "The Bitburg Controversy," in *AJYB*, 1987, vol. 87, pp. 21–37.

2. Remarks of Elie Wiesel at the White House, Apr. 19, 1985, reprinted in Hartman, *Bitburg in Moral and Political Perspective*, 241–44. See also interview with Elie Wiesel, *Der Spiegel*, Apr. 29, 1985, reprinted in Levkov, *Bitburg and Beyond*, 383–85.

3. George Shultz, *Turmoil and Triumph* (New York, 1993), 539–60.

4. On the meeting and correspondence between Seymour Reich and Kohl, see BPA Informationsfunk, Mar. 11, 1989, ACDP, 4/40 B'nai B'rith; B'nai B'rith News, Mar. 10, 1989, and Kohl to Reich, Jan. 8, 1990, BBA, Germany file.

5. Kissinger stated publicly that if the Bitburg visit was scrapped, "It would do enormous damage to our [American] foreign policy." Shultz, *Turmoil and Triumph*, 552; on Ambassador Arthur Burns's attitude, 549–50. See also Arthur Burns's special contribution to the volume edited by Levkov, *Bitburg and Beyond*, 225–26.

6. Howard I. Friedman to AJC leaders on the AJC response to Bitburg, May 9, 1985, Blaustein Library, Bitburg visit file; AJC background memorandum on the Bitburg affair, Apr. 24, 1985, ibid. See also Marc H. Tanenbaum's summary, "The American Jewish Committee at the White House," in Levkov, *Bitburg and Beyond*, 330–34.

7. Arthur Goldberg to President Ronald Reagan, Apr. 16, 1985; Hyman Bookbinder to Howard Friedman, May 13, 1985. AJC Archives, DGX 84–85.

8. Andrew Baker to Harold Applebaum, May 28, 1985, AJC Archives, DGX 84–85.

9. Alois Mertes, who died on June 16, 1985, referred to his address before the AJC on May 2 in his recollections, which were posthumously published in *Rheinischer Merkur/Christ und Welt*, July 20, 1985. ACDP, Press documentations, Alois Mertes file.

10. Menahem Z. Rosensaft, "Reagan Errs on the Holocaust," *NYT*, Mar. 30, 1985. Quoted in Levkov, *Bitburg and Beyond*, 68–69.

11. Michael Wyschogrod, "Reconciliation in Munich," *Congress Monthly* 52 (July–Aug. 1985): 305.

12. Levkov, *Bitburg and Beyond*, 313–14. See also Walter Ruby, "WJC Head Angered by Jews Coming to Reagan Defense," *Jewish World*, May 20, 1985, AJC Records, DGX 84–85.

13. Abraham H. Foxman, "Thoughts After Bitburg," *ADL News*, reprinted in Levkov, *Bitburg and Beyond*, 381. In the same vein, Nathan Perlmutter, ADL national director, May 5, 1985, AJC Archives, DGX 84–85.

14. *NYT*, May 10, 1985, quoted in Lipstadt, "Bitburg Controversy," 37.

15. Statement of Kenneth J. Bialkin, Chairman of the Presidents Conference, May 7, 1985, AJC Archives, DGX 84–85.

16. Israeli Press Highlights, a review of weekend newspapers by the Israel Office of the AJC, Israel and Bitburg, press summary, May 6, 1985. Shimon Peres's statement quoted in the *NYT*, May 7, 1985.

17. According to public statements, it appeared that opposition to Reagan's visit to Bitburg came mainly from the liberal side. William Bole, "Bitburg—Who Spoke Out, Who Didn't," *Present Tense* 12 (Summer 1985): 16–19. Later findings contradicted this assumption. See note 19, below.

18. Lipstadt, "Bitburg Controversy," 31.

19. Findings of the Roper Poll and analysis by Milton Himmelfarb, Oct. 29, 1985, AJC Archives, DGX 84–85. The Roper report on Opinion About Bitburg, Levkov, *Bitburg and Beyond*, 433–38.

20. William Schneider, "Washington Out of Step with Nation on Reagan," *National Journal*, Oct. 5, 1985, p. 2274, Himmelfarb to Gordis, Oct. 30, 1985, ibid.

21. Hajo Funke, "Bitburg und die Macht der Juden," in *Antisemitismus nach dem Holocaust*, edited by Alphons Silbermann and Julius H. Schoeps (Cologne, 1986), 41–52.

22. Fritz Ulrich Fack, "Ein Scherbenhaufen," *FAZ*, Apr. 29, 1985.

23. Shultz, *Turmoil and Triumph*, 554. Teltschik continued to be very critical of American Jewish reactions. In 1989 he warned Marc Fisher, who had just been appointed as correspondent of the *Washington Post* in Bonn, that "the greatest danger Germany faced came not from the Soviet Union or East Germany, but from the Western allies, whose mistrust grew more palpable and painful daily." Marc Fisher, *After the Wall: Germany, the Germans, and the Burden of History* (New York, 1995), 319.

24. Dregger was for many years head of the so-called Stahlhelm faction in the CDU, which distinguished itself by its right-wing nationalistic views. Peter Glotz, a member of the Bundestag and at that time secretary general of the SPD, accused Dregger of damaging the image of the Federal German Republic in the American mind, Apr. 23, 1985. Levkov, *Bitburg and Beyond*, 103–4.

25. Hans-Jochen Vogel, the head of the SPD parliamentary group, criticized the

government's handling of the affair, but the party did not put on a major fight on that issue.

26. Jürgen Habermas, "Defining the Past: A Politico-Cultural Tract," in Hartman, *Bitburg in Moral and Political Perspective*, 43–51. Translated from *Die Zeit*, May 17, 1985, pp. 57–58.

27. Richard von Weizsäcker's speech of May 8, 1985, reprinted in Hartman, *Bitburg in Moral and Political Perspective*, 262–73, here p. 265.

28. Willy Brandt, "Wir brauchen eine neue Phase der West-Ost Politik," in *40 Jahre danach: Nürnberger Friedensgespräch* (Bonn, 1985), 9–14. Also Nuremberg Manifesto of the SPD executive, May 8, 1945–1985, ibid., pp. 61–63.

29. AJC, Post-Bitburg Analysis. National Advisory Panel Minutes, May 22, 1985, AJC Archives, DGX 84–85.

30. Interview with Stuart Eizenstat, in Levkov, *Bitburg and Beyond*, 339–43.

31. Mark Krupnick, "Walking in Our Sleep: Bitburg and the Post-1939 Generation," in Hartman, *Bitburg in Moral and Political Perspective*, 187–90.

32. Michael Walzer, "Bitburg—Looking Back," *Congress Monthly* 52 (July–Aug. 1985): 2, 23.

33. Alvin H. Rosenfeld, "The Holocaust in Jewish Memory and Public Memory," *Dimensions* 2 (Fall 1986): 9–12.

34. Charles Silberman, *A Certain People: American Jews and Their Lives Today* (New York, 1985), 366.

35. Midge Decter, "Bitburg: Who Forgot What," *Commentary* 80 (Aug. 1985): 21–27.

36. Lucy S. Dawidowicz, "In Berlin Again," *Commentary* 82 (Aug. 1986): 32–41.

37. Address of van Well to B'nai B'rith Board of Governors, "German Jewish Relationship after Bitburg," May 21, 1985, ADL Archives, ADL FC Germany; Gerald Kraft, B'nai B'rith president, interview after visit to Germany (late in 1985), probably Jan. 1986, BBA, Germany file.

38. AJC, 1985 Leadership Delegation to Germany, Oct. 12–26, 1985, AJC Archives, AJC Records, Germany DGX 84–85; Ted Freedman to ADL directors, Jan. 22, 1987, ADL Archives, ADL FC Germany.

39. The Burton Joseph Prize for Human Rights was presented to Weizsäcker on Dec. 5, 1989, a few weeks after the breakdown of the Berlin Wall. *B'nai B'rith Record*, Feb. 1990, BBA. In May 1997 the same award was presented to his successor Roman Herzog.

40. Ernest W. Michel, *Promises to Keep* (New York, 1993), 289–93.

41. Andrew Baker, "Reconciliation," 18.

42. FES, *Der Holocaust als Unterrichtsthema in amerikanischen Schulen: Ergebnisse eines Studienaufenthalts deutscher Lehrer in den USA* (Bonn, 1988); also FES, Bonn, note by Peter Schneider about the visit of two German teachers to the United States upon the invitation of the ADL, Fall 1988, FES, Bonn.

43. Joachim Rohlfes, *Juden in den Vereinigten Staaten* (Bonn, 1990). In 1988 the AJC and the Ebert Foundation convened in Bonn a conference on American Jews in German textbooks. News from the Committee, June 6, 1988, Blaustein Library, Germany file.

44. Naomi Pfefferman, "An Eye-Opening Visit to Germany," *Jewish Monthly* 102 (Jan. 1988): 18–19.

45. News Conference on ADL-Sponsored Survey of Anti-Semitism in Germany, Berlin, Technical University, June 9, 1988, Robert Goldmann to A. Foxman, June 10, 1988; ADL news release, New York, June 23, 1988, ADL Archives, ADL FC Germany.

46. Eleanor S. Lazarus to Dagmar Celeste, Dec. 17, 1987, AJC Archives, New York.

47. Atlantik-Brücke/American Jewish Committee, "American Jews and the Federal Republic of Germany: Problems and Opportunities," Report on a Conference in Bonn-Bad Godesberg, Nov. 21–23, 1987, AJC Archives. Quote from Alvin Rosenfeld, p. 15; Executive summary, pp. 37–38.

48. Ibid.; also Second Atlantik-Brücke-AJC Conference, June 18–20, 1988, New York, Draft, Sept. 20, 1988, AJC Archives. The conference dealt mainly with American Jewish perceptions of Israel and German perceptions of American Jews. For German comments, see Günther Gillessen, "Immer wieder Brücken bauen: Neubesinnung auf die deutsch-amerikanischen Beziehungen," *FAZ*, Dec. 29, 1987; Jörg von Uthmann, "Für Israel um jeden Preis? Die amerikanischen Juden und ihr politischer Einfluss," *FAZ*, Feb. 13, 1988; Josef Joffe, "Keine Versöhnung um den Preis der Relativierung: Die erste Diskussion mit Vertretern des amerikanischen Judentums auf deutschem Boden," *Süddeutsche Zeitung*, Dec. 22, 1987.

49. For the *Historikerstreit* see Richard Evans, *In Hitler's Shadow: West German Historians and the Attempt to Escape from the Nazi Past* (New York, 1989); Peter Baldwin, ed., *Reworking the Past, the Holocaust, and the Historians' Debate* (Boston, 1990). Gordon Craig discussed the subject in the *New York Review of Books*, Oct. 8, 1987. Echoes of the Historians' debate resonated at the Atlantik-Brücke-AJC conferences. See also Jerry Z. Muller, "German Historians at War," *Commentary* 87 (Mar. 1989): 33–41; Dan Diner, "The Historians' Controversy—Limits to the Historization of National Socialism," *Tikkun* 2 (1987): 74–78. For a recent succinct German treatment of the debate, see Peter Steinbach, "Der Historikerstreit," *Tribüne* 34 (Sept. 1995): 120–33.

50. The Inaugural Paul Lecture, Johann W. Schmidt, "Those Unfortunate Years": Nazism in the Public Debate of Postwar Germany, delivered on Oct. 15, 1986 (Bloomington, 1987). See also Heiner Lichtenstein, ed., *Die Fassbinder-Kontroverse oder das Ende der Schonzeit* (Königstein, 1986).

51. *Voice of German Americans* 28 (Nov. 1977): 1; JTA Daily News Bulletin, Oct. 11, 1977, p. 4; George Pape, Letter to the Editor, *NYT*, Nov. 21, 1977.

52. German-American and Jewish Leader Denounce Provocations, AJC, received Sept. 28, 1978, AJC Archives, BGX 78, Germany/West; Helmut Kuhn, "Die Deutschen von Manhattan," *Die Zeit*, June 12, 1992, p. 56.

53. "Link between German-American Groups and Holocaust Revisionist Institute Disclosed by the Wiesenthal Center," *JTA Daily News Bulletin*, Jan. 12, 1984, p. 1.

54. Elsbeth M. Seewald to members of the U.S. Congress, Apr. 30, 1985; for her open letter on Waldheim, *Deutsch-Amerikaner*, June 1987, p. 1.

55. *Steuben News* 60 (Apr. 1988): 1, 7.

Chapter 17

1. See chap. 3.

2. AJJDC reports on Berlin, Feb. 21, 1946, #282, and May 31, 1946, #353, quoted in Robin Ostow, *Jews in Contemporary East Germany: The Children of Moses in the Land of Marx* (New York, 1989), 12–13. For the life and problems of the Jews in East Germany I have relied on Erica Burgauer, *Zwischen Erinnerung und Verdrängung: Juden in Deutschland nach 1945* (Hamburg, 1993), Pt. 3 "Jüdisches Leben in der DDR," pp. 137–355; Siegfried Theodor Arndt, et al., *Juden in der DDR: Geschichte-Probleme-Perspektiven* (Duisburg, 1988); Lothar Mertens, "Staatlich propagierter Antizionismus: Das Israelbild der DDR," in *Jahrbuch für Antisemitismusforschung*, vol. 2, edited by Wolfgang Benz (Frankfurt, 1993), 139–53; Constantin Goschler, "Paternalismus und Verweigerung—Die DDR und die Wiedergutmachung für jüdische Verfolgte des Nationalsozialismus," in Benz, *Jahrbuch für Antisemitismusforschung*, vol. 2, pp. 93–117; Angelika Timm, "Die DDR, die Schoah und der offizielle Antisemitismus," and Olaf Groehler, "Die Diskussion um die Judenverfolgung in SBZ und DDR," both in *Antisemitismus und Arbeiterbewegung: Entwicklungslinien im 20. Jahrhundert*, edited by Mario Kessler (Bonn, 1993), 65–77 and 79–94, respectively; Michael Wolffsohn, *Die Deutschland- Akte: Juden und Deutsche in Ost und West, Tatsachen und Legenden* (Munich, 1995). (Wolffsohn's volume contains a great number of relevant quotes from former East German Communist sources, even though one does not have to share that author's interpretations.) There are a number of relevant articles in Werner Bergmann, Rainer Erb, and Albert Lichtblau, eds., *Schwieriges Erbe: Der Umgang mit Nationalsozialismus und Antisemitismus in Österreich, der DDR und der Bundesrepublik Deutschland* (Frankfurt, 1995): Lothar Mertens, "Die SED und die NS-Vergangenheit," pp. 194–211; Olaf Groehler, "Zur Gedenkstättenpolitik und zum Umgang mit der 'Reichskristallnacht' in der SBZ und DDR (1945–1988)," pp. 285–301; Peter Maser, "Juden und Jüdische Gemeinden in der Innenpolitik der DDR," pp. 339–68. See also Jerry E. Thompson, "Jews, Zionism, and Israel: The Story of the Jews in the German Democratic Republic since 1945" (Ph.D. diss., Washington State University, 1978), and Klaus J. Herrmann, "Political and Social Dimensions of the Jewish Communities in the German Democratic Republic," in *Nationalities Papers*, vol. 10 (Charleston, Ill., 1982). For a partly more positive view of the East German Communist regime's relations with the Jewish community, see Mario Kessler, *Die SED und die Juden: Zwischen Repression und Toleranz* (Berlin, 1995). Three detailed monographs appeared after my manuscript had been submitted to the publisher: Angelika Timm, *Hammer, Zirkel, Davidstern. Das gestörte Verhältnis der DDR zu Zionismus und Staat Israel* (Bonn, 1997); Angelika Timm also published a volume in English, *Jewish Claims against East Germany: Moral Obligations and Pragmatic Policy* (Budapest, 1997); Lothar Mertens, *Davidstern unter Hammer und Zirkel. Die jüdischen Gemeinden in der SBZ/DDR und ihre Behandlung durch Partei und Staat 1945–1990* (Hildesheim, 1997).

3. On the Thuringian restitution law see Thomas Schüler, "Das Wiedergutmachungsgesetz vom 14. September 1945 in Thüringen," *Jahrbuch für Antisemitismusforschung*, vol. 2, pp. 118–38; Goschler, "Paternalismus und Verweigerung," 95–99.

4. Angelika Timm, "Israel in den Medien der DDR," *Jahrbuch für Antisemitismusforschung*, vol. 2, pp. 154–73, esp. p. 156.

5. Yachil to Aryeh Levavi, Nov. 4, 1952, ISA, FM Records 2418/13, quoted in Wolffsohn, *Die Deutschland-Akte*, 241, n. 19; Deutschkron, *Israel und die Deutschen*, 184–86.

6. Timm, "Israel in den Medien der DDR," 156–57; Jeffrey Herf, "East German Communists and the Jewish Question: The Case of Paul Merker," *Journal of Contemporary History* 29 (Oct. 1994): 628–61; also his article "Der Geheimprozess," *Die Zeit*, Oct. 7, 1994, pp. 13–16.

7. Olaf Groehler, "Der Umgang mit dem Holocaust in der DDR," in *Der Umgang mit dem Holocaust: Europa-USA-Israel*, edited by Rolf Steininger (Vienna, 1994), 233–45.

8. I dealt with this change of attitude in *Yad Mushetet*, 41–45.

9. See chap. 2.

10. Benjamin Pinkus, *The Soviet Government and the Jews, 1948–1967: A Documented Study* (Cambridge, 1984), 193–201, 232–37. On Israel's early policy toward Communist Eastern Europe see Uri Bialer, *Between East and West: Israel's Foreign Policy Orientation, 1948–1956* (Cambridge, 1990).

11. Report to the World Union for Progressive Judaism, from Rabbi Steven S. Schwarzschild, Apr. 4, 1950, AJA, World Union for Progressive Judaism Records, Manuscript Collection 16, box 5/5.

12. The Anti-Jewish Purge, *AJYB*, 1954, vol. 55, pp. 268–70; Ostow, *Jews in Contemporary East Germany*, 16; Peter Maser, "Juden und Jüdische Gemeinden," 343–47.

13. Z. Shuster's report on East Germany, Forty-sixth Annual Meeting, AJC, New York, Jan. 30, 1953–Feb. 1, 1953, Blaustein Library; News from the Committee, Jan. 27, 1953, YIVO, AJC Records, FAD-1, box 25. See also *AJYB*, 1954, vol. 55, pp. 268–70.

14. For the unsuccessful efforts of the Jewish communities in the field of restitution, see Goschler, "Paternalismus und Verweigerung," 98–106.

15. Joe Gordon to Slawson, on Karlikow's report from Berlin, Apr. 24, 1953, also AJC memorandum, "Communist Antisemitism and Eastern Germany," YIVO, AJC Records, FAD-1, box 25.

16. F. L. Brasloff, On the Position of East German Jewry, Feb. 3–Mar. 6, 1953, CZA, Goldmann Archive, Z6/348. Brasloff concluded that the flight from East Berlin and East Germany was mainly caused by fear and did not result from persecution. The new policy of the East Berlin regime was part and parcel of the general Soviet policy but not the outflow of German antisemitism. F. R. Brasloff, Jan. 24, 1953, ibid., Z2/695. See also Greta Beigel's report, "Recent Events in East Germany," Mar. 30, 1953, CZA, Goldmann Archive, Z6/750.

17. Cp. Groehler, "Der Umgang mit dem Holocaust in der DDR," 242–44; Groehler, "Zur Gedenkstättenpolitik und zum Umgang mit der 'Reichskristallnacht' in der SBZ und DDR," 294–300.

18. Rolf Vogel to F. L. Brasloff, Sept. 11, 1967, CZA, Goldmann Archive, Z6/1176; Declaration of Jewish Citizens of the DDR, *Neues Deutschland*, June 11, 1967; Burgauer, *Zwischen Erinnerung und Verdrängung*, 191–95; Information, Aug. 13, 1982, Stiftung Archiv der politischen Parteien und Massenorganisationen im Bundesarchiv-Berlin (hereafter SAPMO-BA), SED Central Committee, Working Group Church Problems, IV, B/2/14/175.

19. *Neues Deutschland,* Nov. 3, 1956, quoted in Deutschkron, *Israel und die Deutschen,* 190.

20. Wolffsohn, *Die Deutschland-Akte,* 35–36.

21. Herbert Strauss, "The Jews of East Germany," *ADL Bulletin* 21 (Mar. 1964): 4–5.

22. Excerpts from the address of Joachim Prinz, AJ Congress, Washington, D.C., Mar. 17, 1965, AJHSA, AJ Congress Papers, I-77, box 52.

23. A. S. Karlikow to David Geller, Jan. 15, 1973, AJC Archives, Germany East/ Restitution, BGX 73.

24. David Geller to Bertram Gold, Mar. 12, 1973, ibid.; Goldmann to Werner Nachmann, Sept. 2, 1974, CZA, Goldmann Archive, Z6/2466; AJC Draft memo, Aug. 2, 1974, AJC Records, Germany, FAD-E, 74.

25. Ibid. For a summary of the negotiations between the GDR and the Claims Conference from the viewpoint of an East German historian, see Angelika Timm, *Alles Umsonst? Verhandlungen zwischen der Claims Conference und der DDR über "Wiedergutmachung" und Entschädigung* (Berlin, 1996), 19–40.

26. Minutes of meetings held in Washington, Aug. 22, 1973, AJC Archives, Germany East/Restitution, BGX 73.

27. Resumé of Meeting of Jewish Delegation with Assistant Secretary of State Arthur Hartman, July 17, 1974, AJC Archives, July 29, 1974, AJC Records, Germany East/Restitution, BGX 1974.

28. Javits to Kissinger, Dec. 20, 1973, and Marshall Wright, Assistant Secretary of State for Congressional Relations, to Javits, Jan. 22, 1974; Javits to Kissinger, Feb. 25, 1974, and Linwood Holton, Dept. of State, to Javits, Mar. 14, 1974; David Geller to Bertram Gold, Apr. 11, 1974, ibid.

29. Saul Kagan to Claims Conference Board of Directors, Sept. 11, 1974, AJC Records, Germany East/Restitution, BGX 1974; Saul Kagan to N. Goldmann, Aug. 8, 1974; Claims Conference Report on meeting of Rabbi Israel Miller with Scott George, Director of the Office of Central European Affairs, Dept. of State, Aug. 14, 1974; Goldmann to Hartman, Dec. 9, 1974, and Hartman to Goldmann, Dec. 20, 1974; Claims Conference, B. B. Ferencz, Memorandum, Dec. 16, 1974, all CZA, Goldmann Archive, Z6/2469; Claims Conference, B. B. Ferencz, Memorandum, GDR file 1974–1976, AJC Archives, Germany East/Restitution, BGX 76.

30. Otto Funke, AFC, declaration, Nov. 22, 1976, and Saul Kagan to Funke, Dec. 6, 1976, AJC Records, Germany East/Restitution, BGX 76.

31. Claims Conference, Benjamin B. Ferencz, memorandum, Aug. 3, 1977, on meetings in Washington, Aug. 1, 1977, AJC Archives, Germany East/Restitution, BGX 77; Timm, *Alles Umsonst?* 23.

32. Timm, *Alles Umsonst?* 25–30.

33. Delegation of the House of Representatives led by Holocaust survivor Thomas P. Lantos, (D, Calif.), received by Honecker, SAPMO-BA, SED Central Committee, Central Party Archive, Bureau Hermann Axen, IV 2/2.035/113. For Axen's visit to the United States, May 1–8, 1988, ibid., IV, 2/2.035/114.

34. A. S. Karlikow for files, June 15, 1982, AJC Records, Germany East, BGX 82. The definitive negative decision was conveyed by Rozanne Ridgway, Assistant Secretary

of State, to GDR ambassador Gerhard Herder, on Sept. 12, 1988. Subsequent East German protests by Kurt Nier to the American ambassador in East Berlin were in vain. Sept. 23, 1988, SAPMO-BA, Bureau Axen, IV, 2/2.035/113.

35. Note by Axen, Nov. 10, 1988, ibid. On Axen see also Margarita Mathiopoulos, "Hermann Axen—Opfer, Täter, Hofjude," *Menora* 6 (1995): 301–15.

36. *Neues Deutschland*, June 24, 1987, quoted in Burgauer, *Zwischen Erinnerung und Verdrängung*, 224; Minutes of the talk between Honecker and Galinski, June 6, 1988, SAPMO-BA, SED Central Committee, Central Party Archive, IV, 2/1/679. The report on the conversation between Axen and Rabbi Israel Miller, SAPMO-BA, DY30/IV/2/2.035/114, is reprinted in Timm, *Alles Umsonst?* 46–47.

37. Undersecretary of State John Whitehead visited Berlin in 1987 and 1988. He visited the East Berlin Jewish community, among others, in November 1987. *Neues Deutschland*, Nov. 11, 1987, quoted in Burgauer, *Zwischen Erinnerung und Verdrängung*, 226.

38. Haskell L. Lazere, abbreviated report on mission to Germany, Oct. 1–13, 1983, AJC Records, Germany, AJC Leadership Delegations, WTX 83–84; Visit to East Berlin; Meetings of Eugene DuBow with Klaus Gysi and Peter Kirchner, Aug. 7, 1985, DGX 84–85.

39. Report by Rabbi Ernst M. Lorge, "High Holiday Services in East Berlin," AJC Records, Germany, DGX 84–85.

40. Wolffsohn, *Die Deutschland-Akte*, 304–5.

41. The delegation consisted of Dr. Peter Kirchner, the head of the East Berlin Jewish community, and Dr. Irene Runge, a Communist Jewish intellectual. After Germany's unification Dr. Runge lost her job at Humboldt University because of her involvement in East German Stasi (Ministry of State Security) activities. On the nonparticipation at WJC 1981 plenary assembly, see R. Bellmann to Klaus Gysi, Sept. 29, 1980, SAPMO-BA, Church Problems, IV, B 2/14/174.

42. Wolffsohn, *Die Deutschland-Akte*, 329–31, 335–36.

43. Report on visit of Secretary of State for Church Affairs Kurt Löffler, to Israel, Jan. 29–Feb. 3, 1989, SAPMO-BA, Church Problems, IV, B 2/14/176.

44. Minutes of talk between Honecker and Bronfman, Oct. 17, 1988, SAPMO-BA, SED Central Committee, Central Party Archive, IV, 2/1/686; also talk between Löffler and Bronfman, Israel Singer, and Maram Stern, Oct. 18, 1988, note of Oct. 19, 1988, SAPMO-BA, Church Problems, IV, B 2/14/175.

45. *Neues Deutschland*, Oct. 18 and 19, 1988.

46. Bronfman to Honecker, Apr. 14, 1989, SAPMO-BA, DY30/IV 2/2.035/113, reprinted in Timm, *Alles Umsonst?* 49; Information, Apr. 4, 1989, on a talk with Maram Stern, SAPMO-BA, Church Problems, IV, B 2/14/176; G. Jonathan Greenwald, *Berlin Witness: An American Diplomat's Chronicle of East Germany's Revolution* (University Park, Md., 1993), 65, 51; Note of July 18, 1989, SAPMO-BA, Bureau Axen, IV 2/2.035/115. On Avi Beker's talk with Herbert Barth see Angelika Timm, *Hammer, Zirkel, Davidstern*, p. 320.

47. James M. Dorsey, "Party Chief Asks Jews to Oppose German Unity," *Washington Times*, Feb. 21, 1990. Gysi made his remarks during a meeting with Rabbi Zvi Weinman, an Israeli Orthodox rabbi involved in efforts to reestablish Jewish life in East

Germany. Commenting on Gysi's appeal for Jewish financial aid for East Germany to prevent German reunification, Singer stated that the world Jewish community would first have to address the issue of unification before deciding on possible aid.

48. Modrow to Bronfman, Feb. 1, 1990, BAP, DC20.4998, reprinted in Timm, *Alles Umsonst?* 50.

49. *Neues Deutschland*, Apr. 14–15, 1990; protocols of the Volkskammer, July 22, 1990, 27/106.

CHAPTER 18

1. For German unification see Elizabeth Pond, *Beyond the Wall: Germany's Road to Unification* (Washington, D.C., 1992); Konrad Jarausch, *The Road to German Unity* (New York, 1994); Michael R. Beschloss and Strobe Talbott, *At the Highest Levels: The Inside Story of the End of the Cold War* (New York, 1993); Philip Zelikow and Condoleeza Rice, *Germany Unified and Europe Transformed: A Study in Statecraft* (Cambridge, Mass., and London, 1995). These books stress particularly the leading role of the United States in the unification process. For the European context see Peter H. Merkl, *German Unification in the European Context* (Philadelphia, 1993); for Chancellor Kohl's policy, Horst Teltschik, *329 Tage: Innenansichten der Einigung* (Berlin, 1991). James Baker described President Bush's and his own part in German unification in his memoirs *The Politics of Diplomacy: Revolution, War, and Peace, 1989–1992* (New York, 1995), 153–215, 230–59. Cp. also Genscher's reminiscences: Hans-Dietrich Genscher, *Erinnerungen* (Berlin, 1995). For a critical view of the attitude of Germany's neighbors and their public and publicized opinion on German unification, cp. Ines Lehman, *Die deutsche Vereinigung von aussen gesehen: Angst, Becknkeu, und Erwartungen in der ausländischen Presse*, 2 vols. (Berlin, Bern, and New York, 1996–97).

2. Fisher, *After the Wall*, 13. Cp. also Joseph Greenblum, "A Pilgrimage to Germany," *Judaism* 44 (Fall 1995): 478–84.

3. Even before the breakdown of the Berlin Wall, Ambassador Vernon Walters recommended reunification of Germany in peace and free elections. Associated Press, Sept. 3, 1989. See Walters's recollections, *The Unification Was Predictable* (New York, 1992).

4. Arthur M. Hanhardt Jr., "Die deutsche Vereinigung im Spiegelbild der amerikanischen veröffentlichten Meinung," in *Die USA und die Deutsche Frage, 1945–1990*, edited by Wolfgang Uwe Friedrich (Frankfurt, 1991), 407–17. See also Friedrich's introduction, p. 38. Wolfgang Hanrieder's article, "Vom Doppelcontainment zum Umbruch in Europa," appeared in the same volume, pp. 231–58.

5. Teltschik, *329 Tage*, 34–35, 150. See also the documentation of the Shamir-Kohl controversy after Shamir's PBS interview of Nov. 15, 1958, in *Die Welt*, Feb. 1, 1990: Kohl to Shamir, Dec. 1, 1989, and Shamir to Kohl, Dec. 10, 1989.

6. AJC, Statement on German Unification, May 17, 1990, Blaustein Library. Some of the AJC spokesmen, such as Rabbi Marc Tanenbaum, found it "appalling that Jews who seek democracy and freedom for themselves would deny it to East Germans." *Jewish Week* (New York), Feb. 2, 1990, Blaustein Library. On the other hand, Sander L. Gilman, who was in both West and East Berlin in December 1989 after the collapse of the Berlin Wall, voiced his fear of the implications of German unification as a Jew

and an intellectual. In particular he was concerned about the revival of right-wing forces. See his "German Reunification and the Jews," a revised response to the AJC Colloquium on German Reunification, Mar. 7, 1990. *New German Critique* 52 (Winter 1991): 173–91.

7. Seymour D. Reich, "Coming to Terms with a United Germany," *Jewish Monthly* 104 (June–July 1990): 2; German Unification: A Fact Sheet, prepared by Warren Eisenberg, Apr. 12, 1990, BBA, Germany file. Kohl thanked Reich, who also happened to serve as chairman of the Presidents Conference, for his "encouraging words" with regard to future relations between a united Germany and Israel and the Jewish people. Kohl to Reich, Apr. 26, 1990, BBA, Germany file.

8. Abraham H. Foxman, "Why I Cannot Celebrate the Reunification," *ADL News*, Sept. 27, 1990, Blaustein Library, Germany file.

9. Deputy chief of German mission Karl Theodor Paschke addressing an ADL national leadership conference, ADL News, Mar. 19, 1990, ADL Archives.

10. In September 1990 I interviewed Rabbi Alexander Schindler, WJC secretary general Israel Singer, AJ Congress executive director Henry Siegman and also talked to representatives of the JLC and the Simon Wiesenthal Center in New York. *DAVAR* (Tel Aviv), Sept. 29, 1990.

11. Ibid.

12. E.g., James Baker III to Foxman, May 30, 1990, ADL Archives, ADL FC Germany.

13. Cp. chap. 17.

14. Michal Y. Bodemann, "Federal Republic of Germany," in *AJYB*, 1992, vol. 92, pp. 360–62. Edgar Bronfman quoted in *Davar* poll (Amir Neuman), Mar. 2, 1990; Kalman Sultanik, "A Statement on German Unification," *Midstream* 36 (Apr. 1990): 14–15; Reunited Germany Concerns Leaders, Insider, Dec. 1, 1990, BBA.

15. Foxman to Secretary of State James Baker, Aug. 29, 1990, and R. G. H. Seitz to Foxman, Sept. 28, 1990, ADL Archives, ADL FC Germany.

16. E.g., controversy between Kohl and Rabbi Marvin Hier, head of the Wiesenthal Center, *NYT*, Mar. 2, 1990; Rabbi Abraham Cooper, associate dean of the Wiesenthal Center, "For the New Germany, Memory of the Past Must Be Part of Its Future," *New York Post*, Oct. 2, 1990; J. J. Goldberg, "For Jews, Events in Germany Rekindle Dark Memories," *Jewish Week*, Nov. 17, 1989. Henry Siegman reiterated his viewpoint at a conference on American-German relations sponsored by the Armonk Institute and the Atlantik-Brücke, Feb. 1991, New York.

17. Rabbi Simcha Freedman, quoted in *Miami Jewish Tribune*, Feb. 23, 1990. Quite naturally, right-wing extremist Rabbi Meir Kahane opposed any contacts with Germany, "the Amalek of our times"; "Halachic Overview—Germany," *Jewish Press*, Oct. 12, 1990.

18. Elie Wiesel, "I Fear What Lies Beyond the Wall," *NYT*, Nov. 17, 1989; "Germans and Jews: An Interview with Elie Wiesel and Sidney Zion," *Dimensions* 5, no. 2 (1990): 20–22.

19. "The Writers' Call to Conscience," *Washington Post*, Feb. 12, 1990.

20. A. M. Rosenthal, *NYT*, Feb. 4, 1990; also "Sins of the Fathers," a letter to young Germans, *NYT*, Mar. 11, 1990.

21. Michael Lerner, "'No' to German Reunification," *Tikkun* 5 (Mar.–Apr. 1990): 6, 121–22; responding to comments, *Tikkun* 5 (July–Aug. 1990).

22. Alan M. Dershowitz, *Chutzpah* (Boston, 1991), 137–38.

23. Michael Wyschogrod, "Two Germanys Into One," *Hadassah Magazine* 71 (May 1990): 14–15.

24. Charles S. Maier, "Reflections on the Day of Germany Unity," in Friedrich, *Die USA und die Deutsche Frage*, 443–47. For Maier's thought on the Holocaust, see his *The Unmasterable Past: History, Holocaust and National Identity* (Cambridge, Mass., 1988).

25. *Jewish Monthly* 104 (May 1990): 17–20, 51.

26. Dan Diner, *Der Krieg der Erinnerungen und die Ordnung der Welt* (Berlin, 1991). See also his important historical essay, *Verkehrte Welten: Antiamerikanismus in Deutschland: Ein historischer Essay* (Frankfurt, 1993), esp. pp. 155–59. The English translation of that essay appeared in 1996: *America in the Eyes of the Germans: An Essay on Anti-Americanism* (Princeton, 1996).

27. Kent Schiner and Daniel Mariaschin, meeting with German ambassador Jürgen Ruhfus, July 15, 1991, Washington, D.C., note for file July 16, 1991, BBA; Rudolf Seiters to Schiner, Aug. 6, 1991, ibid.; Wolf Calebow, Letter to the Editor, *Commentary* 92 (Sept. 1991): 9–10. Calebow, who together with Trosten had been involved in promoting closer relations between the AJC and the Federal Republic, responded to a critical article on Germany's contribution to the development of Iraq's weaponry that had been published in *Commentary* several months earlier: Michael Ledeen, "Iraq's German connection," *Commentary* 91 (Apr. 1991): 27–30. Most prominent among Jewish opponents of the Gulf War was the International Jewish Peace Union, which was supported by a number of noted left-wing intellectuals. However, *Tikkun* editor Michael Lerner condemned Iraqi aggression and endorsed the American lead in confronting the aggressor in the framework of the UN. *Tikkun* 5 (Sept.–Oct. 1990): 7, 93–94.

28. E.g., Andrei S. Markovits's response to comments during the Gulf War, "Die Linke gibt es nicht—und es gibt sie doch," *Frankfurter Rundschau*, Mar. 7, 1991. In the mid-1980s Markovits had dealt with anti-Americanism in the German Left in an article, "On Anti-Americanism in West Germany," *New German Critique* 34 (Winter 1985): 3–27. In 1992 he again reviewed the debate between pacifists and the so-called bellicists in the German Left, *Frankfurter Rundschau*, Jan. 17, 1992. See also Detlev Claussen, "War of Words: An Intellectual Damage Assessment after the Gulf War," *New German Critique* 57 (Fall 1992): 67–85. Markovits returned to deal with the internal German discussion on that nation's role in the Gulf War and in the Yugoslavia conflict in a recent volume he co-authored with Simon Reich: *The German Predicament: Memory and Power in the New Europe* (Ithaca, N.Y. and London, 1997).

29. Cp. Murray Gordon, "Racism and Antisemitism in Germany: Old Problem, New Threat," *Congress Monthly* 60 (Mar.–Apr. 1993): 3–7. For 1993 see *Antisemitism: World Report 1994* (London, 1994), 38. See also Werner Bergmann, "Xenophobia and Antisemitism after the Unification of Germany," *Patterns of Prejudice* 28, no. 1 (1994): 67–80.

30. Memorandum from Rabbi Andrew Baker, Robert Goldmann, and Warren Eisenberg to Jewish community organizations, Dec. 14, 1992, AJC Records, AJC,

DHX 1988–94, box 2; Adina Voges, "Die Skepsis bleibt, trotz langer Debatte," AJC trifft Zentralratsvertreter zu Meinungsaustausch. *AJW*, Feb. 18, 1993.

31. The agreement was signed in Bonn in October 1992. For the anti-boycott measures, see Ambassador Jürgen Ruhfus to Kent Schiner, July 30, 1992, BBA.

32. AJC, David Jodice, *United Germany and Jewish Concerns* (New York, 1991); Jennifer Golub, *German Attitudes Toward Jews: What Recent Survey Data Reveal* (New York, 1991); Jennifer Golub, *German Attitudes Toward Jews and Other Minorities* (New York, 1994). Professor Ludwig Ehrlich of the Continental District of B'nai B'rith regarded the negative findings of the study as exaggerated, since for many years antisemitism in Germany did not exceed 16 percent of the population. Statement to the Catholic News Agency, Basel, Mar. 10, 1994. Cp. also Rainer Erb, "Jews and Other Minorities in Germany since the 1990s," *Patterns of Prejudice* 27, no. 2 (1993): 13–19.

33. Ignatz Bubis at the Israel-German Society, Apr. 6, 1994, Tel Aviv. Cp. Wolfgang Benz, "Ein Tabu weicht der Schamlosigkeit. In Deutschland zeigt sich immer unge-hemmter der Antisemitismus," *AJW*, Dec. 24–31, 1992. In this context, see also Frank Stern's pessimistic analysis *German Unification and the Question of Antisemitism* (New York, 1993) and the replies of his critics. For an earlier statement of his views, see Frank Stern, "The 'Jewish Question' in the 'German Question': Reflections in the Light of November 9, 1989," *New German Critique* 52 (Winter 1991, Special Issue on German Unification). Professor Michael Wolffsohn, the Israel-born German Jewish historian and political scientist, presented himself as an outspoken defender of Germany, arguing that neither Jews nor the world in general have any reason to fear a united, democratic Germany. See his volume *Keine Angst vor Deutschland!* (Erlangen, 1990).

34. E.g., Michael Stürmer, *Die Grenzen der Macht: Begegnung der Deutschen mit der Geschichte* (Berlin, 1990); Hans-Peter Schwarz, *Die Zentralmacht Europas: Deutschlands Rückkehr auf die Weltbühne* (Berlin, 1994); Christian Hacke, *Weltmacht wider Willen: Die Aussenpolitik der Bundesrepublik Deutschland* (Berlin, 1993); Gregor Schöllgen, *Angst vor der Macht: Die Deutschen und ihre Aussenpolitik* (Berlin, 1993). Israeli historian Omer Bartov, in his review of a volume edited by Peter Baldwin, *Reworking the Past, the Holocaust, and the Historians' Debate* (Boston, 1990), expressed his concern about possible negative repercussions of the Historians' Debate after the reunification of Germany. See his review essay, "Time Present and Time Past: The Historikerstreit and German Reunification," *New German Critique* 55 (Winter 1992): 173–90.

35. E.g., Rainer Zitelmann, *Wohin treibt unsere Republik* (Berlin, 1995). See also his earlier publications: *Hitler: Selbstverständnis eines Revolutionärs* (Stuttgart, 1987); *Adolf Hitler, Eine politische Biographie* (Göttingen, 1989); and the volume he edited together with Uwe Backes and Eckhard Jesse, *Die Schatten der Vergangenheit: Impulse zur Historisierung des Nationalsozialismus* (Frankfurt and Berlin, 1990). The main mouth-pieces of the German "New Right" are *Junge Freiheit* and *Criticon*, but a great many of their spokesmen also contribute to respectable conservative publications such as the *FAZ* and *Die Welt*. For Nolte's efforts to gain a more "objective" appraisal of National Socialism, see his *Streitpunkte: Heutige und Künftige Kontroversen um den Nationalsozialismus* (Berlin and Frankfurt, 1993) and Jürgen Kocka's review "Durch und durch brüchig," *Die Zeit*, Nov. 12, 1993, p. 15. Representative of "New Rightist" thought are a number of contributions to a volume edited by Heimo Schwilk and Ulrich

Schacht, *Die selbstbewusste Nation: "Anschwellender Bocksgesang" und weitere Beiträge zu einer deutschen Debatte* (Frankfurt, 1994). See also Richard Evans's review article, "Prisoners of the German Past," *Patterns of Prejudice* 30, no. 1 (1996): 73–81; Jacob Heilbrunn, "Germany's New Right," *Foreign Affairs* 75, no. 6 (1996): 80–98, and the responses to him: "Mr. Heilbrunn's Planet," *Foreign Affairs* 76, no. 2 (1997): 152–61.

36. Golub, *Current German Attitudes Toward Jews and Other Minorities*, 3. The 1994 poll confirmed the same trend, which was already revealed by the 1990 poll. Jodice, *United Germany and Jewish Concerns*, 3–4.

37. Arnulf Baring, *Deutschland, was nun? Ein Gespräch mit Dirk Rumberg und Wolf Jobst Siedler* (Berlin, 1991), quoted in Klaus Wippermann, "Befreiung vom 'eiternden Stachel der Reue und des Schuldgefühls'," *AJW*, Jan. 28, 1993. Baring, who after 1969 supported the social-liberal coalition in Bonn, turned neoconservative in the latter 1980s. Again, as in 1986, Jürgen Habermas was in the forefront of those who opposed putting aside the memory of the Holocaust because of the immediate confrontation with the vanquished Communist regime in the former GDR. See his essay "Die Last der doppelten Vergangenheit," *Die Zeit*, May 13, 1994, p. 54. See also Horst-Eberhard Richter, "Kein Verbrechen des SED-Regimes darf Auschwitz relativieren," *AJW*, Feb. 6, 1992.

38. The most detailed account is Edward T. Linenthal's account, *Preserving Memory: The Struggle to Create America's Holocaust Museum* (New York, 1995). For the development of the project under the Carter and Reagan administrations see Judith Miller, *One, by One, by One*, 220ff., mainly pp. 254–64, and her article "Holocaust Museum: A Troubled Start," *NYT Magazine*, Apr. 22, 1990. Henry Kissinger feared that the Holocaust museum in Washington would constitute too high a profile for American Jews and preferred building a museum in New York.

39. Marc Fisher, "Germany's Holocaust Fears: Museum Offered Millions to Update Image," *Washington Post*, Mar. 30, 1993.

40. Ibid.; also Judith Miller, "Holocaust Museum: A Troubled Start."

41. One of the permanent critics of Jewish treatment of the memory of the Holocaust and the building of Holocaust museums was Günther Gillessen, a senior correspondent of the *FAZ*. See, for instance, his articles "Bedenkliche Art der Erinnerung," Aug. 4, 1992, and "Mit Gedenkstätten ist es nicht getan," July 18, 1994, both in the *FAZ*. At the AJC-Atlantik-Brücke conference in March 1994 in Jerusalem, he stated that for him the Shoah was a closed chapter; future generations of Germans should not be troubled by feelings of shame; and photos showing the suffering of the victims should be made taboo. Jews in Israel and the Diaspora should look for other substitutes for their national identity instead of the Shoah that happened fifty years ago. Michael Wolffsohn, another committed opponent of the Holocaust Museum in Washington, argued that commemorating the past by photos and exhibits contradicted Jewish religious tradition. See Michael Wolffsohn, "Eine Amputation des Judentums? Einige kritische Fragen zur Washington Holocaust-Gedenkstätte," *FAZ*, Apr. 15, 1993. The quotes from Howard Friedman are from his Alois Mertes Memorial Lecture, Bonn, Oct. 29, 1991, AJC Archives, New York.

42. E.g., in 1991–92 Chancellor Kohl met three times with leading members of the AJC, in March 1991 and February 1992 in Bonn and in June 1992 in New York. ADL

leaders were received by him in January 1993 in Bonn. On November 2, 1991, they met President Richard Weizsäcker, who later discussed the subject of "Learning and Tolerance" at the Second B'nai B'rith Lecture held at Georgetown University on May 23, 1993. Henry Marx, "Helmut Kohl bei jüdischen Vertretern in New York," *AJW,* June 18, 1992; AJC, Office of European Affairs, leadership delegation meeting with Kohl, June 8, 1992; ADL News, June 13, 1993, ADL Archives, ADL FC Germany; "Weizsäcker vor dem B'nai B'rith International in Washington," *AJW,* May 27, 1993. An AJC leadership visit to Germany in February 1995 included visits with Chancellor Kohl and President Herzog.

43. For instance, the conference held in January 1993 in New York devoted much time to xenophobia and antisemitism; the conference held in March 1994 in Jerusalem centered on current issues in German-Israeli relations and the meaning of the Holocaust fifty years later. AJC summaries of the conference in New York, Jan. 17–19, 1993, and in Jerusalem, Mar. 9–12, 1994. See also Josef Joffe, "Alte Besorgnisse, ganz gegenwärtig," *Süddeutsche Zeitung,* Feb. 9, 1993.

44. In July 1994 the AJC executive committee endorsed Germany's candidacy for a permanent seat at the UN Security Council. AJC news release, July 5, 1994.

45. Leslie Goodman, "The First Jewish Delegation to United Germany Explores the Future of German-Jewish Relations," *Jewish Monthly* 105 (Feb. 1991): 20–21, and Reva Price, "Building Bridges," *Jewish Monthly* 106 (Feb. 1992): 17–18; B'nai B'rith News, Mar. 4, 1993 (the mission led by President Kent Schiner visited Germany Mar. 16–21, 1993); ADL mission to Germany, report on Melvin Salberg and Robert Goldmann visit to Bonn, Nov. 5–7, 1991, ADL Archives, ADL FC Germany. See also Report on B'nai B'rith Mission to Germany, Feb. 7–12, 1993, BBA, Germany file.

46. *AJW,* Oct. 28, 1993.

47. For the German Jewish community's post-unification policies see Ignatz Bubis, *Ich bin ein deutscher Staatsbürger jüdischen Glaubens* (Cologne, 1993); also John Rodden, "Ignatz Bubis: An Interview," *Jewish Spectator* 61 (Fall 1996): 21–27. Micha Guttmann, the former executive director of the Central Council, presented a concise summary in an essay, "Macht oder Ohnmacht: Jüdische Politik in Deutschland," *Tribüne* 34 (Sept. 1995): 174–82. For the recent German Jewish cultural developments see Sander L. Gilman and Karen Remmler, eds., *Reemerging Jewish Culture in Germany: Life and Literature Since 1989* (New York, 1994).

48. *WJC Report* 17 (Mar.–Apr. 1993): 1–2. Bubis to ADL leadership mission to Germany in Jan. 1993, quoted in Salberg and Foxman, Chairman's Report on Jan. 1993 Mission to Germany, ADL Archives, ADL FC Germany. See also Warren Eisenberg, Report from Germany: Berlin in the Fall of 1992, BBA, Germany file. On the Central Council's visit to the United States, see "Viele besorgte Fragen beantwortet: Zentralrat Vertreter in USA," *AJW,* Jan. 28, 1993.

49. Cp. chap. 11.

50. Statement by the New York Board of Rabbis Study Commission to Germany, Summer 1994, "A Rabbinic Odyssey to Germany," by Rabbi Daniel Z. Kramer, UJA Rabbinic Cabinet, July 1994.

51. Ismar Schorsch, "To Remember Is Not Enough," *Sh'ma,* Nov. 11, 1994, pp. 1–3.

52. Arthur Hertzberg, Gesher Symposium "Israel and World Jewry at the Cross-roads" (in Hebrew), *Gesher* 41 (Winter 1995–96): 38–42.

53. "Expressing the Inexpressible—Reactions to Steven Spielberg's 'Schindler's List,'" American International Center for German Studies, Humanities Seminar, a special compilation of German and American newspaper editorials and articles, Washington, D.C., May 5, 1994.

54. Jörg Bremer, "Noch nie hat Israel einen lebenden Staatsmann auf diese Weise geehrt," *FAZ*, June 9, 1995; Judith Hart, "Eine Visite ohne Fehl und Tadel," *AJW*, June 15, 1995.

55. The English text of Weizman's address was reprinted in *Congress Monthly* 63 (Mar.–Apr. 1996): 3–5.

CHAPTER 19

1. According to the *1997 Annual Survey of American Jewish Opinion*, 35 percent of American Jews have an unfavorable opinion of Germany, 4 percent a very favorable opinion, and 25 percent a somewhat favorable opinion. However, a substantial majority of American Jews believe that Germany is making a sincere effort to come to grips with the Holocaust (*1997 Annual Survey of American Jewish Opinion*, AJC, New York, May 1997), pp. 24, 36, 75.

2. Helmut Schmidt's "Keine Angst vor den Japanern," *Die Zeit*, Nov. 16, 1984, pp. 9–10.

3. Jonathan D. Sarna, "The American Jewish Community's Crisis of Confidence," in *Policy Forum* 10 (1996) (Institute of the World Jewish Congress, Jerusalem), 7–17. Cp. also Seymour Martin Lipset and Earl Raab, *Jews and the New American Scene* (Cambridge, Mass., 1995), especially pp. 198–207.

4. For American-German relations in the mid-1990s, see Beate Lindemann, ed., *Amerika in uns: Deutsche-Amerikanische Erfahrungen und Visionen* (Mainz, 1994). It includes contributions in English by Steven Muller, "Europe with Germany as Its Vital Center," 45–55, and Paul Nitze, "Reworking the German-American Partnership," 65–85. See also *Der Spiegel Dokument* 4 (1994), *An vorderster Front: Das neue deutsch-amerikanische Verhältnis*, and Werner Weidenfeld's essay, "Wir brauchen die Transatlantische Gemeinschaft: Plädoyer für eine neue Grundlage der europäisch-amerikanischen Zusammenarbeit," *FAZ*, May 9, 1995. For a more critical view cp. Gerald R. Kleinfeld, "The Fragile German-American Community of Shared Values," *German Comments* 14 (Oct. 1996): 21–32. On postunification Germany, see "Germany in Transition," *Daedalus* 123 (Winter 1994).

5. E.g., Matthias Geis, Dossier, "Verschanzen oder Aufklären," *Die Zeit*, Dec. 19, 1997, pp. 9–11.

6. E.g., speech of President Roman Herzog, *FAZ*, May 9, 1995; statement of Chancellor Helmut Kohl, *Süddeutsche Zeitung*, May 6–7, 1995; Wolfgang Schäuble, head of the CDU/CSU parliamentary group, "Trauma und Chance," ibid. May 4, 1995.

7. E.g., Volker Ullrich, "Goldhagen und die Deutschen," *Die Zeit*, Sept. 13, 1996, p. 2.

8. See chap. 8.

BIBLIOGRAPHY

Unpublished Sources/Archival Material

Dean Acheson Papers, HSTL, Independence, Mo.
Jakob Altmaier Papers, AdsD, Friedrich-Ebert-Stiftung (FES), Bonn
American Council for Judaism Papers, AJA, Cincinnati, partial
American Jewish Committee Records, YIVO, New York, and AJC, New York
American Jewish Conference Collection, CZA, Jerusalem
American Jewish Conference Papers, AJHSA, Waltham, Mass., partial
American Jewish Congress Papers, AJHSA, Waltham, Mass.
American Jewish Joint Distribution Committee Archives, New York
Anti-Defamation League of B'nai B'rith, Foreign Correspondence Files, ADL
    Archives and Resource Center, New York
Bernard M. Baruch Papers, Princeton University, Princeton, N.J.
David Ben-Gurion, Diaries and Correspondence, Kiryat Sdeh Boker
Herbert Blankenhorn Papers, BA, Koblenz
Franz Blücher Papers, BA, Koblenz
B'nai B'rith Archives, Washington, D.C.
B'nai B'rith District Grand Lodge #2 Collection, AJA, Cincinnati
Franz Böhm Papers, ACDP, Konrad-Adenauer-Stiftung, St. Augustin
Willy Brandt Depositum, AdsD, FES, Bonn
Heinrich von Brentano Papers, BA, Koblenz
Bundeskanzleramt Records, BA, Koblenz
Collection Büro für Friedensfragen, BA, Koblenz
Emanuel Celler Papers, LC, Washington, D.C.
Central Conference of American Rabbis Records, AJA, Cincinnati

Cincinnati Jewish Community Relations Committee/Council Papers, AJA, Cincinnati
Benjamin V. Cohen Papers, LC, Washington, D.C.
James Bryant Conant Papers, Harvard University Archives, Cambridge, Mass.
Oscar Cox Papers, FDRL, Hyde Park, N.Y.
Abraham Cronbach Papers, AJA, Cincinnati
Thomas Dehler Papers, Archiv des Deutschen Liberalismus, Friedrich-Naumann-
    Stiftung, Gummersbach
U.S. Department of State, Record Group 59, Decimal Files, United States National
    Archives, Diplomatic Branch; Records of the Policy Planning Staff 1947–1953.
    Washington, D.C.
Jacob Diel Papers, ACDP, KAS, St. Augustin
John Foster Dulles Papers, Princeton University, Princeton, N.J.
Felix von Eckardt Papers, ACDP, KAS, St. Augustin
Ludwig Erhard Papers, Ludwig-Erhard-Stiftung, Bonn
Fritz Erler Papers, AdsD, FES, Bonn
Georg Federer, Tagebuchaufzeichnungen, IfZ, Munich
Solomon Andhil Fineberg Papers, AJA, Cincinnati
Felix Frankfurter Papers, LC, Washington, D.C.
Manfred George Papers, Deutsches Literatur-Archiv, Marbach
Nahum Goldmann Archive, CZA, Jerusalem
Israel Goldstein Papers, CZA, Jerusalem
Kurt R. Grossmann Papers, LBI, New York
Friedrich (Fritz) Heine Papers, AdsD, FES, Bonn
Daniel J. Heineman Correspondence (Copy of the James Heineman Collection, New
    York), Stiftung Bundeskanzler-Adenauer-Haus, Rhöndorf
Werner Otto von Hentig Papers, IfZ, Munich
Theodor Heuss Papers, BA, Koblenz
Max Horkheimer Papers, Municipal and University Library, Frankfurt
Israel Foreign Ministry Records, ISA, Jerusalem
Jewish Labor Bund Archives, YIVO, New York
Jewish Labor Committee Collection, Robert Wagner Labor Archives, New York
Jewish War Veterans Archives, Washington, D.C.
Horace M. Kallen Papers, YIVO, New York
Harry M. Kilgore Papers, FDRL, Hyde Park, N.Y.
Julius Klein Papers, JWVA, Washington, D.C.
Heinz L. Krekeler Papers, IfZ, Munich
Herbert H. Lehman Papers, Columbia University, New York
Senator Joachim Lipschitz, Files relating to his visit to the U.S., Landesarchiv, Berlin
Hubertus Prinz zu Loewenstein Papers, IfZ, Munich
Max Lowenthal Papers, Wilson Library, University of Minnesota, Minneapolis
Isador Lubin Papers, FDRL, Hyde Park, N.Y.
John J. McCloy Papers, Amherst College, Amherst, Mass.
Records of the U.S. High Commissioner for Germany, John J. McCloy, Washington
    National Record Center, Suitland, Md.

Henry Morgenthau Jr. Diaries, Presidential Diaries and other papers, FDRL, Hyde Park, N.Y.

National Jewish Community Relations Advisory Council Papers, Waltham, Mass.

David K. Niles Papers, HSTL, Independence, Mo.

Erich Ollenhauer Collection, AdsD, FES, Bonn.

OMGUS Papers (the author used MF 260 microcopy at the IfZ, Munich)

Politisches Archiv des Auswärtigen Amtes, Bonn. Depts. II, III, VII; Files of the Foreign Minister and the State Secretary

Hermann Pünder Papers, BA, Koblenz

Anna Eleanor Roosevelt Papers, FDRL, Hyde Park, N.Y.

Ludwig Rosenberg Papers, AdsD, FES, Bonn

Harry N. Rosenfield Papers, HSTL, Independence, Mo.

Samuel I. Rosenman Papers, FDRL, Hyde Park, N.Y.

Samuel I. Rosenman Papers, HSTL, Independence, Mo.

Fritz Schäffer Papers, BA, Koblenz

Carlo Schmid Papers, AdsD, FES, Bonn

Helmut Schmidt Depositum, AdsD, FES, Bonn

Kurt Schumacher Collection, AdsD, FES, Bonn

SED Central Archive, Stiftung Archiv der politischen Parteien und Massenorganisa-tionen im Bundesarchiv, Berlin

Lou H. Silberman Papers, AJA, Cincinnati

Abba Hillel Silver Papers, The Temple, Cleveland

SPD (Social Democratic Party of Germany), Protocols of the parliamentary group, protocols of the party leadership, AdsD, FES, Bonn

Henry L. Stimson Diaries, Yale University, New Haven, Conn.

Harry S. Truman Papers: White House Central Files, Official Files, President's Secretary's Files, Confidential Files, Post-Presidential Papers, Independence, Mo.

James Warburg Papers, JFKL, Boston

Bruno Weil Papers, LBI, New York

Lewis H. Weinstein Papers, AJHSA, Waltham, Mass.

Stephen S. Wise Papers, AJHSA, Waltham, Mass.

Joel Wolfsohn Papers, HSTL, Independence, Mo.

World Jewish Congress Collection, AJA, Cincinnati

World Jewish Congress British Section Collection, CZA, Jerusalem

World Union for Progressive Judaism Records, AJA, Cincinnati

PRINTED SOURCES (DOCUMENTS, MEMOIRS, CORRESPONDENCE, ETC.)

Adenauer, Konrad. *Briefe*, 1945–1947, 1947–1949, 1949–1951, 1951–1953. Edited by Hans Peter Mensing. Berlin, 1983–1987.

———. *Erinnerungen*. 4 vols. Stuttgart, 1965–1968.

———. *Reden, 1917–1967*. Eine Auswahl. Edited by Hans-Peter Schwarz. Stuttgart, 1975.

———. *Teegespräche*, 1950–1954, 1955–1958, 1959–1961, 1961–1963. Vols. 1–3 edited by Hanns Jürgen Küsters; vol. 4 edited by Hans Peter Mensing. Berlin, 1984–1992.

Adenauer-Heuss. Unter Vier Augen. Gespräche aus den Gründerjahren 1949–1959. Edited by Hans Peter Mensing, Berlin, 1997.

Akten zur Auswärtigen Politik der Bundesrepublik Deutschland. Adenauer und die Hohen Kommissare. Vol. 1: 1949–1951; vol. 2: 1952. Edited by Hans-Peter Schwarz et al. Munich, 1989, 1990. 3 vols.: 1963; 2 vols.: 1964; 3 vols.: 1965; 2 vols.: 1966. Edited by Rainer A. Blasius et al. Munich, 1994–1997.

Akten zur Vorgeschichte der Bundesrepublik Deutschland, 1945–1949. 5 vols. Munich, 1976–1983.

Allensbacher Jahrbuch der Demoskopie (Jahrbuch der öffentlichen Meinung), 1947–1992. 9 vols. Edited by Elisabeth Noelle Neumann et al. Munich, New York, London, and Paris (previously Allensbach and Bonn), 1956–1993.

Archives of the Holocaust. An International Collection of Selected Documents. Vols. 1–22. New York and London, 1990–1993.

Arendt, Hannah. *Eichmann in Jerusalem: A Report on the Banality of Evil.* New York, 1963.

Arendt, Hannah, and Karl Jaspers. *Hannah Arendt/Karl Jaspers Correspondence, 1926–1969.* New York, 1992.

Baker, James A. *The Politics of Diplomacy: Revolution, War, and Peace, 1989–1992.* New York, 1995.

Baring, Arnulf, ed. *Sehr geehrter Herr Bundeskanzler!: Heinrich von Brentano im Briefwechsel mit Kanzler Konrad Adenauer, 1949–1964.* Hamburg, 1974.

Baruch, Bernard M. *Baruch: The Public Years.* New York, 1960.

David Ben-Gurion and Chancellor Adenauer at the Waldorf Astoria, March 14, 1960 (Document). Introduced by Zaki Shalom, *Israel Studies,* vol. 2 (Spring 1997).

Ben-Natan, Asher. *Briefe an den Botschafter.* Berlin, 1973.

Birrenbach, Kurt. *Meine Sondermissionen. Rückblick auf zwei Jahrzehnte bundesdeutscher Aussenpolitik.* Düsseldorf, 1984.

Bisgyer, Maurice. *Challenge and Encounter: Behind the Scenes in the Struggle for Jewish Survival.* New York, 1967.

Blankenhorn, Herbert. *Verständnis und Verständigung: Blätter eines politischen Tagebuchs von 1949 bis 1973.* Frankfurt, 1980.

Blum, John Morton. *From the Morgenthau Diaries.* 3 vols. Boston, 1967.

———. *Roosevelt and Morgenthau: A Review and Condensation of "From the Morgenthau Diaries."* Boston, 1970.

Blumenson, Martin. *The Patton Papers.* Boston, 1974.

Brandt, Willy. *Deutschland, Israel, und die Juden.* Berlin, 1961.

———. *Erinnerungen.* Frankfurt, 1989.

———. *In Exile: Essays, Reflections, and Letters.* London, 1971.

Bronfman, Edgar. *The Making of a Jew.* New York, 1996.

Bubis, Ignatz. *Ich bin ein deutscher Staatsbürger jüdischen Glaubens.* Cologne, 1993.

Buchstab, Günter, ed. *Adenauer: "Es musste alles neu gemacht werden." Die Protokolle des CDU—Bundesvorstands, 1950–1953.* Stuttgart, 1986.

Bulletin des Presse–und Informationsamtes der Bundesregierung, Bonn.

Carstens, Karl. *Erinnerungen und Erfahrungen.* Boppard, 1993.

Cohen, Michael, ed. *The Letters and Papers of Chaim Weizmann.* Vol. 21, series A. Jerusalem, 1979.

Dubinsky, David, and A. H. Raskin. *David Dubinsky: A Life with Labor.* New York, 1977.

DuBois, Josiah E., Jr. *The Devil's Chemists: Twenty-four Conspirators of the International Farben Cartel Who Manufacture Wars.* Boston, 1952.

Eban, Abba. *An Autobiography.* Tel Aviv, 1977.

Eckardt, Felix von. *Ein unordentliches Leben: Lebenserinnerungen.* Düsseldorf, 1967.

Eisendrath, Maurice. *Can Faith Survive? The Thought and Afterthoughts of an American Rabbi.* New York, 1964.

Eisenhower, John S. D., ed. *Dwight D. Eisenhower: Letters to Mamie.* Garden City, N.Y., 1978.

Ferencz, Benjamin B. *Less than Slaves: Jewish Forced Labor and the Quest for Compensation.* Cambridge, Mass., 1979.

From the Diaries of Felix Frankfurter. Edited by Joseph P. Lash. New York, 1974.

Gallup, George H. *The Gallup Poll: Public Opinion, 1935–1971.* Vol. 1: 1935–1948; vol. 2: 1949–1958; vol. 3: 1959–1971. New York, 1972.

Genscher, Hans-Dietrich. *Erinnerungen.* Berlin, 1995.

Goldmann, Nahum. *The Autobiography of Nahum Goldmann: Sixty Years of Jewish Life.* New York, 1969.

———. *Mein Leben als deutscher Jude.* Munich, 1980.

———. *Mein Leben: USA-Europa-Israel.* Munich, 1981.

Goldstein, Israel. *My World as a Jew: The Memoirs of Israel Goldstein.* New York, 1984.

Greenwald, G. Jonathan. *Berlin Witness: An American Diplomat's Chronicle of East Germany's Revolution.* University Park, Md., 1993.

Grewe, Wilhelm G. *Rückblenden, 1976–1951: Aufzeichnungen eines Augenzeugen deutscher Aussenpolitik von Adenauer bis Schmidt.* Frankfurt, 1979.

Heuss, Theodor. *An und über Juden: Aus Schriften und Reden.* Düsseldorf, 1964.

Horowitz, David. *In the Heart of Events.* Jerusalem, 1980.

Hull, Cordell. *Memoirs.* 2 vols. New York, 1948.

Hyman, Abraham S. *The Undefeated.* Jerusalem, 1993.

Israel Foreign Office. *Documents Relating to the Agreements between the Government of Israel and the Government of the Federal Republic of Germany.* Jerusalem, 1953.

Israel State Archives, State of Israel. *Documents on the Foreign Policy of Israel.* Vols. 5–8: 1950, 1951, 1952, 1953. Jerusalem, 1988–1995.

Jelinek, Yeshayahu A., ed. *Zwischen Moral und Realpolitik. Deutsch-israelische Beziehungen, 1945–1965: Eine Dokumentensammlung.* Gerlingen, 1997.

Die Kabinettsprotokolle der Bundesregierung, 1949–1953. Edited by Hans Booms. Boppard, 1982–1989.

Kempner, Robert M. W. *Ankläger einer Epoche.* Frankfurt, 1986.

Kissinger, Henry. *The White House Years.* Boston, 1979.

———. *Years of Upheaval.* Boston, 1982.

Klutznick, Philip M., with Sidney Hyman. *Angles of Vision: A Memoir of My Lives.* Chicago, 1991.

Kubowitzki, A. Leon. *Unity in Dispersion: A History of the World Jewish Congress.* New York, 1948.

In Zentrum der Macht. *Das Tagebuch von Staatssekretär Lenz 1951–1953.* Edited by Klaus Gotto, Hans-Otto Kleinmann and Reinhard Schreiner. Düsseldorf, 1989.

Martin, James Stewart. *All Honorable Men.* Boston, 1950.

McGhee, George. *At the Creation of a New Germany. From Adenauer to Brandt: An Ambassador's Account.* New Haven, Conn., 1989.

Mende, Erich. *Von Wende zu Wende, 1962–1982.* Munich and Berlin, 1986.

Meroz, Yohanan. *In schwieriger Mission: Als Botschafter Israels in Bonn.* Frankfurt, 1986.

Michel, Ernest W. *Promises to Keep.* New York, 1993.

Morgenthau, Henry, Jr. *Germany Is Our Problem.* New York, 1945.

Murphy, Robert. *Diplomat Among Warriors.* Garden City, N.Y., 1964.

Osterheld, Horst. *Aussenpolitik unter Bundeskanzler Ludwig Erhard, 1963–1966: Ein dokumentarischer Bericht aus dem Kanzleramt.* Düsseldorf, 1993.

———. *"Ich gehe nicht leichten Herzens . . ." Adenauers letzte Kanzlerjahre: Ein dokumentarischer Bericht.* Mainz, 1984.

Padover, Saul K. *Experiment in Germany: The Story of an American Intelligence Officer.* New York, 1946.

Pearlman, Moshe. *Ben Gurion Looks Back.* London, 1965.

Peres, Shimon. *Kela David* (David's Sling), in Hebrew. Jerusalem, 1970.

Public Opinion in Occupied Germany: The OMGUS Surveys, 1945–1949. Edited by Anna J. Merritt and Richard L. Merritt. Urbana, Ill., 1970.

Public Opinion in Semi-sovereign Germany: The HICOG Surveys, 1949–1955. Urbana, Ill., 1980.

Riesser, Hans Eduard. *Von Versailles zur Uno: Aus der Erinnerung eines Diplomaten.* Bonn, 1962.

Robinson, Nehemiah. *Indemnification and Reparations: Jewish Aspects.* New York, 1944.

Schmidt, Helmut. *Weggefährten. Erinnerungen und Reflexionen.* Berlin, 1996.

Kurt Schumacher: Reden, Schriften, Korrespondenzen, 1945–1952. Edited by Willy Albrecht. Berlin, 1985.

Sharett, Moshe. *Yoman Ishi* (Personal Diary). 8 vols. (in Hebrew). Tel-Aviv, 1978.

Shinnar, Felix E. *Bericht eines Beauftragten: Die deutsch- israelischen Beziehungen, 1951–1966.* Tübingen, 1967.

Shultz, George. *Turmoil and Triumph.* New York, 1993.

Smith, Jean Edward, ed. *The Papers of General Lucius D. Clay: Germany, 1945–1949.* 2 vols. Bloomington, Ind., 1974.

Söllner, Alfons, ed. *Zur Archäologie der Demokratie in Deutschland.* 2 vols. Frankfurt, 1986.

Die SPD-Fraktion in Deutschen Bundestag. Sitzungsprotokolle, 1961–1966, edited by Heinrich Potthoff. *Sitzungsprotokolle, 1949–1953* and *1953–1957*, edited by Petra Weber. Düsseldorf, 1993, 1994.

Steinberg, Rafael. *Javits: The Autobiography of a Public Man.* Boston, 1982.

Stimson, Henry L. and McGeorge Bundy. *On Active Service in Peace and War.* New York, 1947.

Strauss, Franz Josef. *Erinnerungen.* Berlin, 1990.

Taylor, Telford. *The Anatomy of the Nuremberg Trials.* New York, 1992.

Teltschik, Horst. *329 Tage: Innenansichten der Einigung.* Berlin, 1991.

U.S. Department of State. *Foreign Relations of the United States: The Conference at Quebec, 1944.* Washington, D.C., 1972.

U.S. Department of State. *Foreign Relations of the United States, 1952–1954,* vol. 9. Washington, D.C., 1986.

U.S. Department of State, Office of Public Affairs. *Germany, 1947–1949: The Story in Documents.* Washington, D.C., 1950.

U.S. Senate, Committee on the Judiciary. *Morgenthau Diary* (Germany), 2 vols. Washington, D.C., 1967.

Verhandlungen des Deutschen Bundestages, 1949–. Bonn.

Vogel, Rolf, ed. *Der deutsch-israelische Dialog. Dokumentation eines erregenden Kapitels deutscher Aussenpolitik.* Vol. 1, 3 pts. Munich, 1987–1988.

———, ed. *Deutschlands Weg nach Israel: Eine Dokumentation.* Stuttgart, 1967.

Waldman, Morris. *Nor By Power.* New York, 1953.

Walters, Vernon. *The Unification Was Predictable.* New York, 1992.

Warburg, James P. *Germany: Key to Peace.* Cambridge, Mass., 1953.

———. *The Long Road Home: The Autobiography of a Maverick.* Garden City, N.Y., 1964.

Welles, Sumner. *The Time for Decision.* New York, 1944.

Wilson, Hugh R. *A Career Diplomat: The Third Chapter: The Third Reich.* Edited by Hugh R. Wilson, Jr. New York, 1960.

Wischnewski, Hans-Jürgen. *Mit Leidenschaft und Augenmass: In Mogadishu und anderswo.* Munich, 1989.

Wise, Stephen, S. *Challenging Years: The Autobiography of Stephen Wise.* New York, 1949.

ORAL HISTORY INTERVIEWS

Gershon Avner, Hebrew University, Institute for Contemporary Jewry, Oral History Division, Sept. 30, 1971

Bernard Bernstein, COHC, 1975

AJC, William E. Wiener Oral History Library, Remembering Jacob Blaustein, An Oral History Collection, 1971–1972, comprising oral history interviews. Among them, interviews with David Ben Gurion, 1972; Abba Eban, 1972; Nahum Goldmann, 1971; Saul Kagan, 1971; John J. McCloy, 1972; George C. McGhee, 1972; Rolf F. Pauls, 1972; John Slawson, 1972.

Benjamin B. Buttenwieser, COHC, 1975

Lucius D. Clay, COHC, 1971

William H. Draper, HSTL, 1972

Alexander Easterman, Hebrew University, Oral History Division, March 19, 1971

Theodor Ellenoff, AJC Oral History Collection, 1988

Myer Feldman, JFKL, oral history interview, July 29, 1967

Benjamin B. Ferencz, Hebrew University, Oral History Division, Apr. 1971

Nahum Goldmann, Hebrew University, Oral History Division, Nov. 14, 20, 1961

Abraham S. Hyman, Hebrew University, Oral History Division, n.d.

Saul Kagan, Hebrew University, Oral History Division, March 24, 1971

Herbert H. Lehman, COHC, 1961
Louis E. Levinthal, Hebrew University, Oral History Division, June 29, 1962
Isador Lubin, HSTL, 1974
James W. Riddleberger, HSTL, 1972
Seymour Rubin, Hebrew University, Oral History Division, March 29, 1971
Joseph Schwartz, Hebrew University, Oral History Division, Aug. 14, 1962
Eliezer Shinnar, Hebrew University, Oral History Division, Nov. 18, 1970
Note: The AJC Oral History Collection is now deposited at the New York Public
    Library, Jewish Division.

INTERVIEWS, WRITTEN AND ORAL, BY THE AUTHOR

Asher Ben-Nathan, Dec. 8, 1994, Tel Aviv
Alexander Böker, Aug. 25, 1989, Munich
Richard Cohen, June 6, 1988, New York
Benjamin Grey, May 25, 1988, Los Angeles
Ben Halpern, June 24, 1988, Brookline, Mass.
Friedrich (Fritz) Heine, June 30, 1984, Bad Münstereifel
Philip M. Klutznick, June 15, 1988, Chicago
Heinz L. Krekeler, Sept. 1, 1989, Bad Salzuflen
Henry Morgenthau III, Sept. 23, 1990, Cambridge, Mass.
Emanuel Muravchik, June 19, 1988, New York
Rolf F. Pauls, Aug. 30, 1989, Bonn
Gerhart Riegner, May 15, 1987, New York
Morris U. Schappes, May 28, 1988, New York
Alexander Schindler, Sept. 1990, New York, synopsis published in *Davar*, Sept. 29,
    1990
Henry Siegman, Sept. 1990, New York, synopsis published in *Davar*, Sept. 29, 1990
Israel Singer, Sept. 1990, New York, synopsis published in *Davar*, Sept. 29, 1990
Hans Steinitz, July 9, 1988, New York

NEWSPAPERS, PERIODICALS, AND YEARBOOKS

ADL Bulletin
Allgemeine Jüdische Wochenzeitung (preceded by *Allgemeine Wochenzeitung der Juden in
    Deutschland*)
American Jewish Archives
American Jewish History
American Jewish Year Book
Amerikastudien/American Studies
Annals of the American Academy of Political and Social Science
Atlantic Monthly
Aufbau
Aussenpolitik
Leo Baeck Institute Yearbook
CCAR (Central Conference of American Rabbis) *Yearbook*

Bibliography

Commentary

Committee Reporter

Congress Monthly (preceded by *Congress Bi-Weekly, Congress Weekly*)

Conservative Judaism

Contemporary Jewish Record

Deutschland–Berichte

Dimensions

Foreign Affairs

Forum

Forrerts

Frankfurter Allgemeine Zeitung

German Comments

German Studies Review

Hadassah Magazine

Harper's Magazine

Hazionut

Herzl Yearbook

Historische Zeitschrift

Holocaust and Genocide Studies

Israel Studies

Jahrbuch für Antisemitismusforschung

Jahrbuch zur Geschichte und Wirkung des Holocausts

Jewish Advocate

Jewish Currents

Jewish Forum

Jewish Frontier

Jewish Life

Jewish Monthly (preceded by *National Jewish Monthly*)

Jewish Observer

Jewish Social Studies

Jewish Spectator

Jewish Week

Journal of Contemporary History

Journal of Holocaust Education

Journal of Israeli History

Journal of Reform Judaism/Reform Judaism

JTA Daily News Bulletin

Judaism

Liberal Judaism

Menora, Jahrbuch für deutsch-jüdische Geschichte

Menorah Journal

Midstream

Modern Judaism (preceded by *Journal of Modern Judaism*)

Moment

Neue Gesellschaft/Frankfurter Hefte

Neues Deutschland
New German Critique
Newsweek
New York Review of Books
New York Times
Orthodox Jewish Life
Das Parlament (also *Aus Politik und Zeitgeschichte*)
Patterns of Prejudice
Present Tense
Rabbinical Assembly of America, Proceedings
Reconstructionist
Rheinischer Merkur/Christ und Welt
Sh'ma
Der Spiegel
Studies in Contemporary Judaism
Süddeutsche Zeitung
Survey of Jewish Affairs
Tikkun
Die Tribüne
Vierteljahrshefte für Zeitgeschichte
Vorwärts
Washington Post
Die Welt
Simon Wiesenthal Center Annual
Tel-Aviver Jahrbuch für deutsche Geschichte
WJC Report
Yad Vashem Studies
Yahadut Zemanenu
Yalkut Moreshet
Yiddisher Kempfer
YIVO Annual
Die Zeit
Zionist Quarterly
Note: I have used the American Yiddish daily press mainly according to the *Yiddish News Digest* published by the American Jewish Committee, deposited at the Blaustein Library.

BOOKS

Alteras, Isaac. *Eisenhower and Israel: The U.S.-Israeli Relations, 1953–1960.* Gainesville, Fla., 1993.

Ambrose, Stephen E. *Eisenhower.* 2 vols. New York, 1983.

Backer, John H. *The Winds of History: The German Years of Lucius DuBignon Clay.* New York, 1983.

Balabkins, Nicholas. *West German Reparations to Israel.* New Brunswick, N.J., 1971.

Baldwin, Peter, ed. *Reworking the Past, the Holocaust, and the Historians' Debate*. Boston, 1990.

Barkai, Avraham. *Branching Out: German-Jewish Immigration to the United States, 1820–1914*. New York, 1994.

Bar-Zohar, Michael. *Ben-Gurion: A Political Biography*. 3 vols. (in Hebrew). Tel-Aviv, 1975–1977.

Bauer, Yehuda. *American Jewry and the Holocaust: The American Jewish Joint Distribution Committee, 1939–1945*. Detroit, 1981.

———. *Flight and Rescue: Brichah*. New York, 1970.

———. *Jews for Sale: Nazi-Jewish Negotiations, 1933–1945*. New Haven and London, 1994.

———. *My Brother's Keeper: A History of the American Jewish Joint Distribution Committee*. Philadelphia, 1974.

———. *Out of the Ashes: The Impact of American Jews on Post-Holocaust European Jewry*. Oxford, 1989.

Bauer-Hack, Susanne. *Die jüdische Wochenzeitung Aufbau und die Wiedergutmachung*. Düsseldorf, 1994.

Benz, Wolfgang, ed. *Zwischen Antisemitismus und Philosemitismus in der Bundesrepublik*. Berlin, 1991.

Berenbaum, Michael. *After Tragedy and Triumph: Essays in Modern Jewish Thought and Experience*. Oxford, 1991.

Berger, Elmer. *The Jewish Dilemma*. New York, 1945.

Bergmann, Werner, and Rainer Erb, eds. *Antisemitismus in der politischen Kultur nach 1945*. Opladen, 1990.

Bergmann, Werner, Rainer Erb, and Albert Lichtblau, eds. *Schwieriges Erbe: Der Umgang mit Nationalsozialismus und Antisemitismus in Österreich, der DDR und der Bundesrepublik Deutschland*. Frankfurt, 1995.

Berman, Aaron. *Nazism, the Jews and American Zionism 1933–1948*. Detroit, 1990.

Bialer, Uri. *Between East and West: Israel's Foreign Policy Orientation, 1948–1956*. Cambridge, 1990.

Bird, Kai. *The Chairman: John J. McCloy, the Making of the American Establishment*. New York, 1992.

Birkl, Rudolf, and Günter Olzog, eds. *Erwartungen: Kritische Rückblicke der Kriegsgeneration*. Munich, 1980.

Blasius, Rainer A., ed. *Von Adenauer zu Erhard: Studien zur auswärtigen Politik der Bundesrepublik Deutschland*. Munich, 1994.

Bodemann, Michal, ed. *Jews, Germany, Memory: Reconstruction of Jewish Life in Germany*. Ann Arbor, Mich., 1996.

Bower, Tom. *The Paperclip Conspiracy: The Hunt for the Nazi Scientists*. Boston, 1987.

———. *The Pledge Betrayed: America and Britain and the Denazification of Postwar Germany*. Garden City, N.Y., 1982.

Boyd, Jonathan, and Stephen Ward. *Nazi Gold. The British and Allied attempt to deal with the loot from the Second World War and the implications for the Tripartite Gold Commission*. London, 1997.

Brecher, Frank W. *Reluctant Ally: The United States Policy Toward the Jews from Wilson to Roosevelt.* New York, 1991.

Breitman, Richard, and Alan M. Kraut. *American Refugee Policy and European Jewry, 1933–1945.* Bloomington and Indianapolis, 1987.

Brenner, Michael. *Nach dem Holocaust: Juden in Deutschland, 1945–1950.* Munich, 1995.

Brochhagen, Ulrich. *Nach Nürnberg: Vergangenheitsbewältigung und Westintegration in der Ära Adenauer.* Hamburg, 1994.

Burgauer, Erica. *Zwischen Erinnerung und Verdrängung: Juden in Deutschland nach 1945.* Hamburg, 1993.

Buscher, Frank M. *The U.S. War Crimes Trials in Germany.* New York, 1989.

Chernow, Ron. *The Warburgs: The Twentieth-Century Odyssey of a Remarkable Jewish Family.* New York, 1993.

Clark, Delbert. *Again the Goose Step.* Indianapolis, 1949.

Clark, Ronald W. *Einstein: The Life and Times, An Illustrated Biography.* New York, 1971.

Cohen, Michael J. *Truman and Israel.* Berkeley, Calif., 1990.

Cohen, Naomi W. *American Jews and the Zionist Idea.* New York, 1975.

———. *Encounter with Emancipation: The German Jews in the U.S., 1830–1914.* Philadelphia, 1983.

———. *Not Free to Desist: The American Jewish Committee, 1906–1966.* Philadelphia, 1972.

Dash Moore, Deborah. *B'nai B'rith and the Challenge of Ethnic Leadership.* Albany, N.Y., 1981.

Dershowitz, Alan M. *Chutzpah.* Boston, 1991.

———. *The Vanishing American Jew: In Search of Jewish Identity for the Next Century.* Boston, 1997.

Deutschkron, Inge. *Israel und die Deutschen.* Cologne, 1983.

Diefendorf, Jeffry M., Alex Frohn, and Hermann-Josef Rupieper. *American Policy and the Reconstruction of West Germany, 1945–1955.* Washington and Cambridge, 1993.

Diner, Dan. *America in the Eyes of the Germans: An Essay on Anti-Americanism.* Princeton, N.J., 1996.

Dinnerstein, Leonard. *America and the Survivors of the Holocaust.* New York, 1982.

———. *Antisemitism in America.* New York and Oxford, 1994.

———. *Uneasy at Home: Antisemitism and the American Jewish Experience.* New York, 1987.

Doneson, Judith E. *The Holocaust in American Film.* Philadelphia, 1987.

Donovan, Robert. *Conflict and Crisis: The Presidency of Harry S. Truman.* New York, 1977.

Döscher, Jürgen. *Verschworene Gesellschaft: Das Auswärtige Amt unter Adenauer zwischen Neubeginn und Kontinuität.* Berlin, 1995.

Eisenhower, David. *Eisenhower at War.* New York, 1986.

Ermarth, Michael, ed. *America and the Shaping of German Society, 1945–1955.* New York and Oxford, 1993.

Evans, Richard. *In Hitler's Shadow: West German Historians and the Attempt to Escape from the Nazi Past.* New York, 1989.

Farrer, David. *The Warburgs: The Story of a Family.* New York, 1975.

Feingold, Henry L. *Bearing Witness: How America and Its Jews Responded to the Holocaust.* Syracuse, 1995.

———. *The Politics of Rescue: The Roosevelt Administration and the Holocaust, 1938–1945.* New Brunswick, N.J., 1970.

———. *A Time for Searching: Entering the Mainstream, 1920–1945.* Vol. 4 of *The Jewish People in America,* a series sponsored by the American Jewish Historical Society, Baltimore, 1992.

Felken, Detlef. *Dulles und Deutschland: Die amerikanische Deutschlandpolitik, 1953–1959.* Bonn and Berlin, 1993.

Finger, Seymour Maxwell, ed. *American Jewry During the Holocaust.* New York, 1984.

Fisher, Marc. *After the Wall: Germany, the Germans, and the Burden of History.* New York, 1995.

Foschepoth, Josef, ed. *Adenauer und die deutsche Frage.* Göttingen, 1988.

———. *Die Anfänge der Gesellschaften für Christlich-Jüdische Zusammenarbeit.* Göttingen, 1993.

Fraser, Steven. *Labor Will Rule: Sidney Hillman and the Rise of American Labor.* New York, 1991.

Frei, Norbert. *Vergangenheitspolitik: Die Anfänge der Bundesrepublik und die NS-Vergangenheit.* Munich, 1996.

Friedman, Murray, ed. *Philadelphian Jewish Life, 1940–1985.* Ardmore, Pa., 1986.

Friedrich, Wolfgang Uwe, ed. *Die USA und die Deutsche Frage, 1945–1990.* Frankfurt, 1991.

Fuchs, Lawrence H. *The Political Behavior of American Jews.* Glencoe, Ill., 1956.

Gardner Feldman, Lily. *The Special Relationship between West Germany and Israel.* Boston, 1984.

Genizi, Haim. *America's Fair Share: The Administration and Resettlement of Displaced Persons, 1945–1952.* Detroit, 1996.

———. *Yoetz Umekim: hayoetz latzava haamerikai vesheerith hapleita* (The Adviser on Jewish Affairs to the American Army and Displaced Persons, 1945–1949) (in Hebrew). Tel Aviv, 1987.

Gilman, Sander L., and Karen Remmler, eds. *Reemerging Jewish Culture in Germany: Life and Literature Since 1989.* New York, 1994.

Gimbel, John. *The American Occupation of Germany: Politics and the Military, 1945–1949.* Stanford, Calif., 1968.

———. *Science, Technology, and Reparations: Exploitation and Plunder in Postwar Germany.* Stanford, Calif., 1990.

Giordano, Ralph. *Die Zweite Schuld oder von der Last Deutscher zu sein.* Hamburg, 1987.

Glazer, Nathan. *American Judaism.* Chicago, 1957.

———. *The Social Basis of American Communism.* New York, 1961.

Goldberg, J. J. *Jewish Power: Inside the American Jewish Establishment.* Reading, Mass., 1996.

Goldhagen, Daniel Jonah. *Hitler's Willing Executioners: Ordinary Germans and the Holocaust.* New York, 1996.

Golub, Jennifer. *German Attitudes Toward Jews and Other Minorities.* AJC Working Paper on Contemporary Anti-Semitism. New York, 1994.

Goschler, Constantin. *Wiedergutmachung und die Verfolgten des Nationalsozialismus, 1945–1954.* Munich, 1992.

Gottlieb, Moshe R. *American Anti-Nazi Resistance, 1933–1941.* New York, 1982.

Gotto, Klaus, ed. *Der Staatssekretär Adenauers: Persönlichkeit und politisches Wirken Hans Globkes.* Stuttgart, 1980.

Greiner, Bernd. *Die Morgenthau Legende: Zur Geschichte eines umstrittenen Plans.* Hamburg, 1995.

Grobman, Alex. *Rekindling the Flame: American Jewish Chaplains and the Survivors of European Jewry, 1944–1948.* Detroit, 1993.

Grose, Peter. *Gentleman Spy: The Life of Allan Dulles.* Boston, 1994.

Grossmann, Kurt R. *Germany's Moral Debt: The German-Israel Agreement,* Washington, D.C., 1954.

Grusd, Edward E. *B'nai B'rith: The Story of a Covenant.* New York, 1966.

Guhin, Michael A. *John Foster Dulles: A Statesman and His Times.* New York, 1972.

Halperin, Samuel. *The Political World of American Zionism.* Detroit, 1961.

Hanrieder, Wolfram E. *Germany, America, Europe: Forty Years of German Foreign Policy.* New Haven and London, 1989.

Hartman, Geoffrey, ed. *Bitburg in Moral and Political Perspective.* Bloomington, 1986.

Hattis Rolef, Suzan. *The Middle East Policy of the Federal Republic of Germany.* Jerusalem, 1985.

Heer, Hannes, and Klaus Naumann, eds. *Vernichtungskrieg: Verbrechen der Wehrmacht, 1941 bis 1944.* Hamburg, 1995.

Helmreich, William B. *Against All Odds: Holocaust Survivors and the Successful Lives They Made in America.* New York, 1992.

———. *The World of the Yeshiva: An Intimate Portrait of Orthodox Jewry.* New York, 1989.

Henke, Klaus-Dietmar. *Die amerikanische Besetzung Deutschlands.* Munich, 1995.

Henke, Klaus-Dietmar, and Hans Woller, eds. *Lehrjahre der CSU: Eine Nachkriegspartei im Spiegel vertraulicher Berichte an die amerikanische Militärregierung.* Stuttgart, 1984.

Hentschel, Ludwig. *Ludwig Erhard: Ein Politikerleben.* Munich and Landsberg, 1996.

Herbst, Ludolf, ed. *Westdeutschland, 1945–1955: Unterwerfung, Kontrolle, Integration.* Munich, 1986.

Herbst, Ludolf, and Constantin Goschler, eds. *Wiedergutmachung in der Bundesrepublik Deutschland.* Munich, 1989.

Hertzberg, Arthur. *The Jews in America: Four Hundred Years of an Uneasy Encounter.* New York, 1989.

Hilberg, Raul. *The Destruction of the European Jews.* Chicago, 1961.

———. *Perpetrators, Victims, Bystanders: The Jewish Catastrophe 1933–1945.* New York, 1992.

Hoopes, Townsend. *The Devil and John Foster Dulles.* Boston, 1973.

Isaacson, Walter. *Kissinger: A Biography.* New York, 1992.

Isaacson, Walter, and Evan Thomas. *The Wise Men: Six Friends and the World They Made.* New York, 1986.

Jarausch, Konrad. *The Road to German Unity.* New York, 1994.

Jaspers, Karl. *The Question of German Guilt.* New York, 1947.

Jay, Martin. *The Dialectical Imagination: A History of the Frankfurt School and the Institute of Social Research.* New York, 1973.

Jodice, David. *United Germany and Jewish Concerns.* AJC Working Paper on Contemporary Anti-Semitism. New York, 1991.

Karp, Abraham J. *The History of the United Synagogue of America, 1913–1963.* New York, 1964.

Kaufman, Menahem. *An Ambiguous Partnership: Non-Zionists and Zionists in America, 1939–1948.* Jerusalem and Detroit, 1991.

Kessler, Mario. *Die SED und die Juden: Zwischen Repression und Toleranz.* Berlin, 1995.

Kessner, Carole S., ed. *The "Other" New York Jewish Intellectuals.* New York, 1994.

Kimball, Warren F. *Swords to Ploughshares: The Morgenthau Plan for Defeated Nazi Germany.* Philadelphia, 1976.

Kittel, Manfred. *Die Legende von der "Zweiten Schuld": Vergangenheitsbewältigung in der Ära Adenauer.* Berlin, 1993.

Kloke, Martin. *Israel und die deutsche Linke: Zur Geschichte eines schwierigen Verhältnisses.* Frankfurt, 1990.

Köhler, Henning. *Adenauer: Eine politische Biographie.* Berlin, 1994.

Kolko, Gabriel. *The Policy of War: The World and U.S. Foreign Policy.* New York, 1968.

Kolsky, Abraham. *Jews Against Zionism: The American Council for Judaism, 1942–1948.* Philadelphia, 1987.

Kramer, Jane. *The Politics of Memory: Looking for Germany in the New Germany.* New York, 1996.

Krieger, Wolfgang. *General Lucius D. Clay und die amerikanische Deutschlandpolitik.* Stuttgart, 1987.

Lavy, George. *Germany and Israel: Moral Debt and National Interest.* London, 1996.

Lehman, Ines. *Die deutsche Vereinigung von aussen gesehen: Angst, Bedenken, und Erwartungen in des ausländischen Presse.* 2 vols. Berlin, Bonn, and New York, 1996–97.

Lemkin, Raphael. *Axis Rule in Occupied Europe: Laws of Occupation: Analysis of Government Proposals for Redress.* Washington, 1944.

Levkov, Ilya, ed. *Bitburg and Beyond.* New York, 1986.

Liebman, Arthur. *Jews and the Left.* New York, 1979.

Lindemann, Beate, ed. *Amerika in uns: Deutsche-Amerikanische Erfahrungen und Visionen.* Mainz, 1994.

Linenthal, Edward T. *Preserving Memory: The Struggle to Create America's Holocaust Museum.* New York, 1995.

Lipset, Seymour Martin, and Earl Raab. *Jews and the New American Scene.* Cambridge, Mass., 1995.

Lipstadt, Deborah E. *Beyond Belief: The American Press and the Coming of the Holocaust.* New York, 1986.

Lookstein, Haskel. *Were We Our Brothers' Keepers? The Public Response of American Jews to the Holocaust, 1938–1944.* New York, 1985.

Löwenstein, Stephen M. *Frankfurt on the Hudson: The German Jewish Community of Washington Heights, 1933–1983, Its Structure and Culture.* Detroit, 1988.

Lubell, Samuel. *The Future of American Politics.* 2nd ed., rev. Garden City, N.Y., 1956.

Lüth, Erich. *Die Friedensbitte an Israel: Eine Hamburger Initiative.* Hamburg, 1976.

Maier, Charles S. *The Unmasterable Past: History, Holocaust, and National Identity.* Cambridge, Mass., 1988.

Maier, Charles, and Günter Bischof, eds. *The Marshall Plan and Germany: West German Development within the Framework of the European Recovery Program.* New York, 1991.

Markovits, Andrei S., and Simon Reich. *The German Predicament: Memory and Power in the New Europe.* Ithaca, N.Y. and London, 1997.

Marquardt-Bigman, Petra. *Amerikanische Geheimdienstanalysen über Deutschland, 1942–1949.* Munich, 1995.

Mausbach, Wilfried. *Zwischen Morgenthau und Marshall. Das wirtschaftliche Deutschlandkonzept der USA 1944–1947.* Düsseldorf, 1996.

Mayer, Frank A. *Adenauer and Kennedy: A Study in German-American Relations.* New York, 1996.

Mayers, David Allan. *George Kennan and the Dilemmas of U.S. Foreign Policy.* New York and Oxford, 1988.

Medzini, Meron. *Hayehudiah Hageiah: Golda Meir vachazon Israel,* in Hebrew. (The Proud Jewess: Golda Meir and the Vision of Israel.) Jerusalem, 1990.

Merkl, Peter H. *German Unification in the European Context.* Philadelphia, 1993.

Mertens, Lothar. *Davidstern unter Hammer und Zirkel. Die jüdischen Gemeinden in der SBZ/DDR und ihre Behandlung durch Partei und Staat 1945–1990.* Hildesheim, 1997.

Meyer, Michael A. *Response to Modernity: A History of the Reform Movement in Judaism.* New York, 1988.

Middleton, Drew. *The Struggle for Germany.* Indianapolis, 1949.

———. *Where Has Last July Gone? Memoirs.* New York, 1973.

Miller, Judith. *One, by One, by One: Facing the Holocaust.* New York, 1990.

Mitscherlich, Alexander, and Margarethe Mitscherlich. *The Inability to Mourn: Principles of Collective Behavior.* New York, 1975.

Morgenthau, Henry III. *Mostly Morgenthaus: A Family History.* New York, 1991.

Morse, Arthur D. *While Six Million Died: A Chronicle of American Apathy.* New York, 1967.

Morsey, Rudolf. *Heinrich Lübke: Eine politische Biographie.* Paderborn, 1996.

Mosesson, Gloria R. *The Jewish War Veterans Story.* Washington, D.C., 1971.

Mowrer, Edgar Ansel. *Germany Puts the Clock Back.* New York, 1933.

Naimark, Norman M. *The Russians in Germany: A History of the Soviet Zone of Occupation.* Cambridge, Mass., 1995.

Neumann, Emanuel. *In the Arena: An Autobiographical Memoir.* New York, 1976.

Neustadt, Amnon. *Die deutsch-israelischen Beziehungen im Schatten der EG-Nahostpolitik.* Frankfurt, 1983.

Newton, Verne W., ed. *FDR and the Holocaust.* New York, 1996.

Niethammer, Lutz. *Entnazifizierung in Bayern: Säuberung und Rehabilitierung unter amerikanischer Besatzung.* Frankfurt, 1972.

Nolte, Ernst. *Streitpunkte: Heutige und künftige Kontroversen um den Nationalsozialismus.* Berlin and Frankfurt, 1993.

O'Connor, Richard. *The German Americans*. Boston, 1968.

Ostow, Robin. *Jews in Contemporary East Germany: The Children of Moses in the Land of Marx*. New York, 1989.

Patai, Raphael. *Nahum Goldmann: His Mission to the Gentiles*. Tuscaloosa, Ala., 1987.

Peck, Abraham J., ed. *The German-Jewish Legacy in America, 1938–1988: From Bildung to the Bill of Rights*. Detroit, 1989.

Peterson, Edward N. *The American Occupation of Germany: Retreat to Victory*. Detroit, 1977.

Pinkus, Benjamin. *The Soviet Government and the Jews, 1948–1967: A Documented Story*. Cambridge, 1984.

Pond, Elizabeth. *Beyond the Wall: Germany's Road to Unification*. Washington, D.C., 1992.

Proudfoot, Malcolm J. *European Refugees: A Study in Forced Population Movement*. Evanston, Ill., 1956.

Rabinbach, Anson, and Jack Zipes, eds. *Germans and Jews since the Holocaust: The Changing Situation in West Germany*. New York, 1986.

Raphael, Marc L. *Abba Hillel Silver: A Profile in American Judaism*. New York, 1989.

Rawidowicz, Simon. *Babylon and Jerusalem: Toward a Philosophy of Israel's Wholeness* (in Hebrew). Waltham, Mass., 1957.

Rees, David. *Harry Dexter White: A Study in Paradox*. New York, 1973.

Rendtorff, Rolf, and Hermann Henrix, eds. *Die Kirche und das Judentum: Dokumente von 1945–1985*. Paderborn, 1988.

Richter, Klemens, ed. *Die Katholische Kirche und das Judentum: Dokumente von 1945–1982*. Freiburg, 1982.

Rippley, La Vern J. *The German Americans*. Boston, 1976.

Rischin, Moses, and Raphael Asher, eds. *The Jewish Legacy and the German Conscience*. Berkeley, Calif., 1991.

Robinson, Jacob. *And the Crooked Shall Be Made Straight: The Eichmann Trial, the Jewish Catastrophe, and Hannah Arendt's Narrative*. New York, 1965.

Rohlfes, Joachim. *Juden in den Vereinigten Staaten*. Bonn, 1990.

Rose, Norman. *Chaim Weizmann: A Biography*. New York, 1986.

Rosenfeld, Alvin, and Itzhak Greenberg. *Confronting the Holocaust: The Impact of Elie Wiesel*. Washington and London, 1978.

Rovere, Richard A. *Senator Joe McCarthy*. New York, 1959.

Rupieper, Hermann-Josef. *Der besetzte Verbündete: Die amerikanische Deutschlandpolitik, 1949–1955*. Opladen, 1991.

Ryan, Allan A., Jr. *Quiet Neighbors: Prosecuting Nazi War Criminals in America*. San Diego, 1984.

Sachar, Howard M. *A History of the Jews in America*. New York, 1992.

Sagi, Nana. *German Reparations: A History of the Negotiations*. Jerusalem, 1980.

Saidel, Rochelle G. *Never Too Late to Remember: The Politics Behind New York City's Holocaust Museum*. New York and London, 1996.

Schöllgen, Gregor. *Angst vor der Macht: Die Deutschen und ihre Aussenpolitik*. Berlin, 1993.

Schrenck-Notzing, Caspar. *Charakterwäsche: Die amerikanische Besatzung in Deutschland und ihre Folgen.* Stuttgart, 1965.

Schröder, Gerhard, Alfred Müller-Armack, Karl Hohmann, Johannes Gross, Rüdiger Altmann, eds. *Ludwig Erhard: Beiträge zu seiner politischen Biographie. Festschrift zum fünfundsiebzigsten Geburtstag.* Frankfurt, Berlin, Wien, 1972.

Schwabe, Klaus, ed. *Adenauer und die USA.* Bonn, 1994.

Schwartz, Rabbi Yoel, and Rabbi Yitzchak Goldstein. *SHOAH: A Jewish Perspective on Tragedy in the Context of the Holocaust.* Jerusalem, 1990.

Schwartz, Thomas Alan. *America's Germany: John J. McCloy and the Federal Republic of Germany.* Cambridge, Mass., 1991.

Schwarz, Hans-Peter. *Adenauer: Der Aufstieg, 1916–1952.* Vol. 1. Stuttgart, 1986.

———. *Adenauer: Der Staatsmann, 1952–1967.* Vol. 2. Stuttgart, 1994.

———. *Die Zentralmacht Europas: Deutschlands Rückkehr auf die Weltbühne.* Berlin, 1994.

Schwilk, Heimo, and Ulrich Schacht, eds. *Die selbstbewusste Nation: "Anschwellender Bocksgesang" und weitere Beiträge zu einer deutschen Debatte.* Frankfurt, 1994.

Segev, Tom. *The Seventh Million: The Israelis and the Holocaust.* New York, 1993.

Shafir, Shlomo. *Yad Mushetet: Hasocial demokratim hagermanim veyachasam liyehudim ule Israel bashanim 1945–1967*, in Hebrew (An Outstretched Hand: German Social Democrats, Jews and Israel, 1945–1967). Tel Aviv, 1986.

Shapiro, Edward S. *A Time for Healing: American Jewry since World War II.* Vol. 5 of *The Jewish People in America*, a series sponsored by the American Jewish Historical Society. Baltimore, 1992.

Sheffer, Gabriel. *Moshe Sharett: A Biography of a Political Moderate.* New York, 1996.

Shpiro, David H. *From Philanthropy to Action: The Political Transformation of American Zionism in the Holocaust Years.* Oxford, 1993.

Silberman, Charles. *A Certain People: American Jews and Their Lives Today.* New York, 1985.

Silver, Daniel Jeremy, ed. *In Time of Harvest: Essays in Honor of Abba Hillel Silver on the Occasion of His Seventieth Birthday.* New York, 1963.

Simpson, Christopher. *The Splendid Blond Beast: Money, Law, and Genocide in the Twentieth Century.* New York, 1983.

Sklare, Marshall, ed. *The Jews: The Social Pattern of an American Group.* New York, 1958.

Smith, Arthur L., Jr. *Die Hexe von Buchenwald: Der Fall Ilse Koch.* Weimar, 1994.

Smith, Bradley F. *Reaching Judgment at Nuremberg.* New York, 1977.

———. *The Road to Nuremberg.* New York, 1981.

Smith, Jean Edward. *Lucius D. Clay: An American Life.* New York, 1990.

Spiegel, Steven L. *The Other Arab-Israel Conflict: Making America's Middle East Policy from Truman to Reagan.* Chicago and London, 1985.

Spotts, Frederic. *The Churches and Politics in Germany.* Middletown, Conn., 1973.

Steinbach, Peter. *Nationalsozialistische Gewaltverbrechen: Die Diskussion der deutschen Öffentlichkeit nach 1945.* Berlin, 1981.

Steininger, Rolf, ed. *Der Umgang mit dem Holocaust: Europa-USA-Israel.* Vienna, 1994.

Stember, Charles Herbert, et al., eds. *Jews in the Mind of America.* New York, 1966.

Stern, Frank. *The Whitewashing of the Yellow Badge: Antisemitism and Philosemitism in West Germany, 1945–1952.* Oxford and New York, 1992.

Stock, Ernest. *Chosen Instrument: The Jewish Agency in the First Decade of the State of Israel.* New York, 1988.

Stürmer, Michael. *Die Grenzen der Macht: Begegnung der Deutschen mit der Geschichte.* Berlin, 1990.

Sylke, Tempel. *Legenden von der Allmacht: Die Beziehungen zwischen amerikanisch-jüdischen Organisationen und der Bundesrepublik Deutschland seit 1945.* Frankfurt, 1995.

Tevet, Shabtai. *Kin'at David: The Life of David Ben Gurion* (in Hebrew). Vol. 3. Jerusalem, 1987.

Timm, Angelika. *Alles Umsonst? Verhandlungen zwischen der Claims Conference und der DDR über "Wiedergutmachung" und Entschädigung.* Berlin, 1996.

———. *Moral Obligations and Pragmatic Policy.* Budapest, 1997.

———. *Hammer, Zirkel, Davidstern. Das gestörte Verhältnis der DDR zu Zionismus und Staat Israel.* Bonn, 1997.

Urofsky, Melvin J. *A Voice That Spoke for Justice: The Life and Times of Stephen S. Wise.* Albany, N.Y., 1982.

———. *We Are One!: American Jewry and Israel.* Garden City, N.Y., 1978.

Vollnhalls, Clemens, ed. *Entnazifizierung: Politische Säuberung und Rehabilitierung in den vier Besatzungszonen.* Frankfurt, 1990.

———. *Evangelische Kirche und Entnazifizierung: Die Last der nationalsozialistischen Vergangenheit.* Munich, 1989.

Weiss, John. *Ideology of Death: Why the Holocaust Happened in Germany.* Chicago, 1996.

Wiesel, Eli. *All Rivers Run to the Sea.* New York, 1995.

Wiggershaus, Rolf. *The Frankfurt School: Its History, Theory, and Political Significance.* Cambridge, Mass., 1994.

Wolfe, Robert, ed. *America as Proconsul: The United States Military Government in Germany and Japan.* Carbondale, Ill., 1984.

Wolffsohn, Michael. *Die Deutschland-Akte: Juden und Deutsche in Ost und West: Tatsachen und Legenden.* Munich, 1995.

———. *Eternal Guilt? Forty Years of German-Jewish-Israeli Relations.* New York, 1993.

———. *Keine Angst vor Deutschland!* Erlangen, 1990.

Wyman, David S. *The Abandonment of the Jews: America and the Holocaust, 1941–1945.* New York, 1984.

———. *Paper Walls: America and the Refugee Crisis, 1938–1941.* Amherst, 1968.

Yaffe, James. *The American Jew: Portrait of a Split Personality.* New York, 1968.

Young, James E. *Writing and Rewriting the Holocaust.* Bloomington, Ind., 1988.

Young-Bruehl, Elisabeth. *Hannah Arendt: For Love of the World.* New Haven and London, 1982.

Zelikow, Philip, and Condoleeza Rice. *Germany Unified and Europe Transformed: A Study in Statecraft.* Cambridge, Mass., and London, 1995.

Zimmermann, Moshe, and Oded Heilbronner. *"Normal" Relations: Israeli-German Relations* (in Hebrew). Jerusalem, 1993.

Zitelmann, Rainer. *Wohin treibt unsere Republik?* Berlin, 1995.

Zweig, Ronald W., ed. *David Ben Gurion: Politics and Leadership in Israel.* London and Jerusalem, 1991.

————. *German Reparations and the Jewish World: A History of the Claims Conference.* Boulder, Colo., 1987.

SELECT ARTICLES

Alter, Robert. "The Deformations of the Holocaust." *Commentary* 71 (Feb. 1981).

Arendt, Hannah. "The Aftermath of Nazi Rule: Report from Germany." *Commentary* 10 (Oct. 1950).

Asher, Joseph. "Our Attitude to the Germans—A Time for Reappraisal?" *Pointer* (Summer 1966).

Auerbach, Yehudit. "Ben Gurion and Reparations from Germany." In *David Ben-Gurion: Politics and Leadership in Israel,* edited by Ronald Zweig. London, 1991.

Bergmann, Werner. "Xenophobia and Antisemitism after the Unification of Germany." *Patterns of Prejudice* 28, no. 1 (1994).

Birnbaum, Norman. "Stirrings in West Germany." *Commentary* 37 (Apr. 1964).

Brier, Jean-Paul. "The Holocaust and West Germany: Strategies of Oblivion." *New German Critique* 19 (Winter 1980).

Brinkley, Alan. "Minister Without Portfolio." *Harper's,* Feb. 1983.

Buscher, Frank M. "Kurt Schumacher, German Social Democrats and the Punishment of Nazi Crimes." *Holocaust and Genocide Studies* 5 (1990).

Cahnmann, Werner. "Germany: The Time Has Come for Friendship." *Sh'ma,* Apr. 13, 1973.

Cohen, Elliot. "What Do the Germans Propose to Do?" *Commentary* 10 (Sept. 1950).

"Condition of Jewish Belief." Symposium. *Commentary* 42 (Aug. 1966).

Craft, Robert. "The Furtwängler Enigma." *New York Review of Books,* Oct. 7, 1993.

Dawidowicz, Lucy. "In Berlin Again." *Commentary* 82 (Aug. 1986).

Diner, Dan. "The Historians' Controversy—Limits to the Historization of National Socialism." *Tikkun* 2 (1987).

Dinnerstein, Leonard. "Franklin D. Roosevelt and the Jews: Another Look." *Dimensions* 10 (1996).

Erb, Rainer. "Jews and Other Minorities in Germany since the 1990s." *Patterns of Prejudice* 27, no. 2 (1993).

Evans, Richard. "Prisoners of the German Past." *Patterns of Prejudice* 30, no. 1 (1996).

Falk, Gerhard. "The Reaction of the German American Press to Nazi Persecution, 1933–1941." *Journal of Reform Judaism* 32 (Spring 1985).

Fogelman, Eva. "From Mourning to Creativity: The Second Generation of Survivors in Israel and the United States." *Midstream* 37 (Apr. 1991).

Frei, Norbert. "'Wir Waren Blind, Ungläubig und Langsam': Buchenwald, Dachau and die amerikanischen Medien im Frühjahr 1945." *Vierteljahrshefte für Zeitgeschichte* 35 (1987).

Friedlander, Henry, and E. M. McCarrick. "Nazi Criminals in the United States: Denaturalization after Fedorenko." *Simon Wiesenthal Center Annual* 3 (1986).

Funke, Hajo. "Bitburg und die Macht der Juden." In *Antisemitismus nach dem Holocaust,* edited by Alphons Silbermann and Julius H. Schoeps. Cologne, 1986.

Genizi, Haim. "Philip S. Bernstein: Adviser of Jewish Affairs, 1946–1947." *Simon Wiesenthal Center Annual* 3 (1986).

"Germany 1967." *Atlantic*, May 1967.

"Germany and Jews Today." Symposium. *Midstream* 27 (Oct. 1981).

"Germany in Transition." *Daedalus* 123 (Winter 1994).

Gillessen, Günther. "Konrad Adenauer und der Israel-Vertrag." In *Politik, Philosophie, Praxis: Festschrift für Wilhelm Hennis zum 65ten Geburtstag*, edited by Hans Maier et al. Stuttgart, 1988.

Gilman, Sander L. "German Reunification and the Jews." *New German Critique* 52 (Winter 1991).

Goldmann, Nahum. "Adenauer und das jüdische Volk." In *Konrad Adenauer und seine Zeit: Politik und Persönlichkeit des ersten Bundeskanzlers*, edited by Dieter Blumenwitz. Stuttgart, 1976.

Gordon, Murray. "Racism and Antisemitism in Germany: Old Problem, New Threat." *Congress Monthly* 60 (Mar.–Apr. 1993).

Greenberg, Irving. "The Interaction of Israel and the Diaspora after the Holocaust." In *World Jewry and the State of Israel*, edited by Moshe Davis. New York, 1977.

Griffith, William E. "Die Bundesrepublik in amerikanischer Sicht." *Aussenpolitik* 13, no. 2 (1962).

Grubbe, Hans-Jürgen. "Das Amerikabild Konrad Adenauers." *Amerikastudien* (American Studies) 31 (1986).

Guttmann, Micha. "Macht oder Ohnmacht: Jüdische Politik in Deutschland." *Tribüne* 34 (Sept. 1995).

Heilbrunn, Jacob, "Germany's New Right." *Foreign Affairs* 75 (Nov.–Dec. 1996).

Herf, Jeffrey. "East German Communists and the Jewish Question: The Case of Paul Merker." *Journal of Contemporary History* 29 (Oct. 1994).

Hertz, John H. "The Fiasco of Denazification in Germany." *Political Science Quarterly* 63 (1948).

Hertzberg, Arthur. "Israel and World Jewry at the Crossroads." Gesher Symposium (in Hebrew). *Gesher* 41 (Winter 1995–96).

Jacobs, Paul. "Eichmann and Jewish Identity." *Midstream* 7 (Summer 1961).

Jay, Martin. "The Jews and the Frankfurt School Critical Theory's Analysis of Antisemitism." In *Permanent Exiles. Essays in the Intellectual Migration from Germany to America*. Edited by Martin Jay. New York, 1985.

Jelinek, Yeshayahu A. "John J. McCloy, Jacob Blaustein, and the Shilumim: A Chapter in American Foreign Affairs." In *Holocaust and the Shilumim: The Policy of Wiedergutmachung in the Early 1950s*, edited by Alex Frohn. Washington, D.C., 1991.

———. "Die Krise der Shilumim/Wiedergutmachung—Verhandlungen im Sommer 1952." *Vierteljahrshefte für Zeitgeschichte* 38 (1990).

———. "Political Acumen, Altruism, Foreign Pressure or Moral Debt: Konrad Adenauer and the 'Shilumim.'" In *Tel Aviver Jahrbuch für deutsche Geschichte*, vol. 19, edited by Shulamit Volkov and Frank Stern. Tel Aviv, 1990.

Jena, Kai von. "Versöhnung mit Israel? Die Deutsch-Israelischen Verhandlungen bis zum Wiedergutmachungsabkommen 1952." *Vierteljahrshefte für Zeitgeschichte* 34 (1986).

"Jewishness and the Younger Intellectuals." Symposium. *Commentary* 31 (Apr. 1961).

479

Jick, Leon A. "The Holocaust: Its Use and Abuse in the American Public." *Yad Vashem Studies* 14 (1981).

Joffe, Josef, et al. "Mr. Heilbrunn's Planet." *Foreign Affairs* 76 (Mar.–Apr. 1997).

Klausner, Abraham. "The First Days at Dachau." *Journal of Modern Judaism* 5 (Spring 1985).

Kraushaar, Wolfgang. "Die Affäre Auerbach: Zur Virulenz des Antisemitismus in den Gründerjahren der Bundesrepublik." *Menorah* 6 (1995).

Lavsky, Hagit. "British Jewry and the Jews in Post-Holocaust Germany: The Jewish Relief Unit, 1945–1950." *Journal of Holocaust Education* 4 (Summer 1995).

Ledeen, Michael. "Iraq's German Connection." *Commentary* 91 (Apr. 1991).

Lerner, Michael. "'No' to German Reunification." *Tikkun* 5 (Mar.–Apr. 1990).

Lipman, Samuel. "Furtwängler and the Nazis." *Commentary* 95 (Mar. 1993).

Lipstadt, Deborah E. "America and the Holocaust." *Modern Judaism* 10 (1990).

———. "America and the Memory of the Holocaust, 1950–1965." *Modern Judaism* 16 (Oct. 1996).

———. "The Bitburg Controversy." In *American Jewish Year Book*, vol. 87. (1987).

Lübbe, Hermann, "Der Nationalsozialismus im deutschen Nachkriegsbewusstsein." *Historische Zeitschrift* 236 (1983).

Mankowitz, Ze'ev. "The Formation of the She'erith Hapleita: November 1944–July 1945." *Yad Vashem Studies* 20 (1990).

Markovits, Andrei S. "On Anti-Americanism in West Germany." *New German Critique* 34 (Winter 1985).

Mathiopoulos, Margarita. "Hermann Axen—Opfer, Täter, Hofjude." *Menorah* 6 (1995).

Mayer, Fred A. "Adenauer and Kennedy: An Era of Distrust in German-American Relations?" *German Studies Review* 17 (Feb. 1994).

Miller, Susanne. "Zwischen Konfrontation und Anpassung: Die SPD-Bundestagsfraktion, 1949–1957." *Die Neue Gesellschaft/Frankfurter Hefte* 42 (Jan. 1995).

Moskowitz, Moses. "The Germans and the Jews: Postwar Report. The Enigma of German Irresponsibility." *Commentary* 2 (July 1946).

Muhlen, Norbert. "In the Backwash of the Great Crime." *Commentary* 13 (Feb. 1952).

———. "The Return of Goebbels' Film Makers." *Commentary* 11 (March 1951).

———. "The Shooting in the Moehlstrasse: Is It Nazi Anti-Semitism All Over Again?" *Commentary* 8 (Oct. 1949).

"My Jewish Affirmation." Symposium. *Judaism* 10 (Fall 1961).

Neusner, Jacob, and Richard L. Rubenstein. "Germany and the Jews: Two Views." *Conservative Judaism* 17 (Fall–Winter 1962–63).

Ofer, Dalia. "Defining Relationship: The Joint Distribution Committee and Israel, 1948–1950." In *Israel: The First Decade of Independence*, edited by S. Ilan Troen and Noah Lucas. Albany, N.Y., 1995.

Peck, Abraham J. "'Our Eyes Have Seen Eternity': Memory and Self-Identity Among the She'erith Hapletah." *Modern Judaism* 17 (Feb. 1997).

Penkower, Monty N. "The Bergson Boys." *American Jewish History* 70 (Mar. 1981).

———. "Jewish Organizations and the Creation of the War Refugee Board." *The Annals of the American Academy of Political and Social Science* 450 (July 1980).

————. "The 1943 Joint Anglo-American Statement on Palestine." In *Essays in American Zionism: Herzl Yearbook*, vol. 8, edited by Melvin J. Urofsky. New York, 1978.

Phayer, Michael. "The German Catholic Church After the Holocaust." *Holocaust and Genocide Studies* 10 (Fall 1996).

Rabinbach, Anson. "The Jewish Question in the German Question." *New German Critique* 44 (Spring–Summer 1988).

Robinson, Jacob. "Eichmann and the Question of Jurisdiction." *Commentary* 30 (July 1960).

————. "The International Military Tribunal and the Holocaust: Some Legal Reflections." *Israel Law Review* 7 (Jan. 1972).

Robinson, Nehemiah. "The Luxembourg Agreements and Their Implementation." In *Essays in Jewish Sociology, Labor, and Cooperation in Memory of Dr. Noah Barou, 1889–1955*, edited by Henrik F. Infield. London, 1962.

Rosenfeld, Alvin H. "The Holocaust in American Popular Culture." *Midstream* 29 (June–July 1983).

Ryan, Allan A., Jr. "Attitudes Toward the Prosecution of Nazi War Criminals in the United States." In *Contemporary Views on the Holocaust*, edited by Randolph I. Braham. Boston, 1983.

Sarna, Jonathan D. "The American Jewish Community's Crisis of Confidence." *Policy Forum* (Institute of WJC) 10 (1996).

Scholem, Gershom. "Jews and Germans." *Commentary* 42 (Nov. 1966).

Schorsch, Ismar. "The Holocaust and Jewish Survival." *Midstream* 27 (Jan. 1981).

————. "To Remember Is Not Enough." *Sh'ma*, Nov. 11, 1994.

Shafir, Shlomo. "American Jewish Leaders and the Emerging Nazi Threat (1928–January 1933)." *American Jewish Archives* 31 (Nov. 1979).

————. "Postwar German Diplomats and Their Efforts to Neutralize American Jewish Hostility: The First Decade." *YIVO Annual* 22 (1995).

————. "The View of a Maverick Pacifist and Universalist: Rabbi Abraham Cronbach's Plea for Clemency for Nazi Criminals in 1945." *American Jewish Archives* 42 (Fall–Winter 1990).

Shapiro, Edward S. "The Approach of War: Congressional Isolationism and Anti-Semitism, 1939–1941." *American Jewish History* 74 (Sept. 1984).

————. "World War II and American Jewish Identity." *Modern Judaism* 10 (Feb. 1990).

Siegele-Wenschkewitz, Leonore. "Auseinandersetzung mit einem Stereotyp. Die Judenfrage in Leben Martin Niemöllers." In *Die Deutschen und die Judenverfolgung im Dritten Reich*, edited by Ursula Büttner. Hamburg, 1994.

Smith, Arthur L., Jr. "A View of U.S. Policy Toward Jewish Restitution." *Holocaust and Genocide Studies* 5, no. 3 (1990).

Stern, Frank. "Philosemitism—The Whitewashing of the Yellow Badge in West Germany, 1945–1952." *Holocaust and Genocide Studies* 4, no. 4 (1989).

Strauss, Herbert A. "My Germany—and Yours?" *Sh'ma*, Apr. 13, 1973.

Trepp, Leo. "What Shall We Do About Germany." *Sh'ma*, Apr. 13, 1973.

Walter, Hilde. "German Students Seek Peace with the Jews: Behind the Fight Against Nazi Movie-Makers." *Commentary* 14 (Aug. 1952).

Wetzel, Juliane. "'Mir szeinen doh': München und die Umgebung als Zuflucht von

Überlebenden des Holocausts, 1945–1948." In *Von Stalingrad zur Währungsreform: Zur Sozialgeschichte des Umbruchs in Deutschland*, edited by Martin Broszat et al. Munich, 1988.

"Where Do I Stand Now?" Symposium. *Judaism* 23 (Fall 1974).

Whitfield, Stephen. "The Holocaust and the American Jewish Intellectual." *Judaism* 28 (Fall 1979).

———. "The Real (John J.) McCloy?" *Moment* 8 (Sept. 1983).

Wolffsohn, Michael. "Die Wiedergutmachung und der Westen-Tatsachen und Legende." *Aus Politik und Zeitgeschiche* 16–17 (1987).

———. "Die Wiedergutmachung mit Israel. Eine Untersuchung bundesdeutscher und ausländischer Umfragen." In *Westdeutschland, 1945–1955*, edited by Ludolf Herbst. Munich, 1986.

Young, James E. "Holocaust Memorials in America: The Politics of Identity." In *Survey of Jewish Affairs*, edited by William Frankel. London, 1991.

INDEX

WIDENER UNIVERSITY WOLFGRAM LIBRARY CHESTER, PA